SLAUGHTER
ON THE
SOMME

SLAUGHTER
ON THE
SOMME
1 July 1916

*The Complete War Diaries of the
British Army's Worst Day*

Compiled by

Martin Mace and John Grehan

With Additional Research by
Sara Mitchell

Pen & Sword
MILITARY

First published in Great Britain in 2013
and reprinted in this format in 2016 by
PEN & SWORD MILITARY
An imprint of
Pen & Sword Books Ltd
47 Church Street
Barnsley
South Yorkshire, S70 2AS

ISBN 978 1 47389 269 9

Printed and bound in England by
CPI Group (UK) Ltd, Croydon, CR0 4YY

Typeset in Palatino by
CHIC GRAPHICS

Pen & Sword Books Ltd incorporates the imprints of Aviation, Atlas,
Family History, Fiction, Maritime, Military, Discovery, Politics,
History, Archaeology, Select, Wharncliffe Local History, Wharncliffe
True Crime, Military Classics, Wharncliffe Transport, Leo Cooper,
The Praetorian Press, Remember When, Seaforth Publishing and
Frontline Publishing.

For a complete list of Pen & Sword titles please contact
PEN & SWORD BOOKS LIMITED
47 Church Street, Barnsley, South Yorkshire, S70 2AS, England
E-mail: enquiries@pen-and-sword.co.uk
Website: www.pen-and-sword.co.uk

Contents

Foreword

At 07.30 hours on 1 July 1916, the shrill blasts of hundreds of officers' whistles pierced the air along the eighteen miles of British front line trenches on the Somme. This was the signal for thousands of British soldiers to heave themselves up and over their parapets and to lurch forward into No Man's Land towards the German wire. What happened next, as those men walked headlong into a flailing maelstrom of searing shell fragments and machine-gun bullets – many of them disappearing forever into clouds of swirling dust and smoke – has become the stuff of myth and legend.

Now, for the first time, the details of those events – as recorded by the men who wrote the entries in the official war diaries of the battalions which went 'over the top' on 1 July 1916 – have been painstakingly transcribed from the original documents and brought together in a single volume by Martin Mace and John Grehan. Given the many hours I have spent silently scribbling away, hurriedly copying war diaries in regimental records or the National Archives over the last three decades or so, it is a book I wish I had had on my shelves some thirty years ago when I started visiting the Somme and began researching the stories of the men who had stepped over the parapet of their own trenches with such hope and confidence on that blisteringly hot Saturday in July almost a century ago.

In those far off, pre-digital, days – no laptops, no digital cameras, tight budgets – one had to travel to what was then known as the Public Record Office at Kew, armed only with pencil and paper and either manually copy the war diaries, record them on to a Dictaphone to be typed up later or – the expensive option this – have them photocopied. It was always an arduous task; always racing against the clock and as the time approached to pack up and leave, there was always one more battalion's diary to study. There was never enough time – never enough money! In the years which followed several books were published which dealt with the experience of specific battalions on 1 July 1916, but there has never been a reliable source in which all the war diary entries for every battalion involved in the attack have been collected together. Until now.

Not only does the fruit of the authors' undoubted labours deserve to take its place as an absolutely essential reference for anyone drawn to, or with an interest in the Battle of the Somme and that single, dreadful day in British military history, but it also serves to construct a deliberately unvarnished mosaic from the many fragments – piece by piece, diary entry by diary entry – of what happened along the length of that long and undulating strip of tortured ground on that fateful day. In spending countless hours going through the piles of original diaries and patiently transcribing every single word, what Mace and Grehan have done here is akin to pulling individual family photographs from a pile of old shoeboxes and placing them side-by-side to reveal a greater whole without recourse to any attempt at 'interpretation'.

FOREWORD

What Mace and Grehan present here then, are the myriad individual battalion 'snapshots' of that great British Army of almost a hundred years ago – the hard-bitten regular soldiers, the part-time Territorials and the keen, eager Kitchener volunteers who went into battle side-by-side on 1 July 1916. These then are the immediate 'after action' attempts to record the events of what proved to be a shockingly bloody day in what had, by then, already become a long and bloody war.

Saturday, 1 July 1916, was a day which led to changes in the ways in which the British Army would fight its future battles. It was a day which put paid, once and for all, to any lingering hopes held by the British people for an early, victorious conclusion to that Great European War. But that was for the future. As darkness descended on the battlefield after that 'first day' of the Somme, there had been no stunning, overwhelming British victory. Well–planned and executed operations on some southern sectors had achieved deserved success but these had been more than outweighed by almost complete annihilation and crushing defeat further north and here only chaos and confusion reigned.

What Mace and Grehan succeed in doing wonderfully well is putting us back in the British trenches as darkness fades on the evening of 1 July in the immediate aftermath of that cataclysmic event and, just like the men tasked with completing the daily war diary entries for some proud battalions which, to all intents and purposes, had ceased to exist, we grapple to make sense of the enormity of what has occurred just hours earlier.

True, the war diary entries – and the attached appendices and documents dealing with 1 July, which the authors have also wisely included – are variable in their detail, content and quality. Some entries consist of just a few terse and factual lines whilst others are almost voluminous in their detail; some providing, for example, detailed descriptions of what happened, lists of officers taking part, trench names and trench map locations and including standing orders and messages received. And yet those entries which are sparse should not be seen as inferior to others which provide more detail. As spare as they are they tell their own story and often the truth of what happened can be read between the lines:

'It is difficult to discover exactly what happened', writes the diarist of the 20th (Service) Battalion of the Northumberland Fusiliers (1st Tyneside Scottish), which attacked up Mash Valley north of la Boisselle, 'but though a few reached the 3rd GERMAN line the remaining survivors fell back to our first line under cover of darkness, not a single officer who went forward escaped becoming a casualty.' That it was difficult to discover 'exactly' what happened is understandable given the casualty figures that follow immediately below the entry: 10 officers – including the commanding officer – and 62 other ranks killed, 10 officers and 305 other ranks wounded, 10 officers and 267 other ranks missing.

Such supreme eloquence portrayed in such a simple statement. It is just one telling example of the many that are to be found in the pages that follow.

Jon Cooksey
Editor of Stand To!, *the journal of the Western Front Association*

Acknowledgements

A project of this magnitude would not have been possible without the generous assistance of a large number of individuals and organizations – those who spared us the time to help in our quest to locate the War Diary entry of each and every battalion that went 'over the top' on 1 July 1916. Unfortunately, with so many transcriptions, it is not possible to thank each and every one of those historians, library services, regimental museums and county record offices or archives by name. To you all, though, we extend our grateful thanks.

We are also grateful to Jon Cooksey, editor of *Stand To!*, the journal of the Western Front Association, not only for agreeing to write a Foreword, but also for his assistance in compiling our list of those battalions to be included.

Lastly, without the untiring help of Sara Mitchell, both in the initial research and in the subsequent transcriptions, we doubt that this book would ever have seen the light of day.

Introduction

Towering over the landscape of the Somme battlefield, the Thiepval Memorial has become one of the most tangible expressions of a defining episode in recent British history – the Battle of the Somme in 1916.

This 150 foot high brick and stone structure, visited by tens of thousands of people each year, was designed by Sir Edwin Lutyens and built between 1928 and 1932.[1] Unveiled by the Prince of Wales, in the presence of the President of France, on 1 August 1932 (originally scheduled for 16 May but due to the death of French President Doumer the ceremony was postponed until August) the memorial bears the names of more than 72,000 officers and men of the United Kingdom and South African forces who died in the Somme sector before 20 March 1918, and have no known grave.[2]

The Battle of the Somme, also known as the Somme Offensive, was fought between 1 July and 18 November 1916, on both sides of the River Somme. The battle saw the British Army, supported by units and regiments from nations throughout the British Empire and its Dominions as it was then, including Australia, New Zealand, Newfoundland, Canada, India and South Africa, mount a joint offensive with the French Army. The battle would grind on into the winter, becoming one of the bloodiest military operations ever recorded.

The Somme was the first battle to involve substantial numbers of battalions from Lord Kitchener's New Army. Included were many of the famous Pals battalions that had formed in response to Kitchener's call for volunteers in August 1914. The only non-UK troops attacking on the British sector on 1 July 1916, were units from Bermuda and Newfoundland. Because Newfoundland was still a colony of Great Britain at the time – Newfoundland did not become a part of the Canadian confederation until 1949 – the Newfoundland Regiment was a part of the British Fourth Army on 1 July rather than the Canadian Corps, which was assigned to another part of the Allied line on that day. The regiment was virtually wiped out during their failed attack at Beaumont-Hamel.

It was 07.30 hours on the morning of Saturday, 1 July 1916. As soon as the officers' whistles had fallen silent, they were replaced by the sound of thousands of men climbing out from the relative safety of their trenches and into No Man's Land. Following behind were the men of the 16th (Tyneside Commercials) Battalion Northumberland Fusiliers and, on their left, the 15th (1st Salford Pals) Battalion Lancashire Fusiliers.

These Pals battalions, from the 32nd Division's 96 Brigade, part of X Corps, were just two of the many thrown into action on the opening day of the Battle of the Somme. For the Lancashire men their target, which lay just beyond the first lines of German trenches, was the shattered village of Thiepval, whilst the area just to the south of the village was to be taken by the Newcastle Commercials.[3] Neither battalion achieved its objective.

Apart from a few soldiers who managed to penetrate the German lines north and east of Thiepval, only to be picked off by German soldiers emerging from their well-protected dugouts and literally "never heard of again", the furthest advance that most of the Salford Pals achieved was No Man's Land. Here, faced with uncut German wire and fierce, well-aimed machine-gun fire, the men remained stranded for much of the day, relentlessly fired on by enemy artillery.[4]

The adjacent Northumberland Fusiliers fared even worse. "When the barrage lifted 'A' and 'B' Coys. moved forward in waves and were instantly fired upon by enemy's MG and snipers", recorded the battalion's War Diary. "The enemy stood upon their parapet and waved our men to come on and picked them off with rifle fire. The enemy's fire was so intense that the advance was checked and the waves, or what was left of them, were forced to lie down."[5]

It is perhaps fitting therefore that the area just behind the section of the German front line attacked by these two Pals battalions was chosen for the site of the Thiepval Memorial.

Of the 141 days that comprise the Battle of the Somme, it is the opening day of the offensive that is often seen to most represent the sacrifice of a generation of young men. Before midnight on that fateful first Saturday in July 1916 – almost the middle day of the middle year of the First World War – the British Army suffered no less than 57,470 casualties – a number that comprised 585 prisoners of war, 2,152 men missing, 35,493 wounded and a staggering 19,240 dead.[6]

Even then, however, the chaos and confusion of that day meant that it was some time before those behind the front line appreciated the true scale of the disaster. At 19.30 hours on 1 July, General Sir Henry Rawlinson, commander of the British Fourth Army, considered his casualties to be around 16,000. The figure rose to 40,000 by 3 July and the final tally of 60,000 was not determined until 6 July (although exact figures were still not reached for some time).

The nature of the battles on the Somme meant that many thousands of the dead had to be left on the battlefield.[7] Even when some of the casualties were buried, the fact that these ceremonies often took place close to the front meant that the improvised grave markers were frequently lost or destroyed in the subsequent fighting; the ceaseless pounding of the artillery meant that many of the bodies simply vanished.[8]

A number of sources exist to help an individual understand the events, losses and suffering of 1 July 1916. Indeed, there have been scores of books published regarding both the Battle of the Somme and its shocking first day. The general story of the battle is therefore well known but such was the scale of the engagement there has never been an attempt to record what happened to *every* battalion that went over the top on that day. Whilst brief summaries may exist, they often lack detail and may have suffered the interpretations of historians. What we present here is the only comprehensive and authentic account available – the war diaries of every single British and Commonwealth battalion that actually left the Allied trenches to attack the German positions on that day.

A War Diary is an official daily record of operations, intelligence reports and other events, kept for each battalion by an appointed junior officer. They are not personal diaries. As will become apparent in the following pages, the information and quality of each War Diary varies, often quite substantially. Some diaries will record little more than daily losses and map references whilst others will be much more descriptive. A few contain details about individual gallantry actions. Units of infantry battalion/artillery brigade size were obliged to keep such a record once they were on active service overseas. Often they are the most detailed surviving contemporary record of the movements and activities of a unit.

Many of them were scribbled hastily in pencil and use obscure abbreviations, whilst some are the second carbon copy of the original, so they may be difficult to read. By far, the majority of the war diaries were written by hand, though a small number were typed. Writing such documents in the trenches would have been a difficult enough job in its own right but amid the clutter and confusion of battle it must have been doubly so. It was also the case that in many battalions most of the officers and large numbers of NCOs were killed or wounded on 1 July and the task of writing up the War Diary may have fallen to someone who had had no previous experience at compiling these reports. The result is that many of the war diaries are not easy to read, especially as they are now more than ninety years old and have suffered a degree of degradation. As would be expected, the hand writing of some of the men is best described as 'individualistic'!

What is important is the fact that these accounts (and the accounts, reports and appendices associated with them) were written at the time or immediately after the fighting on 1 July. Some record the unfolding events as they happen, almost minute by minute; others are terse commentaries, the authors no doubt too tired or too shocked to elaborate further or concentrate on the task in hand.

The accounts vary enormously in length and content. Some are brief, factual reports; others are long, highly-detailed accounts including vivid descriptions of the fighting. This is exemplified by the War Diary entry of the 16th (Service) Battalion (Public Schools) Duke of Cambridge's Own (Middlesex Regiment) – see VII Corps. Despite suffering 524 casualties on 1 July 1916, this battalion's War Diary entry gives little indication that the men even "went over the top", though this is confirmed in the Corps' introduction. The historian Ray Westlake, in *Tracing British Battalions on the Somme* (Pen & Sword, Barnsley, 2009, p.223), states that "one source (H.L. Smythe) records that when Beaumont-Hamel was later taken in November the remains, paybooks etc., of some 180 Middlesex men were found at the sunken road in No Man's Land".

Transcribing the War Diary entry of the 15th (Service) Battalion (1st Edinburgh

City) Royal Scots (Lothian Regiment) – see III Corps – was without doubt the hardest task we encountered in compiling this book. The author's handwriting, spelling, grammar and style found us considering his state as he wrote the account. Was he shell-shocked? Had he gone over the top and survived the undoubted horror of the attacks that day? How many of his friends and colleagues had been killed? We could not help but feel that some, even all, of these emotions had found their way on to the pages of the diary.

Despite the inequalities of the accounts we have retained the texts exactly as they have been written. Readers will therefore note the seemingly arbitrary use of capital letters by some diarists and the equally varied abbreviations of regiments and ranks. Spelling mistakes have not been rectified nor have grammatical errors. Question marks in the text have not been inserted by us; they were written by the diarists.

The difficulty we have experienced in reading some of the war diaries means we may have interpreted the names of some individuals (and particularly their initials) and places incorrectly. All we can state is that we have endeavoured to ascertain the correct spellings to the best of our ability. Where we have been completely unable to decipher a word or sentence, despite referring to copies of the war diaries held by various institutions, museums and individuals, rather than trying to guess at its meaning we have declared in the text that the word or words are illegible.

There are also instances where pages of the War Diary remain missing, or where corners and edges have been torn off. Again, in such cases, this has been indicated by us in the text. Any errors in transcription are our responsibility, and for these we offer our apologies.

The biggest difficulty lay in setting parameters for an infantry battalion's inclusion in this book. After much consideration, the decision was taken to examine those battalions which, as a whole or in part, "went over the top" between Zero Hour and midnight on 1 July 1916. In this, a battalion, or elements of it, was required to have left the relative safety of the British front line trenches and stepped out into No Man's Land. There is no necessity for the men to have got any further.

Such stipulations, of course, exclude many infantry battalions that were also involved in the opening day of the offensive – units that were held in reserve, unable to move forward, whose attacks were cancelled and so on. In some cases, these battalions suffered losses and casualties comparable to those of some of the attacking units. Take, for example, the 7th (Service) Battalion Prince of Wales's Volunteers (South Lancashire Regiment). Their War Diary account, descriptive and detailed as it is, reveals their involvement in the opening day of the Battle of the Somme. Despite the fact that they did not "go over the top", its value as a historical record is beyond dispute and therefore worth including here:

"By 1A.M. on the morning of the 1st of July the Battalion had taken up its position in a line of trenches part of which it had dug in the month of May, running N.W. ALBERT. The trenches consisted of two lines, the front line provided with dugouts, the rear line fire stepped and traversed, but with no accommodation [*illegible*] in the nature of dugouts or shelters. For this reason, companies were distributed in depth, so that the relative discomfort of passing the night in the rear line was shared equally by all.

"The disposition of the Battalion both in this line, known as the Intermediate Line, and in the trenches – the TARA-USNA line – to which it was to move on the signal of Zero hour had been previously arranged.'A' Coy on the right with 'B' Coy next to it; their Bombers and Headquarters; then 'C' Coy next to 'D' Coy on the left flank. On the right of the Battalion was the 7th East Lancashire Regt and on the left the 7th Kings Own Royal Lancaster Regt. Brigade Headquarters was situated almost on the extreme left of the Brigade line. The frontage given to each Battalion was small, & men had to sleep in the communication trenches connecting the two lines.

"As soon as the Battalion was settled, unit commanders were summoned to Battalion Headquarters & the Brigade order for the first move to come that morning was read to them and all final instructions were given. Water carts and cookers were being brought up to the line under Brigade arrangements and consequently the time of their arrival was uncertain but in anticipation of their appearance it was arranged to give the men hot cocoa and milk at 5A.M. and to have breakfast at 6.30A.M. This arrangement was carried out.

"At 4am the water carts, Lewis guns limbered [*sic*] wagons and Mess cart were sent back to join the 1st Line transport which was Brigaded in bivouac in No.1 Emergency Road about W.25.A. The cookers remained in the vicinity of the Intermediate Line during the day.

"At 6.21am the first shell from a British field gun streaked across the German lines. It was the single prelude note of the immediate opening chorus of the massed guns which lay concealed on every side. The theme swelled from crescendo to crescendo, and the Battalion moved to its second position through a veritable storm of sound.

"The Brigade operation order of the previous night had implied by inference that 7.30A.M. would be Zero hour, and as that hour drew near preparations were made to move. No definite intimation of the hour, however, was received, and it was discovered only by dispatching an orderly to the Battalion on our right who had obtained its information by sending an enquiry to Brigade Headquarters.

"At 7.45am the leading platoon of 'A' Coy began to move, in rear of the 7th East Lancashire Regt. The route followed was a track, leading from south of the Intermediate Line to Tallest Chimney thence south-west of the Station to North Chimney thence north-east parallel with the railway line crossing it at MARMONT Bridge at W.22.D.6.5 thence south-east crossing the R. ANCRE at W.23.c.2.4 thence north-east along the river valley as far as POND Bridge striking from there up a re-entrant towards OVILLERS POST. The whole route was across the open, and the movement was carried out by platoons keeping 100 yards distance between each other. The heat was already intense, and the burden of the kit, particularly of the trench boards for bridging trenches, carried by the men made itself apparent even before the TARA-USNA line was reached. Beyond these two factors, no difficulty was met with in this march, and there was practically no hostile shelling in rear of the British front line. In the TARA-USNA line the left of the Battalion rested on the three trees at W.18.D.1.9 The distribution was in depth. Brigade Headquarters was situated in the USNA REDOUBT.

"The battalion was in position by 9.15A.M. From that hour until 2.30 in the afternoon the Battalion lay still and rested. Our batteries continued firing with a varying intensity, and answering shells could be seen bursting over the British front line. No accurate information of the progress of the opening assault could be obtained; no orders, no intimation of the probable task of the Battalion, were received. The Battalion lay still and waited.

"The day threw into vivid relief the antagonistic contrast between man and nature. Due west, the valley of the Ancre lay hot and perfect in the sun, its eastern slopes stained scarlet with massed poppies swaying to the breeze. Northwards, could be seen the trees of AUTHUILLE WOOD, unblemished to the distant view. South west, appeared the roofs of ALBERT and above them the gleaming figure of the Virgin Mother, brooding over the town and twisted life below. Overhead, the lark ascended to the sky with its morning song.

"But through the quietness of the day came the constant reiterating rush of shells, and on every [*illegible*] in the trenches which scarred and seared hillside and valley lay men waiting to kill and to be killed.

"At 2.30pm the Brigadier with his Brigade Major came down the trenches and told us to be ready for work at 3 o'clock. The Commanding Officer went with them to Brigade Headquarters to receive orders, and preliminary warning was sent to companies to be ready to move at 3pm and that the probable direction was OVILLERS LA BOISELLE.

"[At 3.05pm] The Commanding Officer returned and gave Company Commanders verbally as much information as he had obtained. OVILLERS was proving an obstacle and the 56th Inf. Bde was ordered to attack just north of it and then bomb towards it from the right. Definite objectives were given – the 7th Loyal North Lancashire Regt was to attack and this Battalion to be in support to it. The move up to the British front line was to be made by trenches, through OVILLERS POST – RIBBLE STREET – PENDERHILL STREET and BARROW STREET.

"[At 3.20pm] Companies moved off in the following order, 'D', 'C', 'B', 'A', the Bombers being in the rear of 'B' Company. The Colonel & Adjutant were at the head of the leading company. The move was exceedingly slow. There were no guides at OVILLERS POST, although these had been promised, and there was

INTRODUCTION

tremendous congestion in RIBBLE STREET, the trench being used for IN and OUT purposes, by fighting troops, stretcher parties, wounded men, orderlies, carrying parties. The heat was intense and the smell almost suffocating. The Germans were using 'Tear' shells and gas goggles had to be in readiness.

"[4.20pm] At the junction of RIBBLE STREET and JOHN O'GAUNT STREET a verbal order came from the Brigadier 25th Brigade passed up from the rear, to halt and stand fast. This was confirmed by a message received from the O.C. 7th Loyal North Lancashire Regiment.

"[5.10pm] The Brigadier & Brigade Major (56th Infantry Brigade) came up and ordered the Battalion to go to UPPER HORWICH Street and to report to G.O.C. 70th Infantry Brigade, 8th Division, under whose orders the Battalion would be.

"Without a guide the Battalion moved to UPPER HORWICH STREET by WENNING STREET and CONISTON STREET to CONISTON POST. The Commanding Officer reported to the Brigadier, 70th Inf. Bde, and arranged to take over the whole of his frontage. The distribution of companies was settled and orders were being written when a message came through to say that the 12th Division would relieve the 8th Division and that this Battalion was to return to the TARA-USNA line. Part of the Battalion had already started out under guides to take over its new frontage and also within three minutes three different routes were given by which it was to return to its former position. The result was that it was impossible to collect all the companies – verbal and written messages were dispatched to them – and the whole Battalion arrived back, from where it had originally set out at 3.20pm., at 8.15 that night.

"The whole movement had been exceedingly tiring, executed under a very hot sun, through crowded trenches, with constant halts; above all, with no achieved object. Consequently men & officers who had been fresh were rendered almost out of count for immediate fighting purposes by fatigue.

"[At 11pm] Orders were received from 56th Infantry Brigade to move to Railway cutting S.W. of ALBERT. 7 S. Lan. R. not to move until relieved by 12th Division. The Staff Captain came with the verbal information that the relief would not take place for 3 hours, and companies were warned accordingly. In fact, the relief did not take place until 7am. on the 2nd inst."

*   *   *

It is the job of the historian not only to assemble facts and present them to the public, but also to interpret those facts. Inevitably, much is gained and, often, lost in such interpretations, everything being dependent upon the inclination of the author. That each new book on any subject can claim to be different from those that preceded it is ample proof of this.

Where then lies the truth? Which interpretation shall be judged the correct one? The answer to these questions is simple; all will have their merits either in accuracy or brevity. However, only one account will be authentic – that delivered by the men who witnessed the events in person.

Battles are notoriously difficult to describe, the individual soldier being unable to see much beyond his immediate vicinity. For each battalion, the war diaries can provide a holistic view of the unfolding events and their possible short-term consequences. It is to those documents that we must turn.

This book makes no attempt at providing a comprehensive history of the events of 1 July 1916. Its sole object is to draw together the War Diary entries of each battalion, with each corps supported by the original official history. What is presented here, therefore, are genuinely authentic and often comprehensive accounts of the fate that befell so many men that day, unsullied by retrospection or by subsequent personal bias.

This, then, is our assembly of facts, raw and untainted from the day that is described as the bloodiest in the history of the British Army.

Martin Mace and John Grehan
Storrington, 2012

NOTES

1. The building work was completed in early 1932. The result was a massive stepped pyramidal form of intersecting arches that culminates in a towering eighty-foot high central arch. Clad in brick, the memorial's sixteen piers are faced with white Portland stone upon which the names of the missing are engraved (other dressings are of Massangis limestone). The original facing bricks came from a brick works near Lille – over ten million bricks and 100,000 cubic feet of stone were used in the construction at an estimated cost of £117,000 (some £6m today). The whole structure sits on a ten foot thick "raft" that was formed from 12,000 tons of concrete.

2. When it was inaugurated, the Thiepval Memorial bore the names of 73,357 officers and men in lettering chiseled by Macdonald Gill on fifty-six stone wall panels. The newly published registers, on the other hand, contained the particulars of 73,077 dead. This discrepancy was due to the fact that between the carving of the panels and the first edition of the registers, the remains of 280 men had been found, usually as the woods and remaining tracts of devastated land on the Somme were cleared or brought under the plough, and these casualties had been buried in a marked grave. In time, as they were no longer missing their names would be removed from the memorial's panels.

3. Chris McCarthy, *The Somme: The Day-by-Day Account* (Brockhampton Press, London, 1998), p.27.

4. Michael Stedman, *Thiepval* (Pen & Sword, Barnsley, 2005), p.70.

5. War Diary 16th Battalion Northumberland Fusiliers, November 1915 to February 1918).

6. Gary Sheffield, *The Somme* (Cassell, London, 2003).

7. Of the 150,000 soldiers of the British and Empire forces who died in the area of the Somme before 21 March 1918, 84,000 of these are amongst those that still have no known grave. They remain 'Missing'. These numbers include 74,000 men from British regiments (including over 800 from the Royal Navy) and over 800 from South African regiments, and their names are recorded on the Thiepval Memorial. Around 90% of these men died in the period of the Battle of the Somme.

8. In most of the fourteen divisions committed to the attack on the German positions that day, the majority of those killed were missing in action. The 56th (London) Division and the 36th (Ulster) Division together had more than 3,000 men killed and of these 74% were never found. The figure was slightly higher in the 8th and 21st divisions, but the highest percentage of missing occurred in the 34th Division, where 84% of the 1,700 that died have no known grave.

List of Battalions

Alexandra, Princess of Wales's Own (Yorkshire Regiment), 2nd Battalion
Alexandra, Princess of Wales's Own (Yorkshire Regiment), 7th (Service) Battalion
Alexandra, Princess of Wales's Own (Yorkshire Regiment), 10th (Service) Battalion
Bedfordshire Regiment, 2nd Battalion
Bedfordshire Regiment, 7th (Service) Battalion
Border Regiment, 1st Battalion
Border Regiment, 2nd Battalion
Border Regiment, 11th (Service) Battalion (Lonsdale)
Buffs (East Kent Regiment), 7th (Service) Battalion
Cheshire Regiment, 1/5th (Earl of Chester's) Battalion (Territorial Force)
Cheshire Regiment, 9th (Service) Battalion
Devonshire Regiment, 2nd Battalion
Devonshire Regiment, 8th (Service) Battalion
Devonshire Regiment, 9th (Service) Battalion
Dorsetshire Regiment, 1st Battalion
Duke of Cambridge's Own (Middlesex Regiment), 2nd Battalion
Duke of Cambridge's Own (Middlesex Regiment), 4th Battalion
Duke of Cambridge's Own (Middlesex Regiment), 12th (Service) Battalion
Duke of Cambridge's Own (Middlesex Regiment), 16th (Service) Battalion (Public Schools)
Duke of Edinburgh's (Wiltshire Regiment), 2nd Battalion
Duke of Wellington's (West Riding Regiment), 2nd Battalion
Durham Light Infantry, 15th (Service) Battalion
Durham Light Infantry, 18th (Service) Battalion (1st County)
East Lancashire Regiment, 1st Battalion
East Lancashire Regiment, 11th (Service) Battalion (Accrington)
East Surrey Regiment, 8th (Service) Battalion
East Yorkshire Regiment, 1st Battalion
East Yorkshire Regiment, 7th (Service) Battalion
Essex Regiment, 1st Battalion
Essex Regiment, 2nd Battalion
Essex Regiment, 10th (Service) Battalion
Gordon Highlanders, 2nd Battalion
Hampshire Regiment, 1st Battalion
Highland Light Infantry, 15th (Service) Battalion (1st Glasgow)

Highland Light Infantry, 16th (Service) Battalion (2nd Glasgow)
Highland Light Infantry, 17th (Service) Battalion (3rd Glasgow)
King's (Liverpool Regiment), 17th (Service) Battalion (1st City)
King's (Liverpool Regiment), 18th (Service) Battalion (2nd City)
King's (Liverpool Regiment), 20th (Service) Battalion (4th City)
King's Own (Royal Lancaster Regiment), 1st Battalion
King's Own Scottish Borderers, 1st Battalion
King's Own Scottish Borderers, 6th (Service) Battalion
King's Own (Yorkshire Light Infantry), 2nd Battalion
King's Own (Yorkshire Light Infantry), 8th (Service) Battalion
King's Own (Yorkshire Light Infantry), 9th (Service) Battalion
King's Own (Yorkshire Light Infantry), 10th (Service) Battalion
King's Own (Yorkshire Light Infantry), 12th (Service) Battalion (Miners) (Pioneers)
Lancashire Fusiliers, 1st Battalion
Lancashire Fusiliers, 2nd Battalion
Lancashire Fusiliers, 15th (Service) Battalion (1st Salford)
Lancashire Fusiliers, 16th (Service) Battalion (2nd Salford)
Lancashire Fusiliers, 19th (Service) Battalion (3rd Salford)
Leicestershire Regiment, 1/5th Battalion (Territorial Force)
Lincolnshire Regiment, 1st Battalion
Lincolnshire Regiment, 1/4th Battalion (Territorial Force)
Lincolnshire Regiment, 1/5th Battalion (Territorial Force)
Lincolnshire Regiment, 2nd Battalion
Lincolnshire Regiment, 8th (Service) Battalion
Lincolnshire Regiment, 10th (Service) Battalion (Grimsby)
London Regiment (Territorial Force), 1/2nd Battalion (Royal Fusiliers)
London Regiment (Territorial Force), 1/3rd Battalion (Royal Fusiliers)
London Regiment (Territorial Force), 1/4th Battalion (Royal Fusiliers)
London Regiment (Territorial Force), 1/5th Battalion (London Rifle Brigade)
London Regiment (Territorial Force), 1/9th Battalion (Queen Victoria's Rifles)
London Regiment (Territorial Force), 1/12th Battalion (The Rangers)
London Regiment (Territorial Force), 1/13th Battalion (Kensington)
London Regiment (Territorial Force), 1/14th Battalion (London Scottish)
London Regiment (Territorial Force), 1/16th Battalion (Queen's Westminster Rifles)
Manchester Regiment, 2nd Battalion
Manchester Regiment, 16th (Service) Battalion (1st City)
Manchester Regiment, 17th (Service) Battalion (2nd City)
Manchester Regiment, 18th (Service) Battalion (3rd City)
Manchester Regiment, 19th (Service) Battalion (4th City)
Manchester Regiment, 20th (Service) Battalion (5th City)
Manchester Regiment, 21st (Service) Battalion (6th City)

Manchester Regiment, 22nd (Service) Battalion (7th City)
Manchester Regiment, 24th (Service) Battalion (Oldham) (Pioneers)
Monmouthshire Regiment, (Territorial Force) 1/2nd Battalion
Newfoundland Regiment, 1st Battalion
Norfolk Regiment, 8th (Service) Battalion
Northamptonshire Regiment, 6th (Service) Battalion
Northumberland Fusiliers, 13th (Service) Battalion
Northumberland Fusiliers, 14th (Service) Battalion (Pioneers)
Northumberland Fusiliers, 16th (Service) Battalion (Newcastle)
Northumberland Fusiliers, 18th (Service) Battalion (1st Tyneside Pioneers)
Northumberland Fusiliers, 20th (Service) Battalion (1st Tyneside Scottish)
Northumberland Fusiliers, 21st (Service) Battalion (2nd Tyneside Scottish)
Northumberland Fusiliers, 22nd (Service) Battalion (3rd Tyneside Scottish)
Northumberland Fusiliers, 23rd (Service) Battalion (4th Tyneside Scottish)
Northumberland Fusiliers, 24th (Service) Battalion (1st Tyneside Irish)
Northumberland Fusiliers, 25th (Service) Battalion (2nd Tyneside Irish)
Northumberland Fusiliers, 26th (Service) Battalion (3rd Tyneside Irish)
Northumberland Fusiliers, 27th (Service) Battalion (4th Tyneside Irish)
Prince Albert's (Somerset Light Infantry), 1st Battalion
Prince Albert's (Somerset Light Infantry), 8th (Service) Battalion
Prince of Wales's (North Staffordshire Regiment), 1/5th Battalion (Territorial Force)
Prince of Wales's (North Staffordshire Regiment), 1/6th Battalion (Territorial Force)
Prince of Wales's Own (West Yorkshire Regiment), 1/5th Battalion (Territorial Force)
Prince of Wales's Own (West Yorkshire Regiment), 1/6th Battalion (Territorial Force)
Prince of Wales's Own (West Yorkshire Regiment), 1/7th Battalion (Leeds Rifles) (Territorial Force)
Prince of Wales's Own (West Yorkshire Regiment), 2nd Battalion
Prince of Wales's Own (West Yorkshire Regiment), 10th (Service) Battalion
Prince of Wales's Own (West Yorkshire Regiment), 15th (Service) Battalion (1st Leeds)
Prince of Wales's Own (West Yorkshire Regiment), 16th (Service) Battalion (1st Bradford)
Prince of Wales's Own (West Yorkshire Regiment), 18th (Service) Battalion (2nd Bradford)
Prince of Wales's Volunteers (South Lancashire Regiment), 11th (Service) Battalion (St. Helen's Pioneers)
Princess Charlotte of Wales's (Royal Berkshire Regiment), 2nd Battalion
Princess Charlotte of Wales's (Royal Berkshire Regiment), 6th (Service) Battalion

SLAUGHTER ON THE SOMME: 1 JULY 1916

Princess Victoria's (Royal Irish Fusiliers), 1st Battalion
Princess Victoria's (Royal Irish Fusiliers), 9th (Service) Battalion (Co. Armagh)
Queen's (Royal West Surrey Regiment), 2nd Battalion
Queen's (Royal West Surrey Regiment), 7th (Service) Battalion
Queen's Own (Royal West Kent Regiment), 7th (Service) Battalion
Rifle Brigade (The Prince Consort's Own), 1st Battalion
Rifle Brigade (The Prince Consort's Own), 2nd Battalion
Royal Dublin Fusiliers, 1st Battalion
Royal Dublin Fusiliers, 2nd Battalion
Royal Fusiliers (City of London Regiment), 2nd Battalion
Royal Fusiliers (City of London Regiment), 11th (Service) Battalion
Royal Inniskilling Fusiliers, 1st Battalion
Royal Inniskilling Fusiliers, 2nd Battalion
Royal Inniskilling Fusiliers, 9th (Service) Battalion (Co. Tyrone)
Royal Inniskilling Fusiliers, 10th (Service) Battalion (Derry)
Royal Inniskilling Fusiliers, 11th (Service) Battalion (Donegal and Fermanagh)
Royal Irish Regiment, 2nd Battalion
Royal Irish Rifles, 1st Battalion
Royal Irish Rifles, 8th (Service) Battalion (East Belfast)
Royal Irish Rifles, 9th (Service) Battalion (West Belfast)
Royal Irish Rifles, 10th (Service) Battalion (South Belfast)
Royal Irish Rifles, 11th (Service) Battalion (South Antrim)
Royal Irish Rifles, 12th (Service) Battalion (Central Antrim)
Royal Irish Rifles, 13th (Service) Battalion (1st Co. Down)
Royal Irish Rifles, 14th (Service) Battalion (Young Citizens)
Royal Irish Rifles, 15th (Service) Battalion (North Belfast)
Royal Irish Rifles, 16th (Service) Battalion (2nd Co. Down) (Pioneers)
Royal Scots Fusiliers, 2nd Battalion
Royal Scots (Lothian Regiment), 12th (Service) Battalion
Royal Scots (Lothian Regiment), 15th (Service) Battalion (1st Edinburgh)
Royal Scots (Lothian Regiment), 16th (Service) Battalion (2nd Edinburgh)
Royal Sussex Regiment, 8th (Service) Battalion (Pioneers)
Royal Warwickshire Regiment, 1st Battalion
Royal Warwickshire Regiment, 1/6th Battalion (Territorial Force)
Royal Warwickshire Regiment, 1/8th Battalion (Territorial Force)
Royal Warwickshire Regiment, 2nd Battalion
Royal Warwickshire Regiment, 11th (Service) Battalion
Royal Welch Fusiliers, 1st Battalion
Seaforth Highlanders (Ross-Shire Buffs, The Duke of Albany's), 2nd Battalion
Sherwood Foresters (Nottinghamshire and Derbyshire Regiment), 1/5th
    Battalion (Territorial Force)

LIST OF BATTALIONS

Sherwood Foresters (Nottinghamshire and Derbyshire Regiment), 1/6th Battalion (Territorial Force)

Sherwood Foresters (Nottinghamshire and Derbyshire Regiment), 1/7th (Robin Hood) Battalion (Territorial Force)

Sherwood Foresters (Nottinghamshire and Derbyshire Regiment), 1/8th Battalion (Territorial Force)

Sherwood Foresters (Nottinghamshire and Derbyshire Regiment), 11th (Service) Battalion

South Staffordshire Regiment, 1st Battalion

South Staffordshire Regiment, 1/6th Battalion (Territorial Force)

South Wales Borderers, 2nd Battalion

Suffolk Regiment, 8th (Service) Battalion

Suffolk Regiment, 11th (Service) Battalion (Cambridgeshire)

York And Lancaster Regiment, 1/5th Battalion

York And Lancaster Regiment, 8th (Service) Battalion

York And Lancaster Regiment, 9th (Service) Battalion

York And Lancaster Regiment, 10th (Service) Battalion

York And Lancaster Regiment, 12th (Service) Battalion (Sheffield)

York And Lancaster Regiment, 13th (Service) Battalion (1st Barnsley)

York And Lancaster Regiment, 14th (Service) Battalion (2nd Barnsley)

List of Maps

Abbreviations

A&SH, A&S Highs	Argyll and Sutherland Highlanders (Princess Louise's)
AAD	Advanced Ammunition Depot
ACI	Army Council Instruction
Actg	Acting
AD, Art. Dpt	Artillery Depot
Adj, Adjt	Adjutant
ADS	Advanced Dressing Station
Adv	Advance or Advanced
AF	Army Form
AG	Anti-gas
Amb	Ambulance
Amn	Ammunition
AO	Army Order
AOC	Army Ordnance Corps
AOD	Army Ordnance Depot
Appx, Appdx	Appendix
Approx	Approximately
ARP	Ammunition Refilling Point
ARS	Advanced Regulating Station
Arty	Artillery
ASC	Army Service Corps
Att, Attd	Attached
BA	British Army
BAC	Brigade Ammunition Column
BAD	Base Ammunition Depot
Bde	Brigade
BEF	British Expeditionary Force
BG, Br. Genrl	Brigadier General
BGGS	Brigadier-General General Staff
BGRA	Brigadier-General Royal Artillery
BGS	Brigadier, General Staff
BM	Brigade Major
Bn, Btn, Batt, Battn	Battalion
BOD	Base Ordnance Depot
Brig	Brigade

BSD	Base Supply Depot
Bty	Battery
Capt, Cpt	Captain
CCS	Casualty Clearing Station
Cdg, Cmdg, Commdg	Commanding
CDS	Corps Dressing Station
CHA	Commander Heavy Artillery
CO	Commanding Officer
Co, Coy	Company
Col, Coln	Column
Comd	Command
Commdrs,	Commanders
Cpl	Corporal
CQMS	Company Quartermaster Master Sergeant
CRA	Commander Royal Artillery
CSM	Company Sergeant Major
CT	Communication Trench
DA	Divisional Artillery
DAC	Divisional Ammunition Column
DAP	Divisional Ammunition Park
DAQMG	Deputy Assistant Quartermaster General
DCLI	Duke of Cornwall's Light Infantry
DCM	Distinguished Conduct Medal
DDMS	Deputy Director Medical Services
Div	Division or Divisional
DLI	Durham Light Infantry
DO	Dug-out
DoW	Died of wounds
DRS	Divisional Rest Station
DSC	Distinguished Service Cross
DSO	Distinguished Service Order
DTMO	Divisional Trench Mortar Officer
DWR	Duke of Wellington's Regiment (West Riding)
Engr(s)	Engineer(s)
Eqpt	Equipment
Est	Establishment or establish
Ey	Enemy
Ex, Excl	Excluding

ABBREVIATIONS

FA	Field Ambulance
Fd	Field
FDS	Field Dressing Station
Fm, Fmn	Formation
FOO	Forward Observation Officer
FSPB	Field Service Pocket Book
Ft	Feet or Foot
Fus, Fusrs	Fusilier(s)
Fwd	Forward
GHQ	General Headquarters
GOC	General Officer Commanding
GS	General Service or General Staff
GSO	General Staff Officer
GSW	Gunshot Wound
HA	Heavy Artillery
HE	High Explosive
HLI	Highland Light Infantry
How	Howitzer
HQ, Hqts, HdQrs	Headquarters
Hr	Hour
HT	Horse Transport
Hy	Heavy
IB	Infantry Brigade
IC	In Charge
2/IC	Second in Charge
Incl	Including or included
Ind, Indep	Independent
Inf, Infy	Infantry
Inf Bde	Infantry Brigade
Infm, Info	Information
Inf Reg, Inf Regt	Infantry Regiment
Int, Intel	Intelligence
IO	Intelligence Officer
Junc	Junction
KOSB	King's Own Scottish Borderers
KOYLI	King's Own Yorkshire Light Infantry
KRRC	King's Royal Rifle Corps
KSLI	King's Shropshire Light Infantry

L.Bdr, L/Bdr	Lance Bombardier
L.Cpl, L/Cpl, L/C, Lce Cpl	Lance Corporal
LF, Lanc Fus, L.Fus	Lancashire Fusiliers
L.G., L. Gun	Lewis Gun
LO	Liaison Officer
L of C, LC	Lines of Communication
L.Sgt, L/Sgt	Lance Sergeant
Lt	Lieutenant
Lt Col	Lieutenant Colonel
Maj	Major
MC	Military Cross
MDS	Main Dressing Station
Med	Medium or Medical
Mg, MG, M.Gun	Machine-gun
MGS	Machine-Gun Section
Min	Minute
MM	Military Medal
MO	Medical Officer
NCO	Non-Commissioned Officer
NF, Northd Fus	Northumberland Fusiliers
Nfld	Newfoundland
OC	Officer Commanding
Off, Offr	Officer
OIC	Officer-in-Charge
OP	Observation Post
OR, O. Rank	Other Rank(s)
Ord	Ordnance
Pdr	Pounder
Pl, Plt	Platoon
Pnr	Pioneer
Posn	Position
Pt, Pte, Prvt	Private
PW, PoW	Prisoner of War
QM, Qr.Mr.	Quarter-Master
QMG	Quartermaster General
QMS	Quarter-Master Sergeant

ABBREVIATIONS

QVR	Queen Victoria's Rifles
QWR	Queen's Westminster Rifles
RA	Royal Artillery
RAMC	Royal Army Medical Corps
RAP	Regimental Aid Post
RB	Rifle Brigade
Rd	Road
RE	Royal Engineers
Rec, Recce	Reconnaissance or Reconnoitre
Recd	Received
Ref	Reference
Reg, Regt	Regimental
Res	Reserve
RF	Royal Fusiliers
RFA	Royal Field Artillery
RFC	Royal Flying Corps
Rfn	Rifleman
Rft	Reinforcement(s)
RHQ	Regimental Headquarters
RIF, R.Ir.F.	Royal Irish Fusiliers
RIR, R.I.Rifles	Royal Irish Rifles
RMO	Regimental Medical Officer
RO	Routine Orders
Rptd	Repeated
RQMS	Regimental Quarter-Master Sergeant
RS	Royal Scots
RSF	Royal Scots Fusiliers
RSM	Regimental Sergeant-Major
RV	Rendezvous
RWF	Royal Welch Fusiliers
RWK	Queen's Own Royal West Kent Regiment
SAA	Small Arms Ammunition
SB	Stretcher Bearer
SC	Staff Captain
Sec	Section
Sec Lt, 2/Lt	Second Lieutenant
Sgd	Signed
Sgt, Sjt	Sergeant
Sig	Signal
Sigmn	Signaller or Signal Man

SL	Start line
SLI	Somerset Light Infantry
SMO	Senior Medical Officer
SO	Staff Officer
SP	Start Point, Strong Point, or support
Spr	Sapper
ST	Support Trench
Sup, Supp	Supply
SWB	South Wales Borderers
Temp, Tempry, T/	Temporary
TF	Territorial Force
Tfd	Transferred
Tho'	Though
Thro'	Through
TM	Trench Mortar
TMB	Trench Mortar Battery
TO	Transport Officer
VC	Victoria Cross
WD	War Diary
Wef	With Effect From
WO	Warrant Officer
Yd	Yard
Y&L	York and Lancaster Regiment

Individual Corps Sections

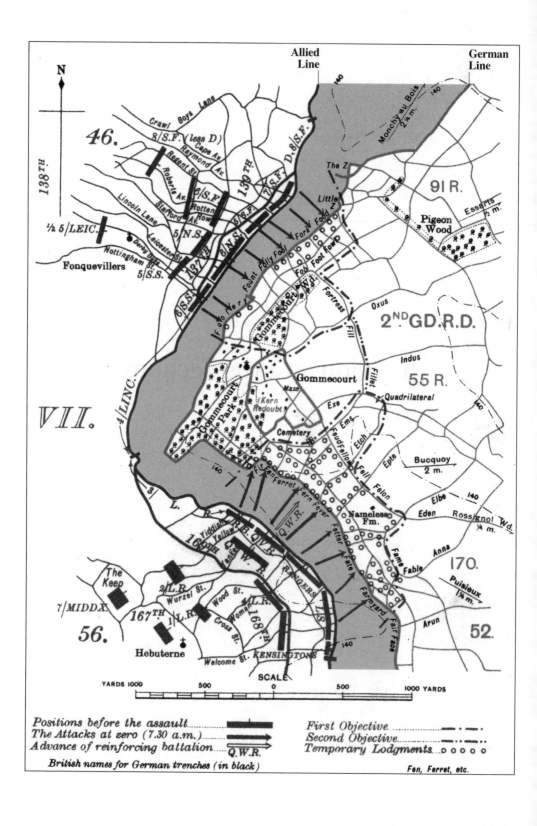

Allied Line

German Line

N

138TH.

46.

Crawl Boys Lane

8/S.F. (less D)
Raymond Av
Regent St.
Roberts Av.
Cape Av
Stafford Av.
6/S.F.
Rotten Row
139TH.
7/S.F. D.8/S.F.
5/S.F.
Little Z
Fork Foot

Monch'au Bois 2¼ m.

The Z

91 R.

Pigeon Wood

Esserts ½ m.

Lincoln Lane

½ 5/LEIC.

Derby Dyke
Leicester St.
5/N.S.
6/N.S.
Fount Folly Fool
Fob Foot Fowp

Nottingham St.

Fonquevillers

5/S.S.
127TH.
6/S.S.
Fo Nero
Gommecourt Wd.
Fortress

Oxus

2ND GD.R.D.

Fold

Gommecourt Pk. Wd.

Fill

Indus

VII.

4/LINC.

Gommecourt Park
Maze
Kern Redoubt
Cemetery

Gommecourt

Exe
Feudfellow
Ems
Etch
Fell
Felon

55 R.

Quadrilateral

Epte

Bucquoy 2 m.

3/L. R.

Fanferret Fern Fever
Q.W.R.

Elbe
Eden
Rossignol Wd. ¼ m.

169TH.
L.R.
R.B. Q.V.R.
Yiddish Yellow
Yankee
W.R.

Nameless Fm.

Fetter Fate

Anna
Fame Fable

170.

Puisieux 1¼ m.

The Keep

2/L.R. Wurzel St.
Wood St.
Woman St.
RANGERS
Farmyard
Fair Face

γ/MIDDX.

56.

167TH.
1/L.R.
Cross St.
168TH.
L.R.
KENSINGTONS
140

Arun

52.

Hebuterne

Welcome St.

SCALE

YARDS 1000   500   0   500   1000 YARDS

Positions before the assault ....
The Attacks at zero (7.30 a.m.) ....
Advance of reinforcing battalion ... Q.W.R.

First Objective ....
Second Objective ....
Temporary Lodgments ○○○○○

British names for German trenches (in black)

Fen, Ferret, etc.

VII Corps

1 July 1916

Part of Sir Douglas Haig's plan was to lengthen the front of attack by a subsidiary offensive against Gommecourt. For this he had renounced the idea of recapturing the portion of Vimy ridge lost on 21 May, having decided that, with the troops available, he had not sufficient forces to undertake both enterprises. The operation against Gommecourt was allotted to VII Corps[1] of the Third Army (General Sir Edmund Allenby). Between it and the left of the main attack against Beaumont Hamel and Serre, carried out by VIII Corps, there would be left a two mile gap, from which no attack was to be made owing to lack of troops. This, as we have seen, was held by two battalions provided by VIII Corps.

It was not until 28 April that General Snow had received orders that an offensive against Gommecourt would be required at the end of May, a date subsequently postponed to the end of June. During the first week in May the 56th and 46th Divisions arrived in VII Corps' area to carry out the operation. By the morning of the 10th they had taken over the trenches allotted to them, part of a very wide front hitherto held by the 37th Division, which then closed on its left. It was, however, asking very much that two divisions new to the ground should attack at two months' notice defences of the strength of Gommecourt, unless a complete surprise without much previous preparation were intended. The enemy salient was in reality a small modern fortress. It required siege operations, or, at any rate as events proved, bombardment by super-heavy guns to destroy its dug-outs, as well as a great amount of trench-work to get within assaulting distance, besides an ample supply of labour for carrying up stores and munitions. For mining there was obviously no time. It must, however, be distinctly borne in mind that in Sir Douglas Haig's plan nothing depended on the capture of Gommecourt.

The object of the attack was "to assist in the operations of the Fourth Army by diverting against itself the fire of artillery and infantry which might otherwise be directed against the left flank of the main attack near Serre". There was no intention of exploiting the capture of Gommecourt by sending a force southwards from the village to roll up the German line or clear the ridge leading south-east behind it. No troops were provided or available for such a purpose. A success at Gommecourt would merely shorten the British line by cutting off an enemy salient.

1

It seems improbable that GHQ realized the strength – and that strength enormously increased by flanking artillery defence – of the Gommecourt salient. If an attack is to be made merely in order to hold enemy troops and prevent their employment elsewhere, a weak or vulnerable part of the enemy's front should be chosen, not the strongest. Further, Gommecourt was particularly easy of defence, and from the shape of the ground it was a most difficult place from which to disengage troops in the event of partial failure or incomplete success.

Neither General Snow of VII Corps nor his Army commander were men of half measures. If the enemy's attention was to be attracted to Gommecourt in order to ensure the success of the Fourth Army, they were ready to take all risks, but they did go to the length of suggesting that a threat from Arras would be more effective and less costly. This, however, would not have prevented the enemy from using the guns which he had in the vicinity of Gommecourt against the northern flank of VIII Corps.

Sir Douglas Haig having decided in favour of the attack on Gommecourt, the divisions of VII Corps were at once set to work on preparations and training on the same lines as those of the Fourth Army. Ill luck seemed to attend on the preparations, and it seemed an evil presage to the troops that an enemy aeroplane at once flew over the practice ground marked out to represent unmistakeably the Gommecourt defences. Lack of sufficient labour units necessitated the employment of all the attacking battalions of the 46th Division and many of those of the 56th, whose sector was not so water-soaked, in the most exacting fatigues up to the very eve of the assault. Probably barely a man of the former division enjoyed a full night's sleep for a week previous to the attack, and there was scarcely a day or night when the rain did not fall consistently and heavily, and working parties were not soaked to the skin.

The ground had an important bearing on events. Gommecourt village stands at the junction of four low ridges with flat tops, which make the outline of a St. Andrew's Cross, its four arms stretching towards Essarts, Rossignol Wood, the western edge of Hébuterne, and the eastern edge of Fonquevillers. The German line on the north-western face of the salient ran slightly below the crest of the western side of the Essarts ridge, with a shallow valley in front of it, on the other side of which was the British line.

Behind this line the ground was nearly level, so that the Germans had complete observation for more than 2,000 yards over VII Corps' area (except over a small portion hidden by the ruins of Fonquevillers and the trees near that village) and the 46th Division had in consequence to dig numerous long and deep communication trenches. On the south-western face of the salient, almost as far south as Nameless Farm, the British and German trenches were nearly on the same level, with a dip, in which there was a hedge, between them; beyond this point both were on the western side of the wide valley between Rossignol Wood and Hébuterne, the British thus being on a forward and the Germans on a reverse

2

slope. The enemy artillery observation posts were on the eastern side of the valley. The approaches on the British side in the 56th Division area were completely hidden from ground view right up to Hébuterne, but were under observation of the German balloons. The chief British observation posts were on the eastern edge of this village and the ridge running south of it. The slope of the valley provided natural drainage, which the very gentle gradients in the 46th Division sector did not.

The defences of Gommecourt were, in consequence of their salient position and a previous unsuccessful French attack on them, stronger probably than any others on the German front, and were specially well provided with deep dug-outs,[2] there being a number of them in the park, where a dense mass of trees still furnished complete cover from view. The eastern portion of Gommecourt village was organized as a large closed work, known as "The Maze", and called by the Germans "Kern Redoubt". As a measure of security the enemy had covered the salient by three retrenchments, known as the 1st and 2nd Switch Lines and the Intermediate Line. These were crossed by numerous communication trenches, and the two systems taken in combination provided a series of defence lines available to block and encircle the British in whatever direction they might penetrate. The garrison of the salient was on 1 July three regiments (nine battalions), with one in reserve.[3]

As finally settled, the plan for the capture of the Gommecourt salient consisted of two convergent attacks against its haunches (first objective). These secured, the attackers were to proceed and join hands in the German 1st Switch Line behind the village, and thus isolate it. The programme gave the infantry thirty minutes from zero to reach this second objective. On the 2,000 yards of front facing the village and park, between the two attacks, there were to be no offensive operations, but wire was to be cut and smoke released as elsewhere. The clearing of the park, the village and the Maze was not to be attempted before zero plus three hours, until which time the fire of the super-heavy and heavy howitzers was to be kept on these targets. There was not sufficient time to undertake mining operations, as No Man's Land was wide, and silent mining under the German trenches was impossible except at fifty or sixty feet, a depth which would much delay the removal of spoil.[4] This was a most unfortunate circumstance, for the explosion of a large charge against the warren of deep dug-outs in Gommecourt Park, or under the Maze, might have proved a determining factor in the action.

The 56th Division was to make the right attack, the 46th the left, while each division furnished a battalion – 1/3rd London (two companies) and 1/4th Lincolnshire were detailed – to fill the intervening gap.

One of the difficulties of attack was the width of No Man's Land, which varied from eight hundred yards in front of the 56th Division to 400-500 in front of the 46th Division. In the case of the former a new line, 850 yards to the front, as well as one communication trench, was, by a well-planned operation, dug by the 167th

Brigade, with the 416th (Edinburgh) Field Company Royal Engineers and a company of the 1/5th Cheshire (Pioneers) attached, along the whole divisional front of attack on the night of 26/27 May.

Warned that such an operation so close to the enemy involved serious risk, Major General Hull decided that it must be taken. Nearly 3,000 men were engaged within four or five hundred yards of the enemy, after the operation had been carefully practised under Brigadier-General F.H. Burnell-Nugent for four days and nights. Two nights before it took place small parties of the London Rifle Brigade were sent to remain out night and day, to keep off patrols.

On the next night the line was pegged out and stringed. To support the operation if things went wrong the whole corps artillery stood ready; and to cover the noise and distract the enemy's attention carts full of empty biscuit tins were driven up and down in Hébuterne. The same covering party, two companies of the London Rifle Brigade, was used each night until the work was finished. The completion of 2,900 yards of trench and 1,500 yards of communication trench was effected at a cost of 8 men killed and 55 wounded.

On the first night (26th/27th) a shallow trench was dug throughout, with parts deepened for detached posts and Major General Hull himself went round it on the morning of the 27th. To prevent the enemy destroying the new trench, which the chalk soil of the area made vividly conspicuous, the Royal Flying Corps kept a 'plane in the air all day to deal with any German aviators who attempted to carry out photography or registration, and arrangements were made for counter-battery fire on any enemy guns which endeavoured to register. No interference, however, took place.[5]

The Germans made no attempt to destroy the new work, although by bursts of fire on subsequent nights they sought to disturb the working parties which completed the trench and added support and other communication trenches. This advance still left No Man's Land 400-500 yards wide. It was intended to reduce it by a further push forward, but this proved impossible owing to the bad weather, which interfered with work and made it necessary for all available labour to be diverted to the upkeep of existing fire and communication trenches.

The situation of the 46th Division was somewhat different. No Man's Land being only 400-500 yards wide, the assaulting troops might be able under the final barrage to creep to within assaulting distance. But before the trenches lay a tangle of thick barbed wire, twenty yards wide, left by the French. To cut gaps through this was no easy task, and the brigade commanders were in favour of making a trench about a hundred yards in front of it. This, however, was not begun until the first week in June, after Russian saps had been run out to its site. The ground in the shallow depression between the opposing front trenches proved however soft and soggy, and little work was done on the first night owing to the mud encountered.

On the following nights artillery fire prevented the trench from being dug to its full depth, so that it did not provide more than 3 to 4 feet of cover. Some communication trenches run out to it later were similarly left at 2½ to 3 feet deep. Then in the bad weather before the battle the trenches fell in and became waist-deep in mud and water, so that on the day of assault some portions of the advanced trench – also of the assembly trenches behind the front line and parts of the communication trenches near them – could not be used by fully equipped troops. Regimental runners stripped themselves to shorts and boots before trying to pass along them. Yet to achieve even these inadequate results the men had been overworked by heavy digging and carrying, and were "dog-tired".

As it was obviously impossible to dig another series of trenches nearer to the enemy, it was finally decided that before zero the troops should crawl out under the barrage to about two hundred and fifty yards from the German trenches. During the night of 30 June/1 July, the 1/4th Lincolnshire (46th Division), holding the portion of the line facing Gommecourt Park between the attacking fronts, dug a shallow trench in front of its position. This so far proved of use that it attracted shells which might otherwise have been directed on its front line or the attacking troops.

In the weeks available, the plan of attack was thought over and elaborated with the greatest care, and at one of the many rehearsals on the dummy trenches smoke was used to accustom the troops to move through it. The employment of gas was considered, but, in view of the difficulty of combining the digging of new trenches with the construction of cylinder emplacements and the labour involved in carrying up the cylinders, the idea had to be abandoned.

The 37th Division, on the left of the corps line, holding 4½ miles as far as Ransart (5½ miles N.N.E. of Gommecourt), was not to attack, but to take such measures as would induce the enemy to believe that it would do so. Early in June it made an advanced trench, as the 56th and 46th had already done; for No Man's Land on its right was 1,000 yards wide, narrowing to five hundred, and obviously too wide for assault. Some smoke and gas were to be released from time to time on its front, and wire-cutting was to be carried out.

During the five days previous to Z Day, it was to concentrate trench-mortar and machine-gun fire south and north of the Monchy salient, increasing in intensity as Z Day approached. Its artillery in particular was to shell vulnerable points and the roads and approaches to Essarts, and part of it was to be prepared to support the 46th Division. Finally, five minutes before zero hour, smoke was to be released. All these measures were duly carried out, but the labour involved, particularly the transport of the gas cylinders, was so heavy that even batmen, grooms and other specially employed men had to be impressed to help.

In consequence of the nature of the operation, VII Corps, with Sir Douglas Haig's approval, made no attempt to hide or disguise the preparations for the attack – in fact, they carried them out ostentatiously with the deliberate intention of attracting attention. The result was immediate and satisfactory; for in mid-June, after the new advanced trenches had been dug, the German 2nd Guard Reserve Division, which was in reserve, was interpolated in the line between the 52nd and 111th Divisions to hold the Gommecourt salient. Thus, without any attack, VII Corps had diverted a division and the six heavy batteries attached to it, which might have been employed elsewhere to stem the main attack.[6] When, four days before the assault, Sir Douglas Haig asked General Snow how he was getting on, the commander of VII Corps was able to reply, "They know we are coming all right".

During the bombardment the whole of the artillery in the corps, except some 18-pounder batteries detailed for wire-cutting, had worked under the command of the GOC corps artillery, but at zero hour on the day of attack, the divisional artillery, except three batteries of 4.5-inch howitzers retained for counter-battery work, reverted to divisional control.[7]

The howitzers and guns available proved altogether inadequate to deal with the German artillery, all of whose heavy batteries were beyond the range of the British 60-pounders and 6-inch howitzers, and still more of the old 4.7-inch guns, and therefore inaccessible to counter-battery work, except by the few super-heavy weapons. The enemy had concentrated against the front of attack the guns of the 2nd Guard Reserve Division, the 52nd Division, and the greater part of those of the 111th (to the north of Gommecourt), including a large number of attached heavy guns.

Both the 46th and 56th Divisions, however, suffered specially from enfilade fire from artillery not on the corps front: the latter from batteries to the south-east near Puisieux (3 miles south-east of Gommecourt) on VIII Corps' front, and the former even more from the very numerous guns on the 37th Division front, in and around Adinfer Wood, some in concrete casements, as was discovered in 1917, which fired a continuous rain of 5.9-inch howitzer shells. The German barrage put down on No Man's Land was more severe than in any other sector.[8] The manner in which the enemy managed to concentrate gun fire from a wide front on to the place where it could be most usefully employed, deeply impressed British staff officers, but even had this not been accomplished, the attack of VII Corps, taking place on the extreme left, with a gap on its right of two miles, would have suffered from all the disadvantages of an offensive on a narrow front. It was the German artillery which proved the main factor in the successful defence.

One special feature of the bombardment of the sector opposite the 46th Division requires mention: the GOC directed that the enemy front trench should not be shelled, but fire kept on the support and reserve lines, as he desired to keep this trench intact for use by his own troops.

The lifts of VII Corps' artillery were arranged to conform with the plan of attack; half the guns in the two Heavy Artillery Groups which were firing on the defences to be attacked were to lift two minutes before zero, and the rest at zero, to the eastern half of the inner flanks of the first objective (Ems and Oxus Trenches, south and north respectively of Gommecourt village). They were then to switch for fifteen minutes on to the second objective, after which the barrage was to be shifted forward to cover the consolidation of that line. The artillery firing on Gommecourt village and park was, however, to continue its task, as already mentioned, until three hours after zero.

The 18-pounder batteries of both divisions had very short lifts, almost amounting to a creeping barrage. In the 56th Division the guns lifted at zero to the reserve trench, and fired on it for four minutes, and just beyond it for six minutes, then swept the communication trenches for twelve minutes, and, shifting inwards, dealt with the second objective for eight minutes. In the 46th Division, the lifts were: at zero to the support trench; at plus 3 minutes to the reserve trench; at plus 8 they covered the reserve trench till plus 20; at plus 25 they lifted to the second objective, on which they fired until plus 30.

On the front of VII Corps, as on that of VIII, there was no surprise whatever: "The new British assault trenches, the pushing forward of saps, the frequent bombardment of important points, the appearance of heavy trench-mortars, and the increasing artillery fire, which from time to time rose to 'drum-fire', left no doubt as to the intention of the enemy".

As if expecting the attack on 1 July, the German artillery at 04.00 hours on that day began shelling the front positions in which the assaulting troops might be expected to be assembled, and continued to do so until 06.25 hours, when the intense bombardment caused them to give attention to the British batteries. But as the hour of assault approached some German guns again opened on the trenches and shelled them so consistently that the leading troops of the 56th and 46th Divisions were glad to advance in order to escape their fire.

Assault of the 56th Division

The 56th (1st London Territorial Force) Division[9] was to attack on a 900-yard front from the southern edge of Gommecourt Park south-eastwards. Major General Hull placed the 168th Brigade (Brigadier-General G.G. Loch) and 169th Brigade (Brigadier-General E.S. D'E. Coke) in the front line. He held the 167th (Brigadier-General F.H. Burnell-Nugent), less two battalions, in reserve round Hébuterne, the 1/8th Middlesex and half of the 1/3rd London being assigned the duties of occupying the front line when the attacking brigades left it and of supplying working and carrying parties.

The objective of the 168th Brigade was the German third trench (Fame-Felon),[10] and strong-points were to be established on the two flanks and in the centre near Nameless Farm. It was also to dig a trench across No Man's Land to protect the right flank. The 169th Brigade was to do more. It was first to reach the third trench (Fell-Fellow-Feud) up to Gommecourt cemetery, on the left of the 168th, and establish three strong-points on its own left flank near the cemetery, in the south-western part of the Maze and at the southern corner of Gommecourt Park. Then it was to swing forward its left to the Quadrilateral, a large strong-point behind the 1st Switch Line, east of the Maze, and later to push out and gain touch with the right of the 46th Division where the Indus communication trench cut the 1st Switch (Fillet-Fill), thus completing the line behind Gommecourt.

The assault of the 56th Division was carried out with the greatest dash, and the failure to capture the Gommecourt salient cannot in any way be attributed to the gallant regiments composing it, for they did practically all that was asked of them. The assault of the 168th Brigade was led by the London Scottish and the Rangers, with the Kensingtons and 1/4th London in support; that of the 169th Brigade by the Queen Victoria's Rifles and London Rifle Brigade, with the Queen's Westminster Rifles in support. The last-named battalion was to pass through the line and capture the Quadrilateral. The 1/2nd London was in reserve. Each brigade had attached to it a section of a field company Royal Engineers (2/1st London and 2/2nd London respectively), and a company of the pioneer battalion (1/5th Cheshire).

At 07.20 hours smoke was discharged from the left of the line, and in five minutes it was down along the whole front. At 07.25 hours, under cover of this, in spite of a heavy enemy barrage falling at the moment on the first and second trenches and the communication trenches, the leading companies clambered over the top and advanced steadily into No Man's Land, to form up on tapes laid there. At 07.30 hours they rose and moved to the assault.

The wire had, as a rule, been well cut – the worst places had been dealt with by Bangalore torpedoes on the previous night, but the enemy was untiring in repairing the damage by means of "concertina" wire and new strands. Some parties had to file through gaps and others went astray in the smoke cloud, but only the Victoria's, and the Queen's Westminster following them, seem to have been definitely delayed by uncut wire. The Londoners were too quick for the enemy by a few seconds and, with comparatively little loss, were in the German front line before they could be seriously opposed. The first objectives, the three front German trenches (or rather what remained of them, for they were nearly unrecognizable with the exception of Nameless Farm, were secured. The first two trenches were easily overrun; the third, manned by German riflemen closely packed on the fire step and assisted by machine-gun fire, was only gained after a fire fight and party rushes, attacks up the communication trenches finally breaking the German resistance.

Nameless Farm was never captured. It had long lain derelict, but its cellars gave protection to the garrisons of a shell-hole position on its site and of the portion of the trench behind the farm; the German defence of it was determined, and without doubt this greatly contributed to tire out the attackers and deplete their supply of bombs.

The progress of the assault was well reported by signals to airmen and by runners to battalion headquarters, and at 09.30 hours boards exhibited in the three German trenches showed that they were nearly all in the possession of the 56th Division, and that the work of consolidation was proceeding whilst nearly three hundred unwounded prisoners were sent back of whom about eighty were killed by German shell fire in crossing No Man's Land. After this unfortunate occurrence the hundreds of prisoners taken were herded into their own deep dug-outs.

The barrage was in fact so severe that the Kensington company detailed to dig the trench to protect the right flank could not do so, and most of the large party of bombers detailed in orders to go forward at 09.30 hours to assist the Queen's Westminster in the next stage of the action, the capture of the Quadrilateral, became casualties in No Man's Land. Several parties of the Queen's Westminsters in vain attempted to reach the Quadrilateral from the third trench but one party of bombers, led by an officer of the 1/5th Cheshire, pushing on via the cemetery, succeeded in doing so, only to meet destruction there.

By this time the assaulting battalions, and two companies of the 1/4th London (168th Brigade) and the Queen's Westminsters (169th), which had gone across to support them, were entirely cut off by the enemy barrage which had been put down on the lost front trenches and No Man's Land. Several attempts to send forward bombs and ammunition only led to the annihilation of the carrying parties, and soon from every side counter-attacking troops were moving towards the 168th and 169th Brigades, whose line, owing to losses, was no longer a continuous one.

Assault of the 46th Division

The assault of the 46th Division was carried out by the 137th Brigade (Brigadier-General H.B. Williams) and the 139th Brigade (Brigadier-General C.T. Shipley). In the front line of the former, on the right, were the 1/6th South Staffordshire and 1/6th North Staffordshire, with the 1/5th South Staffordshire and 1/5th North Staffordshire in support, the 1/5th Lincolnshire (attached from the 138th Brigade) being in reserve and providing carrying parties. In the 139th Brigade, the 1/5th and 1/7th Sherwood Foresters led, the 1/6th was in support and the 1/8th in brigade reserve. The 138th Brigade (Brigadier-General G.C. Kemp),[11] less two battalions, was in divisional reserve. To each of the assaulting brigades was attached a whole field company Royal Engineers (1/2nd and 2/1st North Midland), and the pioneer battalion (1/1st Monmouthshire) was detailed to improve and dig communication trenches.

The first object of the division was to form what the operation orders called "a defensive flank", but was actually a "pocket", in the German position north of

SLAUGHTER ON THE SOMME: 1 JULY 1916

Gommecourt, its trace running from the enemy front trench along the Fonquevillers – Gommecourt road to the north-eastern end of Gommecourt, thence along Oxus communication trench for five hundred yards, and then back in a "dog-leg" via Fortress, Foreign and Ouse Trenches to the British line. Ten strong-points were to be established in the new line.

The second object was to join hands with the 56th Division in the 1st Switch Line by working southwards from Oxus Trench along Fill Trench. At 10.30 hours, three hours after zero, on the conclusion of the bombardment, the clearing of Gommecourt village was to be taken in hand.

The first of the six waves was to start from the advanced trench, but on the right its condition was so poor that the 1/6th South Staffordshire preferred to use the original front line, leaving it well before zero to reach the assault position. Assembly trenches had been dug one hundred and fifty yards behind the front line, but, as already mentioned, they had been damaged by water, and were unusable. Moreover, the ground between them and the front line was covered with a confused mass of old French trenches, so tapes were put out and pegged down on the previous night to give the second and subsequent waves their alignment. At four minutes before zero the second wave was to move out from the front trench and take up position eighty yards behind the first. The other lines were then to leave their trenches and follow over the open.

Ill-luck attended the attack of the 137th Brigade from beginning to end. The smoke-cloud formed was at first very dense, so dense that many men lost their way in it and as a result the advance was not uniform and simultaneous, but within half an hour it had blown back and dispersed. The Germans were fully on the alert,[12] and the muddy state of the ground near the front line and in No Man's Land delayed the attackers – who, by their opponents' account "advanced quietly as at manoeuvres" – so that they were only halfway across No Man's Land when the defenders came up out of their dug-outs. The wire, when reached, was found either intact or repaired, or as some officers reported, cut but not cleared away, merely smashed up and twisted.[13]

Almost before the British artillery lifted the Germans manned the parapet and shell holes; "at the same moment the annihilating barrage fire of the German artillery began". On account of this fire the third wave was ordered to file up the communication trenches instead of advancing over the open, an instruction being added, which led to much confusion, that all "down" trenches were "up" trenches until 09.00 hours. But before this wave got clear of the advanced trench, the enemy barrage came down on No Man's Land, and steadily increased in intensity, a number of guns away to the north joining in.

Particularly effective machine-gun fire came from a pronounced spur held as a salient in the German line north of the left of the attack, and known as "The Z", so that practically none of the rear lines got across. Part of the first three waves even remained in our front line trenches or lay down in No Man's Land. The leading lines of the 1/6th South Staffordshire and 1/6th North Staffordshire, though particularly galled by flanking fire from saps and shell holes to the south, reached the enemy wire, where they were mostly shot down, or wounded by hand-grenades. Only a few determined men succeeded in entering the front trench through gaps, but, receiving no support owing to the failure of the rear waves to come on, these were soon driven out again or destroyed.

The 139th Brigade did better. The first three waves of Sherwood Foresters, with considerable casualties, reached and broke into the German front trench; some parties advanced to the second,[14] but there was some loss of direction on the left, as air observers reported British soldiers in the Z and "Little Z", and this is confirmed from German sources. Their rumoured presence there prevented guns from being turned on to deal with the flanking fire coming from the Z. Here also the succeeding waves were met by heavy fire: the fourth wave never moved forward as a whole, and only small portions of the fifth and sixth got beyond the advanced trench.

Touch with the leading lines was completely lost: the ample means of visual and mechanical communication arranged – telephone, flags, lamps, discs, shutters, pigeons, flares and rockets – all broke down owing to casualties, and no runner could get through. The only signal that came from the front was the lighting of two flares in the second German trench, reported at 11.00 hours from the air.

Behind the Sherwood Foresters, who had effected an entry, the enemy issued from his deep dug-outs, which should have been dealt with by the rear lines. Manning the parapet, these Germans prevented reinforcements from crossing No Man's Land, and all along the line they could be seen bombing the shell holes in which the men of the 46th Division had taken refuge near the German wire.

By 09.00 hours Brigadier-General H.B. Williams was definitely certain that the assault of the 137th Brigade had failed. He realized that this failure must inevitably lead to increased pressure on the 139th Brigade and the 56th Division, and therefore determined to renew the attack with the 1/5th South and 1/5th North Staffordshire, and with the 1/5th Leicestershire (attached), which formed his rear waves and had been held up.

Measures were taken to get the barrage brought back. A second attack by troops already engaged, however, is always hard to organize, and in this case the difficulties in the way of reorganization were many. There was no chance of drawing the men back into the open; they had to be sorted out in the crowded trenches, which being full of mud a foot deep, made all movement slow. Many men were already missing – the 1/5th North Staffordshire could report only two hundred present – and in all units there was a shortage of officers.

Very soon after brigade orders had been issued to prepare for an advance, the two Staffordshire lieutenant colonels (R.R. Rayner and W. Burnett)[15] were wounded, the fall of the latter not becoming known for some time, so that further delay ensued, and this was fatal to any chance of success. The organization of the attack was finally placed in the hands of Lieutenant Colonel C.H. Jones, commanding the 1/5th Leicestershire, and the brigade major and staff captain of the brigade were sent to assist him in his hard task of arranging the men to form four waves.

An unforeseen difficulty then supervened; the men had been carefully trained for weeks to play definite parts in the assault, and it was not easy to make them realize that these roles must now be forsaken and something different done. For instance, a party told to carry concertina wire could not for some time be got to understand that they must drop their loads and help to form an attacking wave. To make matters worse, the rear lines and carrying parties, unable to advance, were blocking the trenches, which, owing to their muddy condition and the enemy bombardment, could only be cleared with great difficulty.

The task of the 139th Brigade was somewhat different to that of the 137th. It had effected a lodgement in the enemy's front, and the problem was to reinforce the troops there and send them bombs and supplies. Brigadier-General Shipley considered that this could not be done without another smoke barrage, for there was not even shell-hole cover, except in the hundred yards in front of the British trenches, and again at 50-70 yards in front of the German line, the 300-400 yards stretch in the centre of No Man's Land being absolutely bare. He therefore decided to wait until bombs to form a smoke cloud could be procured.

It was soon evident that there was no possibility of an immediate further attack or advance by the individual brigades, and the GOC of the 46th Division decided to make the operation a combined movement. He himself co-ordinated the separate preparations of the brigades, and arranged that the divisional artillery and part of the corps artillery should co-operate; he did not allot any fresh troops. The advance was to be made at 12.15 hours, the 137th Brigade attacking afresh, with the aid of smoke, and the 139th sending over one company to stiffen the line and parties carrying grenades and supplies. The corps commander, who visited the 46th Division at this time, approved of the plan.

As the 137th Brigade could not be ready by 12.15 hours, a postponement was made to 13.15 hours, but shortly before this hour the 139th Brigade reported that there were still no smoke bombs, and it did not advance. The 137th, not being ready, conformed. The hour was then fixed for 14.45 hours, when again a postponement was made, as Brigadier-General Shipley reported that the smoke would not be available until 15.15 hours, because chaos reigned in the communication trenches. The time of the advance was then fixed by the 46th Division for 15.30 hours.

Smoke bombs were duly fired from Stokes mortars at 15.20 hours, and a screen, continuous but not thick, was formed in front of the 137th Brigade, but only twenty bombs could be collected for the 139th Brigade, and the smoke barrier on its front was entirely insufficient to hide movement even for a moment. Brigadier-General Shipley therefore sent orders for the advance to be stopped.

The commander of the 1/6th Sherwood Foresters had already come to the conclusion that it was useless to go on: the enemy was on the alert, and of twenty men on the left who did go over the parapet, eighteen were cut down by machine-gun fire and shrapnel in the first twenty or thirty yards.

On the right, the acting commander of the 1/5th South Staffordshire, who had arranged to make a signal to his men to move into position, was wounded shortly before 15.30 hours. Thus no signal was given, and the few officers surviving being inexperienced, everyone waited for someone else to start, and no movement took place.

The commander of the 1/5th North Staffordshire in the front trench, seeing no advance on either side of him, telephoned to Brigadier-General Williams for instructions, and was told to "sit tight". Meanwhile the corps commander, having heard that the 56th Division had been forced back, had sent orders to call off the attack of the 137th Brigade, which reached the brigadiers and Lieutenant Colonel Jones at the very moment the troops in the trenches should have started.

It would have been mere waste of life to have tried to cross No Man's Land after the hour of 15.30 hours had passed; for, warned by the smoke, the Germans had again put down a barrage and the British artillery which had bombarded the German trenches from 15.00 to 15.30 hours had lifted. The thin smoke cloud was rapidly diminishing, and without it, though a 150-yards No Man's Land might have been rushed, to cross 350 yards and more was out of the question. The original attack of the division having failed, the only hope of success lay in an advance by entirely fresh troops, and since the Gommecourt operation was only a diversion it did not seem advisable to employ the last reserves of VII Corps, except to assist a definitely new main attack. Before such could take place the confusion and congestion in the trenches would have to be cleared up, and this would take many hours.

No men of the 1/5th and 1/7th Sherwood Foresters, who had made entry in the German position, had come back during the day but a few returned about 21.30 hours after having lain in shell holes in No Man's Land, and they reported the lodgment as still held, but this does not seem to have been the case.[16] The casualties of the assaulting battalions had been very heavy; in the two Sherwood Forester battalions, nearly eighty per cent, including both Lieutenant Colonels D.D. Wilson and L.A. Hind, were killed.[17]

Loss of the lodgement of the 56th Division

The failure of the 46th Division to do more than make a small entry into the German line with its left brigade had, however, disastrous consequences for the 56th. That division had by careful preparations and a fine advance attained nearly all of its principal objective, and now held on, the divisional and brigade staffs buoyed up by the news that the 46th Division would renew its attack. But very soon after the British assault had been launched at 07.30 hours, it must have become evident to the commander of the *2nd Guard Reserve Division* that he need have no anxiety for the northern face of the Gommecourt salient, and had only the 56th Division to deal with.

As the German accounts show, from north, east and south thirteen fresh companies from the supports and reserves moved down against the lodgement made by the London Scottish, the Rangers, Queen Victoria's Rifles, Queen's Westminster Rifles and the London Rifle Brigade. The method of attack employed by the enemy was intense artillery fire lasting a few minutes, closely followed by bombing attacks. The most deadly fire came in enfilade from a single light gun or pair of guns hidden 3,000 yards to the south-east of the head of Puisieux valley.

Owing to the enemy's barrage, the passage of reinforcements and stores across No Man's Land had from the first been hazardous. About 09.00 hours half a company of the Kensington, with a London Scottish machine-gun crew, got over with difficulty to the London Scottish, whose own parties with those of other battalions trying to bring up bombs and ammunition had all been destroyed in No Man's Land. These were the last reinforcements received, as a very gallant attempt of two companies of the 1/2nd London about 14.00 hours merely led to their being mown down by machine-gun fire from the park and by heavy artillery fire from Puisieux. There were so many wounded now lying in No Man's Land that men of the remaining companies went out to try to bring in some of them. This was countenanced by a German medical officer, who came out with a white flag and said that there was no objection to the removal of wounded on the British side of the wire, so long as no firing took place. Unfortunately this truce was interrupted by an 18-pounder shelling the German front trench.

As long as hand-grenades lasted, eked out by the German stick-grenades found in the dug-outs, the Londoners were able to hold their own, but by midday the supply began to run short, as repeated messages "S.O.S. bombs", "S.O.S. bombs", sent back by "shutters" testified.

Three times a heavy barrage ploughed through the lines of the men of the 56th Division, strong bombing attacks were made on them from the direction of Gommecourt Park, and under this combined pressure they were gradually forced out of the German third line. Little help came to them from their own artillery; news of the enemy counterattacks from Gommecourt never reached corps headquarters, and the guns were employed in barraging the enemy communication and switch trenches down which enemy reinforcements could be seen passing all day.

The information received from aviators as to the situation was not considered sufficiently definite for close support to be given to the 56th Division's front troops. The four 18-pounder batteries and howitzer battery, placed at the call of the GOC 169th Brigade after zero hour, were also dealing with counterattacks coming down the communication trenches. Later when the German front trenches were crowded with troops firing on the men of the 56th Division retreating across No Man's Land, the little ammunition left had to be husbanded, in view of a general counter-attack then appearing imminent.

At 14.00 hours the 168th and 169th Brigades were still holding the second and first lines and the southern part of Gommecourt Park, but from 13.00 hours onwards parties, chiefly consisting of wounded men, began to return to the British trenches, crawling across No Man's Land. Good counter-battery work and an attack by the 46th Division might now have relieved the situation: yet not only was there no sign of movement on the left, but information came in that, on the right, the attack of the VIII Corps on Serre had failed, whilst the 31st Division was back in its own trenches. Although there was now no hope for the troops of the 56th Division still in the German lines, they continued to resist. By 16.00 hours the Germans had retaken the second trench and had one or two footings in the first, and the 169th Brigade collected the last reinforcement, orderlies, clerks and servants, for a final desperate effort to help the Londoners.

At 15.26 hours a message was received by General Snow from VIII Corps that it was intended to make a renewed attack at night. Having two and a half comparatively fresh battalions in the 56th Division and three and a half in the 46th, he ordered them to be prepared to assist VIII Corps by an attack after dark, the hour of which would be notified later. Before night fell, however, the men remaining in the German front lines had been gradually reduced in numbers by bombing, until the lodgement of the 56th Division consisted of a single point in Ferret Trench, a couple of hundred yards from Gommecourt Park, with five officers and 70 men holding it.

The wounded were got away and sections were organized with the remaining Lewis guns to hold the rear edge and parados of the enemy front trench. Finally, the men were driven from their last position inside the German lines to the shell holes near the wire, but it was not until about 21.30 hours, when it became dark, that, ammunition having been expended, the last party came back, suffering heavy loss in the withdrawal.[18]

The operations of VII Corps had left it in the position from which it had started, with only the satisfaction of knowing that it had kept some German infantry and artillery from the main battle. The success of the 56th Division, the more remarkable on account of the failure of the divisions on either side, cost the lives of over thirteen hundred of some of the best infantry in the Armies in France.[19]

In the evening, the 138th Brigade (with the 1/8th Sherwood Foresters of the 139th attached) took over the front of the 46th Division, and Brigadier-General G.C. Kemp determined to make a last effort to gain touch with the men said to be holding out in the enemy's position. Shortly after midnight he sent the 1/5th Lincolnshire to make the attempt, with the 1/5th Leicestershire as a right flank guard. The battalion advanced up to the enemy wire, but found the German trenches strongly held, the wire uncut, and the Germans very much on the alert, so that innumerable light balls and flares immediately lit up No Man's Land. It was obviously useless to persevere, and every man was ordered to lie down and wait. Eventually, by divisional order, the Lincolnshire fell back after suffering considerable casualties, bringing their wounded with them out of No Man's Land.

The attempt "to divert against itself forces which might otherwise be directed against the left flank of the main attack near Serre" cost VII Corps nearly 7,000 casualties.[20]

Owing to fire, the removal of wounded was carried on under difficulties until midnight was past, but as it grew light the German 2nd Guard Reserve Division again chivalrously gave assistance. Early in the morning of the 2nd the Germans hoisted a large red-cross flag on the parapet opposite the 46th Division. Both sides sent out parties to collect the wounded, and nearly all the British were brought in; there was ceremonial saluting on both sides, but no fraternization. This was not, however, the end of a revival of the old courtesies of war: a couple of days later a German aeroplane dropped a list of the prisoners taken at Gommecourt, and in return a similar list was sent by the same means to the enemy.

The German account of Gommecourt

The general effect of the British bombardment was good, so that the "front trenches were levelled and the wire shot away", but the losses in men, in consequence of there being plenty of deep dug-outs, were small. The sector opposite the 56th Division was held by the 170th Regiment, with four companies and the left company of the 55th Reserve Regiment in the front line. Here the smoke completely hid the start of the attack, and, owing to the damage done to the entrances of the dug-outs, the men could not get out quickly enough, and were overrun by the Londoners.

A counter-attack was at once made by one company of the garrison of the un-attacked Kern Redoubt (Maze) (2½ companies and the infantry pioneer company of the 55th Reserve Regiment, and a section of engineers), but the British obtained possession of three lines of trenches. Towards 08.45 hours the commander of the 170th Regiment, with the assistance of his neighbours, got a counter-attack going. Against the right flank and right centre of the lodgement were sent seven companies of the 170th Regiment and two of the 15th Reserve Regiment, whilst four companies of the 55th Reserve Regiment bore down on the left centre and left flank.

The British had consolidated the position and erected barricades, and little was effected against them until the afternoon hours, when simultaneous bombing attacks of all the companies engaged on the counter-attack gradually drove the Londoners back. Two officers and seventy men were taken prisoners.

Opposite the 46th Division the men of the right of the 55th Reserve Regiment and the 91st Reserve Regiment managed to clamber out of their dug-outs in time, and received the advancing lines with heavy machine-gun and rifle fire."In spite of this the British pushed through the broken-down wire and smashed-up front trench, tried to fill up their thinned ranks and press on."A counter-attack from the third trench struck them at the decisive moment. The assaulting British, though they fought stoutly, were, except for a few prisoners (30), annihilated.

The artillery of the 52nd Division and 2nd Guard Reserve Division and some batteries of the 111th Division took part in the defence, those of the 52nd having a considerable number of guns put out of action.

Nearly fourteen hundred British who had fallen in or in front of the position of the 55th Reserve and 91st Reserve Regiments were buried. These regiments claim to have made prisoner, 16 officers and 251 men, and the 170th Regiment, 6 and 150.[21]

NOTES

1. VII Corps (Lieutenant General Sir T. D'O. Snow) comprised: 56th Division (Major General C.P.A. Hull, died 24 July 1920), 167th, 168th and 169th Brigades; 46th Division (Major General Hon. E. J. Montagu-Stuart-Wortley), 137th, 138th and 139th Brigades; 37th Division (Major General Lord Edward Gleichen), 110th, 111th and 112th Brigades. GOC Royal Artillery was Brigadier-General C.M. Ross-Johnson; GOC Heavy Artillery was Brigadier-General C.R. Buckle; Chief Engineer, Brigadier-General J.A. Tanner (killed 23 July 1917).

2. Usually forty feet below ground, lighted with electricity, and provided with kitchens and other amenities. They had several entrances, and were interconnected, passages leading back from the front to the rear lines.

3. 170th of the 52nd Division, 55th Reserve and 91st Reserve of the 2nd Guard Reserve Division. To the north was the 111th Division. The 52nd and 111th Divisions contained three infantry regiments each (two in the line and one in reserve), the 2nd Guard Reserve Division four, the 77th Reserve being north of Gommecourt and the 15th Reserve in reserve.

4. A deep mine at Messines, with a 700-yards gallery, took the best part of a year.

5. The idea at the time was that the German dawn reports must have already gone in, stating"situation unchanged", and, when it got lighter, and the new lines of chalk parapet were seen, no one dared inform higher authority what had happened.

6. For more information, the reader is directed to *Schlachten des Weltkrieges, Somme Nord*, (Reichsarchiv, Oldenburg) i. p.250.

7. The corps' heavy artillery consisted of Nos. 19, 35, 39 and 48 Heavy Artillery Groups, the first two firing on trenches and villages, the latter two being employed as counter-batteries. Howitzers: two 15-inch; two 12-inch; twenty-four 9.2-inch; twenty-eight 6-inch. Guns: two 9.2-inch; two 6-inch, twelve 60-pounders; twelve 4.7-inch. Taking the front as 4,000 yards, this gives a heavy per 47 yards, with a field gun per 27 yards.

8. The 2nd Guard Reserve Division had 6 heavy batteries attached, and the 52nd, 8; the allotment to the 111th is not available. Apparently the enemy, averaging 4 guns to a battery, had a slight inferiority in heavy guns on the actual front of attack, but this does not take into account those firing from the flanks, from Puisieux and Adinfer, which occasioned the heaviest losses.

9. This Territorial division was assembled in France in February 1916. All the infantry battalions were already serving there, having gone out in the autumn of 1914 or early in 1915 to be attached to various Regular brigades to strengthen them, and they had taken part in much fighting. The divisional troops,

except one field company Royal Engineers from Edinburgh, and the Pioneers, 1/5th Cheshire, were London Territorials.

10. It should be noticed that the enemy trenches were given names by the VII Corps on a system: first, on the right, words beginning with Fa, then blocks of Fe, Fi, Fo. The communication trenches had river names beginning with A, E, I, O to correspond. Thus behind Felon Trench was Elbe communication trench.

11. 1/4th and 1/5th Lincolnshire and 1/4th and 1/5th Leicestershire. The 1/4th Lincolnshire was holding the portion of the front line between the attacks of the 46th and 56th Divisions, and the 1/5th Leicestershire was sent to the 137th Brigade to dig a communication trench across No Man's Land parallel to the Fonquevillers – Gommecourt road after the attack had succeeded. This trench, starting from the ruins of a "Sucrerie", was begun, but could not be proceeded with on account of the German gun fire.

12. It seems possible that the digging of the long new trench by the 56th Division was regarded as a feint, and that an attack was expected only from the northern side of the salient, which strategically offered advantages and the possibility of sweeping down the German lines towards the main attack.

13. The records of the German Reserve Infantry Regiment 91, against which the 46th Division attacked, state: "At the places where the British intended to break into our front line the wire was shot to pieces and swept away ... repairs to the wire were undertaken wherever the bombardment permitted, but the trenches were completely levelled and filled up. (This does not agree with the unanimous accounts of officers who got into the German front trench, which was intact, too wide to jump and too deep to get out of without assistance.) Only the dug-outs were still intact, contrary to the expectation of the enemy." The repulse of the 46th Division is attributed to "the annihilating barrage fire of the artillery" and close fighting with hand-grenades. The war diary of the 55th Reserve Regiment, which defended Gommecourt village and park, states that at the hour of attack the front was "ripe for assault, wire swept away and trenches smashed in, but shell holes were occupied at exactly the right moment, and the attackers were received with hand-grenades. The barrage fire called for began at once."

14. The records of the German Reserve Infantry Regiment 91 admit that some of the British reached the second trench in the northern sector of the 46th Division attack.

15. The latter died of wounds two days later. Thirty-six-year-old Lieutenant Colonel William Burnett DSO is buried in Warlincourt Halte British Cemetery, Saulty.

16. An account of the German Reserve Infantry Regiment 91 states that "by about midday, according to the reports of the front companies, the position in its whole entirety was again in our hands." The details of the annihilation of the parties of the Sherwood Foresters who broke into the Z and got as far as the second trench are very circumstantial. One officer and thirty men are claimed as prisoners.

17. Casualties are thus: l/6th South Staffordshire, 14 officers and 205 other ranks (out of 500); l/6th North Staffordshire, 13 officers and 292 other ranks (out of 23 and 740); l/5th Sherwood Foresters, 24 officers and 395 other ranks; l/7th Sherwood Foresters, 18 officers and 391 other ranks (out of 536).

18. The war diary of the 55th Reserve Regiment gives 21.45 hours as the time at which complete possession was regained.

19. Casualties were: London Scottish, 14 officers and 602 other ranks (out of 24 and 847); The Rangers, 17 officers and 447 other ranks (out of 23 and 780); Queen Victoria's Rifles, 12 officers and 448 other ranks (out of 27 and 671); London Rifle Brigade, 19 officers and 535 other ranks (out of 23 and 803); Queen's Westminster Rifles, 28 officers and 475 other ranks (out of 28 and 661); 1/4th London, 16 officers and 324 other ranks (out of 23 and 650); 1/13th London (Kensington), 16 officers and 310 other ranks (out of 24 and 500).

20. The 46th Division suffered 50 officers killed, 71 wounded, 14 missing and 2 prisoner and 803 other ranks killed, 1,340 wounded, 172 missing and 3 prisoner – a total of 2,455. The 56th Division suffered 53 officers killed, 107 wounded, 17 missing and 6 prisoner, and 1,300 other ranks killed, 2,248 wounded, 356 missing and 227 prisoner – a total of 4,314.

21. Of German casualties, British prisoners taken at Gommecourt on the 1st July saw evident signs of heavy losses during the preliminary bombardment in the shape of, literally, "stacks" of corpses, five or six bodies in height, putrefying, whilst awaiting burial.

Index of Battalions

1/5th (Earl of Chester's) Battalion (Territorial Force) Cheshire Regiment

SOUASTRE

7.30 am. 56th and 46th Divisions attacked GOMMECOURT. Disposition of Battalion for operations:'A' Coy attached 169 Bde;'B' Coy attached 167 Bde;'C' Coy attached 168 Bde. Headquarters Specialists and'D' Coy (less one platoon attd to 'B' Coy) formed part of Divisional Reserve and remained in SOUASTRE. The Specialist platoon of'B' Coy remained at HENU with R.E. 168th and 169th Infantry Brigades attacked. The work carried out by 'A', 'B' and 'C' Companies is set forth in Appendix I herewith. Casualties suffered:

		Officers	Other Ranks
Killed		Sec Lieut DAVIES, F.A.	12
Wounded		Lieut LEIGH, H.R.	84
		Sec Lieut SIMPSON, H.C.H.	
		Sec Lieut ANDREWS, E.I.	
Missing		Lieut BASS, P.B.	75
		Sec Lieut ARTHUR, G.S.	
Died of Wounds			1
Total		6 officers	172

Documents Attached to the War Diary

Appendix No.1, an account of the battalion's actions on 1 July 1916, signed by Lieutenant Colonel John E.G. Groves, Commanding 1/5th (Earl of Chester's) Battalion (Territorial Force) Cheshire Regiment:

1st July 1916
Weather – fine
Reference Map GOMMECOURT, 1/5,000
1. 45th and 56th Divisions attack GOMMECOURT. 56th Divisional attack was made by 168th and 169th Infantry Brigades. The object of the attack was for VIIth Corps to establish itself on a line which runs approximately on our present line about 250 yards N.E. of the 16 Poplars – East of Nameless Farm – along a ridge in K.5.a and E.29.c to the little"Z"and thence back to the British line.
    (a). The objectives of the 168th Infantry Brigade were to capture the German

line from FAIR TRENCH about K.11.d.1.3 along FARM, FAME, ELBE, FELON to a point in FELL 50 yards N.W. of the trench junction at K.5.c.5.2 and to establish itself in three strong points:
1. About FARM YARD.
2. About trench ELBE, between ET and FELON.
3. About CROSS TRENCHES of FELL and FELON with EPTE.
'C' Company of this Unit was responsible for the wiring of these strong points. (Lieut. E.M. Dixon in command).
(b). The task of the 169th Infantry Brigade was to be carried out in three phases:
1st Phase: To capture line of German trenches from left of 168th Infantry Brigade along FELL, FELLOW, FEUD, the CEMETRY, ECK, THE MAZE, EEL and FIR and to establish strong points:
(i) From FEUD through EMS to the CEMETRY inclusive.
(ii) About the MAZE.
(iii) About the S.E. corner of GOMMECOURT PARK (i.e. the junction of FIR and FIRM trenches).
2nd Phase: To capture Quadrilateral of trenches in the S.E. portion of K.5.a immediately after the 1st phase.
3rd Phase: To secure the cross trenches at K.5.a.7.8 (where INDUS crosses FILL and FILLET) and joining hands with the 46th Division along FILL.
'A' Company of this unit was responsible for the construction of the strong points mentioned in the 1st Phase and the consolidation of the Quadrilateral. The Company was split up as follows:- 1 Platoon attached L.R.B., 2 Platoons attached Q.V.R., and 1 Platoon Q.W.R.
(c) The 167th Infantry Brigade was in reserve. The tasks allotted to 'B' Company, which was attached to this Brigade were as follows:
(i) 2 platoons under 2nd Lieuts. F.A. Davies and W.F. Smith were to fix boards bearing new names in the captured German trenches.
(ii) 1 platoon of 'D' Company (attached 'B' Company) under 2nd Lieut. H.W. Glendinning was to remove barricades on the HEBUTERNE – BUCQUOY Road. 1 platoon under 2nd Lieut. J.D. Salmon was to remove barricade on the HEBUTERNE – GOMMECOURT Road and bridge trenches.
2. The attack commenced at 7.30a.m. when the first waves of infantry stormed the German positions as indicated above.
(a) 'A' Company went over by platoons in the 3rd wave behind the L.R.B., Q.W.R. and Q.V.R. 2nd Lieut. E.I. Andrews was wounded before reaching the German first line, but went on. Work was commenced upon the strong point running through EMS to the CEMETRY.
Some Bombers, not 5th Cheshires, passing along ECK, accidentally dropped a bomb which exploded and seriously wounded Lieut. P.B. Bass.
Owing to intense Bombing by the Germans, many casualties were inflicted on this Company which had to eventually withdraw from the enemy's position about 8-0 p.m. No Platoon Commanders returned with the Company.

The losses of this Company were as follows:

	Officers	Other ranks
Killed	-	5
Wounded	2nd Lieut. H.C.H. Simpson	34
	2nd Lieut. E.I. Andrews	
Missing	2nd Lieut. G.S. Arthur	74
	Lieut. P.B. Bass.	
Total casualties	4 officers	113

(b) 'C' Company of this unit awaited orders all day in the reserve trenches. One platoon under Lieut. H.R. Leigh was ordered to reinforce the London Scottish but when it reached the German wire this order was countermanded and the platoon returned to the remainder of the Company.
The losses of this Company were as follows:

	Officers	Other ranks
Killed	-	5
Wounded	Lieut. H.R. Leigh	16
Missing		1
Total casualties:	one officer and 22 other ranks.	

(c) The work of 'B' Company in the attack was as follows:
2nd Lieut. F.A. Davies went over in front of his platoon but was killed by machine-gun fire soon after he had entered "No man's land". The leading men were also killed or wounded and the remainder of the platoon was held up.
2nd Lieut W.F. Smith was ordered to go over behind the 3rd London Regiment, which was in reserve. This Battalion was not called upon to go over, so that 2nd Lieut. W.F. Smith with his platoon remained all day in our trenches.
2nd Lieut. H.W. Glendinning proceeded with his platoon to the barricades on the HEBUTERNE – BUCQUOY Road, succeeded in removing one barricade, but was unable to carry on owing to heavy casualties. The barricades in question were in the German barrage fire, which was very intense. Several attempts were made to carry on but the barrage was too intense to work under and the work had to be abandoned.
2nd Lieut. J.D. Salmon succeeded in blowing up the barricade on the HEBUTERNE – GOMMECOURT Road with gun cotton charges and bridged all trenches to the front line, thus satisfactorily performing the task allotted to him.
The losses of this Company were as follows:

	Officers	Other ranks
Killed	2nd Lieut. F.A. Davies	1
Wounded	-	23

Died of Wounds	-	1

Total casualties: one officer and 25 other ranks.

The losses of the platoon of 'D' Company attached to 'B' Company were as follows:

	Officers	Other ranks
Killed	-	1
Wounded	-	11
Total		11

3. 'C' Company and the remnants of 'A' Company returned to billets in SOUASTRE. 'B' Company remained at HEBUTERNE.

The total casualties sustained by the Battalion were:

	Officers	Other ranks
Killed	1	12
Wounded	3	84
Missing	2	75
Died of Wounds	-	1
Total	6	172

A document entitled "Additional Communication", dated 3 July 1916, and signed by Lieutenant Colonel John E.G. Groves, Commanding 1/5th (Earl of Chester's) Battalion (Territorial Force) Cheshire Regiment:

To: Headquarters, 56th Division.

Herewith I beg to forward reports received from various officers, N.C.O's and men of this Unit with regard to the action on Saturday 1st. inst.
I will hold the officer, N.C.Os and men at your disposal for further interrogation should you so desire.

3rd. July 1916.
John E.G. Groves
Lt. Colonel, Commdg. 1/5th. Bn. Cheshire Regiment
No.1878 Corporal H. Wolfenden is of No.2 Platoon of 'A' Company. This platoon was to consolidate junction of trenches INDUS-FILLET. He states:
"It was about 8.0.o'clock when we went over. We set out towards the German Lines and turned to the right as we had rehearsed. We reached the German first line having lost about five men. Stretcher Bearer S. Clarke stayed behind bandaging these men. We got to the 2nd line which was full of Q.V.R. so we could

not get in. We lost about 12 men here and Clarke came up and commenced bandaging these.

We had to stay outside the trench but we looked about to find our way. Then Sergt. Boardman said "Come on boys I've got it" we then went along a communication trench and eventually reached a point where the trench branched off to the left and right and also went straight on (Cpl. Wolfenden, states that the trench on left front was FILLET and the communication trench EMS). He continues – My platoon had to go on up FILLET but we found the bombers in front of us consisting of Q.W.R. with some Q.V.R. We could not get on and we could not reach the point where we were to work. My party, therefore, joined No.1. platoon and worked on the QUADRILATERAL. We blocked the trench leading to the right at a distance of about 15 yards from junction then we went on consolidating. Corporal Radcliffe found a Lewis gun in the QUADRILATERAL and fired on any Germans he could see also snipers.

Some of the Q.W.R. and Q.V.R. went to the left after reaching the junction. There were two Officers of the Q.W.R. dead at this point. After a while the Germans came up behind the block which we had built and started bombing and Corporal Radcliffe turned round the gun and fired in the direction of the block. During this time some of the men were passing up bombs and after a while they could get no more, and as the Germans were still bombing down FILLET, the order came down to retire.

Corporal Radcliffe and myself carried down a wounded man to the German front line and when we got there we were ordered to mount the fire step. The trench was very crowded and I only saw one Officer, 2nd Lt. Arthur. We saw the Germans following down the communication trench and started firing at them. Soon after this the order was passed down "every man for himself", and I saw the men in the trench leave for our trenches. I made for a gap in the German wire and got back safely."

No.1460 Private Brown R.J. No.4 Platoon 'A' Coy. 1/5th Cheshire Regt. Attached 'C' Coy. Q.V.R. Private Brown states:
"We followed up 'C' Company of the Q.V.R. We went over the parapet and got to the German front line and we couldn't see anything of the Q.V.R. so we started letting into the Germans. Then we got to the 2nd line and started letting into the Germans again, but Mr. Bass stopped us and told us to get into the trench and wait orders. We got into the 2nd line trench and sat down. Mr. Bass took the first man and told him to come with him. Whilst Mr. Bass was away we set at work to reverse the parapet. Sergt. Lancely went up to the 3rd line to 2nd Lieut. Arthur, and then we went up to the 3rd line and attached ourselves to 2nd Lieut. Arthur. We started cutting a piece out of the traverse or block for the Q.V.R. and we placed a man on guard in the communication trench.

Whilst he was on guard some Germans came up. We cut the piece out and went down the trench and helped to pass bombs up. We then had orders to retire. I never saw Mr. Bass after he had taken the man away. He went up to report to Captain Cox, of the Q.V.R."

No.171. Sergt. J. Robinson, platoon Sergeant of No.1 Platoon, which was led by 2nd Lieut. Andrews, is not sure whether they got in the QUADRILATERAL, but was delayed owing to 2nd Lieut. Andrews being wounded. He advanced up the trench and found Sergt. Ogden, of his platoon and Corporal Radcliffe with some men working near the QUADRILATERAL. He states that it was half past seven when the first lot went over the parapet. Soon after, 2nd Lieut. Andrews, ordered them to go over. They reached the German lines in the smoke. Whilst they were consolidating, messages were sent down for more bombers and Sergt. Jones went up but was hit in the back of the head.

Sergt. Robinson continues: "I have not seen him since. I have no clear idea of what happened when we retired. I know that we manned the German fire step and found the trench very crowded because it was so narrow. My men were very scattered. The word came along "every man for himself" and we all left the trench. I reached our front line alone. The Q.W.R. bombers could not get enough bombs. Corporal Radcliffe, with a Lewis gunner named Mugan killed many Germans with the Lewis gun."

2382 Private H. Lancashire No.4 Platoon 'A' Company, states:
"My platoon under Lieut. Bass was ordered to consolidate the Cemetery. I went over with the platoon and lost them in the smoke. I got into the first wave with the Q.V.R. and Q.W.R. and opened fire on bombing parties of Germans in the first German trench. I was in a shell hole with a Q.V.R. We got the order to advance and got bombed again so we got down and opened fire near the German front line trench. I looked to my right and saw Lieut. Bass with Private Clifford going over some high ground near the German 2nd line. I made my way to him and found Clifford waiting. He said that Lieut. Bass was reporting to Capt. Cox of the Q.V.R. Lieut. Bass came back and gave orders to three of us, who were there to make a fire step in a trench running through the Cemetery. As we were digging, some bombers passed along and one accidentally dropped a bomb which exploded. Lieut. Bass was hit in the eye and Clifford was wounded. We bandaged them up but could not stop Lieut. Bass bleeding and I went to find some one to report to. An officer of the Q.V.R. said "come along with me". We found Capt. Cox and reported what had happened. I followed the Q.V.R. officer and the men said the Germans were bombing us out. I saw some of our own men but they had not seen my platoon. I then helped to pass up bombs for the Q.V.R. I saw Clifford with some other wounded. The order came down that they were bombing from the right and we passed bombs. It was about 2.30.p.m. I should think and we were still being bombed in the German front trench and were moving to the left to try to get in touch with the L.R.B. We kept on passing bombs and taking turn on look-out and were finally driven into a section of trench about 50 yards long and facing GOMMECOURT PARK. About 7.30.p.m. they started sending whizzbangs. After some time a wounded Captain told us to go back to our own lines and we did so."

No.1464 Sergt. Ogden G.H., No.1 Platoon 'A' Coy. 1/5th Cheshire Regt. states:
"We were attached to 'B' Coy. Q.W.R. My platoon had to consolidate QUADRILATERAL. We went over behind the Q.W.R. and got to the German 3rd line. We were held up there by German fire and manned the trench, while the Q.W.R. bombers, bombed up. We were asked by an officer to go up and help the Q.W.R. and did so. We started consolidating and building blocks. I heard an officer say that the trench in which we were working was EMS. The Germans kept bombing all the time and we replied but were gradually forced back until at last I found myself with many others in a section of German front line trench about 50 yards long. We kept sniping from here and bombing with our own bombs and German grenades. At last the order came along to get back to our own front line; we did so about 8.0 o'clock I should think."

2nd Lieut Glendinning, 'D' Company 5th Cheshire Regiment, attached with No.14 Platoon to 'B' Company 5th Cheshire Regiment, states:
"On July 1st, I received orders to remove barricades on the HEBUTERNE – BUCQUOY Rd., with No.7 platoon of 'B' Company, No.14 platoon of 'D' Company and 5 N.C.O.s and men of the R.E. (total party numbered 55). We assembled in CROSS ST. at 7.30am. the main party being divided into three working parties. At 7.45a.m. I moved off via WURZEL ST. and reached first and second barricades approximately at K.10.c.9.8½ and started to clear them. We were under heavy shell fire which became more intense as time wore on and I found it impossible to continue owing to heavy casualties. One barricade was removed and some shell holes filled in. Between 10 and 11a.m. I returned my party to WURZEL ST. and waited there half an hour. As no change in conditions took place I myself went back to report to the R.E. Major and O.C. 'B' Company and received orders to carry on when possible. I returned to the barricade myself and found conditions were impossible for work. I, therefore, took my men back to the village. About 2.0p.m. I again went to reconnoitre the position, but found that shell fire was too intense to work under. During work on barricades I had 25 to 30 casualties."

No.2333 Sergt. R.N. Prince platoon Sergt. of No.9 Platoon 'C' Coy. states:
"We were attached to the Kensingtons. We arrived at the assembly place with them in WARRIOR ST. at 7.25 a.m. we advanced down WARRIOR ST. with working material. We had great difficulty in advancing owing I think to wounded but when we got into the fire trench my part of the platoon was cut off by some Kensingtons ('A' Coy.). The Brigade Major told us to prepare to fight and we moved the material out of our way. I afterwards learned that the part of the platoon with Mr. Leigh was ordered by the Brigade Major to reinforce the London Scottish in the German 3rd line. They went over the top but on reaching the German wire a Major of the L.R.B. ordered Mr. Leigh to return as the position was being evacuated. Before Mr. Leigh had returned the Brigade Major in the trench had

ordered us to clear the fire trench. A written order was obtained for this and the men returned to assembly place in WARRIOR ST. I sent a runner to my O.C. Company reporting that we had lost touch with Mr. Leigh and I received an order to bring my men back to the Company in CROSS ST. I did so and then went to find Mr. Leigh. He received orders to take the platoon in reserve with the Kensingtons and did so. Soon after this he was badly wounded and then we received orders to rejoin the Company in CROSS ST. where we remained till the Company was sent down."

1/5th Battalion (Territorial Force)
Leicestershire Regiment

FONQUEVILLERS

Midnight. At midnight the Battalion was dispersed thus for battle: 'A' Company Capt. R. Ward-Jackson & 'D' Company Capt. Wyndham-Tomson, were in dug-outs & cellars in FONQUEVILLERS. Battalion Hd.Qrs., 'B' & 'C' Company, Lewis Guns, Bombers were in MIDLAND trench, an Assembly trench running N.& S. about 700 yds West of FONQ. Church. GOMMECOURT was to be attacked. The 46th Division was to advance in S.E. direction, the 56th in N.E. direction – The Park, the point of the salient was to be refused – the intention being to isolate the Park Garrison and to attack it from N.E. & S.E. at 3 p.m.

The position had been shelled by artillery and trench mortars for some days previously, and smoke barriers had been formed. Much wire however was left – dug-outs were not destroyed & M.G. emplacements were free from damage. The village was flattened out & the trees bared and torn down.

The 46th Division was disposed thus: The Notts & Derby Brigade on the left – the Stafford Brigade on right. The attack was to be in 8 waves. The 5th Leicestershire formed a 9th wave behind the Staffords of 'A' Company, 2 Platoons under 2nd Lieuts Hepworth and Salmon were to dig a Communication Trench from the Sucrerie, a ruin in font of our line, to the nearest point in the HUN first line. This work was actually started, Captain Ward-Jackson superintended until he was severely wounded & carried in by C.S.M. Hill.

Artillery had fired all night on enemy's approach lines. At 6.24 a.m. the bombardment of front lines began – at 7.30 a.m. the infantry advanced. The 56th Division reached the 3rd Hun Line and took prisoners, but were driven back. They lost many by the fire from PUISIEUX. A smoke barrier had been formed, but apparently this blew off at the time the 4th or 5th wave was starting across from the 46th Division. The Hun M.G's got into action & the attack of the 46th Division was held up at about 8 a.m.

The remainder of 'A' and 'D' Companies 5th Leics had been organised in carrying parties – ammunition, bombs, R.E. material, water. These parties started but were held up by lines in front which could not advance. 'B' and 'C' Companies with Lewis Guns started at 7.30 with the advance. They were to have taken up position in our old front line, but again were held up by waves in front.

3.30 p.m. A second attack was organised for 3.30 p.m. but it proved impracticable. The recent heavy rains had made the trenches sticky, and the task of sorting the units proved impossible.

3.50 p.m. At 3.50 p.m. orders were given for the 5th Leicestershire to hold our front line, and for the Staffords to withdraw.

4 p.m. This was done and the 5th Leicestershire remained in the trenches that night. The night and the following day were spent in clearing the trenches, collecting the dead and wounded and organising the stores.

1/4th Battalion (Territorial Force) Lincolnshire Regiment

FONCQUEVILLERS

7.30 a.m. Attack on GOMMECOURT, 1st wave 7th and 5th Nott & Derby, 2 Lt. Jelliott killed, 2 Lt. Gowers wounded, 2 Lt. Lee wounded, 2 Lt. Skinner shell shock.

We were relieved at night by 1st & 14th Co of Lon (London Scottish) & Kensingtons. We proceeded to HANNESCAMP trenches 'C' and 'B' Coys in front line and 'A' and 'D' in support. 1 case Diphtheria.

1/5th Battalion (Territorial Force) Lincolnshire Regiment

Very fine day. Daybreak found 1/5 Lincolns in Corps line 1,000yds east of SOUASTRE. But guns registering from 5AM onwards, & at 6.25AM intensive bombardment of the GOMMECOURT salient began. Hostile artillery at once replied and FONQUEVILLERS 1¼ miles away, was soon wreathed in smoke. At 7.20AM huge smoke clouds appeared & at 7.30AM the noise of the attack was heard. At 8.30AM the battn began to leave the Corps Line for the MIDLAND trench, 400yds N of FONQUEVILLERS. Enemy was now putting a heavy barrage on the village & occasional shrapnel on the plain west of it but the battalion marching by platoons at 300yds distance reached the MIDLAND TRENCH without casualties. The day was spent in this trench which was shelled occasionally, 1 O.R. being killed & 1 wounded.

At 8.30PM orders received to send 2 officers to reconnoitre German front line before GOMMECOURT WOOD & at 9PM orders received that the battalion was to attack this line & consolidate it at 11PM, 1/5 Leics R. digging a defensive flank on right back to our lines. It was represented that the 4 Co Commanders were away & that there would not be time to affect the relief of the remnants of 139 I. Bde & to form up for the attack in the time given. Time was, accordingly extended to 12 midnight at which time artillery was ordered to barrage on German second line while battn attacked front line in 4 lines of sections on a 4 Co. frontage.

At 9.30PM. bn began to leave MIDLAND Trench & proceeded through FONQUEVILLERS & then by ROBERTS AVENUE to its position, which was on frontage between WHIZBANG AVENUE & STAFFORD AVENUE.

Owing to congested state of trenches (they were full of dead bodies, badly battered by shell fire, & stragglers & wounded were coming in rapidly from NO MANS LAND) bn did not finally get into position until 12.45AM, 2nd inst.

O.C. Co's were met by battn on way up to trenches & had received their orders by 11PM.

At 11.30PM. orders were changed from 1 to 2 below.

1. Bn would attack & consolidate front line & reconnoitre beyond it getting into touch with any parties of Sherwood Foresters who might have entered hostile trenches on left of battn frontage & there been surrounded.

2. Bn would not consolidate but would retire as soon as in touch with Sherwoods bringing the later back too & in any case bn would retire to our lines before dawn.

Owing to enemy's fire & confusion caused by relief & the presence in all fire & communication trenches of parties of other battalions wounded or stragglers it was found impossible to communicate this alteration in orders before 12 midnight to the left Co.

1/2nd Battalion (Royal Fusiliers) London Regiment (Territorial Force)

HEBUTERNE

The preparations leading up to the attack on GOMMECOURT are detailed in last month's diary, and references are to the map appended thereto.

This morning the attacking troops were assembled in accordance with plans laid down.

5.0 a.m.   Battalion in position in reserve trenches between R. line and HEBUTERNE. Battalion Headquarters in dug-outs in YIDDISH STREET (Map Square K9 6 7.2). Battle police were in position at ends of communication trenches and prisoners of war guards were ready. All ranks were issued with hot pea-soup which had been prepared under orders from Division.

5.30 a.m.   There was considerable shelling on assembly trenches before the intensive bombardment began, but our Battalion suffered no casualties from it.

6.25 a.m.   Guns of all calibre commenced intensive bombardment of German lines.

7.16 a.m.   Smoke was discharged from 'Z' hedge. Assembly trenches now being heavily shelled.

7.25 a.m.   Smoke dense along whole Division front, and assaulting Battalions moved forward under cover of it.

7.30 a.m.   Artillery lifted from enemy's front line system, and assault commenced, lines advanced steadily in excellent formation, and enemy opened barrage fire on all our trenches. Nevertheless our troops reached enemy's trenches with comparatively small losses. Machine Guns in GOMMECOURT PARK opened fire. The enemy manned his parapet in places, but his rifle fire was ineffective. Sec Lt. J.W. Sanders, who had been detailed to take a party of 20 men of 'A' Company and carry 2" trench mortar ammunition to German front line, went over with third wave, but his party had suffered casualties during assembly and only himself and 8 men reached the enemy lines. They waited until it was clear that the trench mortars were not being brought over and then came back.

7.50 a.m.   Left Battalion (L.R.B.) had gained all its objectives and was consolidating.

8.0 a.m.   Company of 3rd Londons were ordered by Brigadier to commence digging a communication trench across NO MAN'S LAND.

8.7 a.m.   L.R.B. had erected name boards in FEN, FIR and FEAST trenches.

8.20 a.m.   Enemy still held FELLOW. Parties of Q.V.R. and Q.W.R. were lining NAMELESS FARM ROAD and were not in touch with Rangers (12th Londons).

8.30 a.m.   On the right, London Scottish (14th Londons) were holding as far as FAME FARM and S.E. corner of strong point K.11.C. Left Battalion of 168 Bde held FELT, FETTER and FATE but was held up at FELON, and its flank companies were reported to have been driven back. Q.V.R. held FEED, FEINT and FELLOW and were pushing forward.

8.35 a.m.   Germans appeared coming towards our lines with hands up; many were caught by barrage fire on NO MAN'S LAND. CEMETERY and FEUD now occupied by our troops, and a few L.R.B. were in MAZE.

9.0 a.m.   Work on new communications trenches across to German lines had not been begun on account of barrage, and 3rd Londons reported that work was impossible. L.R.B's were engaged in vigorous grenade fighting in GOMMECOURT PARK. Their consolidation was being checked by heavy rifle and machine gun fire from the left.

9.30 a.m. Hostile barrage had become very intense. Q.V.R. after hard fighting had taken all their objectives. Q.W.R. were mixed up with Q.V.R. but were making some progress up ETCH and EMS.

10.15 a.m. Enemy bombing down EMS towards FEUD and shortly afterwards seen leaving EMS and collecting North of CEMETERY strong point. Company of L.R.B. in GOMMECOURT PARK had been reinforced by two platoons and were still fighting hard with grenades.

11.15 a.m. Two platoons of Q.W.R. attempted to cross NO MAN'S LAND to reinforce but were stopped by barrage. Parties of hostile bombers had now got between parts of Q.V.R. left company in CEMETERY and others were seen advancing through GOMMECOURT PARK.

11.30 a.m. By this time about 80 prisoners had been taken back by our guards, mostly 170th Regt, with some 55th Regt (2nd Guards Reserve Divn, which had been recently brought up to strengthen the line) Q.V.R's attempted unsuccessfully to get through barrage with further supplies of bombs. Enemy machine-guns now firing from near NAMELESS FARM and ERIN.

11.40 a.m. R.F.C. reported FEUD, FELLOW and FELL strongly occupied by our troops. ETCH and EMS empty of troops. L.R.B's fourth company unable to advance through barrage.

12.30 p.m. Enemy launching vigorous counter-attacks down EPTE, EMS and ETCH and gradually forcing our troops out of his third line. Supply of bombs taken over in assault practically exhausted and German grenades being freely used.

12.40 p.m. Brigadier having stated that communications had failed, four men of our Battalion volunteered to try to get across with a written message from him to bomb up EMS and ETCH and take QUADRILATERAL which would be bombed until 1.30 p.m. Lance Cpl BOYCE and Corporal WERNER were successful in getting across. L/Cpl BOYCE came back with a message that Q.V.R. were retiring. Corporal WERNER decided to take his message as far forward as possible and was last seen entering German front line. He is missing.[1] Our troops were now being forced from enemy front line and were coming back. 'B' Coy was at once ordered to move up to our front line to right of 'Z' hedge and be ready for immediate action L.R.B. seen from our Battn HQ to be sending "S.O.S. – Bombs" on a shutter signalling board.

1 p.m. 'Z' hedge heavily shelled.

1.30 p.m. Brigadier ordered us to send one company with grenades to FERRET trench. 'D' Company ordered to carry this out. Q.V.R. sending back urgent messages for reinforcements.

1.45 p.m. Brigadier ordered us to attack FEN and FEVER and regain FEAST and FEMALE with two companies. 'C' Coy ordered to advance against FEN and 'A' Coy against FEVER.

2.0 p.m.   At this hour Division were holding on the right part of FANCY, west end of K.11.C and FALL. In the centre, isolated posts in German first and second lines. On the left, FERRET, FIBRE and corner of GOMMECOURT Park.

2.30 p.m. 'C' Coy (Captain P.J.A. HANDYSIDE) having moved up communication trenches to our front line at right end of 'Z' hedge, attacked in line across the open, but were met by a very intense barrage; machine gun fire from both flanks was especially heavy. Captain Handyside was wounded about 15 yards from our front line, but crawled forward encouraging his men until a shell burst over him and he was killed. Very soon the company was stopped by the fire, and had lost all its officers. None of the company were seen to enter the German trenches, though several were shot down near their wire. About 50 men, including many wounded, crawled in after dark.

3.0 p.m.   'A' Company (Captain J.R. GARLAND)[2] made a brave attempt to cross No Mans Land but only a few of them succeeded in reaching the German lines. The Company lost its officers; Capt Garland was killed by a rifle bullet. Practically all the N.C.Os were casualties, and about 35 men survived and came in later when the German lines were finally evacuated. O.C. 'D' Coy, who had been ordered to attack FERRET, reported that he had three times attempted to advance, but that the artillery and machine gun fire was too hot to hope to get across in sufficient numbers to make the attack worthwhile. Lieut H.W. Everitt and several men had been hit merely getting out of the trench.

3.15 p.m. Brigadier ordered us not to continue our attempt to reinforce, but to hold Y sector trenches.

3.30 p.m. At this time our troops still held part of K.11.C. on right, and parts of FERRET, FERN, FEN and FIR were being gallantly held by about 100 men of L.R.B., Q.V.R. and Q.W.R.

3.50 p.m. Enemy seen advancing from EPTE against FELL and FELLOW.

4.0 p.m.   Parties of right brigade forced out of German lines. Enemy massing in FISH, FIRM and near CEMETERY were dispersed by our artillery.

4.42 p.m. Orders received to reorganise, and prepare to take over German front line at dusk. 'B' and 'D' Companies were now holding fire trench, Boyan and support lines of Y sector.

5.15 p.m. Enemy seen massing at INDUS-FILLET junction. Parties of our troops continue to crawl into our lines.

6.5 p.m.   Orders to hold German front line tonight confirmed.

7.10 p.m. Verbal orders from B.G.C. to reconnoitre after dusk. He would then decide whether or not German front line should be held. At present the only hold we appeared to have on the enemy trenches was about 70 men in FERRET.

8.0 p.m.   Last survivors in German lines were seen to be coming back.

8.45 p.m. Men coming in state that there are now no unwounded men in the German lines.

9.45 p.m. Artillery on both sides practically ceased fire.

9.50 p.m. Orders received to put out strong covering parties in front of Y47 and Y48 and to occupy Boyan behind these trenches, with posts in front line. Seconds in command, and other officers who had been kept in reserve, rejoined for duty.

10.0 p.m. Survivors of 'A' and 'C' Companies were reorganised & with all available details went out to collect wounded but had not time to get all in before daybreak.

NOTES

1. Corporal Werner is not listed in the records of the Commonwealth War Graves Commission and is therefore assumed to have survived or been captured.

2. Aged 23, Captain James Richard Garland, the son of Richard Edmund and Olive May Garland, of 162, All Souls Avenue, Willesden, London, is buried in Gommecourt British Cemetery No.2, Hébuterne.

1/3th Battalion (Royal Fusiliers) London Regiment (Territorial Force)

HEBUTERNE

Battalion in position in front of HEBUTERNE, area "C" "Y" Sector, north of HEBUTERNE-GOMMECOURT road, to take part in the attack by the 56th Division, on GOMMECOURT. Task allotted to the Battalion is to dig a communication trench across "No Man's" Land, after the attack has been launched, from sap at "Z" Hedge to junction of FIR and FIRM in the German line. (See attached plan). Also to provide working parties to carry forward R.E. material for consolidating captured ground.

The Battalion will come under orders of G.O.C. 169th Brigade for these operations

7.16 a.m. Smoke commenced S.E. corner "Z" Hedge and some distance to the right.

7.25 a.m. Smoke all along the front. Smoke drifted well.

8.0 a.m.   Notified by Brigade that digging of C.T's might begin

10.10 a.m Digging of C.T's found to be impossible owing to the heavy barrage put up by enemy, causing numerous casualties.

1.5 p.m.   "Z" Hedge, occupied by 2nd Lt. Johnson and 15 platoon, heavily shelled.

One machine-gun destroyed, the only survivor being 2nd Lt. Johnson and one man.

1.32 p.m. Ordered to move 350 available men to Y.48.R.

8.25 p.m. Ordered to occupy Y.48.R. and Y.49.R.

9.45 p.m. Our artillery practically ceased fire.

Approximate casualties for the day – 3 Officers and 120 other ranks.

1/4th Battalion (Royal Fusiliers) London Regiment (Territorial Force)

2.45 a.m. The day of the Battle of Gommecourt. About 2.45 a.m. the Germans opened an intense bombardment on all assembly trenches, to which our Artillery did not retaliate and shortly afterwards a portion of the left assaulting Battalion was blown back from their assembly trenches into our area and caused great congestion of traffic.

6.25 a.m. Our intense bombardment began.

7.25 a.m. Smoke was discharged along the whole front.

7.30 a.m. The assaulting columns advanced and the Battalion moved from their assembly trenches into their Battle positions. Two Platoons of 'B' Company, who suffered 26 casualties during the previous bombardment, forming the fifth wave of the assaulting columns.

8 a.m. Communication was extremely difficult owing to the German barrage.

8.45 a.m. Orders were received for the two Companies in our front line to reinforce the Rangers left, in the German front line trench FETTER, and to move up the supporting Company 'D' to our front line. Of six runners dispatched with the message by different routes and two additional runners sent after 15 minutes interval, only one returned, having failed to locate the left Company. The others were all killed.

9.5 a.m. Information was received that the RANGERS and FUSILIERS were in the front line German trench.

10.25 a.m. Information was received that the leading Companies of the Battalion were over in the second line German trench.

10.45 a.m. The Battalion Trench Pioneers were went over.

10.53 a.m. The Brigadier required information of the situation of the left of the Brigade in the German line. Privates Whitehead and Buckingham volunteered to go across and report.

11.50 a.m. A message was received from Captain A.R. Moore (untimed) to say he was still in his preliminary battle position in WH9. A patrol was dispatched reporting on return that Captain Moore's Company had gone forward.

1 p.m.   Information was received from O/C 'D' Company that he had suffered 50% casualties and that the position had become intenable.

1.30 p.m.   The above patrol sent across to the German line returned with the information that the junction of ET and FELT in the second line German trench was held by a party of RANGERS under Lieut Harper and that he was urgently in need of bombs. At that time there were none of our Brigade in the German third line trench. This information was reported to Brigade Headquarters and passed on to O/C Rangers.

1.45 p.m.   A special bomb squad from our Battalion was ordered across but the party were all killed or wounded before reaching the German Line.

2.30 p.m.   The front of the Battalion Headquarters dug-out was blown in by a German high explosive shell which killed 7 men and wounded 7 others who were in the trench outside. The Commanding Officer, Major Moore, the Adjutant and Signalling Officer were in the dug-out at the time.

3.30 p.m.   'D' Company again reported heavy casualties.

3.45 p.m.   The Brigade Headquarters ordered the Company to withdraw to the W.R. line and the withdrawal (with a strength of 20 men) was reported by Captain Stanham at 4.45 p.m.

6.30 p.m.   Brigade Headquarters ordered the Battalion to reform in the W.R. line between WOOD STREET and WOMAN STREET.

The strength of the Battalion on the evening of the 30th June was 32 Officers and 890 Other Ranks, distributed between:

H.Q. and fighting line 23 Officers and 700 Other Ranks.

Transport and Depot 9 Officers and 115 Other Ranks.

Detached as Brigade Carriers 75 Other Ranks.

On the night of 1st/2nd July after the action 7 Officers and 356 Other Ranks answered at Roll Call.

In 'B' Company the clearing party both Officers were wounded and only about 10 men got back from the German line.

'A' Company, most gallantly led by Captain A.R. Moore, reinforced and reached the second German line, losing all its Officers and all but 18 men.[1]

Only two Platoons of 'C' Company got forward as the order failed to reach the Company Commander. This Company was very severely treated by the German Barrage, and was greatly extended owing to the front line trench being so much blown in. This accounted for the order not reaching the left of the line. All its Officers were killed or wounded and the company was brought out of action by Company Sergt Major Davis.

'D' Company, which was in reserve, sat through the most intense artillery bombardment from 2.30a.m. until withdrawn as above stated, by Captain Stanham, who kept them well in hand throughout the day ready to move forward if required.

NOTE

1. A Barrister-at-Law, and the son of Sir John Moore, Physician to H.M. The King in Ireland, 32-year-old Captain Arthur Robert Moore was killed on 1 July 1916. His body was never found or identified and he is commemorated on the Thiepval Memorial.

1/5th Battalion (London Rifle Brigade) London Regiment (Territorial Force)

HÉBUTERNE. July 1.

As already recorded in the previous month's diary, the Battn marched to HÉBUTERNE and took up their position in the assembly and front line trenches in the Y. sector. For the position of Coys, H.Q. etc see operations orders attached, which also gives the troops on our immediate flanks.

The smoke cloud which was most effectual commenced at 7.16 a.m. and at 7.27 a.m. the 1st waves moved forward followed by the remaining ones exactly in accordance with orders. The lines advanced in excellent order and the movements went like clockwork, so much so that by 7.50 a.m. all our objectives were reached. By 8.7 a.m. the work of consolidation had commenced.

Soon after this the first serious opposition was encountered in the shape of strong enemy bombing parties, whose advance was covered by snipers, some of whom were even up trees – heavy M.G. fire was also opened from reserve lines.

Bad casualties began to occur and 'A' Coy in FIR had to be reinforced by a platoon as they were having a hard fight in GOMMECOURT PARK where hostile bombers were particularly active. Bombs now began to run short and German ones were freely used. Owing to the very heavy and accurate barrage across No Man's Land, the reserve Coy although attempting it several times, were unable to get across with reinforcements and extra ammunition and bombs. The situation now became serious as our men were being driven out of the enemy's 2nd and 3rd line trenches by strong bombing parties, and finally men began to withdraw to our own lines.

Later our only hold on the German lines was in FERRET, but at dusk the men there were forced to withdraw so that at 8.45 p.m. we had no unwounded men, except those who had been taken prisoner in the hostile trenches.

It seems probable that although the actual attack was unsuccessful and was very costly, we killed a large number of Germans, but undoubtedly the attack failed on account of the lack of success by the Division on our left and also because we were unable to get the Reserve Coy across with the supply of bombs that were so urgently needed.

At 5 p.m. the officers who had been ordered to remain out of the attack had orders to go up and help reorganise. Major HUSEY during the day was with the 56th Div. H.Q. doing liaison work between the 46th and 48th Divisions.

VII CORPS

Documents Attached to the War Diary

An account by 9849 Sergeant H. Frost, 'A' Company:

Everything went well for the first few hours. We reached the enemy front line quickly and without many casualties, so far as I could see. Our formation was rather broken up owing to the difficulties en route but the corner of the PARK was distinguishable and we all got in somewhere near and spread along the trench allotted to the Coy. This trench was just inside the PARK and hidden by a hedge still thick in parts, especially at the far end. The Germans remaining did not offer great opposition. A number of prisoners were taken and sent across by orders of Capt. SOMERS-SMITH. About 40 more taken during the day were put into dug-outs and had to be abandoned in the final withdrawal. We never succeeded in gaining the whole of the "Strong point", partly because our own Artillery continued to play for some time on that section, and later on, because of the stronger opposition offered by the enemy.

Moreover a few of our men from the far end of our position had to be bent back towards 'C' Company (in the centre) as there was a gap between ourselves and them at that point and Germans were still in sight there. The situation began to get critical about midday and we were attacked more and more by bombers and snipers, causing us a number of casualties. We managed to hold on to our bit of trench however and, in fact, it was the last piece of enemy trench to be evacuated. The credit for this is certainly due to Sgt. LILLEY who worked very hard and courageously throughout the day. I cannot say how much I admired his behaviour. Another who helped greatly was a youngster working the Lewis gun posted in our trench. He kept his cool and never hesitated to expose himself, I do not know his name but McOWAN would. During the afternoon a strong attack was made against the other end of the line, chiefly by bombers. I understand our own supply was exhausted and that our men were using German ones found in the trench.

At 6 p.m. Sgt. LILLEY went and reported to Capt. de COLOGAN that our position was serious. Nothing had been seen of Capt. SOMERS-SMITH or Lt. BAKER for some time. From this moment we could see the other end of the line being gradually driven in towards our L.R.B. bit of trench. Twice we had seen parties leave the trenches and cut across the open. Finally at about 8 p.m. the remainder (possibly 100 of various Regiments) came rushing along to 'A' Coy trench followed by Germans who were showering bombs on them. There was no hope of holding on any longer and our party of 'A' Coy joined in the rush for the open quitting at point 94 ... What a pity we could not get up some supports. We could easily have cleared the PARK then I am sure. The result would have been so different. I was hit in right side of face when leaving the German trench and lost much blood. My body is badly bruised from concussion earlier in the day ... MUNDAY was very good too, helping with the Lewis gun though wounded in the arm.

SLAUGHTER ON THE SOMME: 1 JULY 1916

An extract from a letter written by Second Lieutenant R.E. Petley, 'D' Company (on the right):

"... If you get a chance I should like you to bring his name to the notice of the C.O. As you may have heard (Vide appendix C) I was left with about 30 men in ECK for about 3 hours after every one else had gone, having got the order to withdraw. I only got the order in reply to a message asking for more grenades. On our way back Sergt. Austin was a very great help to me in keeping off no less than four different bombing parties. He managed to hold these parties off while the chaps filed along and we reached the German second line with practically no casualties. It was in the independent rushes across the open that the casualties occurred. I lost sight of Austin during the last dash we had to make after being bombed out of our shell hole, having no bombs or ammunition left ..."

A report by Second Lieutenant R.E. Petley in response to a request by the battalion's C.O., Lieutenant Colonel A.S. Bates:

I will begin my narrative from the time of the assault. It was really magnificent the way every man, cool and collected, strolled out through quite a stiff barrage to the tape I had laid down 150 yards out during the night. The smoke lifted for a few seconds when we were out and I noticed the men were inclined to bunch on the right. I shouted an order and they shook out as if they were on WIMBLEDON Common. We (the first wave) got straight to our objective ECKE without very much trouble and before the whole of 'D' Coy were up I got into touch with the Q.V.R. on our right and with 'C' Coy on our left.

We got our wire out at once and started the work of consolidation immediately. Within a quarter of an hour of our arrival we were seriously troubled with snipers from the PARK and CEMETERY as well as a machine-gun from the rear. All apparently had gone well and Captain de COLOGAN sent several messages to Capt SOMERS-SMITH to that effect. After we had been in our positions about an hour I worked my way along the whole of 'D' Coy to see that the men were digging well etc. I got a slight wound in my shoulder for my trouble, but still things seemed to be going well, and our casualties were comparatively slight. We were then hoping soon to hear that the Q.W.R. and SOUTH STAFFS had reached their objectives.

Then a Q.V.R. man came and reported that he had lost touch with his Regiment and that only about a dozen of his men were on our right, also that they were being bombed. SMITH (Sec. Lt. 'D' Coy) went along to see what he could do and a message was sent back to H.Q. in EXE. I believe a party of Battalion Bombers tried to cut them off in the rear. However it soon became evident to us that the HUNS were bombing uncomfortably near us on the right and Capt. de COLOGAN moved further down ECKE towards EXE. I found myself in a sort of "Cul de sac" and managed to get into the main trench (if it can be so called) by making each man crawl singly over a big mound of earth while we kept the HUNS on our right down with bombs and sniping. As soon as we were all over we turned this mound into a barricade and managed easily enough to hold the Germans back.

I then went along to the left to find Capt. de COLOGAN but could find no trace of the rest of 'D' Coy nor 'C' Coy. I at once sent a message back to advanced H.Q. asking for more bombs and men. I heard from SMITH that this message did not arrive, and that as soon as de COLOGAN reached the front German trench, finding I was not there, he sent two different parties to try and reach us, but they were unable to get near. Apparently Capt. de COLOGAN had passed the order to withdraw down to me before he left ECKE, but as I did not receive it, and as we were holding the HUNS up on the right I could see no reason for withdrawing without orders.

I sent another message back for more bombs about 4 p.m. At 4 p.m. I sent the following to advanced H.Q.:

"I sent a message to you about 2 hours ago to the effect that I am holding on to ECKE with about 40 men including a dozen Q.V.R. and 1 Q.W.R. and that I wanted more bombs. Quite out of touch to right and left. Have held off Germans on our right with barricade. It is quite absurd to lay here at night as we are."

At 4.30 p.m. Sgt. ROBINSON appeared. He explained what had happened and brought me verbal orders to withdraw. I gave him the following message for Capt. de COLOGAN and told him to lead the party out.

"Sgt. ROBINSON brings me verbal orders to withdraw which of course we reluctantly must obey. Sgt. ROBINSON is bringing all the men down to you and Sgt. AUSTIN and I are trying to get Sgt. OLORENSHAW. Should like some hot dinner when we get back."

Sgt. AUSTIN, Cpl. THORPE and myself brought up the rear. Our idea was to try and bring one at least of the wounded back.

As soon, however, as the party started we were bombed rather heavily from FEMALE and of course I had to order all wounded to be left alone. We managed to account for two or three of the HUNS in FEMALE and kept them down until the rear of our party had passed the top of EXE. We worked our way round to about the junction of MAZE and FIBRE, AUSTIN and I bringing up the rear.

We had no less than four different bombing parties to keep off and the whole of my party got to the German second trench with only two or three casualties. It was in the independent rushes across the open, of course, that the casualties occurred, but even then most of us, I believe, got to the German front trench where apparently were the remnants of 'C' and 'D' Coys. and a lot of Q.V.R's. AUSTIN and I lay in a shell hole by the second line to cover as much as possible these final rushes. Our intention was to stay there until dark, but on a bomb bursting in our shell hole we cleared off before the smoke lifted. AUSTIN muttered that he was hit, but we did not wait to argue. We ran in different directions and I have not seen him since. Although the bomb burst practically on us I was unhurt except for a few tiny pieces in my legs.

I worked my way to the German front trench and joined the others. HARVEY, de COLOGAN, SMITH, COX of the Q.V.R., several other officers and about 60 or 70 men. They were being bombed from the right and it was evident that we should have to clear.

Most of the party, I am afraid, were hit in NO MAN'S LAND and I fear HARVEY and de COLOGAN were killed then. SMITH and I with about a dozen others held the HUNS off until the main crowd had cleared and then we rushed for the nearest shell holes. I was then hit in the knee and you can imagine the waiting till dark and crawling in etc.

There is an incident I should like to mention which shows that we had a decent lot of HUNS opposite and which would prove a source of consolation to the relatives of the missing. About 9.45 p.m. (early twilight) a German came out to us, and as I saw his red cross I prevented our men from firing. He came up, saw I had been roughly dressed, and went on nearer to our own lines to attend to one of his own men. Some of our men got up to go and he shouted out and stopped one of their machine guns. I think his action showed pluck and decency and augurs well for our wounded which we had to leave behind.

I have already mentioned Sgt. AUSTIN as being very useful in helping in our miniature rear guard action. Cpl S.A. EBBETTS, who was killed, also rendered me every assistance, and his brother was exceedingly useful in helping me and other wounded back.

I trust by now the Battalion is well back and I hope to be out again before you return to the firing line.

1/9th Battalion (Queen Victoria's Rifles) London Regiment (Territorial Force)

(ST AMAND) HEBUTERNE

Battalion left billets in St AMAND 8.0–9.30 p.m. 30.6.16 and took up position in assembly trenches, Y sector. Attack carried out as per summary being rendered next month.

Casualties:

Officers	Killed	6	Wounded	5	Missing	5
Other Ranks	Killed	51	Wounded	290	Missing	188

Document Attached to the War Diary

A report on operations at Gommecourt, 1 July 1916:

On the night of June 30/July 1 the Battalion moved up into its position of assembly as follows:

'A' and 'C' Companies in Y.4y. and the BOYAU de SERVICE. Attached to 'C' Company were 1 platoon 5th Cheshires and 8 R.E.

'B' Company in Y.4y.L. with ½ section 169th Trench Mortar Battery.
'D' Company in Y.4y.R. in reserve.
Battalion H.Q. at the junction of YELLOW STREET and Y.4y.R.
The objective of the Battalion was as follows:
'A' Coy through FEVER, FEINT, FELLOW, FELL and EPTE (exclusive)
'B' Coy through FERN, EMS (inclusive) FEED & EMDEN to FEUD STRONG
POINT & CEMETERY. As soon as STRONG POINT was established and EMS
was clear 1 platoon of 'C' Coy in FEUD was to occupy EMS getting into touch
with Q.W.R. at QUADRILATERAL. The platoon of 'A' Coy in FELLOW & FELL
were then to move to their left and be in support in FEUD & FELLOW.
'B' Coy through FEVER, FERR to FEINT, FEED.

A further phase to commence 3 hours after the time of the assault consisted in
bombing parties from H.Q. bombers and 'B' & 'D' Companies clearing
GOMMECOURT PARK and VILLAGE. These parties were to clear from STRONG
POINT and CEMETERY as far as the pond S. of the church and S.W. as far as
FIBRE and get into touch with L.R.B.

6.25 a.m. Intensive bombardment of enemy's line began.
7.20 a.m. Smoke began (five minutes too soon) from the 'Z' hedge and at [*sentence
           ends here*].
7.25 a.m. Smoke was issued all along the line and the first two Companies moved
           forward.
7.30 a.m. The Assault commenced, the artillery lifting off the enemy's first line of
           trenches.
           The Assault was carried out in a series of waves as follows:
           1st wave 1 Platoon each of 'A' & 'C' at 4 paces interval.
           2nd wave 2 Platoons each of 'A' & 'C' at 2 paces interval.
           3rd wave 1 Platoon each of 'A' & 'C' at 4 paces interval.
           4th wave 3 sections H.Q. Bombers, 1 Platoon Cheshires, 8 Sappers.
           5th wave 'B' Company at 2 paces interval.
           ½ section T.M.B.
           Signallers.
           As soon as the assault commenced the German Barrage was opened on
           to our trenches, though not severe at first it increased in intensity later.
9.48 a.m. By 9.48 a.m. the assaulting companies had reached their objective and
           occupied FEUD, FELLOW and FELL after heavy fighting. They did not
           however get in touch at EPTE with the Battalion on the right (the left
           Battalion of the Brigade on the right). At the same time the third
           Company was consolidating the German 2nd line. The Germans were
           pressing hard at this time and the shortage of bombs began to be felt.
10.30 a.m. In accordance with the orders as to the 4th phase, 3 sections of bombers

41

with battle police from the reserve company were ordered at 9.30 a.m. to join the companies in the German line. Owing to the congestion in Y.4y.R. and the communication trenches this party did not leave till after 10.30. As soon as the party left the trench they came under heavy machine gun fire and half the party became casualties immediately. This party was unable to get across No Man's Land the enemy's barrage by this time being intense.

11.0 a.m. Shortage of bombs became critical.

12.30 p.m German counter attack increased in force and the companies were
to driven back from the 3rd line to take 2nd line.
1.30 p.m.

2.0 p.m. Companies driven back to German 1st line.
About this time a few wounded men began to reach our lines.

4.30 p.m. The Battalion was ordered to collect all stragglers in our lines and hold Y.4y. strongly.

7.0 p.m. From this time up to about 7.0 p.m. survivors in German trenches kept up their resistance in the 1st line but at 7.0 pm. they were finally driven out and those who got across No Man's Land began to return to our trenches. After dark the Battalion took up the position in Y.4y.L. & Y.4y.R. and remained there for the night and the next day until the afternoon when it withdrew to BAYENCOURT.

1/12th Battalion (The Rangers) London Regiment (Territorial Force)

Report of Action of 1st July 1916
Part I: Diary

3.25 a.m. Reported to Brigade information as to enemy wire in Battalion front except Left Centre Company.

3.37 a.m. Reported to Brigade all Companies except Left Centre Coy in position and all wire to their front cut.

3.38 a.m. Reported to Brigade information as to enemy wire in front of Left Centre Company.

3.40 a.m. Reported to Brigade Left Centre Company in position and our wire cut.

4.30 a.m. Enemy commence shelling our three 'W' lines, and NAPIER.

5.30 a.m. Shelling by enemy slackened.

5.45 a.m. O.C. 4th London Regiment informs me by telephone the enemy had been shelling 'K' line severely.

6.10 a.m.   Right Centre Company reports about 20 casualties including smoke-bomb throwers.

6.15 a.m.   Right Company reports only five smoke-bomb throwers left.

6.25 a.m.   Intense bombardment commenced by our guns.

7.10 a.m.   Situation reported to Brigade by telephone.

7.25 a.m.   Smoke commenced.

7.30 a.m.   Assault started.

7.36 a.m.   German 4.2 still coming on to junction of NAPIER and WOMAN; also machine-gun fire apparently from GOMMECOURT.

7.45 a.m.   Reported to Brigade that Battalion went forward 7.30 a.m. but no reports back yet.

7.50 a.m.   Runner reports that all our four waves have crossed German front line and Fusiliers are occupying our front line, and that an Officer of the Royal Fusiliers was calling for reinforcements.

7.58 a.m.   German rifle fire increased.

8.2 a.m.   Officer from Right Company reports they are checked between German first and second lines by shell fire. Fusiliers have gone forward; reinforcements urgently needed.

8.5 a.m.   Runner reported that Right Company was back in our Boyau trench. Sent Mr Down to collect them and endeavour to advance.

8.10 a.m.   Runner arrived who stated he was sent on by O.C. 4th London Regiment, reported our Left Company had been beaten back by rifle and machine gun fire and bombs.

8.15 a.m.   Corporal Jackman, of 'B' Company, reports they got to first German wire. Our bombers threw a few bombs, Germans got up threw bombs and opened fire with machine-gun.

8.43 a.m.   Rfn. Livesley (runner) reports that Fusiliers and Rangers together are holding our front line.

8.55 a.m.   Arranged with C.O. 4th Fusiliers that when his two reinforcing Companies reach our front line the whole will advance again. Sent orders to my men to this effect.

9.0 a.m.   Reported this to Brigade Major.
            Message B.M. 46 received.

9.15 a.m.   'B' Company runner reports 'B' Company to be in German second line.

10.25 a.m. Runner from 'A' Company reports that Mr Parker is in German second line, and wants more bombs. Sent off carrying parties accordingly.

10.26 a.m. Reported above to Brigade by 'phone.

10.40 a.m. Explained our situation to London Scottish.

10.45 a.m. Liaison Officer rings up R.A. Brigade H.Q. and asks for retaliation on the 4.2, which has crumped junction of WOMAN STREET and NAPIER all the morning.

11.30 a.m. Bombing Officer (Mr.Higgins) reported that about 20 R.F. 4th London

Regiment, in BOYEAU near LONE TREE, and another 50 in support trench. Commanding Officer, 4th London Regiment confirmed this, and said he had been told to keep these men there by Brigade.

11.45 a.m.   Liaison Officer again reported to R.A. Brigade H.Q. that 4.2 was still troublesome.

12.00
Midday.   Reported to Brigade by telephone that situation unchanged.

12.5 p.m.   Explained situation to London Scottish (by telephone).

12.45 p.m.   Reported to Brigade that enemy still placing heavy barrage on "No Man's Land".

1.20 p.m.   Carrying party under C.S.M. Brown started with ammunition and bombs for Left Centre Company.

1.45 p.m.   O.C. 4th London Regiment (R.F.) reported that one of his runners had seen Mr. Parker and 12 men in FALL Trench where it joins the BOCQUOY ROAD and Mr Parker had told him to report this to me. The same man had met our bombers going up, but they were unable to get through enemy's barrage.

1.55 p.m.   Battalion Bombing Officer (2/Lt Higgins) returned and reported that it was quite impossible to cross the barrage on our front line trench.

2.20 p.m.   C.S.M. Brown returned to report was quite impossible to get his carrying party through barrage on our front line.

2.25 p.m.   Brigade Major informed me by telephone that 169th Infantry Brigade were holding enemy front in GOMMECOURT PARK. Also that one Company 1st London Regiment is in "W.R." line, and one Company 1st London Regiment is in Cross Street, and Brigade are asking Division for more counter battery work.

3.45 p.m.   Situation unchanged.

4.5 p.m.   O.C. 4th London Regiment informed me by telephone that he was withdrawing his men from our front line to the "WR" Line.

4.45 p.m.   Situation unchanged.

4.50 p.m.   Brigade Major reported that the entire Brigade had withdrawn to "WR" Line. Sent Battalion Bombing Officer and Battalion Signalling Officer to find, collect and organise our men.

5.45 p.m.   Two Companies 1st London Regiment (R.F.) relieve our men in "WR" Line. Our men moved into NAPIER in support. Sent back to Brigade Store for tools and water. Reported this to Brigade.

6.25 p.m.   Received orders from Brigade to reform Battalion in "WR" Line, and acted accordingly.

8.15 p.m.   Germans appear to be reinforcing with one Company their trenches South of GOMMECOURT PARK under fire from our artillery.

10.30 p.m.   Received orders as to relief tonight.

THE RANGERS 12TH LONDON REGIMENT
Part II: Narrative

The whole Battalion advanced to the assault at 'Zero', after which the sequence of events in each Company was as follows:

Right, 'A' Company

All four waves of this Company crossed the German front line, which was apparently unoccupied.

As the Company began to cross the German second line a small party of Germans came out of a dug-out and threw bombs at our men.

The London Scottish who were moving immediately on our right, threw bombs at these Germans, killing some of them and the German survivors ran back along the short length of FALL Trench which runs in an easterly direction from a point about 30 yards South of BUCQUOY ROAD. Our Company then came under machine-gun enfilading fire from their left, many of them were hit and the rest took shelter in shell-holes on our side of the German second line from which they opened fire on German Bombers who were bombing our two Lewis guns which had got into FATE Trench.

A party of some 15 to 20 men including the two Lewis guns appears to have been all that remained of the Company. This party was under the command of 2/Lt Parker.

It is reported that while this party was being collected a bombing party composed of Kensingtons and London Scottish were observed working along to the left of BUCQUOY ROAD in the direction of FELT.

2/Lt Parker then sent a bayonet man and two bombers along the short portion of FALL which runs in an easterly direction and these men returned and reported all clear; whereupon 2/Lt Parker took his party up that short length of trench and started to consolidate the eastern most end of it, at the same time sending out blocking parties to both his flanks.

This appears to have been the situation somewhere about mid-day.

At about 3.30 p.m. a mixed party of Q.V.R. and Q.W.R. came along from the direction of FELT followed by a party of Germans who were bombing them.

"The Rangers" party collected all available bombs and held their left barricade whilst the bombs lasted.

When the bombs gave out the whole party moved to their right and joined the London Scottish, from whom some bombs were collected and the Germans were again were again held back until all the bombs had been expended.

The Germans then bombed our party back as far as the southernmost communication trench leading from FARM to FARMER. From this point the "Rangers", Q.V.R. and Q.W.R. retired with the London Scottish down that communication trench and the sap continuation of it, and crossed "No man's Land" into our "WR" line, where the "Rangers" remained for the rest of the day.

The total number of unwounded survivors out of the Company is approximately: Officers 1. Other Ranks 49.

Right Centre, 'B' Company

When the fourth wave of this Company was about to reach the wire in front of the German first line they met a party including men of other companies coming back.

Corporal Tombleson of the Right Centre Company and another Corporal of the Left Centre Company collected about 10 men and advanced again, but only Corporal Tombleson and three men succeeded in getting through the wire (which was about 2 feet high) uninjured and they had to take cover in a shell hole between the wire and the first German line. The Corporal states that this shell hole was 25 yards from the German first line.

In this shell hole they found a wounded man of the Left Centre Company who stated that there were no "Rangers" in front of them.

Corporal Tombleson states that he was unable to detect any signs of the German first line being occupied until nightfall when star-shells were sent up from it at frequent intervals. After dark the Corporal and his party returned to our "WR" line.

The total number of unwounded survivors out of this Company is approximately: Other ranks 57.

Left Centre, 'C' Company

All the waves of this Company are stated to have crossed the German first and second lines. Before they reached NAMELESS FARM they came under heavy machine-gun fire.

By this time all the waves had become merged.

The line began to waver and the machine gunners of that Company under L/Cpl Saville opened fire on the German parapet with one Lewis Gun and fired off all their ammunition.

The line was then beaten back and retired to our original front line. The Corporal states that he went back for more ammunition and having obtained it he and Rifleman Bartleman took the gun forward again across the German first line, when they were again met by machine-gun fire which appeared to come from ROSSIGNOL WOOD, NAMELESS FARM, and the German 4th Line.

These two men state that they again returned with their gun to our front line and collected more ammunition and then advanced once more with the 4th London Regiment Royal Fusiliers.

The Corporal state that while crossing "No Man's Land" he was buried by a shell and dazed, and subsequently found himself back in a small dug-out near WOOD STREET with the Lewis Gunners of the 4th London Regiment, with whom he remained.

The total number of unwounded survivors out of this Company is approximately: Other Ranks 63.

Left, 'D' Company
The whole of the Company was held up by uncut wire in front of the German first line and came under enfilade fire from a machine gun on their left. This Company opened rifle fire on the Germans who were standing with their heads and shoulders above their parapets throwing boxed shaped hand grenades.

After about ten minutes nearly everybody in the Company was wounded.

Two Lewis gun teams then arrived and took cover in shell holes and also opened fire on the Germans.

There was a gap of about 20 yards in the German wire through which Major Jones led a party of about eight men until he fell wounded about two yards in front of the enemy's parapet and was seen to crawl into a shell hole.

Rifleman Perkins one of the eight men appears to have been the only one not hit.

He states that he got into the German trench where he was seized by two Germans but managed to beat them off by striking them in the face with a bomb he was holding in his hand. He then got back on to the German parapet and was seen by other men of the Company standing there throwing his bombs into the German trench.

Afterwards a party of three N.C.O.s and nine men (including Rifleman Perkins) returned to our first line where they remained until about 9.30 p.m.

The total number of unwounded survivors out of this Company is approximately: Other Ranks 46.

1/13th Battalion (Kensington) London Regiment (Territorial Force)

HEBUTERNE
After an hours rest in the valley by COIGNEAUX-SAILLY Road the battalion moved on by platoons to HEBUTERNE and arrived in main street at 12.5 a.m. As platoons moved past billet 101 they were issued with hot soup in petrol cans and collected their Lewis Guns and ammunition.

3.0 a.m.   All companies and details were in position in assembly areas by 3.0 a.m.

4.0 a.m.   Enemy began a heavy bombardment of our trenches with field guns 4.2 and 5.9 howitzers.

5.10 a.m.   Enemy has now been shelling our trenches for over an hour continuously and heavily with shrapnel and H.E. Some damage to trenches but nothing serious reported.

5.30 a.m.   Enemy bombardment considerably slackened.

6.25 a.m.   Heavy bombardment commenced by our own artillery this is the intensive bombardment preceding the assault.

7.26 a.m.   Smoke cloud began to be released.

7.30 a.m.   Zero Hour – Assault proceeded.

8.25 a.m.   1 prisoner was brought past Battn H.Q. slightly wounded. He belonged to the 170 Inf. Regt. and was born 7/2/93.

As soon as the smoke cloud was released the enemy began to put a barrage on No Mans Land. This barrage reached great intensity by 7.45 a.m. and was kept up by the enemy for many hours without any slackening. In addition to this, the enemy began with H.E. shells of heavy calibre systematically to blow in the English trenches. He began with the front line and worked back. The communication trenches also he shelled continuously.

The result of this was that 'A' Coy which had been detailed to dig a fire trench across No Man's Land were unable to carry out their task and under orders of Major Dickens parties were organised to go across to assist the London Scottish by carrying forward S.A.A. and grenades.

9.0 a.m.   One platoon of 'A' Coy and one platoon of 'C' Coy had gone forward and disappeared. Capt Ware had led one party and is believed to have been hit in taking them across. A portion of 'D' Coy had also gone across endeavouring to take ammunition to London Scottish.

9.15 a.m.   Casualties to [this] time estimated at 100 all ranks. Including 2 Coy Commdrs Capt TAGART wounded and Capt WARE wounded & missing. 2/Lt   also has been wounded. The clearing party which followed the London Scottish over has sent no report back.

No abatement of hostile shelling.

9.50 a.m.   Read verbal orders over telephone from Brigade that the left support Coy is to go across to fill the gap which exists between London Scottish left and Rangers' right. They are to over run "Fate" & "Form" trenches and hold & consolidate FAME trench.

10.0 a.m.   This order sent by runner to 'D' Coy.

10.30a.m.   Sgt Jones 'B' Coy came back from German trenches he had brought back Lt Penn who was badly wounded. He reports that the clearing party had received heavy casualties probably 50%. Lt Penn & 2/Lt Ball both wounded 2/Lt Pike still all right, but no bombs left.

11.15 a.m. Verbal message from 'D' Coy that 2/Lt Mager is killed & 2/Lt Parry wounded, 2/Lt Clark also believed to be wounded. Company has suffered heavy casualties and is very scattered in trenches; orders to assault do not seem to have reached the Coy by 11.0 a.m.

11.25 a.m. Capt Harris sent forward with orders to collect all available men in W.48 & W.48.S. and take them across to fill gap between Rangers & London Scottish.

11.30 a.m. No abatement of hostile bombardment.

'A' & 'C' Coys still sending small parties out with bombs endeavouring to take them to London Scottish. Casualties heavy, and trenches much damaged.

11.45 a.m. 'B' Coy Lewis detachments and a few bombers sent to occupy W.47.R. 2/Lt Bryce reported wounded.

1.30 p.m. Capt Harris returned to report that only 20 men of 'D' Coy left and these are left under 2/Lt Pilgrim manning W.48.trench. Impossible to take these men across to fill gap.

1.35 p.m. 2/Lt Dawes sent back by Major Dickens to report that there are only left about 50 men of 'A' & 'C' Coys in W.47. & W.47.S.

1.50 p.m. Party of signallers & servants with a few minor shell shock cases collected and sent under Capt Harris to man W.47.R. with 'B' Coy Lewis guns and any other men he could collect. 2/Lt Dawes sent to assist in organising this.

3.0 p.m. 2/Lt Mackenzie reported killed.

Major Dickson reports he has now 13 men with him in W.47. and asks for instructions. He is ordered to bring them to assist in manning W.47.R. & W.48.R.

4.15 p.m. Report received from wounded men that 2/Lt Pilgrim now has 7 men with him.

6.0 p.m. Enemy bombardment considerably reduced in weight.

6.25 p.m. Rec'd orders from Brigade to collect & reform remains of Battalion in W.48.R. and organise defence of that line.

7.0 p.m. 2/Lt Pilgrim killed. 6 men of 'D' Coy came back from W.48. into W.48.R.

7.30 p.m. Brigade H.Q. disconnected from telephone and moved back.

9.50. p.m. Verbal orders received from 167 Inf Bde that 8th Middx Regt is taking over W.Sector and relieving troops at present there. Kensington Battn is to move back to SAILLY where 168 Inf Bde H.Q. are now established.

10.30 p.m. Company of 8th Middx came in to relieve this battalion.

12.00
midnight. Battn arrived outside SAILLY and received orders to occupy the Corps line of trenches, which run just E. of SAILLY.

Casualties suffered on 1st July, 17 Officers & 310 O.R. Numbers taken into action, 24 Officers, 525 O.R. Quartermaster brought to the Battn in the Corps trenches a reinforcement of 100 O.R. from 3rd Civil Service Rifles 15th Londons.

Documents Attached to the War Diary

An account of operations by the battalion on 1 July 1916, written by Lieutenant Colonel W.H. Young:

The 56th Division was formed in January 1916, the infantry, being battalions of

London Territorials which had come out to France in 1914 and early 1915. They had originally been attached to Regular Brigades and several of them had suffered heavily in some of the earlier engagements.

Subsequently they had been withdrawn from the front line and had been employed on L. of C.

The Kensington Battn. was at NEUVE CHAPELLE and had also lost heavily at FROMELLES.

The 56th Division consisted of the 167th, 168th, and 169th Brigades, the 168th Brigade being formed of: 1/4th (R. Fusiliers) Battn. 4 London Regt, 1/12th Battn. London Regt. (The Rangers), 1/13th (Kensington) Battn. London Regt, 1/14th Battn. London Regt. (The London Scottish).

The Division remained in the back area until May when it was moved forward into the line, the front occupied by it extending from HEBUTERNE to a point opposite the western corner of GOMMECOURT PARK. During this period assembly trenches were pushed forward in front of the existing trenches in anticipation of the offensive which eventually started on 1st July.

At the time that I received orders to take over command of the Battalion I was at ETAPLES, and on 27th June a car was sent to fetch me.

The Battn. at the time was in billets at SOUASTRE and on the way there I called at Brigade Headquarters and reported myself to the Brigadier.

I found that the attack on GOMMECOURT was expected to take place on 29th June, also that the Colonel who I was relieving was still with the Battn.

It had been arranged that he was to command the battalion in the attack and that I was to wait with the transport and to take over command afterwards. As I gathered he was being removed from his command the arrangement struck me as being peculiar.

I enquired whether there were any points with regard to the Battn. which required special attention. After some hesitation the Brigadier informed me that the men were not good at digging. I remarked that I was not altogether surprised at this, having regard to the class of man one would expect to find in a London Territorial Battn. but that I would give the matter every attention.

I then asked if he could give me any information about the Company Commanders. He again hesitated and then replied that he really knew very little about them. This appeared to me to be an extraordinary statement as he had been in command of the Brigade for about 5 months. The Brigade had hardly been in action at all, so far as I know there had been no casualties and therefore there could not have been very much change in the Battn. (I knew nothing whatever about the Battalion and was therefore anxious to obtain all the information I could about it, especially in view of the fact that there was every probability of my having to take over command during offensive operations. It will be seen that my efforts were not very successful, the Brigadier volunteering no information or assistance of any kind. In addition it appeared to me that the Brigade Staff consisted of junior and inexperienced officers and altogether the general atmosphere compared most unfavourably with that in the Brigade I had just left.)

With regard to the question of the men not being much good at digging I will mention here a story which I heard subsequently from an independent and quite reliable source. When the Brigade started to dig the assembly trenches the Brigade Major – a young R.E. Officer – calculated the strength of working parties and time required for the work taking as his basis the task which could be done by a trained sapper working under normal conditions.

The men who in civil life were principally clerks, shop assistants, etc had had very little experience of digging. In addition to this there had been a good deal of rain; the ground was wet and stuck to the shovels, making digging very difficult. It is hardly surprising, therefore, that the tasks were not completed in the time allowed. The failure was attributed to slackness on the part of the regimental officers and men and gave rise to a certain amount of trouble.

After my interview with the Brigadier, which I may say had hardly inspired me with confidence, I proceeded to join the Battn. I saw the Colonel and told him what I had come for. I also informed him as to the arrangements that had been made for my taking over. He not unnaturally objected and went off to see the Brigadier. Shortly afterwards I received orders to take over command at once. (I never heard why this officer was removed from his command).

In the meantime orders had been received that the attack was postponed for 48 hours. I was much relieved at this as it gave me an opportunity of looking round the Battn, and also of visiting the trenches. (The 167th Brigade were in the line at the time and I gathered that the Brigadier was being relieved of his command. I do not know on what grounds, but I could not help noticing that his removal was giving rise to a good deal of unfavourable comment among the Regimental Officers of the Division.) As far as the Battn. was concerned I could find very little wrong.

The Brigade moved up to the assembly trenches on the night of 30th June and I reported the Kensington Battn. in position at about 3.0 a.m. on 1st July.

The Brigade was formed up as follows: First Line – London Scottish on the right, Rangers on the left. In Support – Kensington on the right, Fusiliers on the left. The Brigade front and objective are shown approximately on the plan.

The Kensington Battn. was ordered to find a clearing party to go over after the London Scottish and to clear the enemy's trenches behind them. We also had to dig a trench across "No Man's Land" in the position shown by the dotted line.

The following report gives an account of the business so far as the Kensington Battn. was concerned.

A report on operations on 1 July 1916, by 1/13th Battalion (Kensington) London Regiment:

Battalion marched off from SOUASTRE at 8.25 p.m. picked up tools, Grenades, etc, at BAYENCOURT, and arrived in the assembly trenches in front of HEBUTERNE between 1.15 a.m. and 3.0 a.m. on 1st July.

A platoon of the 5th Cheshire Regt. attached for wiring in front of the trench to be dug across "No Man's Land" assembled with 'A' Coy – the Company detailed to dig the trench.

The duties allotted to the different Companies were as follows:

'A' Company (Major Dickens) made up to 187 all Ranks (18 from 'C' Coy, 17 from 'D' Coy, and 17 Battn. Snipers) was detailed to move out from our trenches as soon as information was received from London Scottish that they had occupied the first line German Trench and to dig a Fire Trench across "No Man's Land" joining the British and German first line trenches and protecting the right flank.

'B' Company (Capt. M.R. Harris) was divided up as follows: Two Platoons for clearing party. 36 men Brigade Carrying Party. 12 men to Brigade M.G. Coy, for carrying Lewis Guns and remainder of Company in reserve near Battn. H.Q. under Captain Harris.

'C' Company (Capt. Ware) strength 90 all Ranks were to move forward as soon as the attack was started and to occupy the trenches left by 'A' Company and the right of the London Scottish.

'D' Company (Capt. Taggart) were similarly to occupy the trenches previously held by the left of the London Scottish. A clearing party strength 79 all ranks was to follow the London Scottish and to clear trenches, bomb Dug-outs etc.

4. a.m.	At 4 a.m. the Enemy started a heavy bombardment of our trenches with 5.9 and 4.2 Howitzers.
5.30 a.m.	This bombardment slackened somewhat about 5.30 a.m. Some damage was done to our trenches in places, but nothing serious was reported.
6.25 a.m.	At 6.25 a.m. our bombardment began and while this continued the Enemy's bombardment practically ceased.
7.25 a.m.	At 7.25 a.m. our smoke was started and the enemy at once put a heavy barrage over our first and second lines and also heavily shelled our communication trenches.
7.50 a.m.	At 7.50 a.m. the London Scottish assaulted and 'C' and 'D' Companies moved up and occupied the trenches left by them, and the clearing party went over after the London Scottish. Owing to the smoke it was impossible to see from our trenches what progress the London Scottish had made, and as no message was received from them Lieut. Beggs went out with a patrol to ascertain whether they had been successful in occupying the German first line trench. The patrol became separated in the smoke and Lieut. Beggs went on by himself. He got into the German trench and found that the London Scottish were in the first line and then returned to our lines.

Owing however to the heavy barrage which the enemy kept up over

"No Man's Land"and to Machine Gun fire it was found impossible to dig the trench. At intervals during the morning messages were received from the London Scottish asking for reinforcements and Grenades. Every effort was made to comply. A certain number of each men were got over but I have been unable to ascertain how many. Some boxes of Grenades were also got over at intervals during the morning. Capt. Ware displayed great gallantry in getting a carrying party over.

9.50 a.m. Instructions were received from the Brigade that a Company was to be sent over to FATE, FARM, and FALL trenches to fill a gap between the Scottish and the Rangers. 'D' Company was detailed for this duty and orders to this effect were sent to them.

10.5 a.m. Information received that Capt. Taggart commanding 'D' Coy was wounded.

10.30 a.m. As the front line had now become seriously weakened owing to men sent over in support of the London Scottish and to heavy casualties Capt. Harris was ordered to bring up the Lewis Guns and the remainder of 'B' Coy to trench W.47.R.

11.35 a.m. A message was received from 'D' Coy, that 2/Lieut. Mager was killed and 2/Lieut Parry was severely wounded and that the Company had not got beyond our first line. Capt. Harris was ordered to take command of 'D' Company and to endeavour to get them over. He returned subsequently and reported that only about 20 men of the Company were left, and that it was practically impossible to get over.

12 noon. Officer casualties reported up till 12 noon were as follows:
Killed: 2/Lieut. Mager, 2/Lieut. Sachs.
Wounded: Capt. Taggart, Lieut. Penn, 2/Lieut. Parry. 2/Lieut. Bryce. 2/Lieut. Beggs. 2/Lieut. Ball.

1.30 p.m. Collected 32 men (Signallers, runners, servants and Shell shock cases) and sent them under Cap. Harris to trenches W.47.R.
The bombardment still continued with unabated violence. The trenches in front of the reserve line were now practically destroyed.

3. p.m. Message received from Major Dickens reporting that he had now only 13 men left and that the front line trench had practically disappeared and asking for instructions. I ordered him to get back to the reserve line with his men and to take charge of the defence of it.

3.45 p.m. Major Dickens reported at Battn. H.Q. he had succeeded in getting his 13 men back and had collected some men of the Brigade Carrying Party. Capt. Harris also had been able to collect some men belonging to other battalions of the Brigade which he took up to trenches W.47.R. and W.48.R.

5.30 p.m. Bombardment ceased.
The men holding trenches W.47.R. and W.48.R. were sorted out and

collected in their various units and arrangements were made for holding the trench.

The total casualties incurred by the Battalion during the day in killed, wounded and missing were: 16 Officers, 310 Other ranks.

3-7-16. (sgd) W.H.W. Young, Major. Commdg 1/13th (Kensington) Battalion, London Regt.

Note. The total strength of the battalion when it went into the trenches was 24 Officers and rather over 500 other ranks.

A report on the attack on Gommecourt, 1 July 1916, by C.S.M. A.J. Evans:

I shall always look back on July 1st with pride and sorrow because it was humanly impossible to do more than the Division did, sorrow for the hundreds of gallant Londoners who laid down their lives in a desperate attempt to achieve the impossible.

I have never experienced shell fire to equal that poured by the German artillery into the unfortunate 168 and 169 Brigades. A perfect hurricane of high explosive and shrapnel met the assaulting waves, added to this was the confusion caused by our own smoke barrage, the chocked communication trenches and the terrible casualties, and yet in spite of all this, the attack was pressed home with great determination and the objective reached.

That the ground gained could not be held was due to the cutting off of help and ammunition by the furious and sustained shelling. Stunned exhausted and bitter, the survivors at the end of the day straggled back to their own reserve line, too dazed to wonder how they had come through too tired to care, and worst of all with the cruel sense of failure.

I doubt if the Division has a more glorious page to its history than this fateful day, instead of apparent failure it had most brilliantly attained its object namely, that of holding the Gommecourt front the vital infantry and artillery reserves of which the enemy had such pressing need to withstand our main offensive on the right.

Reinforced and reorganised after the severe fighting of July 1st the Division took part in further heavy fighting on the Somme front in September. Here it maintained a reputation for fighting and endurance of which we shall always be proud.

With hardly a square yard of ground untouched by shell fire, carrying parties, ration parties and reliefs proved an experience never to be forgotten.

I recall an incident which for human endurance would be hard to beat.

A party of 80 under an Officer started away one night about 5 p.m. in full battle order, each man carrying 3 stokes mortars in a sandbag. With a guide from the T.M.B. the party moved slowly forward over the difficult ground. For a time progress was steady but as the darkness increased and with it, heavy shellfire, it became difficult to keep the big party closed up and together.

Nearing the front line a fairly heavy barrage was encountered and finally to cap all, the guide now confessed that he had lost the way. Shortly afterwards in his efforts to recover his direction, he became separated from the party and was not seen again. Without a guide or even an idea as to direction, the men now lay down in the open, whilst the officer and N.C.O.s endeavoured to locate the battery. In this, by rare good fortune, they were successful.

It was afterwards found that the party had narrowly escaped blundering into the German outpost system, a fate which had already overtaken a draft of reinforcements. To do this was quite easy when one remembers the absence of a definite trench system and the uncertain position of our own outposts.

Restarting by some mischance, only about half of the party moved off and they arrived at the Battery safely, but in dumping the mortars they were heard by one of the enemy outposts and heavily fired on, losing several killed and wounded. It was now discovered that half of the party was missing and a N.C.O. was sent to fetch them in, which, after considerable trouble in finding them, he succeeded.

Exposed as they were an immediate start back was made, the reserve area being reached about 7 a.m. the following morning, in what state of exhaustion can better be imagined than described.

The foregoing is typical of what was happening every day and night in this memorable battle.

Of the Division's great part in the capture of such famous places as Combles, Guillemont, Ginchy, Les Boeufs and Morval much has been written.

The spirit shown and maintained must always make London look with pride on the part taken by its sons in the Battle of the Somme.

1/14th Battalion (London Scottish) London Regiment (Territorial Force)

Bn. in action. Assault on German trenches E of HEBUTERNE and 250 yds N of SUNKEN ROAD, HEBUTERNE – PUISIEUX.

Documents Attached to the War Diary

An account of the battalion's actions on 1 July 1916:

30th June

11 p.m. Battalion Scouts examined wire in front of FARMYARD Trench it was found uncut for over 100 yds from the right and Bangalore Torpedoes were successfully placed under it and exploded.
Further N. it was cut, N. of HEBUTERNE-BOCQUOY it was uncut.

SLAUGHTER ON THE SOMME: 1 JULY 1916

1st July

1.30 a.m. Message sent to MACART Group R.F.A. asking "for guns to fire wire cutting fire to clear front thoroughly".

7.28. Right and right centre Companies moved over to Tape which had been placed out on neutral ground overnight to bring our line of men parallel to German lines.

7.30. LONDON SCOTTISH moved forward their 4 Companies side by side 'A' on the right, each on a frontage of 1 platoon.

The smoke was good but it was thicker than in practice & it was hard to keep direction. The smoke barrage put up by the troops on our right until 8.30 a.m. was very good.

8 a.m. Situation:

'A' Coy, Capt SPARKS,

No.2 [*illegible*] missing

No.3 Petrie & 5 men reached FAIR Trench

No.4. went through a gap in line S. of FARMYARD and occupied objective with some opposition.

No.1 Capt Sparks followed & started consolidation there.

Cpl BAIN held Fair, L/Cpl. AITKEN bombed down – pushed back German bombers & R.E. got to work on a block. Capt Sparks, his H.Q. & 2 Lewis guns held CT between Fair and FANCY on a fire trench.

2/Lt. SPEAKE & PETRIE held FARM & blocked FANCY.

Snipers were established in good position. Communication with 'B' Coy established in CT between FARM and FABLE.

'B' Coy, Major F.H. LINDSAY

Occupied objective assigned to them by 7.45 a.m. consolidation began & work of blocking FABLE. This was interfered with by enemy bombing attacks, which were driven off. This was helped by L/Cpl. THOMAS with 1 Lewis gun who chose a good position; and though he only had 3 magazines he did very good work.

'C' Coy, Major C. LOW D.S.O., Lt. H.C. Lamb.

11 Platoon led – 12 next under Major Low the wire was cut. They swept right over and occupied FABLE Trench after some fighting, Major Low was wounded in fighting with his pistol.

9 and 10 Platoon were delayed in German trench line by opposition from Germans who had come up from dug-outs & by the enemy artillery who started firing at FARM & FARMYARD Trenches.

Lt. Lamb took over from Major Low who was taken back to the Doctor. He then took on his two platoons as owing to the smoke & derelict condition of trenches both officers thought they were in FARM.

These platoons reached the NAMELESS FARM Road to the right of

ELBE Trench & were fired on from EDEN they withdrew to their objective by sections the remainder opening covering fire. The smoke had now cleared.

'D' Coy,   Lt. J.C. BROWN CONSTABLE.

Went over but suffered very severely from German barrage fire. No.16 & Lewis gun in reserve lines being entirely knocked out before they reached our wire.

No.13 which led was held up by uncut German wire & bombers & snipers in FATE Trench.

Lt. Constable & No.14 came up and by his skill he got a footing in the German line & reinforced by No.15. they bombed there way up to FALL Trench and northwards along FATE. Suffering severely by rifle fire from loop hole traverses but progress was made by our bombers getting out and rushing them over the open.

Touch was obtained with the RANGERS in FATE Trench, but the enemy remained on our left in FAME & FALL Trenches and made Bombing attacks which were driven off and the trenches blocked.

Clearing party of Kensington Bn. suffered very severely coming over but their remaining parties did good work in FARMYARD Trench.

10.15 a.m.   Situation:

At Bn. H.Q. messages had been received from Capt. WORLOCK at the end of WELCOME St. "20 prisoners have come over, 4 LONDON RANGERS found German Trench fully manned and cannot get in."

From 'C' Coy giving situation, Casualties: 3 Officers, 80 OR

From 'A' Coy giving situation, Casualties: 1 Officer, 50 OR

From 'B' Coy giving situation, Casualties: 50 OR

No message received from 'D' as they had lost all Officers and N.C.O.s and ceased to exist as a separate unit.

From this it was apparent that SAA & Bombs were urgently needed and therefore at 9.15 a.m. 1 Bombing Squad & 1 NCO and 20 Carriers

9.45.   1 NCO & 20 Carriers

10.   1 Bombing Squad & 6 Carriers

3 reserve Lewis Gunners were all sent forward, i.e. 59 N.C.O.s & men in all.

Owing to German Barrage fire on our Trenches on NEUTRAL ground and in FARMYARD Trench only 3 of these men reached the German lines the others were hit.

Situation 2. p.m. Other units.

A missed party of RANGERS, QVR and KENSINGTONS, made a stand at in FALL Trench and in FATE, the former were driven back to FATE by hostile bombers as they themselves ran out of bombs. They made a brave stand in FATE.

Lt. F.S. THOMPSON of the LONDON SCOTTISH Section of the 168th Bde M.G. Coy came over. 1 Gun team arrived & took up its arranged position. Sgt. STRACHAN went back for the other; No.1 has been hit in neutral ground but had gallantly crawled on with his gun to the german lines.

A party of KENSINGTON Bn brought 5 Boxes of Bombs. 1 Officer, 50 men had started through the Barrage.

About 40 German had been captured and had received instructions to go over to our lines through their own barrage.

A message giving situation had been sent to the WARWICKS on our left.

Situation 2.30 p.m.

'A' Coy.   H.E. fire very heavy.

Cpl. BAIN & Cpl. FAIRMAN still held FAIR Trench, & new block made Southern face before FAIR & FANCY was destroyed.

New firing line made in trench "behind" it by the SPEAR.

Covered by 1 Lewis Gun & Lt. THOMPSON & 1 Vickers gun to the South & by 2 Lewis guns to the East.

L/Cpl AITKEN & snipers picked off enemy bombers.

FARM consolidated and good fire steps made.

'B' Coy.   2/Lt. WHITE YOUNG held FAME & part of FALL.

But severe pressure on both flanks with left in the air necessitated a withdrawal to FALL.

A party works on restoring a communication trench to FARMER.

The 2 Lewis guns had good positions in FALL.

Severe losses were inflicted by enemy rifle men some of whom wore a green uniform.

About this time Major Frances Lindsay arranged for Capt SPARKS to rest, but the Major was killed while walking back.

'C' Coy.   Had acted in unison with B.

The re-adjustment was helped by further good work by L/Cp THOMS with a Lewis Rifle.

Sketch B shows the new position.

Situation about 4 p.m.

The troops on our left had withdrawn, Capt H.C. SPARKS who had commanded since Major Lindsay was killed said "I am faced with this position, I have collected all bombs and SAA from casualties, everyone has been used, giving the enemy's continued barrage fire none can be brought to me

I am faced with 3 alternatives:

(a) to stay here with such of my men as are alive; and be killed.

(b) to surrender to the enemy.

(c) to withdraw such of my men as I can.

Either of the first two alternatives is distasteful to me. I propose to adopt the latter."

He therefore gave orders for all wounded to be withdrawn and sent Lt. GAVIN to the Southern Sap in FARMYARD to send them over in small bodies.

After giving them time to withdraw Lt. THOMPSON & the Vickers gun and arranged a methodical evacuation of the position, he did this so coolly that in spite of the fire, and the boldness of the enemy due to our having no ammunition that his arrangements were carried out and there was no confusion.

Capt. SPARKS, SJTS LATHAM, LEGGAIT Cpl. FAIRMAN and WESTON with 1 Lewis gun held the German parapet to cover the withdrawal and remained there keeping off the enemy until all others had got away. His other Lewis gun had been put out of action by his order before moving. Capt. SPARKS himself had to remain in a shell hole 50 yds from the enemy line for 4 hours.

The Battalion was reformed in the old British Front Line just N of the road from HEBUTERNE to PUISIEUX.

There went into Action: 23 Officers and 811 soldiers*, 1 Officer and 36 Medical Staff and S.Bs of these, 5 Officers and 62 O.R. were not ordered to go over to the German lines.

There remained the next morning: 9 Officers and 236 O.R. and 21 Medical Staff and S.B.s

I am sending details of German method, bomber etc later.

Bernard C. Green, Lt. Col., Commanding London Scottish.

A report submitted to 168 Brigade, for the attention of Commander Royal Engineers, 56th Division, dated 7 July 1916:

Report on work of section 2/2 London Field Co R.E. under Lt. VILLA during action on 1st July 1916.

The Section was divided as follows.

Lt. VILLA and 1 N.C.O. 10 men in Reserve,

Remainder divided into 4 parties, each party attached to the Company whose duty it was to block FAIR, FANCY, FACT and FABLE Trenches respectively. They carried tools and demolition material.

In the assault they went with the 3rd wave these attacks to the right Company 'A' reaching their objective, the Bombers being successful they were able to get to work at once on the block in the hostile first line, did it by demolishing 3 traverses & making it very good.

The block in the 2nd Line was also carried out very well under the exceedingly difficult circumstances.

The other 2 parties also got to their objectives, but owing to the very heavy fire, casualties and the failure of the troops on our left they were not able to carry out what they had set out to do and one party with very great gallantry moved over to make a hasty block to protect our left.

Throughout the action the R.E. behaved very well indeed, they carried out their work regardless of the very heavy howitzer fire and rifle fire of the enemy and they earned the very high respect and regard of all those who fought beside them.

Their very fine behaviour must have been largely contributed to by the training and leadership they had received before the action.

I have formed a high opinion of Lt. VILLA's abilities and have recommended No.2431 Cpl. A.E. PERRETT for the Distinguished Conduct Medal.[1]

An extract from a private letter written by Lance Corporal Aitken:

It nearly broke my heart to have to retire from those swine, we had held them easily all day & when they tried to bomb we leathered them & had at last frightened them into silence. It would have helped me greatly had the men picked up and brought to me all the bombs they could find but they were afraid to handle them, this should not be.

Another thing the machine (Lewis) gunners were knocked out & no one there except myself knew how to fire it.

A general lecture on this gun would prove of value as it is very simple & easy to handle.

Please don't think that I am trying to run things but these points struck me at the time & I put them forward for what they are worth.

NOTE

1. The award of the Military Cross to Corporal Perrett was announced in *The London Gazette* of Friday, 1 September 1916.

1/16th Battalion (Queen's Westminster Rifles) London Regiment (Territorial Force)

Attack on GOMMECOURT (detailed report attached). Survivors of the Battn remained in Road Support Trenches at HEBUTERNE during the night July 1st to 2nd.

Casualties – Killed Offs 2, O.R.16, Wounded Offs 9, O.R. 224, Missing Offs 9, O.R. 241, Sick O.R. 1, Other causes 1, Reinforcement 1 O.R.

Documents Attached to the War Diary

An account of operations by the battalion on 1 July 1916, written by the Commanding Officer:

HEBUTERNE

7.30 a.m. The Battalion assembled on the night June 30th/July 1st in the assembly trenches in Y.47. area, and at 7.30 a.m. advanced to the attack following the two leading Companies of the Queen Victoria Rifles – 'A' Company on the right – 'B' Company on the left – in columns of Platoons in line abreast at 30 yds distance; 'C' Company together with the H.Q. Bombers following in similar formation.

'D' Company which had assembled in the old 'R' Line and was in support, was moved forward almost immediately by Captain Glasier to the assembly trenches which our front Companies had moved out of - ready to reinforce or take up material for consolidation.

The enemy first and second line trenches were much more strongly held than had been expected and their deep dug-outs seemed practically all to have been undamaged by the artillery bombardment, and both in front of the front line and of the 2nd line enemy trenches a great deal of the wire was not cut at all, so that both the Victorias and ourselves had, in places, to wait and file in close order through the gaps, and many were hit doing this in both these two German lines. And in both of them a certain number of the enemy who had emerged from their dug-outs or been got out by the Victorias were still engaging their attention. So that, as the advance was being made under heavy Machine Gun Fire from our right from certainly two Machine Guns (one by NAMELESS FARM and one from about 30 yards on the South side of the ETCH communication Trench in the enemy front trench FEVER) and also under rifle fire from FELLOW itself, the losses were heavy before reaching the bank on the enemy side of the GOMMECOURT-NAMELESS FARM ROAD, which the Victorias were lining.

At this point our 3 Companies and the two of the Victorias were joined up and intermixed. As no Officer who got as far as this has returned and only one Sergeant, it is extremely difficult to know in detail what happened and still more difficult because signal communication across "No Man's Land" was never able to be established, and as only one messenger from the Companies on the other side of it ever succeeded in getting through, no information except this one message brought by Rifleman Orchard (Signaller) from the GOMMECOURT-NAMELESS FARM ROAD received at 8.30 a.m. was received until the evening, except what was obtained by observation or given by the Royal Flying

Corps, and some of what was given by the Royal Flying Corps was, as is not hard to understand, not correct. But clear statements say that Captain G.R.COCKERILL Commanding 'B' Coy and Captain H.F. Mott, Commanding 'C' Coy were both killed crossing the 1st Line German trench (FERN) and that Captain F.G. SWAINSON Commanding 'A' Coy was killed shortly after leaving the 2nd Line German Trench (FEED).

It was from this junction of the NAMELESS FARM ROAD with ETCH that 2nd Lieut J.A. HORNE of 'B' Company, the senior Officer left, 2nd Lieut A.G. VYATES and 2nd Lieut A.G. NEGUS and 2nd Lieut D.F. UPTON of 'C' Coy and 2nd Lieut E.H.BOVILL of 'A' Coy, collecting their men together dropped into ETCH Communication trench and bombed up it into and along FELLOW, along which 2nd Lieut UPTON led one bombing party and thence along FEUD nearly to the Cemetery, where some German bombers held them up for a time. When they had in this way cleared these trenches, they put up one of the Battalion sign boards, on seeing which, the men still lining the NAMELESS FARM ROAD, came over the open and dropped into them.

It was by this junction of FELLOW and ETCH that 2nd Lieuts YATES and NEGUS were killed.

2459 Lance Corporal D. Newton, 2613 Rfn A.E. Clark and another bomber tried to bomb up ETCH, but it was too strongly held and they were driven back. They then blocked ETCH and also FELL (the enemy 3rd Line trench to the South of FELLOW) with the assistance of the Platoon of Cheshire Pioneers and of the R.E. Sappers, who are reported to me to have worked most gallantly under the covering fire of a Lewis Gun mounted by 2nd Lieut HORNE and the only gunner left.

8.30 a.m.   By this time some more of 'B' Coy, among them 2969 Corporal F.E. Hayward, 2nd London Regiment attached Queens Westminster Rifles, some of 'C' Coy and some of the H.Q. Bombers worked up by the Cemetery and up EMS and the whole of FELLOW & FEUD were now in our possession.

1799 Sergeant W.G. Nicholls who, after Lieut P. Spencer-Smith had been wounded, after crossing the 2nd German Trench (FEED) had been in command of the H.Q. Bombers Section with some of this section and I believe led by the young Cheshire 2nd Lieut [*illegible*] continuing with others, among them, 1687 Corporal R.T. Townsend 'C' Company, 2936 Lance Corporal W.C. Ide (2nd London Regiment attached 1st Queens Westminster Rifles) 'C' Company, Corporal Hayward 'B' Company, 2755 Rfn F.N. Stow 'D' Company, up EMS undoubtedly did actually reach the QUADRILATERAL, where a strong enemy bombing party met them and the Cheshire 2nd Lieut ordered our party to retire – apparently trying to cover their retirement himself, as he has not been seen since.

9.30 a.m.   SUPPORT COMPANY. This Company was ordered at 9.20 a.m. to send a Platoon up with all the bombs they could carry to reinforce the front, thought then to be still held up on the GOMMECOURT-NAMELESS FARM ROAD with written orders to the Senior Officer present to try and bomb up ETCH, EMDEN and EMS. There was by this time only one Officer left with 'D' Coy and the Coy Sergt Major had also been killed. 1704 Sergeant H.E. Ironmonger tried to get his Platoon across, but the Machine Gun Fire and Artillery barrage made it impossible and he withdrew the few men who were not hit.

11.0 a.m. At this time another attempt was made to reinforce the front Companies with the remaining Platoons of 'D' Coy and to get bombs up to them, but it was not possible to get through the enemy barrage and Machine Gun Fire. The last remaining Officer of 'D' Coy had now been hit.

1.0 p.m. Attempt to reinforce again repeated but it could not be done.

1.30 p.m. It was reported that the front Companies were being driven back from FELLOW. H.Q. Details runners etc turned out to the French trench in front of Cross Street.

9.0 a.m. SITUATION IN ENEMY TRENCHES. These trenches were under heavy
to Machine Gun fire chiefly from our right. A good many enemy dead were
1.45 p.m. found in these trenches. Many of them, at any rate having been killed during the previous night and this morning's artillery bombardment.

12 noon. Soon after 12 noon strong bombing counter attacks were made by the enemy both down EMS but principally from the direction of GOMMECOURT and down FILM. Our own supply of bombs was exhausted as well as the German ones of which a great number were taken from German Prisoners or found in the trenches in which they were stored in large quantities and at 12.30 p.m. 2nd Lieut J.A. HORNE who had displayed the greatest gallantry during the whole morning, organising and directing men all along FELLOW and shooting with a Lewis Gun when all the team had been knocked out, decided to withdraw to the next line of German Trenches (FEED) and it was in covering this withdrawal that he was hit and believed beyond doubt to have been killed. This left only 2nd Lieut E.H. BOVILL, who had been wounded in the nose very early in the morning, but who carried on most gallantly with his Platoon all day – and 2nd Lieut D. UPTON of all the Officers who went over the top in the morning. This 2nd Line of German Trenches becoming also untenable they decided at 1.45 to withdraw further to the 1st German line, most of them to FERRET where they stayed, still hoping at night to be reinforced and able to hold their own, but at 7 p.m. the enemy began to surround them coming in from both flanks and the supply of bombs being entirely used up, as well as all the German ones they could find, they were compelled to retire across the open to our own lines.

2nd Lieut Upton by this time wounded was unable to get away and is missing. He was the Officer who had led the bombing party along FELLOW in the morning and he and 2nd Lieut BOVILL had displayed great gallantry all day in reorganising the men and carrying on the attack and defence as long as they had bombs either of our own or enemy ones that could be got, and later when forced to withdraw in carrying out the withdrawal from trench to trench.

7.30 p.m. 2nd Lieut BOVILL is reported to have been almost if not quite the last to leave the last enemy trench and it was cruelly hard luck that he should have been killed on the very parapet of our own trench, as he was just stepping into it.

MACHINE GUNS

The Vickers Gun which accompanied 'A' Coy got as far as the junction of ETCH, FEED and FEINT and was there brought into action by 2nd Lieut ENGALL (Q.W.R. attached 169. Inf. Bde M.G. Coy) who had only one of his team left with him – he fought the gun himself until he was killed at this spot.

TRENCH MORTARS

Two of the Trench Mortars were taken up to the enemy front line and probably further – one is thought to have been brought back on the retirement and fired from a shell hole in "No Man's Land" but I have obtained no authentic information on this. The other two, as well as those who were to have gone forward to make the smoke barrage up ETCH and EMS were apparently all knocked out during the bombardment previous to Zero hour.

ACTS OF GALLANTRY etc

Owing to there being no Officer returned from the other side many meritorious acts cannot for the present at any rate be brought to notice, neither those done by men killed and wounded, nor by those who came through it, but I desire to particularly bring to notice the most gallant conduct and bearing of 2nd Lieut J.A. HORNE who by his example and leading inspired and helped all who came within his reach. I have every reason to fully believe that his gallantry and leading merit a recommendation for the Victoria Cross. All who are returned speak in glowing terms of his most gallant conduct. I deeply regret to fear that there is practically no chance of he having survived as he was seen to be wounded very severely.

I desire also to specially mention 2nd Lieut E.H. BOVILL who though wounded early in the day carried on with his Platoon most gallantly until the final withdrawal, during which he was killed.

And 2nd Lieut D. UPTON (2nd London Regiment attached 1st Queens Westminster Rifles) who led the bombing party along FELLOW in the morning and who also did gallant service all day long.

VII CORPS

And 2nd Lieut J.B. ENGALL (Q.W.R. attached 169th Inf. Bde M.G. Coy) mentioned above. (Missing and Killed)

Of the N.C.O.s and Men – I have the honour to forward the attached recommendations for immediate reward etc, etc. (See Confidential Papers "Recommendations for Awards.)

A report on the attack on Gommecourt, 1 July 1916, signed by the Commanding Officer:

Headquarters, 169th Infantry Brigade.

Points which occur to me to be worthy of consideration arising out of this day:

1. That nothing like the full value can be got out of Machine Guns if they only have teams of four. The guns so quickly get put out of action through casualties to the personnel. I consider that every Machine Gun should have a team of eight and should go into action with a team of this number.

2. With reference to Lewis Guns, the drum magazine is so easily damaged, and then, of course, becomes unusable on the gun, and is also bulky and inconvenient to carry. Our Lewis Guns in more than one instance appear on this day to have been unable to be kept in action on account of want of ammunition or of damage to the drums which prevented them from being used, but as none of the Lewis Gun Teams have returned I am unable to give authentic information on the point. Perhaps someone else will be able to say definitely whether there is anything in this or not.

3. It is again clearly proved that the only way to get up the number of men who are required for consolidating, and also the stores to do it with, is together with the assaulting troops, otherwise it is impossible to get them up at all. Neither our own Artillery nor the enemy seem able to put in such effective counter battery work as can, on the day of battle, stop the others Artillery barrage.

4. It is again clearly proved how essential it is for the holding of captured trenches that every man should be a qualified bomber and that a sufficient supply of bombs is taken up with the assaulting troops; it is impossible to get them up afterwards.

5. COMMUNICATION. To have any chance of standing up to our own front line trenches, all cable must be either armoured or deeply buried; anything else is futile.

6. R.A.M.C. ARRANGEMENTS. If arrangement had been made to send up 100 fresh bearers with stretchers on the evening of the battle to begin immediately it was dark to look for and collect wounded in "No Man's Land" the whole of the wounded in our Sector could have been collected and evacuated the same night. The Regimental Stretcher Bearers and Volunteers from the survivors worked gallantly and indefatigably as they always do, but there is a limit to what men can do especially after a day of battle and the individual fresh man could have done much more; also there was a considerable shortage of stretchers.

No doubt all these points and others have been already thought out, but I bring them forward just as my own expression of opinion for anything they may be worth.

1/5th Battalion (Territorial Force) Prince of Wales's (North Staffordshire Regiment)

FONQUEVILLERS.

7.30 a.m. Attack on Gommecourt. See copy of"Narrative of Operations"attached. Battalion relieved by 4th Leicesters at 4.30 p.m. and went into Advanced Corps Reserve Line. Lieut. Colonel W. Burnett wounded.

Document Attached to the War Diary

A narrative of operations on 1 July 1916, written by "Captain, Commanding 1/5th Battalion North Staffs. Regt." on 4 July 1916:[1]

Narrative of Operations on July 1st 1916.
1. The Battalion moved into position in assembly trenches and was reported all correct about 4.0 a.m.
2. The bombardment commenced at 6.25 a.m.
3. The attack was launched at 7.30 a.m.
4. The first three waves got well away with few casualties, at proper intervals.
As the 4th wave was reaching the advance trench machine gun fire was opened from the S.W. end of FORD TRENCH and an artillery barrage was opened on our advanced line, support and communication trenches. At this time the 5th wave (consolidating parties) were coming up LINCOLN LANE; many men were hit and dropped their R.E. Material (Chevaux de frise, etc) causing obstruction which seemed to delay this wave. At the same time a party of Monmouths who were at the head of LINCOLN LANE caught it badly from shell fire, many being killed or wounded which created a further blockage.

When the 5th wave arrived at the advance trench they found the 4th wave had not left this line, although considerably overdue; considerable confusion ensued and in spite of all efforts from the officers the 4th wave could not be persuaded to go forward. The 5th wave (less 1 party) therefore, went through the 4th wave and advanced through them towards the German wire; on arriving there this wave had all its officers killed or wounded and a large number of men knocked out. There they were met by a party of the former waves under an officer (unknown Captain who was afterwards killed) who gave the word to retire, a few men managed to get back to the advance trench where they remained.

The 6th wave (Carrying parties) under Captain Wilton was met by these just about the advance trench. Captain Wilton was wounded in the neck (and had to come back) and Second Lieut. Read put his men in the C.T. leading to the advance trench – where he was met by returning party and, in spite of all messages forward, was unable to get his party forward. 2nd Lieut. Watkin who got out of the trench to investigate was immediately killed. 2nd Lieut Scrivener's party could not get further than the front trench owing to the block.

The 8th wave, under 2/Lieut. Lemon, got to our front line and were unable to move forward or backwards owing to the congestion.

The Support Company and 1 Lewis Gun, under Captain Worthington, moved up to the support trench allotted to them.

Lieut Colonel W. Burnett on hearing that the attack was not developing as arranged, personally went forward to the advance trench and with 2nd Lieut. Read and Lieut. E. Robinson, tried to reorganise and push on. Lieut. Robinson's party moved forward but Lieut. Robinson and most of his men were killed; Col. Burnett disappeared and was only found about 1 p.m. seriously wounded in the abdomen alongside a C.T. leading to the advance trench.

Things then got in utter confusion. At 11.0 a.m. Captain Wenger was 'phoned for by the Brigade Major to go out to Adv. Battalion Headquarters and take the situation in hand pending the return of Lieut. Colonel Burnett who, up to that time, could not be traced. At 12 noon Captain Wenger was given orders to re-organise the remaining 5th North Men into two waves using a party of 5th Lincs. [corrected in the diary to Leics.] to form 3rd and 4th waves. The fresh attack was timed for 1.15 p.m. but as the re-organisation was not complete by 1.0 p.m. the time for attack was altered to 3.30 p.m. Captain Wenger was given orders to side-slip and get in touch with 139th Brigade on his left, his left to be directed on the N.W. corner of GOMMERCOURT WOOD, the 5th South to side-slip to the top of LINCOLN LANE and the whole to go over together.

At 3.15 p.m. Captain Wenger 'phoned to the Brigade Major 137th Brigade that the 5th South left had not reached this point and they were not in touch with his right; he received orders to attack without them. In the meantime he went to H.Q. 6th Sherwoods and saw Major Hall of 6th Sherwoods and the Brigade Major, 139th Brigade, who informed him they were not going to attack unless a smoke barrage was put up - this was 'phoned to the Brigade Major, 137th Brigade.

At 3.25 p.m. the 4 waves (two 5th North and two 5th Leicesters) were ready to attack; the 1st wave was on the parapet, the 2nd behind in the front trench and the 5th Leics. in Support Trench behind ready told off. 2nd Lieut. Lemon was on left of 1st wave, 2nd Lieut. Read in centre, Captain Wenger himself on the right, Capt. Worthington with 2nd Lieut. Scrivener in command of the 2nd wave. 2nd Lieut. Lemon was to give the signal when the 139th Brigade were ready at 3.30 p.m. so as to make the attack simultaneous.

At 3.28 p.m. Captain Wenger received word from 2nd Lieut. Lemon that the 139th Brigade had made no preparations and Captain Robinson of the 6th Sherwoods told him they had no orders to attack and were not going over at the time mentioned. Captain Wenger immediately dispatched an orderly to Captain Wilson (Adjutant, 5th North) to 'phone the Brigade Major, 137th Bde, that the 139th Brigade were not going over and were the 5th North to go by themselves;

the Brigade Major's reply was to sit tight. The 5th North remained in that position for half an hour under severe artillery barrage on their front wire and heavy machine gun fire from the right.

About 4.30 p.m. orders came through to man the trench and all 6th North and 5th Leics. to file out.

I have collected the first part of the narrative from Officers and men who survived as I myself was not then present.

NOTE

1. The battalion's Commanding Officer at Zero Hour on 1 July 1916, was Lieutenant Colonel R.R. Raymer. During the attack Raymer was wounded by a shell fragment to the left thigh and was initially evacuated to No.3 General Hospital at Le Treport. From here he was subsequently transferred to a hospital in the UK on 7 July. An operation on 23 July 1916, removed the fragment and some pieces of clothing embedded in the wound. Such were the battalion's losses in the attack, that at the time this report was written it was being commanded by a Captain.

1/6th Battalion (Territorial Force) Prince of Wales's (North Staffordshire Regiment)

Battalion in trenches at FONQUEVILLERS. (Map Ref) X preparatory to an attack on GOMMECOURT WOOD and VILLAGE. Battalion on right, 6th South Staffs Regt, Battalion on left, 7th Notts & Derby Regt. The attack was preceded by an intense bombardment lasting 65 minutes and the infantry assault took place at 7.30 a.m. under cover of a smoke barrage.

The attack was carried out by means of four waves, each wave consisting of one platoon per Company. The 1st wave occupied the assault trench, the 2nd and 3rd waves the fire trench and the fourth wave the retrenchment. These were followed by consolidating and carrying parties, found by the 5th North Staffs. Immediately the smoke appeared the enemy opened heavy machine gun fire and barraged our front line. Whilst the assault was in progress this fire caused heavy casualties, which occurred chiefly in the first four waves. The casualties so depleted the strength of the waves that very few men succeeded in reaching the enemy wire, which was found to be very strong in parts.

Owing to the smoke many men lost direction and were unable to see the gaps in the wire. Previous heavy rain had made the trenches in a very bad condition, especially the assault trench, which was from 2 to 3 feet deep in mud. This caused delay in the waves leaving the trenches. The enemy front line trench was found to be very strongly held and with so few men left it was impossible to advance. After this, those who had not become casualties retired to the assault trench. Nothing of note occurred between this and 5 p.m. when the Battalion was relieved by the 5th North Staffs and proceeded to St. AMAND and billeted.

11th (Service) Battalion Royal Warwickshire Regiment

HANNESCAMPS

6.30 a.m. Intense bombardment on GOMMECOURT Salient. At 7.25 a.m. smoke was discharged all along our line, 2 Divisions on our immediate right attacked at 7.30 a.m. all went well except on right of 46th Divsn. opposite Southern end of FONQUEVILLERS.

Here there was a check. Observation was rendered exceedingly difficult owing to the dense smoke. Our right Company reported having seen some of our men about the hostile trenches which had been attacked. Later it was reported that the 46th Division attacking troops had occupied the hostile third line except for the check already mentioned.

At 3.30 p.m. our artillery again bombarded that sector but apparently our troops could not advance further. In the meantime the 56th Divsn. was reported to have secured its objective. At midnight information came to hand that the 46th Division had been ordered to withdraw to its original front line. We were very fortunate during the bombardment having only 6 casualties (one killed). Weather fine and hot. Wind W.

Document Attached to the War Diary

Extracts from the diary of Brevet-Colonel C.S. Collison, DSO, 11th Royal Warwickshire Regiment – Chapter XI (Extract), The Battle of the Somme:

At 6.30 a.m. our artillery opened an intense bombardment of the German positions about Gommecourt. At 7.25 a.m. smoke was discharged along the fronts of the 37th, 46th and 56th Divisions, and at 7.30 a.m. (zero hour) the two latter Divisions attacked from the N. and S. Up to midnight no really accurate record of the results of these actions is obtainable; but the advance of a Brigade of the 46th Division was stopped, and renewed at 3.30 p.m. I watched this phase from the Divisional line, but was unable to see any progress, though there was some apparently.

The attack of the 56th Division (hidden from us by the bend of Gommecourt Wood) is reported to have been satisfactory – also unsatisfactory. Very heavy fighting was going on here at about 10 p.m. At 1 a.m. (2nd July) information was received that the 46th Division was to be withdrawn to its original line, after attempting to extricate two battalions, which had not been located since the commencement of the attack."

The above account is taken from my diary, under date 1st July, and I only record it as an example of the confused and scanty nature of the information that reaches those whose knowledge of battles is usually confined to what takes place in their immediate neighbourhood. In this case the event in our immediate neighbourhood was the advance of the left brigade of the 46th Division, but the clouds of smoke from our own trenches and from those of the attacking troops, combined with the vapour and dust from the bursting shells, made even this movement very hard to follow. It was, however, apparent to us that the smoke cloud put up at 3.30 p.m. to cover a renewal of the attack on the left, was ineffective. Probably it was found impossible to arrange it effectively in the stress of battle; moreover what wind there was, was not then in the right direction. It had been a day of intense heat and of strenuous fighting against a resolute resistance, and in this part of the field, at any rate, the action seemed to die out during the afternoon.

Our own part in this first phase of the historic battle was naturally a minor one. The German defensive fire was directed almost entirely upon the fronts of the attacking divisions, and our loss was only one killed (Private Wilson) and 2/Lt. Denley and 6 men wounded. At nightfall a strong patrol, under Brocksopp, attacked the ground between the opposing lines, bombed a listening post opposite our front, and returned without encountering any opposition.

Unusual quiet marked the 2nd July in this Sector, and only the thunderous rumblings and mutterings to the South indicated that the struggle was still in progress in the region of Albert, and on the French front. The 46th and 56th Divisions had now withdrawn to the positions they occupied before their advance, and an uncanny silence succeeded to the noise and turmoil of the last week.

1/5th Battalion (Territorial Force) Sherwood Foresters (Nottinghamshire and Derbyshire Regiment)

FONQUEVILLERS
46th Division's attack at GOMMECOURT.
Two Brigades assaulting (137th & 139th), & one in reserve (138th). Two Battalions (5th & 7th) formed first four waves of the assault of the 139th Brigade. 6th Battn was in support & the 8th in Reserve.

The objective of this Battalion was the German 3rd Line from the northern edge of GOMMECOURT WOOD on the right, to a point 250 yards north where ORINOCO C.T. crossed the 3rd Line.

Companies were organised in four waves, the rear Platoon or wave carrying bombs & material for consolidation. 'D' Company was on the right. 'A' Company in the centre, & 'C' Company on the left. 'B' Company was detailed to do the carrying.

The final bombardment began at 6.25 a.m. Smoke bombs were thrown at 7.25 & the first three waves moved to the assault five minutes later.

The enemy set up a triple barrage of Artillery & Trench Mortar fire & concentrated upon the Battalion front very heavy Machine Gun fire. The first three waves attacked with great dash & many are known to have reached the enemy's first trench, but casualties during the advance were very heavy & the enemy opposition strong & well organised. The fourth waves were delayed by their heavy loads & by the muddy state of the trenches due to heavy rains. They moved over the parapet 15 minutes late. The carrying company was delayed still more for similar reasons, & advanced at 8.10 a.m. By this time the smoke had to a great extent cleared & the enemy seeing them poured in accurate & withering fire & completely checking further advance.

From Aeroplane observation it is thought some men reached & for a time held part of the enemy's second system, but it was not possible to send up support, and owing to failure on the part of the Brigade on the right to reach their objective, the right flank of the Battalion was exposed. Efforts were made later in the day to send fresh troops to the assault, but these were without success.

The attack succeeded in its object to the extent that enough troops were held in front of the Division to have altered the whole course of the operations further south.

The Battalion was relieved at 7 p.m. & moved into billets at BIENVILLERS.

After this attack Lt Col D.D. Wilson was reported missing & Major B.H. Checkland assumed command of the Battalion.[1]

Document Attached to the War Diary

A series of notes written by T.F.C. Downman in June 1918:

I joined the 5th Bn. Sherwood Foresters, the 139th Brigade, 46th Division, VIII Corps, Third Army, on 12th June 1916, the Battalion then being at Lucheaux near Doullens. I was posted to 'A' Coy & was put in charge of No.3 Platoon. That day and each day that week the attack was practiced over ground supposed to resemble that which would be the scene of the real action. These practices were continually begun, stopped and sent back and re-commenced. Equipment was altered several times and generally put into a state of muddle.

18th June the Battalion marched to Pommier and took up billets there, from here working parties went up to the front every day. Occasional shelling of the village especially after the batteries of 9.2s had commenced their work. The evening of the 27th the Battalion went into the trenches in support, the attack being timed for 7.30 a.m. on 29th. The trenches were deep in mud and lacking duck boards; this deficiency was begun to be made good on morning of 28th. The evening 28th the Battalion moved out of the trenches back to Pommier. The attack was with held for 48 hours, thereby losing the value of the artillery preparation, enabling the enemy to organise his defences, and spoiling the spirit of our men.

We had already had elaborate instructions as to what to do when we had reached our objectives, and instructions as to flares, Verey lights, and numerous other details. So there being nothing further to learn (?) we spent a quiet time till the afternoon of the 30th June. That evening we moved up to the trenches and again had parties carrying duck boards. My platoon had already been reduced from a strength of 35 to 20, fifteen men being taken as bombers, runners, carriers &c, then during the board carrying a shell wounded my platoon sergeant and 4 men of my platoon, reducing the strength to 15.

SLAUGHTER ON THE SOMME: 1 JULY 1916

At 11 p.m. we moved up to the front line going over the top for some distance. We eventually reached our portion of the line (3 bays for 1 platoon), about midnight. From about 12 to 12.30 a.m. 1st July the enemy machine guns were very active, just passing over the parapet of our front line. After this had died down I sent a small party out, about 6 men who each had wire cutters, to clear the path through our wire; this was soon done and I went out myself right through the gap which was quite well cleared. I attempted to report to my Company Commander who was with Battalion headquarters, but lost my way down a badly battered communication trench (I had only been down this once before and that was in daylight and before the Bosch had bombed it. All our communication trenches were in good condition a week before the attack, but had been systematically bombarded by the Bosch during the last few days). I regained the front line and sat on the firing step until daylight; during this time the trenches were shelled by the enemy with small high explosives. About 3.30 a.m. hot tea with rum mixed in came along, I saw this distributed to my platoon, who each had a cupful, and then passed on to the next platoon.

Soon after this casualties came along, chiefly from the Monmouths who had been out digging an advanced line, a dead man was deposited in my middle bay. At 5 a.m. I went into a dugout and remained there ¾ of an hour. I then returned to my station (the next bay) and waited there. An issue of neat rum came round; each man in my platoon had a small cupful.

After the intense bombardment had started at 6.30 a.m. the enemy replied with shrapnel on my right, but nothing came near me. At 7.25 a.m. the platoon on my left (No.2) were to go out and I was to follow and get behind them (70 yards interval) at 7.28 a.m. I remained to the left of my platoon and in communication with a man of No.2 platoon, at 7.26 a.m. I called to him and asked if No.2 had gone, he replied NO; again at 7.27, 7.28, 7.29 and 7.30 I received the same reply; as I was then 2 minutes overdue I decided not to wait and immediately gave the order for No.3 to go over.

Smoke bombs had been thrown out about 7.20 a.m. and did nothing but make a thick fog of evil smelling and tasting smoke on our own parapet, making it difficult to find the way out and calculated to lose one's sense of direction.

When beyond the smoke I looked for my platoon which should have been lined up in the prone position in front of our own wire, but I could see no one, either to right, left, or ahead. Looking back I saw a party coming out carrying tremendous burdens, offering a good target and moving very slowly. This was No.4 platoon, supposed to bring up wire, steel poles, bombs, flares &c for 'A' Coy.

Without waiting I proceeded towards the German lines alone, taking a direction towards the left, according to instructions. I passed the advanced line, a very shallow and narrow trench and came to a very large shell hole; here I came up with 2 men of my platoon who had evidently gone on without waiting for me. They gave me the direction further to the left and followed me. I was not aware of shells, bullets or other missiles whilst in the open.

On reaching the German wire I found it well cut and smashed up and had no difficulty in getting through. On reaching the German front line I found a trench nearly eight feet deep, very wide and apparently totally blocked at one end and partially blocked at the other. It was quite empty. I jumped in and climbed out the other side, still followed by the two men I met in the open, but I do not remember seeing them after this.

Between the Bosch 1st and 2nd line I was in the open until noticing a communication trench on my left I jumped into it and was going up when I saw head of me two"cheveaux de frises"[sic] lying at the bottom of the trench affecting a temporary barricade. When nearing this about half a dozen bullets hit the side of the trench a yard in front of me, evidently a machine-gun, but fortunately finished a belt or jammed as I got over the obstacle and proceeded.

I soon saw Second Lieut. McInnes of 'D' Coy ahead; he called to me to come on evidently thinking I had brought reinforcements. I reached him in the 2nd German line and found it very badly knocked about on the right resembling sand hills, quite irregular; to the left the trench was in good order, complete with fire step, and dugouts etc. One or two Bosch were firing at us with rifles. Our men (i.e. McInnes' men of 'D' Coy) used our bombs on these Bosch. I fired my revolver in the direction of the Bosch, also towards their third line, which was still under our barrage. We soon ran out of bombs and as there were only McInnes and myself with about 12 to 15 men and no reinforcements came up nor was there any sign of the carrying platoon for either 'A' or 'D' Coy or the carrying company 'B' Coy for the battalion, things were looking serious for us. We thereupon retired towards our centre, i.e. to the left along the Bosch 2nd line.

Of the Staffords who should have been on our right flank there was absolutely no sign, there was also a gap on our left and we were not in touch with 'A' Coy. I attempted to reach 'A' Coy, with which I should have been, but after going some distance without sign of anyone, concluded that they had not reached the 2nd line, so I rejoined Second Lieut. McInnes. Sec.Lt. Callow of No.16 Platoon, 'D' Coy appeared about this time without any men; he went off to the left to touch up with 'A' Coy.

McInnes now got on the fire step in one of the bays to observe what was going on in the German 3rd line, our barrage having lifted from it. He was immediately hit by a bullet on the steel helmet. This dazed him, and he again got up and looked towards the 1st line. Before I could speak to him he was hit again, this time right through the helmet and into the brain. He died immediately.[2]

At this time we should have attacked the 3rd line, but being 2 officers and a dozen men it would have been impossible. In spite of elaborate instructions which we had received regarding distress signals, flares, Verey Lights etc, we were absolutely unprovided except for the very light pistol I carried. I had asked for cartridges, but was not given any. McInnes had sent two runners back for reinforcements. I doubt if they got more than a few yards.

Callow now returned and we were all moving along towards the left. However he said he would go to the left and I was to take all the men left, to the right and try to connect up with the Staffords. I had moved back one bay to the right when the Germans bombed us. The first two bombs exploded near me and wounded me in the left arm and hip. The men scattered immediately and Bosch opened with rifles from the direction in which we had been going. I was hit by a bullet in the left arm, through the bicep, the bullet then struck a steel shaving mirror which I carried in my left breast pocket, and so being turned made a shallow groove across my solar plexus and landed in a box of safety matches in my right breast pocket, igniting them. Most of these details I was not aware of until 2 or 3 days after.

Before I had recovered from the shock of the bomb explosions, all the men disappeared. Where they went to I don't know, but presume some of them were wounded by the bombs but were able to clear out of the bay evidently intending to get cover from further bombs. I think these men left the 2nd line and went towards the 1st German line, but were either killed or wounded (and eventually taken as prisoners) by German rifle fire from the direction in which we had been moving, i.e. from the German 2nd line on our right flank.

However almost immediately after the bombs the trench filled with Germans from both sides, and before I could offer any resistance I was pounced on and my revolver and very light pistol were taken, the latter evoking some comment. Several Germans then lined the fire step and threw a few bombs, there was no reply and they had retaken this portion of their 2nd line effectually scattering our little party. Whilst still lying on the floor of the trench I was threatened with the bayonet and was nearly finished off by one but fortunately this was averted.

A German then bandaged my arm with my field dressing and left me to myself. After some minutes as all the Germans had disappeared I managed to crawl out into a shallow trench going about 10 yards in the direction of the 1st line. Here I remained from 8.20 a.m. to 12.30 p.m. during which time our shells were again very active on the 2nd line, several pieces coming very near me. At 12.30 I thought it advisable to seek better cover and crawled back and found the entrance to a dug-out which I thought was empty. I went down a few steps and sat down.

After 10 minutes or so a German N.C.O. came along and took me down the dug-out, about 40 feet deep. Here there were several Germans in a large dug-out fitted with beds, tables &c. I was given some cold coffee and my belongings were looked at. My revolver ammunition alone was taken away. Shelling of these lines was going on all the time, whilst I was in this dug-out and a shell burst at the mouth and threw large quantities of earth down, covering the pack and equipment of a German who had been neatly arranging them on the steps.

About 2.30 p.m. I was taken to another dug-out some distance to the right and most probably in the 3rd line. This was a large place with several rooms, bedrooms with ordinary iron bedsteads, furniture &c. I was placed at a small table in a passage near an officers' mess. This mess belonged to the 91st Regiment. Here I was given hot coffee, kriegbrot and some sausage meat, also cigarettes.

The Major or Colonel of this Regiment was seated at a large table with all the junior officers around; he commenced reading a long report to them, in the middle he turned round and asked me my name; this by the way was the only question that was asked me. I was not searched or interrogated. I noticed my Very light pistol on the table. This seemed to be regarded with suspicion, so I asked an orderly who spoke English if I could speak to the Colonel. This was quite readily granted, so I explained that the Very light pistol was merely a signal pistol and not a new pocket trench mortar.

This German officer understood and showed me his store of signal cartridges, several thousands and of a variety of colours; they were smaller than ours and looked very much like a sporting cartridge, of not too large a bore. I also noticed some of their pistols which had barrels nearly twice the length of the cartridges, thus accounting for the superiority of their lights over ours of that date.

About 5.30 p.m. I was sent to a dressing station in the trenches, on the way I noticed several of our 9.2" shells lying in the mud at the bottom of the trenches; if all of these had explode the results would have been very useful to us. The dressing station was about 50 feet below the surface and well fitted up with an operating table, equipment, and instruments of all kinds. There were stretchers and beds in various rooms off the passages. After waiting here some time whilst several Bosch were attended to, I was bound up and sent upstairs again. Here I found a string of lightly wounded Bosch and looked round for the sentry, with rifle, who had brought me there, expecting to be escorted somewhere. However the sentry had gone and the wounded Bosch made it plain that I was to join their party. This I had to do being placed second in the single file.

We went down the trenches in this fashion being followed by English 18-pounders. We had to wait and go down a dug-out, full of wounded Bosch, for nearly an hour, then we proceeded still with numerous shells falling near. I understood from the behaviour of the Germans and their evident "wind" that another attack was in progress. However, if there was one it was soon over and did not get anywhere near us.

We proceeded and went some miles zigzagging about; we passed several small parties coming up, about 7 or 8 under an officer; some of them asked me for money, but I took no notice of these requests. We eventually came to a road and got out of the trench and went over the open going back towards some villages behind the lines. This area was swept by spent bullets which whistled through the grass. On reaching the high road probably that between Bucquoy and Puisseaux, our party consisted of myself with about 6 Bosch wounded; the others, about another dozen wounded, had evidently dropped out on the way. This road was being shelled with shrapnel by our field guns. Several transport carts coming along had narrow escapes but none were hit. We reached a village about 9 p.m. by my watch.

*　　*　　*

SLAUGHTER ON THE SOMME: 1 JULY 1916

From my own observation and from information obtained from officers, N.C.O.s and men of the 46th and 56th Divisions I arrive at the following:

Ours was a subsidiary attack and kind of extra to the main attack further South, but at the same time it was intended to be successful and to capture the strong positions made about the Gommecourt Wood.

The attack failed through various causes of which the following are the chief:

The absurdly inadequate strength of some of the attacking units; my own battalion went over between 500 and 600 strong. My own platoon consisted of 15.

Lack of knowledge on the part of the higher commands of the conditions prevailing in the trenches, and of what was likely to take place in an attack on trenches from trenches.

The absurd distribution of equipment; those in 1st waves who got into German lines having to wait for 4th waves who never got there.

Overloading of all attackers, especially "carriers".

Very bad management regarding cutting of German barbed wire; this was absolutely uncut on a 2 battalion front, letting down our right flank and the 56th Division's left flank. The wire on my own front was sufficiently cut owing to the energies of Lt. Lilley who had taken patrols out to do this work, the artillery not being sufficiently competent to do it properly.

Half-heartedness in regard to the attack by Divisional General (46th Division). Only 4 battalions went into attack at 7.30 a.m. They were not supported and no reinforcements were sent. I understood that subsequent attacks by the rest of the division took place during the day, none of which reached the German lines. If these troops had all attacked between 7.30 and 8 a.m. we should have gained our objectives and held them, presuming that the wire was cut.

NOTES

1. One of the officers killed during the attack was 27-year-old Captain John Leslie Green, Royal Army Medical Corps attached to the 1/5th Battalion (Territorial Force) Sherwood Foresters (Nottinghamshire and Derbyshire Regiment). Born at Buckden, Huntingdonshire, the son of John George and Florence May Green, of St. Mark's Lodge, Cambridge, Green had been educated at Felsted School and Downing College, Cambridge. He had not completed his medical studies at Bartholomew's Hospital when war broke out in 1914 but was commissioned into the Royal Army Medical Corps. A veteran of the Battle of Loos, Green was with his battalion at Zero Hour and moved forward with the rear of his battalion as they struggled to reach the German wire. An extract from *The London Gazette*, No.29695, dated 4 August 1916, records the following: "Although himself wounded, he went to the assistance of an officer who had been wounded and was hung up on the enemy's wire entanglements, and succeeded in dragging him to a shell hole, where he dressed his wounds, notwithstanding that bombs and rifle grenades were thrown at him the whole time. Captain Green then endeavoured to bring the wounded officer into safe cover, and had nearly succeeded in doing so when he himself was killed." Captain Green's Victoria Cross, awarded for his actions on 1 July 1916, was presented to his wife by King George V at Buckingham Palace on 7 October 1916. His body was recovered from the battlefield and lies today in Foncquevillers Military Cemetery.

2. Twenty-two-year-old Second Lieutenant John Edward McInnes is commemorated on Pier and Face 10 C 10 D and 11 A of the Thiepval Memorial.

1/6th Battalion (Territorial Force) Sherwood Foresters (Nottinghamshire and Derbyshire Regiment)

FONCQUEVILLERS

139th Bde attacked on a front from N.E. corner of GOMMECOURT WOOD to point of LITTLE Z. 5th & 7th Bns assaulted in 4 waves of 3 Coys, remaining Coys of each Bn carrying Bombs, S.A.A. & material. The 6th Bn also carried – 'A' & 'B' on front in 2 waves to follow 5th & 7th Bn carrying Coys, and 'D' & 'C' in two waves to remain in old front trench & retrenchments until ordered to advance.

The 1st 3 waves of assault carried 1st, & to some extent 2nd & 3rd German trenches under partial cover of smoke, but owing to very muddy state of our trenches, part of 4th wave and greater part of 5th & 7th Bn carrying companies could not get away before smoke lifted, and all attempts to advance by these and 6th 'A' & 'B' Coys were met by heavy artillery and machine-gun barrage.

The attack (as also that of 137th Bde against GOMMECOURT WOOD) therefore failed with heavy losses to assaulting Battns, but the main object was achieved of containing enemy forces near GOMMECOURT.

About 8 p.m., the Bn was relieved in trenches by 8th Bn Sherwood Foresters, and remained the night near LEFT BATTN HDQRS, FONCQUEVILLERS.

Casualties:

Killed: Officers – Lieut E.M. JELLICOE.
               Other Ranks – No 158 C.S.M. GODDARD; 1443 L/Sgt
               ALLCOCK; 2206 L/Sgt S.SHARMAN; and 17 others.

Wounded: Officers – Capt F.M. DICK; CAPT & ADJ C.B. JOHNSON; CAPT
               V.O. ROBINSON, CAPT F.B. ROBINSON (att 139th Bde M.G.
               Coy) died of wounds 3.7.16.; LIEUT R.D. WHEATCROFT, died
               of wounds 3.7.16.; 2nd Lt H. SIMPSON, died of wounds; 2/Lt
               F.R. OLIVER (at duty); 2nd Lt F.W.A.STUBBS; 2nd Lt J.E.
               BARKER.

Other Ranks   140.
Total casualties   170.

Documents Attached to the War Diary

A series of corrections sent to Headquarters, 139th Infantry Brigade, signed by Lieutenant Colonel G.D. Goodman, Commanding 6th Battalion Sherwood Foresters, and dated 3 July 1916:

In accordance with Brigade Operation Orders my Battn was, in the early morning of the 1st inst disposed as follows: 'A' & 'B' Coys in 1st Support Line with some bombers, remainder of bombers and 4 Brigade Machine Guns in a small trench behind.

SLAUGHTER ON THE SOMME: 1 JULY 1916

The remaining two Companies 'C' & 'D'* occupied 3rd Support Line in order from right. *(read 'D' & 'C'). Owing to the muddy state of the trenches it took considerably longer than had been expected to get this wave into position and it was not completed before 3.15 a.m.

At 5.45 a.m. I moved to LEFT ADVANCED HEAD QRS (7th Battn).

About 7 a.m. Major HIND, his Adjutant and Medical Officer left. He stated he was going to new front trench to watch the waves out and then go himself.

At *8.45 a.m. *(7.45 a.m.) I and my Adjutant went along GREEN STREET towards REGENT STREET to watch my leading Companies advance and to follow them.

I found GREEN STREET congested and waited a long time trying to get men forward but found it impossible as the front line was blocked. During this time the enemy's bombardment was very heavy with shrapnel and H.E., the latter being distributed around advanced Headquarters of both Battalions. My Adjutant was wounded beside me.

At 7.45 a.m. Capt ROBINSON, Commanding my Right ('A') Coy had a report from his runners that the 5th Battn Carrying Company was moving. He lead his Company forward but was checked by the 5th Carring [sic] Coy who said they were checked by the 4th wave who had not cleared. *It was 8.45 a.m. before the head of my 'A' Coy was in the old front line trench and partially ready to move. (All the men could not get into this trench).

*At 8.45 a.m. Lieut Wheatcroft at head of his platoon crossed our wire. All but Sgt Wagg being hit, and withdrew to old sap.

Capt ROBINSON reported the block to Major CHECKLAND who pushed on 5th Carrying Company. By this time the smoke had almost gone.

The left platoon of 'A' Coy (or most of them) then got over the parapet under Lt R.D. WHEATCROFT and the right of the Company endeavoured to advance up No.3 sap and "C" C.T.

The Barrage was very heavy and Lt Wheatcroft was almost at once badly wounded. There were many casualties and the men withdrew for shelter to the saps and other trenches.

The same thing happened on the left when my 'B' Company was kept back by the 7th Carrying party. Capt F.M. DICK Commanding my Company was hit in the leg as soon as he got over the parapet and his Coy Sergt Major was killed at his side. The survivors accordingly took cover.

I sent messages to Coy Commanders to organise men in old front trench and retrenchments.

When I found it was impossible to get my men forward owing to the congestion I returned to left HEADQUARTERS about 9.30 a.m. and reported by telephone to Brigade. At my request the Assistant Adjutant 7th Battn went to the new front trench for information and I received a verbal message from Capt SCOTT M.O. 7th Battn that he was in that trench with a good many men.

9.45 a.m. received telegraphic message from Brig Genl that Naylor of 5th in

German front line trench required help. I sent message to Capt Robinson to organise advance from new Front line trench and went to No.3 sap where I conferred with Capts KERR & ROBINSON who said Naylor was back and advance impossible.

The enemy's fire (chiefly rifle) on that (new front) trench was very heavy and accurate. No.3 Sap (to which I went) was covered by enemy's rifle fire.

About 12.30 p.m. I received orders to attack with two Companies of my Battalion at 1.15 p.m. under cover of smoke. There was no smoke however and I did not attack. Another attack was ordered for 2.30 p.m. also under cover of smoke which however was not ready, and orders were received to the effect that the smoke would be at 3.25 p.m. and I was to advance at 3.30 p.m.* (Read 3.30 and 3.35 p.m. 1,200 men of 137th Bde were also attacking.)

A Staffird [sic] Officer came to confer and I settled that my right should advance on ORKNEY, my left on OUSE C.T.s. A small carrying party was organised and bombers collected. About 3.30 p.m. a small film of smoke appeared but in no way interfered with the view of the enemy trenches. I accordingly at 3.35 p.m. ordered the men not to go over the parapet.

There was a very heavy and extremely accurate barrage and also considerable rifle fire. I was and am, quite satisfied that there was no possible chance of reaching the objective and no result could have been achieved. As a matter of fact, owing to a mistake a party of 20 did leave the trench, most of them were struck down at once.

An "additional report" sent by the OC 1/6th Battalion (Territorial Force) Sherwood Foresters (Nottinghamshire and Derbyshire Regiment) to Headquarters, 139th Infantry Brigade, signed by Lieutenant Colonel G.D. Goodman at 15.15 hours on 3 July 1916:

From: O.C.6th Sherwood Foresters.
To: H.Q. 139th Infantry Brigade.
I should like to add to my report of this morning a statement with regard to the smoke and state of our trenches on the 1st inst.
1. I had anticipated that the state of the trenches would add materially to the time required by the rear waves for deploying into the open. Shortly before 8.30 a.m. I sent a message to the right of the line (to Capt Robinson) that the smoke must be prolonged if required and was subsequently informed that Major Checkland had given orders to the Officer in charge of the Smoke party. However, when shortly after, I was waiting in GREEN STREET for my carrying party to move up I found a small party of LINCOLNS with an officer coming down the trench. They said they had orders to go back. I ordered them back to continue the smoke, and they complied but I believe there was not much material left. All reports agree that the smoke has practically gone when the 4th wave was about to start.
2. The greatest difficulty was the mud in the trenches. The C.T.s were even more difficult to pass than on the preceding days as the water was subsiding and thick

mud being formed. It was immensely difficult for the carrying Companies to get along with their loads and the men were much fatigued.

But the men were all very keen and did their utmost, and I am confident that all would have gone well had they not been impeded by the condition of the trenches.

1/7th (Robin Hood) Battalion (Territorial Force) Sherwood Foresters (Nottinghamshire and Derbyshire Regiment)

FONQUEVILLERS

Battalion in Trenches, 5th Bn Sherwood Foresters on its right, and was ordered to attack Enemy Trenches, commencing at 7.30 a.m.

Report to Major E.H. Spalding on the attack of July 1st 1916, by the 7th (Robin Hood) Battn Sherwood Foresters.

In accordance with the Brigade orders the 7th Battn (S.F.) Robin Hoods attacked the German Lines, the objective being the capture and consolidation of the German Trenches from the point of the LITTLE Z to the junction of FONT and C.T. ORINOCO.

The Battalion was detailed to attack in 5 waves, the first four waves were composed of 'A','B','C' Coys in lines of Platoons, the 5th wave 'D' Coy being a carrying and digging Company.

The first wave was formed up in our new front line trench, the 2nd and third waves in our old front line trench, the 4th wave in the 1st retrenchment and the 5th wave in GREEN ST.

As detailed in orders the smoke was discharged at 7.27 a.m. and at the same time the 2nd wave commenced to file through the gaps in our wire. The first wave moved out at 7.30 a.m. from the new advanced trench; the 3rd wave commenced to move out through the gaps in our wire when the second wave got clear.

Owing to the density of the smoke these three waves were soon lost to sight from the old front line. Out of these 3 waves only about 12 men reached the German 2nd Line, they found the wire was sufficiently cut to enable them to get through; this small party was in the second line until the smoke cleared, and finding they were not supported by any other of our men and that a number of Germans were approaching them from dug-outs, they fell back on the German 1st Line Trench, about 5 reaching it.

In this trench were about 24 of our men who had been endeavouring to make some sort of fire position; before this could be done the Germans made a bombing attack, both from the right and the left, our men were unable to offer much resistance, their rifles in some cases being muddy, and having no supply of bombs, eventually those that were left retired and took shelter in shell holes, immediately WEST of the German wire remaining there until dark.

A small party of bombers under the Battalion Bomb Officer 2Lt C.H. Burton worked their way up the C.T. and advanced beyond the German 2nd Line, bombing several dug-outs on the way, and accounting for a number of Germans, this party however had to fall back eventually.

In the meantime the 4th wave moving up from the retrenchment, their advance being delayed by the state of the trench, moved out from the fire trench, but found when reaching the new advance trench the smoke had cleared and (though a number of men attempted and a few succeeded) it was practically impossible to advance owing to the machine gun fire.

The 5th wave (the carrying and digging party) were delayed in getting into position in the fire trench, by the state of the C.T.s. The trenches by this time were subjected to a very heavy enfilade artillery fire from the direction of Monchy, and the carrying company when getting over the parapet and moving through the wire suffered heavy casualties, the O.C. Company was killed and the only two subalterns wounded, very few of this wave advanced beyond the old fire trench.

The smoke was quite clear between the German 1st Line and our new advanced trench by 7.55 a.m. and this seriously affected the advance, efforts were made to get the remaining portions of the 4th wave and carrying Coy to advance on the expected resumption of the smoke but no more was sent over.

The artillery fire was kept up on our trenches all the morning and accounted for a great number of casualties amongst the men occupying them.

In accordance with orders a party was organised to carry boxes of bombs, formed up in two waves to follow a company of 6th Sherwood Foresters, the advance to take place under cover of smoke at 3.30 p.m. This advance however did not take place.

The following casualties occurred during the foregoing operations:

Major	L.A. HIND	Comdg Officer	Missing believed killed
Captain	R.M. GOTCH	Adjutant	Missing believed killed
"	W.E.G. WALKER	Sig Officer	Killed
"	A.A. WALTON	O.C. 'C' Coy	Wounded
"	W.H. ROUND	" 'D'"	Killed
"	T.H. LEMAN	" 'A'"	Missing believed killed
Lieut	J. MACPHERSON	" 'B'"	Killed
2/Lieut	C.W. SHELTON		Wounded
"	S.E. CAIRNS		Wounded
"	S.L. LANCASTER		Wounded
"	C.H. BURTON		Missing
"	M.D. HEMPTON		Wounded
"	S.E. BANWELL		Wounded
"	J.E. GARNER		Wounded
"	J.F. BISHOP		Missing
"	W.E. FLINT		Missing believed killed
2/Lieut	H. WILKINS		Missing believed killed

"	J.H.C. FLETCHER	Missing believed killed
"	A. CHARLES	Missing believed killed

Casualties: Other Ranks

Killed	43
Missing believed killed	27
Missing believed wounded	10
Missing	116
Wounded	189
Wounded at Duty	39
Total	424

9-11 p.m. Battn withdrawn and marched to BIENVILLERS, being relieved in Trenches by 8th Bn S. Foresters Regt.

1/8th Battalion (Territorial Force) Sherwood Foresters (Nottinghamshire and Derbyshire Regiment)

FONCQUEVILLERS

1.15 a.m. Battalion began to move up from FONCQUEVILLERS to take its place in trenches allotted to Reserve Battn.

3.15 a.m. Battn was in position except for carrying parties taking up breakfast to front line troops of 5th, 6th & 7th Battns, which rejoined later.

6.25 a.m. Intense bombardment began & lasted until 7.30 a.m.

7.25 a.m. Smoke discharged & continued for one hour.

7.30 a.m. 5th & 7th Battns moved off to the assault. Heavy barrage on our front lines & some on rear positions.

8 a.m. to Companies began to move forward to Support lines, which however in
10.30 a.m. many cases were blocked by troops or blown in & little progress was made. The troops in front had not got on successfully – communication with German front line had not been made before smoke had all cleared away.

11am to Little action of any kind - & very little information received as to
3.0 p.m. progress made by assaulting Battns.

3.0 p.m. Fresh bombardment began on right brigade front.

3.30 to Bombardment continued by us, with a view to fresh attack being
4.15 p.m. launched by 2 Co's of 6th Battn which however, was cancelled.

5.5 p.m. Orders were received to send out daylight patrols to ascertain [*illegible*] positions. These were sent out, but could not get far, though they brought back some useful information.

6.10 p.m. Orders received to relieve Battn in old front line & advanced line. 5th, 7th & part 6th Battns withdrew & 'A' Coy took over line, with 'D' on left, 'C' Coy in Support Lines & 'B' Coy at SNIPER'S SQUARE.

9.30 p.m. Orders received that 5th Lincs would attack from our line at midnight. Co's were accordingly re-arranged & 'A' Coy's area taken over by 5th Lincs.

1/6th Battalion (Territorial Force) South Staffordshire Regiment

FONQUEVILLERS
Operations, 1st July, 1916.

The 137th Infantry Brigade having been ordered to attack GOMMECOURT WOOD and VILLAGE, the Battalion took up their position in our old front line trenches between the FONQUEVILLERS – GOMMECOURT ROAD and LEICESTER STREET (E.28.a.5.3.) at 1 a.m. on 1st July.

The attack was ordered to commence at 7.30 a.m. in four waves – the Companies advancing by Platoons in depth at a distance of 80 yards – in conjunction with the 1/6th Battn North Staffordshire Regiment and two Battalions of the 139th Infantry Brigade on our left.

The assault was preceded by an intense bombardment of the supporting artillery commencing at 6.25 a.m. and was also covered by a smoke barrage which opened five minutes before the attack was launched. During the course of this bombardment the enemy replied vigorously with howitzers and field guns upon our front line and communication trenches and at intervals he directed short bursts of machine-gun fire on our parapet and exits from the direction of our front and right front.

At 7.30 a.m. the four platoons of the leading wave having moved out to the new front line, under cover of the smoke advanced to the assault of the enemy's position and were followed by the succeeding waves.

The fourth wave was delayed for about five minutes by the casualties which blocked the communication trenches leading to the front line and by the heavy load which they were carrying. The disposition of the Companies from right to left was 'C', 'A', 'B', 'D' and of these the only Company which was able to penetrate the enemy's line in any strength was 'D' Company on the left, who found that the wire was well cut on their frontage: three platoons of this Company obtained a footing in the front line and some men are reported to have gone further but they were outnumbered and accounted for by the enemy. The remaining three Companies on the right, 'B' 'A' and 'C' were held up by the enemy's wire which had not been so well cut, and although small parties were able to enter the enemy's line they could not obtain a permanent footing there.

Eighty men returned within an hour to our front line where they remained until noon, when they were ordered to occupy our supports, and they were subsequently withdrawn from the trenches.

Casualties were 239, out of a fighting strength of 523.

The Battalion was then relieved by 1/5th Leicester Regt., and marched to ST. AMAND.

The Battalion rested at ST. AMAND.

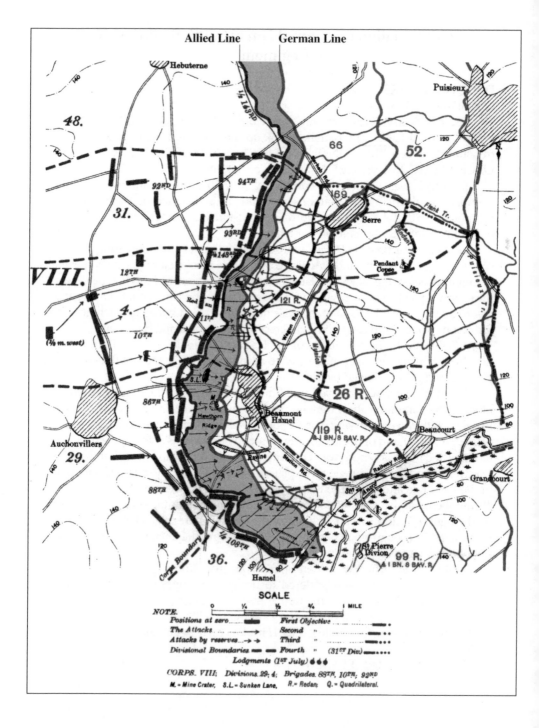

Allied Line   **German Line**

SCALE

VIII Corps

1 July 1916

The upper waters of the Ancre flow westward to Hamel (where as already mentioned it makes a southern bend) through a narrow valley, with the villages of Miraumont, Grandcourt, Beaucourt and St. Pierre Divion on its banks. On the northern side of the bend are a series of large spurs projecting south-eastwards towards the river: the Auchonvillers spur (with an eastern under-feature known as Hawthorn Ridge); the Beaucourt spur which runs down from Colincamps; and the Grandcourt spur which has the village of Serre at its northern end.

Between the three spurs are shallow valleys: in that which separates the Auchonvillers and Beaucourt spurs lie Beaumont Hamel village and the road to it from Auchonvillers. This valley has a branch, called "Y Ravine", which cuts into the southern side of Hawthorn Ridge. The other valley, known as the Beaucourt valley, is marked by the beginning of the Beaucourt – Puisieux road and passes southward of Serre.

The front of VIII Corps[1] facing Beaucourt – Serre had therefore a succession of ridges and valleys before it, and the ends of Y Ravine, Beaumont Hamel valley and Beaucourt valley, trending westward, penetrated into it. The Colincamps – Beaucourt spur, where it crossed the front line, was known as Redan Ridge.

The German front line ran first on the eastern slope of Auchonvillers spur, passed round the head of Y Ravine to Hawthorn Ridge, crossed the shallow Beaumont Hamel valley, and continued across to the Beaucourt spur (Redan Ridge), and over the slight depression, the head of Beaucourt valley, between this and the small knoll of the Grandcourt spur on which Serre stands. The intermediate line, known as Munich Trench, started from Beaucourt Redoubt above Beaucourt and going north included Serre village; the second position ran from Grandcourt to Puisieux, with the third position, as elsewhere, three miles behind it.

No Man's Land was wide in the southern sector, averaging 500 yards, but only 200 yards in the northern; it was open and bare of cover, except for a sunken lane, running north from the Auchonvillers – Beaumont Hamel road, and a small bank between this lane and the German line.

The German front position was a formidable one. It was well traced with a number of minor salients and flanks, and a large flanking bastion in the shape of the head of Y Ravine. There was natural cover available for supports and reserves in the succession of valleys behind it, besides unusually good artificial cover in dug-outs and cellars of the villages, to which secure entrances had been made on the reverse slopes. The miniature fortress of Beaumont Hamel completely commanded the valley parallel to the front which VIII Corps must cross in an advance,[2] and the Beaucourt ridge overlooked the whole with excellent observation for artillery.

The battle-ground formed a kind of amphitheatre: VIII Corps seemed confronted with tiers of fire and was under complete observation by the enemy, so that even its field artillery suffered from the German counter-batteries, as, though well dug in, the flashes of the guns were visible. Its own position, sloping to the front, gave it no more than command of the German front line and support trenches; observation – and most of the artillery observers had to be near the front line – was limited by the ridges beyond; there were thus many places close to the front on which ground observation was impossible. Moreover, the convex shape of the slope on the British side made it difficult to bring heavy gun fire on the enemy front position, and there were therefore parts of it which were hardly touched by the preliminary bombardment.

The corps had three of its four divisions and two battalions of a brigade of the fourth, in line. On the right, the 29th Division, of Gallipoli fame, held the eastern face of the Auchonvillers spur, with Beaumont Hamel in the valley in front of it, its right immediately north-east of the Hamel – Auchonvillers (St. John's) road, and the left near the head of the Beaumont Hamel valley. The 4th Division, of the original B.E.F., continued the line across the upper, east and west, portion of the Beaucourt spur to beyond the Mailly Maillet – Serre road. Brought up to strength with the finest of recruits – for the last time from the battalions' own recruiting areas – the division was as "fighting fit" as it was at any time of its existence. The 31st Division (New Army) on the left, lay along the forward slope of the dip between Serre and Colincamps (2½ miles west of Serre), facing the former village, which stood undestroyed – many of its houses still had their roofs on – amid a mass of trees, conspicuous on its knoll, 1,000 yards away, completely overlooking the position of the division.

The plan of attack was that the 29th and 4th Divisions should advance due eastwards into and across the Beaumont Hamel valley on to the Beaucourt spur, where lay the German intermediate line. Thence they were to press on to the German second position. The 31st Division, on the left, as the advance progressed, was to form a defensive flank, including the village of Serre, pivoting on its left, which was to stand fast at John Copse, whilst its right, swinging forward, kept touch with the 4th Division. The 48th (South Midland) Division, Territorial Force, was to be in corps reserve at Bus les Artois; but two battalions, the 1/7th and 1/5th Royal Warwickshire, of its 143rd Brigade (Brigadier-General B.C. Dent),[3] were in the line on the left next to VII Corps. From the two-mile front which they held no attack was to be made, although preparations for one were to be simulated, and the enemy wire cut. On the day of battle these two battalions were not to advance, but smoke was to be discharged from their trenches shortly before zero hour, as on other parts of the line. Nevertheless, no assembly trenches were dug, and no passages cut through the British wire, so that the inertness of this sector must have been evident to the enemy.

The 29th and 4th Divisions were allowed three and a half hours – not long enough as later experience proved – in which to reach the German second position, an advance of 4,000 yards. On arrival there they were to send parties with Lewis guns a short distance forward to a sunken road which they were to consolidate for defence. The 31st Division would find for the general line of its defensive flank an existing German communication trench, known as Flank Trench, which led from Puisieux Trench past the north of Serre village to the German front trenches.[4] Since the width of No Man's Land varied, the leading lines were to leave the front parapet at such times before zero as would enable them to reach a position one hundred yards from the German trench by zero.

The orders given to VIII Corps[5] laid down six lifts for the artillery: off the front trench at zero; off the first objective, at fifteen or twenty minutes after zero, varying with its distance from the front line; off the second objective at forty or forty-five minutes after zero (but at one hour and twenty minutes for the flank near Beaucourt); and three hours and thirty minutes after zero off the third objective, Puisieux Trench – at which hour as already mentioned the infantry was to reach it – with intermediate lifts at one hour and thirty-five minutes and two hours and forty minutes. These times applied to the field artillery. In each case the heavy artillery was to lift five minutes earlier and straight on to the objective. A definite attempt to get a creeping barrage formed by the divisional field artillery was ordered, the words used being: "At the commencement of each infantry attack the divisional artillery will lift 100 yards and continue lifting at the rate of 50 yards a minute to the objective, firing three rounds per gun at each step."

It was added in explanation: "The rate of advance of the infantry has been calculated at 50 yards a minute. Infantry must not arrive before the times shown on the map [provided to the officers], as the artillery will still be firing on these points. It is the intention of divisional artillery to assist the infantry forward by lifting very slowly 50 yards each minute, i.e. at the same rate as it is calculated the infantry will advance.

"The times once settled cannot be altered. The infantry therefore must make their pace conform to the rate of the artillery lifts. If the infantry find themselves checked by our own barrage, they must halt and wait till the barrage moves forward.

"The success or otherwise of the assault largely depends on the infantry thoroughly understanding the 'creeping' method of the artillery."

These instructions were repeated in the divisional orders.

To the 4.5-inch field howitzers of the division was left the destruction of machine-gun nests and shelters near the front. Unfortunately their power was insufficient for the purpose, and their consequent failure may have contributed to the ill-success of VIII Corps.

Each division in front line was ordered to have two 18-pounder batteries ready to move forward at short notice, and routes for the purpose were reconnoitred. No portion of the divisional field companies Royal Engineers was to take part in the assault; one section of a company was as a rule placed at the disposal of the commander of each assaulting brigade, but it was not to be ordered forward until the objective had been gained. The remainder of the Royal Engineers were held back for work on and improvement of forward roads and water supply, as well as for consolidation of strong-points at night.[6]

In addition to the usual arrangements made to keep up signal communication with the assaulting columns by visual, runners, screens, flares and signalling to contact aeroplanes, a French type of lamp, which had a wide beam, and therefore did not require accurate aligning, was employed, and bombers carried red and yellow flags to show where the front lines of their battalions were.

Assault of the 29th and 4th Divisions

The preparations on the front of the 29th Division included the excavation of three shallow tunnels under No Man's Land: one to be opened up as a communication trench to the sunken lane, and the others dug to within thirty yards of the German front trench. The extremities of the latter two, at 02.00 hours on the morning of the assault, were opened up to the surface as emplacements for batteries of Stokes mortars.[7]

A mine of 40,000lbs of ammonal had also been prepared and charged by 252 Tunnelling Company Royal Engineers under Hawthorn Redoubt, a strong-point in the German front line on the crest of Hawthorn Ridge, immediately opposite Beaumont Hamel village, commanding the head of the valley. This mine had important and direful consequences.

The G.O.C. VIII Corps originally wished to fire it four hours before zero, so that the redoubt, which flanked No Man's Land, should be blown up and the crater consolidated and occupied before the assault, but long enough before the latter to ensure that any general alarm on the enemy's side should have died down. G.H.Q., on the advice of the Inspector of Mines, forbade this, on the grounds that British troops had never yet "made a good show" at occupying a crater, whereas the Germans were extremely proficient in that art, and would therefore at zero probably be found in possession of the crater. The Inspector of Mines insisted that zero was the proper time.

On 15 June 1916, the Fourth Army had issued an order that all mines were to be fired between zero and eight minutes before zero, and, as a kind of compromise, VIII Corps suggested ten minutes before zero, and this was agreed to and sanctioned by G.H.Q., although eight or ten minutes would equally give the enemy warning. It seems to have been in the minds both of Sir Douglas Haig and General Rawlinson that, even if the mine – the only one north of the Ancre – did give the alarm, it might be to the advantage of the attacks of the XIII and XV Corps on the right.

Their success was all important, and it might be helpful if the attention of the enemy could be drawn to the situation north of the Ancre before they were launched. It is said that some apprehension was felt in the 29th Division that if the mine were fired at zero the attacking infantry might be injured by falling fragments. As a matter of fact, although some dust remains in the air, all material that might inflict injury comes down, as is demonstrated by photography, within twenty seconds of the time of firing, and no further cracks in the ground, a most alarming feature of the explosion, are formed.[8]

The permission to fire the mine at 07.20 hours still allowed arrangements to be made in accordance with the original idea of occupying the crater before the main assault, but the decision to do so at once created difficulties. It was obvious that the heavy artillery barrage could not be continued on Hawthorn Redoubt and the neighbouring trenches whilst the infantry was seizing the crater. The whole of VIII Corps' heavy artillery, not merely that supporting the 29th Division, was therefore ordered to lift at 07.20 hours, ten minutes before the assault. At this hour "the howitzers firing on the first line lifted to the reserve trenches, and at 07.25 hours were joined there by the howitzers which had been firing on the support trench."[9]

The thin 18-pounder shrapnel barrage of the field artillery was to lift at zero off the front line, but in the 29th Division, "in order to avoid a pause at 0000 (zero), at -3 (minutes) in each field battery, one section (of the two engaged) will lift on to the support line, where it will remain until 0002." Thus on that division's front not only would there be for ten minutes no heavy artillery fire, but for three minutes only half the 18-pounder fire.

At 07.20 hours the mine under Hawthorn Redoubt was blown, the heavy barrage lifted, and the Stokes mortars in the advanced emplacements, and four in the sunken lane in No Man's Land, to which two companies of the 1/Lancashire Fusiliers pushed forward, opened a hurricane fire on the German front trench, giving confirmation to the Germans, if any were needed, that the assault was about to take place.

Under cover of this fire, the leading companies of the assaulting infantry began to leave their trenches and form up in No Man's Land. Two platoons of the 2/Royal Fusiliers, with four machine-guns and four Stokes mortars, rushed forward to occupy the mine crater. They reached the near lip, not without a number of casualties, and at once came under heavy machine-gun and rifle fire from the German trenches on either flank and from the far lip of the crater, which the Germans had immediately occupied.[10]

SLAUGHTER ON THE SOMME: 1 JULY 1916

The explosion of the mine ten minutes before the assault undoubtedly prejudiced the chances of success,[11] as it warned the Germans to be on the alert.

It immediately brought down the enemy barrage, and within five minutes it seemed that every enemy machine-gun along the front was shooting incessantly. The divisions were caught forming up. Even before the heavy barrage lifted at 07.20 hours, Germans appeared in the front line; after that hour, with hardly a British shell or bullet striking the parapets, most of them fired standing in the remains of the trenches. Others sprang out to the front, some into shell holes, rifles and machine guns in hand. They received the leading infantry lines with very heavy fire directly these tried to advance across No Man's Land to their assault position one hundred yards from the German front line, whilst the party on the far lip of the mine crater, armed with machine guns and light trench mortars, simply shot right and left as it pleased.

The lack of surprise, however, cannot be attributed entirely to the mine being fired at 07.20 hours. Lanes had been cut in the British wire and bridges laid over the rear trenches some days before. A bombardment had been fired every morning, beginning at 05.00 hours, for a week. With the Germans the only question was, which day would be zero day. The mine announced not only the day, but almost the minute. Directly it was fired, without any appreciable pause, the enemy machine-gun fire became terrific; for the simultaneous lifting of the heavy gun barrage made it perfectly safe for the Germans to man their defences. The British creeping barrage moved on at zero, to the exasperation of the infantrymen, who were left to their fate.

The bombardment, as a whole, was considered to have been successful, the wire effectively cut, and the enemy defences demolished; in some units there was a little anxiety because their raids had been unsuccessful. It turned out that the counter-battery work had failed to make much impression, and the first indication of this fact was the shelling in the early hours of 1 July of the trenches of the 31st Division, which were crowded with men. A hit on a 6-inch water-main flooded the trenches of the 4th Division.

The enemy had a further surprise in store. The corps had been given to understand that there were only fifty-five heavy guns in position to oppose it, yet at zero the Germans opened a number of new batteries which had not previously fired, and had not therefore been located. A total of sixty-six batteries (including guns on the unattacked front immediately north of VIII Corps, which fired in semi-enfilade) are reported to have come into action against the three divisions of VIII Corps. The volume and accuracy of their fire disorganized the attack at the very outset.

Across the front of the 87th Brigade (Brigadier-General C.H.T. Lucas), on the right, ran Y Ravine, with only its edge, not its hollow, visible from the British line. The German front trench followed first the edge of the Beaumont Hamel valley and then the lip of the ravine, thus forming in front of the brigade a deep re-entrant, which ensured cross fire. Both here and along the whole front of the 29th

Division, owing to the convexity of the slope, the German wire was not generally visible from the British trenches, and much of it was found uncut.[12]

The 1/Royal Inniskilling Fusiliers, on the right attacking south of the ravine, moved forward down the slight slope in admirable order, in spite of heavy casualties. Lieutenant Colonel R.C. Pierce was among the killed. However, the greater part of the men who reached the German front defences were held up by uncut wire.

Half-a-dozen parties here and there managed to get through it, then across the front trench and even beyond it down into the valley: they were not, however, in sufficient numbers to make good. Fired at from behind by machine-guns, brought up from dug-outs which they had overrun without"mopping up", all were either killed or taken prisoners.

The 2/South Wales Borderers, on the left opposite the ravine, was unable to reach the German position (except some of the left company who were shot on the German wire), owing to the intensity of the fire from three German machine-guns – all that was visible of the defenders – which, unhindered by barrage or covering fire, raked its lines. By 07.35 hours nothing remained of the Borderers but some scattered individuals lying within a hundred yards of the German trench.

The German field batteries behind Beaucourt ridge at about 2,000-2,500 yards' range, and the heavies in rear of them, placed a severe and most accurate barrage along the British front, support and reserve trenches, almost as soon as the rear companies of the leading battalions advanced. From this shelling and the machine-gun fire, the supporting battalions, the 1/King's Own Scottish Borderers and 1/Border Regiment, also suffered heavily as they came up to the front trench, and whilst crossing the bridges over it into No Man's Land, Lieutenant Colonel A.J. Ellis of the Border being severely wounded. They had advanced over the open, timed to enter No Man's Land at 08.05 hours, according to programme, all the battalions in support and in reserve moving in accordance with a time-table fixed by the corps. It being obvious that the German machine-guns had not been subdued, both commanding officers had suggested a pause for further bombardment, but, misled by the enemy firing white flares, which were to have been the British signal that the first objective had been reached, the brigadier ordered them to proceed.

The lanes cut through the British wire were rather narrow and difficult to find, the men"bunched"badly, and, the barrage having gone on, the German machine-gunners, already ranged on the passages, caused further heavy losses, until the dead lay literally in heaps at these places. The survivors nevertheless continued their advance from shell hole to shell hole until only a few small isolated parties were left. Finally these were compelled to come to a halt well in front of the German position, which was not entered anywhere.

Very soon after 08.00 hours the advance of the 87th Brigade had melted away, and was at a complete standstill. When troops meet with unexpected resistance, the quickest and most effective way to help them is by artillery fire, but owing to the rigid orders regarding the barrage all power to modify the distribution of fire had been voluntarily abandoned, and the barrage went on, leaving the infantry to its fate.

The assault of the 86th Brigade (Brigadier-General W. de L. Williams), which was to carry the village of Beaumont Hamel, hidden in the bed of the valley, fared no better, fire being opened as soon as the men left the trenches five minutes before zero.

The 2/Royal Fusiliers, on the right (less the half company that had gone to Hawthorn Redoubt mine crater), suffered very heavy casualties, including Lieutenant Colonel A.V. Johnson wounded. Thirty or forty men, diverging to the left, entered the mine crater and held on there, but the few who penetrated into the German front trench were killed.

The attack of the 1/Lancashire Fusiliers, on the left, was led by two companies (with a special bombing party one hundred strong, two machine-guns and four Stokes mortars) which had gone forward by the sap to the sunken lane half-way across No Man's Land. Although supported by a simultaneous advance of the rest of the battalion from the British front trench, their attack, as a whole, failed not many yards from the sunken lane: in fact the Lancashire men were mown down directly they showed above the dip in which the lane lies, and only a party of about fifty reached the low bank beyond it.

Here again, as soon as the leading battalions of the 86th Brigade advanced, the German artillery placed a barrage on the British front trenches. Returning wounded, afoot and on stretchers, delayed the advance of the supporting battalions, the 1/Royal Dublin Fusiliers and 16/Middlesex,[13] which were ordered to move along the communication trenches. They crossed the parapet, however, shortly before 08.00 hours, and, as they advanced, they could see much of the wire entanglement still uncut, and the various gaps in it choked with dead or wounded. Heavy machine-gun fire, particularly from "The Bergwerk",[14] on the Beaucourt ridge immediately behind the northern end of Beaumont Hamel, at once swept them down. Except for some 120 of the 2/Royal Fusiliers who made their way to the Hawthorn mine crater, none of the 86th Brigade reached the German position, and in trying to reorganize the advance, the brigade-major, the staff-captain and a second brigade-major were all wounded.

Following the Gallipoli practice, all the infantrymen of the 29th Division, in order to assist the artillery in spotting the front line, wore a triangle cut from a biscuit tin, which was sewn on the haversack carried on the back. With the sun's rays shining, the plaque certainly showed up the position of the men lying on the ground, but as it was thought to have increased the casualties, it was never worn again.

The reports of the fighting that now reached divisional headquarters unfortunately exaggerated the strength of the parties of the 87th Brigade which had been seen by observers moving down into the valley to the German support line, while the report made by a brigade that white flares had been seen gave false confirmation to many wild rumours. General de Lisle, under the impression that his right brigade had gone on unchecked to its objective, and that the supporting battalions were only temporarily held up by a few machine-guns, ordered his reserve brigade, the 88th (Brigadier-General D.E. Cayley) to move up its two leading battalions behind the 87th Brigade, leaving the others still at his disposal.

After assembling them in a trench along the Hamel – Auchonvillers road, the forward trenches being blocked, Brigadier-General Cayley was to send them to attack on a frontage of 1,000 yards between the divisional right boundary and the western extremity of Y Ravine. There would be no artillery support, but they would be covered by a barrage from the 88th Machine Gun Company.

At 09.05 hours only the 1/Newfoundland Regiment,[15] the left battalion, advanced over the open. It did so independently by brigade orders, as the start of the 1/Essex on its right had been delayed by the complete congestion of the trenches with the bodies of dead and dying, in places piled one on the other, through which it was attempting to move. No sooner had this isolated and doomed attack of the Newfoundlanders left cover than their ranks were swept with bullets from the German position around Y Ravine.

Dropping dead and wounded, as an artillery observer reported, at every yard, nevertheless the battalion pressed on, never faltering. The majority of the men were hit before they had gone much beyond the British wire, but some got across No Man's Land and actually reached the German trench and disappeared into it before they were finally shot down. The battalion suffered over seven hundred casualties, and was literally annihilated, losing every one of its officers, actually three more than the number it should have taken into action.

The 1/Essex coming up later, also suffered very heavily as soon as it left the front trenches, both from artillery on the right and machine-gun fire, particularly on the left. The fourth company was held back. Nevertheless, here too a few men reached the German position before they were killed. The survivors of both battalions remained lying out in No Man's Land.[16]

At 10.05 hours, as soon as General de Lisle had heard of this disaster and of the severe casualties suffered by the two leading brigades,[17] he directed that for the moment no more troops should be sent forward. The artillery barrage, by now across the Beaumont Hamel valley and on the fourth objective, was brought back, but only three or four hundred yards, as no one knew exactly where our men were, and, although a new artillery programme was issued, the results of it helped the infantry but little.

The 4th Division also sustained disastrous losses in its assault. On the front of this formation it was reported that the wire was well cut and the trenches well battered. Unfortunately the enemy's deep dug-outs had not been touched. Some of the entrances had been hit, but, as every dug-out had several, this was of small importance. The 11th Brigade (Brigadier-General C.B. Prowse) led the way from its assembly trenches, deep "slits" off the communication trenches, with three battalions in front line and three in support,[18] on the whole divisional frontage of fifteen hundred yards. It was to capture the first and second objectives, after which the 10th and 12th Brigades were to pass through it and assault the third.

Even during the final intense bombardment German machine-guns had fired intermittently, but at 07.20 hours, almost as the heavy artillery lifted, actually whilst the infantry was beginning to form up in No Man's Land in front of its trenches, the German machine-gun fire grew continuous. Deadly enfilade fire came from Ridge Redoubt on Redan Ridge in the centre of the front line opposite the division, and frontal fire not only from the defenders of the front line, but over their heads from reserves in the trenches on the Beaucourt spur, where they seem to have been massed in anticipation of a coming attack.

At the same time the enemy batteries, both heavy and field, as elsewhere, placed a barrage on No Man's Land, subsequently lifting it on to the British front trenches. This barrage was put down in "crumps" on a small length of trench, and after about ten minutes shifted to another. So severe were its results that for fifty yards behind the front no solid ground was left, nothing but a wilderness of shell holes.

At 07.30 hours, as soon as the final advance began, a few bold German machine-gunners put their weapons on the remains of the parapet and kept sweeping the line. The 1/East Lancashire, on the right, and the right of the 1/Rifle Brigade, in the centre, suffered especially, although the Riflemen were at the wire directly the shrapnel barrage lifted. The two machine-guns on the German parapet fired till the last moment, while another two in Ridge Redoubt, never silenced on this day, swept all No Man's Land and the front line systems. They not only shot down the leading battalions, but slaughtered the supporting ones, and prevented reinforcements and supplies from crossing.

The wire having been well cut by the field artillery, those of the leading platoons who survived reached the German front trench. Some even penetrated to the support trench, only to be at once surrounded and killed or taken prisoners: only two men returned. The other lines were unable to reach the German trenches, and took what cover they could. The left company of the 1/Rifle Brigade, and the right of the l/8th Royal Warwickshire, together with the supporting companies, were on the swell of ground formed by Redan Ridge, where, although exposed to enfilade fire from Ridge Redoubt, they received little direct fire. They were now able to penetrate separately into the German position, and enter the "Heidenkopf" better known as the Quadrilateral Redoubt.[19]

Crossing the front line they gained the support trench beyond it on a frontage of six hundred yards. The left of the l/8th Royal Warwickshire at first made good progress, and also entered the German front trench, but, its left flank exposed by the failure of the troops of the 31st Division, it encountered heavy machine-gun fire, especially from the direction of Serre, in front of which village it was suspected that the Germans had concealed or camouflaged machine guns under the remains of some burnt haystacks. The rear lines were stopped, and only small parties of the front lines reached the German support trench.

At 07.40 hours, according to the time-table, the three supporting battalions of the 11th Brigade began to move across No Man's Land. On the right, the 1/Hampshire, like the greater part of the 1/East Lancashire in front, was unable to reach the German lines, and, taking cover in the mass of shell holes between the opposing fronts, became mixed with the latter battalion. In the centre, the 1/Somerset Light Infantry was forced to incline to the left, for Redan Ridge, which should have been crossed, was now continuously swept by machine-gun fire, but, pressing on, the survivors reinforced the companies of the Rifle Brigade and Warwickshire in the Quadrilateral.

Small parties of the Rifle Brigade and Somerset Light Infantry then fought their way on for another quarter of a mile to the furthest trench of the German front position, and occupied three hundred yards of it. On the left the 1/6th Royal Warwickshire, moving up in support of its sister battalion, passed the Quadrilateral, and the right companies of both Warwickshire battalions then went on and gained touch with the advanced position of the Rifle Brigade and Somerset Light Infantry, but the companies on the left, suffering heavy losses from the fire of the camouflaged machine-guns near Serre, were unable to make any progress.

From the Serre direction, too, came a bombing counterattack on the Quadrilateral. It was evident that the 31st Division had not reached the village, and from the battle headquarters of the infantry brigadiers of the 4th Division, some four hundred yards behind the front line, offering a view from Beaumont Hamel to Serre, the falling back of the 29th Division was actually witnessed. But the exact situation of the leading battalions of the 4th Division was not known, as the signal for "stopped by uncut wire", one white flare, and that for "objective gained", three white flares, proved too much alike to be decisive.

In the meantime the 10th Brigade (Brigadier-General C.A. Wilding), and the 12th Brigade (Brigadier-General J.D. Crosbie), moving from the reserve trenches across the open in artillery formation, were approaching the British front line, timed to leave it at 09.30 hours. In view of the manifestly heavy losses of the 11th Brigade, signal messages had been sent at 08.35 hours from divisional headquarters directing the 10th and 12th Brigades, notwithstanding the corps timetable, to refrain from crossing the front line to the assault until the situation became clearer. These instructions did not, however, arrive in time for the leading battalions of either brigade, which were a little ahead of the clock, to be stopped, but those in rear were held back.[20]

About 09.30 hours, therefore, another considerable advance – four and a half battalions in extended lines on a front of fifteen hundred yards – began from the British front line, the 2/Royal Dublin Fusiliers and 2/Seaforth Highlanders of the

10th Brigade on the right, and the 2/Essex and 1/King's Own with half of the 2/Lancashire Fusiliers (12th Brigade) on the left. The leading companies of the Dublin Fusiliers at once came under heavy fire not only from Ridge Redoubt and the adjacent trenches, but from Beaumont Hamel, and only a few men reached the German position. The commanders of the rear companies, seeing the situation and discovering that most of the East Lancashire and Hampshire were immediately ahead of them in No Man's Land, halted their men in the front trenches.

The Seaforth and the Lancashire Fusiliers, by inclining to their left, got some shelter under the north side of Redan Ridge, and were able to avoid the machine-gun fire from Beaumont Hamel. Crossing the German front line south of the Quadrilateral, they pressed on and reinforced the advanced units of the 11th Brigade. As they approached they were received with shouts of welcome which were at first mistaken by them for cries of defiance from the enemy and caused a momentary pause. However, some of the 10th Brigade went on and even entered Munich Trench, five hundred yards beyond.

The 2/Essex and 1/King's Own, advancing on the original frontage of the left wing of the Rifle Brigade and the 1/8th Royal Warwickshire, suffered heavily from artillery fire in No Man's Land, and two small mines were fired under the King's Own. Nevertheless they crossed the German position, Major J.N. Bromilow (King's Own) being killed, and Lieutenant Colonel Sir George Stirling (Essex) severely wounded soon afterwards, and they sent reinforcements to the furthest trench occupied by the 11th Brigade. Small parties of the same battalions, too, entered Munich Trench and passed beyond it to the edge of Pendant Copse; in fact it was reported to the division that some infantry had been seen entering Serre.

Observation of troops, on account of smoke and dust, was extremely difficult, and although two contact patrol aeroplanes displayed amazing daring, flying along the front sometimes only fifty feet above the troops under heavy small-arm fire, no definite information could be obtained. It seemed certain that a considerable portion of the 4th Division had successfully broken through the German front position, and this was confirmed by reports from the 31st Division on the left. It is now known that a large number of men who had thus penetrated the enemy's front were shot down by Germans, who came in behind them from the trenches on either side, which the 29th and 31st Divisions on the right and left had failed to capture.

Assault of the 31st Division towards Serre

The 31st Division[21] was to form a defensive flank facing north-east, keeping in touch with the left of the 4th Division. This entailed an advance on the right of some 3,000 yards. Major General Wanless O'Gowan detailed for the operation the

93rd Brigade (Brigadier-General J.D. Ingles), and the 94th Brigade (Brigadier-General H.C. Rees, commanding temporarily in the absence of Brigadier-General G.T.C. Carter-Campbell), retaining the 92nd Brigade (Brigadier-General O. de L. Williams); the last remained in reserve in the support trenches all day.

The heavy artillery bombardment on this sector of the enemy front had not been successful, but the wire had been effectively cut and blown into thick heaps, and the defences much damaged. Still the Germans from their excellent observation posts in the partially destroyed village of Serre overlooked the British position.

At 07.20 hours, as elsewhere on VIII Corps' front, when the first waves of infantry clambered over the parapet, and began passing through the narrow passages in their own wire to lie out in No Man's Land preparatory to the advance, heavy machine-gun fire was opened on them. The German batteries, heavy artillery from a hollow south-east of Puisieux, and field guns from about Serre, also laid an accurate barrage on the British front trench, extending to fifty yards in front of and behind it.

In spite of the British counter-battery fire and the hurricane fire of the Stokes mortars during the last ten minutes before zero, there was no falling off in the volume of the enemy reply. In fact, at 07.30 hours, as soon as the leading waves rose, his fire increased in intensity, and Germans were seen to man the front trench, some standing up clear of it, whilst others, carrying machine-guns, ran out into the shell craters in No Man's Land in order to fire more effectively. Here also the barrage had passed on, and there were no guns available to deal with the enemy.

Only a few isolated parties of the 31st Division were able to reach the German front trench, where they were in the end either killed or taken prisoner. The extended lines started in excellent order, but gradually melted away. There was no wavering or attempting to come back; the men fell in their ranks, mostly before the first hundred yards of No Man's Land had been crossed. The magnificent gallantry, discipline and determination displayed by all ranks of this North Country division were of no avail against the concentrated fire-effect of the enemy's unshaken infantry and artillery, whose barrage has been described as so consistent and severe that the cones of the explosions gave the impression of a thick belt of poplar trees.

On the front of the 93rd Brigade, the 15/West Yorkshire, leading, was almost annihilated by frontal fire and deadly enfilade fire from the sides of the re-entrant it was attacking. All the officers (including Major R.B. Neill, commanding, who was severely wounded), became casualties in the first few minutes, and the survivors of the lines of companies lay down in No Man's Land.

The 16/West Yorkshire, with one company of the 18/Durham Light Infantry, detailed to take Pendant Copse, on its right, advanced from the support line across the open and suffered very heavily even before reaching the front trenches. Major

C.S. Guyon was killed, and only a few men crossed over into No Man's Land, but some of the Durhams actually entered Pendant Copse. The 18/West Yorkshire, in support, was unable to make any headway. The 18/Durham Light Infantry (less one company), in reserve, was kept back.

The 94th Brigade,[22] assaulting on a two-battalion frontage, with the 11/East Lancashire (whose Lieutenant Colonel, A.W. Rickman, was killed) and the 12/York & Lancaster, encountered from the outset an almost equally heavy fire. Much of this came from the left flank, where the German position to the north, which was not being attacked, had not been neutralized, as was expected, by a smoke-screen. Nevertheless, the right company of the East Lancashire broke into the German front line.

Reports from various observation posts stated, about 08.30 hours, that a party of this company[23] had been seen first lying down in line and later advancing into Serre village, and at 09.15 hours an artillery observing officer, specially detailed to watch the progress of the infantry, reported that he distinctly saw some eighty to one hundred men rise from a trench near Serre and disappear into the village. About this time the Germans were reported to be shelling the village,[24] but it is clear that, whatever temporary success it may have gained, the whole of this party was either killed or taken prisoner within a few hours.

A number of men of the right company of the 12/York & Lancaster also succeeded in entering the German front trench, and a few eventually entered Serre.[25] The bulk of the battalion was held up in No Man's Land, where it occupied the Russian sap which had been made and opened up to afford flank protection, but many men reached the German wire entanglement only to find that, in spite of gaps, it still formed a sufficient obstacle to prevent them from reaching the German trench under fire.

Efforts made to reinforce the party of the East Lancashire reported to be in Serre village were of no avail; the gap in the German front trench where the East Lancashire had broken through had been filled by Germans, who came out of the dug-outs to mount machine-guns after our men had passed on. Here, as on the front of the 93rd Brigade, the supporting battalions suffered heavily from the German artillery barrage, which was at once put down when they made any movement and was obviously directed by observation. The leading companies of the 13th and 14th York & Lancaster were badly mauled by it, the supporting companies stopped short; orders were therefore given to suspend the attack.

About 09.00 hours the Germans opposite the 93rd Brigade appeared to be concentrating for a counter-attack, and, regardless of divisional orders, at the instance of Brigadier-General Ingles, the 170th Brigade Royal Field Artillery brought back its fire to disperse them.

A little later the rest of the 12/King's Own Yorkshire Light Infantry (Pioneers) was moved up to support the 93rd Brigade. The situation in the trenches of the 31st Division, after the initial attack had failed, with a heavy 5.9-inch barrage falling on them and almost continuous machine-gun fire sweeping them, certainly invited counter-attack. Fortunately the enemy in front remained quiet for the rest of the morning, and by noon fire had almost come to an end. At intervals Germans showed themselves above the parapet of their front trench to snipe the men lying out in front of the wire entanglements, but they were checked by machine-gun fire from the British trenches. Similarly, any movement in or over these trenches was spotted by the enemy and artillery fire fell on them.

Endeavours to renew the assault of VIII Corps

The first reports received at corps headquarters at Marieux (ten miles west of Serre)[26] were most encouraging and rose-coloured. It seemed certain, as was indeed the case, that the 4th Division had broken through, although it was not realized for some time that the assault as a whole had gone amiss. The first unfavourable sign was the total absence of prisoners.

Then news, scanty and uncertain, began to trickle in. Throughout the day the information received from the front, particularly as regards the situation at Serre, was poor in spite of the measures ordered to ensure a good supply. So many senior regimental officers were killed or wounded that the usual channels of communication failed. It was most difficult to decide what course of action to take, with the result that a great deal of the fire of the heavy artillery was wasted on back areas.

At 10.25 hours, however, General Hunter-Weston, the corps commander, though he still hoped to exploit the success which had been achieved, came to the conclusion that any thought of attacking the German second position, Puisieux Trench, must for the moment be abandoned. He ordered that all efforts should be directed to gaining and consolidating the German intermediate position, Munich Trench.

To support the centre and left of the 4th Division, reported in that locality, he directed that the remaining two battalions (4/Worcestershire and 2/Hampshire) of the 88th Brigade, in 29th Division reserve, and the right of the 4th Division should carry out a combined converging attack through Beaumont Hamel village and across the head of the valley.

By this time the artillery brigade commanders had brought the fire of most of their batteries back without orders, having seen, from their observation posts, when their barrage was 1,000 yards ahead, that the enemy in places was obviously in his front trenches. The divisional artillery was therefore ordered to begin a fresh bombardment of the German line in the sector selected, and lift at 12.30 hours; the heavy artillery was to turn its fire on to the front line at 12 noon and lift at 12.25 hours.

At 12.30 hours the infantry was to attack: the two battalions of the 88th Brigade against Station Road and Beaumont Hamel from the south-west, and the 10th

Brigade (4th Division) eastwards against a frontage of 1,000 yards immediately north of the village. From 11.00 hours onwards, however, owing to the enemy barrages, signal communication forward to the front trenches – in spite of all cables being buried six feet deep for 5,500 yards behind the front line – became as uncertain as communication back from the fighting front, and there were heavy casualties among runners who attempted to take messages across to the units in the German position.

The difficulties which the runners encountered also prevented supplies of hand-grenades and ammunition being carried up. On the front of the 29th Division the garrison in the Hawthorn Redoubt crater, short of ammunition and assailed by trench-mortar bombs, hand-grenades and machine-gun fire from both sides, was driven out before noon, and an effort made shortly afterwards by the 1/Lancashire Fusiliers, reinforced by the "10 per cent reserve" from the front line, to advance from the sunken lane broke down under machine-gun fire.

On the front of the 4th Division by this time the troops which had broken through and reached Munich Trench and even a trench beyond it, were much reduced in numbers. Running short of hand-grenades, and driven to rely on rifles only, as could be seen from artillery observation posts, they were gradually forced to retire; the enemy, soon after 11.00 hours, were working forward and round the flanks by the use of shell craters with which the whole of this ground was now scarred. At the same time strong parties of enemy bombers attacked down the trenches from the north, and from near Serre, against the flank and rear of the British advanced troops.

A little before 11.00 hours the remaining two companies of the 2/Lancashire Fusiliers and a company of the 2/Duke of Wellington's (12th Brigade) had been able to reinforce the garrison in the Quadrilateral and the adjacent front trenches, but otherwise little assistance could be given. Thus by noon the remnants of the advanced troops, short of bombs and ammunition, were falling back to this redoubt.[27] The 4th Division was now considerably disorganized, and its trenches crowded with wounded, the 11th Brigade, and the two battalions of the 143rd with it, alone having lost ninety officers and 1,948 other ranks out of approximately 4,500 of all ranks who had gone into action.[28]

In these circumstances, although Lieutenant General Hunter-Weston contemplated using his reserve division, the 48th, to back up the 88th and 10th Brigades, and moved it up to Mailly Maillet, two miles behind the battlefront, the renewed attack ordered had much less chance of success than the original assault. Nor could it be organized in time. Owing to the greatly congested state of the trenches, the order for the attack did not reach the two battalions of the 88th Brigade until 13.30 hours. The hour of assault was postponed, and at 13.45 hours the orders for their taking part in the operation were cancelled. Instructions were issued for the reorganization of units of the 29th Division and the clearing up of the front trenches.

The attack of the 10th Brigade in like manner failed to materialize. The Seaforth Highlanders, already in the German trenches, and such men of the leading companies of the Dublin Fusiliers who were with them, were to take part, but the message to the Highlanders never reached them, and the rest of the Dublin Fusiliers had lost so heavily that they could not be reorganized in time for attack.

At 13.00 hours the 1/Royal Warwickshire, a supporting battalion of the 10th Brigade, was ordered to take the place of the Dublin Fusiliers with a company of the 1/Royal Irish Fusiliers in support, but every attempt to cross the British front trenches into No Man's Land was met by intense enemy machine-gun fire and further attempts were abandoned. After dark, however, the company of the Royal Irish Fusiliers crossed over to the Quadrilateral.

At 14.55 hours Major General Lambton reported to corps headquarters that his division had suffered heavy casualties, and that no further attack was possible that day.[29] He ordered the scattered units of the 11th Brigade to be collected and re-formed as a divisional reserve, and the 10th and 12th Brigades to take over the defence of the British front line, the 12th Brigade being also entrusted with the defence of the German trenches about the Quadrilateral still in British hands. At the same time, the field batteries occupying offensive positions near the front line were ordered to withdraw after dark to previously prepared positions further back.

On the left, in view of the continued rumours that Serre village was in the hands of British troops, the 31st Division, at 12.15 hours, had ordered the 94th Brigade to make another effort to get forward and confirm this success. Brigadier-General Rees replied that it would be better to postpone any further action until more definite news was received, but this, owing to all communication with parties in the German position being cut off, never came.

At 16.07 hours an aeroplane observer reported that Serre village and adjacent portions of Munich Trench and Pendant Trench (thought to be held by the 4th Division) were unoccupied, and that there were only small British parties in the trenches between the German front line and Serre. The 94th Brigade was nevertheless again ordered to prepare an attack with any available men against the German front on the left opposite John Copse, with a view to establishing communication with the British parties supposed to be in the neighbourhood of Serre.

However, after subsequent consultation with the commanders of the 93rd and 94th Brigades, Major General Wanless O'Gowan came to the conclusion that these two brigades, in view of their heavy losses[30] – to which, late in the day, was added Lieutenant Colonel M.N. Kennard, a cavalry officer commanding the 18/West Yorkshire – and the mixture of their units in the trenches, were not fit to undertake any further offensive operations that day.

He reported his opinion to VIII Corps headquarters at 18.00 hours, and General Hunter-Weston thereupon directed the front trenches to be cleared up and the units reorganized. At the same time, he ordered two battalions of the 92nd

Brigade, in divisional reserve, to be moved forward to deliver an attack, under cover of darkness, at 02.00 hours, for the purpose of clearing up the situation and gaining touch with any British troops still within the German defences.

Later however, at 21.50 hours, after further consideration, this attack also was cancelled. The wisdom of this decision cannot be questioned; for it would have been nearly impossible to bring up organized troops until order had been restored in the communication trenches and front position. Success, too, even if gained, would probably have been in vain; for during the night a number of wounded and unwounded men returned from No Man's Land and from the German lines, and, from their statements, it was gathered that, although so far all counter-attacks had been repulsed, there were no longer any men of the 31st Division left in the German defences capable of holding out against a renewed attack.

Thus at the end of the day VIII Corps had nothing to show for its very heavy losses except a footing in and near the Quadrilateral, and this had to be abandoned next morning.[31]

There had been no surprise, except what the enemy achieved in his display of guns and machine-guns; the bombardment had made little impression on the German defences, having been too much distributed in depth, and counter-battery work had failed. The enemy's machine-guns, when the barrage moved on prematurely, emerged to mow down the attacking infantry, their fire causing such heavy losses in officers that the general movement was disorganized; the second line of battalions was engaged too soon, and it was impossible to stop its advance; and the various parties of British, principally of the 4th Division, who managed to cross the enemy's front defences were in many cases shot down from behind by Germans who appeared from dug-outs which had not been "mopped up".

Finally, owing to the enemy's barrage, it had been impossible to exploit the breach made in his defences by the 4th Division, and the failure of the division on either side made it impossible, as in the case of the 36th Division, to hold on to the ground gained.

Under cover of darkness the battle front of VIII Corps was cleared and the defence reorganized, but the front line had been so obliterated that it could only be held by posts, with a continuous defence in the support, or the third line. On the right, facing Y Ravine and the head of the Beaumont Hamel valley, the 29th Division arranged to hold the front with the 88th Brigade and the survivors of the 86th. The 87th Brigade moved back into divisional reserve, but only until the next night, when it went into the line again to take over the part of the 36th Division front north of the Ancre. In the centre, across the swell of ground between the Beaumont Hamel and Beaucourt valleys, the 4th Division held the front, including the Quadrilateral, with the 10th and 12th Brigades, whilst the 11th Brigade was withdrawn into divisional reserve. On the left, before Serre, the remnants of the 93rd and 94th Brigades, 1,436 all ranks, were reorganized, the 18/Durham Light Infantry and 13/ and 14/York & Lancaster holding the front defences. The 92nd

Brigade was marched back to Bus les Artois to join the corps reserve.

The 48th Division (less the 143rd Brigade, two battalions of which had held defensively the northern sector of the corps front north of John Copse throughout the day, and two had attacked with the 4th Division) remained in the Mailly Maillet area, to which it had moved, in a position of readiness throughout the day and the following night.

The clearing of the battlefield of VIII Corps, apart from the great number of casualties (over 14,000, heavier than in any other corps) presented many difficulties. The trenches were crowded with dead and wounded, and whilst lying in them and in No Man's Land many of the wounded were further injured or killed by the German barrages; all day and well into the night there was a stream of walking wounded to the collecting station at Acheux, which was difficult to control.

During the pause after midday, until 16.00 hours when British guns reopened fire, the Germans allowed stretcher-bearers to work in No Man's Land, but from that hour until about 22.30 hours machine-gun and field-gun fire prevented any movement.

All through the night artillery, engineers, the field ambulance bearers (although it was not their proper work) and battalion parties assisted to bring in the wounded. As it was impossible to carry stretchers up the communication trenches owing to their being very narrow and having many traverses, the trenches were bridged and they were borne over the top. However, even the advanced dressing stations were shelled, particularly a bearer post near Auchonvillers, known as the "White City", where in a hollow road a number of dugouts had been cut in the chalk. Here Lieutenant Colonel C. Howkins, Royal Army Medical Corps (Territorial Force), was severely wounded.

On the morning of the 2nd there was an informal truce, and the enemy offered no objection to the collection of wounded, provided parties did not come too close to his wire. The work was resumed at night, the searchers being sometimes guided by the cries of the wounded, but some of these kept still as death for fear of being picked up by the Germans. The dead were also brought in as far as possible, but not till forty-eight hours after the evening of 1 July could it be said that most of the wounded had been removed, and another twelve hours elapsed before No Man's Land could be reported cleared.

The Germans opposite VIII Corps

The German account of the fighting on VIII Corps front agrees generally with the British.[32] Considerable stress, however, is laid on the damage done by the bombardment:

"Entanglement wire torn to pieces, trenches filled up, and most of the shelters

(*Unterstände*, not the mined dug-outs, *Stollen*) crushed in. Crater touched crater. Only a few miserable remnants of walls of Beaumont Hamel remained."

As soon as the British left their parapet, the Germans manned what remained of the trenches and opened fire. They had been sheltering in "great, deep-mined dug-outs like tunnels, painfully constructed during the winter of 1914-15. Whole companies found shelter in them." In the sector of the 119th Reserve Regiment, besides the dug-outs in Beaumont Hamel, there were others in Y Ravine (called by the enemy "Leiling Schlucht"), and south of the village the great "Leiling" and "Bismarck" mined dugouts.

In the sector of the 121st Reserve Regiment, opposite the 4th Division, the British arrived so quickly that there was not time for all the men to climb out of the deep dugouts. At Hawthorn Redoubt, the mine blew up "more than 3 sections", and the shelters of 1½ platoons were crushed in, so that barely two sections escaped. The rest of the company in question was in a large mined dug-out, but the four entrances were covered up by the explosion, and the inmates imprisoned until the British retired. Nothing is said about the British breaking through anywhere, but it is admitted that "the situation at the mine crater became extremely critical. If the enemy broke in there, the whole position of the 119th Reserve Regiment was gone."

A counter-attack by two platoons, which worked from crater to crater, combined with grenade fighting, finally drove the British back. It is claimed that "in an hour, with the exception of the ground gained in Heidenkopf Redoubt (the Quadrilateral), the position was clear of the enemy . . . and in the course of the night the redoubt was cleared after bitter close fighting". The 169th Regiment, opposite the 31st Division, also made a counter-attack with two companies, and expelled the attackers who had entered the front system, taking thirty-four prisoners – the only ones mentioned.[33]

NOTES

1. VIII Corps (Lieutenant General Sir A.G. Hunter-Western) comprised: 29th Division (Major General H. de B. de Lisle), 86th, 87th and 88th Brigades; 4th Division (Major General Hon. W. Lambton), 10th, 11th and 12th Brigades; 31st Division (Major General R. Wanless O'Gowan), 92nd, 93rd and 94th Brigades; 48th Division (Major General R. Fanshawe), 143rd, 144th and 145th Brigades.; G.O.C. Royal Artillery, Brigadier-General T.A. Tancred; G.O.C. Heavy Artillery, Brigadier-General D.F.H. Logan; Chief Engineer, Brigadier-General G.S. Cartwright. Lieutenant General Sir A.G. Hunter-Weston had commanded the 29th Division and VIII Corps at Gallipoli, and, after sick leave, had returned to France (he had commanded a brigade of the 4th Division there in 1914) in March 1916.

2. Beaumont Hamel was not captured until 13 November 1916, and then only with the aid of tanks and a new form of gas projection.

3. The other two battalions of the brigade were attached to the 4th Division, and attacked with it.

4. The German force opposing VIII Corps consisted of the 119th Reserve and 121st Reserve Regiments, all Württemberg troops, of the 26th Reserve Division, and the 169th Regiment of the 52nd Division, their sectors corresponding roughly to those of the three attacking divisions of the VIII Corps. Part of

the 66th of the 52nd Division was in reserve behind Puisieux. The boundary between the 26th Reserve and 62nd Divisions was just one hundred yards north of the line of demarcation between the 4th and 31st Divisions. Each regiment had two battalions in the front defences, with the third battalion in the intermediate line. The main German artillery positions were on the reverse slope of the Beaucourt spur in rear of Munich Trench, and also on the reverse slope of the Grandcourt spur in rear of Puisieux Trench.

5. The heavy artillery of the corps consisted of five groups, the 1st, 4th, 16th, 17th and 36th, comprising – Howitzers: three 15-inch; two 12-inch; twelve 9.2-inch; sixteen 8-inch; twenty-four 6-inch. Guns: six 6-inch; thirty-two 60-pounders; eight 4.7-inch. A "groupe" of 75mm of the French 37th Artillery Regiment was attached. This works out at about one heavy gun per forty-four yards. The divisional artillery had a field gun per twenty yards.

6. The 29th Division attached one whole field company (1/1st West Riding, 1/3rd Kent and 1/2nd London) to each of its three brigades, but, owing to the heavy fixed duties mainly in connection with communications and water supply, only a small portion of each company was available; the 4th Division attached only one section (7th, 1/1st Durham and 1/1st Renfrew); the 31st Division attached three sections (210th Field Company) to the 94th Brigade, which hoped to consolidate its objectives by daylight, keeping the rest of the divisional Royal Engineers (211th and 223rd) in reserve, as the 93rd Brigade preferred to wait until night before bringing up its engineers.

7. Two communication tunnels, known as "Cat" and "Rat", were also made on the 4th Division front, and the exits, ten yards from the enemy, were opened at 23.00 hours on 30 June. A Lewis gun was mounted in each at 07.25 hours. Both guns were hit by machine-gun fire within ten minutes, and German bombing parties occupied the ends, which were then blocked. An attempt to construct similar tunnels on the 31st Division front was detected by enemy patrols, who blew them in when about half-way across No Man's Land, but a sap to form a defensive flank was tunnelled between the front trench and the enemy trenches on the left. It was blown open on the morning of the 1st, and known as "Russian Trench".

8. This was well known in France from the experience in the minor actions earlier in the year. Thus at the action of the St. Eloi craters, thirty seconds', and finally sixty seconds', interval had been allowed, but in the end the infantry started actually at zero. In the instructions for the Messines offensive in 1917, it was stated "all material comes down within twenty seconds".

9. Report of the G.O.C. Heavy Artillery, VIII Corps. The war diary entry states: "The assault was launched at 7.30 am, and the artillery lifted at 7.20 and 7.25 in accordance with operation orders." VIII Corps' operation orders of 15 June state that the orders to the artillery were "issued to artillery only". No copy can be found. That the barrage lifted before the time expected was noticed by a number of infantry officers.

10. The account of the 119th German Reserve Infantry Regiment states: "During the intense bombardment there was a terrific explosion which for the moment completely drowned the thunder of the artillery. A great cloud of smoke rose up from the trenches of No.9 Company, followed by a tremendous shower of stones, which seemed to fall from the sky over all our position. More than three sections of No.9 Company, were blown into the air, and the neighbouring dug-outs were broken in and blocked. The ground all round was white with the debris of chalk as if it had been snowing, and a gigantic crater, over fifty yards in diameter and some sixty feet deep (actually 130 feet in diameter and 58 feet deep) gaped like an open wound in the side of the hill. This explosion was a signal for the infantry attack, and everyone got ready and stood on the lower steps of the dug-outs, rifles in hand, waiting for the bombardment to lift. In a few minutes the shelling ceased, and we rushed up the steps and out into the crater positions. Ahead of us wave after wave of British troops were crawling out of their trenches, and coming forward towards us at a walk, their bayonets glistening in the sun."

11. *Schlachten des Weltkrieges, Somme Nord,* (Reichsarchiv, Oldenburg) i. p.32, states that the Germans "were warned of the coming attack by the firing of the mine".

12. It has been stated that in the 29th Division, having been reconstituted after Gallipoli, many of the battery commanders were inexperienced and could not manage the difficult task of cutting wire with shrapnel.

13. Originally a Public Schools battalion, which had already given some 1,450 men to be commissioned, it had come into the division to replace the 1/Royal Munster Fusiliers, transferred to the 16th Division.

SLAUGHTER ON THE SOMME: 1 JULY 1916

Every officer but one was killed or wounded on 1 July.

14. That is "The Mine". It was a system of caves and underground passages which had been excavated in days long past to obtain hard chalk locks for building purposes, and used as refuges by the inhabitants in time of war. There were many such in the Somme area, and they provided splendid shelter for the German supports and reserves.

15. The regiment was composed entirely of native-born Newfoundlanders. The 1st Battalion (the 2nd was draft-finding) landed at Suvla in September 1915 to join the 88th Brigade of the 29th Division, and accompanied the division to France. In all, 6,339 men were accepted for service in it, 4,984 being sent overseas; 1,232 were killed, 2,314 wounded and 174 taken prisoner.

16. The casualties were: 1/Essex, three officers killed, eleven wounded, and one missing, with fifty-seven other ranks killed, 156 wounded, and one missing – a total of 229 men. The Newfoundland Regiment suffered fourteen officers killed and twelve wounded, with 219 other ranks killed, 374 wounded and ninety-one missing – a total of 710.

17. The 86th Brigade casualties were: 2/Royal Fusiliers, six officers killed, fifteen wounded and two missing, with 158 other ranks killed, 334 wounded and forty-six missing – a total of 561. 1/Lancashire Fusiliers, eight officers killed and ten wounded, with 156 other ranks killed, 298 wounded and eleven missing – a total of 483. 16/Middlesex, twenty-four officers killed and eight wounded, with 177 other ranks killed, 301 wounded, ten missing, and twenty-nine PoW – a total of 549. 1/Dublin Fusiliers were six officers killed and ten wounded, with 70 other ranks killed and 219 wounded – a total of 305. The Machine-Gun Company and Trench Mortar unit losses amounted to one officer killed and fourteen wounded, with seven other ranks killed, thirty-seven wounded and twelve missing – a total of seventy-one. Therefore, the brigade losses were 613 killed, 1,246 wounded, eighty-one missing and twenty-nine PoW – a total of 1,969.

The 87th Brigade casualties were: 2/South Wales Borderers, nine officers killed, six wounded and two missing, with 141 other ranks killed, 212 wounded and two missing – a total of 372. 1/King's Own Scottish Borderers, eleven officers killed and eight wounded, with 145 other ranks killed and 388 wounded – a total of 552. 1/Inniskilling Fusiliers nine officers killed and eleven wounded, with 236 other ranks killed, 308 wounded, three missing, and one PoW – a total of 568. 1/Border Regiment were ten officers killed and six wounded, with 173 other ranks killed, 362 wounded, twenty-two missing and two PoW – a total of 575. The Machine-Gun Company losses amounted to two officers missing, with two other ranks killed, seven wounded and eleven missing – a total of twenty-two. Therefore, the brigade losses were 736 killed, 1,308 wounded, forty-two missing and three PoW – a total of 2,089.

Including the casualties to divisional troops, the total for the division on 1 July was 223 officers and 5,017 other ranks.

18. Its own four and the l/6th and l/8th Royal Warwickshire lent from the 48th Division, in corps reserve.

19. The Quadrilateral, named "Heidenkopf" after a local commander, lay on the Serre – Mailly road. It was the remnant of a former German line which once ran through Matthew Copse and Touvent Farm. In previous fighting the Germans had been pushed back closer to Serre, but the Heidenkopf had held firm, and consequently now formed a pronounced salient in No Man's Land. The Germans had realized that in the event of a general offensive the work, owing to its prominent position, could no longer be permanently held, and they had therefore mined it with the idea of blowing it up as soon as the British entered. On the morning of 1 July the Heidenkopf was only defended by one machine-gun and by a few engineers who were to fire the mine. At the moment of assault, however, the machine-gun jammed, and, by some error, the engineers blew the mine too soon, with the result that they and the machine-gun crew were blown up with the redoubt before the British reached it. The effect of the explosion was greater than calculated, for it blocked up many of the German dug-outs nearby, so that the assaulting infantry were able to overrun the whole position of No. 3 Company, the right company of the 121st Reserve Regiment, which held this sector of the defences. One effect of the mine was to obscure all view of Serre and Puisieux from the front line for quite a long time.

20. The messages did not reach brigade headquarters till about 09.00 hours, and then had to be sent by runner, as the battalions were on the move.

21. The original 31st Division was formed in November 1914. In April 1915 it was broken up into independent brigades for draft-finding purposes, and a new 31st Division formed from the original

106

38th. Its infantry came from Hull (four battalions), Leeds, Bradford (two), Accrington, Sheffield, and Barnsley (two), with one Durham battalion (the first raised at the expense of a county). The pioneer battalion was the 12/King's Own Yorkshire Light Infantry (miners). The division was concentrated at Ripon and its first commander was Lieutenant General E.A. Fanshawe. It was sent from Britain to Egypt in December 1915, but was almost at once ordered to France, where it landed in March 1916. It had not yet been in action.

22. A company of the 12/King's Own Yorkshire Light Infantry (Pioneers) was attached to each attacking brigade, and the company with the 94th followed its first wave.

23. Distinguishing marks were worn by each unit taking part in the attack, such as coloured badges or ribbons, sacking covers to the steel helmet, etc., so that units could be identified.

24. Probably the fire of the 170th Brigade R.F.A.

25. Bodies of men of the 12/York & Lancaster were found in the northwest corner of the village when it was entered during the unsuccessful attack of the 3rd Division, with the 31st Division on its left, on 13 November 1916.

26. There was a corps observation post, with a General Staff officer in it, in Jacob's Ladder, just south of Hamel.

27. It was at this period of the fighting that Drummer W. Ritchie, 2/Seaforth Highlanders, gained the Victoria Cross. He repeatedly stood up on the German parapet and sounded the "charge" in order to encourage successive parties of men without leaders, who were falling back to the British trenches, to go forward again.

28. Including the Brigadier, Brigadier-General C.B. Prowse (died of wounds), who, as no information came back, left his headquarters to find out what was happening, and was hit, and of the six battalion commanders who fought under him, Lieutenant Colonels Hon. L.C.W. Palk (Hampshire), J.A. Thicknesse (Somerset Light Infantry), D. Wood (Rifle Brigade) and E.A. Innes (l/8th Royal Warwickshire), were killed, and J.E. Green (East Lancashire) and H. Franklin (l/6th Royal Warwickshire), wounded.

29. The 10th Brigade suffered twenty-eight officers killed, twenty-five wounded and two missing (a total of fifty-five), and 222 other ranks killed, 643 wounded, twenty-five missing and eighteen PoW (a total of 908). The 11th Brigade (six battalions) suffered seventy-three officers killed, sixty wounded and twelve missing (a total of 145), and 1,113 other ranks killed, 1,753 wounded, 112 missing and fifty-six PoW (a total of 3,034). The 12th Brigade suffered thirty-four officers killed, forty-nine wounded, one missing, and one PoW (a total of eighty-five), and 405 other ranks killed, 1,008 wounded, fifty-three missing and thirteen PoW (a total of 1,479). The Divisional Troops suffered one officer killed and seven other ranks killed, twenty-five wounded, and thirteen missing. Overall divisional losses were 1,883 killed, 3,563 wounded, 218 missing and eighty-eight PoW – a total of 5,752.

30. The 93rd Brigade suffered thirty-seven officers killed, fifty-three wounded and four missing (a total of ninety-four), and 561 other ranks killed, 1,144 wounded, twenty-four missing and one PoW (a total of 1,730). The 94th Brigade suffered twenty-nine officers killed, twenty-four wounded and two missing (a total of fifty-five), and 676 other ranks killed, 824 wounded, thirty-seven missing and seven PoW (a total of 1,544). The 12/KOYLI (Pioneers) suffered one officer killed and three wounded, and forty-five other ranks killed, 109 wounded and five missing. Other Divisional Troops suffered three officers wounded and one missing, along with nine other ranks wounded and one missing. Overall divisional losses were 1,349 killed, 2,169 wounded, seventy-four missing and eight PoW – a total of 3,600.

31. The sector of the German front line about the Quadrilateral was held tenaciously throughout the afternoon by men of the Lancashire Fusiliers and Seaforth Highlanders, and parties of the 11th Brigade, under Lieutenant Colonel J.O. Hopkinson of the Seaforth, but, although they were reinforced after dusk by a company of the 1/Royal Irish Fusiliers (10th Brigade), they were gradually driven back, and by midnight only the company of the Irish Fusiliers remained in the German front line, the others having been ordered to evacuate it, to avoid a disaster. This company, which did not receive the order, withdrew successfully at 11.30 hours on the following morning, bringing back its wounded and three German prisoners.

32. *Schlachten des Weltkrieges, Somme Nord*, (Reichsarchiv, Oldenburg).

33. The losses on the 1st July of the three regiments engaged are given as – 119th Reserve Regiment: eight officers killed and three wounded, and ninety-three other ranks killed, with 188 wounded; 121st Reserve Regiment: seven officers killed and nine wounded, and 192 other ranks killed, with 282 wounded and seventy missing; 169th Regiment: five officers killed and four wounded, with 136 other ranks killed, 215 wounded and two missing.

Index of Battalions

Border Regiment, 1st Battalion
Duke of Cambridge's Own (Middlesex Regiment), 16th (Service) Battalion
(Public Schools)
Duke of Wellington's (West Riding Regiment), 2nd Battalion
Durham Light Infantry, 18th (Service) Battalion (1st County)
East Lancashire Regiment, 1st Battalion
East Lancashire Regiment, 11th (Service) Battalion (Accrington)
Essex Regiment, 1st Battalion
Essex Regiment, 2nd Battalion
Hampshire Regiment, 1st Battalion
King's Own (Royal Lancaster Regiment), 1st Battalion
King's Own Scottish Borderers, 1st Battalion
King's Own (Yorkshire Light Infantry), 12th (Service) Battalion (Miners) (Pioneers)
Lancashire Fusiliers, 1st Battalion
Lancashire Fusiliers, 2nd Battalion
Monmouthshire Regiment, (Territorial Force) 1/2nd Battalion
Newfoundland Regiment, 1st Battalion
Prince Albert's (Somerset Light Infantry), 1st Battalion
Prince of Wales's Own (West Yorkshire Regiment), 15th (Service) Battalion (1st
Leeds)
Prince of Wales's Own (West Yorkshire Regiment), 16th (Service) Battalion (1st
Bradford)
Prince of Wales's Own (West Yorkshire Regiment), 18th (Service) Battalion (2nd
Bradford)
Princess Victoria's (Royal Irish Fusiliers), 1st Battalion
Rifle Brigade (The Prince Consort's Own), 1st Battalion
Royal Dublin Fusiliers, 1st Battalion
Royal Dublin Fusiliers, 2nd Battalion
Royal Fusiliers (City of London Regiment), 2nd Battalion
Royal Inniskilling Fusiliers, 1st Battalion
Royal Warwickshire Regiment, 1st Battalion
Royal Warwickshire Regiment, 1/6th Battalion (Territorial Force)
Royal Warwickshire Regiment, 1/8th Battalion (Territorial Force)
Seaforth Highlanders (Ross-Shire Buffs, The Duke of Albany's), 2nd Battalion
South Wales Borderers, 2nd Battalion
York And Lancaster Regiment, 12th (Service) Battalion (Sheffield)
York And Lancaster Regiment, 13th (Service) Battalion (1st Barnsley)
York And Lancaster Regiment, 14th (Service) Battalion (2nd Barnsley)

1st Battalion Border Regiment

FRONT LINE

7.30am   The Btn (less 10%) advanced just SOUTH of BEAUMONT HAMEL, their objective being BEAUCOURT REDOUBT.

The 2nd S.W.B.s, whose objective was the first two GERMAN LINES, were wiped out by MACHINE GUN fire in our own wire.

The 1st Btn The BORDER REGT then went over the top from our support line, and over our first line, the bridges over our front trench having been ranged by the GERMAN MACHINE GUNNERS the day previously, we met with heavy losses, while crossing these bridges & passing through the lanes out in our wire. The men were absolutely magnificent, and formed up as ordered outside our wire, made a right incline, and advanced into"NO MAN'S LAND" at a slow walk, also as ordered. The advance was continued until only little groups of half a dozen men were left here and there, and these, finding that no reinforcements were in sight, took cover in shell holes or where ever they could.

8am   The advance was brought entirely to a standstill.

8.15am   Enemy re-opened his bombardment on our trenches, for which our guns retaliated.

9.15am   LIEUT-COL ELLIS having been wounded and brought in by No.8409 PTE. NEWCOMBE, MAJOR MEIKLE JOHN (who had been in command of the 10 [illegible]) assumed command of the BTN, and collected all the men he could in the support line, as ordered by the BRIGADIER.

10.30am   The 10% ordered back to reserve line, where they stayed until next morning. Advance definitely given up in this sector.

The BTN. strength of those who took part in advance was OFFICERS 23.[1] OTHER RANKS 809.[2]

NOTES

1. The War Diary lists the following officer casualties – Killed: Captain F.R. Jessup and Captain T.H. Beves; Missing Believed Killed: Second Lieutenants W.K. Sanderson, J.Y. Baxendine, A.E. Fraser and L. Jackson; Wounded and Missing: Second Lieutenants H.L. Cholmely and W.P. Rettie; Wounded: Lieutenant Colonel A.J. Ellis, Captain J.G. Heyder, Lieutenant J.B. Sinclair, and Second Lieutenants G.W.N. Rowsell, F.H. Talbot, H.W.H. Barnes, D. Bremner, H.F. Sampson, F.T. Wilkins, D.C.R. Stuart and D. Cargill.
2. Other ranks casualties are listed as sixty-four killed, 411 wounded and 144 missing.

18th (Service) Battalion (1st County)
Durham Light Infantry

FRONT LINE

7.30am   Beginning of Battle of Somme. Objective of 18th D.L.I. line running S.E. of SERRE.

Battle of SERRE
18 DURHAM LIGHT INFANTRY

4.50am   Battn reached Assembly Trench, MAITLAND. H.Q. near WARLEY-MAITLAND junction. 11 EAST LANCS on left, 2nd WEST RIDING on right. 18 WEST YORKS in LANGUARD EAST of MAITLAND, Bde H.Q. in LEGEND.

6.0am   German guns appear to be inferior to our artillery. Our aircraft patrol lines effectively.

7.20am   Mine sprung at BEAUMONT HAMEL by BRITISH.

7.30am   Men are crossing to GERMAN lines carrying artillery disc, but smoke prevented good observation.

9.20am   Brigade instruct Battn to move to line Monk Trench to support 18 WEST YORKS.

9.47am   'A' Co leave MAITLAND & advance to MONK.

10.00am   'B' Co leave MAITLAND & advance to MONK with 'C' Co in MAITLAND ready to advance. Lancs. H.Q. in MAITLAND between BLENEAU & GREY.

11.0am   'A' & 'B' Cos heavily shelled in the open between MONK & MAITLAND.

11.30am   GERMAN artillery very effective & appearing to predominate.
Brigade instructs 'B' Co to reorganise in DUNMOW. [*illegible*] parties proceed to Sap A to report to 15 WEST YORKS.

11.57am   Message to Bde reporting disposition. 2 Platoons 'A' Co in MONK, 1 Platoon 'A' in FLAG, 1 Platoon 'A' in MAITLAND, 'B' Co WEST of MONK, 'C' Co in MAITLAND. Btn H.Q. as at 10a.m.
Heavy casualties in all Cos.

12.32pm   Bde instructs 'B' Co to hold SACKVILLE in conjunction with 4th Div, LEGEND also held by 4th Div.
Bde instructs Cdg Off to hold NEW DUNMOW.

1.53pm   'C' Co with 60 men of 18 WEST YORKS in NEW DUNMOW, 'A' & 'B' Cos garrison MAITLAND with bombing parties on right & left of NEW DUNMOW & LANGUARD, and Lewis guns NORTH and SOUTH of NEW DUNMOW.

3.11pm   1 Co 11 EAST YORKS move to MAITLAND & are under O.C. 18 DURHAM L.I. to cover 159 [*possibly 189*] Bty R.F.A.

3.40pm   O.C. 18 DURHAM L.I. moves 11 EAST YORKS from MAITLAND to take over defence of LANGUARD.

3.43pm   'C' Co report (1) front line trench blown out of existence as fighting trench, (2) front line full of EAST & WEST YORKS, (3) recall of bombing parties working with 15 WEST YORKS.

3.50pm   18 WEST YORKS are collected by 18 DURHAM L.I. in NEW DUNMOW. 'A' & 'B' Cos are being reorganised. Stragglers of 16 WEST YORKS are being collected.

Casualties approximately (less 'D' Co) 5 Officers wounded, 11 O.R. killed, 126 O.R. wounded. 4 Officers 'D' Co wounded, 17 O.R. 'D' Co reported Btn H.Q.

18 DURHAM L.I. instructed by Brigade to hold Front Line for the night & to expect counter attack. 'C' Co manned front line, 'A' & 'B' in MAITLAND, 16 WEST YORKS in DUNMOW. 'C' Co has bombing parties Sap A & Sap B.

5.45pm   11 EAST YORKS reported in position in LANGUARD.

6.30pm   Major TILLY reported at H.Q.

16th (Service) Battalion (Public Schools) Duke of Cambridge's Own (Middlesex Regiment)

Battalion in action 7.30am from support trenches.
Casualties:

Officers	Killed	3	Wounded	10	Missing believed Killed	6	Missing 5
O.R.	Killed	19	Wounded	306	Missing believed Killed	37	Missing 138

10.15am   Balance of Battalion took over front line trenches AUCHONVILLERS sector.[1]

NOTE

1. Other than the losses sustained, this War Diary entry gives little indication that the battalion "went over the top", though this is confirmed in the Corps' introduction. The historian Ray Westlake, in *Tracing British Battalions on the Somme* (Pen & Sword, Barnsley, 2009, p.223), states that "one source (H.L. Smythe) records that when Beaumont-Hamel was later taken in November the remains, paybooks etc., of some 180 Middlesex men were found at the sunken road in No Man's Land."

2nd Battalion Duke of Wellington's
(West Riding Regiment)

For the past month or six weeks the Bn had been busily engaged preparing for an attack on the German trenches. The VIII Corps under (Gen Sir A. Hunter Weston), to which the Bn belonged, was to attack the German trenches between HAMEL & SERRE. The Divisions comprising the Corps & their positions for attack were as follows, Right Division: 29th Div, Centre Division: 4th Div, Left Division: 31st Division & Reserve 48th Div has two battalions.

The 4th Div to which Bn belonged was to attack between the villages of BEAUMONT HAMEL & SERRE and gain the PUSIEUX Ridge.

The dispositions of the division for the attack were as follows, the 11th Bde with two battalions from the 48th Div were to make the first assault and capture the 1st and 2nd German lines supported by the 10th Bde on the right and the 12th Bde on the left. The Support Bde were to go through the leading Bde and push on & capture the PUSIEUX Ridge.

The Bn formed the left support battalion of the 12th Bde. The KINGS OWN & ESSEX were the leading Bns with left and right respectively. The LANCS Fus formed the right Support Bn. The chief role of the Bn was to carry up R.E. material to consolidate the captured position, consequently two Coys No's 2 & 4 were nearly all carrying R.E. material. Besides this each Bn had to provide 125 O.R. to act as Bde carriers for carrying up Rations, Ammunition, Bombs etc.

2am	Bn in position for the attack in assembly trenches South of SUCERIE.
5.30am	Breakfasts, hot tea & vegetable & meat ration.
8.55am	Leading Coys move out of assembly trenches & commence to advance.
9.25am	Bn received orders to halt. Runners sent forward to order Coys to halt.(up to this time casualties in Bn had been light), No.4 Coy halted but No's 1, 2 & 3 Coys went on to avoid barrage & gained German front line, some men reached the 2nd line, for some time no information was received from any of the Coys. Bn H.Q. had meanwhile been established in TAUPIN Tr. Later from Bn H.Q. our troops could been seen entering into what appeared to be the German 2nd Line, here they were reorganised & the remnants of the 11th Bde and the leading Bn of the 12th Bde pushed forward again, eventually this force was forced to retire owing to enfilade machine gun fire from SERRE & BEAUMONT HAMEL. A party of our troops, made up from men of various units, remained in the QUADRILATERAL till dusk and then came back to our trenches. One party of Irish Fusiliers remained till next morning.
3.30pm	About 3.30pm the C.O. (Lt Col R.N. BRAY) was sent for by the Brigadier (Gen J.D. Crosbie) from whom orders were received to reorganise and

hold front line. The section to be held by the Bde was from junction of DELAUNAY & WOLF Trs. to CAT ST. with H.Q. in VALADE Tr. The C.O. was given command of the KINGS OWN, ESSEX & DUKES for this purpose. The trenches held by Bn were BURROW, WOLF & LEGEND. Lts DAVIS & SUGDEN being in command. The men of the KINGS OWN & ESSEX had no officers with them. The other officers with the Coys were 2/Lts HOMFRAY, HARRY, JOHNSTON & MAUNDER.

During the night the Bn took over a little more of the line from the 1st Rifle Brigade. The night was comparatively quiet no counter attacks being made.

Total casualties during the day were:

Officers: 3 killed, 11 wounded, missing nil.

Other ranks: 18 killed, 251 wounded, 40 missing.

Officers killed were: Capt C.L. HART , Lt N.W. HADWEN, 2/Lt C.H. BOWES.

Wounded: Capt K.J. MILLN, Lts A.F. HEMMING, L.C. ADYE, S.R. LORD, D.M. BROWN, H.R. THELWELL, C.R. SANDERSON, E.S. PLUMB, S.B. KINGTON, C.W.G. GRIMLEY, C.D. JOHNSTON.

1st Battalion East Lancashire Regiment

The plan of the attack on the German lines detailed for the above date was as follows:

3 Coys were placed in the front line; each Coy on a front of 2 Platoons taking up their positions thus:

'C' Coy under Captain THOMAS on the right, stretching from the junction of 10-11 to the junction of 13-14.

'A' Coy joined 'C' on the right, holding the line to the junction 16-17, 'B' Coy thence to the junction 19-20.

On the Bn right the 1st LANCASHIRE FUSILIERS were entrusted with the capture of BEAUMONT-HAMEL, and on the left the 1st RIFLE BRIGADE protected our flank.

The 2nd line took up their position in MINDEN TRENCH - GREEN TRENCH and LUDGATE STREET.

'D' Coy were in Bn Reserve in CHATHAM trench.

During the previous night the wire in front of our trenches was systematically cut in order to allow for the progress of the attacking force.

Throughout the night the bombardment was carried out in salvos, and at 6AM increased in intensity culminating in a bombardment, which (according to prisoners) exceeded even that at Verdun.

At 7.26AM in accordance with the plan, the 6 leading platoons left the trenches and took up their position in "No Man's Land". This was accomplished almost without loss.

At 7.30AM. the guns lengthened and laid down a barrage on the enemy's support lines and communications.

At the same time our front line pushed forward, and the supporting platoons left our original front line trenches.

They were met with very heavy artillery and machine gun fire, some of 'A' & 'B' Coys did reach the German front line at 7.35AM, but were captured by the Germans who came out of their dug-outs and surrounded them. This caused the loss of Capt's PENNY and BROWNE, 2nd Lt's MALLET and JONES. Capt THOMAS, LTS FISHER & NEWCOMBE, 2Lt's C.P. WATSON, C.E.S. WATSON, SADDLER and THOMPKINS were unfortunately killed on the way across.

At 7.32AM 'D' Coy and Bn H.Q. left CHATHAM trench, but were hung up by reason of the intense machine gun fire, as were the 1st Hampshire Regt, who followed in support.

About 8.30AM the 1st Royal Warwickshire Regt who had been detailed to go through our objective were definitely warned to stand fast at TENDERLOIN TRENCH.

About 10.30AM. Lt Col J.E. GREEN D.S.O., who was in a depression near the German barbed wire was hit by a bullet which pierced his shoulder. He did not come in to have his wounds dressed, but lay there with the Adjutant (Capt S.J. HEATH), awaiting orders.

Captain WHIGHAM the M.O. who had been doing splendid work in "No Man's Land" was also wounded in the shoulder about the same time and had to leave the line.

The Bn continued to hold the line of shell holes in front of the German barbed wire, but it was seen that the strongholds of the enemy lines were too strongly fortified to be taken.

At 6PM Captain HEATH was severely wounded in trying to crawl back to the line. Colonel GREEN came in at 8.30pm badly shaken up and suffering from his wound. He was taken to the dressing station at the WHITE CITY.

Orders were received an hour later that the Battalion was to withdraw and retire to MAILLY-MAILLET, the 1st Royal Warwickshire Regt being detailed to cover the retirement.

11th (Service) Battalion (Accrington)
East Lancashire Regiment

The assembly trenches for the attack on Serre extended from MARK COPSE to MATTHEW COPSE inclusive with the 12th Battn York and Lancaster Regt on the left and the 93rd Brigade on the right. The 13th and 14th Battn York and Lancaster

Regt were in support of the 11th E. Lancs Regt & 12th York and Lancs Regt. The Battalion was ordered to go forward in 4 waves accompanied by details from the 94th Machine Gun Company and the 12th Battn K.O.Y.L.I. (Pioneers), the hour for attack being 7.30a.m.

When the infantry advanced heavy rifle and machine gun fire was opened from in front an enfilade from the direction of the POINT and GOMMECOURT Wood. A heavy artillery barrage was also placed on our front line trenches. From information brought back by wounded it appears that only a few reached the enemy front line and were able to enter their trenches owing to the intensity of the machine gun and rifle fire. Small parties penetrated as far as the German fourth line, but were not heard of again. During the day the unwounded men who returned were utilised to occupy our front line trenches.

The Battalion remained in the front line until 1a.m. on the 2nd July. When relieved by the 13th Battn York & Lancaster Regt.

Report on Operations June 30th to 9.40pm July 1st – Battle of the Somme

7pm, 30.6.16   The 11th East Lancashire Regt marched off according to timetable along the prescribed route at 7pm 30.VI.16 and reached Courcelles at 8.30pm where tea was served to the men.

9.40pm   After synchronising watches at 9.30pm the head of the column left Courcelles 9.45pm and marched as directed to Central Avenue. The trench was in a very bad state and over the knee deep in mud which had become glutinous.

12.20am, 1.7.16. As the fork in Central Avenue had not been reached by 12.20am – I proceeded to the head of the 2nd wave and ordered them to go overland. I reported this to 94th Brigade at entrance to Central Avenue. After crossing to the batteries the Regiment had to proceed in the trenches owing to the batteries firing. I reached with the head of the column the front line system of trenches at 2.40am where I found that orders had been issued by higher Command that Sap D & Sap C were not to be occupied by any troops. Accordingly I had to make fresh dispositions for the accommodation of my first wave. I accommodated No.1 and 11 Platoon or Company between [illegible] Avenue and 29.A.93. No.5 & 6 platoons X Company between this point & Mark Copse inclusive [illegible] the positions from which the 1st wave would start. They were accommodated in partially blown in fire bays in Traffic Trench. The wave being under Command of Capt Tough. The 2nd wave was under command of Capt Livesey and was accommodated in Copse Trench. The 3rd wave under 2/Lt Williams in Campion.
4th wave in Monk under Capt Riley.
Head Quarters at mouth of Sap C.
During the night & early morning there was a constant bombardment.

	Attention was paid to Rob Roy and the front line.
7.20am	At 7.20am the hurricane bombardment opened and the first wave crossed into no man's land. The Germans opened almost immediately with M.G. & Rifle fire putting on a few minutes later an intense barrage.
7.22am	The 2nd wave proceeded to follow the 1st wave into no man's land.
7.23am	Two platoons 13Y & L crossed following my 2nd wave
7.29am	I saw my 3rd & 4th waves advancing from Campion & Monk respectively. By this time there was intense Rifle M.G. Fire and a very heavy barrage of artillery fire.
	They crossed into no man's land" crossing the front line about 7.32am
7.39am	I reported by runner via Mark Copse 1st two waves crossed according to time table.
	Heavy M.G. & Rifle Fire still coming from German 1st line intense fire of all description.
7.42am	I reported by runner intense fire of all descriptions.
7.50am	I reported by runner all four waves have gone forward. M.G. Fire still coming from the North. Report from Lt Gay, left Platoon through 1st line Lt Gay wounded.
	M.G. Fire much less intense.
	I sent Lt Macalpine to establish telephone communication between Mark Copse & my H.Q. Lt Macalpine returned & informed me all communication was cut & it was not re-established all day.
8.10am	I reported M.G. fire still coming from the North traversing from beyond Mark Copse over Sap C.
	Capt Gurney 13th Y & L arrived with only 9 men in his two platoons.
	I further reported I could see odd groups in my front believed to be wounded, also that I could not see any of my waves.
	No further report from waves.
	Heavy Artillery Barrage on front line.
8.22am	Machine gun fire still coming from direction of Mark Copse.
	Heavy Artillery Barrage front line.
	No information from any waves.
	R.7. line not entered about 8.35.
	Very little rifle fire to my front. Heavy M.G. fire still coming from my left over Mark Copse. And now and then a burst from Right.
	No information from my waves.
9am	Report from Corpl Rigby wounded, belonging to 1st wave, states that only 7 of his platoon got into 1st line.
	They held it for about 20 minutes. Bombing Germans back till Bombs were exhausted. Capt Livesey was with Corpl Rigby & was wounded. Corpl Rigby saw remains of 2nd wave in front of our barbed wire. Germans still holding out.

Saw no sign of 3rd or 4th wave

Heavy Barrage on front line.

Capt Currin 13 Y & L reported arrived.

Capt Smith 13 Y & L was informed was going forward to 2nd line German trenches.

10.1am　No report from my waves Eczema heavily shelled & Capt Roberts R.A.M.C. wounded. Message from O.C. 13 Y. & L that 'C' Company 13 Y & L Capt Currin was going forward to occupy German 1st line trenches. Heavy barrage front line trenches M.G. fire from Right.

Capt Currin is putting his company into front line from Matthew Copse to Sap C, 10 wounded men. 11th E. L. have returned & they state front line still in German hands.

11.25am　No information from any waves.

Pte. Glover 1st wave [*illegible*] Capt Livesey states 1st wave encountered heavy M.G. Rifle and grenades & Bombs & artillery fire on crossing no man's land

Capt Livesey 1st wave with remnants of 2nd wave, together with 3rd wave charged German trenches led by Capt Livesey. Lt Thompson also entered German trenches.

Lt Ashwell wounded.

Between 1st & 2nd line German trenches Captain Livesey sent back a message for reinforcements. This never reached me.

Captain Currin is holding from Matthew Copse to Sap C. 18th W. Yorks pushing his line to the South.

A number of wounded in Sap C & in Eczema. Field dressings urgently required.

11.50am　Capt & Adjt Peltzer & Lt Rydon wounded.

Lt Rydon remained on duty.

No reports from my waves except statements of wounded men.

I asked for reinforcement of one company as only a few of Capt Currin's party arrived.

Was promised Company HXQ – they never arrived.

12noon　I proceeded to put front line in state of defence as far as possible against counter-attack. Sap C which had been opened up was blocked by bomb stops. I asked Staff Capt for Supply of Bombs which arrived later.

3.10pm　The Trench Mortar 92nd Brigade occupying Sap C were withdrawn and put in emplacements on right & left of Sap C. I went along my whole front line and reported there were very few bays defensible – Men mostly driven out of them and are located in Eczema. 93rd Brigade have withdrawn their men and I have only left 1 officer & 25 O.R. of my own Regiment available. 2 Stokes Guns in position and details of KOYLI and Capt Currin & Capt Gurney and about 30 men 13 Y & L. 12th Y & L are in Mark Copse & have no one except their HQ and that they are not in touch with any of their waves I am holding mine head by means of Bomb Stops.

3.50pm   R.18. Very intense bombardment of my front line. All posts drawn in by artillery fire. Men accommodated in Eczema. Urgently require more men. Bombardment still intense especially from [*illegible*].
Lt Ryder severely wounded.
R.19. I have 55 men in all some of whom are wounded. 2 Lewis Guns only. Five men to work them one of whom wounded. Posts filled by officer's servants.

R.20.

9.20pm   I beg to report that at 9.20pm I saw 2 German removing our wounded back to their lines from no man's land. As regards numbers I have at present 50 men including Stokes Mortars & HQ [*illegible*]. I have also 1 Officer 25 men 18th West Yorks, holding 3 posts in 93 area. 1 & 2 posts opposite [*illegible*] Avenue.
Then there is a gap until you come to Capt Gurney who holds 4 posts [*illegible*] S of Sap C. I have one post between Sap C & Mark Copse.
There are no Lewis or M.G. in line.
I am getting the wounded evacuated as soon as possible but there are a good number yet to be attended to.
I have 5 Red Rockets at Sap C & 12 Y & L have their Rockets.

1st Battalion Essex Regiment

TRENCHES
List of Officers who took part in the attack on July 1st 1916: Lt Col A.C. Halahan, Capt F.C. Dinan, Capt A.D. Henderson (W), Capt G.A.M. Paxton, Capt T.A.C. Brabazon (W), Capt A.N.W. Powell, Lieut H.A. Harvey, Lieut R.E.G. Carolin, Lieut F.F. Cooke (W), 2/Lieut W.R. Cheshire (K), 2/Lieut R.B. Horwood (K), 2/Lieut E.T.H. Hill (W), 2/Lieut H.A. Jackson (W), 2/Lieut A.J. Morison (W), 2/Lieut B.O. Warner (W), 2/Lieut W.J. McLean, 2/Lieut A.P. Chawner, 2/Lieut C.R. Lawson, 2/Lieut G.A. Apps, 2/Lieut M.C.W. Kortright, 2/Lieut A. Grant, 2/Lieut B. Hull, 2/Lieut F.R. Wheatley, 2/Lieut J.T. Broomfield, M.O. Capt F. Saunders, 2/Lieut A. Coucher (Battle Police). Other Ranks 840.

3.30am   Took up position in ST. JOHN'S ROAD (ref Trench map) as follows: W Coys right on FRENCH Trench. Z, Y & X. X Coys left being on UXBRIDGE ROAD. Men much fatigued by long time, (9pm. 30th – 3.30am 1st) it had taken to get into position and heavy equipment carried.

6.0am   Intense artillery bombardment commenced.

7.20am   Mine exploded under HAWTHORNE REDOUBT.

7.30am   86th & 87th Brigade left our 1st Line trenches, to assault their objective. Heavy artillery and machine-gun fire, and difficulty of getting through our own wire caused these Bdes very heavy losses. Very few men survived long enough to enable them to reach half way across "NO MAN'S LAND".

8.40am   Orders received cancelling our previous objective and ordering ESSEX & N.F.L.Ds to advance and clear up german 1st Line trenches. Worcs and Hants remaining in reserve.

N.F.L.D. were ordered to advance to the attack from their positions in ST. JOHN'S ROAD. ESSEX owing to ground between ST. JOHN'S ROAD and our front line, being under heavy fire, were ordered to advance via communication trenches and take up a position in our front line from which to commence the assault. ESSEX and N.F.L.D. Regt. to advance to the assault independently as soon as they were ready.

8.45am   Orders issued to Coys to take up the following positions: - Y Coy with its right on point 100 yds N. of MARY REDAN. X Coy to prolong to the left. W and Z Coys being in support trenches. N.F.L.D. on the left were seen to advance from ST. JOHN'S ROAD and immediately came under very heavy Arty & M.G. fire which practically wiped them out before they had gone many yards beyond our front line.

10.50am   Y Coy reported that they were in position in touch with W Coy. Z Coy had taken up a position between X and Y Coys owing to the congestion of the trenches due to being chocked with wounded and badly damaged by shell fire, it had taken Coys two hours to get into position. Orders issued to Coys to attack. Coys came under heavy Arty M. gun barrage immediately they appeared over the parapet, causing heavy losses. Report received from O.C. X Coy, that our wire on his front was uncut, that further advance was impossible, and that he had suffered heavy casualties. Z Coy in centre was able to make better progress. One platoon under 2/Lt CHAWNER getting about halfway across "NO MAN'S LAND". W Coy attempted to support, but were unable to make much progress

11.10am   Lt SKITT R.F.A. attached, learned from his group, that a bombardment of the 1st German line was ordered from 11.10am to 12.30pm. Orders were immediately given to cease attack and reorganise in ST. JOHN'S ROAD, but it was only possible to convey the message to Z Coy.

11.30am   Communication established with Bde and orders received to renew the attack at 12.30pm.

11.55am   Orders issued to Coys to reorganise for the renewal of attack at 12.30pm.

12.20pm   Message received from Bde postponing the attack to 12.45pm.

Brigade informed that owing to casualties and disorganisation, it was impossible to renew the attack until we had had time to reorganise. Subsequent orders received, cancelling the attack and ordering us to hold the line MARY REDAN – NEW TRENCH – REGENT STREET. Getting in touch with the Worc. on our left and the 36th Div. on the right and be prepared to repel counter attack. Bn. occupying above position with one Coy in support in ST. JOHN'S ROAD.

3.30pm Orders received that 7th Worcs were to relieve us in the firing line. Coys on relief were to go into ST. JOHN'S ROAD.

10.30pm Head of Worc arrived at KNIGHTSBRIDGE and Coys notified and ordered to move.

11.40pm Relief cancelled and Coys ordered to resume their previous positions.

2nd Battalion Essex Regiment

BERTRANCOURT

Zero hour was given out as 7.30AM and 65 minutes before that hour our artillery commenced a heavy bombardment of the German trenches, this lasted until 20 minutes before zero when the bombardment became intense.

At 10 minutes before zero a mine was fired and at zero the leading lines of the 11th Brigade advanced. At 8.36AM 'A' and 'D' Companies advanced from their assembly trenches and immediately came under very heavy machine gun fire and artillery barrage. At about 9.30AM the 10th Brigade were holding a line about 50 yards short of the German 2nd line and some parties had forced their way through and got as far as PENDANT COPSE. The main line tried to consolidate themselves in the line of craters but this work was practically impossible owing to the intense machine gun fire brought to bear on them from the direction of SERRE on the left flank and BEAUMONT-HAMEL on the right. Later a screen of Bombers advanced against them and the Brigade on the left retiring, left their left flank in the air.

About 4.0pm the line was forced to retire to the German front line, where a small body consisting chiefly of SEAFORTHS, ESSEX and WARWICKS with Captain A.G. de-la-Mare and 2/Lieut L.J. Ward of the ESSEX made a long stand in the Quadrilateral until 1.0AM on the 2nd inst when they were relieved by the Royal Irish Fusiliers. The fighting in the Quadrilateral was entirely by bombing and our men were hampered by an inadequate supply of bombs although they used the bombs found in the German trenches. At one time our Heavy Artillery also began to shell the Quadrilateral, but was stopped before doing any harm by means of an Electric lamp found by a signaller.

Communication was also kept with our front line by means of visual signalling and in this way bombs were asked for but the difficulty of getting them across "No man's land" through the fire was very great.

Casualties: 22 Officers and about 400 other Ranks.

1st Battalion Hampshire Regiment

Great Offensive begins – at 7.30am the whole line assaulted. The Brigade front line consisted of EAST LANCS and SOMERSETS and the second line of the HAMPSHIRES and RIFLE BRIGADE. We had 'A' Company, half 'C' and 'B' Coys in the front line – half of 'C' Coy to look after an enemy trench on right flank and 'D' Company in reserve. As soon as our troops left their trenches heavy machine gun fire was brought to bear on them from all directions and it was impossible even to reach the GERMAN front line. Our casualties in Officers amounted to 100% and was also very heavy in Other Ranks. After lying about in shell holes all the day the men came back to their original front line.

That night the remains of the 11th Brigade were relieved by the 10th Brigade and went back to billets in MAILLY.

1st Battalion King's Own (Royal Lancaster Regiment)

Owing to the fact that there are so few Officers and men now with the Battalion who made any substantial progress in the attack on the 1st July it is neither possible to give an accurate nor detailed account of the operations.

This account is based on information obtained from Officers and men who took part in the attack and are now serving with the Battn. Also on different categories of casualties sustained by different companies according to their different dispositions.

ASSEMBLY AREA

1.30am July 1st.

> The Battalion was present in its assembly area at 1.30am 1st July. Casualties amounted to 6 up to this period.
>
> Dispositions of Coys in the attack. Each Coy had a frontage of one platoon i.e. Battn. had a frontage of 4 platoons (approximately 500 yards) exact disposition of Coys as shown on diagram below.

8.41am The Attack. An Officer's patrol consisting of 1 Officer (2/Lt. C.C. MacWalter) and 20 O.R. advanced as a screen extending over the whole Battn. front at 8.41am.

8.46am Leading sections of the Battn. advanced from their Assembly Area. Directly the advance commenced the Battn. came under heavy machine gun fire and there seems no doubt that a large number of casualties occurred before reaching our own front line. The two left Coys, seemed to have suffered most heavily up to this point. The advance still continued, however, a large number of casualties being sustained in NO MAN'S LAND from both machine gun and shell fire; this is proved by the fact that a large number of killed and wounded were brought in from NO MAN'S LAND. The two left Coys again seemed to have suffered most heavily.

As regards the left Coy, owing to the fact that the right Battn. 31st Division had been unable to make any headway, few of them reached the front line.

There seems to be a general opinion that the Battn. lost its direction to a certain extent, advancing too much to its left as men of the left Coy state that when they crossed our front line there were men of the 31st Division in our front line at this point.

LEG END

4.00pm (about). The Brigadier of the Right Brigade 31st Division checked any further advance and ordered what men remained to form up in LEG END. This seems to have been about 4.00pm but the exact time is uncertain.

120 men remained at the end of the day and were ordered to form up in their former Assembly trenches (GREEN TRENCH area).

Only a small number of these Coys, reached the German front line, the two right Coys seemed to have made substantial progress. Some men state that they actually saw men crossing the German second line. The casualties in missing of these two Coys, are considerably greater than in the two left Coys.

An officer of the left centre Coy who was only able to reach the German front line owing to his having so few men left, states that he saw no one advancing on his left, but that to his right he could see men advancing (most of these men appeared to belong to the Seaforth Highlanders). He further states that the enemy were holding their second line directly in front of him and to his left front very strongly and that they had machine guns in the open just in front of their second line on his left front. German 2nd line 12.30pm. Those men of the two right Coys, who are now with the Batt. state that in the German second line there was a mixed force of all Regiments and that at about 12.30pm these men retired with the remainder of this force, first of all back to the German first line, and shortly after, thence to our front line, owing to the strong bomb attacks made by the enemy which they were unable to meet owing to the shortage of bombs.

Critique of Scheme and Time Table for the Attack:

Speaking from observation on the extreme right of the 4th Division as well as from accounts received from left of the Division there seems to have been:

1. Lack of weight.
2. The fact that 11th Brigade and 31st Division were unable to capture and

consolidate their first objectives, enabled the enemy in places to man these objectives and with rifle and machine gun fire inflict heavy losses on the Battns. advancing in rear before they could even reach their own front line. They were thus by the Time Table unable even to act as a support to the 11th Brigade.

3. Whilst not in a position to state whether any batteries were detailed as "Swingers" had such Batteries been able to fire on points where the enemy in rear of their front line were seen to be using both machine gun and rifle fire, the advance would have been probably more effective. As it was it appeared that the Artillery barrage worked strictly according to programme as was intended, thereby giving little "Artillery support" to the rear Battns. of the Division.

4. Such strong points as the village of SERRE, the RIDGE REDOUBT which commanded the advance inflicting heavy casualties with machine gun by cross fire must be captured before a considerable advance can be made. No doubt, owing to the fact that the 31st Division were unable to make any advance most of the machine guns in SERRE, by that time unmolested by Artillery fire were able to concentrate on the advancing troops to their left front.

5. There seems to have been an impression in the Batt. that there would be no advance by the 12th Brigade until SERRE and THIEPVAL were taken, which of course would have been the case had the programme worked out satisfactorily.

6. The Time Table was strictly adhered to throughout, and the advance carried out as a drill movement.

7. If a proportion of Officers could be kept in mine dug outs near the front line and sent up to their units directly the troops have entered the enemy trenches, or at the discretion of the Brigadier General, control could be efficiently established, and the positions captured, thoroughly consolidated and held.

Casualties:

Killed. Capt J.F.H. Young, 2nd Lt H.P. Melly, 2nd Lt R.R. Minor, 2nd Lt C.C. MacWalter, 2nd Lt P. Clegg, 2nd Lt J. Rowley, 2nd Lt G.R. Hablutzel.

Wounded. Capt A.H. Read 3rd Batt. Sussex Regt., Capt S.S. Skeats, 2nd Lt H.S. Sever, 2nd Lt J.P. Robinson, 2nd Lt L.L. Mortlock, 2nd Lt F.A. Markham, 2nd Lt C.O. Wright, 2nd Lt E.H. Hallett, 2nd Lt A.P. Myers (Shell Shock), 2nd Lt W.R. Thompson, 2nd Lt L.A. Hall (Shell Shock), 2nd Lt C.S. Whitworth, Capt F. M. Barnes R.A.M.C.

Missing. Major J.N. Bromilow, Capt A. Weatherhead, 2nd Lt A.H.W. Hudson.

1st Battalion King's Own Scottish Borderers

FIRING LINE

0200. Bn in the line as previously arranged. 'D' Company in BROOK STREET, 'B' Company and T.M. Section in PICCADILLY, 'A' Company and Machine Gun Section in ST JAMES' STREET, 'C' Company and a Platoon ½ Monmouth Regiment in BUCKINGHAM PALACE ROAD.

2/Lt GOW 'C' Company killed while getting his platoon into position and 2 men 'C' Company wounded. Bn Head Qrs in DUGOUT at Junction PICCADILLY, BOND STREET.

0733. 1/Royal Inniskilling Fusiliers commenced attack from front line trenches, Bn to advance when last wave of 1/R.I.F. reached German wire.

0740. 1/R.I.F. held up by Machine gun fire.

0752. 1/R.I.F. attack not progressing. Bn moved out under heavy machine gun fire.

0810. Our attack not progressing owing to intense enemy machine gun fire. Attack on left observed to be equally unsuccessful.

0831. Advance still going on but being constantly checked.

0838. Enemy heavily shelled MARY REDAN.

0845. The attack ceased.

0900. Capt Ainslie sent message to say he was collecting all wounded and unwounded men in trenches N of MARY REDAN.

0940. Newfoundland Regiment and 1/Essex Regiment advanced, the Newfoundland Regt on the left and the Essex in support of Bn. Both attacks failed.

1020. Bn Reserve under Major G.Hilton arrived and took up their position in front line trenches.

1137. Our front line and support trenches very heavily shelled by enemy.

1600. Orders received for the Bn and Bn Reserve to re-organise at FORT JACKSON on relief.

1730. Bn relieved by 1/Essex Regiment. Assembled and re-organised in FORT JACKSON.

2300. 1 Officer and 20 men digging a grave at KNIGHTSBRIDGE. Heavy bombardment by enemy on front line trenches at night, but undisturbed at FORT JACKSON.

12th (Service) Battalion (Miners) (Pioneers) King's Own (Yorkshire Light Infantry)

MOLLINGHAM.

Battalion reported present at assembly posts at 5.50am.

Battalion reassembled at assembly posts at 4.30pm.[1] Approximate casualty list 197 all ranks, including one officer killed and three wounded.[2]

NOTES

1. Prior to the attack, five saps were dug along the 31st Division's front, each running from the front line to within thirty or forty yards of the German trenches. One hour before the assault, all the saps were to be opened up. Once the attacking troops had reached their objectives, two companies of the 12th (Service) Battalion King's Own (Yorkshire Light Infantry) were to commence digging communication trenches from these saps across the last stretch of No Man's Land to the German line. Two platoons of 'A' Company, meanwhile, were instructed to follow the 12th York and Lancaster Regiment and 11th Battalion East Lancashire Regiment across No Man's Land. This was a costly instruction: as many as four out of every five men from these two platoons were wounded or killed. A little more detail of the attack on 1 July 1916, can be found in the War Diary under the following day's entry: "Lts W.H. ROBERTS, H.D. GAUNT and 2nd Lts W. BAIRD, L. FORSDIKE especially showed coolness & energy during the attack 1/7/16. C.S.M. R.E. FREAKES displayed splendid discipline and pluck, & stopped a tendency among a few men to retire, he was assisted by C.Q.M.S. R. KEER who also displayed pluck & energy. Sgt. A. ADAMS was reported by his officer as splendid, though wounded early on."

2. The return of eight missing men on 4 July brought the number of casualties down to 189. The officer killed was 20-year-old Lieutenant James Stanley Lightfoot Welch, who lost his life while leading his platoon forward across No Man's Land. In a letter describing Lieutenant Welch's death, the battalion's Commanding Officer, Lieutenant Colonel E.L. Chambers, wrote: "He was a brave officer, and died gallantly leading his platoon against the enemy. He was wounded first of all by a bullet and fell, but he was killed immediately afterwards by a shell. He died instantaneously, and could have suffered little pain. His last words to his platoon were: 'Never mind me; carry on.' I am deeply affected by his death, and we all give you our heartfelt sympathy in your sorrow. He was an excellent officer, and always did his duty, and did it well." (See the *Wakefield Express*, 15 July 1916). The son of the Rev. Edward A. and Edith Marion Welch, of Southchurch Rectory, Southend-on-Sea, he had been born in Toronto, Canada. He is buried in Queens Cemetery, Puisieux.

1st Battalion Lancashire Fusiliers

Account of action & messages see Appendix. The battn was badly cut up by enemy's M.G. fire suffering 508 Casualties & 21 officers casualties. At dusk we returned to our trenches but held & consolidated Sunken Rd. The battalion fought nobly, but had no chance of success against enemy's M.G. fire.

Document Attached to the War Diary

Appendix: Account of action, 1 July 1916, and the attack on Beaumont Hamel:

At 7am. Battn. H.Q. moved from White City to Sunken Road, & at the same the enemy began to shell the Sunken Road with 77cm guns, & inflicted about 20 casualties. They had probably spotted the communication trench leading from the end of the tunnel into the road.

0720. The mine under HAWTHORNE REDOUBT was fired, & though it was not visible from the road, all felt the ground shake. 'B' & 'D' Coys were now lining up in position for the assault. 'D' Coy had to be careful not to expose themselves as the Northern end of Sunken Road is shallow, & 'B' Coy had to carefully select their exits, as the bank is overhung & lined with trees at the Southern end. 86th Stokes gun battery opened hurricane bombardment on german first line.

07.30. The leading sections of 'B''D' & bombing Company dashed forward in extended order, being led by 2/Lt's CRAIG, GORFUNKLE & SPENCER, 'B' Coy by 2/Lt's PRESCOTT, EDWARDS, & KERSHAW, at the same moment 1 platoon 'B' Coy under Lt. WHITTAM & 2 platoons bombers left our trenches S. of BEAUMONT road. 'A' Coy began to leave front line trenches in support of 'B' & 'D' Coys.

The leading 2 lines of 'B' & 'D' Coys had a few moments grace, & then the enemy M.G. opened & a storm of bullets met the attack. The third & fourth lines of 'B' & 'D' Coys were practically wiped out within a few yards of Sunken Road & only some wounded, including Capt's NUNNELEY & WELLS the two Company Commanders managed to crawl back.

'A' Coy had also suffered in their advance to Sunken Road, the three subalterns all being hit & many men. Capt MATHEY reached the road & dashed on with the men who entered near Northern end.

'C' Coy caught the M.G. fire as soon as they left the trenches Capt DAWSON & C.S.M. NELSON being hit on the parapet, when giving orders to Coy to advance. 2/Lt CASEBY & about 60 OR reached the Sunken Road, but one platoon under 2/Lt Jones got blocked in the communication trench by wounded.

The bank into the Sunken road is a steep drop of about 15 feet, & men encumbered with coils of wire, mauls etc rolled down this to the bottom. There now ensued some delay whilst 'C' Coy & remainder of 'A' Coy who had entered down steep bank were collected & sorted from the 100 wounded who had by now collected in Sunken road, preparatory to further advance.

Sgt CAULFIELD a Lewis gunner had located a M.G. behind some debris in the village, & he pointed this out to C.O. Two Lewis guns were established toward N. flank to put it out of action, but the german artillery observation was very quick & they were immediately shelled by 77cm guns, & 1 gun hit. Still the M.G. ceased firing from that position.

0815. It took nearly half an hour organising the further advance, & at 0815 the C.O. ordered the Stokes guns to open a rapid burst under cover of which 2/Lt Caseby led forward about 75 OR who had been collected.

126

This reinforcement was launched from the N. end of the road to try & gain a footing toward Northern end of village, where the ground is higher.

All ranks dashed forward bravely, but on topping the crest, just 10 yards from the Sunken Road they were met by the same heavy M.G. fire & only 2/Lt Caseby & about 100 OR reached the german wire.

It was now 08.30, & no reports had come from the front, & it was not possible to see from Sunken Road what was happening on the flanks, so C.O. returned to our trenches to get news there.

Major UTTERSON reported that besides the 10% reinforcements, who were holding front line system there were about 30 men who had not gone over the top owing to being blocked by wounded. These were collected.

Very little movement could be seen in the german lines, & the village was certainly not occupied by our troops, & fire had died down. Around HAWTHORN REDOUBT about 25 germans under an officer could be seen working round the crater. One of our M.G's opened on them, but had to cease almost at once as enemy artillery blew in the parapet by them in under 3 minutes.

0945.   Returning to the Sunken road there was nothing to be done, as we had no reinforcements – at about 0945 there was a sudden retirement on our Right or Southern flank, presumably Royal Fus & Middlesex. Everyone thought for the moment the Germans were counterattacking, & nothing seemed more possible from our point of view. We had over 100 wounded in the Sunken road & they tried to make a rush for the tunnel. This was soon [illegible] & about 50 fit men were made to line the bank at either end.

25 under Sgt Green began digging in at the Southern end & making a barricade & about 35 did the same at the Northern end.

11.45.   Time passed & at 11.45 G.S.43 (1) from GOC 86th Bde was received – G.M. 17/1 (2) sent in reply – (copies attached).

There was no time to receive an answer to G.M.17/1 & orders were given to Major UTTERSON that at 1230 he was to advance with his 25 men viz all that were available in our front trenches exclusive, exclusive of 10% who were not under our orders.

The remaining men in Sunken road were got ready to advance, if Major Utterson's reinforcements reached the road.

Although there was no chance of achieving anything on our own front, there were about 700 men in our trenches opposite the Hawthorne Redoubt, & to help them it seemed necessary to attract as much M.G. fire as possible on ourselves.

Unfortunately only Major Utterson & 4 OR reached the road, & the troops on our right never moved, so our sacrifice was in vain. Still it showed us that the enemy still held the village & that his M.G's were intact.

There was nothing now to be done except to hold on to Sunken Road. Further steps were taken to improve entrenchments already begun, & the wounded who could move by themselves were allowed to crawl back to White City via the Tunnel.

1pm.   Received BM1. copy attached - & reply CM.15/1.

1.50pm.   CM16/1 despatched.

2.10pm.   Capt FULTON (attd to Bde Staff) arrived & talked over situation, & informed me that Sunken Road must be held at all costs.

Nothing else changed the situation for the remainder of the day, except the German shells which dropped into Sunken Road caused a few more casualties, & the Germans sniped at & killed a good many of our wounded, whenever they moved or tried to put on their field dressings.

At 6pm   Remainder of men except 1 officer & 25 withdrew from Sunken road, & at night all available stretcher bearers & men searched the field for wounded.

The day had cost the battalion many valuable lives. Casualties were 7 officers killed 14 wounded & 500 OR's. The battalion fought well, but the enemy was ready for us & had plenty of M.G's & against them no troops with a strength of only 1½ men per yard can hope for success.

2nd Battalion Lancashire Fusiliers

12.15am   The Battalion passed the starting point East of BERTRANCOURT for the Assembly Trenches.

2.50am   Battalion was settled in, in Assembly Trenches at Q.1.A.

7.30am   The 11th Bde attacked the German front line System.

(See Operation Orders by Lt Col. G.H.B. Freeth CMG DSO dated 26/6/16)

8am   Battalion moved out of Assembly Trenches in Artillery formation. This being done everyone lay down and awaited further orders.

8.30am   Battalion Advanced, directing flank moving at 50 yards a minute. Nothing retarded the advance until shortly after 9am when the head of the Battalion passed over the line of Vallards Trench.

Directly the small parties crossed the above line they became subject to heavy Artillery, Machine gun and Rifle fire.

A particularly heavy barrage had to be passed through on our front line and on all "NO MANS LAND".

However the advance was still carried on, naturally faster than the 50 yards a minute.

9.15am   About 9.15am the Head of the Battalion crossed over our front line trench. The Casualties in Officers and O.R. were by then fairly numerous.

About 9.45am the front companies had reached the third line of the German Front Line System.

As it was impossible to advance further, owing to the entire lack of support on either flank an attempt was made to consolidate the position.

The advance then began to telescope. The front two companies and parts of the rear two collected in the German lines.

The remainder collected in our old front line and fed the forward line as well as possible with bombs.

Owing to the Germans not being entirely driven out of their front line the ground occupied by our troops closed in round the area of the Quadrilateral.

This area was successfully held by the use of Grenades, Stokes Mortar, Machine guns, rifles and bayonets until the order was given to evacuate the position about 4am the following morning.

This evacuation was carried out successfully and with few casualties.[1]

Document Attached to the War Diary

Diary entry of Lieutenant V.F.S. Hawkins, 2nd Battalion Lancashire Fusiliers, detailing the events of 1 July 1916:

THE ATTACK

At 6.30am the artillery fire became rapid until 7pm. [*sic*] when it became intense. It was the most extraordinary sight. The Bosch line could not be seen for smoke and bursting shells. Bosch still hardly answered at all. The first mistake was made at 7.25am when the Beaumont Hamel line under the Hawthorne Ridge Redoubt went up. This gave the Germans 5 minutes to consolidate the crater which they made use of. Zero hour was at 7.30am.

At 7.30am the first waves went over and then things began to happen. In spite of the six days bombardment German machine guns got going from every direction.

Beaumont Hamel opposite the 29th Division was a veritable fortress. The 29th Division never got near the Hun Front Line. The 93rd Brigade of the Division on our left never got more than half way over No Mans Land, although the left Brigade of that Division did get into Serre that day.

SLAUGHTER ON THE SOMME: 1 JULY 1916

The 11th Brigade got the first line fairly easy. Gen. Prowse left the Headquarters too soon and was killed rushing a machine gun. He was shot in the stomach and died at Maueux Corps Headquarters that evening. The losses of the Brigade were awful. The C.O.s of the Hampshires, The Rifle Brigade and the Somerset Light Infantry were killed and most of the Officers were knocked out. They finally got held up somewhere in the 2nd line.

Meanwhile we were waiting in Brigade Headquarters for news. The Essex and Kings Own were going over first with the Lan. Fus. and Dukes in support. The Kings Own and Essex were wonderful. The Kings Own got very nearly to Pendant Copse and the Essex to Munich trench. Martineau the Brigade Signalling Officer went off to raise a forward signal station which he did somewhere on 63 over and over again we got a message back from him saying the Essex were bombing in Munich trench and wanted more bombs. Of the Kings Own we never heard a word, beyond from the Adjutant who came in to Headquarters with a cracked head. This was the first action in which Steel Helmets were worn and they undoubtedly saved many lives.

Just before the Brigade went over the Division wired us to stop the Battalions and also stop the 10th Brigade. Runners were immediately sent to the Kings Own and Essex, Lan. Fus, Dukes.

They were too late however. The Kings Own and Essex were right on. The Lan. Fus. were mostly in the quadrilateral and one Coy of the Dukes was in the Bosch line.

The result of all this was that the 93rd Brigade having failed on the left and the 29th Division on the right, the German came down from either flank and the Kings Own and Essex were practically missing. Major Bromilow has not been heard of since. (His body was found in August 1917.) Col. Stirling the C.O. Essex was wounded twice at the beginning and got away. Cadic the Adjutant of the Essex and the Adjutant of the Kings Own were both wounded.

Fighting went on all afternoon. Some of the Seaforths of the 10th Brigade got over and joined up with the Lan. Fus. in the quadrilateral. The C.O. of the Seaforths, Hodge, Bertie Ravenscroft, Hall, Watkins, Mansell and Rougier in the Quad with him and stayed there till 2am July 2nd. bombing the whole time. C.S.M. Laverick and Sgt. Albon were in there too. These to found a stokes gun and although they had never seen one before worked it till they ran dry of ammunition.

B. Farrow was killlled in No Mans Land on his way back having been with the others all the time.

The Roman Road on the afternoon of July 1st was ghastly, wounded in every place conceivable coming up all the time. Macdonald with a bullet in his chest and a Bosch Helmet was the only one of the Officers I saw from the Regt. He was quite happy.

I heard nothing of Brain or Firth till well into the afternoon. They reported in writing that they were somewhere near the Quadrilateral and did we know where the others were, they lost each other at the beginning of the show.

The attack finally ended as far as the Division was concerned at 2a.m. July 2nd, when the last of our people came back from the Quadrilateral.

The sum total of the attack was a bad hammering and no ground captured, but from all accounts Bosch lost heavily too.

The following casualties and Officers in the 2nd Lan Fus.: Sayers, Charlie Robeton, Farrow, Nipper Kennion, Gammon, and Maciver – Killed.

Bertie Ravenscroft, Rougier, Williams, Gregory, Bowes Collis-Browne, Macdonald, Anderson – wounded. Daies Missing reported (prisoner). Firth, Brain, Hodge, Mansell, Watkins, Rougier and Hall came through.

Of these Sayers, Robertson, Bowes and Collis-Browne were hit before reaching our own front line.

The other Battalions except the Dukes had lost worse than we had. The 110 Brigade practically did not exist.

While the 10th Brigade except for the Seaforths, had been stopped by the Division and had not lost so badly.

The Bosch showed his fighting powers that day, and he put up a grand fight. It was however nearly all his Officers. The machine Guns in our vicinity were nearly all manned by Bosch Officers and all the prisoners told us the same. The prisoners No.15 all Wurtenburgers from the Regt.

I first saw Brain about 5pm the evening of the 12th, he seemed pretty broken up, but had not been hit. John Carr, the C.O.'s orderly of course hadn't cared a hang for anything. Clegg Brains orderly got wounded.

The Bosch had put up a very fine Barrage of 5.9 H.E. and Shrapnel. He put up every gun in a clump on to one small bit of the front, using his machine guns elsewhere. After 10 mins or so he would shift all his guns to another small portion of the front and so on always having a machine gun Barrage where his guns were not firing. It was most effective. He also blew a couple of mines in No Mans Land under our first wave.

NOTE

1. The War Diary lists six officers as having been killed on 1 July 1916, along with nine wounded and one missing. There were twenty-four other ranks killed, 273 wounded, seven died from wounds and forty-eight were missing. Total casualties were sixteen officers and 352 other ranks.

1/2nd Battalion Monmouthshire Regiment
(Territorial Force)

MAIILY WOOD
'Z' Day.   The attack started at 7.30am at that hour.
'A' Co.   Began to move up to the front line along the Old BEAUMONT ROAD.

The Bombers, under LT W.M. SANKEY proceeded up the SUNKEN ROAD to clear the way for three platoons of the Coy who were to carry bombs into BEAUMONT. They were held up by machine-gun fire at a distance of 100 yards from their objective. Attempts were again made to get along into BEAUMONT, but the Infantry had not cleared the enemy front trenches & at 9am it was still strongly held.
Casualties:
Killed – O.R. 3.
Wounded – Officers 1 (Lt HUNT), O.R. 10.

'B' Co.   At 7.50am Nos 5 & 6 Platoons proceeded to 1st AVENUE TUNNEL via YELLOW LINE, TIPPERARY & 1st AVENUES. At the same time Nos 7 & 8 Platoons proceeded to MARY TUNNEL via WITHINGTON AVENUE. The work of the Co was to dig communication trenches from the Bastion ends of 1st AVENUE and MARY TUNNELS respectively. Great difficulty was experienced in trying to get to their respective positions owing to the congested state of the trenches & the enemy's barrage. 5 and 6 Platoons were unable to get to the eastern end of the TUNNEL at 1st Avenue, it being full of wounded & signallers & orderlies trying to get thro. This party remained in the support trench all day & suffered considerably from the enemy barrage.
7 and 8 Platoons after two attempts found it impossible to get out to No Man's Land to start digging, as the enemy's trenches had not been taken. Later in the day the party did manage to get out & do a little sapping – 10 yards – towards the enemy's trenches, but suffered considerably from the enemy's barrage.
Casualties:
Killed – 3 O.R. (including Co. S. Maj)
Wounded – O.R. 21.

'C' Co.   In YELLOW LINE, this company was intended for consolidating the 3rd objective when captured by 88th Brigade, owing to the failure of the attack on the first objective the Co remained standing by in the position of readiness until 7pm when it was ordered to rejoin Battalion.
Casualties: nil.

'D' Co.   No.13 Platoon, sections 1 & 2 attached to 'C' Co Lancashire Fus. (the Consolidating Co) laden with stakes & wire these sections went over the parapet in rear of the Co & turned up the SUNKEN ROAD. There they were ordered to dump all material and advance across the open. They got to within 50 or 60 yards of the enemy's front line and lay there under cover of a slight ridge and "dug in". The Co had Stokes guns & 2 Lewis guns, these were used, but orders were given to cease fire as it was thought hostile fire would be drawn & position rushed by the enemy. The party consisted of about 150. They withdrew about 10pm.into

TENDERLOIN having a bombing party behind to cover them.
Casualties:
Killed – O.R. 2.
Wounded – Officer 1 (Lt. T.E.R. WILLIAMS), O.R. 8.
Missing – O.R. 2.

Sections 3 & 4 Attached to 'B' Co 16th MIDDLESEX REGT. & went over the parapet in rear of the Co carrying coils of French wire and two BANGALORE TORPEDOES. They advanced in rear of the Co towards the enemy's front line & laid down. In the meantime some of the Middlesex had got into the enemy's front line. The enemy bombed them and they retired. Over 2 sections retired into our front line.
Casualties:
Killed – O.R. 1.
Wounded – O.R. 12.

No. 14 Platoon Sections 5 & 6 attached to ROYAL FUSILIERS were split up amongst the different sections of the Co they were attached to, & there does not appear to be a clear account of what happened other than the attack was a failure & when the R.F. withdrew into our front line our men were collected and placed in a deep "dug out" & remained there until ordered to rejoin the Battalion.
Casualties:
Killed – O.R. 1.
Wounded – O.R. 2.
Missing – O.R. 3.

Sections 7 & 8 Attached to the DUBLIN FUSILIERS and carried material up to our front line. They were ordered into "deep dug outs" in rear of our front line when it was found the enemy's front line had not been taken. They carried wounded back during the day & bombs & ammunition to our front line from the reserve dump in AUCHONVILLIERS. They also acted as a ration party during the early hours of the 2nd.
Casualties:
Wounded – O.R. 1.

No. 15 Platoon Attached to 1st BORDER REGT. This platoon got over the parapet from FETARD ST each man carrying 8 full water bottles in a sand bag & also signalling material. They filed over the parapet thro our wire, then got into extended order, to cross our front line, they again got into file until clear of our wire. They then lay down as the advance was checked. After being in this position about 2 hours a withdrawal into our front line was made. This platoon after assisting the wounded retired into dug-outs in JOHN STREET.
Casualties:
Wounded – Officer 1 (CAPT A.C. Sale). O.R. – 7.
Missing – O.R. 3.

No.16   Attached to 'A' Coy K.O.S.B. (1st Bn). They advanced in rear of the Coy
Platoon   over the open from JAMES STREET to our front line near MARY
REDAN. By the time our front line was reached the companies in front
had got mixed up & the platoon could get no information about 'A' Coys
movements and no orders having been given they found CAPT COX 'B'
Co of this Battalion & assisted on work in MARY TUNNEL. About
8.30pm. orders were given for this sap to be closed.
Casualties:
Killed – O.R. 2.
Wounded – O.R. 13.
Missing – O.R. 1.

6pm.   Orders received from 29th Div that the Battalion was to be collected &
reformed in MAILLY WOOD and a small working party under an officer
detailed to clear & keep clear each of the main communication trenches.
The Battalion Reserve of 10% was used for this purpose & divided up
into 3 parties of 9 & 3 do. of 10, each under an officer & were sent to
1st, 2nd and 3rd AVENUES, BROADWAY, WITHINGTON & GABION.
The trenches were found to be comparatively little damaged & the work
of clearing was done with out incident, enabling the parties to return to
camp between the hours of 3 and 5 am on the 2nd. Reformation of
Battalion in MAILLY WOOD was completed by midnight.

Document Attached to the War Diary

*Report to 29th Division General Staff detailing the battalion's actions on 1 July 1916,
and subsequent duties until 3 July 1916, signed by Lieutenant Colonel A.J.H. Bowen,
O/C 1/2nd Battalion Monmouthshire Regiment:*

The Battalion was ordered to take part in the Operations by using the two
companies ('A' & 'B') to dig 4 Communication Trenches across "No Man's Land",
after the enemy front line had been taken, and two companies ('C' & 'D') were
allotted to Brigade for carrying and consolidation work, the Battalion was split up
in "ACHEUX WOOD" and moved off from there.

DRESS AND EQUIPMENT.
Men carried equipment with 120 rds. S.A.A. Rifle and Bayonet, 2 Sandbags in belt
front, 2 Mills Bombs, one in each bottom pocket of tunic. Haversacks were carried
on the back with Mess Tin Rations and Iron Rations inside. Water Bottles were
carried as usual. 80% of the men carried Shovels and 20% Picks. These were
carried on the back slipped under the equipment, and were found to be quite
comfortable.

SPECIALISTS.

Regimental and Platoon Bombers carried 50 rds. S.A.A. and 20 Bombs. (These were rather too many for a long march).They also carried Picks and Shovels and were used for digging. Runners wore an Armlet Badge and carried 50 rds. S.A.A. All ranks carried 2 Smoke Helmets and Tear Mask, Identity Disk, Field Dressing, and Waterproof Sheet.

Officers were equipped like the men except that the Revolver was carried on the left side and no Ammunition Pouches were worn. Officers wore Mens'Tunics with Badges of rank on the shoulders and Puttees.

200 of the men wore Steel Helmets, the remainder wore a Service Cap.

COMMUNICATION.

Communication was arranged with 2 Companies digging the Communication Trenches, and with the Company attached to the 88th Brigade by Runners to HEADQUARTERS, and these worked satisfactorily. The only communication arranged with 'D' Coy (allotted to the 87th [*corrected to 86th*] Brigade) was by checking if a man came back through the Communication Trenches.

The reason for this was that the Company was so split up that the Communication was impracticable, for example one Battalion had 16 men allotted to it for carrying and they were allotted, one man to each section of the Consolidating Company.

FORMING UP AREA.

'A', 'B' and 'C' Coys left ACHEUX WOOD by small parties on the night 30th June 1916 at 23.00 hrs at one minute intervals and proceeded to their forming up of areas.

'A' Coy to 86th Trench.

'B' Coy to Yellow Line between FORT WITHINGTON and FORT ANLEY.

'C' Coy to Yellow line between GABION AVENUE and FORT WITHINGTON.

Latrines and Cooking Places had previously been made in these trenches and Camp Kettles and Water Bottles taken up on the previous day. 'C' Coy had also taken up the consolidating material and left a guard over it. In consequence of the good arrangements made by Company Commanders, every man in 'A', 'B' and 'C' Coy's had Hot Tea, fried bacon and bread and jam for breakfast on Z morning 1st July. In addition Half-a-pound of Chocolate was brought and issued to each man, and every man also had a big Sandwich of Boiler Bacon in his Haversack.

'A' Coy.   Strength:

        Officers 5.

        Other Ranks 140.

        MAJOR A.H. EDWARDS Command, LIEUTS L.L. WILLIAMS. E.V. HUNT. 2nd LIEUTS W.M. SANKEY. W.D. HOWICK. (4th R.W.F.)

        On 'Y' Night No.2 platoon proceeded from ACHEUX WOOD to Sap 7 to dig a trench from there to the SUNKEN ROAD. (Q4d36 to Q.4-d,5.6.) 7 yards long. This was finished by 2.30am.on Z day. They then rejoined the remainder of the Company in trench 86. Where the company remained until 7.30am. The Company moved up to the front line along the Old BEAUMONT ROAD. The Bombers under LIEUT W.M. SANKEY proceeded up to the SUNKEN ROAD to clear the way for three platoons of the company who were to take bombs into BEAUMONT. They were held up by machine-gun fire at a distance of 100 yards from their objective. Attempts were again made to get along into BEAUMONT-HAMEL with bombs but the infantry apparently had not cleared the enemy front trench, which at 9.0am. was strongly held.

Casualties:

Killed - O.R. 3.

Wounded – Officers 1. Lt HUNT, O.R.10.

'B' Coy.   Strength:

Officers 5.

Other Ranks 138.

Capt C. Comely, Command. Capt C.W.H. Cox. Lieut A.L. Coppock (3rd Welsh). 2nd Lieut's W.S. Bartlett, E.F. Lawlor.

The Company remained in the Yellow Line until 7.30am 1/7/16. Breakfast and Rum were issued before moving off. At 7.30am the assault was commenced. At 7.50am Nos 5 & 6 Platoons proceeded to 1st AVENUE TUNNEL via YELLOW LINE, Tipperery and 1st AVENUES. At the same time Nos 7 & 8 platoons proceeded to MARY TUNNEL via WITHINGTON AVENUE.

The work of the Company consisted of digging Communication Trenches from the Eastern Ends of 1st Avenue and Mary Tunnels respectively. On reaching their respective positions (which was done under great difficulty owing to the congested state of the trenches and the enemy's barrage.) both half Companies found after 2 attempts that it was impossible to get out onto "No Man's Land" to start digging as the enemy's trenches had not been taken. 5 & 6 Platoons, the left half Company at 1st AVENUE TUNNEL was unable to get to the Eastern End of the Tunnel as it was full of wounded, Signallers and Orderlies trying to get through. This party remained in the Support Trench during the day, during which time it suffered considerably from the enemy's barrage.

7 & 8 platoons, the right half company at MARY TUNNEL were able to do a little Sapping (10x) towards the enemy trenches but suffered considerably from the enemy's barrage. At about 7.0pm the 10% of the Company which had remained behind, came up to clear the

Communication Trenches and the main parties of the Company were ordered to withdraw and proceed to MAILLY WOOD to reform.
Casualties:
Killed – 3 O.R. (including the Coy S. Major).
Wounded – 21 O.R.

'C' Coy. Strength:
Officers 4.
Other Ranks 136.
Capt H.W.E. BAILEY, Command. Lieuts M.F. Turner, G.E. FOSTER. 2nd Lieut B.D. WILLIAMS. This Company was intended for consolidating 3rd objective which captured by the 88th Bde.
The Company moved to the YELLOW LINE by FORT WITHINGTON and had breakfast. Owing to the failure of the attack on the first objective, the Company remained standing by in the position of readiness all 1st July until 7.0pm. it was ordered to rejoin the Battalion in MAILLY WOOD.
Casualties: nil.

'D' Coy. Strength:
Officers 4.
Other ranks 135.
Capt A.C. SALE. LIEUT T.E.R. WILLIAMS. 2nd Lieuteants J.D. SIMPSON, H.B. DAVIES.
No.13 Platoon. Sections 1 & 2 of this platoon were attached to 'C' Coy of the 1st Lancs. Fus. which was the Consolidating Company.
On the morning of the 1st loaded with stakes and wire they went over the parapet in rear of 'C' Coy and turned up the SUNKEN ROAD. There they had orders to dump all material and advance across the open. They got to within 50 or 60 yds of the enemy's front line and lay there under cover of a slight ridge and "Dug-in". They had Stokes Guns and 2 Lewis Guns. These were used but orders were given to cease fire as it was thought that fire would be drawn and position rushed by the enemy.
The party consisted of about 150. They withdrew at night about 10.0pm into TENDERLOIN leaving a Bombing Party behind to cover their withdrawal.
Casualties:
Killed – O.R. 2.
Wounded – Officers 1, O.R. 8.
Missing – O.R. 2.

Sections 3 & 4. Were attached to 'B' Coy of the 16th Middlesex Regt. and went over in rear with coils of French wire and 2 BANGALORE TORPEDOES.
They advanced in rear of 'C' Coy and got ¾ of the way across towards the German Front Line where they laid down. In the meantime some of the Middlesex had got into the enemy's front line. The enemy

Bombed them and they retired. These 2 Sections retired into our front line and on receipt of an order returned to MAILLY WOOD.

Casualties:

Killed – O.R. 1.

Wounded – O.R.12.

No.14 Platoon. Sections 5 & 6 of this Platoon were attached to the ROYAL FUSILIERS, and were split up amongst the different Sections of the Company they were attached to. There does not appear to be any clear account of what happened other than the attack was a failure and when the R.F.s withdrew into our front line our men were collected and placed into a "Deep Dug-out" until they were ordered to return to MAILLY WOOD.

Casualties:

Killed – O.R.1.

Wounded – O.R.2.

Missing – O.R. 3.

Total – 6.

Sections 7 & 8. Were attached to the DUBLIN FUSILIERS and carried material up to our front line. They were ordered into "Deep Dug-outs" in rear of our front line when it was found that the enemy's front line had not been taken. They carried wounded back during the day and Bombs and Ammunition to our front line from the Reserve Dump in AUCHONVILLERS. They also acted as a ration party during the early hours of the 2nd.

Casualties:

Wounded – O.R. 1.

No.15 Platoon. Attached to 1st Border Regt. On the morning of the attack they got over the Parapet in FETARD ST. each man carrying 8 Full bottles in Sandbag and also Signalling Material. They filed over the Parapet through our wire and then got into extended order. To cross our front line they again got into file until clear of our Wire. They then laid down as the advance was checked. After being in this position for about 2 hours a withdrawal into our front line was made. This platoon after assisting the wounded retired into Dug-outs in JOHN ST. and then at night returned to MAILLY WOOD.

Casualties:

Wounded – Officers 1, O.R. 7.

Missing – O.R. 3.

Total – 1 Officer and 10 O.R.

No.16 Platoon. Attached to the 1st K.O.S.B. and on morning of attack moved in rear of 'A' Coy. They advanced over the open from St. JAMES ST. to our front line near the MARY REDAN.

By the time that our front line was reached the Companys in front had got mixed up and this Platoon could get no information as to 'A' Coy's movements and no orders having been given they joined Capt. Cox of 'B' Coy and assisted on work in MARY TUNNEL.

Casualties:

Killed – O.R. 2.

Wounded – O.R. 3.

Missing – O.R. 1.

Total – 6.

About 8.30pm orders were given for the Sap to be closed and they returned to

MAILLY WOOD.

In the evening of the 1st July the Battalion was ordered to reform in MAILLY WOOD. This was completed at 10.0pm. Working Parties were found at night to clear Communication Trenches. GABION and TIPPERARY, 1st AVENUE, BROADWAY, 2nd and 3rd AVENUES. This was done the trenches not having been badly damaged except near Junctions with support and front trench.

At 6.15am on the 2nd July orders were received that the Batt. with the 1st Hampshire Regt. and the 4th Worcester Regt. of the 88th Brde. would be attached to the 48th Div. The Commanding Officer called on the G.O.C. 88th Bde. and received instructions for the Battalion to take part in an attack on the German Trenches from pt.78.28. to pt. 60. (Q.10.b.72. to Q.11.c.6.0.) at 3.15am on the 3rd July 1916. The Batt. was to be in support and if the objective (the first 3 lines of enemy trench system) was taken, it would be used for consolidating if the trenches had not been taken the Batt. would be used for attack. About 9.30pm the Batt. moved up into FETARD ST. by Companies. The enemy bombarded the trenches with Tear Shells which were very irritating. Masks were put on and in the darkness it was exceedingly difficult to see in the trench. Many Telephone Wires were hanging loose and obstructing movement.

'A' & 'D' Coys went in by WITHINGTON AVENUE (and up trench) in the rear of the 48th Div. They were about half way up when the Infantry in front turned about and passed them, consequently 'A' and 'D' Coys were held up for 3 hours while these troops retired. The Lewis Guns Bombers 'B' and 'C' Coys reached the trenches at midnight and received orders that Operations were cancelled. There was a heavy bombardment of FETARD ST. from 1.0am to 3.0am 3rd July but the men being in deep dugouts no Casualties were caused. At 6.0am orders were received that the Batt. was to reform in MAILLY WOOD. This was completed by 8.30am. At 5.0pm 3rd July the Batt. went up to clear the communication trenches and repair firing line.

'A' Coy proceeded to MESNIL and up JACOBS LADDER and firing line of K.O.S.Bs and S.W.Bs. 'B' Coy to GABION and WITHINGTON AVENUES and firing line of 1st Hants and 4th Worcesters.

'C' Coy to Tipperary and 1st AVENUE and BROADWAY and firing line of the 4th Worcesters.

'D' Coy to 2nd and 3rd Avenues and firing line of 1st DUBLIN FUSILIERS.

A great deal of work was done in the firing line; the communication being fairly good except at junctions which had been heavily shelled. The Companies returned to MAILLY WOOD at about 4.30am 4th July.

The casualties for the Battalion for the period 1st to 3rd July were as follows:

Killed	Officers	nil
	Other ranks	11
Wounded	Officers	4
	O.R.	81
Missing	Officers	nil
	O.R.	10
Total casualties	Officers	4
	O.R.	102

1st Battalion Newfoundland Regiment

TRENCHES
ST. JOHNS ROAD
CLOMMEL AV.
General attack all along the line.

0600– Intense bombardment.
0730

0730. 86th & 87th Brigades attacked 1st system of enemy trenches. 88th Bde, under pre-arranged orders were to move forward at 0840 to attack 3rd line system of trenches. About 0820 received orders not to move until further orders. Presumably the first attack not having been successful.

0845. Received orders on telephone to move forward in conjunction with 1st Essex Regt. and occupy enemy's first trench – one objective being point 89 to just north of point 60 and work forward to Station Road clearing the enemy trenches - and move as soon as possible. Asked Brigade if enemies 1st trench had been taken and received reply to the effect that the situation was not cleared up. Asked Brigade if we were to move off to attack independently of Essex Regt. and received reply in affirmation.

0915. Reported to Brigade that Newfoundland Regt. was moving off. It was subsequently found that the Essex Regt. did not attack until 0955 i.e. after our attack had failed.

The Regiment moved off in previously arranged formation i.e. 'A' & 'B' Companies ('A' on left) in 1st line in lines of platoons in file or single file at 40 paces interval and 25 paces between sections – followed by 'C' & 'D' Coys ('C' on left) in similar formation at 100 yards distance. 'C' Coy had been specially detailed as consolidating company and therefore carried additional equipment.

The advance was made direct over the open from the rear trenches known as St. John's Road and Clommel Avenue. As soon as the signal for advance was given the regiment left the trenches and moved steadily forward. Machine gun fire from our right front was at once opened on us and then artillery fire also. The distance to our objective varied from 650 to 900 yards.

The enemy's fire was effective from the outset but the heaviest casualties occurred on passing through the gaps in our front wire where the men were mown down in heaps. Many more gaps in the wire were required than had been cut. In spite of losses the survivors steadily advanced until close to the enemies wire by which time very few remained. A few men are believed to have actually succeeded in throwing bombs into the enemy's trench.

A report by Capt. G.E. MALCOLM commanding 'D' Co. 1st K.O.S.B's which formed part of the first attack carried out by the 87th Bde is attached.

0945.	The C.O. reported personally at Bde Battle H.Q. 100 yards behind our firing line that the attack had failed. Shortly afterwards enemy opened an intense bombardment of our trenches with heavy artillery which was kept up for some time.

During the night and evening unwounded survivors managed to crawl back to our own lines and by next morning some 68 had answered their names, in addition to stretcher bearers & H.Q. runners. During the afternoon the 10% reinforcements under Capt. FORBES-ROBERTSON arrived in the trenches and orders were received to occupy the support trench in the right subsector known as St. James' Street, where we remained on July 2nd.

Summary of Casualties on July 1st 1916:

Officers	Killed	11
	Wounded	12
	Died of Wounds	2
	Missing (Believed killed)	1
Other Rank	Killed	66
	Wounded	362
	Died of Wounds	21
	Missing (Believed killed)	209

Document Attached to the War Diary

Copy of a report from Captain G.E. Malcolm, O.C. 'D' Company, 1st Battalion King's Own Scottish Borderers, to the Adjutant, 1st Battalion King's Own Scottish Borderers, dated 5 July 1916:

Sir, I have the honour to make the following report.

On the morning of 'Z' day at 0.20. 'D' Coy received the whistle signal to advance. On leaving the trenches they came under very heavy machine gun fire. The Company moved forward in line of Platoons in column of sections in single file. No.13 Platoon on the left and No.16 on the right. At 60 yards from our own trenches I gave the signal to lie down as I intended to make the right wheel on to our objective at that point and 'C' Coy and the Border Regt were not yet in position. Owing to casualties I had 3 men of No.13 (2 wounded) and 1 of No.14 platoon left, I could see no one of the other platoons.

At 0.35 I sent a message to the Adjutant 1st K.O.S.B. by Private Douglas stating estimated casualties.

At 1.00 a company of Newfoundland Regt. 40 strong came up without officers. I gave the signal to my company to advance and took command. I hoped to get a footing in the enemy trenches and so hinder the machine gun fire.

I was wounded 60 yards from the enemy trenches. The advance ceased 20 yards further on.

I should like to congratulate the Newfoundland Regiment on their extreme steadiness under trying conditions.

1st Battalion Prince Albert's (Somerset Light Infantry)

Z day. Fine and warm. After a very intense bombardment, at 7.20am a large mine was exploded under the HAWTHORN REDOUBT.

Practically no casualties were suffered while in Assembly trenches.

At 7.30am the attack was launched. The 11th Bde advanced in magnificent style in following order, from right to left:

> 1st East Lancashire Regt,
> 1st Rifle Brigade,
> 6th Warwicks.

For second line 1st Hampshire Regt, 1st Somerset L. Infy, 8th Warwicks. Battn advanced on a front of One Coy.

Leading Battn advanced in lines, 2nd line of Battn in lines of Sections.

The Battn advanced in four lines.

1st line, 2 platoons	'A' Coy on right.	2 of 'B' on left.

2nd line, 2 platoons	'A' Coy on right.	2 of 'B' on left.
3rd line, 2 platoons	'C' Coy on right.	2 of 'H' on left.
4th line, 2 platoons	'C' Coy on right.	2 of 'H' on left.

The 10th & 12th Bdes were behind 11th Bde. The advance was carried out excellently to start with, and a severe barrage was not encountered. Shortly after heavy rifle fire was opened & machine guns from both flanks. The 1st East Lancashire & 1st Hampshire Regts were unable to get beyond the enemy's wire. The battn had to ease off to the left, owing to the ridge which it should have crossed, being swept by machine guns and quite impossible, and found itself in the German trenches in the neighbourhood of the Quadrilateral. The Warwicks gained their objective, but were unable to hold on there.

The 4th Division was greatly handicapped owing to the fact that the 31st Division on the left was unable to make progress, and that the 29th Division on the right was unable to capture BEAUMONT HAMEL. It is impossible to get a detailed account of the fighting that ensued, but the situation after the first hour or two was that men of various battns in the Division were holding part of the Quadrilateral and were engaged in a fierce grenade fight. Our men were for some time severely handicapped by shortage of grenades, but these were afterwards sent up.

Capt HARINGTON & Lieut GREATHAM were only officers of the Battn there. Both left wounded about 1.30P.M.

C.S.M. CHAPPELL was then in command of men of the Battn in the Quadrilateral. Previous to this R.S.M. PAUL came across with the Bde Carriers under a heavy fire. Sergt IMBER & Pte HODGES did excellent work in signalling from German trenches for grenades, Barrage etc.

After dark, men of the 11th Bde were relieved by Royal Irish Fusiliers & withdrew to our own lines. Major MAJENDIE arrived about 4.30 with Reinforcement Officers and took command of the Battn; which had been collected together in Assembly trenches by R.S.M PAUL. Orders were received about 10pm for 11th Bde to return to MAILLY MAILLET as Div Reserve. 10th & 12th Bdes to hold line. The Battn lost very heavily.

With the exception of 2nd Lieut MARLER, Bde Dump officer, no officers with the exception of Capt ACLAND RAMC, who formed up in Assembly trenches, returned unscathed at the end of the day.

Lt. Col. THICKNESSE & Capt FORD (Adjutant) were both killed before our trenches were passed.

Battn Casualties were 26 Officers and 438 O.R.[1]

NOTE

1. The following is the list of officer casualties – Killed: Lieutenant Colonel J.A. Thicknesse and Captain C.C. Ford. Missing believed killed: Captain R.J.R. Leacroft (killed), Captain G.H. Neville (killed),

Lieutenant E.C. MacBrigan (killed), Second Lieutenants G.P.C. Fair (killed), J.A. Hellard (killed), J.A. Johnston (killed), A.V.C. Leche (killed), R.E. Dunn (killed) and W.H. Treasure (killed). Wounded and missing: Second Lieutenants H.M. Tilley (missing) and F.A. Pearse (killed). Missing: Lieutenant V.A. Braithwaite (killed), Second Lieutenants G.C. Winstanley (killed), H.E. Whitgreave (killed), and T.M. Doddington (killed). Wounded: Captains W.W. Llewellyn and A.J. Harington, Lieutenants G.V.C. Greatham, R.W.Shannon, and C.J.O. Danbery, Second Lieutenants R.C. Strachey, H.L. Colville (died of wounds 6 July 1916), A.H. Collins, and A.R. Waugh. Brigadier General Prowse died of wounds.

15th (Service) Battalion (1st Leeds) Prince of Wales's Own (West Yorkshire Regiment)

IN THE FIELD

7.30am. The Battle of the Somme commenced.

The attack was launched in successive waves. Every wave was met by a very severe sweeping M.G. fire. There had been an hours intense artillery bombardment of the enemy's front lines and a 10 minutes intense "hurricane" trench mortar bombardment but when the advance was made the enemy front line was thick with men.

The 94th Brigade advanced on our left and were reported at one time to be in possession of the village of SERRE. Large numbers of our men were casualties long before reaching the German wire. Some were reported to be over the front enemy trenches and in their first objective.

The 4th Division advanced on our right. Fighting was hard & shelling heavy. Machine gun fire was intense. Our casualties were 24 officers and 504 other ranks.

The killed officers were: Capt & Adjt S.T.A. Neil, Capt G.C. Whitaker, Lt J.G. Vause, Lt E.H. Lintott, 2nd Lt's J.A.R.R.E. Wikey, J.P. Everitt, M.W. Booth,[1] V. O'Land, C. Saunders and T. Humphries & Lt S.M. Bickersteth.

The wounded officers were: Major R.B. Neill in command, 2nd Lts P.H.L Mellor, D.S. Wells, J.S. Jones, A.M. Hutton, R.H. Tolson, J. Gibson, Leek, Briley, A. Liveridge, L. Foster & James. 2nd Lt Stanley sprained his ankle & was admitted to hospital.

By the end of the day we were holding our own front line. The attack succeeded in the South at THIEPVAL where there was continuous hard fighting for several days. The final advance in the South was highly successful Major J.C. Hartley took command.

40 reinforcements of the Battalion were brought up. Dead & wounded were being brought in from No mans land for several days.

NOTE

1. Major William Booth (Major was his Christian name, not rank) had played cricket for Yorkshire between 1908 and 1914. In 1913 he made over 1,200 runs and took 181 wickets in first-class matches –

the highest number of wickets by any bowler that season. He was named one of Wisden's Cricketers of the Year in 1914. Booth also played test cricket for England during the 1913-14 tour of South Africa. On 1 July, one of the successive waves of troops contained another famous cricketer, Abraham "Abe" Waddington who also would play for Yorkshire and England. Waddington was wounded by shrapnel during the attack at Serre and took shelter in a crater in No Man's Land. The mortally-wounded 29-year-old Booth lay in the same crater and would soon die in Waddington's arms, an experience that would haunt the latter for the rest of his life. Booth's body lay on the battlefield until the following spring when it was finally recovered. He lies in Serre Road No.1 Cemetery.

16th (Service) Battalion (1st Bradford) Prince of Wales's Own (West Yorkshire Regiment)

COLINCAMPS
The Bn. which had marched from BUS the previous evening was in its appointed place in the assembly trenches, N and S. MONK (also called NEW MONK) and BRADFORD by 3.0am. A preliminary bombardment was opened by our artillery on the enemy lines which as the hour for attack drew near developed into an intense bombardment. Just before the infantry assault the medium & light trench mortars joined in, but they did not prevent enemy machine gun fire opening at 7.30am.

7.30am. The Infantry assault commenced but owing to the large casualties including the loss of all officers, no detailed narrative was possible.

The following Statements have been made by survivors:

STATEMENT BY SERGEANT-MAJOR CUSSINS:
The Bn. left Colincamps about 10.10pm Friday night June 30th & went up to the trenches, via Southern Avenue. Until arriving at Sackville Street the casualties were very slight; on leaving Sackville Street, by the various communication trenches we lost more men.

We arrived at our position in the assembly trenches between 2.30 and 3.0am.

When we got in position, between 2.30 and 3.0am. the enemy were shelling our portion of the line heavily. From the time elapsing between the Battalion entering the assembly trenches, up to zero, the Battalion lost very few men. Five minutes before 7.25, the enemy Machine Gun, Rifle Fire, and Shrapnel were directed against the parapet of our Assembly trench – the Southern half of Bradford Trench – causing us to suffer considerably. A lot of men never got off the ladder, but fell back; and many fell back from the parapet, in getting over.

On getting out of the trenches to take up our position in front, we lost heavily through the line of shrapnel, machine gun, and rapid rifle fire; by the time we attained our position in front of Bradford trench, most of the Officers, NCOs and many men were knocked out.

SLAUGHTER ON THE SOMME: 1 JULY 1916

At zero we advanced, and continued to advance until the Company Headquarters, with which I was, found ourselves in front of the Battalion – all in front having been hit. We found ourselves then half way between "Leeds" and the front line. At this point I continued the advance – Capt Smith having been knocked out –and I carried on until we got to the front line.

In our advance, we passed the majority of 'A' Co. half way between Leeds trench and the front line, lying on the ground, killed or wounded. I found in the front line, a good many of the 15th W. Yorks, what was left of the D.L.I. Co. attached to us, also a few of the K.O.Y.L.I. I found no Officers or NCOs of any of the above regiments, or of my own regiment.

The order came to "eaze off to the left" – I proceeded to do this, and found Lt. Jowett, of my Regiment, who ordered me to try to collect and organise the few men who were left, with a view to advancing again. At this moment, the enemy started shelling our front line, very heavily, with Shrapnel and High Explosive – this would be nearly one hour after zero, but, of course, I cannot give correct time.

Within a very short time, all the men we had collected were knocked out – including Mr. Jowett, who gave me instructions to make my way back to Brigade Headquarters and report that there were no men left. He told me that he had already sent back to Battalion Headquarters 3 or 4 times, but without success. This would all be about one hour to an hour and a half after zero, and I could make out that some of our men were then advancing towards the enemy lines, and must have been quite close up to the German parapet, as I saw some of the Germans show themselves over the parapet, shoot at, and then throw bombs at, what must have been some of our men still advancing.

I made my way to what I took to be Brigade Headquarters, as I saw a notice board to that effect, but it turned out to be the 94th Brigade – who telephoned my information to the Division, and also gave me orders to proceed to the 93rd Brigade Headquarters. This took some time, and on getting to Sackville Street, I was ordered, with others, to line that trench, with a view to quelling a German counter attack which had just started. As soon as the necessity for this was over, I reported myself to the 93rd Brigade Headquarters, who told me that what was left of the 16th West Yorks were being collected in Sackville Street, and I was to return there and look after them.

In the day – somewhere between 3 and 4 in the afternoon – I was ordered to form up the remainder of the Battalion in Legend Street, near Brigade Headquarters. After two hours I was ordered to take the 16th down to "Dunmow" trench, which I did.

During the wait at Brigade Headquarters, I took the names and numbers of the men of the regiment that I had with me – about 50 in all. Just as I was going down to Dunmow trench, first reinforcements in the form of 6 Officers and NCOs arrived. Until the arrival of these reinforcements, I had no NCO above the rank of Lance/Corporal.

STATEMENT BY PRIVATE DRAKE (PLATOON RUNNER ATTACHED TO 13 PLATOON 'D' COY):

Two men were hit before the company took up the position in "Bradford" trench. (This statement was subsequently corrected by Drake asserting that two men were not actually hit, but became casualties through shell shock). 'D' Co. therefore, so far as Drake is aware, reached "Bradford" trench without casualties.

The Company got out of the trench, up the ladders, close on zero, without casualties; there was no gun fire on them at all – only Machine gun fire, which did not affect the Company.

'D' Co. got into their first position, outside "Bradford" trench, without loss, so far as Drake is aware. Drake was then despatched to Battalion Headquarters with a message; message timed 8am from Capt. Clough, and reads as follows:

"To C.C., 16th West Yorks, From C.C. 'D' Co.: 'D' Co. advancing – Casualties unknown" (Sgd) Alan Clough, Place: In front of Bradford trench. Time: 8am, 1/7/16"

I found no-one at Battalion Headquarters and therefore I returned with the 18th W. Yorks Rgt. still without casualties. Got the order to move forward; walked up to front line, and contracted a few casualties on our way to the front line. My own section were wiped out as we went into No-man's Land. Got about 60 yards into No-man's land. We were 70 yards out, and I saw Capt. Clough on my left, and further on our left was our other gun. We went out, and over the parapet, at a very slow double. Met a man of the 15th W. Yorks, and he said that no-one had passed him advancing – the rest dropped through traversing machine gun fire. I looked at the German front line trench and saw no Germans.

We stayed there sometime – until approximately 2pm. In the meantime my No.1 had crawled back (I hear he is still alive). I crawled into B sap entrance and waited there until the middle of the night, then I crawled out and got into "Sackville" trench and finally reported to Battalion Headquarters.

I saw Capt Clough wounded in No-man's land – probably in the left wrist; he appeared to try to move backwards, and I think he was hit again.[1]

Of the machine-gun section, to which I was attached, five of the six got into No-man's land before being knocked out.

TO O.C. 16th WEST YORKS. 3/4/16, STATEMENT SUBMITTED BY 2nd LT. C.F. LAXTON:

Sir, My duty as INTELLIGENCE OFFICER is not yet finished; I must try to let you know what went on up to the time of my being hit. At 5 minutes to zero, Major Guyon, Ransome, and myself left our headquarters for the front line, followed closely by our retinue. We had only been by Sap A about two minutes when Major Guyon was struck through the helmet, by a bullet. Ransome and I were alongside at the time, and bandaged him up, though unconscious, and apparently dying, the wound being in the temple.[2] We were obliged to leave, as things did not appear to be going well. We urged the men on, and saw the columns advancing over "Leeds" trench, one being led by Capt. Pringle.

Things seemed to stop, men were falling and no-one advancing over our front line. Stead was in the front line with a few men, which we scraped together for a rush. Stead and I scrambled out, and the men tried to follow, but were mown down by machine gun fire. I got about 15 yards before being hit by a bullet, in the left knee and a piece of shrapnel in the right thigh; and managed to crawl to a shell hole about five yards in front, where I found Stead, shot dead.[3]

After staying there for about 15 minutes, I tried to regain our trenches, leaving all surplus kit, and gained a shell hole a few yards nearer. Ransome evidently saw me, and came out to my assistance. I sent him back to find the nearest place where I could crawl into the trench, which he did, and I followed. This was the last I saw of him, but afterwards heard he was suffering from shell shock, with Hoffman. About any other Officer or Men I know nothing. I don't think our rear two Companies ever reached our front line, owing to the sweeping machine gun fire. I think these are all the details I can supply, and hope things are going alright; and that our final objective was gained. I have seen no 16th W. Yorks Officer as yet, but hear that Auty, Grey and Hepworth were on the same train that I was, but could not get about to see them. I am very comfortable, and hope soon to be in England, I hear that Major Moore has just left this ward, for England.

Hoping all is well. Your obedient servant, (Signed) C.F. Laxton 2nd Lt. I.O.

STATEMENT SUBMITTED BY ACTING O.C. 'A' COMPANY:

INFORMATION TAKEN FROM ABOUT 20 MEN OF 'A' COMPANY WHO TOOK PART IN THE ACTION OF 1.7.16.

1. Observations of Enemy movements during preliminary bombardment: – Nil.
2. Fire: a) Men came under Machine Gun and Rifle fire as soon as they left NEW MONK TRENCH.

    b) Artillery fire was heaviest at SAP A.
3. Position of Machine Guns: An NCO reports one gun in the enemy third line 20 yards left of SAP A. All men state that there were a large number of guns in the SOUTHERN POINT of SERRE WOOD.
4. Numbers of Enemy: These cannot be given, but large numbers came up the communication trenches from SERRE.
5. Enemy Front Line: About 10 feet deep. Quite roughly made, and very wet. Very little damage done to them. Men seen in these trenches were not armed – it is thought they were Machine Gun Teams, or Bombers.

    Bombers all came from the third line, over the open, and threw bombs from the back of the first line. Most men are of the opinion that SAP A was thought to be a strong point.

There was a difficulty about keeping direction, as the Battalion drifted to the left, i.e. to the NORTH.

6. The Platoon on the Right; had least casualties, so that most of the information came from this Platoon, which was in NEW MONK , between BLENEAU and FLAG trenches.

(Sgd) F.C. Burnley. 2nd Lt. i/c 'A' Co. 16th W. Yorks.

I came across men – both of my own Company, and the Company immediately behind the front line trench, on the left of "Flag" trench; I did not notice any men until I got up close to the front line. The order came from the Brigadier to move to the left. A good number of men of 'C' Co., 'D' Co., and also of the 15th West Yorks were alive in the front line trench. Came across the Adjutant moving along to the right. Went down to help to man a bay off "Warley" trench. Sometime later – I do not know how long – I went back, and on my way I heard the order to retire. Helped stretcher bearer to carry out a wounded man, and finally reported to "Legend" trench where the Battalion was reformed.

STATEMENT BY PRIVATE PRICE (MACHINE-GUN):

The gun was carried behind the last line (i.e. the last platoon) with orders to follow up the Battalions 'D' Co. Got into "Bradford" trench without casualties to their Machine Gun Team.

I was last out of the Company, went along "Bradford" trench from left to right, and there were no wounded in the trench. Got into the preparatory position; saw Capt. Clough on the centre with Company headquarters. Went forward to the next trench in front of Bradford – no casualties up to then. Got the order to move forward, and reached the Leeds trench.

No.2.   BRADFORD trench from "FLAG" to "WARLEY" was occupied by 'B' Co. on the right and 'D' Co. on the left.

No.3.   Battalion Headquarters were situated in the DUG-OUT in "SOUTH MONK", between "BLENEAU" and "FLAG" TRENCHES.

No.4.   The 15th West Yorks occupied the Assembly trench, "LEEDS" east of NORTH and SOUTH MONK.

No.5.   The 18th West Yorks occupied the Assembly Trench, "DUNMOW", west of "BRADFORD", and,

No.6.   The remainder of the D.L.I. occupied the Assembly trench "LANDGUARD" – west of "DUNMOW".
The Battalion, after having had a meal in the ORCHARD N.W. of COLINCAMPS, moved forward into the trenches at 10pm June 30th, and the Battalion was in position in the Assembly trenches at between 2.30 & 3am.

SLAUGHTER ON THE SOMME: 1 JULY 1916

STATEMENT BY CAPTAIN WATLING:

At about 3.30pm July 1st I left BUS and reported to Brigade Headquarters in "LEGEND STREET" at about 5.45pm. I was told by Capt. Kayll that the remains of the Battalion were in "LANDGUARD". I also saw a few men of the 16th West Yorks in "LEGEND STREET".

I collected the men, as far as possible, and with the assistance of Lt. ARMITAGE and 2nd Lt. BURNLEY we endeavoured to put "LANDGUARD" into a state of defence. I secured ammunition and water from the Battalion dump. At about 7.30pm I received instructions to move the Battalion forward to "OLD DUNMOW" trench – between "BLENEAU" and "WARLEY". At this time there appeared to be anything up to 120 men of the Battalion. MAJOR H.H.KENNEDY (2nd in Command) now assumed Command of the Battalion.

REPORTS BY NCOS AND MEN OF 'B' COMPANY ON THE OPERATIONS OF 1 JULY 1916:

1. No-one seems to have made any observations during the preliminary bombardment.
2. The enemy swept our parapet with very heavy Machine Gun fire, ten minutes before end of our bombardment. This fire was enfilade from both flanks; Barrages of our front line and heavy curtain fire all up communication trenches. The artillery fire came from both flanks, but the bulk was from the left.
3. Positions of Machine Guns not noted.
4. Enemy front trenches and communication trenches seemed to be crowded.
5. General Observation: Main artillery fire seemed to be from left.
6. No.8 Platoon got as far as our own front line. No information regarding other Platoons. The principal enemy tactics noticed was a very quick COUNTER ATTACK on our left flank.
   (Sgd) A.A. Gibson 2nd Lt., 'B' Co.

REPORT SUPPLIED THROUGH SERGEANT IREDALE ON THE PART TAKEN BY 'C' COMPANY IN THE OPERATIONS OF 1 JULY 1916:

1. Came under heavy enemy shell fire about Leeds trench; H.E. and Shrapnel.
2. Enfilade fire from Left mainly, otherwise front fire.
3. Nothing known as to the positions of enemy Machine Guns.
4. Positions of enemy front line held. Numbers doubtful.
   The Battalion moved forward & arrangements were made for the defence of "DUNMOW" nothing of importance took place during the night excepting that we were subjected to a few rounds of Shrapnel & a certain quantity of H.E. – probably from 77 cm guns. On the morning of the 2nd July at about 4am. we noticed a small quantity of black Lachrymatory gases.
   During the day there was intermittent shelling, probably in reply to intense bombardment of the German lines by our artillery at 3 to 3.30pm & 6.30 to 7pm the remainder of our tour in the trenches was uneventful except at about

4.0am on the 4th, when rifle fire was heard on our right, but cannot say by whom was this fire. It was followed by a good deal of machine-gun fire from the Germans, but we sustained no casualties. At about noon there was a severe thunderstorm which flooded a great portion of "OLD DUNMOW" between "BLENEAU" and GREY.

REFERENCE HEBUYERNE TRENCH MAP 1/10000
The Battalion received instructions to move up to the trenches on the 30th June, & moved off from its billets at BUS by half Companies, Half Company of 'A' moving off at 6.35pm. strengths of the Coys was as follows:

Headquarters 46, 'A' Coy 133, 'B' Coy 114, 'C' Coy 130, 'D' Coy 130. Bombers 9, Machine Gun 101, Medical Staff 19. In addition the Battalion supplied the following carrying party under Lts Hoffman & Gibson – 68. The officers who went into action with the Bn were divided amongst Coys as follows: Headquarters 5, 'A' Coy 4, 'B' Coy 4, 'C' Coy 4 , 'D' Coy 4 , MG 3, Dump 2, Medical Officer 1.

One Coy of the 18th D.L.I. & 100 of the K.O.Y.R.I [*sic*] were attached to the Bn for the operations. The places assigned to us were the following assembly trenches: 1. N. and S. MONK from FLAG AVENUE to GREY STREET, in which were placed 'A' & 'C' Coys 1 between FLAG and DELAUNEY. 'D' Coy of the 18th D.L.I. Company were under Machine Gun fire – coming from N.E. – immediately on leaving NEW MONK trench. Snipers from front line seemed to return at 7.45am numbers about one dozen, each Sniper had apparently a loader. Bosches returned from front line & did not hold it during the afternoon.

'D' COMPANY'S REPORT ON OPERATIONS OF 1 JULY 1916:
1. As the Coy was in dead ground no enemy movement could be observed.
2. The first wave got over the top of "BRADFORD" trench & at once came under heavy Shrapnel and H.E. fire, but this did not cause the Coy many casualties, on coming up to & over, our front line, the Coy came under heavy Machine Gun fire from half left, & it is this fire that caused most of our casualties.[4]
3. It is thought that the Machine Gun emplacements were in the German 2nd & 3rd lines & the enemy had automatic rifles (as our Lewis gun) in their front line, & it is thought that there were a great many of these guns.
4. The enemy were observed in large numbers opposite MATTHEW COPSE.
5. The bridges over the assembly trenches appear to have presented a very good target for the enemy artillery & received a great deal of attention.
    (Sgd) A.C. Parker, 2nd Lieut.

NOTES

1. The son of Henry Smith Clough, and Elizabeth Clough, of Redbolt, Keighley, 21-year-old Captain Alan Clough is commemorated on the Thiepval Memorial.

2. Listed by the Commonwealth War Graves Commission as a Lieutenant Colonel, George Sutherland Guyon, of the 2nd Battalion Royal Fusiliers but commanding the 16th (Service) Battalion (1st Bradford) Prince of Wales's Own (West Yorkshire Regiment) was 42 years old at the time of his death on 1 July 1916. He is commemorated on the Thiepval Memorial.

3. Formerly of the 19th Battalion Royal Fusiliers, 31-year-old Second Lieutenant Ralph Stead, from Necton near Swaffham in Norfolk, was buried in Serre Road Cemetery No.1.

4. The following list of the Casualties is given as having been sustained by the battalion during the operations on 1 July 1916 – Officers: ten killed, one died of wounds, one not accounted for and ten wounded. Other ranks: fifty-eight killed, eleven died of wounds, 111 not accounted for, and 313 wounded. Total casualties were sixty-eight killed, twelve died of wounds, 112 not accounted for and 313 wounded; a total of 515.

18th (Service) Battalion (2nd Bradford) Prince of Wales's Own (West Yorkshire Regiment)

IN THE FIELD

4.30am. Battalion in position in assembly trenches. Some casualties en route and whilst in these trenches.

8.20am. Message received from Brigade to the effect that the 16th West Yorks. were held up, and ordering the C.O. to go to Sap "A" to investigate. Lt-Col Kennard accordingly went forward, but was killed about 8.30am by artillery.[1]

8.40am. Battalion left assembly trenches. Under heavy machine gun fire from the time of leaving dead ground up to our front line trenches, and an intense barrage of shrapnel and H.E. Casualties very heavy. Brigade advance was held up in front of German wire, but 15th, 16th, 18th W. Yorks. and one Company of 18th D.L.I. advanced as if on parade. One platoon of 'B' Company reported to have reached the German wire, under Lt. Akam. The rear platoon of the Battn. got as far as our front line. The Adjutant, Capt. T. Williams, and O.C. 'A' Coy (Capt. C.H.C. Keevel) were wounded early on, and the casualties amongst officers were severe.

Owing to the unexpected resistance of the enemy the Brigade was compelled to retire, and a verbal message to this effect was received. For a time the first and second line were vacated, and the Battalion was broken up in retiring through our trenches.

The majority of our casualties occurred between LEEDS trench and our own wire, and were due chiefly to machine gun fire from flank and front. Three very heavy barrages were formed along our line, which hampered the advance and caused other casualties before reaching LEEDS trench. A number of casualties were also caused by indirect frontal machine gun fire caused by indirect frontal machine gun fire.

Approx. total casualties: 16 Officers, 400 Other ranks.

Further details with regard to the attack are given in the reports from O.C. Coys.

4pm.　　Major H.F.G. Carter under instructions from Divisional H.Q., reported to Brigade H.Q. LEGEND, and took over command of Battn, vice Lt Col M.N. Kennard, killed. Battalion at that time very broken up and separated, and being collected under Lt Col Bowes, 18th Durham L.I.

4.30pm.　About 60 of Battn in DUNMOW and OLD DUNMOW.

4.35pm.　Major Carter went round GREY, BRADFORD, MONK, E. BLENEAU, Nos 1, 2 and 3 Posts and 'A' Sap in search of remainder of Battalion. Except for a few wounded these trenches were entirely evacuated at this time.

8.45pm.　Received orders from Brigade to occupy and hold MONK TRENCH. This was done from WARLEY to BLENEAU. 'C' Coy 18th D.L.I. and some machine guns holding front line. Battn H.Q. established at Bomb Dump, MONK TRENCH. At this time Battalion consisted of 6 officers and about 120 O.R. (Officers – Major Carter, Lieut Cross, Lieut Howarth, 2/Lieut Whitaker, 2/Lieut Stephenson, and (at ration dump) 2/Lieut Thornton)

9pm.　　Guides sent to meet reinforcements bringing rations from EUSTON DUMP, under 2/Lieut Thornton.

9.30pm.　2/Lieut Peace reported and was ordered by C.O. to return to Q.M. BUS, for the night as he was wounded and looking terribly ill.

12 midnight.　Telephone communication established with Brigade H.Q.

COPIES OF REPORTS BY COMPANY COMMANDERS ON OPERATIONS OF JULY 1st, 1916.

By O.C. 'A' Company (Lieutenant R.S. Cross. Commanding No.4 Platoon):
During the advance of the first platoon of the leading regiment a rapid rifle fire was opened on them directly they got out of the dead ground wherein the assembly trenches were dug, and this was followed by heavy machine gun fire from direction of front line trenches South of SERRE RD judging by the strike of the bullets. In some cases they were observed to strike the back of the trench (BLENEAU) about half way down, and I judged some of the guns to be a good distance back. By the time I took my platoon out an intense bombardment was in progress on our front line and support trenches, canister bombers and heavy H.E., also shrapnel, catching all the men as they reached the support line. This curtain of fire was extended to our assembly trenches. The heavy guns appeared to be working from PUISIEUX and shrapnel from SERRE. My platoon was in DUNMOW and my line of advance about 20 yds S. of 'A' Sap.

　　Our artillery seemed to me to have been concentrated mainly on German trenches, with good effect in smashing up trenches, but evidently did not smash up their dugouts, judging by the rifle fire.

SLAUGHTER ON THE SOMME: 1 JULY 1916

Report by O.C. 'B' Company (Lieutenant A. Howarth):
We came under heavy machine gun fire on leaving LANDGUARD trench, and heavy artillery fire on reaching S. MONK. The position of the enemy machine guns appeared to be from the SOUTH and was cross fire. Most of the artillery came from PUISIEUX, and was a remarkable curtain of fire.

The position of enemy's machine guns was not actually located, and numbers not able to find out.

The Company started from LANDGUARD to left of GREY, our assembly trenches, and advanced towards 'A' Sap.

It seemed to me that the artillery played too long on the enemy's front line instead of putting out the Huns' guns, owing to the wonderful dugouts used by the Huns. Also the tape to be put out overnight to enable us to keep direction was not done, which seemed to be at fault in places.

By O.C. 'C' Company (Second Lieutenant A.D. Stephenson):
The Company did not pass our front line, and were therefore in dead ground as far as field of view went. We were first shelled before leaving our assembly trench at about 1.20 after zero, the shrapnel doing considerable damage on our left.
On getting out into the open we ran into the zone of H.E. just in front of DUNMOW.

Direction of shrapnel shells from SERRE; H.E. shells from direction of PUISIEUX.

Most of the machine gun fire seemed to come from the direction of the QUADRILATERAL, enfilading our advancing lines from the South after they had left our front line.

No enemy seen in large numbers, but there were several seen on the enemy front line parapet. These must have had good cover in their front line during our bombardment, either in dugouts or tunnels.

This company was the last to leave the assembly trenches, and all four platoons reached our first line.

The enemy artillery was a great surprise to our troops, who had expected to find most of the enemy guns put out of action.

The enemy infantry standing on their parapet firing at our advancing troops seemed to consider themselves quite safe from our guns. Could our advanced troops not have lain down while our guns shelled them down with shrapnel?

Had our machine guns not all been used in the advance, they might have been of some use in enfilading the German parapet or in combating their machine guns.

Further remarks of O.C. 'C' Company on movements of Company (Second Lieutenant A.D. Stephenson):
The platoons each moved off in four lines, but owing to lack of bridges and width of trenches after bombardment, these lines had to close in on each other at every

trench crossed. More bridges over each of the trenches to be crossed would have obviated this.

The Companies in front seemed to have completely lost their direction, possibly owing to the 16th W. Yorks pushing too far to the left.

By O.C. 'D' Company (Second Lieutenant F. W. Whitaker):
Owing to our assembly trenches being in dead ground, I saw nothing of the enemy during the preliminary bombardment.

We came into heavy enemy fire about 100 yards in front of the assembly trench which my Company occupied, i.e., DUNMOW, between BLENEAU and FLAG AVENUE. This was machine gun fire from the right, apparently from the German front line from SERRE RD. South. If these guns had been put out of action my Company would have reached the curtain of fire with very few casualties.

I also observed machine gun fire from the left, N.E. of our line of advance, evidently firing at a very long range.

The curtain of fire fell on our first line trenches, and consisted of shrapnel, apparently coming from behind SERRE village, and H.E., which seemed to come from PUISIEUX.

The enemy machine guns were placed all along the line, and I noticed no particular emplacements.

I saw nothing of the enemy in front, but a small number advanced on my right flank for about 200 yards in the neighbourhood of SERRE RD, and were enfiladed by machine guns which were attached to my party.

I think that the guns immediately behind our assembly trenches attracted fire to our position in the assembly trenches.

My platoon was in the rear platoon of the Company on the right flank of the Battalion, and formed the garrison for "F" strong point. It reached the front line (British).

NOTE

1. Formerly a Captain in the 6th Dragoon Guards (Carabiniers), 32-year-old Lieutenant Colonel Maurice Nicholl Kennard MC, three times Mentioned in Despatches, is commemorated on the Thiepval Memorial. He had been wounded in November 1914. In his book *The Bradford Pals* (Pen & Sword, Barnsley), David Raw writes: "Less than a hundred yards in front of Dunmow trench they came under a heavy cross fire from machine guns firing from their right, probably from the Quadrilateral Redoubt and south of the Serre Road. Almost everyone dropped flat on their stomachs to escape this murderous scythe, except their commanding officer, Lieutenant-Colonel M.N. Kennard. Standing calm and erect amid the crack and whine of bullets and carrying only a walking stick he called out 'come on boys, up you get', turned and began to walk at an easy gait towards the enemy. The Battalion rose to their feet and followed him. As they came out of the dead ground in which their assembly trenches were dug they were additionally engaged by a rapid fire from the front. Casualties were heavy, particularly amongst the officers and including Lieutenant-Colonel Kennard, who was killed by a shell which burst close by him."

1st Battalion Princess Victoria's (Royal Irish Fusiliers)

IN THE FIELD

1am.   Battalion arrived at Assembly trenches in SUNKEN ROAD at 1A.M. without a single casualty in spite of a few heavy shells 5.9 which fell just beside the Battalion when halted on the MAILLY-AUCHONVILLERS ROAD.

9.10am   Report of Operation commencing 1st July. Ref Map 57D. N.E. 3&4

At 9.10am being the hour at which the Battalion was due to advance, the leading platoon advanced from their Assembly Trenches in battle formation (Coys 90yds interval 100yds distance between platoons which were in fours).

At this moment a telephone message was received from the 10th Brigade, that the Battalion were not to advance beyond the line TENDERLOIN-MOUNT JOY until further orders.

This was at once sent on to Companies and reached them as the leading platoons were just crossing the line named.

9.40am   From 9.40am until about 2pm the Battalion remained about K.35.b.5.0. under considerable shell and machine-gun fire.

2pm   About 2pm I received an order from the Brigade to send support to Lt.-Col. HOPKINSON who was holding the QUADILATERAL in K.35.a. with the remnants of the SEAFORTH HIGHLANDERS and some details of other regiments. I sent forward my left Coy 'C' under Capt. E.R. WILSON.

11pm   At 4pm I received a message from the 10th Brigade saying that the Company of my Battalion ordered to the QUADILATERAL had not arrived there. (It was afterwards found that Capt. WILSON'S Company could not advance across the open owing to heavy machine gun and Rifle Fire. Capt. WILSON being wounded while gallantly leading his Coy over the open.)

'D' Coy under Capt. G.W.N. BAREFOOT was then ordered to the QUADILATERAL.

Capt. BAREFOOT led his Coy by a circuitous route and entered the QUADILATERAL from the south with 2 platoons, leaving 2 platoons in immediate support in our own front line and placed himself under orders of Lt. Col. HOPKINSON, 2nd SEAFORTH HIGHLANDERS.

4pm   From this time the QUADILATERAL was held by the SEAFORTH HIGHLANDERS, ROYAL IRISH FUSILIERS and various details of 11th & 12th Brigades and 48th Division.

About 8.15pm.   The disposition of the Battalion were, 'A' & 'B' Coy about K 35 b 5.0. 'C' Coy about K 34 d 8.4. 'D' Coy in the QUADILATERAL less 2 platoons in British Front Line immediately opposite the QUADILATERAL.

8.30pm   At 8.30pm Capt. & Adjt. W. CARDEN ROE returned from the Brigade Hd.Qrs. with orders to the affect that:

1. 'D' Coy were to hold the QUADILATERAL at all costs, all other troops in the QUADILATERAL under the command of Lt. Col. HOPKINSON to be withdrawn.

2. The remainder of the Battalion was to hold our own front line from K.34.d.8.2 to K.34.d.8.7. Acting on this Capt. CARDEN ROE proceeded to the QUADILATERAL and gave the orders to Lieut. Col. HOPKINSON who then withdrew. Capt. BAREFOOT assuming command in the QUADILATERAL.

The remainder of the Battalion proceeded to take up the position in the line allotted to them. This was effected under difficulty owing to the heavy barrage on both our front and support lines, and the relief was successfully complete by 2a.m.on the 2nd of July. Hd.Qrs. moving into the ROMAN ROAD.

Meanwhile at 11.35pm I received orders that all troops were to be withdrawn from the QUADILATERAL and our own front line to be held and consolidated.

I immediately despatched two runners to Capt. BAREFOOT in the QUADILATERAL ordering him to withdraw his Company into our front line and to consolidate there. This message never reached him.

1st Battalion Rifle Brigade (The Prince Consort's Own)

In the Field.
Battalion assaults German front line trenches. Report by Maj. Barclay attached. Relieved on night of 1st-2nd July by 2nd R.W. Riding Regt (Dk of Wellingtons). Proceeded to billets in MAILLY MAILLET.[1]

Document Attached to the War Diary

Copy of a letter written by Second Lieutenant G.W. Glover and sent to Major G.W. Barclay:

My dear Barclay,

I hear I am booked for England so I shan't have any opportunity of seeing you for some time and I want to give you some of what we did yesterday and how things went. I was in the trench we held till the last, and was the only officer in it just at the end. Trevor was there and Billington, and Trevor was killed by a shell a couple of yards from our own front trench as he and I were coming back, being both wounded and ordered back by the Seaforths Colonel who was in charge. Billington is in this place with me.

We started out as arranged, and things seemed going quite well till we, or rather our first wave, reached the German front line; they slowed and we bunched rather and the most fearsome hail of rifle and machine gun fire with continuous shelling, opened on us. Most of us seemed to be knocked out. There were some Germans in the trench near and Sgt. Smith, Corpl. Halls, and myself started to bomb, but the Germans cleared out to our right. What was left of us now seemed to get into the trench and a few Somersets came along and joined, a few going on farther but getting into shell holes just beyond. As far as I can judge we were in the German second trench about in "A" Coys area.

I now found I was with C.S.M. Selway and Sgt. Hunt, and together with them and Sgt. Smith tried to strengthen our position, as we had no touch on the right and there was no possibility of going on.

We were enfiladed too from the left but some Warwicks came up, and apart from shelling we were fairly comfortable. Trevor turned up and Greetham of the Somersets and we decided to carry on, stretch out our right as far as we could, with the Bn bombers, about half a dozen, on our right flank.

We were attacked by the German bombers and resisted them falling back slightly, then they seemed to work round to our right rear.

However, we kept up a look out on that side and a Lewis Gun on the parapet of a communication trench running back domminated the open. A Captain Martin of the 8th Warwicks kept the men as well as he could at strengthening our left, but it was hard work, the men seemed dazed and careless. With rifle fire we drove off an attack on the left front; and we managed by scraping shallow trenches to get in some of the men from the shell holes beyond; Others came in over the top – or didn't. Gradually our bit of trench filled in with a great many of the 12th Bde. and some of the 10th. I afterwards learnt that of the 10th had stayed in the front line, but didn't know till about 5 p.m., otherwise we should have tried to make connection. We were a fearful squash in the trench, everybody in the way of everybody else and it was extremely difficult to move or dig. I did try, but not very successfully to spread the 11th out to the right, and Capt. Martin also tried to get the 10th and 12th to the left, but they were held back and we couldn't get along the single trench. Suddenly our right seemed to be rushed by German bombers, and the men up to our Bn bombing squad rushed back; the bombing squad was apparently cut off.

This was about 11 a.m. to 12 noon, and we were short of bombs, and the Lewis Guns were more or less out of action. All the bombs we had and could spare from the left were passed up and with the help of a Corpl. I managed to get together about four throwers who absolutely kept the trench for us for hours. They were a magnificent lot, and splendid fellows, they deserve any praise or reward. There was another even finer, the runner of the Colonel of the 8th Warwicks, I believe. (But I have all their names, only unfortunately I left it with the things to be returned to my kit; but I will let you have the names when I get my kit and want you, if you can, to do what you can for any who are left). This runner made the trip between that trench and our own at least 20 times, bringing bombs and L.G. ammunition. He did more than any single individual to keep things going. Then towards 2 p.m. or 3 p.m. Trevor passed me up a message from the Colonel of the Seaforths to hold on, he would send on bombs. But for the runner even that would have come too late. The throwers were dog tired and the Germans full of energy; by persuasion we managed to get a team of about half a dozen who carried on manfully, also carriers and men to keep the fire step just there. Some others would have done so had they not been wounded. By way of precaution we built a barricade, leaving about 35 yards of straight trench with a L.G. on top of a traverse commanding it, but held on in our original position till we were suddenly rushed and retired behind the barricade about 4.30 p.m. For a long time the Germans threw into the stretch of trench and on both parapets but never showed up. All seemed to be going well, and by a miracle of good luck all the other people seemed suddenly to disappear from the trench behind us, or the last rush would have been most terrible. They crawled, apparently into the first trench. All seemed perfectly alright, there was a look out on both sides as well as along the straight, and the Germans never reached us with their bombs. Hearing an officer call from a dugout, I went and spoke to him, staying possibly 3 minutes, and as I came up the end came with a rush. How they managed it I don't know, possibly they had worked into a trench near our front, but the Germans suddenly threw bombs, some of which fell on the traverse by the L.G., and drove our men out of the trench. An attempt to make a stand at the next traverse was unsuccessful. In the new trench – the front line – the base of the Quadrilateral – there seemed to be no definite plan, except that they were manning it facing left. Some of the men there and some of ours – out of the advanced trench, I mean, not necessarily R.Bs. – got put and back to our trenches. Some lay on the parapet facing the Germans who put some heavy shells into the middle of them, more went back.

I thought at first there were only about 50, so with Sgt. Charters got some manning the rear parapet that is the one nearer us with a view to a proper retirement if necessary. Then the Staff Captain turned up giving instructions to the C.O. of the Seaforths whom I now saw for the first time with a quantity – about 200 – of troops. He sent out of the trench all who were wounded, including Trevor and Myself. On coming to this new trench I found Capt. Martin, Trevor, Billington, C.S.M. Selway, Sgt. Hunt, Sgt. Charters, Carty and one or two others.

The whole day was hopeless, both flanks in the air, continuous bombardment from the Germans, and our guns doing nothing. When we saw aeroplanes we burnt flares but it made no difference. The German counter-attacking party sent up Very lights at short intervals and their artillery changed to a nicety. Why couldn't ours have held our right flank and put a barrage beyond? We should have held out then.

Why didn't they go for the German guns? They were silent all day instead I think the Germans managed their M.G. fire by putting up mounds of earth between the third and fourth trenches so as to shoot over their own parapets and sweep the whole surface of the ground. They did it wonderfully but it was the cruellest slaughter.

I saw none of our own officers but those I have mentioned. Captain Martin really did help; also less so, 2nd Lt Ward of the Essex. For the rest there was the most awful jumble in the trench, R.Bs. and Somersets very few even then, Essex, Warwicks, Seaforths, Lancs. Fusiliers, some of every regiment in the Division. Some were gorgeous out of each regiment most seemed dazed and indifferent. But all were firm to stay there till the end.

I have written this rather for your own information than as an official report. I have had to put in myself a lot, because I know only what I myself did, so this is quite probably a picture of what happened only our right flank. But I was there from the beginning and all day to the end, and I think nobody could give you just the account I can. The right flank was the weakest point; those bombers and carriers who held were really the heroes of the day with the Warwicks runner.

NOTE

1. A nominal roll of officer casualties on 1 July 1916, was included in the War Diary. It states that the officers killed were: Lieutenant Colonel D. Wood, Captain (Adjutant) G.T. Cartland, Lieutenant (Temporary Captain) A.W. Henderson, Lieutenant (Temporary Captain) R. Fraser, Second Lieutenant G.G. Trevor Jones, and Second Lieutenant J.P. Morum. The officers who died of wounds were Second Lieutenant (Temporary Captain) H.F. Russell Smith and Second Lieutenant N. Fagan. The officers missing believed killed were listed as Temporary Lieutenant G.C.L. Dewhurst, Lieutenant M.G. White, Second Lieutenant C.A. Clark and Second Lieutenant A.G. Clarke. The officer shown as wounded and missing was Lieutenant (Temporary Captain) W.H. Beever, whilst those listed as missing are Second Lieutenant F.W. Kirkland and Second Lieutenant C. Volkers. The wounded were: Second Lieutenant H.L.G. Kensington, Second Lieutenant R.A. Patterson, Second Lieutenant M.F. Bulles, Second Lieutenant G.W. Glover, and Second Lieutenant L.E. Cording.

1st Battalion Royal Dublin Fusiliers

FIRING LINE AUCHONVILLERS
Reached our allotted positions in trenches via BROADWAY at 01.00. 'W' Coy (on right) & 'X' Coy (on left) in ESSEX ST. with 'Y' Coy (on right) & 'Z' Coy (on left) in 88th TRENCH. Casualties during move 2 O.Ranks slightly wounded. Bombardment became more intense from 06.30 to 07.30 at which hour the Attack was launched.

The 2/Royal Fusiliers (on right) & 1/Lancashire Fusiliers (on left) advanced against the Germans 1st Line Trenches. In front of Lancs a large mine was exploded by us near BEAUMONT HAMEL at 07.20. Immediately the 2/R.F. & 1/L.F. advanced we commenced to move up to our Front Line Trenches. 'W' Coy with 'Y' Coy in support up F. ST. & BROADWAY and 'X' Coy with 'Z' in support up

BLOOMFIELD & 2ND AVENUE ready to move out against the German Second Line System of Trenches in BEAUCOURT RIDGE, S.E. of BEAUMONT HAMEL. The Bn. was supposed to move out behind the 2/R.F., by Coys, and reform at STATION RD. (also by Coys) ready for the assault of the enemy Second Line System; but this could only be done after the 2/R.F. had obtained their objective, the enemy Front Line System, and this the 2/R.F. were unable to accomplish.

It was very difficult for Coys to move up to the Front Line owing to the trenches being blocked by a number of men of the Bn. in front (2/R.F.), 86th Bde M.G. Coy & consolidating parties. Consequently it was 08.00 before W & X Coys were able to begin moving out over the parapet. Our own barbed wire was cut at intervals of about 40yds and by this time the Germans had M.G's trained on these gaps, the result being that our casualties were very heavy & only a few of our men ever got through our wire & still fewer of these succeeded in advancing more than 50yds or 60yds before being shot down. 'W' Coy & 'Y' Coy both behaved exceptionally well under fire.

At noon the attack here was abandoned and we were ordered to hold & consolidate our own front line –'X' Coy on Right & 'Z' on left.

At 09.00 we were ordered to recover 4 Stokes Trench Mortars abandoned near the German Line (on lip of mine crater at HAWTHORN REDOUBT). Capt. W.P. OULTON with 20 men went out at dusk & succeeded in recovering all 4 guns – without suffering any casualties.

Our total casualties for the day numbered:

Officers: 4 Killed – Capt. E.R.L. MAUNSELL 1/R.D.F.; 2/Lt. A.J.W. PEARSON 14th Royal Fus.; 2/Lt. C.F. GREENLEES 9th Queen's; and 2/Lt. A.A.M.B. ROSE-CLELAND 1/R.D.F.

7 Wounded – Lt. R. ELPHICK 1/R.D.F.; 2/Lts. T.W.R. NEILL 9th R.S. Fusiliers (seriously), W.J. ROBERTSON 9th R.S. Fusiliers, H.V. Spankie 1/R.D.F., R.G.S. DURWARD 14th Royal Scots, J.E.B. Maunsell 1/R.D.F. and M.H. TIGHE 1/R.D.F.

1 Missing – 2/Lt. D.R. WARNER 1/R.D.F.

Roll of O.R. casualties not yet completed, but estimated 300.

Taken off strength 4 officers killed, 1 officer still missing, 18 O. Ranks killed, 63 O.R. missing, 1 O.R. died.

2nd Battalion Royal Dublin Fusiliers

At 9.0am The Battalion left its Assembly trenches and advanced in the following formation: 'A''B' and 'C' Coys 4 lines of platoons, each platoon in sections of file, the lines 100 yards apart.

'D' Coy in Reserve 200 yards in rear of 45 line, this Coy was in diamond formation, each platoon being in column of fours.

Immediately after leaving their assembly trenches, each line came under a heavy enfilade fire from machine guns in BEAUMONT-HAMEL even the Reserve Coy having casualties, as they left YOUNG STREET.

9.5am.　The order "Stand Fast" was received followed immediately by message "Your Battalion not to go beyond English front line trenches till further orders." Two runners were immediately sent after each Coy and the C.O. personally went to 'A' Coy and was just in time to catch a Sergt. who was a little in rear of the 4th line; he doubled forward with the verbal message. These messages were only delivered at our first line trenches, and the Advance was there stopped.

In the meantime the Battalion had lost heavily not only from machine gun fire from BEAUMONT-HAMEL but from heavy rifle and machine gun fire from the German 1st Line trenches on our immediate front, also from shell fire.

It had been impossible to stop all the Platoons and some had got into the ground between the enemy and our own trenches – these without exception became casualties including 5 officers.

12noon.　Orders as follows were received: "You will attack the German trenches and consolidate line from point 86 to 88 inclusive. The Seaforth Highlrs. are attacking north of THE REDAN. Point 59 is held by our own troops. The 29th Divn. are attacking BEAUMONT-HAMEL at 12.30. Take care of your left flank as there are still some Germans in position opposite THE REDAN."

It was found impossible to collect more than 60 men.

During the Advance out of 23 officers and 480 men going into Action 14 officers and 311 men had become casualties. The Advance having been in lines of sections on a front of 400 yards the remainder were scattered about in the trenches, and mixed up with those troops which remained of the 11th Brigade. The C.O. was therefore ordered to collect all the men possible and put them into the original assembly trenches. This was done, during the evening the carriers and the 10% reinforcements rejoined the Battalion.

2nd Battalion Royal Fusiliers
(City of London Regiment)

BEAUMONT HAMEL

From early dawn until 07.20am bombardment was very fierce. The big mine opposite HAWTHORNE REDOUBT was then exploded and 'Z' Company rushed forward to occupy crater, but were immediately met by heavy machine gun fire and artillery barrage. 5 minutes after this (Zero time) the general attack along the whole front was launched. Very few of our men reached as far as the enemy barbed wire.

Owing to our artillery persistently shelling the 2nd and 3rd line of the enemy's first system, the Germans were enabled to freely use their own front line, and therefore resisted all attacks upon it. This continued to about 12 midday, when the few remaining men in "no mans land" were forced to retire.

1pm Major H.H. Cripps was ordered to Brigade Headquarters to take over the duties of Brigade Major, but was seriously wounded within two hours. Lt Colonel R.V. Johnson was [*page torn*] in the front line trench by one of our own High Explosives and severely shaken. Major G.S. Guyon was killed leading the 16th Bn. West Yorkshire Regt.

Casualties were:

Officers:	Killed	3
	Wounded	12
	Wounded & Missing	1
	Missing	4
	Missing believed killed	4
Other Ranks:	Killed	54
	Wounded	276
	Missing	140

1st Battalion Royal Inniskilling Fusiliers

FIRING LINE

Z Day. In accordance with Orders the Battalion advanced on the objective, which consisted of the first three lines of German Trenches, the Batt advancing in lines of Platoons in single file in the following rotation 'B', 'A', 'D', Coys 'C' Company being held in Reserve in our original front line trench. Immediately our lines appeared on the parapet the enemy brought heavy Machine gun cross fire to bear which heavily decimated the Advance, none being able to gain further ground than the enemy's Wires. Under the circumstances the Advance failed in the Sector allotted to the Batt. as it was also found impossible to bring up Reserves.

Strength of Battalion on entering the Action:

Officers   36
Other Ranks   916

Casualties:

Officers   Lieut Colonel Pierce, (Temp) Captain French, Lieut. Harboard and 2 Lieut. Porter killed. Missing 4. Wounded 11.

Other Ranks   Killed 50. Missing 225. Wounded 265.

Remainder of Batt. rallied in our Front Sector, near St. JOHNS ROAD.

1st Battalion Royal Warwickshire Regiment

ASSEMBLY TRENCHES
See copy of Operation Orders attached.

Document Attached to the War Diary

Copy of a report on the action of battalion operations 22 June 1916, to 1 July 1916, written "in the field" on 5 July 1916, and signed by Lieutenant Colonel G.N.B. Forster, Commanding 1st Battalion Royal Warwickshire Regiment:

The Battalion took up the whole Front Line of the 4th Division on the 22nd JUNE 1916 – Four Companies in the Front Line from BESS STREET on the North to Q4/12 Trench on the South. The Preliminary bombardment commenced at 5-30 A.M. on the 24th JUNE 1916.

On the night of the 24th JUNE at 10 P.M. Gas was discharged from our Front Line Trenches K 34/4 to 7 and lasted till about 12-30 A.M. – The wind became unfavourable shortly after 10-30 P.M. and blew the Gas back over our Line – One cylinder being broken by Shell Fire – The Germans put up a very heavy barrage for about 1 hour and continued an intermittent bombardment till about 1 A.M.

On the night of 25th JUNE 1916 – Gas was again discharged at 2 A.M. till 4-30 A.M. The Gas cloud went over the German Line but wind conditions again turned unfavourable and it returned over our line – The enemy bombarding our line heavily again.

On the night 26th JUNE a raiding party of 2 Officers (Lieut J.L. SHUTE and 2nd Lieut R.W. GORTON) and 20 men at 11.40 P.M., after a bombardment, attempted to cross and raid German Trenches at K35 c 2.4. but the Germans put such a heavy barrage up in front of and on our front line the party were unable to leave our line and the Raid was abandoned.

There was an intermittent reply by the German Guns to our preliminary bombardment day and night.

On the night 26/27th JUNE the Battalion was relieved by the 11th Inf. Bde. On the night 30/1st JULY the battalion left BERTRANCOURT at 9.5P.M. via MAILLY MAILLET to Assembly Trenches in the SUNKEN ROAD between 3rd and 5th AVENUES, being in position by 1-15 A.M.

At 9-10 A.M. 1st JULY the Battalion advanced in small column formation from Assembly Trenches across the open in support of the 2/R. DUB.FUSILIERS – 1/R.IRISH FUSILIERS being on their left.

At 9-15 A.M. received an Order that the Battalion was to halt and reform at the TENDERLOIN – arrived and reformed there by 10 A.M. – The left Coy 'C' had advanced to a position just in rear of the front line before the order to halt reached them.

At 1-5 p.m. received an order to make an attempt to reach the German Line at Point 27 (K 5 c) as British Troops were reported in and about Point 59.

I sent a strong Patrol under Lieut R.R. WATERS from 'A' Coy to try and make a lodgment at Point 27 – moving across by WATLING STREET. This Patrol got across to about Q 4 b 8½.2., where they were stopped by intense Machine Gun Fire from BEAUMONT-HAMEL and had to return, arriving back in our line at 2-15 P.M.

My intention was that if this patrol could have made a lodgment at point 27, to send over the remainder of 'A' Coy in small parties, with supply of Bombs and bomb along the German Line.

At about 1-45 P.M. an order was received to stop any attempt to gain a lodgment at Point 27 – I cancelled the order but too late to stop the patrol.

At 2-30 P.M. sent 1 Company up to the front line to hold our original line about Q 4 b 4.5 to fill up a gap in the line at this point.

At 7 P.M. had orders to relieve the troops along our Front Line from MAXIM TRENCH (inclusive) to Q 4/12 (inclusive) on the South – 2 Coys in the Front Line remainder of Battalion in support. The relief being complete by 11-30 P.M.

The casualties of the Battalion during this period were 8 Officers and about 250 Other ranks from Shell fire and Gas.

1/6th Battalion (Territorial Force) Royal Warwickshire Regiment

7.40am. Battalion left their assembly trenches 10 minutes behind the 1/8th R War R – heavy casualties about 80 before crossing our own lines – mingled with 1/8th R War R immediately on reaching German lines and worked up as far as the third line - first and second wave Battalions on the right had advanced no further –31st Division on left also hung up certain units reaching SERRE – Enemy's opposition a well distributed barrage and very severe cross machine gun fire – 12th Inf Bde followed but were unable to advance further than line held by 11th Inf Bde.

The one officer unhurt (2/Lt J.G. Cooper) returned with a message to Brigade H.Q. between 11 and 12am. The line which was being consolidated was severely pressed on the flanks and forced to withdraw to the Quadrilateral, from where the few remaining men were sent back to our lines about 7pm. All that could be collected were taken back to MAILLY at midnight.

Estimated Casualties: 120 Killed and Missing. 316 Wounded.

Officers Killed: Capt A.B. RABONE. 2/Lieut J. BALKWILL. 2/Lieuts S.J. WINKLEY, H.L. FIELD, R.V. ROSE. Lt. J.E. B.DIXON. 2/Lt R.C. MARTIN.

Missing believed Killed: 2/Lt W.P. WHEELER, 2/Lt R.R. RICE, 2/Lt C.T. MORRIS DAVIES

Wounded and Missing: 2/Lt A.E. CLARKE
Wounded: Lt. Col. W.H. FRANKLIN, Maj. F.H. DEAKIN, Capts. A.B.
TURNER, J.N.G. STAFFORD, E.W. JONES. Lieuts A.D. WILCOX,
W.H.B. BAXTER, K. BROWN, F.L.MORGAN. 2/Lieut A.N. DOWNING,
K. HERNE.

1/8th Battalion (Territorial Force) Royal Warwickshire Regiment

2.0am	Battalion reported present in forming up trenches.
4.0am– 7.0am	Reported that everyone had a good breakfast. Artillery bombardment was intense & not a lot of retaliation from Bosch. Artillery increased in intensity enemy replying with field guns & 15cm.
7.0am	Very intense artillery on both sides.
7.25am	Enemy machines guns opened all along line. Three minutes later our troops are lying on parapet ready to advance.
7.30am	Advance begins. Enemy first line reached & passed very quickly as also was the second. Only in one or two cases were any enemy seen in these two lines. Having plenty of casualties from machine gun fire in enemy third and fourth line.

At the third line we were temporally held up by machine gun fire but took it by rushes, from this point the fighting was all with bombs along trenches. We reached our objective probably 35-40 minutes from Zero hour (7.30am) & at once commenced consolidating & clearing rifles under the direction of Capt Martin & 2/Lt Turner.

By this time the next Battalion was arriving but had had so many casualties that they could not go through us so helped consolidating. This happened with all Battalions following us. Many times we were bombed from this position & regained it until bombs ran out.

We had to retire to the 3rd line, line the parapet & hold on with machine & rifle fire. Parties were detailed to collect as many bombs as could be found (both English & German) & when we had a good store we again reached our objective. No supply of bombs were coming from rear so could not hold on & retired again. Enemy machine guns & snipers were doing a great amount of damage all the while. Enemy artillery opened but fortunately there range was over. Held on to this position until relieved, by a battalion from rear. All through the action no troops were seen on our right or left. This had a great deal to do with the inability to push past our objective.

11.0pm	Arrived at Mailley-Mailley & were put into billets.[1]

NOTE

1. The officer casualties are listed in the War Diary as follows. Killed: Lieutenant Colonel C.A. Jones, Major A.A. Caddick, Captain S.W. Ludlow, Lieutenants C. Hoskins, J.G. Fussell, and A. Proctor, and Second Lieutenants F.N. Noreham and F.B. Key. Wounded: Major J.A. Townsend, Lieutenants H.V. Nash (RAMC), D.R. Adams, L.N. Anster, and H.M. Jones, Second Lieutenants J. Teague, E.R. Shuttleworth, J.N. Pepper, F.N. Heath, R.H. Fish, L. Griffiths. Wounded and Missing: Second Lieutenant F.B. Freeman. Wounded and Prisoner of War: Second Lieutenant F.A. Brettell. Other Ranks losses were fifty-seven killed, 255 wounded and 251 missing.

2nd Battalion Seaforth Highlanders (Ross-Shire Buffs, The Duke of Albany's)

A very fine day! The 4th Division had an objective to take at a distance of about 3,000 yards away. The objective was the ridge running between GRANDCOURT and PUISIEUX-au-MONT. The 11th Brigade which went forward first had as its objective the last trench of the German Front system – named MUNICH TRENCH. The 10th and 12th Brigade had to move forward at a given time after the 11th Bde had had sufficient time to gain their objective, to pass through the 11th Bde, and gain the final objective along the Ridge.   The whole attack was arranged by time, working in hours from Zero. The 29th (Gallipoli) Division attacked on our right, and the 31st (New Army) Division on our left.

Zero was arranged for 7.30am. From 5.30am, onwards there was a very intense bombardment concentrated on the german trenches in front. At 7.30am the 11th Brigade moved forward from our front line trenches in waves.

By 8.45am, no message had come through from the 11th Brigade, nor from Bde H.Q. However it was time for us to move forward, so the patrols under Lt Harrison left the assembly trenches and advanced. Almost at once heavy hostile machine gun fire commenced, fire coming chiefly from the direction of BEAUMONT-HAMEL, and 2/Lt Harrison was badly wounded. (He died of wounds 5 days later at DOULLENS).

Our telephone wire to Brigade H.Q. being at that time out of order, two orderlies were sent there for orders. As they had not arrived back by 9.0am – the hour appointed for the battalion to advance – the Remainder of the Battalion moved forward. 'A' Coy in the centre – 'C' on the left – 'B' on the right moved in waves of platoons. 'D' Coy followed as company in Reserve. The 12th Brigade advanced on our left, the 2nd Essex being next to us. The 2nd Royal Dublin Fusiliers did not move forward with us; and hung back, awaiting further orders from the Brigade.

On coming into view of the german trenches, the Battn came under heavy machine gun fire from the front and the direction of BEAUMONT-HAMEL. A gun firing from the front trench opposite the REDAN was later silenced by our Lewis gunners from behind, but owing to its fire, the rear company was ordered to cross the german trenches about 150 yards South of the REDAN.

After passing the German Front, parties pushed forward and reached the 3rd Line between points 62 and 94.

Other parties of our men may have reached MUNICH TRENCH but there was no possible communication and none returned. It will be understood, the 11th Brigade had failed to reach their objective owing to very heavy machine gun fire, and by this time we were right in among them. Their casualties were very severe, and they had already lost their Brigadier-General Prowse (died of wounds) and all four Commanding officers (killed).

The Germans were holding their 1st, 2nd, and 3rd lines on our right and left. Attempts were made to consolidate the ground gained. The enemy however made determined bombing attacks on both our flanks. These attacks were held in check as long as the supply of bombs lasted, and it was not until heavy losses had been inflicted on our advanced parties that the 3rd line was given up. This took place about 1.0pm.

By 11.0am there were only 5 officers left with the battalion, and casualties were proportionately heavy in the ranks. During the evacuation of the 3rd line a large number of men of various Regiments went right back to our trenches. It was at this juncture that No.68 Drummer Ritchie repeatedly jumped onto the parapet of a german trench, and sounded the Charge, with the idea of encouraging those waverers who had lost their leaders. This gallant action in addition to his gallant conduct throughout the whole day, gained him the Victoria Cross.

The next position held was about point 77. While there, Lt Buckworth, one of the Regiment but attached to the 10th Bde M.G. Coy, came up and reported that he had 2 Machine Guns and 1 Stokes gun in action just South of point 92 on our left. From there he was able to enfilade the germans in their front line trenches north of point 87. It was soon after this that Lt Buckworth was severely wounded and last seen.

While holding the above position near point 77 as many bombs as possible were collected from casualties and messages were sent back for further supplies; but as none arrived and the enemy continued to bomb our flanks, the line was finally withdrawn at about 5.0pm to the original german front line position extending from pt. 56 to pt. K.35.c. 5.8.

At this time there were about 40 men of this Battn left, in addition to two platoons of the right 'B' coy which were unable to advance from our trenches on the South side of the REDAN. On arrival in the german front line the trench was consolidated by double blocking the flanks, and at about 5.30pm a supply of bombs arrived by carriers, and bomb depots were established on the flanks. After this the enemy made no serious attack and was easily driven back when he attempted to bomb us. Orders were received at 5.15pm to return to our line as soon as possible – after dark if necessary. It was considered best to wait till dark before leaving in order to avoid casualties and to enable us to evacuate as many wounded and as much material as possible. A message was also sent back asking for stretcher bearers to be sent up. Several of the wounded were evacuated before dark, and also a number of men from other battalions of the 11th & 12th Brigades returned to our lines.

At about 7.0pm 2 platoons of the 1/Royal Irish Fusiliers arrived with a good supply of bombs, and the right flank which we had consolidated was handed over to them. The other 2 platoons which were to follow went astray and got hung up by the enemy's artillery barrage which was laid across 'No Man's Land' from about 10.0pm – 11.30pm.

At about 9.0pm two messages – J22 and H18 – were received from the 10th Brigade. The first contained orders to hold on at all costs and the other contained orders to return to our own lines. These messages were not timed, but both were brought by the same orderly. It was decided that J22 was the later of the two as the 1/RIF had been sent up to relieve us. We therefore waited for the remaining 2 platoons of the 1/RIF to arrive. This they did about 1.0am on the 2nd, and we returned to 1 SUNKEN ROAD in Q.3.a. as previously ordered, taking with us what wounded we could find in the dark and all the material the men could carry. At this time the enemy were quite inactive so that the relief was completed without further loss.

Document Attached to the War Diary

A section of a report on the action of the 2nd Battalion Seaforth Highlanders written by Captain J. Laurie DSO, Adjutant:

Meanwhile the 1st Reinforcements left BERTRANCOURT at 8pm and following the same track as the Battalion from BEAUSSART, arrived in the TENDERLOIN about 10pm. They remained there for an hour or more, awaiting further orders, and then moved back to the SUNKEN ROAD. The men were put in a trench running along the east edge of the Road about 300 yards S. of the SUCRERIE. Colonel Hopkinson, who had during the latter part of the day been wounded in the face and the shoulder, Captain Laurie the adjutant, and Captain Gordon O.C. 'B' Coy with what remained of the Battalion arrived at this point on the SUNKEN ROAD about 2am.

Very great tribute was paid to the Battalion by all who took part in the day's fighting, and very particularly to Colonel Hopkinson, the Adjutant, and Captain Gordon, who hung on for several hours, commanding and encouraging men not only the remaining few of their own Battalion, but also men of every unit in the Division who having lost their own leaders, left themselves in charge of Col Hopkinson, and fought most gallantly. In due course the Colonel and the adjutant were awarded the D.S.O., Captain Gordon the Military Cross and also C.S.M.'s [*name unclear*] and Aitken of 'B' and 'D' Companies respectively, whereas Sgt K. McLeod of 'A' Company, who was left very early in the day as the senior N.C.O. in his Company, when all his officers and senior N.C.O's had been killed, was awarded a truly well earned D.C.M.[1]

The Casualties were very heavy, and the proportion of killed among the officers was particularly severe. The very large majority of the casualties especially those of the officers occurred during the first two hours of the days fighting.

The Casualties among officers were:

Killed: Capt C.E. Baird, 2/Lt W. Shaw, 2/Lt Gourlay J.N., 2/Lt Sillars (3rd A & S Highs), 2/Lt Buchanan. D., 2/Lt Williamson. J., 2/Lt Broom F.G., 2/Lt Harvey, 2/Lt Crum S.A., 2/Lt F.A. Conner, 2/Lt M.H. Blackwood, 2/Lt T.E. Lancaster. (12)
Died of wounds: 2/Lt W. Harrison (3rd Gordons). (1)
Wounded: Capt. A.W. Somerville. 2/Lt A. Banthorne. 2/Lt A. Phillipps, 2/Lt J.A. McKinnel, Capt. H.B. Golding RAMS, Lt. A.S.C. Jameson. (6)
Wounded and duty: Lt. Col. J.O. Hopkinson. (1)
Wounded and missing: Captain M. MacWatt. 2/Lt. R. MacKenzie. (2)
59 O.R. killed, 255 wounded, 1 missing believed killed, 53 missing, 5 wounded (at duty)

In addition to the officer Casualties serving with the battalion, the following officers, who belonged to the Battn but were [*illegible*] became casualties:

Captain G.N. Alison killed 10th Bde M.G. Company.
Lieut C.R. Beckworth wounded and missing believed killed 10th Bde M.G. Company.
Lieut J.N. Lowe wounded & missing believed killed 10th Bde M.G. Company.
Lieut R.S. Paterson wounded 10th Bde Grenade School.

The bodies of Captain Alison, 2/Lts Williamson, Broom, Buchanan, Blackwood, and 25 other ranks were collected in due course and were side by side in a large British cemetery 200 yards N.W. of the SUCRERIE K.32.d.[2]

NOTES

1. Another gallantry award made to a member of this battalion was the Victoria Cross to 24-year-old Drummer Walter Potter Ritchie. *The London Gazette*, No.29740 published on 8 September 1916, carries this account of his actions: "For most conspicuous bravery and resource, when on his own initiative he stood on the parapet of an enemy trench, and, under heavy machine gun fire and bomb attacks, repeatedly sounded the 'Charge', thereby rallying many men of various units who, having lost their leaders, were wavering and beginning to retire. This action showed the highest type of courage and

personal initiative. Throughout the day Drummer Ritchie carried messages over fire-swept ground, showing the greatest devotion to duty."Though many contemporary accounts and illustrations depict Ritchie playing a drum, he, in fact, was using a bugle – Drummer was the title of the post he held, sixteen to a battalion, comprising the Corps of Drums under a Sergeant Drummer. The Victoria Cross was presented to him personally by the King at Buckingham Palace on 25 November 1916. Ritchie survived the war despite being gassed twice and wounded on two other separate occasions. He died in Edinburgh in 1965 aged 73.

2. Born in Bermuda, 26-year-old Captain George Newdigate Alison and his comrades are still buried in a cemetery at Sucrerie – more specifically Sucrerie Military Cemetery, Colincamps. The cemetery is just over a mile south-east of Colincamps on the north side of the road from Mailly-Maillet to Puisieux. The cemetery was begun by French troops in the early summer of 1915, and extended to the West by British units from July in that year until, with intervals, December 1918. It was called at first the 10th Brigade Cemetery. Until the German retreat in March 1917, it was never more than a mile from the front line; and from the end of March 1918 (when the New Zealand Division was engaged in fighting at the Sucrerie) to the following August, it was under fire. The 285 French and twelve German graves were removed to other cemeteries after the Armistice, and in consequence there are gaps in the lettering of the Rows. There are now 1,103 First World War casualties commemorated in this site. Of these 219 casualties are unidentified.

2nd Battalion South Wales Borderers

FIRING LINE

05.00	During the night Coys moved up to their positions ready for assault in Firing & Support line. Our artillery was active all night. Morning fine but misty. Men were given hot tea at 11.0pm last night and again at 6.0am.
06.30	Our artillery commenced steady bombardment of Eys front line trenches increasing to heavy bombardment & at 07.00 Field Artillery commenced a barrage on Eys front line.
07.20	Mine under HAWTHORN REDOUBT fired & Coys immediately commenced getting out of the trenches & through our wire. (Bn H.Q. moved to Bomb T in B St at 07.10). As the leading Companies reached the outer edge of our wire machine gun fire was opened on them which rapidly increased in intensity, Enemy also opened percussion shrapnel on the advancing lines. By about 07.30 the leading companies had lost nearly all officers and about 70% of the men. 'A' Coy reached a point about 20 yds from Eys front line just south of the nose of the salient where they were held up by M.G. fire & bombs from the trench. 'C' Coy crossed the hollow by sunken road & reached a point about 60 yds from Eys wire where they were under M.G. fire from their right flank. 'D' Coy reached a point about 300 yds from our wire. Position of Coys was roughly as follows:

Reserve Coy 'B' Coy left support trench at 07.30 moving over the top & across the fire trench by bridges. This coy came under Ey machine-gun fire while passing through our wire. They advanced steadily across the open till practically all men were hit. Capt Hughes was last seen about 6-8 yds from the Ey wire leading 6 or 7 men forward all these men were knocked out a few yds further on. H.Q. moved forward with 'B' Coy.

According to original arrangements our Art barrage lifted off Eys front line at 07.30. Ey at once lined his parapet and M.G. fired [*page damaged*].

08.15   1/Border Regt advanced from our support trenches (FETHARD ST) to support the Bn but were caught by Ey Machine Guns before reaching our front line, this Bn lost very heavily & only a few men got up near our forward line & none actually reached the forward line.

Later the Newfoundland Regt advanced but were similarly held up by M.G. fire, a few men only managed to get along the sunken & joined up with the right of 'C' Coy.

During the remainder of the day no further attempt to advance was made, the Enemy fired heavy shrapnel over the wounded & men lying out in the open, also intermittent M.G. fire. Prior to the attack it had been arranged that Coys on reaching Eys trenches should fire Very's lights to let the Brigade know, but shortly after we advanced the Ey put up lights & for some time it was thought that we had taken the front line & also pushed on, consequently our barrage was not put back onto the Eys front line.

09.30   The 10% officers & men left behind at ENGLEBELMER moved up to the front line & afterwards went to ST. JOHNS ROAD.

The actual strength of the Battn as it moved forward to the attack was:

Officers   21
O.R.   578

Casualties were as follows:

	Killed	Wounded	Missing	Missing believed Killed	Total
Officers:	2	4	5	4	15
Other Ranks:	21	160	203	-	384

None reached the Enemy's trench & it was impossible to bring the bodies in, practically all those reported missing were probably killed.

A few wounded & others managed to get back to our trenches during the day and several returned after dark.[1]

NOTE

1. The following is the list of officer casualties – Killed: Second Lieutenant D.F. Don (13/Sherwood Foresters attached 2/South Wales Borderers – SWB) and Second Lieutenant F. Rice (3/SWB attached 2/SWB). Missing: Captain R.J. McLaren (14/Cheshire Regiment attached 2/SWB), Second Lieutenants J. Robinson (3/SWB), G.H. Bowyer (2/SWB), T.W.M. Wells (2/SWB), J.C. Murray (9/SWB attached

2/SWB). Missing believed killed: Captain A.A. Hughes (2/SWB), Captain F.S. Blake (15/King's Liverpool Regiment attached 2/SWB), Lieutenant H.P. Evans (2/SWB) and Second Lieutenant J.B. Karran (9/SWB attached 2/SWB). Wounded: Captain and Adjutant D.H.S. Somerville (2/SWB), Lieutenant C.D. Fonkes (2/SWB), and Second Lieutenants W.M. Mason (9/SWB attached 2/SWB) and W.H. Kelly (2/SWB).

12th (Service) Battalion (Sheffield) York and Lancaster Regiment

COLINCAMPS SECTOR

1.40am.   Battalion Headquarters consisting of Major A. Plackett, Commanding; Major A.R. Hoette, second-in–command; Captain and Adjutant N.L. Tunbridge, Lieutenant H. Oxley, Signalling Officer, and other Headquarters' Details arrived at JOHN COPSE. All quiet. Nothing seen of 'A' and 'C' Companies.

1.55am.   Captain Clarke reported our own wire cut on our front and tapes laid out in front of our line, vide Battalion Operation Order No.15, para.2 (a,b,c,d.) Laying of tape completed about 12.30am. Report sent to Brigade Hdqtrs in DUNMOW.

2.40am.   The first and second waves of 'A' Company reported in position in the Assembly trenches. Company Hdqtrs established in the front line near its junction with JORDAN.

3.45am.   Lieut. ELAM reported Battalion in position in the Assembly trenches. Reports not yet received from 'B" C' and 'D' Coys, however.

3.50am.   'D' Coy reported in position.

4.5am.   Enemy started shelling JOHN COPSE and front line.

4.25am.   Report sent to 94th Infantry Brigade. Battalion in position in Assembly trenches.

6.0am.   'C' Coy report our own guns firing short on the front line between JOHN & LUKE COPSES causing casualties. Reported to Brigade by runner telephonic communication being cut.

6.30am.   'C' Coy reported Bays 31 to 38 heavily shelled. 8 killed and 6 wounded – principally No.12 platoon. Reply sent "Report again at 7.0am. Nothing can be done at present."

7.0am.   'C' Coy reported no further casualties, but that our guns had been firing short, and had been hitting our own parapet in the front line. This was reported to Brigade.

Notes: The Communication trenches i.e. NORTHERN AVENUE, PYLON & NAIRNE were in an exceedingly bad condition owing too the heavy rain; in places the water was well above the knees. This caused great fatigue to the men and consequently delayed assembly of Battalion in the trenches at least 2½ hours.

The Eastern end of NAIRNE was found to be considerably blown in, but was passable. The front line was badly smashed up throughout its length; also the Traffic trench. COPSE Trench was also badly smashed up. MONK & CAMPION were in a bad state, but this was due to the weather rather than to the enemy shelling.

From the outset telephonic communication with the Brigade was cut, and the only means of communication throughout the day was by runner.

The enemy artillery continued shelling heavily from 4.5am, until the attack commenced. In view of the fact that the enemy artillery became active as soon as it was daylight, it would appear likely that the enemy was warned of the attack by observing gaps cut in our own wire and tapes laid out in No Man's Land, thus obtaining at least three and a half hours warning of the attack.

A' Coy reported no sign of the tape which was laid during the night; it had, apparently, been removed. It served no purpose at all except to give the enemy warning.

The wire in front of our lines had been cut away too much and as the gaps were not staggered, our intention to attack must have been quite obvious to the enemy.

7.20am.   The first wave of 'A' and 'C' proceeded into No Man's Land and laid down about 100 yards in front of out trenches under cover of intense bombardment by Stokes Mortars and Artillery. Casualties were not heavy up to this point.

7.29am.   Second wave moved forward and took up a position about 30 yards in rear of the first wave. The third and fourth waves left CAMPION & MONK and advanced in section columns. The enemy started an artillery barrage commencing at MONK and gradually rolling forward to the front line, where it finally settled.

7.30am.   Barrage lifted from the German front line and first and second waves moved forward to the assault. They were immediately met with very heavy machine gun and rifle fire and artillery barrage. The left half of 'C' Coy was wiped out before getting near the German wire, and on the right the few men who reached the wire were unable to get through. As soon as our barrage lifted from their front line, the Germans, who had been sheltering in Dug-outs immediately came out and opened rapid fire with their machine guns. Some were seen to retire to the second and third lines. The enemy fought very well throwing hand grenades into his own wire.

Notes: A great many casualties were caused by the enemy's machine guns; in fact the third and fourth waves suffered so heavily that by the time they had reached No Man's Land they had lost at least half their strength.

Whole sections were wiped out.

The German front line wire was found to be almost intact, particularly on the left.

A few men of both 'A' and 'C' Coys managed to enter the German trenches on the right of the attack, but in all other parts of the line men were held up, being shot down by the Germans in front of them. The few survivors took shelter in shell holes in front of the German wire and remained there until they could get back under cover of darkness.

The failure of the attack was undoubtedly due to the wire not being sufficiently cut. Had this been cut the enemy's machine guns could have been dealt with by the men who managed to reach the front line. As it was, they could not be reached and there was no means of stopping their fire. Bombers attempted to silence them with grenades but could not reach them – consequently succeeding waves were wiped out and did not arrive at the German wire in any strength.

10.30am. Major Hoette wounded in JOHN COPSE. No reports from Coys yet to hand. Reported to Brigade.

1.0pm. Battalion Hdqtrs moved to MARK COPSE, as JOHN COPSE was full of wounded. Still out of touch with Coys; reported to Brigade.

8.21pm. Reply sent to B.M.41, enquiring as to strength, ammunition, bombs, Lewis guns, &c., in front line: "Strength of Battalion – 10 men unwounded. These are runners and Signallers. Have no Lewis guns, 3000 S.A.A. 350 bombs. Lewis pans—nil."

10pm. Message received from Brigade that we should be relieved by the 13th and 14th S. Battalions, York and Lancaster Regiment, in the front line; The Battalion to withdraw to ROLLAND trench. Hdqtrs withdrew from MARK COPSE at 10.15am and was established in a deep sap in ROLLAND. During the night message received from Brigade to say that information had been received that about 150 of our men had penetrated the enemy front line opposite MARK COPSE, and were still maintaining their position in the German front line. Every endeavour was made to get into touch with them and withdraw them.

13th (Service) Battalion (1st Barnsley) York and Lancaster Regiment

WARNIMONT WOOD

5am Battalion formed up in Assembly Trenches ready to advance.

7.30am Attack on German Lines and village of SERRE commenced. The Battalion being Right Reserve Bn. and following in close support of the

11/E. Lanc. R. Two Platoons of 'A' Company under Lt. Maleham (clearing up party) followed the 2nd wave of the 11/E. Lanc. R.

7.40am   'B' Coy under Major Guest followed their 4th wave, with orders to advance to the 4th German Line, while the remaining 2 platoons of 'A' Company under Captain Gurney advanced over our trenches into our Front Line. The advance was carried out in perfect order under a terrific hostile artillery bombardment and machine gun fire; Major Guest and all his Officers, as well as those of the "clearing party" being killed or wounded before reaching the first German line. Although this advance had to be carried out under a perfect tornado of fire all ranks advanced as steadily as if on a drill parade. Major Guest, Lt. Heptonstall and three men of 'B' Coy reached the German front line. Major Guest and the three men were killed and Lt. Heptonstall was wounded in the side but fell into a shell crater where he remained till nightfall when he managed to crawl back to our lines with information as to what had occurred.

9am   Orders were received for 'C' Company (Captain Currin) and 'D' Company (Capt Smith) to advance to & hold the 1st & 2nd German Lines respectively, as a support to our first four waves who were then thought to have succeeded in reaching the German 4th Line. While these two Companies were moving forward they were stopped by verbal orders from the Brigadier who had now received information that all our preceding waves had been decimated and had consequently not reached their objective. 'C' & 'D' Companies were then ordered to re-organise in MONK TRENCH and Lt. Colonel Wilford was ordered to collect what men he could of any units and organise the defence of this trench as our second line as a German counter-attack was feared.

11am   The situation at 11am was as follows:

A few men of 'A' Company under Captain Gurney assisted by stragglers from other units were holding our original front Line trench which had been practically levelled to the ground while 'C' & 'D' Companies and small parties of other units were holding MONK TRENCH as a second line, the 92nd Brigade which had been in Divisional Reserve in SACKVILLE STREET and HITTITE TRENCH having just received orders to withdraw from the line into Corps Reserve.

All afternoon and evening our trenches were subjected to a very heavy bombardment with heavy H.E. & Shrapnel which lessened at dark.

5pm   'C' Company was sent to relieve the survivors of 'A' Company who had been holding our front Line and they were withdrawn to MONK TRENCH. The available strength of the Battalion at this time was about 280 all ranks.

The night was spent in collecting wounded & dead within our line and from NO MANS LAND, and in repairing our much battered trenches and consolidating our position.

Captain Currin and volunteers from 'C' Company did splendid work in rescuing wounded from NO MANS LAND under continued fire. Several wounded and unwounded managed to return from NO MANS LAND under cover of darkness from shell craters in which they had been hiding.

14th (Service) Battalion (2nd Barnsley) York and Lancaster Regiment

IN THE FIELD

Events up to 11.50am are shown in the separate account attached to the previous volume.

12.45pm. The Commanding Officer attended a conference with the Brigadier & instructions were received to hold 2 platoons in readiness to proceed to German trenches on a bombing expedition. 2 Platoons of 'C' Coy were ordered to hold themselves for readiness, but they were not called upon.

Orders were subsequently received that the Battalion would be responsible for holding the line from NAIRNE ST (incl) to LE CATEAU (excl) the 13th Y&L prolonging the line to our right & troops of the 48th Division to our left.

'D' Company were detailed to hold the front line with 'C' Company as support in MONK. The front line trenches were practically non-existent only one in two bays here & there remaining intact, & the front line was therefore held very thinly during the daytime & the posts strengthened at night.

At dark parties were sent out in search of wounded & missing. Several wounded were brought in & some dead bodies recovered. Some men got back unaided from shell holes in NO MAN'S land in which they had been taking refuge during the day.

The enemy's artillery was rather active during the night enfilading our front line.

Document Attached to the War Diary

An account of the part played by the 14th (Service) Battalion (2nd Barnsley) York & Lancaster Regiment in the attack on Serre on 1 July 1916. Written on 7 July 1916, and signed by Lieutenant Colonel W.B. Hulke, the battalion's CO:

ASSEMBLY

At 7.15pm on 30th June 1916, the evening before the attack, the Battalion commenced to move from Warnimont Wood. At 9pm a halt was made just west of Courcelles where tea was provided for the men. At 10.40pm the Battn moved on & the leading Company entered Northern Avenue Trench at 12 midnight. Owing to the very slow progress made by the Battalion in front, Pylon Trench was not reached till 2am, Wagram at 2.35am and Roland at 3.5am.

The whole Battalion was in position in assembly trenches, without casualty, at 4.30a.m.as follows:

A COMPANY
Under Captn Roos, with 2/Lieuts Hirst, Anderson and Kell, (and including detachment of Machine Gun Corps with two Vickers guns), in file in front end of Nairne Trench and along Traffic Trench from Nairne to John Copse, where the leading men of the Company connected with the left flank of first wave of 12th Bn York & Lancaster Regt.

Duty: To proceed in file across"No Mans Land"immediately following assaulting waves. To consolidate and hold German Trench K30a 4085 to K23a 7510, and to construct and hold strong points A and B along that line.

B COMPANY
Under Captn Houston. Two platoons (Lieut Forsdike & 2nd Lieut Strong) in Copse Trench.
Duty: To follow second assaulting wave & clear first, second & third German trenches.

TWO PLATOONS
(Lieut Fairley and 2/Lt Lovinsky in file along Nairne following 'A' Company.
Duty: To file into Russian Sap, convert it into fire trench facing north and hold it.

C COMPANY
Under Captn Edmeades, with 2/Lieuts Johnson & Holmes in Roland Trench.

D COMPANY
Under Captn Robin, with 2/Lieuts Goodburn & Mason in Babylon Trench.
Duty: 'C' & 'D' Companies to be reserve Companies.

HEADQUARTERS
In Roland. C.O., 2nd in Command Adjutant, Signalling Officer and Bombing Officer.

BEFORE THE ATTACK
Zero had been fixed for 7.30am. At 5.20am report was received from O.C. clearing party in Copse Trench that they were being heavily shelled but had sustained no casualties.

5.50am   O.C. Russian Sap party reported all correct.

7.10am   2nd in Command, under orders from C.O. proceeded to front line to see 'A' & 'B' Companies out & to report progress to Battn HQrs.

From time of assembly until zero, assembly trenches, particularly from Rob Roy to Fire Trench were very heavily shelled by the Germans. Just before zero the condition of the front trenches was as follows:

Ravine Trench: From a point about 10 yds east of Jones, this trench was completely levelled and so much exposed that it appeared to form part of "No Mans Land".

Traffic Trench & Fire Bays: (Nairne to John Copse) very much damaged and in places levelled.

John Copse: viewed from front of Nairne resembled a heap of debris.

Copse Trench: Completely blocked at Nairne end. No communication except over the top.

CASUALTIES BEFORE ZERO

On the left flank, particularly between Nairne and John Copse it is estimated that 30% of the assaulting, consolidating and clearing parties became casualties before reaching our parapet. The majority of these were caused by shell fire from direction of positions opposite 48th Divn from which point, traffic and fire trenches could be enfiladed. Many casualties were also caused by M.G. & rifle fire to which 'A' and 'B' Companies were much exposed owing to levelling of Nairne etc.

THE ATTACK

At ten minutes before zero a smoke screen from candles & bombs was started from the front line trenches immediately to the left of Nairne.

The wind was from the West and had a speed of some two miles per hour. The smoke made rather slow progress across "No Mans Land" but volume & direction were good.

At the first sign of smoke, machine gun & rifle fire was opened by the Germans in the trenches opposite 48th Division. This fire rapidly increased in intensity and by zero several machine guns appeared to be in position there. At 10 minutes after zero 'A' Company were clear of Nairne, but the two platoons of 'B' Company (Russian Sap party) were held up in the most exposed part of Nairne by a block in front. Information was received that the block was due to orders having been passed back for the men to proceed at three paces intervals. If this had been adhered to, the two platoons of 'B' Company would have been held up in the most exposed portion of Nairne, under heavy fire, for some time, and would undoubted have suffered casualties amounting almost to annihilation. There was also a great risk that in the broken state of the trenches the suggested intervals would have resulted in men losing touch with those in front, and throwing out all those behind them. Orders were therefore given that the men must push on as quickly as possible, and without intervals, to the Russian sap, and Captn Houston worked his way past the men to see the order carried out. As a result the file commenced to move at a fair pace at 7.52am and at 7.58am Nairne was clear of our men. At 8.5am, no man of the two companies, not a casualty, was in sight between Nairne and John Copse, though some may have been hidden by parts of the Traffic Trench & Fire Trench still intact. Despite our intense bombardment, several enemy snipers were in position almost immediately after zero, and many casualties were caused, particularly in Nairne from their fire.

Just before 8.10am a line of men got over the parapet and advanced in quick time across "No Mans Land". It was thought they formed part of the first wave of second bound. Owing to the higher ground in front of John Copse it was not possible from exposed position of Nairne, to see beyond the seventh man from left of this line. The men advanced in good dressing to middle of our wire when the [*illegible*] came apparently under machine gun fire and commenced to fall. No man of those on the left, got further than a yard or two beyond our wire. Four had commenced to crawl back when a shell burst in the middle of them. No report or message of any sort was received back from 'A' or 'B' Companies once they had left Nairne.

From reports by wounded men who got back from "No Mans Land", very great casualties were sustained by 'A' & 'B' Comps while crossing toward the German wire, on the left flank of attack. As estimated earlier possibly less than 70% were able to leave our parapet and of those it would appear that barely 20% were able to reach the German first line. A portion of 'A' Coy undoubtedly reached the commencement of their objective, while some of the 'B' Coy clearing party, including, Lieut Forsdike, were seen to enter the first German trench. While 'A' & 'B' Companies were endeavouring to carry out their allotted tasks as above, the movements of the two reserve Companies were as follows.

At five minutes after Zero 'C' & 'D' Companies moved forward in lines of sections over the open: 'C' Company from Rolland to Campion and 'D' Company from Babylon to Monk,

They sustained a few casualties from machine gun & rifle fire.

9.30am An officer of the Russian Sap party, 2/Lieut Lovinsky, returned badly wounded and reported that all officers with that party were "knocked out" and that two new platoons must be sent. This officer's injuries were too severe for him to give any more detailed information. Two platoons of 'C' Coy under 2/Lieut Johnson were then ordered to proceed to the Russian Sap to reinforce original party, or, if original party could not be found, to consolidate and hold the Russian Sap. On these two platoons reaching the exposed portion of Nairne the Officer went forward to reconnoitre. He reported that there were no signs of Sap or Trench and that it must have been destroyed by German fire. After personal investigation by the Commanding Officer it was decided that it was quite impracticable for these two platoons to reach where the Russian Sap should have been, from Nairne, without great risk of total destruction, and they were withdrawn, pending an Officers reconnaissance of another route via Mark Copse. Orders were then received from the Brigadier to hold 'C' & 'D' Companies in readiness for his disposal and this was done.

11.50am   information was received by runner that the 12th Battn York & Lancaster Regiment had removed their Head Qrs from John Copse. It was understood that they had gone forward and in accordance with previous arrangements, the Battn HdQrs of this Battalion proceeded to move from Roland to John Copse.

It was found impossible to get beyond Rob Roy (or Jones) and a return to Rolland HQrs was made.

No further movements were made by this Battalion in connection with the attack. All subsequent operations being in reference to the holding of our trenches.

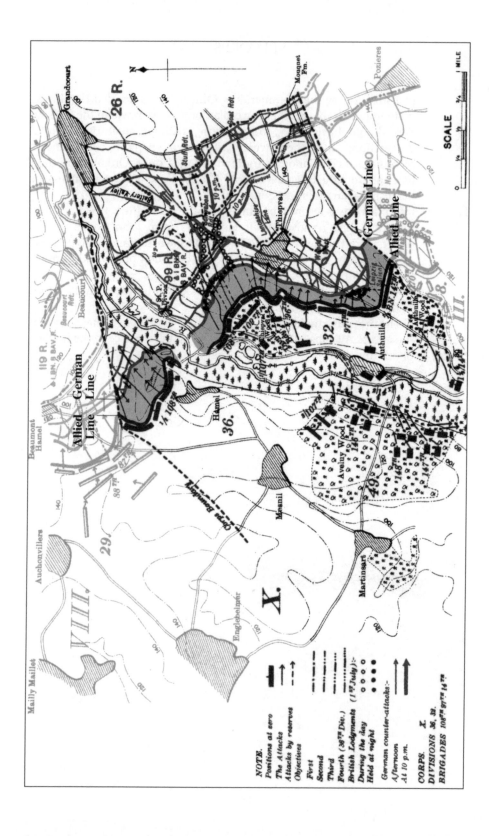

X Corps

1 July 1916

The Thiepval plateau stands out like a great buttress at the western end of the Pozières ridge, overlooking the river Ancre, to which it slopes down steeply on the west and north. From its southern, or rather south-western, face project three spurs on which stand respectively Ovillers, Thiepval and Thiepval Wood, with Nab Valley (later called Blighty Valley), leading up to Mouquet Farm, between the two first.

The front line of X Corps[1] from its boundary with III Corps at Authuille Wood in the centre of Nab Valley, lay for 2,500 yards on the lower slopes of the western face of the Thiepval spur, with the Ancre behind it, then passed over the Thiepval Wood spur, along the front of the wood, and crossed in front of Hamel to the western bank of the Ancre, continuing for 1,000 yards across the Auchonvillers spur to the right flank of VIII Corps.

The German front defences here, held by eight battalions,[2] descending from the Ovillers spur, fell back a little up Nab Valley, and then ran forward in a sharp salient, so as to include the upper slopes of the western edge both of Thiepval spur and plateau, to St. Pierre Divion in the Ancre valley. Beyond the river a minor valley separated the hostile lines. Thus, as a whole, the Germans overlooked the British position. Owing, however, to the convexity of the chalk slopes, much of the Ancre valley was dead ground, and Authuille and Thiepval Woods on the left side of the stream, and the great Aveluy Wood on the right, still a lovely mass of green, afforded cover from view. In spite therefore of the advantages of the enemy line, the British assembly positions could be constructed unobserved, and the troops concealed after they had been concentrated.

The German position was one of great strength. Thiepval village, opposite the centre of X Corps front, stood high on the spur within the German front defences, approximately at the point where the spur merges into the higher ground of the plateau. It had consisted of a cluster of over sixty buildings, chiefly dwelling houses, with a church and chateau, but at the conclusion of the bombardment, with the exception of part of the battered walls of the chateau, hardly one brick rested on another, so that the 32nd Division headquarters, which had been opposite Thiepval some months, had every confidence that the attack would be a success.

Thus no plan had been settled as to what should be done if Thiepval proved too tough a nut to crack. The houses, however, had large cellars which, now covered with a mass of fallen brick and debris, gave cover against all but the heaviest shell. The concentrated bombardment on the village both before and during the action did not find the machine-gun nests, and proved therefore to be of very little avail. The nests were not only well hidden but well protected.

Excellent shelters and ammunition stores for machine-guns to be used in the open were provided by the cellars. A group of these on the western side of the village had been organized as a series of interconnected machine-gun emplacements, forming what was known as Thiepval fort, which was not unmasked until after the attack had been launched. The ruins of the chateau at the south-western corner of the village were similarly turned into a strong machine-gun post. The machine-guns in the Thiepval fort and the chateau were able between them to sweep almost the entire upper part of the western slope of the Thiepval spur. To the south they could enfilade any attack up the slopes from the Ancre valley down to Authuille, whilst to the north they covered the open ground in front of the British trenches along the eastern edge of Thiepval Wood.

Further south, astride the Thiepval spur, the flanks of Leipzig Redoubt,[3] at the tip of the Leipzig Salient, a huge strongpoint with numerous machine guns, completely commanded No Man's Land to the south and west. This space was generally very wide, being at some points as much as six hundred yards, only near the western face of Leipzig Redoubt narrowing down to two hundred.

In the German third or reserve line there were four specially strong self-contained works, designed to flank it. "The Wonder Work" ("Wundtwerk"),[4] in the south above Leipzig Redoubt, was sited slightly on the reverse slope of the Thiepval spur, in order to avoid direct artillery observation, and was in a position to check any advance across the top of the spur if the front defences were broken through. The second was organized in the rear portion of Thiepval village. The third, "Schwaben Redoubt" ("Feste Schwaben"), a great triangle of trenches with a front face of three hundred yards, stood on the top of the plateau[5] with a good command of Thiepval village and the whole length of Thiepval spur. The fourth strongpoint, St. Pierre Divion, guarded the flank on the river.

In addition to these defences on the position directly opposite X Corps, both flanks beyond it provided valuable cross-fire. Any attack against the Leipzig Salient could be enfiladed from a strong machine-gun nest, on the Ovillers spur across Nab Valley opposite the Nab, known as the "Nord Werk" which appears to have escaped attention from the heavy artillery, whilst on the northern flank another strong work, Beaucourt Redoubt ("Feste Alt Württemberg"), in the intermediate line on the north bank of the Ancre, commanded, with St. Pierre Divion, the greater part of the northern and north-western slopes of Thiepval plateau.

The German second position ran from Mouquet Farm to Grandcourt, with an intermediate line in front of it, of which the two portions known as "Mouquet Switch" and "Hansa Line" were connected with Schwaben Redoubt. The third position was three miles in rear of the second. Altogether, from its natural position and the skill with which the defences had been developed in eighteen months' work, the sector was of extraordinary strength, requiring all the art of the gunner and of the engineer to dislocate and destroy its strongpoints and obstacles before there could be any hope of a successful infantry assault.

So far from being cowed by the bombardment and keeping quiet as elsewhere, the Germans on X Corps' front had given ominous signs of life, and their guns for six days before the assault had frequently shelled the British front position, which could be enfiladed from the north, causing considerable losses and preventing sleep. Battalions, however, which reported that the enemy machine-guns had not been silenced were told by the divisional staffs that they were scared. In a final message to his men, one of the infantry brigadiers said: "I am convinced that the German lines are full of men, but they will be in their dug-outs", and it was with this hope that the troops attacked.

X Corps was required to capture the whole of the Thiepval spur and plateau in its first onslaught. The task was big, but the prize was also great; for success at this point would enable the attackers to overlook and menace a great part of the German front: northwards to Serre and southwards to Pozières and Contalmaison.

On the right, the 32nd Division was to assault the German defences along the Thiepval spur between the Leipzig Salient and Thiepval village, both inclusive. The 36th Division was to capture all that part of the plateau between Thiepval village (exclusive) and St. Pierre Divion (inclusive). After securing The Wonder Work, Thiepval village and Schwaben Redoubt, the two divisions were to cross the spur and summit of the plateau to the German intermediate position, that is Mouquet Switch on the front of the 32nd, and Hansa Line on the front of the 36th Division. After capturing this position they were to consolidate it, whilst their reserve brigades were to pass through and attack the German 2nd Position, the Mouquet Farm – Grandcourt line.

By the time-table, this line was to be reached and assaulted at 10.10 hours – that is two hours forty minutes after zero hour. The attack had, as in other corps, been carefully practised over dummy trenches, so much so that an officer of the Ulster Division records that the men carried on even when the officers had fallen.

The 49th Division, in corps reserve, but earmarked to come under General Gough as part of the "army of pursuit" as soon as the 32nd and 36th Divisions had captured their objectives, was to move before daylight on the day of assault to a position of readiness in Aveluy Wood, and a number of bridges, with causeways across the marshy ground on both sides of the Ancre, had been constructed so as to ensure a rapid passage of the river.[6]

The heavy artillery of the corps consisted of two heavy artillery groups to support the divisions, and two counter-battery groups under one commander.[7]

Six field batteries of the 49th Division were attached to the 32nd and 36th Divisions, and a "groupe" of the French 20th Artillery Regiment to the 36th.[8] The field guns were in good pits dug in the chalk, with three or four feet of earth supported on steel joists and timber over them. Excluding from the frontage the gap in the line near the Ancre, there was one heavy gun per fifty-seven yards and one field gun per twenty-eight yards.

There were to be six lifts of the heavy artillery, the super-heavy guns (15-inch and 12-inch) lifting seven minutes before the others. No arrangements were made for any sort of creeping barrage, but the 18-pounders were to search from trench to trench in ten lifts: the 4.5-inch howitzers were to fire on selected strongpoints, moving back to others further in rear, keeping time with the 18-pounder barrage.

Unfortunately, as it proved, the infantry got very little assistance from the guns. The barrages, the first lift of which at zero was from the front trench on to the reserve line (The Wonder Work – Schwaben Redoubt – St. Pierre Divion), ran away from the troops and had eventually to be brought back; meantime, owing to stringent orders for the barrages to go on until countermanded by higher authority, it was impossible for the batteries to comply with the demands of the infantry that they should knock out machine-guns which were giving trouble. Of the two 9.2-inch howitzers specially detailed to destroy machine-gun nests in and about Thiepval, one had a premature burst which not only put it out of action, but its companion also. After midday there was much individual shooting by batteries, but as forward observing officers were not at first allowed to accompany the infantry, and later all communication wires were cut, there was no properly observed artillery fire.

The long spur extending from Auchonvillers to Mesnil and Aveluy Wood provided excellent distant observation, and in a trench dug on it, particularly in the part called Brock's Benefit,[9] in front of Mesnil, there were many artillery observation posts. Observation, owing to a little extra height, was better in the northern portion than in the southern, where Aveluy Wood also interfered with the view, and the general opinion was that more damage had in consequence been done in the enemy's defences opposite the 36th Division than in front of the 32nd. It was thought that the wire, though thoroughly cut north of Thiepval and fairly well cut at the Leipzig Salient, was still a considerable obstacle between those localities.

Shortly before the final bombardment began at 07.00 hours, gas was released from cylinders placed in No Man's Land during the night, and drifted slowly towards Thiepval. The German gas alarms at once sounded, but there was little or no fire in reply. Once the British infantry began to show themselves the German machine-guns opened as if there had been no bombardment.

The Assault on the Thiepval Spur by the 32nd Division

The 32nd Division,[10] whose advanced report centre was on the high ground 1½ miles west of Aveluy Wood, was assembled on the lower slopes of the Thiepval spur from Authuille Wood to Thiepval Wood.[11] The assembly trenches had been dug only a few days before, and the men were tired – "dog-tired" according to some accounts – from the labour of digging in the chalk and carrying up stores. The two front brigades, the 97th and 96th, were to assault the whole western face of the spur from the Leipzig salient to Thiepval village (both inclusive), and then advance eastward crossing the upper part of Nab Valley.

The southern face of the salient was not to be assaulted, for it was expected that, being taken in reverse by the above advance, it would fall automatically. The front opposite it was merely held by two companies of the 2/Manchester (14th Brigade). Thus, as III Corps had neglected the southern side, neither side of the Nab Valley re-entrant was to be attacked. Yet their trenches commanded and flanked considerable stretches of No Man's Land. It proved unfortunate that such a vital point as a valley should have been fixed as the boundary of two corps.

The 97th Brigade (Brigadier-General J.B. Jardine), on the right, was deployed on a frontage of eight hundred yards, with its right directed on the blunted point of the Leipzig Salient. The 17/ and 16/Highland Light Infantry were to lead the assault, supported by the 2/King's Own Yorkshire Light Infantry, and as soon as these battalions had overrun the Leipzig defences, the 11/Border Regiment, assembled in Authuille Wood opposite the southern face of the spur, was to cross No Man's Land and clear up the trenches, the whole brigade then advancing with its right on Mouquet Farm.

The leading companies of the 17/Highland Light Infantry moved out from the British front trench at 07.23 hours and, by order of Brigadier-General Jardine, crept forward to within thirty or forty yards of the German front line.[12] At 07.30 hours the bombardment lifted, and, the wire being effectively cut, the Highland Light Infantry in one well organized rush overran the front of the Leipzig Salient and obtained possession of its head, known to the British as Leipzig Redoubt.

The defenders were taken prisoners before they could emerge from their dug-outs in the chalk quarry, which covered an area of about sixty yards by forty, around which the redoubt was formed. Without delay, the companies moved on against Hindenburg "Strasse" or Trench, one hundred and fifty yards beyond, but, in crossing the open slope, machine-guns in The Wonder Work caused such heavy casualties that the attackers were compelled to halt.

Lieutenant Colonel A.S. Cotton, commanding the 161st Brigade Royal Field Artillery supporting the 97th Brigade, telephoned this information to Brigadier-General Jardine from his observation post, adding, in reply to a question, that the barrage was still going forward, and neither in the 32nd Division nor in III Corps on the right did any troops appear to be following it. Brigadier-General Jardine therefore ordered him to take two batteries out of the barrage and switch them on to the defences in rear of the Leipzig Redoubt, and this, though contrary to higher orders, was done. Under cover of the artillery fire the Highland Light Infantry managed to withdraw to the Leipzig Redoubt.

SLAUGHTER ON THE SOMME: 1 JULY 1916

The right of the 2/King's Own Yorkshire Light Infantry, moving close behind in support, now arrived and assisted in consolidating the position in the redoubt. Renewed efforts to advance across the open failed, however, with heavy loss, and bombing detachments sent from the flanks of the redoubt to work along the German front trenches to the east and north into Hindenburg Trench and Lemberg Trench ("Strasse") behind it, were equally unable to make progress.

At 08.30 hours, according to the time-table, the 11/Border Regiment, in reserve, moved out from Authuille Wood. Unable, in the smoke and dust, to see the actual situation, and believing the advance to be going according to plan, the battalion expected to find the southern face of the salient in British hands. It came at once under heavy enfilade machine-gun fire from the Nord Werk sector to the south. In spite of this fire which caused devastating casualties, including Lieutenant Colonel P.W. Machell, killed, with practically all the officers, the lines of companies continued their efforts to cross No Man's Land. Small parties on the left succeeded in reaching Leipzig Redoubt, where they joined the 17/Highland Light Infantry, but the majority were unable to get forward, and the survivors were reassembled during the day in Authuille Wood.

The left of the 97th Brigade, the 16/Highland Light Infantry with the left half of the 2/King's Own Yorkshire Light Infantry in support, which was to have overrun The Wonder Work, failed to break into the German front trench. Although the shelling of Thiepval village had been apparently very effective, the front trenches and wire were not much damaged. Even during the period of final intense bombardment, as the 16/Highland Light Infantry crept forward to its assault positions close in front of the enemy wire, machine-guns had opened from these trenches and the chateau. Directly the men rose to charge, the fire increased in volume: there was the stabbing clatter of machine-guns in action but no gun was to be seen from the artillery observation posts. Held up at the wire, every gap in which was covered,[13] many of the Highland Light Infantry were shot down and Lieutenant Colonel D. Laidlaw was wounded.[14] Small parties on the right succeeded, like those of the 11/Border, in joining up with the 17/Highland Light Infantry in Leipzig Redoubt, but the centre and left were unable to get forward, and remained lying out in No Man's Land. At any sign of movement rapid machine-gun fire from the chateau was opened, and this checked any effort to resume the attack here.

The two leading battalions of the 96th Brigade (Brigadier-General C. Yatman), the 16/Northumberland Fusiliers and 15/Lancashire Fusiliers, met with disaster at the outset, the immediate cause being the machine-guns in Thiepval fort.[15] The Northumberland Fusiliers, who followed a football drop-kicked by an eminent North Country player, assaulted the southern and central parts of the village, but were held up by a continuous hail of bullets not far from their front trenches. They, too, had to halt in No Man's Land, and so intense and accurate was the machine-gun fire that whole lines of men were swept down dead or wounded at every further attempt to get forward by rushes. It was said, with some truth, that only bulletproof soldiers could have taken Thiepval on this day.

The success of the machine-guns in stopping the leading companies gave time for the enemy to climb out of his dug-outs. The German infantry, some standing on the parapet as the barrage had moved on, then added rifle fire to that of the machine-guns against the supporting company, when it tried to carry forward the attack. The remaining company of the Northumberlands was therefore ordered to man the fire-step of the front line and open covering fire.

The 15/Lancashire Fusiliers, on the left, suffered almost as heavily from the machine-gun fire from Thiepval fort, though the survivors of the leading companies succeeded in entering the enemy front trench before the Germans had time to emerge from underground. Without waiting to clear the dug-outs, however, about a hundred Fusiliers went on past the northern side of Thiepval village; immediately afterwards the Germans swarmed out of their shelters and manned the front trench in time to overpower the survivors of the supporting waves as they arrived.

Going on, the men of the leading companies swung left-handed and joined up with the right of the advancing 36th Division south of Schwaben Redoubt, but throughout the day – on the strength of air reports[16] that British helmets were moving about in Thiepval, confirmed by a message from the 32nd Division that its men had entered the village – it was believed at X Corps headquarters that they had entered and were holding the eastern portion of Thiepval. About 10.30 hours, however, in view of the heavy enemy fire on the front trenches and on No Man's Land, orders arrived from the 32nd Division for the brigades to hang on where they were, as measures were being taken to turn Thiepval from the north.

The mistaken belief that Thiepval, or at any rate part of it, had been occupied by troops of the 32nd Division resulted in the artillery leaving the village alone throughout the day.

The Capture of the Schwaben Redoubt by the 36th Division

The assault of the 36th (Ulster) Division[17] against the German front position was entirely successful, except on the left near the Ancre. At 07.00 hours, in addition to the intense artillery bombardment, forward sections of field guns in Thiepval Wood and Hamel came into action; three 2-inch (stick) trench-mortar batteries, and a 9-inch mortar firing 200lb bombs lent by the French, in Thiepval Wood, continued wire-cutting; and the Stokes mortars opened a hurricane fire on the German front trench, sending showers of earth and débris from it high into the air all along the line.

At 07.15 hours, under cover of this fire, which from German accounts was most destructive,[18] the leading battalions of the 109th Brigade (Brigadier-General R.G. Shuter) and 108th Brigade (Brigadier-General C.R.J. Griffith), which were to lead the assault, left their trenches and crept forward through the gaps in the British wire to within a hundred yards of the German position.[19]

At 07.30 hours buglers in the front trench sounded the "advance", and the assaulting lines rose and moved forward at a steady pace with the precision of a parade movement, watched anxiously by the officers of their battalion staffs who, by divisional instructions, were not to go further than their battle headquarters. The front companies were in four extended lines at fifty paces' distance, followed by the supporting companies in artillery formation, lines of platoons in fours.

The scene with the mist clearing off and the morning sun glistening on the long rows of bayonets was brilliant and striking enough. In no formation was religious feeling deeper than in the Ulster Division; all ranks felt that they were engaged in a Holy War, under Divine guidance and protection, and the remembrance that the day was the anniversary of the battle of the Boyne[20] filled every Ulsterman's heart with certainty of victory.

On the right, in the 109th Brigade, the 9/ and 10/Royal Inniskilling Fusiliers[21] carried all before them, though they had to cross the greater part of No Man's Land, 300-450 yards wide, and success was a matter of seconds. As the lines of these two battalions crossed the débris of the wire entanglement, groups of Germans were already appearing from the deep dug-outs, and in places their light machine-guns were being hurriedly propped up into firing positions. However, the wire had been so well cut by the artillery and trench mortars that, rushing forward without a check, the Ulstermen were able to reach and disarm the Germans before they could open fire.

The front and support trenches were taken with few casualties, but on approaching the reserve trench, five hundred yards beyond, some machine-guns in Thiepval, previously fully occupied in repelling the assault of the 32nd Division, now turned their attention to the 36th Division advancing eastwards past their flank along the skyline of the plateau. This fire caused heavy loss to the 9/Royal Inniskilling Fusiliers on the right. Nevertheless, the advance was not checked, and by 08.00 hours the reserve trench, including the front face of Schwaben Redoubt, had been entered.

A number of Germans came out of the deep dug-outs of the redoubt, dazed and bewildered, and surrendered without offering opposition. Over four hundred prisoners had already been captured, and they were sent back in groups, sixteen Germans to each escorting soldier; so anxious were they to reach shelter that many ran back towards the British lines, outpacing their escorts.

From now on, machine-gun and rifle fire increased both from the right, from the direction of Thiepval, and from the left, from St. Pierre Divion, and Beaucourt on the far bank of the Ancre; in front few Germans could be seen, and the advance was continued successfully to Mouquet Switch and the eastern salient of

Schwaben Redoubt, where Hansa Line ran into it. These positions were reached at 08.30 hours, after a total advance of nearly a mile from Thiepval Wood.

The right battalion of the 108th Brigade, the 11/Royal Irish Rifles, was equally successful. Assisted by a smoke screen formed by 4-inch Stokes mortar batteries of the Special Brigade Royal Engineers in the Ancre valley, which covered the advance from the view of the German machine gunners on the northern bank of the river, the battalion reached the part of Hansa Line immediately north of the Thiepval – Grandcourt road in close touch with the 109th Brigade, south of that road.

The remainder of the 108th Brigade, on either side of the swampy bed of the Ancre, was, however, unable to make progress. German machine-guns in St. Pierre Divion, brought up from deep dug-outs there, inflicted terrible losses on the 13/Royal Irish Rifles on the left bank, and the few survivors of the battalion who got through joined up with the 11/Royal Irish Rifles in Hansa Line. Had St. Pierre Divion been taken in the first rush, the results of the day might have been different; for it would then have been possible to push up the Ancre valley and turn the German position.

The 9/Royal Irish Fusiliers and 12/Royal Irish Rifles, on the right bank of the Ancre, were to advance in conjunction with the 29th Division on their left to Beaucourt station and north of it. The two battalions left their trenches two minutes before zero, and suffered loss whilst going through their own wire.

At zero the survivors had six hundred yards of No Man's Land to cross, and men fell continuously all the way. The advance in lines ceased and efforts were made to gain ground by rushes. Fifty yards from the German wire there remained only a few small parties; one after another of these were seen to fall, only a few men actually reaching the front trench, but these pushed on until they fell.[22] A young artillery officer who was in an observing station alongside his major said "Why do they stop there? Why don't they move?" "They will never move more", replied the more experienced officer. Permission was then asked to bring back the barrage; although this was formally refused, the embargo on change of programme was disregarded and fire again turned on to the German front line.

By 08.30 hours the reports that had reached X Corps headquarters at Senlis[23] were sufficient to show the general trend of the fight. On the front of the 32nd Division, the right of the 97th Brigade had occupied Leipzig Redoubt and the German front trench adjoining it on a frontage of less than three hundred yards. The left of the 97th and the right of the 96th Brigade had been checked in No Man's Land, and suffered heavily. The left of the 96th Brigade had, however, broken through, small parties of the 15/Lancashire Fusiliers being reported to the north and east of Thiepval village.

On the front of the 36th Division two battalions of the 109th and one of the 108th Brigade had successfully carried the German front defences and were advancing on Hansa Line. The other three battalions of the 108th Brigade, astride the Ancre, had failed to make any progress.

SLAUGHTER ON THE SOMME: 1 JULY 1916

At 08.32 hours Major General Nugent asked X Corps headquarters whether his reserve brigade, the 107th (Brigadier-General W.M. Withycombe),[24] should, according to plan, move through the 109th Brigade against the German second position, the Grandcourt line, in view of the fact that the divisions on his right and left were not yet up in line, and that consequently both his flanks were already in the air. There was delay in getting a reply, General Morland being in his observation tree at Englebelmer, and during this interval the reports which reached X Corps from III and VIII Corps, to the south and north, were unsatisfactory, neither corps having achieved any progress.

General Morland therefore, at 09.10 hours ordered the 36th Division to delay the attack of the 107th Brigade on the German second position until the situation on the flanks had become clearer. The 107th Brigade had, however, gone on beyond recall. By 09.15 hours the leading lines of its three battalions, in spite of their heavy losses whilst deploying and crossing No Man's Land, were passing through the front units of the 108th and 109th Brigades in Mouquet Switch and Hansa Line. After a short wait there to reorganize, carrying small parties from both these brigades with them, they set off to attack the 2nd Position, the Grandcourt line, six hundred yards ahead. Advancing sooner than was intended, the leading lines of the 107th Brigade were by 10.00 hours within a hundred yards of the second position, and ran into the British barrage, which was not to lift from that line until 10.10 hours. Heavy casualties were suffered in consequence, and the extended lines had to lie down on an open stretch of rank grassland, which offered no cover.

The war diary of the 9/Royal Irish Rifles states,"if it had not been for the barrage we could have taken the D (Grandcourt) line sitting". The delay, however, was fatal. It gave time for the available Germans,[25] who, in the smoke and dust of battle, had at first been uncertain whether the troops approaching were friend or foe, to man the line and get the range. Thus within a few minutes heavy machine-gun and rifle fire was opened on the Ulstermen from their left rear, from Beaucourt Redoubt, and from Grandcourt.

Nevertheless, at 10.10 hours, as soon as the barrage lifted, some fifty men on the extreme right entered the second position about "Stuff Redoubt" ("Feste Staufen"), which was found unoccupied. Another party entered the position three hundred yards further north, worked up the trench and blocked it towards Grandcourt.

On the left, about two hundred men managed to reach the emplacements of a former German battery position in the upper part of Battery Valley, a depression immediately in front of the second position, and took what cover they could find there. The remainder of the brigade continued to lie in the open grassland under heavy fire.

In this precarious position, with both flanks exposed, the brigade held on. As no news came back, about noon the seconds-in-command of the 9/Royal

Inniskilling Fusiliers and 11/Royal Irish Rifles went forward to endeavour to find out the exact situation. When they eventually returned, they both reported that the position gained could not be held unless Thiepval was captured, and that ammunition was running short.

Almost at the moment that the 107th Brigade was leaving the British front line, reports of the 109th and 108th Brigades gaining their objectives had arrived at brigade headquarters on the west side of Thiepval Wood and at the divisional report centre at Martinsart (behind Aveluy Wood). Soon after, Major General Perceval (49th Division), who was at the moment with Major General Nugent and had heard from him of the failure of the 32nd Division to reach Thiepval, suggested that his whole division should be employed to support the 36th and exploit its success.

Feeling that there was not a moment to be lost, he himself went to Englebelmer, two miles away, to urge this course on General Morland. The corps commander, he found, had just ordered his division to send one brigade to replace the 107th Brigade in Thiepval Wood, where it was to be ready to support either the 36th Division or the left of the 32nd Division, as required. He declined General Perceval's suggestion, being more interested in helping the latter division, as will be seen.

Further fighting on the front of the 32nd Division

In the meantime preparations were being made by the 32nd Division to clear the Germans from the Thiepval spur between Leipzig Redoubt and Thiepval village. At 09.10 hours Major General Rycroft ordered the 96th Brigade, opposite the village, to push forward supports round the northern edge to reinforce the survivors of the 15/Lancashire Fusiliers, who were reported both by artillery and air observers to be in and beyond the village.[26] He added that the reserve battalion, the 2/Royal Inniskilling Fusiliers, could be used for this purpose.

Brigadier-General Yatman had already assembled the two left companies of the 16/Lancashire Fusiliers at "Johnson's Post", the easternmost corner of Thiepval Wood (the other two were with the 16/Northumberland Fusiliers), and had given them orders to advance through the northern edge of Thiepval and gain touch both with the 15/Lancashire Fusiliers in the village, and with the right of the 36th Division about "Crucifix", at the southern end of Schwaben Redoubt.

At 09.15 hours, as soon as these companies left Johnson's Post, violent machine-gun fire from Thiepval fort swept their ranks. After making several vain attempts to cross No Man's Land and suffering heavy casualties, they were compelled to report their failure to Major General Rycroft. For a time action in this part of the battlefield came to a standstill.

On the right of the division, the 14th Brigade (Brigadier-General C.W.

Compton), the reserve brigade detailed to pass through the others and capture the German intermediate position, Mouquet Farm and Mouquet Switch, had during this time moved forward according to timetable from shelters near Aveluy and Authuille in two columns, and reached Authuille Wood. No counter-orders reaching them and believing that all was going according to plan, at 08.45 hours the leading battalion of the left column, the 1/Dorset, moved forward in artillery formation preceded by lines of skirmishers.

However, on leaving the shelter of the wood it was at once assailed by heavy fire from the Nord Werk, on its right flank, of the same machine-guns that had so thinned the ranks of the Border Regiment a quarter of an hour earlier. As a result of this fire, Lieutenant Colonel J.V. Shute was wounded, and only about six officers and sixty men of the two leading companies were able to reach Leipzig Redoubt, where they joined the elements of the 97th Brigade already established there. The other two companies of the Dorset were unable to get forward, and remained in the wood and the neighbouring trenches of the British original front line.

Lieutenant Colonel J.M.A. Graham, commanding the 19/Lancashire Fusiliers, which was following the Dorset, seeing the situation, asked the brigade trench-mortar section (4-inch Stokes), which was near at hand, to place a smoke curtain across No Man's Land to cover the right of his battalion. Having obtained this assistance, he directed his three leading companies to continue the effort to reinforce Leipzig Redoubt. They moved out into No Man's Land in waves of thirty or forty at a time, but, in spite of the smoke curtain, they suffered very heavy casualties, and only about two officers and forty men reached the redoubt.

Finding no officer unwounded, Captain G. Hibbert of the Lancashire Fusiliers assumed command, and he sent back word by runner that, as the redoubt was congested with a mixed collection of men, and dead and wounded, no further reinforcements should be sent. Fortunately two Russian saps had been run out towards the redoubt, one to serve as a trench, the other as a tunnel; these were now opened out, and sure communication was established through them.

The right column of the 14th Brigade, having seen what had happened on its left, had waited in Authuille Wood. On the receipt of Captain Hibbert's message, Brigadier-General C.W. Compton ordered its battalions to stand fast and not to leave the shelter of the wood until further orders.

At 11.40 hours Major General Rycroft discussed the situation with the corps commander by telephone. He explained the position of his brigades as far as was known, and suggested that renewed efforts should be made to get round the northern edge of Thiepval, and thence, working south behind the village, to take in reverse the German position along the spur, including Thiepval village and the Wonder Work, and to cut across "Zollern Graben" and other communication trenches leading to Courcelette (eight miles east of Thiepval). He further suggested that part of the 49th Division, in corps reserve, might be employed in this operation to follow up the 2/Royal Inniskilling Fusiliers, which was already preparing to work past the northern end of Thiepval village. The 14th Brigade in Authuille Wood would co-operate by reinforcing the British troops already in Leipzig Redoubt, and thence, simultaneously with the movement behind Thiepval, would attack both Hindenburg and Lemberg Trenches from the south and west. He asked that an artillery barrage, including fire of heavy howitzers, might be placed on the further side of Thiepval spur, particularly on the Wonder Work, the trenches across Nab Valley and the Nord Werk.

General Morland agreed to this plan, and the bombardment by X Corps artillery was ordered to begin at 12.05 hours and to cease at 13.30 hours, when the infantry attack was to develop. The advisability of including the front face of Thiepval village and the chateau in the bombardment was also discussed, but Brigadier-General Yatman (96th Brigade) asked that it might be deferred, on account of the 15/Lancashire Fusiliers which was still believed to be in the neighbourhood of the village.

Nothing resulted from this somewhat complicated scheme. The bombardment, spread over so large an area, was indefinite and ineffective; in no way did it diminish the resisting power of the Germans along the Thiepval spur position itself. Two companies of the 2/Royal Inniskilling Fusiliers, with various parties of men of the 96th Brigade, moved out from Thiepval Wood at 13.30 hours against the north-west corner of the village, but again the machine-gun fire from Thiepval fort and the ruins of other buildings at once increased to such an intensity that, after heavy casualties, the effort was abandoned.

On the right, the unengaged half of the 2/Manchester of the 14th Brigade, having moved from Authuille Wood by communication trenches, approached Leipzig Redoubt from the left of the line held by its other companies, thereby escaping the enfilade fire from the Nord Werk. By 13.45 hours it had, with little loss, reinforced the troops of the 97th Brigade in the redoubt with two companies. Attempts to bomb forward to Hindenburg and Lemberg Trenches were, however, again checked by German bombing parties who had blocked the communication trenches, and little progress was made.

The trenches about the Leipzig Salient were now so packed with British troops that it was difficult to move along them. A deadlock ensued throughout the afternoon, and it proved a difficult and slow process to discover the actual situation either on the flanks or in front of the redoubt.

The action of the 49th Division in Corps Reserve

The 49th Division had marched during the night from its billets in the Contay – Senlis zone, five miles behind the battle front, and reached its assembly trenches in Aveluy Wood at 03.00 hours. These trenches were in three groups, a group for each brigade, in the eastern part of the wood on the slope of the right bank of the

Ancre. Here, hidden from view, the three brigades awaited orders.

At 07.30 hours the period of intense bombardment gave way to a prolonged rattle of machine-gun and rifle fire, denoting that the assault of the 32nd and 36th Divisions had been launched. At 08.55 hours (warning message, 08.35 hours), the 146th Brigade (Brigadier-General M.D. Goring-Jones) was ordered, as already mentioned, to move to Thiepval Wood in readiness to support either the left of the 32nd or the right of the 36th Division, as required. The brigade moved northwards in column along the railway which follows the Ancre valley, in dead ground, and abreast of Thiepval Wood crossed the reedy swamp of the valley bottom by two duck-boarded causeways: the 1/5th and 1/6th West Yorkshire by South Causeway, the 1/7th and 1/8th West Yorkshire by North Causeway. The movement was observed by the Germans, and came under machine-gun fire from the German trenches north of Hamel. This fire forced the men to cross by small parties at a time, and caused a slight delay, but by 11.35 hours the battalions had completed the passage, and reached the assembly trenches in Thiepval Wood.

The second brigade of the 49th Division, the 147th (Brigadier-General E.F. Brereton), was ordered at 10.55 hours (warning order 10.05 hours), to cross the Ancre to replace the 14th Brigade, which had moved forward into Authuille Wood to support the operations in the Leipzig Salient. The brigade crossed the Ancre swamp by two undamaged bridges near Authuille, the move being completed with few casualties by 12.45 hours. The battalions then took shelter in the two groups of dug-outs, originally occupied by the 14th Brigade, north-east of Aveluy and south of Authuille respectively, on the left bank of the river.

When, therefore, Major General Rycroft (32nd Division) suggested to the corps commander that part of the 49th Division should be used in a movement round the north of Thiepval, the division was already much scattered: the 146th Brigade in Thiepval Wood, the 147th between the Ancre and Authuille Wood – where it remained for the rest of the day – and only the 148th Brigade (Brigadier-General Rodolph Ladeveze Adlercron) was still in Aveluy Wood.

General Morland, however, ordered one battalion of the 148th Brigade to be placed at the disposal of the 108th Brigade (36th Division), on the extreme left of the corps front, opposite St. Pierre Divion, and the 1/5th York & Lancaster was sent from Aveluy Wood along the right bank of the Ancre to Hamel. By corps instructions, Major General Perceval (49th Division) at once went to 32nd Division headquarters, east of Bouzincourt, to discuss with Major General Rycroft the method of employing the 146th Brigade. The latter suggested that it would be best to place the brigade at the disposal of the 36th Division, in order to exploit the success gained on the front of that division by attacking southwards from about Schwaben Redoubt along the intermediate line (Mouquet Switch) behind Thiepval. It was decided, however, to take no immediate action until further information had been received regarding the attack of the 96th Brigade (16/Lancashire Fusiliers and 2/Inniskilling Fusiliers), reported to be developing against Thiepval village; for it seemed that it was more artillery rather than more infantry that was wanted.

At 14.26 hours Brigadier-General Yatman (96th Brigade) reported that the attack of his left against Thiepval village had failed, and that the 2/Inniskilling Fusiliers was about to be moved further north into the 36th Division zone to cross No Man's Land opposite the cemetery, and attack the village from the north. It was then agreed by telephone between Major General Rycroft and X Corps headquarters that this renewed attack should be combined with a frontal attack on the village by the 146th Brigade from Thiepval Wood; further, that the rectangle of German trenches on the western side of the village, including the chateau and Thiepval fort, should be bombarded by all available heavy howitzers for half-an-hour, from 15.30 to 16.00 hours, when the infantry would assault. The orders for this operation were issued from X Corps headquarters at 14.45 hours.

Again from lack of sufficient guns, the bombardment was not effective, and even whilst it was in progress a number of Germans could be seen above the parapet of their front trench and among the ruins of Thiepval village, evidently ready to meet another onslaught. Owing to the congestion in the British front trenches, the 2/Inniskilling Fusiliers was unable to move northwards to the 36th Division zone, and stayed where it was. The order to attack at 16.00 hours reached Brigadier-General Goring-Jones (146th Brigade) at 15.00 hours, and he acted on it without a moment's delay, but the battalion commanders had to be informed and his own orders issued. This did not leave time for the assaulting companies to get into position, and at 16.00 hours only the 1/6th West Yorkshire, on the left about Johnson's Post, with one company of the 1/8th, was in its place.

The leading lines then moved out from the wood across No Man's Land in column of route. Even after the day's firing the German wire in this area was mostly intact, and rapid machine-gun fire from Thiepval fort, from the ruins of the western cottages of the village, and from the intact machine-gun emplacements at once swept the ranks of the Yorkshire-men. They quickly lost half their strength, including Lieutenant Colonel H.O. Wade, wounded; those who survived returned as best they could to the cover of the wood, where they were reorganized as brigade reserve.

In the circumstances, it seemed a waste of life to send forward more troops, and therefore the attack by the remaining companies and by the 1/5th West Yorkshire was, after some confusion and difficulty, stopped, as the men were moving forward in attack formation.

Brigadier-General Goring-Jones – in view of information that the Germans were about to launch a counter-attack – then ordered his battalions to man the front trenches in Thiepval Wood, which they knew, having held them in the preceding February. But on the urgent request of a major of the 36th Division, who showed him a brigade order in which it was stated that two battalions of the 146th Brigade were attacking to help the 36th Division, he instructed the 1/7th West

Yorkshire to send forward two companies. The explanation of the statement was that at 15.58 hours, just before the hour of the attack of the 146th Brigade, General Morland had instructed the 49th Division by telephone to place any battalions of the brigade not already employed in the attack on Thiepval at the disposal of the 36th Division, whose front troops were reported to be withdrawing from Hansa Line and Schwaben Redoubt under pressure of a German counter-attack. This instruction was not sent on to the 146th Brigade as it was obviously too late to stop or change the destination of any of the battalions.

It was still General Morland's belief that the 2/Royal Inniskilling Fusiliers was near Thiepval cemetery in a position to attack the village from the north, and also that many of the 96th Brigade, particularly troops of the 15/Lancashire Fusiliers, were in the eastern part of the village. When therefore he heard that the frontal attack of the 146th Brigade had been held up, at 17.10 hours he ordered two battalions of the 148th Brigade, his reserve, still in Aveluy Wood, to be put at the disposal of the 96th Brigade. Brigadier-General Yatman was to continue the effort to capture Thiepval, and there would be a further bombardment as soon as the time of the attack was notified by him.

Subsequently a telephone conversation between General Morland and Major General Rycroft (32nd Division) took place, as a result of which it was finally decided that the 146th Brigade and the remainder of the 148th Brigade should be placed at the disposal of the 36th Division. No orders were given as regards the 147th Brigade, still in the Authuille and Crucifix Corner shelters. Owing to the confusion, it was not until nearly 21.00 hours – after a barrage had been put down on the northern part of Thiepval and St. Pierre Divion, whence flanking fire was coming – that one-and-a-half battalions of the 146th Brigade, the 1/5th and the remainder of the 1/7th West Yorkshire, moved out from Thiepval Wood to assist the 36th Division.

Meanwhile Brigadier-General Yatman had been able to unravel the actual situation opposite Thiepval village. He found that the survivors of the 2/Royal Inniskilling Fusiliers and 16/Lancashire Fusiliers were back in their starting trenches, and that no British troops were either in the village or the cemetery.

At 18.15 hours therefore he telephoned to Major General Rycroft that, in his opinion, a frontal attack against the village, even if undertaken with two battalions, could not succeed; nor did he consider it feasible to push forward troops from Johnson's Post across No Man's Land to the cemetery to gain touch with the right of the 36th Division about "Crucifix". He also expressed his doubts as to the 36th Division being still around Schwaben Redoubt, as the corps seemed to think. On this being reported, General Morland suggested that the attempt to capture Thiepval should be made under cover of darkness. He emphasized the importance of covering the right flank of the 36th Division, open now, as it had been all day, to attack from Thiepval, and of gaining touch with companies of the 15/Lancashire Fusiliers still believed to be in the eastern part of the village.

Brigadier-General Yatman, after conferring with Brigadier-General Adlercron (148th Brigade), decided to carry out the enterprise at midnight, with the 1/4th and 1/5th King's Own Yorkshire Light Infantry.

At 22.30 hours General Morland definitely ordered an attack on Thiepval, but Brigadier-General Yatman replied that it was too late to change his plans or to issue fresh orders on the subject. At 23.30 hours reports were received to the effect that the 36th Division had abandoned the German intermediate line, and was moving back from Schwaben Redoubt to its original front trenches. General Yatman thereupon cancelled the intended operation, and the 1/4th and 1/5th King's Own Yorkshire Light Infantry returned to Aveluy Wood. The piecemeal employment of the 49th Division by X Corps headquarters had accomplished nothing.

Late at night Brigadier-General Yatman called upon the 146th Brigade for a company to fill a gap on the left flank of the 96th Brigade. Brigadier-General Goring-Jones regretted he could not comply, as from the latest information to hand the effective strength of his brigade had dwindled to little more than that of a company.

Further fighting on the 36th Division's front

The 36th Division had by a splendid effort broken in between the enemy strongholds of Thiepval and St. Pierre Divion and carried in its first assault the entire Thiepval plateau; further its reserve brigade, the 107th, had pushed ahead through the two leading brigades against the German 2nd Position, which some of its men had reached. The general formation of the division then resembled a head and shoulders thrust into the German position, the head represented by a line round Schwaben Redoubt, the shoulders by the Thiepval – St. Pierre Divion trench line on either side, with a hand stretched towards Stuff Redoubt.

Here in a perilous position, on the open plateau, taking shelter where possible in the enemy trenches and dug-outs, the remnants of the battalions spent the rest of the day, under constant artillery and machine-gun fire from three sides; for, owing to the failure of the divisions on the right and left, the enemy was able to concentrate all his efforts on the Ulstermen. In the lulls of the firing, the position was partly consolidated, strongpoints were begun by the Royal Engineer sections, and the trenches leading to the front and flanks blocked.

It was obvious that until Thiepval village was captured no further advance was practicable. Moreover, as the enemy had only the narrow front of penetration by the Ulstermen to deal with, he was able to put down a severe artillery and trench-mortar barrage on Thiepval Wood, the fighting base of the 36th Division, showering it sometimes, like the other woods, with lacrymatory shell, and reducing it to naked tree trunks.

SLAUGHTER ON THE SOMME: 1 JULY 1916

The difficulties of communication back across the original No Man's Land increased: from Thiepval and St. Pierre Divion the enemy gradually built up a barrier of bullets, the machine-guns in Thiepval in particular maintaining constant fire down the Thiepval road, a sunken track leading towards Hamel through No Man's Land, subsequently known as Bloody Road, owing to the mass of dead heaped up in it at the end of the day. The value of constructing strongpoints had been fully appreciated, and the corollary that the enemy strongpoints must be captured, but it had not been realized that the German works would prove of such enormous resisting strength, and be practically unharmed by British shells.

Thiepval and St. Pierre Divion had done the work they were intended to do – shoot in the back and flanks any attackers who might break in between, and force them to retire under a cross-fire of machine-guns. Even for single messengers the passage of No Man's Land was practically impossible, so that most of the men sent forward singly or in groups from Thiepval Wood with ammunition and supplies for the units in Schwaben Redoubt became casualties, whilst as fast as signal wires were repaired they were cut again in many places. The pioneer battalion attempted to dig communication trenches forward from Thiepval Wood, but it was impossible to do so by daylight.

Accordingly, whilst General Morland was concentrating his efforts on the capture of Thiepval village by direct assault, the 36th Division remained unsupported and stationary, its numbers diminishing, its grip on the Thiepval plateau weakening as the day wore on. Ammunition was running short, and all the companies were asking for reinforcement.

During the morning officers' patrols had been sent by the 107th Brigade from the Crucifix road junction towards Thiepval and Mouquet Farm. They were driven off by fire and bombs from the village, but reported that Mouquet Switch was all clear as far as they had gone, that is, to within five hundred yards of Mouquet Farm. It may be that a great opportunity was offered. What opposition would have been encountered, one cannot know; a successful advance in strength down the Mouquet Switch towards Mouquet Farm would have taken in reverse the entire German position along the Thiepval spur, including Thiepval village.[27]

The instructions that no officer of the battalion or brigade staffs was to go forward with the assaulting troops now had dire consequences. No provision had been made for such a movement in the rehearsals, no reserves were sent up to carry it out, and probably not one of the company officers knew of the happy effect produced at Loos by the 2/Welch of the 1st Division moving down in rear of the enemy's defences. At any rate nothing was done.

The British delay in taking advantage of the favourable situation created by the success of one portion of the assault was, as on so many other occasions, utilized by the enemy, although not with his usual decision and celerity.

What happened at Schwaben Redoubt will best be gathered from the enemy's account. About midday a heavy bombardment was opened on it, and shortly after

14.00 hours two infantry attacks developed. The right[28] attack in two portions coming down the Ancre valley from Grandcourt, took in flank the Ulstermen lying out in Battery Valley, and compelled them to retire, which, on the evidence of artillery observers trying to cover them with a barrage, they did with steadiness and in good order. However, the majority were killed as they withdrew across the open, or were cut off and taken prisoners.

The attackers then moved on, and reached the lower part of Hansa Line at 15.00 hours, whence they sent bombing parties along the trench up the hill in the direction of the redoubt. They succeeded in clearing it to within six hundred yards of their objective, but were then checked.

The enemy left attack[29] approached from the other side, from Goat Redoubt in the second position and the Zollern Graben. After killing or capturing on the right the Ulstermen who were in Stuff Redoubt or lying out in front of the second position, where they were out of sight of Schwaben Redoubt owing to the lie of the ground, the Germans continued on, but they were met by machine-gun and rifle fire as they came into view, and stopped about two hundred yards from the redoubt. During the next three hours they made several attempts to storm the work, assisted by the bombardment which still went on, only to be repulsed with heavy casualties, although with each successive attack they steadily drew nearer.

By this time the casualties of the Ulster Division had become extremely heavy, many battalions having lost all the officers with them, and, owing to the impossibility of sending carrying parties across the original No Man's Land, bombs, ammunition belts and water for the Vickers guns were all very short; indeed the guns were only kept going by the use of rifle cartridges.

As the evening drew on the resistance in Schwaben Redoubt began to weaken, and walking wounded and stragglers to drift back. Soon after 17.30 hours messages were received to the effect that two battalions of the 146th Brigade (49th Division) were moving up to assist, and that aeroplanes had reported the enemy's counter-attack to be only in very weak strength. As related above, two companies of the 1/7th West Yorkshire were actually on the way, but they seem to have gone too much to the left and, finding no one, took possession of the trenches in the reserve line north-west of Schwaben Redoubt. It was not until nearly four hours later that the remainder of the two battalions started out from Thiepval Wood.

No help appearing, the senior surviving officer in Schwaben Redoubt, a major who had conducted with great personal gallantry the defence of the southernmost corner of the redoubt near the Crucifix road junction, came to the conclusion that, with hand-grenades running short and of range inferior to the enemy's, with both flanks in the air, and with the enemy still in Thiepval village and St. Pierre Divion, the position, a target for all available German guns, had become untenable. When, therefore, about 22.00 hours the German infantry attacked again simultaneously from north, east and south, and almost succeeded in reaching the redoubt,[30] in order to avoid being surrounded he gave the order for retirement to the old German front position. The withdrawal was carried out in good order without interference by the enemy until the Ulstermen were well clear, when they were followed by rifle fire. The possibility of breaking the German front, but the impossibility of holding the captured ground when of small area, if the Germans were not inclined to permit it, had been once more demonstrated.

Part of the 146th Brigade (1/5th West Yorkshire, two companies of the 1/7th West Yorkshire and two companies of the 1/8th West Yorkshire), sent forward from Thiepval Wood about 21.00 hours, began to reach the redoubt at this time, but it was too late to alter the decision to retire, and by 22.30 hours the whole work had been abandoned. The majority of the survivors were withdrawn to Thiepval Wood under cover of darkness, only a few small parties remaining in the German original front and support lines, with the detachment of the 1/7th West Yorkshire still north-west of Schwaben Redoubt.[31]

Situation of X Corps after nightfall

The withdrawal of the 36th Division from Schwaben Redoubt decided the corps commander to put an end to any further efforts to capture Thiepval village. The remainder of the night was spent in reorganizing the scattered units, whilst the men of the 96th and 97th Brigades still lying out in No Man's Land were able to get back to the British lines under cover of darkness.

On the front of the 32nd Division the position in the Leipzig Salient – the only gain of the day which was retained – was strengthened with engineer assistance, and its defence was now taken over by the 2/Manchester (14th Brigade) and two companies of the 2/King's Own Yorkshire Light Infantry (97th Brigade). The 17/Highland Light Infantry and the parties of the 16/Highland Light Infantry (97th Brigade) were withdrawn. Several enemy bombing attacks against the flanks of the salient were repulsed. The front of the 96th Brigade, opposite Thiepval village, was handed over to two of its battalions, the 16/Lancashire Fusiliers and 2/Inniskilling Fusiliers.

In the 36th Division, orders were issued at 23.30 hours for the recapture of Schwaben Redoubt by units of the 146th and 148th Brigades (49th Division), supported by the survivors of the 36th Division. These orders, however, were subsequently cancelled, as the brigadiers were agreed that it would be impossible, even if the redoubt were retaken, to hold it in daylight, unless Thiepval village were also in British possession. The front trench along the north-eastern edge of Thiepval Wood was re-garrisoned by units of the 36th and 49th Divisions. It was not known at 36th Division headquarters that any men remained in the German position, and it was not until next morning that preparations were made to reinforce the small parties which still held out in the German front line and west of Schwaben Redoubt. The two battalions of the 108th Brigade which had occupied the trenches on the north bank of the Ancre throughout the day, after their failure to get forward to Beaucourt, were informed at midnight that they would be relieved by the 29th Division (VIII Corps).

The total of the casualties of the three divisions of X Corps on 1 July had been over 9,000, more than half of them in the Ulster Division.[32]

The collection of the large number of wounded was a long and painful process, not completed until 3 July. The artillery and the engineers and pioneer battalions – the two last named had themselves suffered heavily in trying to keep communications open and water supply pipes repaired – gave assistance during the night, blankets being used in the absence of sufficient stretchers. But here, as elsewhere, there was no difficulty in caring for and removing the wounded once they reached the divisional dressing stations.

Owing to the congestion of the roads it was impossible to bring rations up as usual by regimental transport to the east side of the Ancre, and most of the water points had been damaged. The difficulties of supply were increased by the enemy enfilading the Ancre valley with a high-velocity gun brought up at night on the Grandcourt – Beaucourt railway just far enough to fire southwards. Thus the troops went short both of food and water.

The Germans opposite X Corps

The sector opposite the 32nd Division was held by I and II Battalions of the 99th Reserve Regiment of the 52nd Reserve Brigade,[33] each with three companies in the front line.[34] Regimental headquarters were in Mouquet Farm. The success of the defence is attributed "essentially" to: "the wonderful effect of the machine-guns, which, without exception, thanks to the well built machine-gun emplacements, were all able to go into action when the attack began".

The 3rd Company, 180th Regiment, which was in Leipzig Redoubt, was practically exterminated in hand-to-hand fighting. The defenders of Thiepval were sheltered in the cellars of the chateau and of the houses in the village, which had been enlarged and improved, and they emerged in time to meet the attack, some of the men half-dressed. The British 96th Brigade is described as coming on in "solid lines without gaps, in faultless order, led by its officers carrying little flags and sticks. Wave after wave was shot down by well aimed fire … a wall of dead British was piled up on the front".

Opposite the 36th Division the German line was held by the III Battalion of the 99th Reserve Regiment and the I and III of the 8th Bavarian Reserve Regiment (attached to the 52nd Reserve Brigade), two companies being in Schwaben Redoubt, with the II Battalion in reserve.[35] The artillery in the 36th Division sector had achieved better results than it had in the 32nd.

"The position had suffered quite exceptionally under the long bombardment; the trenches had been practically wiped out, wire swept aside, and dug-outs mostly battered in. The 9th Company of the 99th, west of Schwaben Redoubt, suffered particularly severe losses. There the enemy assault therefore found favourable conditions."The attack advanced with such rapidity that the machine-guns were able to fire only a few rounds; one machine-gun in the redoubt was knocked out by a direct hit shortly before the attack. It is claimed that the redoubt was entered from the rear.

News of the break-through soon reached Major General von Soden, commanding the 26th Reserve Division, it having been observed from Beaucourt Redoubt. Immediately, at 08.05 hours, he issued orders to the II Battalion, 8th Bavarian Reserve Regiment, his sole divisional reserve, with a machine-gun company and a platoon of an automatic rifle company, to counter-attack and retake Schwaben Redoubt. The battalion had been at Irles (five miles north-east of Thiepval) since 05.30 hours, and only received the order at 09.00 hours.

Lieutenant General von Stein (XIV Corps) did not get the report of the break-through until 09.40 hours, and directed the 26th Reserve Division to counter-attack at once without waiting for the II Battalion of the 8th Bavarian Reserve Regiment. Meanwhile the commander of the 51st Reserve Brigade (180th and 121st Reserve Regiments)[36] had grown impatient and ordered all companies not engaged, two each of I and III Battalions of the 8th Bavarian Reserve Regiment and the 180th Recruit Battalion, to counter-attack from Goat Redoubt and Grandcourt, but he had no sooner done so than Lieutenant Colonel Bram, the officer commanding the 8th Bavarian Reserve Regiment, arrived, and at 11.15 hours the latter was placed in charge of the counter-attack.

There was a terrible state of confusion, owing to lack of communications, and great difficulty in getting the movement under way. Contact could not be established with the Grandcourt group (180th Recruit Battalion) or with the II Battalion of the 8th Bavarian Reserve Regiment, delayed on its way from Irles by artillery fire. Finally Lieutenant Colonel Bram, shortly after 13.00 hours, ordered the counter-attack to be begun by the companies of the I Battalion of the 8th Bavarian Reserve Regiment already at Goat Redoubt; two companies of the II Battalion soon arrived to support them, and the Grandcourt group also started.

When, by order of the divisional commander[37] the assault on Schwaben Redoubt was repeated at 17.00 hours the survivors of the Goat Redoubt detachment did not take part, owing to a false report that the Schwaben had been evacuated. The attack at 18.15 hours seems to have been occasioned by the arrival on the left of a small contingent of two groups of the 99th Reserve Regiment, actually sent up for reconnoitring purposes to find out how far the British had progressed.

After the failures, the artillery bombardment was increased, and towards 22.00 hours "the batteries began to smash the last remains of the fortifications of the high-standing redoubt". The Germans, now supported by two battalions of the 185th Regiment,[38] again pressed on, working up all the trenches round the redoubt. They failed to enter it, but shortly afterwards they saw "thick lines moving westwards from the redoubt on a broad front towards the place where the enemy originally broke through. The doubt whether they were our own troops was solved by light balls sent up from Thiepval. British steel helmets were recognized. ... The Schwaben Redoubt was German again."

According to the narrative, the total number of battalions employed east of the Ancre against X Corps was only 8½, and two of these did not arrive on the scene until after 22.00 hours. The number of enemy machine-guns cannot be ascertained. The German losses are not given.

NOTES

1. X Corps (Lieutenant General Sir T.L.N. Morland) comprised: 32nd Division (Major General W.H. Rycroft), 14th, 96th and 97th Brigades; 36th Division (Major General O.S.W. Nugent), 107th, 108th and 109th Brigades; 49th Division (Major General E.M. Perceval), 146th, 147th and 148th Brigades; G.O.C. Royal Artillery, Brigadier-General C.C. Van Straubenzee; G.O.C. Heavy Artillery, Brigadier-General H.O. Vincent; Chief Engineer: Brigadier-General J.A.S. Tulloch.
2. X Corps was faced by the centre portion of the 26th Reserve Division, whose sector, from Ovillers to Beaumont Hamel, overlapped it.
3. This was the original German name; later when it became one large shell hole it was renamed "Granatloch" (shell hole).
4. Named after General v. Wundt, commanding the 51st Reserve Infantry Brigade, which had built the defences on this sector of the front.
5. Just above where the tower of the 36th (Ulster) Division War Memorial now stands.
6. The swampy state of the valley bottom was due to the banks of the canalised course of the Ancre, at a higher level than the original course west of it, having been damaged by shell fire.
7. With a total of the following – Howitzers: two 15-inch; two 12-inch; twelve 9.2-inch; twelve 8-inch; twenty 6-inch. Guns: twenty-eight 60-pounders; four 4.7-inch.
8. Total of field artillery in action: 128 x 18-pounders; 36 x 4.5-inch howitzers, 36; 12 x 75-mm.
9. So called after the G.O.C. Royal Artillery 36th Division, Brigadier-General H.J. Brock. The artillery of the 32nd Division was commanded by Brigadier-General J.A. Tyler.
10. This New Army division had arrived in France, under its original commander, in November 1915, when its 95th Brigade was exchanged for the 14th of the 5th Division. Its units – the infantry was raised by local effort in 1914 – came from the north of England, but included three Scots battalions, with the 17/Northumberland Fusiliers as Pioneer battalion.
11. One section of the 206th, 218th and 219th Field Companies Royal Engineers was attached to the 14th, 96th and 97th Brigades, respectively; the remainder of the companies were kept in divisional reserve.
12. Brigadier-General Jardine was one of the officers attached to the Japanese Army in the Manchurian War, and had noticed that the Japanese pushed close in under cover of gun-fire before assaulting.
13. A raiding party a few hours before was held up and shot in the wire, the enemy having a machine-gun covering every gap in it. Two Royal Engineer parties, carrying Bangalore torpedoes, were therefore attached to each of the leading companies for the purpose of cutting gaps. None of them survived.
14. The losses were nineteen officers and 492 other ranks.
15. The 16/Lancashire Fusiliers, divided into half battalions, was in support, and moved up into the front trenches. The 2/Royal Inniskilling Fusiliers was in reserve in the Ancre valley.
16. The smoke from the barrages obscured the trench systems. The air information was of little use

except for the movement of German reinforcements well behind the line.

17. This division of the New Army had arrived in France in October 1915. All units, except the artillery, were raised in Ulster in 1914; the artillery was recruited in the suburbs of London from May 1915 onwards.

18. For further detail, see *Schlachten des Weltkrieges, Somme Nord*, (Reichsarchiv, Oldenburg).

19. Each brigade had two sections of a field company Royal Engineers, furnished by the 150th and 122nd, respectively, attached. The 107th had one section of the 121st Company.

20. The anniversary is now kept on the 12th.

21. The 11/Royal Inniskilling Fusiliers and the 14/Royal Irish Rifles were in support and moved up to the front trenches.

22. It was subsequently discovered that a machine-gun which had done much damage was used from the top of a shaft, entered by a tunnel from the bank alongside the railway in the Ancre valley. Like many others, this emplacement was not unmasked until the attack had been launched.

23. General Morland himself was in an observatory in a tree at Englebelmer, three miles west of Thiepval Wood, connected with his headquarters by telephone.

24. The 8th, 9th, 10th and 15/Royal Irish Rifles; the last was attached to the 108th Brigade for the day. The 107th Brigade had proceeded to the front from its assembly place in Aveluy Wood by the right bank of the Ancre, and then through rides in Thiepval Wood. The 10/Royal Irish Rifles, on the right, where the foliage was thin owing to the bombardment, came under machine-gun fire and lost its commanding officer, Lieutenant Colonel H.C. Bernard, who had disobeyed orders as to remaining at battle headquarters, in order to make sure of the deployment of his battalion.

25. A recruit battalion of the 180th Regiment, and, in Grandcourt village, a machine-gun company.

26. These may have been detachments of the 15/Lancashire Fusiliers, but, whoever they were, they subsequently joined up with the right of the 36th Division south of Schwaben Redoubt.

27. The Germans expected that an enveloping movement of this kind would be carried out.

28. The recruit battalion of the 180th Regiment, and two machine-gun companies. The drafts for regiments were at this time trained at the front in battalions so as to be immediately available.

29. By five companies of all three battalions of the 8th Bavarian Reserve Regiment.

30. Two battalions of the 185th Regiment of the corps reserve had arrived.

31. Here it remained until withdrawn on 3 July. Corporal G. Sanders, who led the survivors, received the Victoria Cross (see his battalion entry for further detail).

32. The losses were – 32nd Division: fifty-three officers killed, ninety-nine wounded and six missing, with 1,230 other ranks killed, 2,453 wounded, 102 missing and six PoW (a total of 3,949). 36th Division: seventy-nine officers killed, 102 wounded, seven missing and one PoW, with 1,777 other ranks killed, 2,626 wounded, 206 missing and 164 PoW (a total of 5,104). This division's losses include 142 men from the ranks of various machine-gun and trench-mortar companies. The 49th Division: five officers killed and forty-one wounded, with 126 other ranks killed, 412 wounded, five missing and one PoW (a total of 590).

33. *Schlachten des Weltkrieges, Somme Nord*, (Reichsarchiv, Oldenburg), i. pp.46-9.

34. The 99th Reserve, a four-battalion regiment: the other regiment of the brigade, the 119th Reserve, was north of the Ancre.

35. The position of the 8th Bavarian Reserve Regiment was ascertained after the sketches, derived from *Somme-Nord*, had been printed.

36. The 121st Reserve was in the line north of the Ancre opposite the 4th Division of VIII Corps.

37. The order ran: "The Englishman still sits in Schwaben Redoubt. He must be driven out of it, out of our position. The attack is to be pushed with all energy. It is a point of honour for the division to recapture this important point to-day. The artillery is to co-operate with all possible strength."

38. These battalions were in corps reserve at Beugny (twelve miles E.N.E. of Thiepval). General von Stein put them at the disposal of the 26th Reserve Division at 11.00 hours, but the leading battalion arrived at divisional headquarters at Courcelette (three miles east of Thiepval) only at 18.30 hours, and it was 22.00 hours before it got to the German second position.

Index of Battalions

Border Regiment, 11th (Service) Battalion (Lonsdale)
Dorsetshire Regiment, 1st Battalion
Highland Light Infantry, 15th (Service) Battalion (1st Glasgow)
Highland Light Infantry, 16th (Service) Battalion (2nd Glasgow)
Highland Light Infantry, 17th (Service) Battalion (3rd Glasgow)
King's Own (Yorkshire Light Infantry), 2nd Battalion
Lancashire Fusiliers, 15th (Service) Battalion (1st Salford)
Lancashire Fusiliers, 16th (Service) Battalion (2nd Salford)
Lancashire Fusiliers, 19th (Service) Battalion (3rd Salford)
Manchester Regiment, 2nd Battalion
Northumberland Fusiliers, 16th (Service) Battalion (Newcastle)
Prince of Wales's Own (West Yorkshire Regiment), 1/5th Battalion (Territorial Force)
Prince of Wales's Own (West Yorkshire Regiment), 1/6th Battalion (Territorial Force)
Prince of Wales's Own (West Yorkshire Regiment), 1/7th Battalion (Leeds Rifles) (Territorial Force)
Princess Victoria's (Royal Irish Fusiliers), 9th (Service) Battalion (Co. Armagh)
Royal Inniskilling Fusiliers, 2nd Battalion
Royal Inniskilling Fusiliers, 9th (Service) Battalion (Co. Tyrone)
Royal Inniskilling Fusiliers, 10th (Service) Battalion (Derry)
Royal Inniskilling Fusiliers, 11th (Service) Battalion (Donegal and Fermanagh)
Royal Irish Rifles, 8th (Service) Battalion (East Belfast)
Royal Irish Rifles, 9th (Service) Battalion (West Belfast)
Royal Irish Rifles, 10th (Service) Battalion (South Belfast)
Royal Irish Rifles, 11th (Service) Battalion (South Antrim)
Royal Irish Rifles, 12th (Service) Battalion (Central Antrim)
Royal Irish Rifles, 13th (Service) Battalion (1st Co. Down)
Royal Irish Rifles, 14th (Service) Battalion (Young Citizens)
Royal Irish Rifles, 15th (Service) Battalion (North Belfast)
Royal Irish Rifles, 16th (Service) Battalion (2nd Co. Down) (Pioneers)
York And Lancaster Regiment, 1/5th Battalion

11th (Service) Battalion (Lonsdale) Border Regiment

AUTHUILLE WOOD

Zero time 7.30am. Battalion advanced from assembly trenches at 8am and came under very heavy Machine Gun fire – suffering over 500 casualties. The following officers were killed:

Lt Col P.W. Machell cmg DSO, Capt R. Smith, Capt A.E. Corbett, Capt C. Brown, 2/Lt A.E. Monkhouse, 2/Lt J.C. Parkes, 2Lt G. Coe, 2/Lt G.P. Dunstan, 2/Lt W.S. Paton, Lt F.A. Rupp.

Officers Wounded:
Major P.G.W. Diggle, Capt B.C. Harrison, Capt C.P. Moor, Lieut W.A. Hobson, Lt C.H. Walker, Lt C.W. Margerison, Lt J.H. Hogkinson, Lt M. Gorden, Lt M. McKerrow, 2/Lt J.R.S. Borman, 2/Lt J.W. Moor, 2/Lt W. Green, 2/Lt G. Black, 2/Lt F.M. Ranson, 2/Lt L. Machell.

1st Battalion Dorsetshire Regiment

12.50am. Arrived at BLACKHORSE SHELTERS.

6.30am. Finished breakfasts. (Zero time for attack 7.30am)

7.10am. Started to leave BLACKHORSE SHELTERS by platoons at 100 yards interval, proceeding through AUTHUILLE WOOD along DUMBARTON TRACK in order to attack the enemy in accordance with orders. Captain KESTELL-CORNISH and about ten other ranks were wounded by machine-gun fire as the Battalion was proceeding along DUMBARTON TRACK. After waiting about fifteen minutes in AUTHUILLE WOOD the O.C. 'C' Coy (the leading Company) received information from our liaison party attached to the 11th BORDER Rgt (97th Inf. Bde.) that the latter regiment had commenced its advance; 500 yards behind the rear platoon of 11th BORDER Rgt the leading platoon of 1st DORSET Rgt advanced from AUTHUILLE WOOD in accordance with orders previously received. The remainder of the Battalion followed by platoons or sections (The 96th and 97th Infantry Brigades had attacked the hostile trenches just previous to the 1st DORSET Rgt – the leading Battalion of the 14th Infantry Bde – leaving AUTHUILLE WOOD. They had not however been able to attain their objectives; this fact was not known until later although it was apparent that matters were not progressing quite as favourably as had been anticipated.)
Immediately the leading platoon left AUTHUILLE WOOD very heavy and extremely accurate machine-gun fire was opened by the enemy

from some point on our right not definitely ascertained. As this fire concentrated mainly on the point at the edge of the wood where DUNBARTON TRACK ends – and past which the whole Battalion had to go – we endeavoured to find some other exit from the wood, but could not do so, barbed wire and other obstructions preventing.

The whole Battalion, therefore, advanced from this point by sections, and it was during the dash across country from AUTHUILLE WOOD to our own front line trench about 100 yds ahead that at least half our total casualties were sustained. By the time half the Battalion had left the wood, the end of DUMBARTON TRACK and the ground up to our front line trench was covered with our killed and wounded; yet the men continued to jump up and advance over their fallen comrades as the word to go was given.

Four Lewis guns were lost here by the men being wounded; other men following who stopped in the endeavour to pick up the guns and take them forward, were also killed or wounded.

On arrival in our front line trench we found it to be already occupied by the 11th BORDER Rgt. (numbering approximately 100 to 150 other ranks without any officers). Machine gunners, carrying parties and other details also occupied this trench and the shell craters in front and rear of it. Numbers of killed & wounded added to the congestion and lateral movement was practically impossible, except over the top, until we managed to organise matters somewhat and move the men further to the right.

Six officers and about sixty men went forward almost at once into German front line trench. Part of this was found to be occupied by British troops and part by Germans. A few men of 11th BORDER Rgt. were already there with a considerable number of 17th H.L.I. on the left; some of the 19th Lancashire Fusiliers reached the same place later. All these six officers were wounded - one very slightly who remained at duty – and out of the sixty men who went forward to the German front line trench only about twenty-five actually reached there. Parties were organised to bomb down the enemy trenches to the right and when further advance became impossible barricades were built. The enemy made several attempts to bomb our troops out of their trenches and we lost some officers and men in this way, although the enemy were repulsed. Our bombs ran out and German grenades found in the captured trench were used.

Meanwhile the Dorsets, Borders & Lancashire Fusiliers in our front line trench had become organised. Major J.V.SHUTE had been wounded and Capt. LANCASTER being in the German trench (he had also been reported wounded) the Adjutant assumed command of both 1st Dorset and 11th Border Rgt. Arrangements were made for a concerted attack upon the German position at a given signal; a patrol being first sent out to ascertain exactly which part of the German trench was in our hands and which was still held by the enemy. Also as our own guns were still firing on the German trench it was necessary to wait till this barrage lifted before we advanced. Before this plan of attack could be carried out the Officer commanding the Right Column decided to withdraw the 19th Lancashire Fusiliers and 11th Border Rgt. from our front line trench, leaving the 1st Dorset Rgt. to hold the line. At that time we had – in addition to the Adjutant – three 2/Lieutenant's and eighty-five other ranks actually in the trench. Soon after 1pm these men were sorted out into companies, a commander allotted to each company, sentries were posted, the two remaining Lewis guns in action, and we became again a definitely organised unit. We were unable to get into touch with anyone on our right or left. During the early part of the afternoon sixty more unwounded men rejoined – these having become detached in other parts of our trenches.

The enemy's artillery bombarded us continually all the afternoon and at 5pm. his fire became so intense and accurate that our position became almost untenable. Thirty of the remaining men were either killed or wounded and the trench so damaged as to make communication very difficult.

Soon after 5pm. Major H.D. Thwaytes came up and took command; a message was received from Brigade saying that 15th H.L.I. would relieve 1st Dorset Rgt. and by 2am on the 2nd July we were clear of the front line trench. Party in German trench also ordered to withdraw.

15th (Service) Battalion (1st Glasgow) Highland Light Infantry

CRUCIFIX CORNER

2am	Message fixing zero time for the offensive reached Coys about this time. Zero time – 7.30am.
6.30am	Battalions fell in on AVELUY – AUTHILLE road.
7.30am	'A' Coy set off in Artillery formation, platoons at 100 yards interval, in close touch with the rear of the 2nd MANCHESTER REGT. Progress was much checked and it was 9am before 'D' Coy which was in rear of battalion was clear of CRUCIFIX SHELTERS. 2/LT. WALKER ('A' Coy) wounded (shell shock).

Composition of battalion going into action on this date:

Bn. HQs: Lt. Col. C.G. BEAUCHAMP
Capt & Adj, N.I. HUNTER
Intelligence Officer, 2nd Lt W.A. ALLAN
M.G.O., Lt. H.M. WILLIAMSON
Grenadier Off., Lt. G.D.A. FLETCHER
R.S.M., T. McGREGOR.
O.Rs = 38

'A' Coy   O.C. Major W.M. MACFARLANE
2nd Lt J.C. THOMSON.
2nd Lt E.J. NICOL.
2nd Lt W.H. THOMSON.
2nd Lt F.W. WALKER.
C.S.M. W. HARTERY.
O.Rs = 183

'B' Coy   O.C. Lt. A.D. HUTTON
Lt. A. LYALL
Lt. A. GRAHAM
2nd Lt. D. MARTIN
C.S.M. J. SMART
O.Rs = 192

'C' Coy   O.C. Capt. D.K. MICHIE.
Capt. W.T. MITCHELL.
2nd Lt. R.S. MACFARLANE.
2nd Lt. J.W. WILSON.
2nd G.M. CLEGHORN.
C.S.M. A. CONNELLY.
O.Rs = 170

'D' Coy   O.C. Major D. ANDREW
Lt. D.J. NICOL
Lt. J.T. LYALL
2nd Lt. J. MICHIE
2nd Lt. W. WHITE
C.S.M. J. HARKNESS
O.Rs = 164

Details, including Transport, which did not actually go into action on 1st July, were at BOUZINCOURT under MAJOR GRANT. Over and above these totals a certain number of men were in action, but not with the Battn, being attached to Trench mortar Batteries etc for carrying purposes.

On 1st July 1916 the Battn moved in artillery formation from shelters at CRUCIFIX CORNER to AUTHUILLE WOOD as supporting Battn to the 14/INF BDE, in its attack on German trenches south of THIEPVAL. The Battn moved about

9am, but was checked in the wood, as the troops in front were held up. The two leading Companies, 'A' & 'B', then occupied the Assembly trenches in the wood, and the two rear companies, 'C' & 'D', dug themselves in. On the evening of the 1st and during the night 1st/2nd July, 'A' Coy occupied the fire trenches in the British Line, between MERSEY ST (X.I.B.4/2) and BOGGART HOLE CLOUGH (X.I.A.3/3), 'B' Coy being in support at WOOD POST (X.I.C.5/6). There were about 40 casualties in the Battn during the period it was in AUTHUILLE WOOD on 1/7/16. Included in these was 2/LT. J.W. WILSON (wounded). All the casualties were caused by shell fire, a large proportion of one platoon (No.3) being knocked out by a tear shell which landed in its midst.

During the night 1st/2nd July 'A' Coy patrolled "NO-MANS-LAND" in front of the trenches held by it, under the direction of O/C. Coy (MAJOR MACFARLANE). 42 British wounded, including one officer were brought in. This Coy suffered 10 casualties during the night, 2 of which were caused to the rescuing party.

Document Attached to the War Diary

Appendix "A", a report on the village of Thiepval and the nearby Mouquet Farm:

THIEPVAL

There are 66 houses in THIEPVAL, chiefly farms. Most of these have rain water cisterns.

The Chateau, facing West, is an important building the cellars of which are very large and are used by the Germans for lodging soldiers, and are always full.

THIEPVAL farm is used as a grenade store.

The village is in ruins but from latest reports and from aeroplane photographs it may be deduced that many of its less fragile buildings are still so little damaged as to afford valuable protection against attack.

The following are a few particulars of the buildings that may have escaped our gun fire. The rest may be taken as mere flimsy barns "torches" (unbaked clay and chopped straw):

1. GRIBEAUVAL farm. Brick, some cellarage – say 20 men.
2. Maison MORONVAL. A small brick house with cellars for 15 men.
3. Maison OBIN. A "torches" house which, however, has been sandbagged by the Germans, and has good cellars which are protected by barrels of earth. A small fort for about 40 men.
4. Maison CATHELAIN. A large strongly built house (brick) of seven rooms. Its cellars will hold about 50 men and the whole has been fortified.
5. Maison BARNS which has been strengthened by the enemy.
6. Maison The Cures house (presbytery). A substantial little building of brick with cellars in which 62 people lived for 40 days.

7. Maison SOREL. A small farm with indifferent cellarage.
8. Maison BENJAMIN. A brick house with excellent cellars capable of holding 40-50 men.
9. A sandbagged farm.
10. Maison BAUDELOQUE. A poor house which has been fortified. It has cellars for 10-15 men.
11. Maison DARCHEZ. A "torches" farm with cellars for 20-30 men. It has a good well.
12. A cafe burnt down in 1915. Excellent cellars 30-40 men.
13. A small house with a good well.

Tower in THIEPVAL WOOD, 300 metres North of the Chateau and 80 metres S.S.W. of HAIE, the most Westerly building on the THIEPVAL – St. PIERRE DIVION road and North of it, is loopholed and contains an O.P.

It is estimated that there is accommodation for 1500 men underground.

There are 3 wells (communales), depth about 30 metres, containing good water. There are also wells to be found in most of the farm houses. The water supply of the Chateau is considered abundant. The well in the square North of the Church was mined and had a gallery running towards the Church.

There is a deep walled-in village pond.

Telephones. Behind a wall on the Eastern side of the square by the Church.

FERME DE MOUQUET[1]

The farm was built about 60 years ago, and is very strong for this part of FRANCE. It belongs to M. GONSE who is living at the Chalet Rosa, Berck Plage, P.de C., and has let to M. Vanderdriessche, a Fleming, who is at Brucamps, at the corner of the road to Ailly.

There are 2 supply dumps and an Artillery dump in it or its vicinity. There is a pipe line from the FERME DE MOUQUET to THIEPVAL.

The farm contains several wells. The telephone exchange is situated here.

Under the two barns are 4 big cellars, with windows about a metre square above the ground, from which men standing in the cellars could fire or work Machine Guns (good field of fire). The cellars are capable of holding 40 men.

The Right wing was burnt down in Sept. 1914.

There are several small clusters of trees N., N.W., S.W. an S. of the farm in which batteries are placed.

NOTE

1. Mouquet Farm itself was a heavily defended German position half-way between Pozières and the German strongholds around Thiepval village. Intended to have been captured on 1 July 1916, the farm was the site of nine separate attacks by three Australian divisions between 8 August and 3 September 1916. Although the farm buildings themselves were reduced to rubble, strong stone cellars remained

below ground which were incorporated into the German defences. The attacks mounted against Mouquet Farm cost the 1st, 2nd and 4th Australian Divisions over 11,000 casualties, and not one succeeded in capturing and holding it. The British advance eventually bypassed Mouquet Farm leaving it an isolated outpost. It finally fell on 27 September 1916.

16th (Service) Battalion (2nd Glasgow) Highland Light Infantry

The 16th H.L.I .with 25 Officers and 755 other ranks, relieved the 2nd K.O.Y.L.I. on the night of 30th June/1st July, 1916, taking over from them the trench system extending from SKINNER STREET, point R.31.a.14. to TYNDRUM STREET, point R.31.c.05. (approximately 500yards of front).

Casualties during relief:
1 Other Ranks killed; 2 Other Ranks wounded.

Before midnight, Lieut BOGUE and 2 other ranks reconnoitered the German wire, and found that the wire was very much broken down, and that there were numerous gaps in it. They reported that they anticipated no difficulty in getting through the wire.

During the whole night we bombarded the enemy's trenches heavily, to which he retaliated feebly. At 6.25am the bombardment prior to the advance commenced, and continued until ZERO Time at 7.30am. During that time our front line and communication trenches were badly shelled with H.E. Shrapnel, and Minenwerfer. The advance commenced at 7.30am.

'A' Company leading on the right, with 'C' Company in support, and 'B' Company on the left, with 'D' Company in support. On our right were the 17th H.L.I., and on our left the 16th North'd Fusrs. The 2nd K.O.Y.L.I. were in Support, and the 11th Border Regt. in Reserve.

The enemy opened heavy Machine Gun and Rifle Fire as soon as our men jumped over the parapet, and manned their parados with bombers, with men at 2 yards interval. Our Platoons advanced in waves in extended order, and were simply mown down by the Machine Gun Fire, and very heavy casualties resulted. On the left the Support Company got close up to the German wire, but were unable to advance. On the right we succeeded in entering the German trenches, where we were in touch with the 17th H.L.I. and where we remained until relieved by the 2nd Manchesters.

On our left the men took what cover they could in Shell holes, firing upon the enemy whenever he showed himself. One of our Lewis Gunners fired 24 Magazines of Ammunition, when it was finished, being the only one of his section left he crawled back under cover of darkness, bringing the gun with him.

During the day all available men were organised into Bombing Posts, and were prepared to offer every resistance should the enemy have made any attempt to counter attack. The Artillery were informed of our position, and during the afternoon bombarded the front line opposite us very heavily. The Germans were very active with Machine Gun, Rifle Fire, Bombs and "Oil Cans" on "No Man's Land" sniping at any man who made any movement.

In retaliation to our bombardment in the afternoon our trenches were heavily shelled. This decreased during the night, but was renewed again between 3 and 5am.

Numerous flares were sent up during the night, including many red and green. The enemy were very much on the alert, and kept "No Man's Land" under continuous fire. We were in touch with the 15th Lancashire Fusrs. on our left, and with the 2nd K.O.Y.L.I. on our right.

Colonel Laidlaw having been wounded was evacuated about 8am and Major Kyle joined the Battalion and took over Command about 5pm.

Our casualties during the day were 20 Officers, and 534 other ranks.

17th (Service) Battalion (3rd Glasgow) Highland Light Infantry

12.30a.m.. 'A' Coy report explosion of Mortar Bomb store which caused 'B' Company six casualties – including C.S.M. Reith – all wounds. In addition "B" Coy had six men wounded thro' shell fire about this time.

Zero time was fixed for 07.30AM. This was communicated to Coy Commanders but the men were not told until after daylight.

7.23a.m. 'A' & B' Coys started crawling across "No mans land". Our 'C' Coy on the right of 'A' and 'A' Coy 16th H.L.I. on left of our 'B' Coy. This Coy of the 16th when only 100 yards out got seriously dealt with by Enemy Machine Guns, tho' two platoons got up to the wire they found the latter very strong & new. Lieut. McLaren and a few men joined our 'B' Coy and eventually proved to be the only men of the 16th H.L.I. to penetrate the enemy line.

7.30a.m. 18-pounder Barrage lifted and our men entered the enemy front line. The leading lines pressed on while the moppers proceeded to clear the dugouts. A number of prisoners were taken. The advance across the open was splendidly carried out all ranks behaved magnificently – as indeed was the case throughout the entire action. Captain Mitchell and 2nd Lieutenant Beckett were both wounded before reaching the enemy front line as was Lieut Miller on the right of 'C' Company.

8a.m. Leipzig Trench was taken and the leading lines advanced against

Hindenberg Trench these however were mown down and by 08.15AM every Company officer was a casualty.

9a.m.　The 2nd KOYLI came up but did not go beyond Leipzig Trench. It now became obvious to Col Morton that Leipzig Trench must be held as without reinforcements no further advance could be made both flanks being exposed as the 8th Division on our right had been driven back. The left was particularly exposed and parties under Sergt Macgregor and Sergt Watts were organised and sent to strengthen the left and left centre respectively where 'B' & 'D' Coys had been almost annihilated. Our casualties now amounted to 22 officers and 400 other ranks.

9.30a.m.　The 11th Bn. Border Regt. debouched from Authuille Wood and were absolutely wiped out by Enemy Machine Gun fire, while his artillery barraged the valley E. of the Wood very heavily.

9.40a.m.　Our bombers were holding the flanks successfully. The bomb supply was excellent, the bombers under 2nd Lieut Morrison being entirely responsible for this.

10.10a.m.　The Brigade wired us to push on when the guns lifted off Hindenberg Trench but the redoubt on our left made this movement impossible unless we were in possession of it and in spite of persistent bombing we were unable to take it.

11.15a.m.　The flanks still held but the entire line very weak.

12noon.　The 1st Dorsets came up on our right flank and relieved the tension there. A forward movement initiated by them was to be prolonged by us but the Dorsets were unable to make any progress.

12.38p.m.　2nd Manchester Regt. got orders to attack Hindenberg Trench.

2.11p.m.　Situation is still unchanged, bombing parties worked hard. 2nd Lieuts Morrison and Marr worked throughout all this period with energy, courage and without the least regard of personal safety and to them is due the entire organisation of the parties which held our line against enemy bombing counter-attacks.

3.45p.m.　The Bde asked us for information of the 16th H.L.I.'s location.

4.7p.m.　The 2nd Manchesters reinforced our flanks with one Company on each. This greatly relieved our left which had been badly threatened. Just at this time our line wavered a little in the centre but control was immediately gained. The large number of men of other units without officers or NCOs made control very difficult.

4.15p.m.　Situation easier.

4.20p.m.　Bde were appreciating our desperate position but urge us to give the Manchesters every assistance in a forward movement.

4.47p.m.　Manchesters in position on our flanks but all idea of forward movement given up.

4.55p.m.　Ordered to consolidate ground taken.

In the evening the enemy again delivered two strong counter-attacks which were, however, easily repulsed by our men.[1]

At 9.30 we began to be relieved by two companies of the Manchesters but the relief was not wholly carried out until near midnight. In addition to the Manchesters a hundred men from the K.O.Y.L.I. were sent as reinforcements.

The majority of our battalion was relieved by 11.30 pm, but several bombing parties belonging to the 17th were unable to be relieved till well on towards midday of the following day. The 17th fell back to Campbell Post and held the line in that sub-sector.

1. One of those in the battalion who displayed the highest gallantry on 1 July 1916, was 32-year-old Sergeant James Youll Turnbull (his middle name is also given as Yuill), a pre-war player for Cartha Queens Park Rugby Football Club. An extract from *The London Gazette*, No.29836 dated 24 November 1916, records the following:"For most conspicuous bravery and devotion to duty, when, having with his party captured a post apparently of great importance to the enemy, he was subjected to severe counter-attacks, which were continuous throughout the whole day. Although his party was wiped out and replaced several times during the day, Serjeant Turnbull never wavered in his determination to hold the post, the loss of which would have been very serious. Almost, single-handed, he maintained his position, and displayed the highest degree of valour and skill in the performance of his duties. Later in the day this very gallant soldier was killed whilst bombing a counter-attack from the parados of our trench."The son of James and Elizabeth Turnbull of Glasgow, Turnbull is buried in Lonsdale Cemetery, Authuille.

2nd Battalion King's Own (Yorkshire Light Infantry)

TRENCHES 300 YDS E. OF AUTHUILLE VILLAGE.

Z day. The day of the attack. The Brigade was drawn up in the following position (see map) prior to the assault: The two leading Battns were 17th H.L.I. on the right the 16th H.L.I. on the left. The 17th H.L.I. were on a frontage of 2 platoons from CHOWBENT STREET to KILBERRY STREET and the 16th H.L.I. on the left from KILBERRY STREET to SKINNER STREET. The 2nd K.O.Y.L.I. were the supporting Battalion and formed up in KINTYRE and CAITHNESS TRENCHES some 400 yds in rear of the leading lines as follows – from right to left 2 platoons of 'C' Coy, 2 platoons of 'D' Coy, 'A' Coy, 'B' Coy, 2 platoons 'D' Coy, 2 platoons of 'C' Coy. The 2 platoons of 'C' Coy on each flank were intended to consolidate strong points when the line reached the 2nd objective and the platoons of 'D' Coy were carrying material, wire etc for them.

The officers commanding companies on this day were 'A' Coy Captain C.K. Butler, 'B' Coy Capt T. Wells, 'C' Coy Capt G.A. Gantle, 'D' Coy Captain E.J Millin.

SLAUGHTER ON THE SOMME: 1 JULY 1916

'A' & 'B' Coys were ordered to follow close behind the centre of the attack i.e. the left of [*illegible*] H.L.I. and the right of 16th H.L.I. and [*illegible*] on the 16th, 17th H.L.I. gaining the 3rd objective 'A' & 'B' Coys ('A' on right 'B' on left) were to pass through them and capture the 4th objective prolonging the line of the 11th Border Regt who were coming up on our right from AUTHUILLE WOOD. The 11th Border Regt were allotted the task of capturing the FERME DU MOQUET. The time for the assault was fixed for 7.30am. At 6.25am our artillery put an intense barrage on hostile front line trenches which lasted for 65 mins and under cover of a smoke screen the leading infantry advanced at 7.30am, Zero time at which hour the artillery barrage lifted on to hostile support line was fixed for 7.30am.

At 7.30am the 2nd K.O.Y.L.I. left their assembly position in KINTYRE and CAITHNESS TRENCHES and advanced at a steady pace across the open. On reaching the ridge just behind our own front line the left of the attack i.e. 'B' Coy, 2 platoons 'C' Coy and 2 platoons of 'D' Coy came under a very heavy machine gun fire from the direction of THIEPVAL and suffered many casualties. On reaching our own front line these companies came up with the 16th H.L.I. who had attempted to advance but owing to the terrific machine gun fire had been compelled to fall back again to our front line leaving many dead and wounded behind in "NO MAN'S LAND".

Capt Wells commanding 'B' Coy led his men forward to the attack but was wounded just as he left our parapet. 2nd Lieut E. Hicks R.G.A. who volunteered to accompany Capt Wells as forward observing officer gallantly continued to lead the men of 'B' Coy forward until he also was wounded. 2nd Lieut H.G. Walker 'C' Coy who had been previously wounded but refused to go back continued to lead his men and jumping over the parapet shouted to his men to come on when he was instantly killed.

The hostile machine gun and shell fire was so intense that all efforts to cross the fire swept zone between the opposing lines failed and the survivors where forced to remain in our own front line. Capt E.J. Millin was killed attempting to advance in this part of the field.

Meanwhile the right of our attack consisting of 'A' Coy (Capt C.K. Butler) 2 platoons 'C' Coy and 2 platoons 'D' Coy had been able to advance with less difficulty and following close on the heels of the 17th H.L.I. captured the german front line trench in the LEIPZIG SALIENT (see map) and passing over it established themselves near the Quarry in german support line opposite FORT HINDENBURG where the enemy was established in some strength. Here we established ourselves firmly and the fighting developed into a series of bombing attacks and close fighting. Captain G.A. Gantle commanding 'C' Coy brought a Lewis gun into action at close range and did great execution on the enemy until he was severely wounded in the face.

Captain C.K. Butler cmdg 'A' Coy gallantly led a bombing attack up a communication trench leading from the hostile support line to the reserve line.

Here he was killed by a bullet wound through the head. The position held by us in the LEIPZIG SALIENT was isolated as the troops on the right & left had been unable to make headway however we established ourselves firmly & drove off several hostile bombing attacks. Bn H.Q. consisting of Lt Colonel E.H. Rigg D.S.O. commanding the Battn, Capt G.H. Kent adjt, 2nd Lt E.D. Donnell and 2nd Lieut H. Gresham, Lewis gun officer with 2 Lewis guns as a Battn reserve, moved forward up CAMPBELL AVENUE and across "NO MAN'S LAND" to the german front line in LEIPZIG SALIENT to find out the exact situation which at that time was somewhat obscure.

This was about 9.30am. The situation at that time, in the LEIPZIG SALIENT was roughly as follows; Portions of 'C' 'A' and 'D' Coys numbering about 150 O.R. were established in the german support line intermingled with men of the 17th H.L.I. This detachment was to a large extent isolated for both on the right & left flanks and in front were strong parties of germans still holding out and attempting to bomb us back whilst we attempted to bomb up the communication trenches & push the enemy further back. This however was found to be impossible without further reinforcements and accordingly the position was consolidated as far as possible and defensive flanks formed. The officers left with this detachment were Lieut M.H. Garrard 'C' coy who assumed command after Capt Butler and Capt Gantle had become casualties and did most excellent work throwing bombs himself for several hours, 2nd Lieut A.R. Ramsden 'A' Coy who also did good work in leading bombing attacks throwing bombs himself for a long time and 2nd Lieut P. Lambert 'D' Coy.

About 11am the supply of bombs and ammunition began to run short and accordingly all available men such as regt Sappers (under Cpl. Druggill), cooks, servants etc who had been left behind under Regt Sergt Major Wall were organised into carrying parties and by this means a steady flow of bombs, ammunition, food and water was sent across to the detachment in the LEIPZIG SALIENT who from this time onwards until they were relieved 36 hours later were kept well supplied. These carrying parties deserve special mention for their work was carried out under heavy fire and they were called upon to make repeated journeys across the open under fire in order to get the supplies across. In this connection Coy QR MR Sergt C. Healey did particularly good work, continually going up to his company with supplies as also did Corpl. W. Druggill with the Regt. Sappers. Sergt Major Wall ably supervised the whole system of supplies and ammunition and did very good work. Meanwhile in the LEIPZIG SALIENT itself the position remained practically unchanged throughout the day. Our detachment was reinforced during the day by some men of the 1st Dorset Regt (14th Brigade).

The enemy made no serious counter attack and there was no very heavy shelling during the day but there was a continuous bombing duel. Bn. H.Q. moved back again during the day to CAMPBELL POST. Late in the evening 2 Coys of the 2nd Manchester Regt. under Lt Colonel Luxmore came up to reinforce our detachment in the LEIPZIG SALIENT which was then placed under his orders – some of our bombing posts were then relieved by the 2nd Manchester Regt and our men remained in close support. The night passed without special incident and in the morning the position was unchanged.

At night the detachment of 17th H.L.I. in the LEIPZIG SALIENT were withdrawn to our own lines which were then held by portions of 16th H.L.I., 17th H.L.I. and 2nd K.O.Y.L.I. our detachment consisting of the survivors of 'B' Coy and of the 2 platoons of 'D' Coy and 2 platoons of 'C' Coy who had originally formed the left of our attack which had been hung up.

The officers left with this detachment were 2nd Lieut J.W. Woods who was left in command of 'B' Coy, 2nd Lt A.O. Pardon 'C' Coy, and 2nd Lieut W.A. Smith 'C' Coy. This detachment suffered very heavily during the day & night from shell fire & our own front line became untenable and was practically non existent, accordingly on the morning of the 2nd July this party numbering in all about 100 O.R. was ordered to fall back to our support line. Even here they suffered heavy casualties from shell fire and their numbers became considerably reduced. Many gallant deeds were performed by individuals during the time they were holding our line.

Many wounded men were lying out in shell holes in No Man's Land where they had fallen in the attack. They were unable to move and if they attempted to do so were promptly fired on by enemy snipers and machine guns. In spite of this fire volunteers were not lacking to go to their rescue and a large number were thus brought in – in some cases it was only possible to bandage them up during the day and fetch them in after dark. L/Cpl. A. Holding in particular did very gallant work in this respect saving many lives and there were many others. The Regt. Stretcher bearers behaved with great gallantry in bringing in wounded under heavy fire & in very difficult circumstances.

15th (Service) Battalion (1st Salford) Lancashire Fusiliers

THIEPVAL Subsector.

1.0am.   Battn. arrived and took up positions for Attack.

7.30am.   Zero time. Battn. attacked as ordered. Disposition of Companies was as follows:

'A' Coy under command of Captain A LEE-WOOD formed the Right half of attacking line.

'C' Coy under command of Lieut C.H. WRIGHT formed the Left half of attacking line.

'B' Coy under command of Captain G.Y. HEALD formed the Support to 'A' Coy.

'D' Coy under command of Captain E.C. MACLAREN formed the

Support to 'C' Coy.

Lieuts NOYES, FREEMAN and CLEGG led platoons of 'A' Coy.

Lieuts DONCASTER, JACKSON led platoons of 'C' Coy.

Lieuts LODGE and AIRD led platoons of 'B' Coy.

Lieuts ROBINSON, WRONG, HAMPSON, AUDAER, led platoons of 'D' Coy.

Lieuts CROSSLEY, MARTYN, MARRIOTT, P.J. SMITH were all wounded almost immediately and Capt H. LEE-WOOD killed.

All the rest got forward some considerable distance, and either fell before or after reaching the German lines. Certain officers, NCO's, and men penetrated the line, and passed into the third line trench probably, where it is almost certain they were seen later by one of our aeroplanes, in an isolated position. It is presumed that they gave a good account of themselves, and hoped that some were taken prisoners probably after being wounded, and received good treatment.

After, a leading line or two had got into the front line trench leaving mopping up parties. The Germans reoccupied the front line, coming up from our Right, and overcame the mopping up parties - It is probable that one or two mopping up parties had been wiped out on the way over - When the later lines followed on it was found that the German front line was occupied - It was known that the earlier lines had penetrated - all attempts to get forward by the later lines resulted in the instant killing, or wounding of the party moving forward. It was obvious by 9.0am. that further efforts in this direction were only useless waste of Life. By this time only the Adjutant and Lewis Gun officer, and some 20 or 30 men remained as a collected body under the CO. In the course of the next 3 or 4 hours, these were withdrawn to more sheltered positions, and individuals gradually collected, until by evening some 120 NCO's and men had been got together. Including stretcher bearers the result at 8.0pm. was 3 officers and 150 men remaining, out of a total of 24 officers and 600 odd who attacked in the morning.

Casualties ultimately worked out as follows:

	Officers	Other Ranks
Killed.	2	17
Wounded.	4	144
Missing.	15	288
Total	21	449

16th (Service) Battalion (2nd Salford)
Lancashire Fusiliers

AUTHUILLE

The frontage of the 96th Bde in the attack was from SKINNER ST to QUEENS X ST Trenches R.31.3 to R.25.14, including in the enemy's lines the whole of the defences of THIEPVAL & the strong position South of the village. We had the 97th Bde on our right and the 36th Divn. on our left. The assaulting Batts of 96th Bde were the 16th N.F. & the 15th L.F. My Batt was ordered to support the assaulting Batts & to form two strong points in rear of THIEPVAL. My Coy's were about equal in strength, 120 each including L.G. teams & I had 40 men with Batt H.Q. including messengers, ammn carriers & a small party of bombers.

The Batt left BLACKHORSE dug out about 11pm (June 30th) & moved to places of assembly as under:

    'A' & 'C' Coy's to support Right Assembly Bn   FRENCH TRENCH
    'B' & 'D' Coy's to support Left Assembly Bn   QUEENS X BANK

'C' & 'D' Coy's were to construct strong points & carried R.E. materials for this purpose, they each sent a small party with leading platoon of 'A' & 'B' Coy's respectively to mark out strong points & get ready for construction parties. Lieut Grant 206 Co R.E. & party joined these Coy's in assembly for this work.

'B' Co lost 4 men killed, 1 off & 6 men wounded getting into position but no casualties were suffered whilst in assembly trenches.

Zero time was 7.30am.

Lieut A.N.ALLEN, commanding 'A' Coy, received no message from his officer sent forward, who was badly knocked about by the bombardment, so at 7.55 he moved forward to GEMMELL TRENCH where he met the reserve Coy of the 16th N.F. moving to the front line; at 8.10 he moved into the front line & sent No.1 platoon over the parapet under 2/Lieut W.E. FOSS. The N.F. attack was making no progress & so Lieut ALLEN kept the rest of his Co in the front line. 'C' Coy were now in GEMMELL & Capt KNOTT seeing that he would be wanted to support the attack ordered his men to deposit R.E. material & went to see Col W.H. RITSON C.M.G. Comdg 16th N.F. in front line. Later he brought his Coy into the front line. 'A' & 'C' Coy's held the front line until relieved at 11pm by 2 R. Innisk. Fus. who held as far as GREENOCK my 'C' Co moving to the right as far as SKINNER ST. The casualties suffered by these Coy's were mostly from shells whilst holding the front line which was much battered about & gave little protection.

On the left 'B' Co were better placed for observation & the 15th L.F. were seen to advance in good order & the 36th Div. on our left to be making good progress. At 8 o'clock the first line of 'B' Co advanced but came under M.G. fire whilst crossing QUEENS X BANK, the other lines & 'D' Co followed. The front line reached the cross roads beyond HAMMERHEAD SAP but had suffered severely from M.G. fire from direction of THIEPVAL, Capt TWEED reckoning that his Coy was only about 40 strong at this point.

Word was sent to Capt TWEED that the three officers of 'D' Co had all been knocked out & he went back to instruct 2/Lieut TOWES not to bring the rest of 'D' on until 'B' Co could make better progress. Capt TWEED then went back to the front line & tried to get men forward by various means. He ordered a section to rush forward to a bank that promised protection but all were mowed down; a few men crawling met the same fate.

The other officers of 'B' Co were wounded & as advance was impossible Capt TWEED signalled to the remainder of the men to get under the bank of HAMMERHEAD SAP while he crawled forward to see if it would be possible to get through the wood that way. This was equally impossible & as nothing could be seen of the 15th L.F. advance, I ordered Capt TWEED withdraw his men & reorganise in QUEENS X ST. This was done with a few further casualties & the remains of 'B' & 'D' Co were ready to move again as ordered. Two further attacks were attempted during the afternoon by the 2. R. Innisk. Fus. & later by the 8. W. Yorks but it was found impossible to get beyond our wire. The 2. R. Innisk. Fus took over the front line & 'B' & 'D' Coy's were withdrawn after nightfall.

It is evident that the bombardment failed to dislodge the protected M.G.s in the THIEPVAL defences and it is probable that some of these were in advanced positions nearer to our lines than we had supposed; there must also have been some M.G.s with a high command, for men crawling were instantly detected & fired on. During one bombardment before the attack enemy M.G.s could be heard firing from several positions.

19th (Service) Battalion (3rd Salford) Lancashire Fusiliers

THIEPVAL
Battn. took part in "Attack of 4th ARMY on German Positions"

Documents Attached to the War Diary

A report on operations carried out by 19th (Service) Battalion (3rd Salford) Lancashire Fusiliers from 1st to 4th July 1916. Dated 6 July 1916, and signed by Lieutenant Colonel John Malise Anne Graham DSO:

At 9.30pm on the evening of the 30th June 1916, the Battalion left billets at SENLIS and proceeded to BLACKHORSE BRIDGE SHELTERS, arriving there between 1.0 and 2.0 a.m. on the 1st July.

Here were assembled the Right Column, consisting of:
1st DORSET REGIMENT.

14th BDE. T.M. BATTERY (less 2 Sections)
4 STOKES GUNS.
19th LANCASHIRE FUS.
½ Section 206th COY R.E.
Under command of Lieut-Col J.M.A. Graham DSO 19th Lancs Fus.

At 7.10am the order to advance was given and the columns moved off in the above order. The advance was carried out in columns of platoons in fours, with 100 yards interval between platoons.

The line of advance was along the river bed of the ANCRE [*some of this page is missing*].

On arrival at WESTERN EDGE of AUTHUILLE WOOD, information was received that the 1st DORSET REGT. was experiencing heavy casualties, emerging from WOOD. The 19th LANCASHIRE FUS. continued to advance until the whole Battalion was in columns of route along DUNBARTON TRACK, immediately in rear of 1st DORSET REGT.

Owing to the severe casualties on leaving the WOOD, the O.C. RIGHT COLUMN brought up 2 Trench Mortars to point X.1.C.35/75, and also established 2 LEWIS GUNS, and under cover of the fire of these guns the advance was continued. The open space in front of point X.1.C.35/75 was crossed by squads in rushes of 30 to 40 yards – the men taking cover in shell craters.

'A''B' and half of 'C' Companies then crossed the open spaces between point X.1.C.35/75 and our front line trench, heavy enfilade fire being experienced the whole way across, causing many casualties.

At this juncture, a message was received from LIEUT HUXLEY, Commdg. 'A' Coy stating that the first line trench was so crowded with the remnants of all preceding regiments that it was inadvisable to send any more men across until the congestion was relieved.

This having been communicated to H.Q. 14th INF. BDE. the advance was discontinued by the remaining half of 'C' Coy and 'D' Coy and orders were given that these companies were to move round by ROCK STREET to CHEQUERBENT STREET and effect an exit from the head of the latter street; but owing to the excessive crowding in all these front line trenches, it was found impossible to make any progress, and orders were received from BDE. H.Q. to "STAND FAST".

In the meanwhile 'A''B' and part of 'C' Coys had continued their advance from the front line trenches in waves of 30 or 40 men. The leading wave, lead by LIEUT HUXLEY, got within 10 yards of the German Trench but out of forty men only four remained and they could get no further.

CAPTAIN HIBBERT led the next wave and succeeded in getting into the German trench. He was followed by LIEUT MUSKER and 2/Lieut GEORGE with all the men that could be collected. These were the only three officers left with the two and half Companies that had advanced, the remaining officers having been killed or wounded.

The names of those officers killed or wounded in this advance were:

2/Lieut	H.W.HUXLEY	(Wounded but remained at duty)
-	E.C.E. CHAMBERS.	Killed
-	A.N. DUSSEE.	Killed
-	E.D. ASHTON.	Killed
Lieut	J. HEWITT.	Wounded
2/Lieut	L.N. MIDDLETON.	Wounded
Lieut	R.C. MASTERMAN.	Killed
2/Lieut	J. SHIELS.	Wounded

Captain G. HIBBERT then took command of all available men belonging to the Battalion and proceeded to hold the N.W. angle of the LEMBURG SALIENT – the DORSET REGT. being on his Right. Throughout the day this line of German trench was held in spite of continual bombing attacks by the enemy from a large mine crater on the left flank.

The supply of bombs carried over was soon exhausted, and CAPTAIN HIBBERT very soon found it necessary to make use of all the German bombs in the trench – some 700 or 800 being used.

Seven or eight Germans were found hiding in the dug-outs, and these were sent down in the course of the afternoon to BLACKHORSE BRIDGE, by means of making use of the RUSSIAN SAP opposite SANDA STREET.

At 9.30pm on the evening of the 1st July orders were received for the 19th LANCASHIRE FUS. to retire on AUTHUILLE being relieved by the MANCHESTER REGT. All wounded men belonging to the Regiment were brought down, but the withdrawal had to be conducted very slowly owing to the heavy hostile artillery fire on this section of our front line. The remainder of the Battalion retired down DUNBARTON TRACK on to the AVELUY – AUTHUILLE ROAD. AUTHUILLE VILLAGE was reached at 1am on the morning of the 2nd July, and the Battalion proceeded to man the defences.

On the night of the 2/3 July, the Battalion was ordered to relieve the 15th H.L.I. then holding our front line trench from MERSEY to CHEQUERBENT STREET. The relief was effected by 11pm and this sector was held by the Battalion until the night of the 3rd July, when it was relieved by the 11th Cheshire Regiment.

During the night of the 2/3 July and throughout the morning of the 3rd July, the line was subjected to an intense bombardment causing several casualties – the following officers being wounded: Captain G. HIBBERT. Lieut R.R. EVANS. 2/Lieut H.W. HUXLEY. [2/Lieut] W.R. NIGHTINGALE.

Throughout these operations the Battalion behaved with the greatest steadiness, and the advance was carried out without hesitation on the part of the men – in spite of the intense artillery and machine gun enfilade fire.

The greatest difficulty was experienced in trying to advance from our own front line trench on the morning of the 1st July.

SLAUGHTER ON THE SOMME: 1 JULY 1916

This was due to the fact that when the trench was reached, it was found to be blocked by men of the preceding units of the attacks, and consequently it was found to be almost impossible to keep any direct hold on the men, as they were immediately swallowed up in the melli [*sic*] found in the first line trench, but in spite of this the men moved forward and crossed the trench without hesitation.

The Battalion returned to billets at SENLIS on the night of the 3/4 July.

During these operations the Battalion experienced two hundred and sixty-eight casualties – that is to say 50% of its fighting strength – having 20 officers and 577 other ranks when going into action.

Attached is list of officers who went into action on the morning of the 1st July:

	Lieut-Col.	J.M.A.	GRAHAM DSO.
	Major	J.	AMBROSE SMITH.
	Lieut & Adjt.	A.R.	MOXSY.
	Lieut	G.B.	SMITH.
'A' Coy	2/Lieut	H.W.	HUXLEY.
	2/Lieut	E.C.E.	CHAMBERS.
	2/Lieut	A.N.	DUSSEE.
	2/Lieut	E.D.	ASHTON.
'B' Coy.	Capt.	G.	HIBBERT.
	Lieut	J.	HEWITT.
	2/Lieut	R.L.	GEORGE.
	2/Lieut	L.N.	MIDDLETON.
'C' Coy.	Capt.	W.G.	HAYWOOD.
	Lieut	H.	MUSKER.
	Lieut	R.C.	MASTERMAN.
	2/Lieut	G.H.	DYKES.
'D' Coy.	2/Lieut	H.R.	NIGHTINGALE.
	2/Lieut	I.	JONES.
	2/Lieut	H.B.	CARTWRIGHT.
	2/Lieut	J.	SHIELS.

One Lewis Gun was carried over into the German trenches, but of the others, the carriers were either killed or wounded.

Of the bomb-carriers very few got across the fire-swept zone with their buckets. This was due to the fact that the men could not advance quick enough with the loads they had to carry, and they probably being more conspicuous, were singled out.

The smoke barrage thrown out on our Right flank on the morning of the 1st July considerably aided our advance, and that, together with the machine and Lewis Gun fire from point X.1.C.35/75 certainly helped in reducing our casualties.

Soldiers of 'C' Company, 1st Battalion Lancashire Fusiliers fixing their bayonets prior to the attack on Beaumont Hamel. Photographed by Lieutenant Ernest Brooks, who was looking south with Hawthorn Ridge in the distance, these men are wearing fighting order, with the haversack in place of the pack, and with the rolled groundsheet strapped to the belt below the mess-tin which contained rations. Though this picture is often stated as having been taken on 1 July 1916, research by the historians Alastair Fraser, Andrew Robertshaw and Steve Roberts (detailed in their book *Ghosts on the Somme*) suggests that it was in fact taken the day before. One 'C' Company veteran, Corporal George Ashby, recalls that the men were given "a tot of rum and a packet of cigarettes" in return for posing for the photographer. Company Sergeant-Major Edward Nelson can be seen front right – he would be wounded in opening day of the Battle of the Somme. (HMP)

British troops, believed to be the 2nd Battalion, Gordon Highlanders crossing No Man's Land near Mametz on 1 July 1916. The trench lines are clearly marked by the white chalk excavated during their construction. (HMP)

The 103rd (Tyneside Irish) Brigade, part of the 34th Division, pictured advancing from the Tara-Usna Line to attack the village of La Boiselle on the morning of 1 July 1916. The 34th Division suffered heavier losses than any other British division that day. (HMP)

The tiny figures of soldiers of the 16th Battalion, Middlesex Regiment are pictured as they head back down the slope after having reached the crater on Hawthorn Ridge, which is on the centre of the horizon. The original Imperial War Museum caption states that this image was taken at 07.45 hours on 1 July 1916, though more recent research suggests that it was actually taken at about 10.00 hours when the Royal Fusiliers and Middlesex Regiment abandoned their positions around the crater. (Imperial War Museum; Q755)

The calm before the storm. Troops pictured waiting, some still asleep, in a support trench shortly before zero hour near Beaumont Hamel. (HMP)

The explosion of the mine under Hawthorn Ridge Redoubt – a photograph of the moment that the cinematographer Lieutenant Malins captured on film. The film footage that Malins took of this eruption lasted about twenty-three seconds, with a slight pause as the cloud of dust and debris expands. The mine caused a crater 130 feet across by 58 feet deep. (HMP)

A drawing depicting the moment that Private William "Billy" McFadzean, 14th Battalion Royal Irish Rifles, was killed on 1 July 1916. His Victoria Cross is displayed at The Royal Ulster Rifles Museum, Belfast, Northern Ireland. (HMP)

An artist's depiction of Lieutenant Geoffrey St. George Shillington Cather, 9th Battalion The Royal Irish Fusiliers, during the actions for which he was awarded the VC. His Victoria Cross is displayed at the Regimental Museum of The Royal Irish Fusiliers, Armagh, Northern Ireland. (HMP)

Captain Eric Norman Frankland Bell, 9th Battalion Royal Inniskilling Fusiliers, depicted during the action for which he was awarded the Victoria Cross on 1 July 1916. His medal was presented to the Royal Inniskilling Fusiliers Museum in February 2001. (HMP)

Troops supposedly "going over the top" at the start of the Battle of the Somme in 1916, photographed by Canadian official photographer Lieutenant Ivor Castle. This photograph was widely published as a portrayal of an actual British attack. However, it is now believed that it was in fact taken during a training exercise behind the lines. (HMP)

A New Army battalion pictured resting whilst heading towards the front. (HMP)

This image, purported to show British soldiers moving forward through the wire at the start of the Battle of the Somme, 1 July 1916, is a still from the British film *The Battle of the Somme*. Despite now being one of the most recognizable images from the First World War, this scene is generally considered to have been staged for the camera, possibly at a Trench Mortar School well behind the lines. Nevertheless, it is regularly used to represent British troops "going over the top" at the start of an assault on the Western Front. (Imperial War Museum; Q70168)

The German trenches near La Boisselle shown under bombardment shortly before the British assault on 1 July. It was across No Man's Land like this that so many British soldiers would struggle, faced by the likes of unbroken wire and heavy machine-gun fire. Many have an image of the Western Front being a sea of mud, but, as these photographs testify, this wasn't the case for the first day of the Battle of the Somme. (Imperial War Museum; Q23)

Troops sheltering in a trench as a shell explodes in the background. (HMP)

A ration party, believed to be from the Royal Irish Rifles, pictured on 1 July 1916. (HMP)

Having filmed the explosion of the Hawthorn Ridge mine and the subsequent activity on the slopes of the ridge, Lieutenant Geoffrey Malins and photographer Ernest Brooks made their way to an area of the British trenches known as Tenderloin. They found it full of wounded men. Having moved a little closer to the New Beaumont Road, Malins filmed and Brooks photographed two injured men crawling on their hands and knees towards the junction of Marlborough Street trench and the road. The two soldiers seen here are on the New Beaumont Road itself, and are probably Lancashire Fusiliers who were wounded earlier that morning. (IWM Q752)

Another still from the British film *The Battle of the Somme*. The image is part of a sequence introduced by a caption which reads "British Tommies rescuing a comrade under shell fire. (This man died 30 minutes after reaching the trenches)". The scene is generally accepted as having been filmed on the first day of the Battle of the Somme, 1 July 1916. This image, and the film sequence from which it is derived, has been widely published to evoke the experience of trench warfare, the heroism and suffering of the ordinary soldier, and the huge casualties sustained by the British Army during the initial assault on German lines. In spite of considerable research, the identity of the rescuer remains unconfirmed. The casualty appears to be wearing the shoulder flash of 29th Division. (Imperial War Museum; Q79501)

Some of those who remained; men of the 1st Battalion, Lancashire Fusiliers pictured in the trenches at Beaumont Hamel on the afternoon of the first day of the Somme. Those that have survived the attacks on Y Ravine and Hawthorn Redoubt crater participate in what must have been a saddening roll-call. (Imperial War Museum; Q734)

As night fell – and there were only six hours of darkness in July – many survivors of the attacks of the first day of the battle began to make their way back to the British trenches, whilst stretcher-bearers went out in search of the wounded. Despite the risks, many bearers and medical staff continued to operate on the second day and beyond. This is a typical view of the Somme battlefield in 1916 – a shattered and torn countryside. (HMP)

The Thiepval Memorial and, in the foreground, the Thiepval Anglo-French Cemetery, pictured from the air. The memorial will be found on the D73, next to the village of Thiepval, off the main Bapaume to Albert road. (Courtesy of Aero Photo Studio)

Standing on the Somme battlefield not far from the Thiepval Memorial, the Ulster Tower is a memorial to the men of the 36th (Ulster) Division. Officially opened on 19 November 1921, the memorial is a copy of Helen's Tower which stands in the grounds of the Clandeboye Estate in County Down. Many in the division trained on the estate before departing on their journey to the Western Front. It was in the surrounding area of the tower seen here that two of the Victoria Cross holders commemorated on the Thiepval Memorial – Private William "Billy" McFadzean and Lieutenant Geoffrey St. George Shillington Cather – gave their lives. (HMP)

A short distance from the Ulster Tower, off the track that runs from the junction of Mill Road and Thiepval Road, are these remains of a German observation post. They stand on what would have been the rough location of the German front line on 1 July 1916. A number of trench maps of the time show a strong-point, known as the "Pope's Nose", existing in the German line in this area. Thiepval Wood can be seen in the background. This image illustrates how close together the two front lines were. (HMP)

The construction of the Thiepval Memorial under way in the 1930s. The memorial is actually hollow, built of engineering brick with the large flat roof sections created by set-backs constructed of reinforced concrete. (Courtesy of the Commonwealth War Graves Commission)

An aerial photograph of the Thiepval Memorial's unveiling ceremony on 1 August 1932. The French Guards of Honour, both foot and mounted, can be seen at the bottom of the photograph. Note the shell-cratered field just beyond the memorial. (HMP)

Preserved trenches at the Beaumont-Hamel Newfoundland Memorial. In the background, situated on a mound surrounded by rock and shrubs native to Newfoundland, stands the Newfoundland Regiment Memorial, an impressive bronze caribou which was the emblem of the Newfoundland Regiment. The area of the memorial park was purchased by the Newfoundland government in 1921, and it was officially opened, and the memorial unveiled, by Field Marshal Earl Haig on 7 June 1925. (Courtesy of the Historial de la Grande Guerre)

Two minutes before zero hour on 1 July 1916, the largest mine exploded on the Western Front in the First World War, the Lochnagar mine, tore through the German lines south-east of La Boisselle. This is the resulting crater pictured as it is today. The buildings of the rebuilt village of La Boisselle can be seen in the background. (HMP)

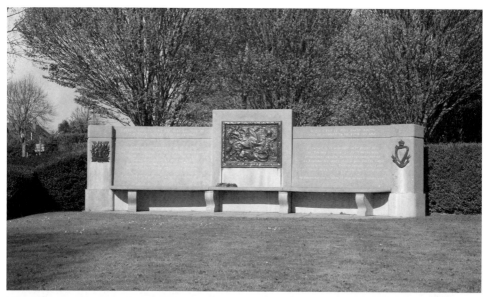

The memorial seat, outside La Boisselle, which commemorates the 34th Division's Tyneside Scottish and Irish Brigades. (HMP)

Located just west of Serre, and in the area where the British front line was located on 1 July 1916, is the Sheffield Memorial Park. Opened as a memorial park in 1936, the site still exhibits the scars of the fighting and shelling that occurred here. An information board near the front of the park contains a map showing the positions of the various battalions here on the opening day of the Battle of the Somme, along with the German trenches and machine-gun positions they advanced against. Also at the front of the park is a shallow depression marking the course of a front line trench from 1 July 1916. (HMP)

Within the Sheffield Memorial Park is a memorial to the Barnsley Pals. The funds for this black granite stone memorial were raised by businesses, the council and individuals from Barnsley, and it was unveiled in 1998, seven years after the last veteran of the Barnsley Pals had died. (HMP)

A picture taken from the main Albert-Bapaume road at La Boisselle of the British front line as of 1 July 1916, looking towards the area known as Usna Hill. The top of the hill represents the approximate location of Usna Redoubt. Lochnagar Crater is on the other side of the village to the left. The sign is part of the Somme's Circuit of Remembrance Tour. The tour runs from the town of Albert to Péronne, and important points along the well sign-posted circuit are each marked with a highly-visible symbol of a poppy. For more information on the Circuit of Remembrance, or to download audio guides, visit: www.visit-somme.com.

X CORPS

A report on operations from 1st to 4th July 1916:

2.0am.   The Battalion arrived BLACKHORSE SHELTERS, drew tools etc, & was ready to move at 3.0am.

Zero time for commencement of operations – 7.30am.

7.10am.   1st DORSET REGT. (leading Battn. of Right Column) moved off from BLACKHORSE SHELTERS by platoons at 50 yards interval.

7.35am.   Leading platoon of 'A' Coy 19th Lancs. Fus. moved off & followed route as detailed in Operation Orders No.37.

8.10am.   Battalion held up by leading Battalion being unable to leave exit of WOOD owing to heavy flanking fire of enemy machine guns. This "hold up" was overcome by advancing in short rushes.

9.35am.   Battalion closed into Column of Route on DUMBARTON TRACK, immediately in rear of 1st DORSETS and moved up to the exit of WOOD.

10.30am.   1st party of 'A' Coy 19th Lancs Fus. left exit of WOOD followed closely by parties of 'B' and 'C' Coys. Casualties during this move severe; all caused by machine gun fire.

11.5am.   Message from O.C. 'A' Coy with information that BRITISH front line trenches were congested with remnants of preceding Battalions and dead & wounded.

C.O. delayed advance of 'D' Coy which was ordered to move up by communication trench – ROCK STREET, meanwhile parties of 'A' 'B' and 'C' Coys, under Capt. G. HIBBERT, advanced to the enemy front line, which was lightly held by personnel of 1st DORSETS.

11.15am.   Troops in front line (British trenches) were organised into their units & prepared to advance in support of troops in enemy trenches, but under orders of G.O.C. 14th Bde. remnants of this Battalion & 11th BORDER REGT. were ordered to withdraw.

1.30pm.   Battalion took up position in old FRENCH TRENCH by ROCK ST. NORTH of DUMBARTON TRACK, re-organised into Coys; roll was called and 7 Officers & 182 other ranks were present; remainder killed, wounded, missing or in German trenches.

Estimate of casualties during 1st 6 hours fighting – 8 Officers 150 other ranks. Lewis Gunners and bombers suffered heavily.

The advance from our own front line was carried out in waves;

1st Wave, led by 2nd Lieut H.W. Huxley, failed to reach enemy trench owing to heavy casualties.

2nd wave under Capt. G. Hibbert, and

3rd Wave under Lieut H. Musker and 2/Lieut R.L. George succeeded in entering enemy trenches.

Capt. Hibbert took command of men of 19th Lancs. Fus. in German line and held the RIGHT flank – with 1st DORSET REGT. On Left – by bombing.

227

Enemy several times attempted bombing counter-attacks but were repulsed.

The supply of bombs in these trenches was short, and Captain Hibbert had to resort to Boche bombs, which were used most effectively.

3.30pm.   Lieut Musker returned to Battalion H.Q. (via RUSSIAN SAP) and reported situation and position held by our troops. 2nd Manchester Regt. had now come up to occupy this captured portion of the line.

7.30pm.   Nothing of importance occurred until 7.30pm when Battalion was ordered to withdraw to AUTHUILLE DEFENCES.

This was carried out and completed at 10.30pm with the exception of Capt. Hibbert and party, who were relieved at 12.30am 2/7/16.

2nd July.

AUTHUILLE DEFENCES – Coys. were re-organised & casualties estimated at 7 Officers & 375 other ranks.

3.30pm.   Defences were heavily shelled & 'B' Coy suffered further casualties.
to 5pm.

9pm.   Battalion moved to relieve 15th H.L.I. in the line – MERSEY ST. to CHEQUERBENT ST. 'D' Coy, held the line, with 'A' 'B' 'C' Coys. in support at WOOD POST. Battn. H.Q. at WOOD POST. 2nd Manchester Regiment on our LEFT; 9th Royal Fusiliers on RIGHT.

Relief completed at 11.30pm at which time Operation Orders from 14th Inf. Bde.

Intelligence report on operations by the battalion between 1st and 3rd July 1916. Signed by Lieutenant G.B. Smith, battalion Intelligence Officer:

July1st.

7.30am.   The Battn. left BLACK HORSE SHELTERS and proceeded via DUMBARTON TRACK to AUTHUILLE Wood.

'A' 'B' 'C' Coys advanced across open from AUTHUILLE Wood to our front line at x.i.a. [*indistinct*] 6/4. Owing to hostile M.G. fire the advance was made by short rushes. Casualties were heavy.

11.30am.   Orders were received from 14th Bde. to proceed via ROCK ST to front line. This was done by 'D' Coy. Front line was found to be impassable. 'D' Coy and men of other Coys still in front line were withdrawn and reformed in AUTHUILLE WOOD.

A portion of 'A' 'B' 'C' Coys had continued to advance to hostile front trench in LEIPZIG SALIENT about R31 2/1 [*indistinct*]. Here a bombing fight was already in progress. They held the enemy trenches already captured, in support of 1st DORSET REGT. until relieved in the evening. Casualties heavy in "NO MAN'S LAND".

9.30pm.   Orders were received from 14th Bde. to man AUTHUILLE defences. This was done, and Battn. remained there until evening of July 2nd.

Enemy Artillery. There was little hostile shelling encountered before noon July 1st. Enemy artillery then became more active against our front line, AUTHUILLE WOOD and communication trenches, with shrapnel 5.9 and lachrymatory shells. This continued for the rest of the day. AUTHUILLE was bombarded with shrapnel. Some casualties.

2nd Battalion Manchester Regiment

Senlis

The Bn. left Senlis on the evening of the 30th ulto. proceeding to Authuille Wood preparatory to going into action on the morning of the 1st July. A detailed report of the Bns. movements is attached covering the 2nd & 3rd July. The Bn. was relieved on the evening of the 3rd July and proceeded to billets at Senlis.

1st July – At 7.30am the Battalion left CRUCIFIX CORNER (AVELUY) and proceeded towards DUMBARTON TRACK (ATHUILLE WOOD). Upon reaching TRAMWAY CORNER it was found that the 1st Dorsets and 19th L. Fus. were not yet clear and the Bn. halted in the road. During this halt information was received from the batteries that the first line trenches had been taken, and from the wounded coming down that the 2nd line trenches (support) had been taken and that the troops were moving on to the third line.

At 9.0am the Bn. moved forward again up DUMBARTON TRACK in column of fours with 10 paces distance between Coys. Half way through AUTHUILLE WOOD the column was again halted (9.15am). Here information was received from the front that the Dorsets had gone over and that the 19th L.F. were just following. Also that a Machine Gun was playing on the edge of the Wood and this part would have to be rushed.

At 9.30am orders were received from the 14th Inf Bde. not to move forward until further orders. At the same time information was received from Capt. W.W. Smith who had been with his Coy in ROCK ST. that the 11th Borderers, 1st Dorsets, and ½ the 19th L.F., had been mown down on leaving the Wood by a hostile Machine Gun. He suggested moving forward to our trenches through ROCK ST. and BURY AVE. instead of across the open. This information and suggestion was forwarded to the Brigade. The way up ROCK ST. and BURY AVE. was reconnoitred and found to be clear and passable. It was also found that our front line was full of 1st Dorsets and 19th L.F. and Borderers who were under the impression that they were in the enemy line.

On the return journey from BURY AVE. the remaining Coy of the 19th L.F. was met making its way to the front trench. This information was passed on to Brigade. The enemy had in the meanwhile commenced to heavily shell the Wood with 10.5cm and 15cm shells, and Lachrymatory shells, and the Bn. moved to the

Assembly Trenches in the Wood. At 10.30am the Colonel was sent for to the Brigade, and an attempt was made to re-organise the Bn. and attached units in the Assembly Trenches.

At 12.15pm the Colonel returned, and a conference of Coy Commanders was held. At this conference the Colonel informed us that the 8th Division on our immediate right had failed to reach the enemy's trenches, and had been badly cut up, that the 96th and 97th Bdes held portions of the enemy's front line. He informed us that we were to be attached to the 97th Bde who held the NAZE and the LEIPZIG LINE and were expecting a counter attack. We were to move at once to reinforce and to bomb our way up the trenches towards the HINDENBURG REDOUBT.

An Artillery Barrage had been established on this Redoubt and would be kept on till 1pm. As it was impossible to get the Coys up in time a message was sent asking for the barrage to remain on until 1.30pm. 'A' and 'B' Coys were ordered to proceed up ROCK ST. to the front line and onto SANDA ST. and to advance across the open to the S.W. face of the NAZE RECTANGLE. The remaining two Coys were to remain in ROCK ST. Two Machine Guns were to go forward with 'A' and 'B' Coys, and the remainder of the attached units and 'B' Headquarters to wait in the Assembly Trenches. Headquarters then moved forward to take up a position at the head of SANDA ST.

ROCK ST. was found to be blocked with troops and it was therefore decided to go down BURY AVE. and along HOUGH ST. to OBAN AVE. this route was found to be clear. 'B' Coy had been disorganised in the Wood and only 2 platoons were found in ROCK ST. As the time was pressing these 2 platoons were taken along with Hd Qrs. and instructions left for the remainder to follow on. These two platoons were sent over the top at the point X.1.a.3.5. and reinforced the 17th H.L.I. in the NAZE at 1.45pm. Unfortunately the point at which these platoons went over was rather too far South, and the platoons came under Machine Gun fire. Only a few casualties however, resulted. These two platoons when reaching the NAZE were directed to the left flank and within 10 minutes had bombed forward, established bombing posts, held back the enemy's advance, and captured 19 prisoners. These platoons went over under 2/Lieut Culley.

The trenches at the NAZE were found to be packed with 17th H.L.I., 2nd K.O.Y.L.I., 1st Dorsets and 11th Borderers and 19th L.F. Only 4 Officers were present and the whole were in a complete state of demoralisation.

At 3.15pm 'A' Coy was sent over to reinforce followed at 3.30pm by the remaining 2 platoons of 'B' Coy, and at 3.45pm by 'C' Coy. 'D' Coy was held in reserve in our original front line, and utilised for carrying forward bombs.

At this time an effort was made to find out exactly how much of the enemy's trench we actually held, the information that we had received being evidently wrong. The trenches however, were so packed with troops that it was impossible to move about or to locate the position of our own neighbouring bombing posts. Information was however, received that we had none of our own troops on either of our own flanks.

At 3.45pm two Machine Guns were sent forward which established themselves in the enemy's original front line. Our men had by this time established a steady bombing barrage which broke the enemy's attack and forced him slowly back.

At 6.0pm the Bn was ordered to take over the NAZE and release the 17th H.L.I. and odd troops keeping only 90 men of the K.O.Y.L.I.

At 6.30pm Bn H.Q. moved forward. When the trenches had been cleared of superflour [sic] troops a German map of the trenches was found, and we were able to realise the position we actually held. It was found that we occupied the Western corner of the salient through points R21c44. – R31c52.15. – X1a52.87. and that the enemy occupied the LEIPZIG LINE. Consolidation of this line was then commenced.

At 8pm orders were received to dig trenches from TYNDRUM ST. and LIME ST. to join the salient with our original line, 1 section R.E. and a part of 17th N.F. were to assist in this work. 'C' and 'D' Coys were detailed respectively for this work.

By this time the RUSSIAN SAP had been opened up and a good deal of the traffic which had originally to go over the top was diverted down this passage. This was fortunate as the overland track had by now been marked down by Machine Guns and snipers, and we were incurring considerable losses. Fourteen more prisoners had by now come through, and five more wounded ones remained in the enemy's trench.

Considerable enjoyment was given to our troops by Lieut Robertson who made the prisoners run across the open through their own Artillery Barrage, upon reaching our line these men were kept out of our dugouts by the sharp end of a bayonet.

The work of joining up our new and original lines was commenced at 10pm but very little work could be done owing to the enemy's Machine Gun fire and Artillery Barrage. The consolidation of the enemy's original line was, however, carried on.

The evacuation of the wounded was carried on throughout the night over the open in spite of the Machine Gun fire and snipers. This evacuation was done by Coys, as our Stretcher Bearers were all occupied throughout the whole night bringing in and collecting the wounded of the Borderers, Dorsets, and 19th L.Fs. from the front of AUTHUILLE WOOD to WOOD POST. Too much praise cannot be given to the heroic efforts of all these men.

16th (Service) Battalion (Newcastle) Northumberland Fusiliers

THIEPVAL SECTOR

Zero time was fixed for 7.30am and at -4 'A' & 'B' Coys moved forward to about 100 yds behind our barrage. 'C' Coy moving into the front line trench. When the barrage lifted 'A' & 'B' Coys moved forward in waves & were instantly fired upon by enemy's M.G. & snipers. The enemy stood upon their parapet & waved to our men to come on & picked them off with rifle fire. The enemy's fire was so intense that the advance was checked & the waves, or what was left of them, were forced to lie down.

On observing this, 'C' Coy, the Support Coy, moved out to reinforce the front line, losing a great number of men in doing so. Bn. H.Q. was moved to the front line trench about 50 yds S. of junction of Hamilton Av at 7.40am & on seeing the position orders were given for 'D' Coy the reserve Coy to advance. Getting over the parapet the first Platoon lost a great number of men & the remainder of the Coy was ordered to "stand fast" & hold the line.

At 8am Brigade H.Q. was advised of the position & at 10.42am orders were received that we had to hang on where we were as they were trying to turn the N. of THIEPVAL.

At 8.20am we asked the 16th LANCASHIRE FUSILIERS to reinforce us in the front line trench & they sent up two Companies. One Coy took up a line from MAISON GRISE Sap to HAMILTON AV. the other Coy remaining in GEMMEL ST. arriving there about 10a.m.

At 9.30am a message was received from O.C. 96th Bde. STOKES MORTAR Battery; whose gun had been unable to fire from 8.15am owing to lack of ammunition, that a fresh supply had arrived. He was ordered to continue firing on the enemy front line in conjunction with our artillery.

The Enemy's artillery continued firing on "No Man's Land" & our front line trench all day, which no doubt accounted for a large number of the casualties amongst the Coys that were lying out. Our artillery continued to fire all day but it was only very occasionally that it appeared to be heavy & effective. The Enemy M.G. fired whenever a movement was shown in the line.

Bn. H.Q. moved back to GEMMEL ST. at 5pm.

Orders were received from Bde. H.Q. at 9.00pm to withdraw the men who were lying out as it was dark & that we would be relieved by the 16th L.F. and 2 R.I.F. after which the Bn. would proceed to the BLUFF.

The relief was completed at 11pm and the remnants of the Bn. 8 Officers & 279 O.R. marched into the BLUFF at about 1.30am.

'A' Coy of the 2 R.I.F. commanded by Capt. WILLIAMS rendered excellent work in carrying back the wounded men who were lying out. Our S.B. also did good work all day as did everybody who took part in the attack. The men of the attacking Coys moved forward like one man until the murderous fire of the Enemy's M.G. forced them to halt. Not a man wavered & after nightfall we found in several places, straight lines of ten or twelve dead or badly wounded as if the Platoon had just been dressed for parade.

1/5th Battalion (Territorial Force) Prince of Wales's Own (West Yorkshire Regiment)

AVELUY WOOD

Until 10am.	Battalion in assembly trenches.
10am.	Battalion moved to assembly trenches in THIEPVAL WOOD.
4pm.	Battalion assembled for attack on THIEPVAL VILLAGE, attack was counter ordered and Battn ordered to occupy BRITISH front line trenches. Battn was withdrawn and ordered to occupy SCHWABEN REDOUBT. REDOUBT reached by small party including Lt. Col Wood, Major Thompson, Lt & Adj Casebourne, Lt Jameson and 2/Lts A.B. Lee, Dresser, Clough, remainder of Battn moved to JOHNSTONES POST. Casualties 2/Lts Ablitt, Brown and White wounded. O.R. killed 5 wounded 53.

1/6th Battalion (Territorial Force) Prince of Wales's Own (West Yorkshire Regiment)

AVELUY WOOD

6.30am.	Heavy bombardment by our Artillery of enemy trenches. Battalion moved across the RIVER ANCRE and took up a position in THIEPVAL WOOD.
3.30pm.	Received orders to attack THIEPVAL along with 1/5 West Yorks Regt at 4.0pm. Very hot day.
4.0pm.	'C' and 'D' Companies went over the parapet to the attack but owing to heavy Machine Gun Fire and Artillery Fire had to retire to our own trenches. At about 3.45pm Lieut Colonel H.O. WADE (Commanding Officer) was wounded, 2/Lieut N. DODD (Signalling Officer) killed, Capt A. HAMILTON (Medical Officer) wounded. Capt J.L. HESELTON (Commanding 'D' Coy) was also wounded.

1/7th Battalion (Leeds Rifles) (Territorial Force) Prince of Wales's Own (West Yorkshire Regiment)

AVELUY WOOD

9a.m.	Orders were received for the Battalion to move to Assembly trenches in THIEPVAL WOOD. This movement was completed by 12 noon without loss.

3.30pm. The 146 Infantry Brigade ordered an attack on THIEPVAL VILLAGE by the 5th & 6th Battns. W. York. Regt. with the 8th Battn. in support and the 7th Battn. in reserve. The 7th Battn then moved into Assembly trenches in the vicinity of BELFAST CITY in THIEPVAL WOOD but was immediately ordered to reinforce the original British front line.

On completion of this move 'C' & 'D' Companies were ordered to reinforce the 36th Division in the captured German 'A' lines but retired from these lines under orders received from the 36th Division, during the night 1/2 July 1916.[1]

NOTE

1. This rather brief description belies the bravery and dedication shown by so many on 1 July 1916. One of those who displayed "the most conspicuous bravery" was 3203 Corporal George Sanders. An extract from *The London Gazette* of 9 September 1916, includes the following account of his actions during the early days of the Battle of the Somme: "After an advance into the enemy's trenches, he found himself isolated with a party of thirty men. He organised his defences, detailed a bombing party, and impressed on his men that his and their duty was to hold the position at all costs. Next morning he drove off an attack by the enemy and rescued some prisoners who had fallen into their hands. Later two strong bombing attacks were beaten off. On the following day he was relieved after showing the greatest courage, determination and good leadership during 36 hours under very trying conditions. All this time his party was without food and water, having given all their water to the wounded during the first night. After the relieving force was firmly established, he brought his party, nineteen strong, back to our trenches." Corporal George Sanders was invested with his Victoria Cross by King George V at Buckingham Palace on 18 November 1916. On 27 June 1917, Sanders was awarded a commission with the 2nd Battalion of the West Yorkshire Regiment. In April of 1918 the West Yorks were involved in bitter fighting at Mount Kemmel during the German Spring Offensive. Acting Captain Sanders was awarded the Military Cross to go with his VC during this action and was then taken prisoner of war on 25 April – he was posted as wounded and missing having been last seen with leg and right arm injuries but carrying on with his revolver in his left hand.

9th (Service) Battalion (Co. Armagh) Princess Victoria's (Royal Irish Fusiliers)

HAMEL
(Department of the SOMME)
Report of action attached.
On the right of our division was the 32nd division making an attack on THIEPVAL village – on our left the 29th division attacking BEAUMONT HAMEL and BEAUCOURT villages.

The general direction of our attack was up the right bank of the river ANCRE (a tributary of the river SOMME) from HAMEL village to BEAUCOURT station.

The Ulster division attacked astride the river ANCRE. Working up the left bank,

234

as indicated above, was the 108th Brigade (less 2 battns) – it consisted of ourselves and the 12th Battn Royal Irish Rifles. On the right bank of the river ANCRE, attacking from THIEPVAL Wood in the direction of GRANDCOURT were the remaining 2 battns of the 108th Brigade, the 11th & 13th Bn Royal Irish Rifles also the whole of the 109th Brigade - with the 107th Brigade in support

The remaining details of this memorable day will be found in the document attached (A1).

Document Attached to the War Diary

A report on the actions of 9th (Service) Battalion (Co. Armagh) Princess Victoria's (Royal Irish Fusiliers) on 1 July 1916:

COMPOSITION AND FORMATION FOR ATTACK.

The Battalion moved at 12.5am from MESNIL to take up its position for the attack, in the Right of the HAMEL Sector, no special assembly trenches had been prepared, and existing trenches were occupied.

The Battalion was on a 4 Company [*changed to Platoon in Diary*] front in the following order: Right Company "A" Captain C. ENSOR, Right Centre Company "B" Major T.J. ATKINSON, Left Centre Company "C" Captain C. M. JOHNSTON, Left Company "D" Captain J.G. BREW, each Company being on a platoon front, making 4 waves: each wave advancing at 60 yards distance. The two leading waves assembled in the front line trench.

The 3rd wave consisting of supporting platoons in communication trenches
The 4th wave consisting of consolidating platoons in 2nd line trench.
Lewis Guns accompanied the leading wave.
2 Stokes Mortars accompanied the second wave.
5 Vickers M.Guns accompanied the third wave.

The Battalion was reported in position at 3am. Between which hour and the hour it moved out the Battn suffered some 50 casualties from large H.E. shell.

Four lengths of Bangalore tubes accompanied the leading waves of each Company.

OBJECTIVES

The German 1st, 2nd and 3rd line trenches from Railway Sap to A 25 in 1st line – BEAUCOURT STATION and the Trench N of it and some detached houses near this station, the left boundary being a line drawn from A 25 to one of these detached houses thence S.E. to the River ANCRE.

TROOPS ON FLANK OF BATTALION

2 Platoons of 12th R.I.R. on Right flank.

3 Coys of 12th R.I.R. on Left flank.
2 Platoons of 12th R.I.R. in support of 9th R. Ir. Fus.

APPARENT EFFECT OF ARTILLERY BOMBARDMENT IN ENEMY'S POSITION
(a) Wire cutting was well carried out and effective lanes were cut.
(b) The enemy's trenches composing the objective of both 9th R. Ir. Fus and 12th R.I.R. did not suffer materially from the previous bombardment.

NATURE OF THE GROUND
The opposing lines of trenches were approximately 400 apart, with a Ravine some 70 yards in width about half way between the opposing trenches, the banks of which were 15 ft to 20 ft high in places and steep. The whole terrain sloping towards the RAILWAY SAP.

THE ADVANCE
Owing to the distance to be traversed and the necessity of the leading wave being within 150 yards of the German line at Zero time (7.30am), the
    1st wave crossed the parapet at 7.10am.
    2nd wave crossed the parapet at 7.15am.
    3rd wave crossed the parapet at 7.20am.
    4th wave crossed the parapet at 7.30am.
The 1st wave suffered little loss getting through our wire, lanes in which had been previously cut, but during the advance to the Ravine casualties were numerous, more especially on the left, from M.G. fire from the flanks.
    The 2nd wave suffered more severely crossing our wire, and also came under the M.G. fire from the flanks.
    The majority of the officers of the 2nd left Companies were casualties before reaching the Ravine, where the two leading waves were reorganised in one line and the advance continued.
    The 3rd and 4th waves were caught by a severe M.G. fire both frontal and flanking, and also by an artillery barrage which the Germans had now placed between our wire and the Ravine, and were practically annihilated.
    Some 150 yards from the German line the assaulting line again came under heavy M.G. fire and suffered severely: not withstanding this, small bodies of men of the Right and two left Companies reached the German wire and charged the trenches, in places the Germans held up their hands to surrender, but realising there were no supporting troops resumed the contest till there were only a handful of our men left.
The Right Centre Company appears to have suffered less severely, and was seen to penetrate the 3 German lines and a small body of them was reported to have reached BEAUCOURT STATION.

Owing to the intensity of the fire only 1 Runner got through, he came from the Left Centre Company Commander, from a spot about 30 yards short of Ravine, with the message "Cannot advance without support".

The Supporting platoon of 12th R.I.R. was sent out but was wiped out.

INFORMATION

Previous to the attack the Intelligence Officer Captain MENAUL and 5 Battalion Scouts proceeded to SHOOTERS HILL whence a view could be obtained of all the attacking ground up to the front line, except on the extreme right. This Officer kept Battalion H.Q. accurately informed of the progress of events by means of his Scouts acting as Runners from 7.30 a.m. to 4p.m. this information was at once passed on to Brigade H.Q. by telephone as soon as received.

ACTION BY THE ENEMY

The main features of the Enemy's defence were the handling of his M.Guns whereby he brought an accurate cross fire on the lanes cut in our own wire and on the gaps made by our own artillery in his wire and subsequently the artillery barrage he placed between our front line and the Ravine.

ACTION AGAINST POSSIBLE COUNTER ATTACK BY THE ENEMY

When the extent of our casualties was realised, every available man left in the Battalion was sent under the command of Major PRATT to hold the front line: the situation was reported to Bde H.Q. and a request made for reinforcements, and 2 Coys York and Lancs Regt were sent up to assist in holding the line against a possible German counter attack.

ACTION SUBSEQUENT TO JULY 1ST

During the night of July 1st-2nd the remnants of the Battalion were withdrawn into the village of HAMEL, the front line being held by 2 Coys 5/6 York and Lancs Regt.

Several parties were organised to search NO MAN'S LAND to bring in casualties, their search was continued by parties sent up to HAMEL on nights of July 2/3, 3/4, 4/5. On July 2 while carrying out this duty Lieut & Adjt G. CATHER was killed.

Early on July 2 orders were received to hand over the line to the 87th Bde and for the Battalion to withdraw to MARTINSART.

GENERAL REMARKS

The outstanding feature of the day were the fine leading by the Company Officers, and the gallant spirit and magnificent dash by the men which carried them on in spite of the severity of the casualties.

STRENGTH

The numbers advancing to the attack were:[1]

Officers[2]   15

Other ranks   600 (approximately)[3]

NOTES

1. A list of officer casualties is also included in the War Diary. They are given as: Captain C.M. Johnston (killed in action); Lieutenant and Adjutant G. St.G.S Cather (killed in action, 2 July 1916). The following were wounded on 1 July 1916: Captains J.G. Brew and C.H. Ensor; Lieutenants H.K. Jackson, J.E. Gibson, T.G. Shillington and E.M. Smith; Second Lieutenants G.E. Barcroft and A.A. Andrews. The following are listed as "missing believed killed" on 1 July 1916: Major T.J. Atkinson; Lieutenants R.S.B. Townsend and A.C. Hollywood; and Second Lieutenants R.T. Montgomery and A. Seggie. Second Lieutenant W.J. Stewart is listed as missing on 1 July 1916, and Second Lieutenant G.D. Craig as suffering from shell shock.

2. On the evening of 1 July, search parties were organized to go back over No Man's Land to look for their missing comrades. As battalion adjutant, Temporary Lieutenant Geoffrey St. George Shillington Cather led one of the parties. He went out at 19.00 hours and continued until midnight searching the area under constant machine-gun and artillery fire for his wounded comrades. The announcement of his award of the Victoria Cross, published in a supplement to the *The London Gazette* of Friday, 8 September 1916, provides an insight into his actions: "From 7pm till midnight he searched No Man's Land, and brought in three wounded men. Next morning at 8am he continued his search, brought in another wounded man, and gave water to others, arranging for their rescue later. Finally, at 10.30am, he took out water to another man, and was proceeding further on when he was himself killed. All this was carried out in full view of the enemy, and under direct machine-gun fire and intermittent artillery fire. He set a splendid example of courage and self-sacrifice." Born on 11 October 1890, at Streatham Hill south-west London, Geoffrey Cather was just 25 years old when he was killed. His formative years were spent at Hazelwood School at Limpsfield in Surrey followed by higher education studies at the famous Rugby School. In September 1914, just after the outbreak of hostilities, he enlisted in the University and Public Schools Corps and was then commissioned into the 9th Battalion Royal Irish Fusiliers in May 1915, the battalion landing at Boulogne in October of 1915. Cather became Assistant Adjutant in November and Adjutant a month later. Cather was buried where he fell, though, like so many others, his body was never recovered from the battlefield. His Victoria Cross is displayed at the Regimental Museum of The Royal Irish Fusiliers, Armagh, Northern Ireland.

3. The other ranks suffered the following casualties: Killed, 56; Wounded, 303; Missing, 159. A total of 518.

2nd Battalion Royal Inniskilling Fusiliers

Battn. was relieved by the 15th Lanc. Fus. and 16th Northumberland Fus. in trenches in THIEPVAL Subsector on night 30 June/1 July.

Arrived at the BLUFF at 3.30am 1st July to be in reserve to 96th Infy. Bde. during attack on THIEPVAL which commenced at 7.30am on 1st July. At 10am Bn. Hd.Qrs. and two Companies moved to JOHNSTONS POST, and one Coy to FRENCH ST at 8.55am. One Coy remained at the BLUFF, but was sent to JOHNSTONS POST at 11.3am.

At 11.50am orders were sent to two Coys to attack well to the North to try and turn THIEPVAL. At 1pm the attack started on a two platoon frontage, but was held up by machine gun fire, and unable to get on.

At 3.30pm orders were received to support the left flank of the 49th Div, (which was to attack at 4pm) and to fill the gap between the 49th and the 36th (Ulster) Division. This attack did not take place on the left, so one Battn. of the 49th Division only arrived up at 4.15pm.

At 6.30pm the Battn. occupied the trenches on the right of the 49th Division, and remained in these trenches till relieved by the 75th Bde, 25th Div, about 5.30am on 3rd July.

9th (Service) Battalion (Co. Tyrone) Royal Inniskilling Fusiliers

IN THE LINE.
On the 1st July, an old landmark in the history of ULSTER, the day so long looked forward to, and prepared for – the Great Offensive by the combined English & French armies in the SOMME – commenced.

The attack was preceded by the most formidable artillery preparation employed as yet in the History of the War, lasting as it did 7 days & 7 nights. The Battalion was allotted Pride of Place in the attack about to be launched, being the leading Battn on the Right of the Division. On our Right was the 32nd Division on our Left the 10th (S) Battn R. Inniskilling Fusiliers while our supporting Battalion was the 11th (S) Battn R. Inniskilling Fusiliers.

Our objective was the point christened LISNASKEA for the occasion. R20.c 7 4 Ref Map 57°S.E. in the German Third Line. No.1 Coy under the Command of Captain H.C. MACLEAN was on the Right of the Battalion & was supported by No.2 Coy led by Captain P. CRUICKSHANK. On the Left was No.3 Coy led by Captain W.F.H. PELLY & supported by No.4 Coy under the Command of Captain J.C. MURIEL.

At 6.25am the final artillery preparation – the intense Bombardment of the enemy lines – commenced. It was of a very furious description while it lasted & appeared so far as we could ascertain at the moment to be very effective. It was at first confined to the enemy's first Line, afterwards lifting as the Infantry advanced to the enemy's successive LINES at given periods of Time.

At 7.15 am after all our consolidation material, Rations, water & ammunition supplies etc. etc, had been seen to & got ready, our men debouched from our trenches in THIEPVAL WOOD under cover of our artillery fire & took up their position in front of our wire through which lanes had been cut. Every Officer & man was eager for the fray & determined to do their utmost that day. All Ranks realised that the great test had arrived & that the Honour of ULSTER & the reputation of their Regiment was at stake, everyone knew his position & the individual part he was to perform & this in itself inspired all Ranks with the greatest confidence.

At 7.30am the Bugle sounded the assault. The two leading companies advanced immediately in perfect line followed by the supporting Companies in Artillery formation. The discipline maintained by all was magnificent the advance being carried out as if it was a parade movement.

On reaching the SUNKEN ROAD in NO MAN'S LAND heavy machine gun & shell fire was encountered, the former from the village of THIEPVAL (afterwards alluded to by the Germans prisoners as THIEPVAL FORT) and the ranks began to thin, men falling by the score. The Calm & deliberate advance however, still continuing. On reaching the German "A" Line those still standing swept on with irresistible determination, charging the machine guns which the enemy had mounted on their parapet. On they pushed towards the "B" Line known as the CRUCIFIX Line. Sweeping over the "B" line with men falling fast at every step, but with magnificent courage they still went on. The enfilading machine gun fire from the Right became more intense & the fire from the machine guns in front from the "C" Line more accurate.

The remnant of the Battalion however steadily advanced towards the "C" Line & succeeded in reaching their objective LISNASKEA. A mere handful of men under 2/LIEUT McKINLEY head on to latter point for about an hour in face of superior numbers.

The Division on our Right was held up & so our Right flank was open & unprotected. The Germans then attempted to cut the party off. Our men were forced to withdraw to the CRUCIFIX LINE where the supporting Battalions were endeavouring to establish themselves.

Here throughout the day the men toiled consolidating the position to meet the inevitable counter-attack. This position was under constant M.Gun fire from THIEPVAL & casualties were numerous. Ammunition & bombs soon began to run short. Messengers were sent for supplies but owing to the murderous fire concentrated on NO MAN'S LAND it was impossible to get stores across. Many of the brave messengers themselves were KILLED or wounded. At 10 o'clock in the morning Major PEACOCKE faced the merciless fire in NO MAN'S LAND & succeeded in reaching the enemy LINES in safety & took charge of the situation. At about 3pm in the afternoon the enemy fiercely bombarded the piece of trench we were holding with High Explosives & Shrapnel attacking at the same time with bombs on our Right. Our bombs were at this time almost exhausted, nevertheless we held on to about 10pm that night, when we were compelled to face back to the German "A" Line & thence to our own trenches. During the night all that was left of the Battalion was reorganised & parties were sent out to succour the wounded lying in NO MAN'S LAND.

To particularise is perhaps invidious, so magnificently did all behave but one cannot help alluding to a few individual achievements. Major Peacocke worked magnificently. He crossed No Mans Land at a time when the fire sweeping it was most intense. He organised and rallied our troops in the enemy lines. He fought hand to hand with the enemy, repeatedly leading his men to repulse their bombing attacks. He was the life and soul of the defence and it was entirely due to his example of coolness and gallantry that our unsupported troops held on to this position for the length of time they did.

2nd Lieut R.W. McKinley with a remarkable determination of purpose forced his way with his small band to LISNASKEA our ultimate objective. He gallantly held on as long as possible and successfully withdrew his men when the position became untenable. He then, although much exhausted, rendered splendid assistance to Major Peacocke.

Sergt Major Chapman although wounded early in the action continued to advance with his company and throughout the day fought with great coolness and gallantry.

Sergt Kelly whilst holding the CRUCIFIX line, volunteered to cross a piece of ground swept by the enemy fire in order to endeavour to get in touch with the troops on our right. He achieved his purpose and later during the day when all of the officers of the Company had fallen he rallied his men and handled the situation with great gallantry and coolness working and fighting with untiring energy until wounded.

Lance Corporal Lyttle D. found himself isolated with a Lewis Gun and Vickers Gun, he fought the Lewis Gun until all his ammunition was exhausted killing many of the enemy. He then destroyed both guns and bombed his way back to our main body near the CRUCIFIX.

Pte. Gibson J.G. on reaching the German wire saw three Germans manning a machine gun from their parapet. Single handed he attacked and killed all three with the butt of his rifle. In many cases, during the attack isolated groups of 3 or 4 of our men attacked the enemy in his dug-outs, causing separate bodies of from 12 to 20 to surrender.

Casualties: As already indicated the casualties suffered by the Battalion were unfortunately very heavy. The Officer Casualties were as follows.

KILLED[1]

Captain H.C. MACLEAN O.C. No.1 Coy, Capt. P. CRUICKSHANK O.C. No.2 Coy, Captain W.F.H. PELLY O.C. No.3 Co, Captain J. WEIR Junior Captain No.4 Coy, Captain H.C. MULKERN R.A.M.C. (M.D. attached), 2/Lieut L.W.H. STEVENSON, 2/Lieut F.P. FOX & 2/Lieut W.A. HEWITT.

WOUNDED

Captain J.C. MURIEL O.C. No.4 Coy, 2/Lieut W.E. McCARTER, 2/Lieut W.H. LONG & 2/Lieut J.L. GRAHAM.

MISSING
2/Lieut A.H. GIBSON & Lieut E.A. TROUTON.

MISSING believed KILLED
Lieut W.M. CROZIER & 2/Lieut J.S.M. GAGE.

The Casualties amongst Other Ranks were as follows:

KILLED	51.
WOUNDED	252.
MISSING	124.
MISSING and WOUNDED	26.
MISSING believed KILLED	4.
Suffering from Shell Shock	4.
TOTAL:	16 Officers and 461 Other Ranks.

NOTE

1. One casualty not listed in the War Diary is Temporary Captain Eric Norman Frankland Bell. Aged 20, the son of Captain E.H. Bell, of 22 University Road, Bootle, but a native of Enniskillen, Bell was attached from the battalion to 109th Light Trench Mortar Battery. His unit was on the right of the assault and just before Zero Hour crept out into No Man's Land, waiting for the barrage to lift. An extract from *The London Gazette*, dated 26 September 1916, records the following: "He was in command of a Trench Mortar Battery, and advanced with the Infantry in the attack. When our front line was hung up by enfilading machine gun fire Captain Bell crept forward and shot the machine gunner. Later, on no less than three occasions, when our bombing parties, which were clearing the enemy's trenches, were unable to advance, he went forward alone and threw Trench Mortar bombs among the enemy. When he had no more bombs available he stood on the parapet, under intense fire, and used a rifle with great coolness and effect on the enemy advancing to counter-attack. Finally he was killed rallying and reorganising infantry parties which had lost their officers. All this was outside the scope of his normal duties with his battery. He gave his life in his supreme devotion to duty." These actions led to the posthumous award of the Victoria Cross, the medal being presented to his family by King George V at Buckingham Palace on 26 November 1916.

10th (Service) Battalion (Derry) Royal Inniskilling Fusiliers

Report on Operations culminating in the Allied Advance on 1.7.16.

In the first place it must be understood that this account only purports to deal with events concerning this Battalion particularly, either directly or indirectly. It will therefore be advisable to summarise shortly the movements and dispositions of the Battalion for a short period immediately preceding the date of the Advance.

For some weeks previous to Wednesday 14th June the Battalion had been lying at LEALVILLERS on which date it moved up to AVELUY WOOD where it bivouaced alongside the rest of the 109th Brigade being employed in the preparation of Assembly Trenches etc, in THIEPVAL WOOD.

On Saturday 24th June it moved back to MARTINSART WOOD from whence it was preparing to move up to THIEPVAL WOOD on 28th June when information was received that the Advance had been postponed for two days and that the Battalion was to move back to FORCEVILLE in the interim. As all material for the advance had been issued to the men it was decided to withdraw the heavier stuff and store it at MARTINSART so as to avoid overtiring the men on the seven mile march which they would eventually have to do from FORCEVILLE to the front line trenches.

Eventually these stores – bombs – Lewis Guns, extra ammunition etc, were dumped near MARTINSART alongside the road by which the battalion advanced to the trenches and were picked up with their parties by the main body as it marched through. This arrangement worked well in spite of the darkness and crowded state of the roads but necessitated a great deal of careful preliminary work.

On Friday 30th June we received orders to march out of FORCEVILLE at 9.15pm en route for Assembly Trenches which had been carefully reconnoitred and fixed upon beforehand. The start was made punctually by platoons at 100 yards distance going through AVELUY WOOD which was very dark and muddy. The Commanding Officer Lieut-Colonel Ross Smyth had the misfortune to slip and sprain his leg and had to be sent back on an Ambulance. Command was then taken by Major F.S.N. Macrory.

Some enemy shelling was experienced from this [*word missing*] on but the battalion was fortunate in reaching its Assembly trenches without Casualties. By the time all Coys and details were in position it was after 1am as the trenches were crowded and progress difficult and slow. Luckily the weather kept fine and the men were in good spirits.

Finally arrangements for the assault were now made and the four gaps in our wire entanglement (which had previously been cut) were inspected and labelled, look out men being posted close to them to direct all troops as to their position. The practical dispositions for the attack may now be provincially summarised.

The 10th Bn. Royal Inniskilling Fusiliers occupied a front of approximately 200 yards from the top of INVERNESS AVENUE on the right to the top of ELGIN AVENUE on the left. The objective was the German "C" line from a point C9 (OMAGH) exclusive – Map Reference R.20.a.7.4 on the left to a point R.20.c.6.6 on the right. This included one strong point known as B.16 (DUNGANNON) which had to be consolidated when captured. As supports, were the 14th Bn. Royal Irish Rifles whose orders were to assist us in holding the "C" line. On our right were the 9th Bn. Royal Inniskilling Fusiliers with the 11th Bn. Royal Inniskilling Fusiliers in similar support. On our left was the 108th Brigade whilst in reserve was the 107th Brigade with orders to pass through us after the "C" line was taken and capture the German "D" line.

SLAUGHTER ON THE SOMME: 1 JULY 1916

The battalion dispositions were that 'A' Coy should lead the attack on the right supported by 'C' Coy, whilst 'B' Coy, led the attack on the left supported by 'D' Coy. Each Coy carried picks, shovels and a proportion of R.E. consolidating material and had attached to it a Machine Gun and team from 109th Brigade Machine Gun Coy, as well as strong parties of Bombers and "cleaners up" from the 14th Bn. Royal Irish Rifles.

By 6am there was every probability of a bright sunny day. An issue of rum was served round to the men in the trenches. Our bombardment which had been intense all night now became terrific, the enemy retaliating with terrible vigour.

At 7am the Stokes Trench Mortars opened a hurricane bombardment on the enemy front trench with very great effect, showers of earth and debris being thrown high into the air all along this trench. The uproar of the explosions coming from all sides was now so great that it was difficult to make ones-self heard, but our men preserved their usual cheerful and almost stolid demeanour through everything, grinning happily if one paused to speak to them. A reference to the map will show that our advance had been made at an angle practically half-right to our front line trenches. The famous "sunken road" in "NO MAN'S LAND" just in front of our line is however practically at a direct right angle to the line of advance and it had been carefully impressed on all ranks that to keep the true direction the "sunken road" would be used as a preliminary forming up place for all our lines. This arrangement was well adhered to by our leading lines but in the excitement of the assault some of the rear "waves" of men advanced straight out of our front trenches and at right angles to them by which error these supporting "waves" reached the german lines much too far to the left which partly counts for the mixing up of battalions that finally ensued.

A more serious error which occurred later was that the leading companies twice ignored the time table of our Artillery barrage and in consequence through their eagerness to advance suffered heavy loss from our own artillery fire. It is unfair to blame anyone in particular for this regrettable incident as all the senior officers with these companies had fallen at the time and though all ranks knew the time table they quite forgot about it in the impetuous ardour of their assault. It is unfortunately not the first time that this accident has happened through the course of the war and its liability is rendered greater by any special gallantry in the troops employed.

At 7.15am on a beautiful summer morning the two leading companies began to issue by platoons through the gaps of our wire into "NO MAN'S LAND" and formed into extended line with about 3 paces interval and in this formation crept cautiously up till the leading line was within 100 yards of the german "A" line, where it lay down to wait the signal for assault.

The three following lines similarly advancing and lying down at distances in rear of about 50 yards successfully. Meantime the supporting Coy's 'C' and 'D' moved forward through THIEPVAL WOOD from their Assembly trenches to the front line trenches just vacated by the leading companies where they prepared to issue in lines of platoons in fours directly the advance was sounded.

At 7.30am sharply the hurricane bombardment of the Stokes Mortars ceased and from our front trench came the regimental bugle call followed by the "ADVANCE". Simultaneously Coy and Platoon leaders blew their whistles and the lines of men jumped up and advanced at a steady march towards the enemy trenches. The spectacle of these lines of men moving forward with rifle sloped and the morning sun glistening on their fixed bayonets, keeping their alignment and distance as well as if on a ceremonial parade. Unfaltering, unwavering – this spectacle was not only impressive it was extraordinary.

Hardly a man was seen to fall in this earlier stage of the advance. On our left the 108th Brigade had advanced slightly before the time but they had a longer distance to come so that the total alignment was not affected. On our right the 9th Inniskillings, less fortunate than ourselves suffered as they advanced from enfilade machine gun fire coming from the Thiepval Direction but never failed to preserve their alignment. Every credit is due to our artillery who had done all they had promised us in the matter of cutting the enemy's wire and levelling his front trenches.

Not a single man of our battalion had occasion as far as one can learn to use his wire cutters of which each Coy carried a supply. In the "A" line the leading Coy's, were reinforced by the two supporting Coy's, and our barrage having lifted the men sped forward towards the "B" line having killed the few Germans who had so far appeared. The supporting Coy's suffered more in the first part of the advance than the leading ones, the enfilading machine gun fire from Thiepval having increased in intensity.

Enemy prisoners now began to come in, most of them having evidently been concealed in deep dug-outs in the german support trench which runs close behind their front trench. They seemed for the most part dazed and bewildered by the fury of our bombardment and were only too glad to surrender and throw down their arms. They were sent back under escort to our trenches – about 16 prisoners to each escorting soldier. The first batches of these prisoners were so anxious to reach the shelter of our trenches that they had outstepped their escort in the dash across the open and meeting our reinforcing lines coming forward were bayoneted by them in the heat of the moment. Some reached our trenches and were there shunted by the few of our men remaining in our front line who were somewhat uncertain as to the true state of affairs in "B" Line which was captured with comparatively little opposition.

About 8am a considerable number of prisoners was taken and the dug-outs were thoroughly bombed whilst waiting for the barrage to lift from "C" line. It was here that 2nd Lieut Spalding 'B' Coy was killed by a regrettable mistake. He had descended to bomb a dug-out and was re-ascending when he was shot by a man of one of the rifle regiments who mistook him for a german.

A start was next made towards "C" line. The advance was checked for a time owing to the right flank 9th Royal Innis. Fus. being held up by enfilade machine gun fire from Thiepval. And during this check we also suffered a great many casualties from the same cause. On resuming our advance a section of our line pushed forward to repel and got cut up by our own artillery fire causing further casualties. Directly the barrage lifted from "C" line our men pushed forward and captured the trench. This was about 9 a.m.

They found a large number of dead and wounded germans in this line which was at once consolidated by our troops. All available Lewis and Vickers Guns being placed in defensive positions.

By this time men from the supporting Battalion (14th Royal Irish Rifles) were beginning to reinforce our men and shortly after the line was further stiffened by the arrival of some of the 107th Brigade.

Our right companies were now largely distributed about the "Crucifix" which they assisted the 9th Royal Innis. Fus. to consolidate. Portions of the left Coys were apparently at least 200 yards too far to the left of their objective owing to having kept a wrong direction from the start as explained before. In fact by this time the men of our battalion were more or less intermingled with representatives of all other Brigades of the Ulster Division. It was extremely difficult to locate any position accurately owing to the battered condition of the trenches. Capt Miller ('D' Coy) had already been brought back to our lines severely wounded in the face with shrapnel. Capt Proctor ('C' Coy) was leading his men towards the Crucifix when his leg was shattered by shell fire and he lay in the trench for many hours, but it proved impossible to get him back owing to heavy fire.

Eventually Capt Knox who went forward with reinforcements about 5pm carried him back as far as the "A" line where Cap. Proctor died. About noon Capt Robertson ('B' Coy) and Lieut Wilton ('A' Coy) were endeavouring to locate their position in "C" line with a map when they were simultaneously struck by rifle fire. The former being wounded in the chin and shoulder and the latter in the chest. Lieut Wilton was assisted back to our lines by one of our N.C.O'S – Sergeants PORTER ('B' Coy) was endeavouring to get Capt Robertson back when a bursting shell killed Porter and both fell. No news can since be obtained of Capt Robertson. It will thus be seen that all four Coy Commanders were wounded or killed during the morning but in spite of this the remaining officers and N.C.O's rallied and organised the men throughout the long and trying day.

There could be no doubt that from noon onwards considerable confusion existed and contrary orders were passed from one flank to another. At some time probably about noon some of our men in conjunction with men of the 107th Brigade attacked and carried a portion of the german "D" line which was held for some time till the enemy artillery found the range and inflicted terrible loss on them. They then fell back to the "C" line and were again decimated by artillery fire.

An order was given by the senior officer on the spot to retire some ten or twenty yards in order to take up a position in a more sheltered trench. The order was taken up wrongly and many men who had gallantly held positions rendered almost untenable by artillery and Machine Gun fire for hours undoubtedly got the impression that they were ordered to fall back on Thiepval Wood. A scattered stream of men began to arrive back in our front line, some wounded and all much exhausted by the terrible ordeal they had come through, the time being then about 5pm. At this juncture an urgent message was received at Battalion Headquarters from the right flank where Lieut McClure of 'C' Coy was in command of the remnants of our men and was still holding the Crucifix. Reinforcements, ammunition, bombs were all called for and perhaps the most important of all – water.

The stragglers were hastily rallied and sent forward to the Crucifix under Capt Knox – some 30 men in all. 6 four gallon petrol tins full of water were also sent with a spare party. This party was severely shelled on its journey across "NO MAN'S LAND" and lost several.

The survivors were unable to find Lieut McClure's party and handed the water over to men of different Battalions in the "C" line. Capt Knox and his party also failed to find Lieut McClure as great confusion reigned in that district accentuated by terrible shelling and machine gun fire from Thiepval.

Many casualties occurred and eventually late in the evening a retirement became inevitable. Our front trenches were now being manned from ELGIN AVENUE westward to the river ANCRE by the 16th Royal Irish Rifles (Pioneers). 5th West Yorkshire regiment and apparently some coy's, of one of the West Riding Regts men of the 10th Royal Inniskilling Fusiliers as they returned to our trenches were collected and sent back to their Assembly trenches. A party was sent to Paisley Dump to draw rations and another party to SPEYSIDE for water and the men were made as comfortable as circumstances permitted.

At 4pm on 2nd July the order was received to move the battalion back to Martinsart Wood and this was accomplished happily without further loss.

Of 22 officers and 742 other ranks who went into Thiepval wood on the 30th June 1916 – 10 officers and 336 other ranks returned to Martinsart Wood 2nd July 1916. In addition to the officers whose names have been already mentioned as casualties the following were wounded during the course of the fighting: Lieut's J. Douglas, McKenzie, and Gibson. The wounded and missing Officers included Lieut's McClure, Shannon and Kemp.

The hope that these officers be still alive is unfortunately very faint as is also in the case of Capt Robertson.

11th (Service) Battalion (Donegal and Fermanagh) Royal Inniskilling Fusiliers

THIEPVAL WOOD
"Z" Day. At 6.30am an intense bombardment commenced. At 10 minutes to Zero time the Battalion moved up in support of the 9th Rl Inniskilling Fusiliers.
At Zero time the Battalion went over the parapet, 'A' Company suffered severely

as they as they were getting out from Machine Gun Fire from THIEPVAL. The remaining companies on reaching the German wire came under Machine Gun Fire from the same direction.

As far as can be ascertained up to the present we have suffered severely, 7 Officers being reported wounded. Signallers and telephones were knocked out almost as soon as they crossed the parapet. 4 Scouts and 4 Runners were afterwards sent out at intervals to try and get in touch with the Battalion, 2 of these were returned wounded, the remainder were not able to pass the Barrage. Extra Signallers were sent out but did not return.

'D' Coy reached their objective (THE CRUCIFIX) and remain there, the remainder of the Battalion is distributed in "C" Line.

The above is a copy of Situation report forwarded to Bde H.Q. on the first at 9.25pm.

Total Casualties were estimated at 600.

Documents Attached to the War Diary

A report from Lieutenant Colonel George Howard Brush, Officer Commanding 11th (Service) Battalion (Donegal and Fermanagh) Royal Inniskilling Fusiliers, regarding operations from Tuesday, 27 June 1916, to 5 July 1916:

On the evening of the 27th June, the Battalion left FORCEVILLE and were billeted in MARTINSART for the night 27/28th June. As the Battalion entered the town, there was some shelling which continued during the night, but without casualties. Wednesday 28th June.

On the 28th June, the Battalion moved up to THIEPVAL WOOD and took over the Sector of trenches held by the 9th Batt. Royal Inniskilling Fusiliers. The relief was completed by 11.50pm. Despite heave [sic] shelling during this operation there were no casualties.

Thursday 29th June.

From 3 to 5am on the morning of the 29th June there was an intense bombardment by the enemy, his fire being chiefly directed against GORDON CASTLE, the assembly trenches below GORDON CASTLE and the approaches to THIEPVAL WOOD. During the day the enemy bombardment was intermittent with bursts of Machine Gun fire from THIEPVAL village.

Throughout this bombardment the Front line was held by three double sentry posts and two Lewis Guns with relief in the service trench; the supporting being in WHITCHURCH STREET. The remainder of the Battalion was distributed in forward assembly trenches. These dispositions in my mind casualties.

During the day the Battalion was employed in keeping communication trenches open, repairing ramps, and improving the assembly trenches to be occupied by the battalion.

During the night 29/30th June, the enemy continued bombarding heavily, particularly between the hours of 3am and 4.30am on 30th June.

Friday 30th June.

Work was continued on the 30th June, on the same lines as previous day. The enemy sent over a large number of Lachrymatory shells, principally around GORDON CASTLE and back assembly trenches.

During the afternoon of 30th June, I withdrew my Front line Company and placed them in their assembly trenches replacing them by my 4 sections of Bombers who were to go forward with the 9th Bn. Rl. Innis. Fusrs. The remainder of the Battalion were settled at intervals during the afternoon in their assembly trenches. All material required for the Advance was distributed amongst Platoons and arrangements for the Advance completed before dawn.

During the night 30th June/1st July, the 9th R.Innis.Fus. assembled in their forward assembly trenches and took over the Front line.

During the 29th and 30th June, my casualties were 4 Killed and 15 wounded.

Saturday 1st July.

At 7.20am on the 1st July the battalion left their assembly trenches and took over the trenches occupied by the 9th R. Innis. Fus.

At 7.30am the battalion moved over the parapet 'A' and 'D' Companies leading.

The leading companies were at once exposed to the heavy barrage which was on our front line and also searching machine gun fire from the direction of THIEPVAL village.

These companies and those following suffered severely and most of their officers and N.C.O's were knocked out before reaching the SUNKEN ROAD the Battalion pushed on to the enemy "A" Line and crossed it, led by Captain W.T. SEWEL who at this point was seen to fall whilst calling to his men to follow him. By this time only one officer, Lieut GALLAUGHER, was left and with the survivors passed on to "B" Line, some remaining there to assist in consolidating the CRUCIFIX whilst the remainder went forward under Company Sergeant Major BULLOCK to the "C" Line.

There was not a great deal of opposition encountered in entering the "B" Line, any Germans met with quickly threw up their hands.

Lieut. GALLAUGHER having barricaded the communication trenches leading to the CRUCIFIX, then started making fire steps to shoot from. He then returned to "A" Line to collect men and material. On his arrival at "A" Line he found part of it occupied by the Germans, so he arranged a bombing party and cleared the enemy out of the trenches towards his right erecting a barricade which he left in charge of a Lance Corporal and 6 men. From there he sent a message reporting the situation as he found it. This message miscarried but I believe was received by the 9th R. Innis. Fus. He then collected all the available men in "A" Trench and shell holes and took them forward to the CRUCIFIX. There were none of my battalion among them as they had evidently gone forward. Lieut GALLAUGHER from this onwards, in conjunction with Lieut. McKINLEY 9th R.Innis.Fus. worked under the orders of Major PEACOCK of the 9th R. Innis Fus. until they were forced to withdraw about 9.30pm.

The Signallers who went forward with the Battalion with telephones etc. were almost immediately knocked out and during the day I tried continually to get into touch with the battalion by runners, scouts and signallers but all were wounded except one.

During the afternoon there was some confusion owing to troops retiring from our left. This at one time appeared serious and our front line was not occupied, but owing to the energy of Captain MOORE, Lieut GORDON and R.S.M. G. BLEAKLEY of this battalion together with Captain MULHOLLAND of the 14th Rl. Irish Rifles, this situation was soon got in hand, these men being placed in the assembly trenches. The situation at this time was very difficult to understand and many German prisoners were mixed up with these men and many more Germans coming over the parapet. R.S.M. Bleakley at once organised a party and occupied our front line and things quickly resumed a normal aspect.

Lieut. GORDON and R.S.M. BLEAKLEY gave me very great assistance during the day. Both of these organised parties for ammunition and water and succeeded in getting water across to the enemy "A" Line. Lieut GORDON also arranged carrying parties for wounded and during the early morning of 2nd July, with the assistance of C.Q.M. Sgt. T. Johnston brought up rations for the battalion to the assembly trenches.

Capt. MOORE and R.S.M. BLEAKLEY were invaluable in controlling the traffic in the ELGIN AVENUE, the control system having completely broken down. This Officer and Warrant Officer stood on the parapet for hours making the supporting battalions coming up get out of this trench into the open to clear the way for the continuous stream of wounded who were being carried down.

Lieut. KNIGHT, the Battalion Bombing Officer also rendered much assistance regulating the supply of bombs and clearing the communication trenches.

Privates Hunter and Smith, Headquarters Orderlies were invaluable and never failed in delivering their messages.

I wish to specially bring to notice the devotion to duty and the excellent work done by Capt. D.E. CROSBIE, R.A.M.C. under very trying circumstances. He was 5 days and 5 nights continuously at work in the Advanced Aid Post in ELGIN AV., and during this time organised several parties and went up to the front line trenches, searched there for wounded men which he brought back. About 1000 cases were dealt with at this Aid Post and each wounded man when dressed was given cocoa or soup and cigarettes. I wish also to mention the work done by the Stretcher Bearers under Capt. Crosbie.

Lieut & Qr. Mr. J. Firth never failed us in sending up supplies of food and water as the water supply in ELGIN AVENUE had failed, the tank having been hit by a shell.

I should also like to mention Lieut. McCorkell Transport Officer and Corporal Warren, Transport Corporal, for the work done by them.

The Orderly Room Staff, consisting of Sergt. Beaty, Corpl. McDougall and L.Cpl. F. Kee did excellent work.

On the night of 3rd/4th July, a party consisting of Capt. W.M. Moore, Lieut. H. Gallaugher and 20 Other ranks, volunteered to proceed to THIEPVAL WOOD and rescue wounded men from NO MAN's LAND. This party after a successful search returned safely, having rescued 28 wounded men.

On the night 4/5th a small party under Capt. CROSBIE R.A.M.C. and Lieut G.M.F. IRVINE and 4 Other Ranks went to THIEPVAL WOOD for the same purpose but were unable to leave the front line as an attack by our troops was imminent.

In conclusion I wish to draw your attention to the gallantry and devotion to duty of all Officers, N.C.O's and men in the Battalion under my Command during a very trying time.

This Battalion has been in the Line now for nearly 6 months and when not actually holding the front line have been supplying working parties, and even this did not seem to damp their ardour.

Report by Captain D.E. Crosbie RAMC, Medical Officer 11th (Service) Battalion (Donegal and Fermanagh) Royal Inniskilling Fusiliers. Dated 6 July 1916:

I took over the Regimental Aid Post at ROSS STREET and ELGIN AVENUE in THIEPVAL WOOD in conjunction with Lieut. GAVIN of the 14th R.I.R. and Capt. PICKEN of 10th R. INNIS. FUS. on the night of 28th June.

Nothing eventful happened until the night of 30th June, when we passed nearly 100 wounded through our hands.

My stretcher Bearers remained with their Companies until the attack started when I gave them orders to collect any wounded they could find belonging to any unit and bring them to the nearest dressing station. This was carried out and the Stretcher Bearers working continually night and day we were relieved, bringing wounded back from the SUNKEN ROAD, No Man's Land and the Wood, under continual shell and machine gun fire.

We located many wounded men in dug-outs and holes in the front line which our Stretcher Bearers carried in. The difficulty in keeping the post clear of wounded was our great trouble as there seemed a great want of both R.A.M.C. Stretcher Bearers and Stretchers, so that on several occasions we had to resort to using the Regimental Stretcher Bearers to evacuate wounded to the collecting post which was great hardship to them. All wounded got hot cocoa or soup and cigarettes when they were dressed, for which they were very grateful.

I wish specially to mention the gallant work done by L. Corpl COOPER, Pte. MEGAGHY, Pte. TOLAND, Pte. BROWNE, Pte. ELLIOTT of 'A' Coy, and Pte. WILSON of 'C' Coy, Pte. ROBB of 'B' Coy and Pte. FENWICK, 'D' Coy.

These men worked continually, Corporal Cooper remaining in the trenches eight hours after the battalion was relieved to bring in a wounded man from the Front Line Trench.

The great assistance given by Lieut. Gavin, 14th Rl. Ir. Rifles made it possible to cope with the enormous number of cases which were dealt with. He went on several occasions to the dug-outs in the front line and located many wounded, and although his feet and ankles were swollen with the continual standing, still continued his work.

Captain PICKEN also worked with splendid pluck and devotion.

The Orderlies and men of 14th R.I.R. and 10th R. In. F. in conjunction with my men gave very great assistance.

At one period the conjection [sic] the Aid Post became so great that I sent up to Colonel BRUSH to ask for assistance to evacuate wounded. He sent 2nd Liut. HANNA who collected a number of men and gave me valuable assistance in clearing the Communication Trenches.

Special Order of the Day issued by Lieutenant-General Sir T.L.N. Morland KCB, DSO, on 3 July 1916:

On the withdrawal of the 36th Ulster Division into reserve after the desparate [sic] fighting of the last few days, the G.O.C. Xth Corps wishes to express to the G.O.C. and all ranks his admiration of the dash and gallantry with which the attack was carried out which attained a large measure of success under unfavourable conditions.

He regrets the heavy and inevitable losses sustained and feels sure that, after a period of rest, the Division will be ready to respond to any call made upon it.

Special Order of the Day issued by Major-General O.S.W. Nugent DSO, Commanding 36th (Ulster) Division, 3 July 1916:

The General Officer Commanding the Ulster Division desires that the Division should know that, in his opinion, nothing finer has been done in the War than the attack by the Ulster Division on the 1st July.

The leading of the Company Officers, the discipline and courage shown by all Ranks of the Division will stand out in the future history of the war as an example of what good troops, well led, are capable of accomplishing.

None but troops of the best quality could face the fire that was brought to bear upon them and the losses suffered during the advance.

Nothing could have been finer than the steadiness and discipline shown by every Battalion, not only in forming up outside its own trenches but in advancing under severe enfilading fire.

The advance across the open to the German line was carried out with the steadiness of a parade movement, under a fire both from front and flanks which could only have been faced by troops of the highest quality.

The fact that the objects of the attack on one side were not obtained is no reflection on the Battalions which were entrusted with the task.

They did all that man could do and in common with every Battalion in the Division showed most conspicuous courage and devotion.

On the other side, the Division carried out every portion of its allotted task in spite of the heaviest losses.

It captured nearly 600 prisoners and carried its advance triumphantly to the limits of the objective laid down.

There is nothing in the operations carried out by the Ulster Division on the 1st July that will not be a source of pride to all Ulstermen.

The Division has been highly tried and has emerged from the ordeal with unstained honour, having fulfilled in every particular, the great expectations formed of it.

Tales of individual and collective heroism on the part of the Officers and Men come in from every side, too numerous to mention, but all showing that the standard of gallantry and devotion attained is one that may be equalled, but is never likely to be surpassed.

The General Officer Commanding deeply regrets the heavy losses of Officers and Men. He is proud beyond description, as every Officer and Man in the Division may well be, of the magnificent example of sublime courage and discipline which the Ulster Division has given to the Army.

Ulster has every reason to be proud of the men she has given to the service of our country.

Though many of our best men have gone the spirit which animated them remains in the Division and will never die.

Order of the Day issued by Brigadier General R.G. Shutter DSO, 109th (Ulster) Brigade, 3 July 1916:

The Brigadier General Commanding wishes to express his warm congratulations and high appreciation to all ranks of the Brigade on their gallant bearing and conduct during the great attack on the 1st July.

The advance of the Brigade was so dashing, so resolute and determined that it was entirely irresistible [*sic*] and carried all before it, chasing the enemy in all directions and taking approximately 400 prisoners.

Each Battalion of the Brigade as was anticipated by all those who knew the grit and sterling qualities of the men of the Ulster Division vied with each other in deeds of personal gallantry and bravery, and the Brigade carried out to the letter the task which was entrusted to it of taking the "C" Line. In so doing the Brigade covered itself with undying fame and glory and its dashing determined advance and behaviour will undoubtedly go down to history as its share of the work of the great Ulster Division of Irish men.

Unfortunately we have sustained grevious [*sic*] casualties but the Brigadier General hopes that when the ranks are presently filled with drafts, that wherever these may come from, the survivors of the original Brigade will do their utmost to instil their own magnificent fighting spirit into the new arrivals, as by doing this they will be offering the most fitting tribute to their gallant dead comrades and friends who have fallen in honour on the Field of Battle, and who have left behind them such a splendid fighting record for those who come after them to live up to and emulate.

Letter sent from City Hall, Belfast, on 20 July 1916. Forwarded to battalion by Captain Ken M. Moore, Staff Captain 109th Infantry Brigade on 31 July 1916.

CITY HALL,
BELFAST, 20th July 1916.

Sir, I have the honour to transmit herewith the enclosed Copy of Resolutions, which were unanimously passed by the Belfast City Council at their Meeting on the 19th inst,
I have the honour to remain, Sir, Your obedient Servant,
[*Signed*] R. MEYER, Town Clerk.

Moved by THE LORD MAYOR,
Seconded by ALDERMAN DORAN, and unanimously
Resolved –"That we, the Lord Mayor, Aldermen, and Citizens of Belfast, acting by the Council, do hereby esteem it our honour and privilege to convey to the Officers, Non-Commissioned Officers and Men of the Ulster Division of his Majesty's Army our high admiration of their magnificent conduct in the successful attack on the German Lines in France, which began on Saturday, 1st July, when they were put to the supreme test, with the result known to the world –Vix., that they covered themselves with glory, the Officers leading their men with a gallantry to which justice cannot be done, and the men vieing with their Officers in deeds of heroism. The citizens reverently pay homage to the heroic dead – young men in the prime of manhood"who have laid down their lives and resigned the bright hopes of youth, and love, and ambition, to save their country from the fate of Belgium, Serbia, and Poland". To those who have been bereaved by the loss of their dear ones this Council tenders its most respectful and deepest sympathy, and prays that God will wipe away their tears and give them consolation. To the wounded the Council send their congratulations on their escape from death, and hopes for their speedy and complete recovery. To the Ulster Division and all sons of Ulster in his Majesty's armies this Council sends greeting and encouragement

to uphold and strengthen the reputation they have already made on the battlefields of France and Flanders.

Moved by Councillor WHITE,

Seconded by Councillor WORKMAN, and unanimously

Resolved –"That those of us at home, keeping before us as an example the self-sacrifice of our gallant soldiers and sailors, should do all in our power by increased devotion and sacrifice on our part to carry the War to a successful issue, and so bring it to pass that our noble dead should not have died in vain".

9th Royal Innis. Fus.

10th Royal Innis. Fus.

11th Royal Innis. Fus.

14th Royal Irish Rifles.

109th Machine Gun Coy.

109th Light Trench Mortar Batty.

For information and transmission to all concerned.

8th (Service) Battalion (East Belfast) Royal Irish Rifles

At dawn Stores and Bombs were issued to Companies, we were shelled intermittently but suffered no casualties.

5am.   Batt marched from AVELUY WOOD to a position at Speyside, THIEPVAL WOOD and remained there during the intensive bombardment which lasted 1½ hours. The Batt behaved remarkably well during the bombardment. Our casualties while at Speyside were 8 killed and 15 wounded.

7.30am.   Batt marched from Speyside to ELGIN AVENUE, and up the side to NO MAN'S LAND, picking up R.E. Stores en route at GORDON CASTLE, THIEPVAL WOOD.

Deployed in NO MAN'S LAND and advanced in rear of 9th R. I. Rifles, while marching along Speyside a group of German prisoners were marched past us, this made the men more enthusiastic than ever, if that were possible.

9.40am.   German 'B' Line was reached (Reference 10th Corps, special map.) and numerous prisoners captured. Direction was lost and the Battalion found itself too far to the left. This was corrected during next advance.

10.10am. Reached 'C' Line and moved straight on and laid down between 'C' and 'D' Lines.

11.0am.   Entered 'D' Line trenches, the barrage having lifted. Heavy casualties occurred during the advance from 'C' to 'D' Line owing to enfilade Machine Gun fire from BEAUCOURT REDOUBT and Machine Gun and Rifle fire almost in reverse from THIEPVAL. 'D' Line was entered at point D.9.

11.8am.   Barrage shortened and made 'D' Line untenable. Battalion therefore returned to between 'D' and 'C' Lines. As many of our shells were falling short, the battalion retired to 'C' Line and took up the line C.9. C.10. and C.11. Capt J.D.M. McCallum reconnoitred the S.E. face of SCHWABEN REDOUBT, and found some of the 9th R. I. Rifles at B.14. under Major Gaffiken. He then worked to the right and found Lieut Sanderson and 2 Machine Guns of 107th Bde Machine Gun Coy at 68. He sent Lieut Sanderson to reconnoitre towards THIEPVAL. Lieut Sanderson worked down trench running from R.20.c.8.2. to R.26.a.2.3., and at the latter point encountered the enemy, and ascertained that THIEPVAL was in their hands. He then returned and reported to Captain McCallum.

12.6pm.   Trenches from midway between C.11. and C.10., the S.E. face of SCHWABEN REDOUBT, from C.10. nearly to B.14., and also the trench running N.E. from C.9. along the THIEPVAL-GRANDCOURT ROAD were heavily shelled by heavy guns from the N.E. and rendered untenable.

Heavy casualties occurred and the Battalion was withdrawn to the line B.14-B.13-B.15 with the exception of a party that remained holding C.11.

12.30pm.   Garrison of C.8. and trench between C.8 and B.14 withdrawn to the triangle B.13. B.14. B15. by order of Major Gaffiken.

Capt McCallum then finding the men too thick in this triangle withdrew the men of the 8th R. I. Rifles to the N.W. face of SCHWABEN REDOUBT, and consolidated the line between B.18 and C.11.

1.55pm.   Capt McCallum found that there was a shortage of bombs and sent to ask for a fresh supply.

3.30pm.   Enemy (about half Battalion) emerged from trees in R.13.b.8.8. and advanced against C.11. Our artillery however got on to them and practically wiped them out.

3.50pm.   Enemy made three bombing attacks.

(1) Along trench running along GRANDCOURT-THIEPVAL ROAD from D.10. which was driven off on reaching R.20.b.27.

(2) From C.12. to C.11. which was driven back by L/Cpl T.J. Allen 8th Bn. R. I. Rifles who bombed them right back to C.12. single-handed. He was killed about 10 minutes after his return to C.11.

(3) From trench running from R.14.c.45. to R.20.a.5.9. (this trench runs from there to B.15., although not shown on the map.)

This attack worked along as far as R.19.d.6.7. when it came in contact with a blocking party of ours. But the enemy outranged our men with his handle bombs and things were looking bad, when Lieut Sanderson 107th Bde M.G. Coy, collected 8 or 9 men at B.18. and charged across the open.

Lieut Sanderson was killed. 2nd Lieut Brown 8th Bn R. I. Rifles also took a party from R.19.b.6.1. and bombed the trench where enemy bombers were, and no more annoyance was caused. 2nd Lieut Brown was wounded.

4.45pm.   Two more bombing attacks were made by the enemy against C.11. from C.12. both of which were driven off.

About this time our guns opened fire on the trenches near C.11 and it was noticed that some troops in the 'B' line were displaying their yellow flags. Our contact aeroplane came over very low and our yellow flags were shown and flares burst, and soon the shelling ceased.

7.15pm.   Enemy's heavy guns heavily bombarded the triangle B.13-B.14-B.15 for an hour.

8.30pm.   Capt McCallum and Sgt Lowry went to investigate and worked along from B.17.-B.15.-B.13-B.14. to B.16. and found trenches unoccupied.

An enemy bombing attack was heard near C.9. so Capt McCallum and Sgt Lowry returned to B.17.

He found none in the 'B' line and as his party at C.11. was dangerously isolated he withdrew them and established himself in the line A.14. A.16. A.17.,where they found a party of between 20 and 30 men under Lieut Stewart (107th Bde M.G. Coy) Here the Battalion reorganised, a blocking party put out to the left, and a patrol sent out to reconnoitre to the right. The patrol returned after half an hour, and reported having found no men of either side for a considerable distance.

10pm.   Several enemy bombing attacks were launched from the neighbourhood of the CRUCIFIX and a strong one from THIEPVAL which came in contact with our blocking party at A.14.

We only had about 12 bombs left, but these sufficed to drive off this attack.

10.20pm.   Another bombing attack came from THIEPVAL working up both 'A' front and support lines.

Having no bombs and very little ammunition left our men withdrew to the 'A' front line, south of A.14 to A.15. to avoid being cut off.

Here 100 men of the W.Yorks were found, who had ammunition but no bombs and no water.

10.45pm.   For the next half hour or so about 100 men came in, in twos and threes from various points, who were collected and reorganised.

11.15pm.   Strong parties of enemy were found to be collecting near the CRUCIFIX and B.17. so 3 red flares were fired for artillery support but without result.

11.30pm.   Several bombing patrols approached which were driven off with rifle fire.

11.45pm.   Having practically no ammunition left it was decided to withdraw to our lines and the men were divided up into six parties which were led independently across our lines.

9th (Service) Battalion (West Belfast) Royal Irish Rifles

THIEPVAL WOOD 'A' 'B' 'C' & 'D' lines.

Battalion moved off from AVELUY WOOD in Column of Route at 5.30am and moved into Speyside about 6am and waited on Speyside Bank until 7.30am. From here please read narrative attached.

From 10.30pm to 7am the remnants of Battalion were resting and holding FRONT LINE THIEPVAL WOOD. Rations were brought up during the night to PAISLEY DUMP by Capt J.C. Douglas Batt T.O. Lt J.A. McConnell was acting as Bde T.O. Lt Stealy drew rations for the Batt from Paisley Dump.

Document Attached to the War Diary

A narrative on the actions of the battalion on 1 July 1916. Dated 7 July 1916, the report is signed by Lieutenant Colonel S.W. Blacker, Commanding 9th (Service) Battalion (West Belfast) Royal Irish Rifles:

7.30am.   The Battalion moved off from SPEYSIDE in column of route, the locality had proved a well chosen one.

A check occurred on the way up owing to the bridges allocated to the Battalion being used by other troops, across SANDY ROW and ELGIN. The bridges over slits and fire trench were intact having been repaired just previous to the Battalion advance by 2/Lieut. Haigh and the Battalion pioneers.

7.45am.   Scouts reported rear Battalions 109th. Brigade moving off.

8.0am.   Whole Battalion in position for advance lying down east of sunken road in line of close column of platoons in fours.

About half a Company 15th. Royal Irish Rifles and Captain Tate crossed into NO MAN'S LAND by our bridge; after crossing Sunken Road they moved half left to clear the Battalion.

8.5am.   Noticed 10th. Royal Irish Rifles formed up for advance but could not see or hear of Colonel Bernard, who was to give pre-arranged signal for the joint advance of both Battalions.

Gave order for whole line to advance.

A good number of prisoners coming in across NO MAN'S LAND unarmed with hands up, these were chased down the ride alongside ELGIN AVENUE.

Immediately on passing GORDON CASTLE R.E. stores were picked up by rear platoons.

On reaching WHITCHURCH STREET it was obvious that THIEPVAL VILLAGE was still occupied, machine gun fire was being brought to bear from this locality and trench mortars were at work from the same place but were not reaching our column.

Captain Byrne, 2/Lieuts. Pomeroy, Jackson and McKee and two Company Sergeant Majors became casualties near the Sunken Road, about 40 men were also hit in NO MANS LAND.

8.10am. Proceeded to Battle Hd.Qrs. with Adjutant.

8.50am. Received a report from O.C. Left Company that [word(s) missing] passed 'B' line and that he was mixed up with lost [word(s) missing] (11th. Royal Irish Rifles).

9.2am. Left Centre Company reported arrival at 'C' line [word(s) missing] mixed with 11th. Royal Irish Rifles at 8.23am.

9.15am. Scouts reported machine guns from THIEPVAL causing considerable casualties.

Communication with Companies by cable not being established linesmen went out to repair line where possible; cable communication was never established with Companies owing to lines being cut, 7 linesmen were killed or wounded in endeavouring to repair the line.

9.50am. Right Company arrived at 'C' line. The runner stated trenches much knocked about and advised that runners sent to Companies should go by way of A.16 and A.17 to B.17 to avoid enfilade fire from THIEPVAL.

10am. The battalion in the open between 'C' and 'D' lines, machine guns in action also Lewis guns, Companies re-organising preparatory to advance on 'D' line.

When barrage lifted unto 'D' the two platoons as arranged went forward but it was difficult to keep the remainder of the Battalion back. Captains Berry and Sinclair were hit at about this time.

The loads of wire etc. had to a great extent been destroyed by this time but the Lewis gun magazines were carried forward.

Major Gaffikin reported that the wire to his front at 'D' line was sufficiently cut to allow the passage of troops but the wire in front of the Right Company was reported not so well cut.

About 35 men got into 'D' line from the two Right Companies; they found 'D' line strongly held and a great number of them became casualties through hand grenades. The trench had evidently also been held by Machine Guns and these had been moved to the flanks.

10.20am. The left of the Battalion went back and started to consolidate B14 – B16 – C9. On the right of the Battalion Lieut. Saunderson, Brigade Machine Gun Company, and late of this Battalion, was in action in the open, taking advantage of shell holes, the Lewis guns were also in action. The Stokes guns were not in action. A catapult carried up by the Right Company was doing good work outside the Divisional area down the trench running from C6 to 'D' line.

10.40am. A portion of the Right Company was still in 'D' line under Corporal Shortt, 'A' Company, he was subsequently killed.

2/Lieut. Gould and 2/Lieut. Morton who were in charge of the amonal torpedoes were hit in front of 'D' line and had to be left there.

10.50am. A message was received at Battle Hd.Qrs. from Major Gaffikin asking that any spare Lewis gun magazines might be sent up, Lieut. Garner sent 5 buckets of magazines up and proceeded to B line with a small party to search for discarded magazines and incidently to look for a suitable Battalion Hd.Qrs. and Signallers dug-out.

Sergeant Moore (Signalling Sergeant) proceeded to CRUCIFIX and endeavoured to establish visual communication with Brigade O.P., but was unable to do so owing to Machine Gun fire, he reported one gun in action close to the CRUCIFIX but concealed.

At this time trench mortar activity became very general from THIEPVAL and the enemy shelled our own front line considerably with heavies.

10.55am. A belated message received at Battle Hd.Qrs. from Left Company (Captain Berry) saying that he was badly enfiladed by machine gun fire from between D.10 and D.11 and could not get on and that he proposed to dig in where he was, half way between 'C' and 'D' lines.

11am. A runner brought in a message from Major Gaffikin saying that our front line was badly enfiladed from direction of BEAUCOURT on the left side and from THIEPVAL on the right.

12Noon. Information not having come through from the front, two Intelligence Scouts were sent out to report on the situation but these men never returned.

12.30pm. Right Company and men from several Battalions retired to line C6 – C7 – C8 – B14, this line was consolidated so as to form a defensive flank.

The line B16 – B14 – B13 and 100 yards south of the CRUCIFIX was at this time being consolidated by mixed troops under Major Gaffikin, Major Peacock, 9th. Inniskilling Fusiliers, was also in the vicinity. Left Company had not dug in between 'C' and 'D' line but at this time had taken up a position between C9 and B16 (inclusive). This position proved to be a very bad one as the field of fire towards 'D' line was interrupted by large mounds of excavated earth thrown up from the trench and on the East side of it; it was also badly enfiladed from D10 – D11 by machine gun fire.

12.50pm. Major Gaffikin sent for Captain Montgomery and they jointly surveyed the line in process of consolidation; they also inspected the line B14 – B15 – B17 – B 18 and 200 yards North towards C11.

The line C11 – C12 was found to be in process of consolidation by our troops.

It became apparent that THIEPVAL, not having been taken was the crux of the situation; a report to this effect was received at Battalion Hd.Qrs. by a runner.

1.30pm. Runner arrived from Major Gaffikin asking for grenades and S.A.A.; these were sent up to B17.

1.45pm. A runner was despatched to Battalion Hd.Qrs. by Major Gaffikin stating that his Right flank was in the air and that his Left flank almost so but this runner was wounded and delivered the message late at night.

2pm. The two remaining Company Commanders (Major Gaffikin and Captain Montgomery) came to the conclusion that the best thing to do was to give orders to hang on to what they had got and to send back for a large supply of grenades and S.A.A.

The chief difficulty at this period and onwards was that runners could not get through, telephonic communication was cut and visual communication was impossible.

2.45pm. The first signs of enemy advancing in small bodies at wide intervals observed. Two men were seen to jump into a trench and immediately afterwards wave a white rectangular board, white on the enemy side and of a neutral tint facing us which they then planted on the parados. This suspicious movement was reported by three different runners to Battalion Hd.Qrs. but none of the messages got through.

3.15pm. A patrol under 2/Lieut. Campbell previously detailed by Captain Montgomery to reconnoitre down the trench to B12, returned, and reported having got almost to B12 from which place the Germans were seen firing on the firestep towards THIEPVAL WOOD; rapid fire was opened on these men and this had the effect of causing some confusion and consternation as the burst of fire was one of surprise.

3.45pm. Some sand bags were observed being thrown up by the enemy at B16; very heavy bombing had been heard from this direction just previous to this; it was evident that they were endeavouring to make a barricade. Fire was immediately opened on this point by our sentries at barricade at B14. This was the beginning of a German bombing counter-attack, well planed and standing out as an example of what can be done in the attack by mutual support.

4pm. At a point 70 yards east of B14 we had established a blocking post in the line B14 – C9; this point was forced, mainly due to the Germans out-throwing our men with hand grenades.

It is important to remember that a block of 50 yards at least is required to stop enemy bombing parties armed with handle grenades and it appears that our bombers were out- ranged, possibly owing to many of the men throwing their grenades instead of bowling them, they thus got easily tired.

At this juncture a catapult did good work and demonstrated the usefulness of this weapon; without which no Company should be without as a portion of its equipment and I am sure if the men are taught to look after the catapult in the same way as they look upon their Lewis gun great good would come of it.

During this period and onwards the Lewis guns and gun teams came into their own and proved that they are a most useful weapon in attack as well as defence, especially in trench fighting of this description.

Whatever the men dropped they hung on to their magazines. Magazines were refilled in both 'A' and 'B' lines under arrangements which had been made by Captain Montgomery.

4.15pm.   To return to the actual trench fighting, the enemy was prevented from adding to his barricade at B16, for some time owing to the action of Lewis gun team but subsequently this Lewis gun was knocked out, and the barricade was re-built very cleverly a little further away by throwing the bags round a corner. Immediately this was seen 2/Lieu. Smeeth was sent with 4 men over our barricade at B14 with orders to go up the trench and bomb the enemy away from their sand bags and hold the corner; a small party being told off to support him.

This party went forward most gallantly and got about half way down the trench when they were themselves bombed most unexpectedly either from a dugout or recess, or some such place. 2/Lieut. Smeeth and one man were wounded but brought in and the whole re-crossed our barricade.

4.30pm.   The enemy now started a long burst of machine gun fire from B16 down the trench to B14 and drilled a hole through our sandbags killing a Lewis gunner and destroying the loophole. This long burst of fire appears to have been the signal for a determined bombing attack from the North, South and East, the whole converging into B.14.

It was at this period that news came to hand that about 15 minutes previous Lieut. Saunderson, 107th Brigade Machine Gun Company, and his party had been wiped out, fighting hard to the end at C.7. He had previously, with a very few men, reconnoitred down MOUQUET SWITCH to a point between C.4. and C.2. which he reported clear as far as he got.

At this period 2/Lieut. Harding, Battalion Intelligence Officer, had proceeded alone to the front line to make a personal reconnaissance as news was not coming in either often or quick enough and it was impossible at this time to tell in any way accurately at Battalion Hd.Qrs. what was going on.

2/Lieut. Harding returned about 4.15p.m and said that German bombing attacks were going on, that he had seen Major Gaffikin and Captain Montgomery but that, providing the supply of hand grenades was kept up, the situation should not become critical, but he pointed out that machine gun fire from THIEPVAL had made the position which was being held by the Battalion an impossible one; he proceeded to Brigade Hd.Qrs. to personally report.

Lieut. Finlay, Battalion Bombing Officer, at this stage collected odd men together and sent them up to 'B' line by the less exposed route, though somewhat longer, under command of Sergeant Cully, the provost sergeant, who was the most dependable N.C.O. I could put my hand on at the time; shortly after this Lieut. Finlay was himself wounded by shrapnel. These grenades were dumped at B.17.and Sergeant [*illegible*] Cully reported afterwards.

The buried cable to Brigade Hd.Qrs. was cut but I was in hopes that the report which 2/Lieut. Harding would be able to give would elucidate the situation better than I could ever write second hand.

4.45pm.	B.14. was forced after fierce fighting; this post was held by 10 men of 'A' Company but none returned.
6pm.	No news was coming through from the front, so 15 men belonging to the Battalion and Stokes Battery were sent up under Rifleman Martin (C.O's Orderly) each man carrying 10 bandoliers of S.A.A. but for some unknown reason they were turned off their objective by a Major of another Corps.
6.30pm.	Trench Mortars were very active from THIEPVAL at this period and the front line trench was also shelled, I surmised that the enemy were preventing the arrival of reinforcements.

2/Lieut. Harding returned from Brigade Hd.Qrs. and informed me that two Companies, 4th Battalion West Yorkshire Regiment, were on their way up to reinforce the front line; but I had previously been informed by Brigade that reinforcements were coming up and this information had been sent on to the senior officer present in the firing line, by three different runners, but as a matter of fact Captain Montgomery did not receive this message till 9p.m.

7pm.	2/Lieut. Harding again went up to the firing line with orders to intercept the two Companies 4th. West Yorks and guide them to the best place. Captain Montgomery states that he never saw these men but 2/Lieut. Harding actually put them into 'B' line, it is quite possible however that they may have been missed but they undoubtedly were fighting.
9.40pm.	2/Lieut. Harding returned at 9.40pm and although he stated that heavy grenade fighting was in progress he did not convey the impression that the men were in any way at their last gasp, but however he emphasised the importance of sending up water and ammunition to 'B' line as soon as possible and for this purpose Lieut. Garner organised a carrying party of 20 men which he took charge of himself and conducted to 'B' line by

the less exposed way; as the water had to be got from SPEYSIDE it never got further than 'A' line but 10,000 rounds got to B.17.

2/Lieut. Harding brought back word that Major Gaffikin had been hit and that Captain Montgomery was in command

At this time 2/Lieut. Harding turned in to have a sleep having arranged to guide me up to 'B' line after dark.

At about this time four reinforcing columns of Germans were seen by Captain Montgomery from B.15. advancing from the direction of FARM DU MOUQUET, Lewis guns were turned on them and they scattered and loss was inflicted thereby.

The German bombing parties were now converging steadily on to B.15. and the men were very much fatigued, so much so in fact that in many instances they were unable to do anything.

At B.15. 2/Lieut. Campbell was hit by a hand grenade where he died.

Reinforcement Officers were sent up to the senior officer present at the front and of these 2/Lieut. Richardson was killed in 'B' line and Lieut. Hone, who had taken a small party to endeavour to bomb from B.15 to B.14. has not been since seen.

9.45pm. Somebody on the left shouted at this time "They are on us from the left" and the men remaining in 'B' line got into 'A' line. Major Peacock, 9th. Inniskilling Fusiliers, and Captain Montgomery of the Battalion under my command, were at the time consulting together, the former shouted to the latter pointing to the right "Try and rally those men there"; Captain Montgomery did succeed in rallying a few remnants but the men were absolutely done and had they stayed there would have been useless for defence so they returned to our lines.

Captain Montgomery reported to me at 10.30pm in a state of collapse, I sent him on down to Brigade and he was evacuated, the wound on his head was not so serious as at first thought, his life being undoubtedly saved by his steel helmet, he was labelled for England, but rallying, prevailed on the Medical Officer to allow him to return to the Battalion where he arrived on the night of the 3rd. July.

10.30pm. Nothing now remained to be done save to organise the defence of our own fire trench which was done.

10th (Service) Battalion (South Belfast) Royal Irish Rifles

SPEYSIDE THIEPVAL WOOD.

6am. Battalion formed up prior to moving up for the attack

6.53am. Battalion moved off; coming under machine gun fire from THIEPVAL VILLAGE a few minutes late.

ROSS CASTLE.

7.10am.   The Commanding Officer Colonel H.C. BERNARD was killed by a shell. The Battalion continued to advance though suffering heavily from shell and machine gun fire, the ground being much cut up and difficult to cross.

7.45am.   The Battalion went over our front line trenches and forward up in NO MAN'S LAND in artillery formation in support of 109th Inf. Bde. By this time many of the officers and senior N.C.O's had been hit. Up to this point Captain J.E. SUGDEN (Adjutant) had commanded the Battalion. At 10.30am MAJOR W.R. GOODWIN assumed command of the Battalion.

8.0am.   The Battalion commenced to advance to the attack over the open ground under heavy enfilade fire (machine gun) from THIEPVAL VILLAGE.

12.30pm. The Battalion reached German support line. After this the Battalion became mixed up with other units & as most of the officers & N.C.O's were killed very few reports were sent in.

5.30pm.   'D' Company reported to be in German 1st line and sent for more ammunition.

8.35pm.   MAJOR PEACOCK 9th R. Inniskilling Fusiliers took command of the remainder of the Battalion at the CRUCIFIX.

11.15pm. LIEUT BENNETT the only surviving officer of the Battalion reported that the Division had retired into THIEPVAL WOOD.

11th (Service) Battalion (South Antrim) Royal Irish Rifles

THIEPVAL WOOD

7.15am.   Battn left assembly trenches to take up its position in line of Deployment for attack. From assembly trenches to no mans land there was very heavy shelling shrapnel & H.E. & one platoon each of 'B' and 'D' Companies were practically annihilated four men only of the 'B' platoon and 3 in 'D' remaining. Captain O.B. Webb commanding 'D' Company was wounded at this period in the stomach and subsequently died.

7.28am.   Battn formed up in no mans land deployed for attack.

7.30am.   Advance began.

7.32am.   First wave of 'A' and 'B' Coy struck German front line trench & passed it without many casualties.

7.35am.   Advance continued & 'A' line taken. There was no organised resistance one or two Germans only seen shooting. Clearing up parties were left to bomb dugouts, where all the Germans were found & many taken prisoner.

7.48am.	Advanced to within 50 paces of German 2nd line & awaited left of our barrage.
7.50am.	German 2nd line captured without much opposition & few casualties. Bombing parties left to clear out any remaining enemy. At this time connection was established with The 10th Innis. Fus. but nothing was seen of The 13th R. IR. Rif. on our left either at this or any other time during the battle & in consequence or left flank was always unprotected.
8.am.	Report received at Battn H.Q. in THIEPVAL WOOD from Major Jenkins at 8.15am stating that 'B' line was occupied & the strong point of CLONES was being consolidated.
	Also from Captain Coling [*name unclear*] who was commanding the left Co in the attack.
8.5am.	Advance continued to German third line but owing to the impetuosity of the attack some of our men were caught in our own barrage & had to retire about 100yds to wait until it had lifted.
8.18am.	Another advance & our barrage was once again encountered. The officers present decided not to attempt a further advance until the barrage of our guns had lifted from its line to German 3rd line.
8.46am.	At this hour the advance was again started & the German third line was occupied. The attack had progressed so far without organised opposition & few casualties once out in the open, but from now on heavy machine gun & shell fire was opened from both flanks & was continuous throughout the day.
9.30am.	Reports from Major Jenkins & Capt. Craig by runner received at H.Q. at 10am stating that their Companies had occupied & were consolidating the German 3rd line where suitable the immediate vicinity of OMAGH proving unsuitable. No other consolidation was attempted as carrying platoons had ceased to exist & material was scarce. Much work was however done with the entrenching tool.
	There were sent Vickers and Lewis guns supporting the attack two vickers firing down a communication trench from the 2nd to 3rd German lines & the Lewis guns in the flanks.
	As units had become intermingled at this juncture our men were ordered by Major Jenkins to move to the left & those of 109th Bn. to the right.
11am.	Units of 107th Bde attacked 'D' line but were driven back owing to no support on either flank.
11.30am to 2pm.	A period of quiet now ensued & consolidation was proceeded with. First period of heavy shelling by enemy occurs.
3.30pm.	Counter attack developed by enemy on our front and left extending down to R. ANCRE. Enemy moved in extended order at about 2 paces

interval. This attack was dispersed by our artillery & machine guns but undoubtedly small bombing parties got into communication trenches as enemy bombing attacks became frequent from this time onwards.

4.30pm to 5pm. By our repulse of the afore mentioned attack our positions were revealed to the enemy & heavy continuous shelling resulted causing a gradual retirement to the second or 'B' line

We had been fighting now for 10 hours, there was no water & the men were becoming exhausted.

7.30pm. The second line which had been consolidated by the 15th R.I R. Rif. was held up to 9.45pm when the remnant of its defenders were shelled out.

8.30pm. An enemy counter attack was made on the second line from the right or THIEPVAL direction. It was repulsed, but bombing attacks continued from that flank.

10.30pm. During this period a gradual retirement was made to the first line where some troops of the 49th Div were found in possession.

11.45pm. A retirement was made to our own lines the troops being utterly exhausted.

12th (Service) Battalion (Central Antrim) Royal Irish Rifles

HAMEL SUB-SECTOR
Full account of attack attached.

Document Attached to the War Diary

A short account of the attack by the 12th (Service) Battalion (Central Antrim) Royal Irish Rifles on 1 July 1916. Written by Lieutenant Colonel G. Bull, Commanding 12th (Service) Battalion (Central Antrim) Royal Irish Rifles:

The bombardment, which had lasted seven days without ceasing reached its climax at 6.25a.m. on the morning of the 1st July, and from 6.25am until 7.30am the German trenches were treated to a perfect hurricane of shells. The companies, who had already been in the trenches (HAMEL Sub Sector) two days, were in the following order:

'B' Company had one platoon (No.8.) on the right made responsible for the marsh, immediately on its left was another platoon (No.6.) responsible for the RAILWAY SAP. The other two platoons of 'B' Coy were in support behind the 9th Royal Irish Fusiliers. The 9th Bn Royal Ir. Fus. were in between 'B' Coy and 'C' Coy; 'C' Coy being on their immediate left, 'C' Coy had 'D' Coy on its left and 'A' Coy was on the left of 'D' Coy.

SLAUGHTER ON THE SOMME: 1 JULY 1916

Starting from the platoon on the right, the attack, as far as it has been possible to gather from the information of eye witnesses remaining went as follows:

RIGHT PLATOON

During the last ten minutes or so of the intense bombardment, No.8 Platoon under Sergt. HOARE left the CROW'S NEST and lay outside their own wire. At Zero and under cover of the Barrage of smoke put up by Trench Mortar Officer they commenced the advance. This platoon was divided into three parts, one under Sergt. Hamilton who went to the left, one under Sergt. Bennison who went to the right and one under Sergt. Hoare who remained in the centre. This platoon was heavily shelled going out and while out were under very heavy Machine-gun fire from both right and left, and Sergt. Hoare's party soon all became casualties.

The left party under Sergt. Hamilton also suffered very heavily but he managed to get into the German Sap with three or four men, but owing to the heavy Machine-gun fire were unable to remain and had to leave the Sap.

On the right Sergt. Bennison was killed and this party with its Lewis Gun came under very heavy Machine-gun fire from the right and were unable to get forward at all. The casualties were heavy, and Sergt. Hoare sent back a man to Lt. Col. Blacker for orders as he could not advance. He received orders to retire; he did so with what was left of the platoon.

No.6 PLATOON

This platoon was under Lieut. Lemon and was made responsible for the RAILWAY SAP. The Platoon left our own trenches before Zero at the same time and on the right of the 9th Royal Ir. Fus. but before reaching the RAVINE the whole Platoon with the exception of Lieut. Lemon and twelve men, were all casualties.

On reaching the RAVINE Lieut. Lemon looked for some supports, but as none were available he advanced with his twelve men to enter the Sap. When he reached the Sap he had only nine men left, but he entered the Sap at the Railway bank. L.Sergt. Millar and three men moved to the right to bomb down the Sap, but these were soon all casualties. Lieut. Lemon and the remainder of the men advanced up the main Sap. The thick wires running into the first large tunnel was cut by Rfmn. Gamble who was the first bayonet man. There was a Machine-gun firing across the Sap from the small tunnel. Lieut. Lemon, however, climbed above the small tunnel with some bombs in order to catch any Germans who might come out and sent the men on. Lieut. Lemon was then shot by two German Officers who fired their rifles at him from the top of a dug-out which apparently led into the tunnel. The two German Officers were immediately afterwards killed by a bomb which exploded right at their feet. The remaining men got cut off between the 1st and 2nd German line and only two of them escaped.

Nos. 7 AND 5 PLATOONS

No.7 Platoon advanced behind the 9th Royal Ir. Fus., but as the Fus. were held up, this platoon only got just beyond our own wire. No.5 was the carrying platoon and did not leave our own wire. Capt. C.S. Murray was in command of these two Platoons, but was wounded at the very start.

The two Machine guns which caught No.6 Platoon so badly were right outside the German trench and the shelling was also very severe in the RAVINE. The Lewis Gun Team which was with No.6 Platoon became casualties before reaching the RAVINE and the Gun was put out of action by Shrapnel. Corpl. Burgess and Rfmn. McNeilly were the two men who escaped from the Sap. Rfmn. McNeilly lost Corpl. Burgess on the way back and reported himself to two N.C.O's of the 9th Royal Ir. Fus.

'C' COMPANY'S ATTACK

Before Zero, 'C' Company who were on the left of the 9th Royal Ir. Fus. left our wire and immediately came under very heavy Machine Gun fire. At Zero the company advanced led by No.10 Platoon and followed by No.11.

No.10 were held up by the wire, which had only two small gaps cut in it at this point. No.10 Platoon at once split in two, each half going for a gap. Some of this party succeeded in getting into the German line, but as there was a German Machine Gun opposite each gap the casualties were very heavy.

No.11 Platoon immediately reinforced No.10 and at once rushed the gaps and a few men succeeded in getting through. The casualties were very severe, but Captn. Griffiths collected Nos.9 and 12 Platoons and gave orders to charge. He was killed immediately he had given the order. At the same time an order came to retire.

The remaining men retired with the exception of Sergt. Cunningham, Corpl. Herbison and L.Cpl. Jackson who remained and fired at the Germans who were standing on their parapet firing and throwing bombs at our men. They killed or wounded at least ten Germans. Rfmn. Craig with a Lewis Gun kept up a good fire by himself, all the rest of the team having been killed or wounded. L. Cpl. Harvey then rallied all the men he could find and rushed the gaps again, but had to retire for the third time. The company had then to retire to the SUNKEN ROAD. Sergt. Cunningham and Corpl. Herbison again did good work by helping wounded men to get under cover in the SUNKEN ROAD. The ROAD was being shelled very heavily all the time.

'D' COMPANY'S ATTACK

'D' Company's attack was led by 2/Lieut. Sir E.H. Macnaghten, Bart., and No.16 Platoon. Sir Harry was on the right of his Platoon and Sergt. McFall on the left.[1] At Zero this Platoon rushed the German front line and entered it. Sergt. McFall found some dug-outs on the left and detailed two bombers to attend to each. The German second line was very strongly held and the Machine-gun fire from the Salient on the left (Q.17.B.) was very heavy. The Germans stood up on the parapet of their second line and threw bombs into the front line, while they kept a steady fire up against the other advancing platoons (13,14,and 15) These suffered very heavily as they approached the German wire and line.

No.14 Platoon lost half its men before No.16 had gained the German front line. An order to retire was shouted out and Sir Harry got out of the trench to order the men not to retire but to come on and just as he got out he was shot in the legs by a Machine Gun only a few yards away, and fell back into the trench.[2] Rfmn. Kane who was quite close to Sir Harry bayoneted the German who was firing the Machine Gun. 'D' Company then fell back behind the RIDGE and were at once reassembled with the remains of 'A' Company by 2/Lieu. Dickson, who ordered a second charge at the German trenches. He was very severely wounded almost as soon as he had given the order, but carried on for a time until he fell, and then Sergt. McFall at once rallied the companies and they advanced a second time. The Machine gun fire from the Salient was very severe and their casualties were very heavy, and they had to eventually fall back on our own trenches.

'A' COMPANY'S ATTACK

'A' Company, who were on the extreme left of the Battalion front, were in touch with the 29th Division. They left their new Trench before Zero and assembled along SUNKEN ROAD. At Zero they began to advance, and at once came under very heavy Artillery and Machine Gun fire.

No.4 Platoon led the attack, and was badly cut up, but what remained entered the German front line they were closely followed by No.3, who at once reinforced themselves. The wire was well cut here, but there were two Machine Guns on each side of the gap and three or four in the Salient, as well as a Company bombing party.

Lieut. McCluggage at once collected his men and tried to rush on to the German second line but was killed in the attempt. The Germans in the front line it was noticed all wore caps while those in the second line wore helmets. The German second line was full of men and there was a very considerable number at the back of the large mound on the left. All these men fired at Nos.1 and 2 Platoons while they were advancing and threw bombs at Nos.3 and 4 while in the German front line. The men of Nos.3 and 4 Platoons bombed three Dug outs and shot a good many Germans.

All these four Platoons suffered very heavily from an exceedingly intense Machine gun fire. An order to retire was passed along, and as there were no supports on the spot 'A' Company did so. Lieut. T.G .Haughton had been wounded in the leg soon after leaving our front line but led his platoon on. He was wounded a second time during the retirement and killed. The Company then retired to the SUNKEN ROAD when 2/Lieut. Dickson, who was the only officer left, assembled the men there and ordered another advance. He was immediately wounded. The men advanced again but were met with a terrific fire from all the Machine guns in the Salient (Q.17.B) and had to ultimately retire to the new Trench. Rfn. McMullen, being the only man left of his team of Lewis Gunners, entered the German line with the Gun and two magazines and fired from his shoulder at the germans in the second line. He retired with the Company and brought the Gun with him.

All companies had now been badly cut up, and had very few men left. We were ordered to attack again at 10.12am with what men we could collect. Major C.G. Cole-Hamilton DSO took command of the front line collected all the men he could find, about 100, assembled them in the New Trench and prepared to launch the attack. Sergt. McFall and S.A. Smith of 'D' Company and L. Cpl. W. Harvey of 'C' Company were conspicuous for their coolness and skill under a very heavy fire in helping Major C.G. Cole-Hamilton DSO to form up the men and carry out the attack.

The attack was made under very heavy shrapnel fire from the time of assembly, and was finally stopped by Machine gun fire. When in advance of the SUNKEN ROAD the same three N.C.O's did magnificent work in steading the men, while L.Cp. Harvey brought a wounded man in on his back.

About 11am another attack was ordered for 12.30pm in conjunction with the 29th Division. Every available man was collected and assembled in the New Trench. The total number this time was 46. The men went forward before 12.30pm and were lying under cover by 12.30pm. Major C.G. Cole-Hamilton DSO finding that the 29th Division did not launch an attack at 12.30pm and not having sufficient number of men to carry out an attack sent a message to the Commanding Officer to this effect. The Commanding Officer ordered the men to be brought back and the front line to be re-organised and held. Sergt. McFall, Sergt. A. Smith and L. Cpl. W. Harvey again did splendid work in getting the men back and re-organised under very adverse conditions.

By 2pm all the men were back and sentries were posted all along the line. This state of affairs continued until the few men who were left in the line were relieved by the York and Lancs. at 6.30pm.

NOTES

1. Twenty-year-old Second Lieutenant Sir Edward Harry Macnaghten, 6th Bart, the son of the late Hon. Sir Edward Charles Macnaghten, 5th Bart., KC, DL, of Dundarave, Co. Antrim, and of the Hon. Lady Macnaghten, of Sandhurst Lodge, Berkshire, was a member of the Black Watch (Royal Highlanders) attached to the 12th Battalion, Royal Irish Rifles. Macnaghten was killed in action on 1 July 1916 (see note 2) and he is commemorated on the Thiepval Memorial. His brother, Sir Arthur Douglas Macnaghten, 7th Bart, also fell on the Somme (15 September 1916) whilst serving with the Rifle Brigade.
2. In the early hours of 2 July 1916, it was reported that Lieutenant Harry Macnaghten, the platoon commander, was missing and Quigg volunteered to go out into No Man's Land to try to locate him. He went out seven times to search for the missing officer without success; on each occasion he came under machine-gun fire but managed to return with a wounded colleague. On one of his forays it was reported that he crawled to within yards of the German position to rescue a wounded soldier whom

271

he dragged back on a waterproof groundsheet. After seven hours of trying, exhaustion got the better of him and he had to rest from his efforts. *The London Gazette*, No.29740 published on 8 September 1916, includes the following: "He advanced to the assault with his platoon three times. Early next morning, hearing a rumour that his platoon officer was lying out wounded, he went out seven times to look for him under heavy shell and machine gun fire, each time bringing back a wounded man. The last man he dragged in on a waterproof sheet from within a few yards of the enemy's wire. He was seven hours engaged in this most gallant work, and finally was so exhausted that he had to give it up." Quigg received his Victoria Cross from King George V on 8 January 1917, at York Cottage, Sandringham. Quigg passed away in 1955.

13th (Service) Battalion (1st Co. Down) Royal Irish Rifles

THIEPVAL
From 5 to 6.30am the men had breakfast, with hot tea & a rum ration. They got out over the parapet about 15 minutes before zero time, 7.30am & laid down on the tape, they moved off a couple of minutes before time, so as to get within 150 yards of the German line before the barrage lifted – as soon as they were over the crest of the hill the German machine guns could be heard firing & the action was started. For account of this action see Appendix 1.

Document Attached to the War Diary

A narrative of the events of 1 July 1916, in respect of 13th (Service) Battalion (1st Co. Down) Royal Irish Rifles:

To 108th Infy Bde.
I have the honour to forward here with a narrative of the events on the 1st July. Very little, almost no information was sent in, this was due in the first place to most of the officers becoming casualties, and the difficulty of getting men across the fire swept zone of NO MAN'S LAND.

Signalling wires had previously been laid out, by the signalling officer of the Bn but all attempts by the signallers to take a line forward were useless. I had 10 signallers killed and wounded.

I append a list of the officers casualties by companies 2/Lieut Fullerton of D Coy is the only officer, who went over, who has come back unwounded, and has very little information to give about his company.

W.H. Savage Col.
Cmdg 13th R. IR. Rifles.

NARRATIVE OF EVENTS ON THE 1ST JULY 1916.
5-6am.   The men had hot tea for breakfast and a rum ration before they got out to the attack, at about 6.30am. they paraded and filed up to the three

gaps in our parapet, being on the steep hillside they were under cover from view & fire & there were no casualties, at a quarter before zero, they moved out & lay down on the tape, they moved off a couple of minutes or so before zero time, so as to be within 150 yards of the German trenches at the lift.

Directly the start was made the German M.Gs could be heard firing at once.

From this time I received no messages, & the Companies were lost.

8.6am. Capt Matthew Comdg 'A' Coy on my right sent in a note to say he was held up in A line and asking for Vickers gun.

Capt Davidson whose guns were in reserve was then sent out.

9.20am. Getting no news from the front, I thought affairs could not be going according to programme, I tried to get reinforcements from 15th R. Ir. Rifles but they could give none, & said their right Coys are through B line and the Companies on the left are in difficulties. After this letter, I asked 108th Infy Bde for reinforcements but none were forthcoming.

10.20am. Capt I.S. Davidson 1008th MG Company reported "Am in B line & have got up 2 Vickers guns, am consolidating both. Cannot say how many Infantry are in line, but in this part, there are only about 30 men of 13th 11th & 15th Royal Irish Rifles. We cannot possibly advance & reinforcements, ammunition & bombs most urgently needed."

This report was sent on to 108th Inft Brigade Major with further request for reinforcement.

Somewhere about this time I sent out 2nd Lieut N.B. Marriott Watson – the intelligence officer to see if any information was forthcoming, he knew the ground well as he was battn scout officer. He however was wounded & admitted to hospital.

The situation was quite confused & very conflicting reports were coming in.

12.40pm. A message from Capt Davidson 108th MGC arrived "I am holding the end of a communication trench in line A with a few bombers & a Lewis gun. We cannot hold much longer. We are being pressed on all sides and ammunition almost finished."

12.50pm. I then sent up the few remaining battn staff, the orderly room sergt, 2 officers servants, two Coy Q.M. Sergts with ammunition, these men were unable to cross No Man's Land two were killed, three were wounded.

1.5pm. 270 Bombs were also sent up with a party & a man who knew the way. 2/Lieut Findlay went out about this time for information & returned wounded later on.

1.40pm. 2/Lieut Dale sent in a note to say he was installed in a German trench 50 yds or more to the left of Captain Davidson, firing on German

Bombing party. This officer returned later on, gallantly saving his two guns & bringing in an extra tripod he found.

3pm.   The situation was confused & no information was available. I received Bde [*word illegible*] No.108/660 regarding party of Germans advancing on ST PIERRE DIVION.

3.20pm. I replied with my No.2 of 1st saying I had no men & reinforcements were required. Rn. J. Blakely came in from the sunken road & reported that Capt Davidson had been wounded in the knee & while he & another man were carrying him out, he was shot dead between them.

3.50pm. 2 Coys of the York & Lancaster Bn. arrived about this time, when Bde [*word illegible*] information re the German counter attack arrived & these two Companies held the N.W. edge of Thiepval Wood.

Several batches of German prisoners came in under escort parties of the Ulster Division from A & D lines of German trenches.

After this time the two Coys of the Y&L Battn. were holding the front line & by night, I had a party of 40 men, gathered up from the men who returned, to hold the left flank of Peterhead & Waterhead Sap.

A prisoner was captured on this flank after dark, which read in conjunction with a note from Capt Porvell R.F.A. looks as if some Germans were coming in to give themselves up, but went away. The message was "Wounded man reports Germans advancing down marsh". The night was quiet except fairly heavy shelling. Men kept coming in, wounded men & others so tired, that they lay down, just were they were.

COMPANY NARRATIVES:

'A' Coy.   From narratives received from the survivors, it appears that 'A' Coy on the right reached A.1. German trench with 1 & 2 Platoons with very few casualties, then advanced on to A.2. trench. During this time 3 & 4 platoons were held up outside A.1. trench and lost a great number of men by machine gun fire, from the direction of St. Pierre DIVION, also bombs thrown from A. trench, which was not cleared. The remaining men of 3 & 4 then advanced and reinforced No.1 & 2 in A.2. trench.

They then proceeded to bomb their way to B. line where they joined up with an officer of the 11th R. IR. Rifles as we had lost all our officers. This trench was held for a considerable time, but owing to our bombs giving out & not getting any reinforcements we were ordered to retire back.

'B' Coy.   No. 6 & 8 platoons advanced to A.1. trench, but suffered very heavily before reaching it, most of the casualties being due to severe machine gun fire from the left. In this trench, they found a large number of the enemy who surrendered & were sent back without escort to our own trenches. They then proceeded to A.2 trench but met with determined opposition & had to retire to A.1. again. They blocked the A.1. trench on the left, as they found the enemy advancing from that side & they succeeded in holding this against the enemy. Subsequently a party from these platoons advanced up communication trench to A.2. line & held a portion of that line by blocking the trench both to right & left. Bombing parties of the enemy continued to harass them continually until they were withdrawn in the evening.

No. 5 & 7 Platoons lost very heavily near the sunken road, but the remainder went on and entered the A.1. trench. They then went on & entered communication trench near the point when it enters A.2. trench. They found considerable opposition at this point from the enemy bombing parties & were driven back to A.1. trench.

They subsequently succeeded in bombing the enemy back up this communication trench into the A.2. lines & put up a barricade at this point, which they held until after 8pm. When they received orders to retire to our own trenches.

Capt Johnston who was in command of No. 5 & 7 Platoons was seriously wounded near A.2. trench early in the proceedings.

'C' Coy.   No. 10 & 12 platoons went in support of 'A' Coy & No. 9 platoon was following as a carrying platoon. No.12 platoon crossed the first line and almost reached the wire of the 2nd line trench, when they were held up by a strong point on their left, which appeared to be a bomb store, & also a machine gun post. Just about this time Lieut Rogers was mortally wounded, after having given the order for bombers to go to the left flank. The Platoon Sergt, Sergt Love, was also killed and the platoon was commanded by Sergt BURNS, who got them into the 2nd line up the communication to the right. Here they met Capt Davidson, who took command of this section of trench until wounded for the 2nd time, when Sergt BURNS & Sergt PIKEMAN 'A' Coy divided the Command between them.

They consolidated this sector and kept bombing the strong point on the left and supporting a party of the 13th R.IR. Rifles until ordered to retire.

No.10   Platoon under 2nd Lt. ARMSTRONG followed No.12, but coming under M.G. fire from the strong point on the left, went off to the right (as far as I can ascertain, as there are few survivors) and bombed their way up a communications trench into the 2nd line. 2nd Lt. ARMSTRONG was wounded here but continued to control his men & organized a sort of strong point near a dugout. They held this until forced to retire to the 1st line again.

No.9   Platoon came on under the command of Capt W.H. SMYTH, who was killed almost immediately, they were the carrying platoon and some of them reached the first line with material, which after dumping there or carrying to second line was not required, as all the time was spent consolidating, holding the line and helping the fighting platoons.

'D' Coy. In the advance 14. 15. 16. Platoons reached the sunken road with few casualties, but from then to A.1 line, we lost very heavily. I (2nd Lt. Fullerton) arriving there with about 16 men, we then proceeded to bomb dugouts from there to the left for about 150 yards & we took about 70 prisoners. Then we were held up by a bombing party of the enemy, but held on & succeeded in gaining another 50 yards. Owing to our bombs giving out we had to barricade ourselves, & signalled for Bombs & reinforcements but the enemy started to bomb us & we withdrew up the trench & barricaded ourselves again, but the enemy still continued to bomb us & I, having only a few men left, we had to withdraw back into our own lines.

14th (Service) Battalion (Young Citizens) Royal Irish Rifles

ELGIN AVENUE-THIEPVAL WOOD

12.15am. I watched the Battalion until the last man had entered ELGIN AVENUE at its junction with PAISLEY AVENUE & sent them all into their assembly trenches on the right of ELGIN AVENUE: here tools etc were issued & the men got settled down as best they could.

1.10am. I proceeded to Brigade Hd.Qrs. in PAISLEY AVENUE and reported the Battalion present in their assembly trenches. The Brigadier gave Zero time and having set & compared watches I departed. Tear shells were very prevalent in this area and I had to fix my goggles, this hampered my progress considerably and brought me into wide contact with projecting obstacles. As I passed the assembly trenches I gave Zero time to all officers, watches were set and final instructions given. At this time a lull seemed to settle over all the earth, as if it were a mutual tightening up for the great struggle shortly to commence. A water hen called to its mate midst the reedy swamp, and a courageous nightingale made bold to treat us with a song.

3.0am. The spell of comparative calm is broken by the enemy shelling the N edge of THIEPVAL WOOD in a line with WHITCHURCH STREET. The shells were falling all around and the candles in the Battalion Hdqrs. kept going out.

6.15am. Our intense bombardment has opened and shells of all sizes, including the big trench mortars are raining upon the Hun lines which are covered with smoke and dust. It is marvellous how anything can live under such a hail of shells.

7.0am. Enemy returns our artillery fire and the wood is getting uncomfortable.[1]

7.30am.   Zero time; the advance of the 109th Brigade has commenced, from the right 9th & 10th R. Inniskilling Fus. supported by the 11th Innis. Fus. & 14th Roy. Ir. Rifles on a frontage of 500 yds, 10 minutes before Zero time the 14th Ir. Rifles moved up from their assembly trenches in order to get into touch with the 10th Innis. Fus. When the clock reached 7.30am the four battalions moved over the parapet & as the 14th moved off, I received a written message from Captain Slacke O.C. 'A' Coy, stating that they were moving, this was the last I ever heard from him. The Brigade moved off as if on parade, nothing finer in the way of an advance has ever been seen, but alas no sooner were they clear of our own wire, when the slow tat tat of the Hun machine guns from THIEPVAL VILLAGE and BEAUMONT-HAMEL caught the advance under a deadly cross fire, but nothing could stop this advance and so on they went.

7.45am.   The first enemy prisoner passed down ELGIN AVENUE, he was in a great hurry to get out of the straffe and discarded his equipment and belongings at this moment I received a report from C.S.M. LOWRY of 'C' Coy, that they had reached the SUNKEN RD, known afterwards as the BLOODY ROAD (as the corpses were piled high here).

8.10am.   Received a message from CAPT. WILLIS 'D' Coy "we are consolidating in front of B line – boys behaved splendidly". A most gallant soldier WILLIS, his coolness and clear headedness throughout the day tended greatly towards the success of the operations. I regret that he is reported missing, a great loss to the battalion – a born leader of men.

8.15am.   More Hun prisoners passing down the trench. Obtained shoulder badges of German Regiments Nos. 55 and 135.

8.45am.   I then received a message by runner that the 107th Brigade had passed through us to the attack of D Line.

9.20am.   Enemy knocking my Batt Hdqrs. Dug out about with 5.9's, great trouble in keeping the candle alight especially as matches were hard to obtain before the battle. Direct hit on our Dug out – still alive.

9.30am.   Lieut Gracey reports that our shells are falling into his trench. I doubt this.

9.33am.   A message comes through to say that the 32nd DIVISION are badly held up in front of that heap of brick dust THIEPVAL VILLAGE – no wonder our attack got enfiladed. I sent down to GORDON CASTLE for ammunition to be sent up.

10.30am.   Lieut LACK my cheeriest and best of the Intelligence officers came back from the enemy lines with 25 prisoners. I asked for reinforcements to be sent up as the German fire was heavy on our people in front, but they did not come. I did not see the reinforcements until late that afternoon.

10.35am.   2nd Lieut WEDGWOOD killed, he was only a child, but had the heart of a lion. Very heavy enemy barrage down about 100 yds back from the edge of the wood, trees knocked down & stones & splinters flying. Kipling said "Fir noise never startled the soldier" he wrote that when his experiences were based on Frontier warfare he might have been in the CALDRON of HELL on that bright July morning he would have undoubtedly been impressed. Enemy still shelling the front of the wood.

11.45am. Message received from 'C' Coy that a heavy barrage had been put down on them, I could hear the 5.9's walloping down on them.

12.45pm. I received a message from 'C' Coy by runner asking for reinforcements urgently, which I passed to the Brigade.

1pm. Enemy looks like counter attacking.

1.20pm. The situation is now serious, a mixed force of the Brigade is holding C Line but are enfiladed heavily from THIEPVAL.

2pm. A message received to say that a train has come into GRANDCOURT with reinforcements.

2.5pm. A message from Lieut Hogg that he is digging a line between C and D Lines with all available men and says he is about to be attacked and asks for reinforcements.

2.10pm. 2nd Lt. WRIGHT my bombing officer is killed by a shell and 2nd Lt. LACK wounded going to the rescue of 2/Lt. RADCLIFFE.

3pm. A big stream of men going down the trench wounded and the wood is stiff with shrapnel.

4pm Received a message from Capt. WILLIS that he was hard pressed but was hanging on and asking for reinforcements, about this time I had a message from Brigade saying reinforcements were coming up, I conveyed this message to Capt. WILLIS and directed him to hold on for all he was worth, he did this right gallantly, ably supported by his 2nd in command Lieut Monard another very tenacious officer.

6pm. Met a company of a Territorial Battn. going down along the top of ELGIN AVENUE, on enquiries been made I found they were my love list and much sought after "REINFORCEMENTS" going the wrong way. The boy in command did not know in what direction he was to go, so I put him right and gave him orders that he was to reinforce the remnants of the 109th Brigade in B and C Lines and to hang on to the S. end of FORT SCHWABEN at all costs.

About 7pm. Lieut GALLAGHER of the 11th Innis Fus came to me at Batt Hdqrs and reported that the whole line had given way, this was corroborated by Lieut Monard and shortly afterwards by Major Peacocke 9th Innis Fus.

8pm. No doubt about this, the trench ELGIN AVE. was full of men so orders were issued and a new line of defence taken up at once in WHITCHURCH STREET by the remains of the 14th and all men that could be gathered together at the time. The young officers who joined just about this time from the Transport lines were told off to supervise and control this new line during the night - and such a night of tumult, in which the telephone took a prominent part. The situation was now as follows:

9.0pm. 9th R. Innis Fus holding Eastern end of WHITCHURCH STREET. 14th ROY. IR. RIF, the western end, together with the 10th R INNIS FUS on their left down towards the ANCRE.

So passed the night into dawn & daylight, & a few bare poles of trees, looking out on the morning, that were once a wood, bore eloquent testimony to the severity of the fire.

NOTE

1. It was at 06.45 hours on 1 July 1916, when Private William "Billy" McFadzean gave his life to save his friends. It was as the German shells sought out the Ulstermen's position that Billy McFadzean was involved with the distribution of bombs. He picked up a box of grenades and cut the cord around it. The announcement of the award of his Victoria Cross describes what happened next: "While in a concentration trench and opening a box of bombs for distribution prior to an attack, the box slipped down into the trench, which was crowded with men, and two of the safety pins fell out. Private McFadzean, instantly realising the danger to his comrades, with heroic courage threw himself on the top of the Bombs. The bombs exploded blowing him to pieces, but only one other man was injured. He well knew his danger, being himself a bomber, but without a moment's hesitation he gave his life for his comrades." McFadzean smothered the bomb blasts and only two (not one) of his comrades were wounded, one of whom, Private George Gillespie, had to have a leg amputated. MacFadzean was quite literally blown to bits and some accounts say that when his remains were later carried away on a stretcher the men removed their helmets in salute to their brave colleague. Many openly wept. His body too, was never recovered but is thought to have been buried in the woods at the back of Connaught Cemetery. William Frederick McFadzean was born in Lurgan, County Armagh, on 9 October 1895. He joined the 14th Battalion Royal Irish Rifles (Young Citizens) as a private on 22 September 1914. This was in response to the call for volunteers to join a division which was to become the 36th (Ulster) Division. He sailed to France with the division in October 1915. McFadzean's commanding officer, Lieutenant Colonel F.C. Bowden wrote to his father, who was a Belfast JP, with the following words, which are recorded in Gerald Gliddon's book *VCs of the First World War*: "It was with feelings of deep pride that I read the announcement of the granting of the V.C. to your gallant son, and my only regret is that he was not spared to us to wear his well-earned decoration. It was one of the very finest deeds of a war that is so full of big things, and I can assure you that the whole battalion rejoiced when they hear it ..." McFadzean's father was presented with his son's VC by King George V in Buckingham Palace, London on 28 February 1917. The king reportedly said to him that, "nothing finer has been done in this war for which I have yet given the Victoria Cross, than the act performed by your son in giving his life so heroically to save the lives of his comrades." His Victoria Cross is displayed at The Royal Ulster Rifles Museum, Belfast, Northern Ireland.

15th (Service) Battalion (North Belfast) Royal Irish Rifles

THIEPVAL

Arrived assembly trenches in Thiepval wood about 12.15AM. 583 all ranks. One man slightly wounded. Zero time 7.30.AM. 15th in support of 108th Brigade. At 6.30.AM. C.O. of 11th R I Rif asked me to closely support him owing to his heavy casualties. At 7.45 & 7.50AM. 'A' & 'B' Coys on the Right of line reported having reached German A Line & estimated casualties at 60 men. 'C' (extreme Left) & 'D' Coys held up by infalade [sic] machine gun fire from St.Pierre Divion & being pressed on L & by Germans who had come up out of dugouts after previous waves had passed over. Capt Chiplin (B Coy) slightly wounded. 7.55. B line captured & C line attacked on the Right.

8.15AM. 'C' & 'D' Coys captured A line on Left. Casualties very heavy. Called for replacements but none available. About 10a.m. large quantities of prisoners, maps, papers etc began to come in. Communication completely broke down owing to German barrage for five hours. One Coy alone sent 14 runners back only one of which got through. In the meantime on the Right C line had been captured and D line penetrated. Capt Chiplin was severely wounded ditto Capt Tate & Capt O'Flaherty killed also Lt Hind. The machine gun infalade fire from both flanks (the 29th & 32nd Divisions having failed) caused very heavy casualties & bit by bit drove us back.

At 8.30pm Lieut Lepper returned & informed me he had only 8 N.C.O's several of which were wounded & a bare half doz men of mixed units left & that both flanks being unprotected he had had to return. Shortly afterwards Lieut Malone with one Sgt and one Rifleman from further to the R came in. At 11pm. Lieut Tiptaft came in with a handful of men & informed me a message to retire had reached him at 6pm but acting on orders received from me to hold on at all cost he had done so till he found himself isolated & short of ammunition when he had retired with his entire force which by now consisted of eleven men included wounded of mixed units. During the day I sent a large quantity of bombs & S.A.A. forward but only a small quantity reached the fighting line. I also sent half of my Batt Bombers (the only reserve I had kept in hand) to reinforce at A.16. owing to a very urgent call. They were practically speaking wiped out. With the attack three lines of cable were run out but immediately broken by the bombardment. Finding attempts to mend the wire only meant casualties & instant severing of connection I gave up the attempt. Six newly joined officers came up to Batt HQ as reinforcements one of whom had to be sent away at once with shell shock.

16th (Service) Battalion (2nd Co. Down) (Pioneers) Royal Irish Rifles

AVELUY

5.30am. Moved to our place of assembly for the battle, starting an hour early, as I knew the enemy would probably know our hour of attack, & I wished to avoid their curtain fire, ordered to assemble at LANCASHIRE Dump, but no shelter there & road being heavily shelled, so took Bt to some slit trenches I had found by a reconnaissance previous night, about 200 yds W of pt named. Left [*illegible*] under a shelter (built previous night) at LANCASHIRE Dump.

6.   At 6am the most tremendous bombardment, hotly replied to by enemy; owing to precautions mentioned in last para, had no casualties.

7.30.   [*Illegible*] charged. It was very difficult to see owing to smoke & dust & mist, but we [*illegible*] no one faltered, & they were soon over 1st & 2 lines of trenches.

8.40.   Sent No.1 Co. to HAMEL to repair St PIERRE-DIVION Rd, No.2 to cut trench across No Man's Land from No.5 Sap to enemy 1st Line. No.1 found road in possession of enemy so garrisoned our 1st Line at HAMEL, & organised party to bring in wounded of 9 R. In Fus who were lying out under heavy fire. Brought in about 60 to 70, but lost 12 men in doing it. No.2 made several most gallant efforts to cut the trench required, but got shot down as they left sap each time, lost about 20 men before desisting. As [*illegible*] I brought No.3 Co. to reinforce No.2. About 9pm, as they were starting the trench at whatever cost, our men returned from enemy 1st Line, Capt Chase showed great calmness + military skill in helping to make arrangements for holding our 1st Line lest the enemy should attack. All THIEPVAL WOOD was now under very heavy shellfire & the scene was beyond description.

1/5th Battalion York And Lancaster Regiment

AVELUY WOOD

3.45am.   Whole battalion in Assembly trenches AVELUY WOOD.

6.20am.   Intense bombardment commenced and lasted for one hour – no retaliation on the Wood.

9.45am.   146 Bde moved up to support 36th Div. and at 11.30am 147 Bde. moved across the ANCRE and took up original position of 14 Bde. Bombardment still sounded intense especially round THIEPVAL.

1.30pm.   Battalion left the Assembly trenches to support 108 Bde (36 Div). 'A' & 'B' Coys under Major Shaw moved to N. side of ANCRE and 'C' & 'D' Coys under Lt. Col Rendall moved to S. of ANCRE.

On N. side of ANCRE 108th Bde were holding original front line which was then taken over by 'A' & 'B' Coys. Capt G.A.G. Hewitt retired to hospital suffering from shock.

4.30pm.   'C' & 'D' Coys proceeded through THIEPVAL Wood by CROMARTY AVENUE and arrived at SPEYSIDE the Hq of the 13th R.I.R. – the wood had been very badly knocked about and bodies, kit and equipment strewed the tracks and trenches. A few casualties sustained from shell fire – [*illegible*] had been ordered by R.I.R. to proceed up CROMARTY

Av. – bad mistake. It was impossible to obtain any information as to the position of the 108th Bde as no reports had been sent back to the Hq at SPEYSIDE. At last a wounded Irish Rifle officer appeared and stated that we had retired from the German "C" line and that the Bosch was pursuing in force – He was very excited and not much notice was taken of his statement – 'C' Coy was ordered to occupy the British front line on edge of WOOD until the situation could be ascertained. A large number of German prisoners coming over the crest were mistaken for the pursuing Bosch and a composite company of a few 'C' Coy, a few 'D' Coy and Hq advanced through the Wood and eventually reached the original British front line. During this advance the enemy had kept up his heavy barrage on the top of the wood causing many casualties. The shelling of the ANCRE VALLEY was particularly heavy with "Tear" shells. The composite company under Captain Fisher advanced to the German "A" line where he was unable to get any information as to which line the 108 Bde was holding. On reconnoitring Capt Fisher found a remnant dug in on a line running N. & S., N. of SCHWABEN REDOUBT and W. of "C" line. The Coy was then brought up to reinforce this line and an attempt was made to bridge the gap between this and our troops in "C" line.

6.30pm. About 6.30pm the enemy were seen advancing to counter attack from the direction of GRANDCOURT in open order. M. Guns and artillery opened on them and they disappeared. The remnant of 108 Bde then withdrew from "C" & "B" lines and Capt Fisher was forced to follow them and man the "A" line.

About midnight the order was given by an officer of the 108 Bde to withdraw – our men repulsed a small bombing attack while the 108 Bde withdrew to the original British front line.

About midnight the last of the 108 Bde were withdrawn into dug outs in THIEPVAL WOOD.

III Corps

1 July 1916

The position of III Corps between Bécourt and Authuille, lay on the forward slopes of a long low ridge between Albert and La Boisselle, marked by Tara and Usna Hills, a continuation of the spur of the main Ginchy – Pozières ridge on which the village of Ovillers stands. Behind this ridge the divisional artillery was deployed in rows, one brigade behind the other, dug in on bare and open ground. The observers were on the crest, with a perfect view of the whole German position spread out before them like a map, each trench shown up by its chalk parapet. The enemy first position, with its front line higher than the British, lay across the upper slopes of the three spurs which reach out south-westwards from the main ridge towards Albert.

The distance between the opposing lines varied from 800 to 50 yards, the trench nearest to the enemy, opposite La Boisselle being known as "Glory Hole".

The right of the corps faced the western slope of the long Fricourt spur; its centre, the La Boisselle spur, with the village of that name almost in the German front line; whilst in front of its left was the upper part of Ovillers spur, with the village within the German front defences. The depressions running into the enemy position between the three spurs were known as Sausage Valley and Mash Valley. Neither was more than 1,000 yards wide, so that, being bare and open, any advance up them could be effectively met by crossfire from both sides, whilst the spurs themselves were covered with a network of trenches and machine-gun nests. The great Thiepval spur – actually opposite X Corps, next on the left – overlooked practically all the first belt of ground over which the divisions of III Corps had necessarily to advance.

The German defences consisted of a front system with four main strongpoints in its southern half: Sausage Redoubt (or Heligoland), with Scots Redoubt behind it, Schwaben Höhe and La Boisselle village. A fifth, Ovillers, was situated centrally in its northern half. Behind the front defences were two intermediate lines: the first from Fricourt Farm to Ovillers, and the second, incomplete, in front of Contalmaison and of Pozières. Behind these again was the second position from Bazentin le Petit to Mouquet Farm, consisting of two lines. The third position was three miles in rear of the second. Owing to the enemy's front position being on the forward slopes, it was completely exposed to fire, except the front trenches

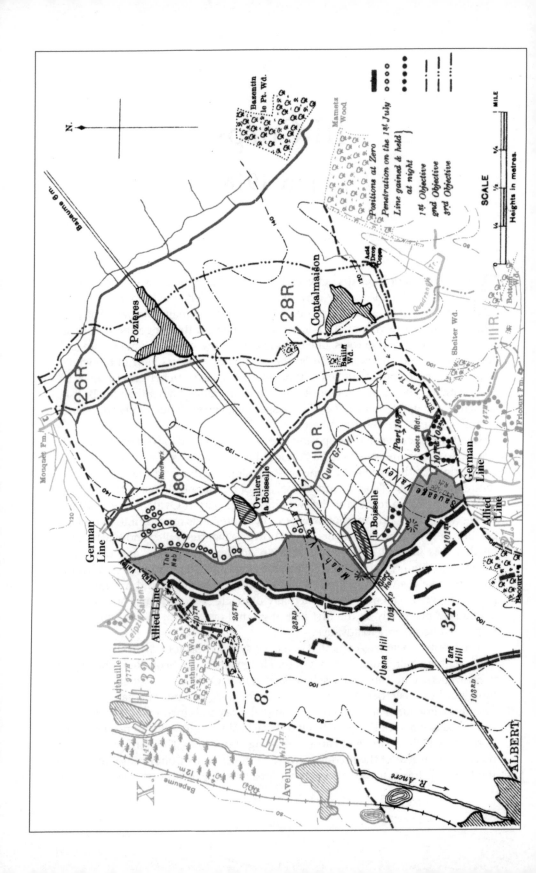

N.

Bapaume 6 m.

X.

Pozières

26R.

Mouquet Fm.

Leipzig Salient

Authuille 97m

Authuille Wd.

32.

Nordwerk

80

Ovillers la Boisselle

110 R.

Quer Gr. VII

The Nab

Ov'ley

Aveluy

Bapaume 6m.

R. Ancre

8.

25TH

104TH

23RD

The Mash

Glory Hole

109TH

Usna Hill

III.

100

Tara Hill

103RD

ALBERT

Bazentin le Pt. Wd.

Contalmaison

28R.

Bailiff Wd.

Acid Drop Copse

Mametz Wood

Sausage Valley

la Boisselle

Part 100

Scots Rdt.

101ST

102ND

101ST

German Line

German Line

Allied Line

Allied Line

Quarangle

Shelter Wd.

III R.

647M

Fricourt Fm.

Bottom Wd.

Becourt

Tree Tr.

Positions on the 1st July

Penetration on the 1st July

Line gained & held at night

1st Objective
2nd Objective
3rd Objective

SCALE

0   ¼   ½   ¾   MILE

Heights in metres.

near La Boisselle and these were not only very near our own front line but difficult to reach with shell fire owing to the configuration of the ground. It will be observed, however, how singularly well the front line was adapted to defence, being sited, as the ground demanded, as a series of salients and re-entrants, the La Boisselle and Thiepval salients being particularly strong.

The high road Amiens – Albert – Pozières – Bapaume cut through the centre of III Corps' front. In its straight course from Albert up to the Pozières ridge it ascends aslant the northern slope of the La Boisselle spur, and thence rises steadily to Pozières. This highway was roughly the line of demarcation between the two divisions which were to make the assault, the actual dividing line being at first about five hundred yards to the left of it, but near Ovillers passing to the right. The 34th Division, on the right, was to attack and capture the German defences on the Fricourt spur and astride Sausage Valley as far as La Boisselle (inclusive). It was then to advance to the line Contalmaison – Pozières (exclusive), halting some eight hundred yards in front of the German second position. The 8th Division, on the left, was to capture the German front defences north of the Bapaume road, including the whole western slope of Ovillers spur and the village. It was then to push forward to a line facing the German second position between Pozières (inclusive) and Mouquet Farm.

The two assaulting divisions had thus to capture two fortified villages and six lines of trenches, and to advance into the German position to a depth of roughly two miles on a frontage of 4,000 yards – a formidable task.

The 19th Division, in corps reserve, but with its guns in action under the other divisions, was to be in a position of readiness in an intermediate position north of Albert, and as the 34th and 8th Divisions moved forward to the assault, the two leading brigades of the 19th Division were to take their places in the Tara-Usna line, ready to move forward to relieve them when they had secured their objectives.

The corps artillery – mostly concentrated on both sides of the Amiens road, just west of Albert – comprised 98 heavy guns and howitzers, in addition to the divisional batteries, and a "groupe" of French 75-mm of the 18th Field Artillery Regiment to fire gas shell. It was organized in five groups, two working with each of the assaulting divisions and the other, composed of the heavier natures, covering the whole front.[2] This gave a heavy gun to every forty yards, and a field gun to every twenty-three yards.

As the infantry commanders were by no means satisfied with the results of the bombardment of La Boisselle and Ovillers, a battery of eight Stokes mortars was told to shell the former at zero. It was speedily knocked out by shell fire, but before this happened considerable effect appeared to have been produced on La Boisselle.

The programme of fire for 1 July provided for eight lifts of the heavy artillery, and laid down that "after the assault the subsequent movement of the infantry will be assisted and regulated by a system of barrages which will move back slowly" in accordance with a timetable.[3] In this programme the sixth lift, to fall behind Contalmaison and Pozières, took place 1 hour and 25 minutes after zero, and the final lift, roughly 1,000 yards further back, 22 minutes later. The "slowly" referred to the general pace of the advance of the barrage, which was about two miles in 1 hour and 47 minutes. It was made in "jumps" by the heavy artillery as in XIII and XV Corps: the divisional artillery barrage, on the other hand, was to go back "very slowly", and the instructions issued in the 34th Division artillery (Brigadier-General A.D. Kirby) made clear what was intended. They state:

"Lifts are timed to commence at the same time as the Heavy Artillery. But instead of lifting straight back on to the next line, divisional artillery will *rake* back gradually to the next line." The rake, however, the speed of which was given in an appendix, was not continuous, but a series of short lifts of 50, 100, or 150 yards. It was further said that "the speed at which the rake goes back to the next line will be calculated so that the shrapnel barrage moves back faster than the infantry can advance". There was not therefore a creeping barrage, but only an attempt to deal with every small intermediate trench.

There were frequent complaints of bad gun ammunition during the preliminary bombardment and on 1 July, for, as in XV Corps, the field-gun ammunition proved to be very faulty, causing numerous premature bursts with consequent casualties as the guns were ranged in several lines. Many of the heavy howitzer shells fell short, and many failed to burst: an officer with the successful right wing of the corps reported "a dud shell every two or three yards over several acres of ground". On the other hand, it should be mentioned that the twelve-inch railway gun, firing at zero from behind Albert at thirteen miles' range, drove the headquarters of the German XIV Corps out of Bapaume.[4]

Two very large mines, to be fired two minutes before zero, were laid by the 179th Tunnelling Company Royal Engineers under the shoulders of the salient formed by the trenches round La Boisselle in order to destroy any flanking arrangements, and by the height of their lips to prevent enfilade fire along No Man's Land on either side. The southern one, known as "Lochnagar", under Schwaben Redoubt, contained 60,000lbs of ammonal;[5] the other, "Y Sap", 40,600lbs of ammonal.[6] As mine warfare had been going on in the La Boisselle area, infinite precautions were necessary to prevent the discovery of this new enterprise, especially as there was no continuous front trench along the mine-field, which was only held by a series of posts covering the mine shafts.[7]

34th Division: The assault on La Boisselle Salient

The full weight of the twelve infantry battalions of the 34th Division was to be thrown in the first assault, by successive waves, against the German position.[8] It was to attack in four "columns", each column three battalions deep on a frontage of four hundred yards. Between the third and fourth columns opposite La Boisselle there was to be a gap.

Unlike Ovillers in the 8th Division area, La Boisselle, the key of the front system owing to its salient position, was not to be attacked directly; the two left columns, passing on either side of it, were, as they advanced, to send into it special bombing parties (amounting in all to one platoon), supported by Lewis guns and Stokes mortars, to clear it from both flanks. Brigade and battalion commanders who expressed doubts as to the feasibility of this course were reminded that the commander of the Fourth Army had said the village would have been rendered untenable and the Germans in it "wiped out" by the preliminary bombardment, while the flanking shoulders on either side of it would be destroyed by the great mines.

On 30 June, however, the front line troops had found the garrison very much on the alert, for parties put over the parapet to clear passages through the wire in front of it were fired upon. It was arranged, therefore, that at zero when the barrage lifted, the bombardment of the village should be continued by trench mortars until the flanking parties could enter. To deal with Sausage Redoubt, a dangerous flanking work, during the night an emplacement for a trench-mortar battery was dug in No Man's Land – there 500 yards wide – and its fire proved very effective until all its personnel were killed or wounded. It was subsequently discovered that the damage done by the bombardment was superficial, and that none of the deep dug-outs had been injured. In one of them an overhearing station had remained in action to the last. At 02.45 hours it had picked up part of a telephoned British order which pointed to an assault in the morning.[9]

The two right columns which assembled in the Tara-Usna trenches were formed of the 101st Brigade (Brigadier-General R.C. Gore),[10] each having one battalion in front and one in support with a battalion of the 103rd Brigade (Tyneside Irish, Brigadier-General N.J.G. Cameron[11]) in rear. The two left columns were similarly composed of the 102nd Brigade (Tyneside Scottish, Brigadier-General T.P.B. Ternan), with the two remaining battalions of the 103rd Brigade in rear. As the 103rd Brigade contained, as did the division as a whole, a large number of miners, extensive galleries had been dug in Tara hill for the first assembly of its battalions.

At the hour of assault all four columns were to advance in extended order in lines of companies, each in column of platoons at 150 paces' distance. Brigadier-General Gore ordered the headquarters (Lieutenant Colonel, second-in-command, adjutant, etc.) of his battalions to stand fast when the troops advanced, and not to go forward until ordered by the brigade. They therefore remained intact and available to reorganize their commands at night, whilst practically all the other battalion staffs became casualties.

The first objective of the two leading lines of battalions was the German front system, consisting of four trenches. The fourth trench, requiring an advance of about 2,000 yards, was to be reached forty-eight minutes after zero hour, i.e., 08.18

hours. The second objective was the German second intermediate line, the *Kaisergraben*, in front of Contalmaison and Pozières villages. This line was to be reached by 08.58 hours, when the 101st and 102nd Brigades were to halt and consolidate. The 103rd Brigade, forming the third line of battalions and following close in rear, would then pass through the 101st and 102nd Brigades, capture Contalmaison village, and advance to the third, and final, objective of the division, a line close to the outer or eastern edge of that village and Pozières. This line, to be reached by the 103rd Brigade at 10.10 hours, was to be put into a state of defence preparatory to a subsequent assault on the German second position, which lay eight hundred yards beyond.[12]

At zero hour the whole infantry of the division, except the head of the second column, rose as one man, the front line going "over the top" and the rear lines moving down the slopes of Tara-Usna ridge, even the reserve battalions of the 103rd Brigade leaving their trenches. In a matter of ten minutes some 80 per cent of the men in the leading battalions were casualties; for directly the artillery barrage lifted off the German front line, an ever-increasing number of machine-guns – mostly in rear of the front line, well sited and hidden, and untouched by the bombardment – came into action, sweeping No Man's Land, which was 200-800 yards wide, and the front slopes of the Tara-Usna ridge.

There was no surprise: the Germans were ready. Warned by the order which had been overheard, and well drilled at manning the parapet, they came up out of their deep dug-outs as if by magic directly the barrage moved, and established a rough firing line before the British had got across No Man's Land.

The four assaulting columns met with misfortunes of varying nature, accentuated by the fact that all the battalions of the 103rd Brigade left the Tara-Usna line at zero when the leading troops went "over the top". Thus, in most cases, as soon as the latter were held up, the tail of each column telescoped on its head, with the result that composite parties formed of men of all battalions were to be found nearly everywhere, thus presenting splendid targets to the enemy. The right column was faced by the steep convex slope of the long western side of the Fricourt spur. The front companies of the 15/Royal Scots moved forward to within two hundred yards of the German front trench before zero hour, covered by the final bombardment and trench mortar fire.

On the barrage lifting, they overran with great steadiness and with little loss the German front trench which lay along the upper part of the slope, the pipe-major in the first wave playing the pipes, which, however, were soon punctured. At this early stage flanking machine-gun fire from Sausage Valley and La Boisselle forced the leading companies of the 15/Royal Scots, which were ahead of those of the second column, from their proper direction, and practically destroyed the left wings of the rear companies and of the lines of the 16/Royal Scots, which were following. The intended line of advance lay north of east, but owing to the hail of fire from the left the lines instinctively veered due eastward, moving straight up instead of aslant the rising slope, leaving parties of the 15/Royal Scots to clear up the German trenches in their sector, which included Sausage Redoubt. This divergence was maintained and accentuated as the advance progressed, carrying the right column into the zone of XV Corps. Thus by 07.48 hours the 15/ and 16/Royal Scots were well on the top of the Fricourt spur, but had left uncaptured both Sausage Redoubt and Scots Redoubt.

The error of direction was not discovered until half-an-hour later, when, after advancing nearly a mile and crossing the German first intermediate line, the Royal Scots reached Birch Tree Wood beyond the Sunken Road, in the depression leading down to Fricourt village and ran into units of the 21st Division (XV Corps). The remains of the two Scottish battalions, now considerably intermingled, edged away therefore to their left, northwards, to rectify the mistake.

Those of the 15/Royal Scots moved along Birch Tree Trench, in the German second intermediate line, towards Peake Woods, and those of the 16/Royal Scots took up a position in support along the Fricourt – Pozières road (the "Sunken Road" of XV Corps' sector), two hundred yards in rear.

Before this northward movement along Birch Tree Trench was completed, the enemy[13] attacked from the direction of Peake Woods, chiefly with bombing parties along the trench. Simultaneously heavy machine-gun fire was opened from the left flank and rear by German parties in the third and fourth trenches, and by a party in Scots Redoubt. This counter-attack caused heavy loss, and forced the Royal Scots to withdraw southwards, the 15/Royal Scots along Birch Tree Trench to a position just inside XV Corps' sector, about Birch Tree Wood – Shelter Wood, and the 16/Royal Scots, with men of the 27/Northumberland Fusiliers, and 11/Suffolk from the next column, to the vicinity of Round Wood. They then initiated a movement towards Wood Alley and Scots Redoubt, being joined by men of various battalions, amongst them a captain of the 11/Suffolk, who had been wounded. Finding only a second lieutenant with the Royal Scots, he took command, and both objectives were secured – Scots Redoubt in an almost undamaged condition and most valuable as a flank support.

The Royal Scots were now astride the Fricourt spur, even a little beyond their first objective along the eastern side of it, and faced the Contalmaison spur 1,000 yards away across the valley. One party of the 16/Royal Scots, according to German accounts, actually penetrated the village and was there annihilated. The 27/Northumberland Fusiliers, which was to follow close behind the 16/Royal Scots, was stopped by the intense and accurate machine-gun fire which dominated No Man's Land. Parties got through to the Fricourt – Pozières road, and some men, with others of the 24/Northumberland Fusiliers of the next column on the left, reached Acid Drop Copse and the outskirts of Contalmaison. But such isolated advances could not change the fortune of the day.

On learning what the situation was, Brigadier-General Gore selected the battalion quarters of the 16/Royal Scots (Lieutenant Colonel Sir G. McCrae) to go forward and take command. The position reached by the Royal Scots was consolidated, and as it flanked the eastern side of the Fricourt spur towards Contalmaison, it formed a strong defensive flank on the left of XV Corps.[14]

On the left of the second column, opposite the gap of two hundred yards which divided it from the third, the Lochnagar mine (the double mine) was successfully exploded at 07.28 hours, blowing up the German garrison and causing a great crater ninety yards across and seventy feet deep, with lips fifteen feet high. Immediately south of the mine, however, the German front trench, following the contour of Sausage Valley, formed a pronounced re-entrant and the infantry of the second column, delayed five minutes by order in view of the mine explosion,[15] was not only behind the columns on either side in crossing No Man's Land, but had further to go than that on its left.

The barrage had of course lifted and the Germans thus had plenty of time to man the position deliberately, including Sausage Redoubt, the northern face of which flanked the advance. Their fire, combined with that of the flanking machine guns in Sausage Valley and La Boisselle, turned first on to the right column and then on to the second, was fatal to the success of the 34th Division. Within two minutes of zero hour, before the lines of the 10/Lincolnshire had cleared the front trench, machine-gun fire raked them and those of the 11/Suffolk following. The latter unit, in addition, suffered from a weak artillery barrage placed on the British trenches by the German batteries soon after the assault had been launched. Men fell fast, and the lines were gradually reduced to isolated small parties.

On the extreme right, a party which tried to storm Sausage Redoubt was burnt to death by flame throwers as it reached the parapet but some of the Suffolks got through and joined, as we have seen, the Royal Scots of the first column on top of the Fricourt spur. Still the courageous efforts of the mass of the Lincolnshire and Suffolks to cross the five hundred yards of No Man's Land were unavailing, and the 24/Northumberland Fusiliers following them was ordered to halt in the front trenches.[16]

The survivors took any cover available in the open fire-swept zone; some men, from all three battalions, reached and consolidated a position in the Lochnagar crater. The party of the 15/Royal Scots left by the right column to deal with Sausage Redoubt attempted to bomb northwards into it, but was not strong enough to do so. Two attempts made by the 27th Field Company Royal Engineers and a company of the 18/Northumberland Fusiliers (Pioneers) to reinforce this party across No Man's Land also failed owing to machine-gun fire; it was obvious that until the Germans could be cleared out of the redoubt, the troops of the second column lying out in No Man's Land could neither be reinforced nor relieved during daylight.

The third column of the 102nd Brigade formed of the 21st, 22nd and 26th Northumberland Fusiliers, the last battalion belonging to the 103rd Brigade, tried to pass immediately south of La Boisselle, but north of the Lochnagar crater.

Starting immediately the mine was fired, and having less than two hundred yards of No Man's Land to cross, it succeeded in overrunning the trenches of Schwaben Höhe. The leading lines then moved along the western side of Sausage Valley, immediately below La Boisselle village, and crossed the next two lines of trenches (Kaufmanngraben and Alte Jägerstrasse). Their right flank was, however, exposed owing to the failure of the second column to advance at zero.

Detachments of bombers were sent out towards La Boisselle, but were unable to make progress. Up to this time, that is twelve minutes after zero hour, the bombardment of the village had been continued by trench mortars, so as to cover the advance of the assaulting columns to the north and south of it, but this did not prevent the Germans from emerging from the deep dug-outs under the ruins. They opened machine-gun fire, as has been seen, on the columns and enfiladed the lines of infantry moving past the southern front of the village, and they drove back the bombing parties.

Very heavy losses were incurred by all three battalions of the third column at this stage. Nevertheless Quergraben III, the German first intermediate line, astride the Contalmaison road, was reached in places, some men being reported as far east as Bailiff Wood, in the second intermediate line, only five hundred yards from Contalmaison itself. But, as elsewhere, it is difficult to discover how far units penetrated, for the leading men were only too often killed or taken prisoner. The Germans now counter-attacked southwards along Kaiserstrasse and Quergraben III, and the Tyneside Scottish, unable to retaliate effectively owing to a shortage of bombs, withdrew to the remains of the third German front trench (Kaufmanngraben). Reduced to seven officers and about 200 other ranks, they held and consolidated this trench on a front of four hundred yards, their right on the road up Sausage Valley.

The fourth column, the left of the 102nd Brigade, which was to pass by the northern side of La Boisselle – while the "Glory Hole" between this column and the third was held by a company of the pioneer battalion – was led by the 20/ and 23/Northumberland Fusiliers (1st and 4th Tyneside Scottish), with the 25th (2nd Tyneside Irish) following. Here, too, the German front line followed the contour of Mash Valley, forming a pronounced re-entrant, so that on the left nearly eight hundred yards of No Man's Land had to be crossed. All depended on the bombardment having obliterated the defences near the two villages, and upon the chance that the defenders, demoralized by it and the firing of the Y Sap mine, would surrender freely.

In spite of the successful firing of the mine,[17] immediately the Tyneside Scottish left the British trenches they encountered cross machine-gun fire, not only from Ovillers on their left front, but at short range from La Boisselle and its trenches on the right, besides some shelling. The two leading battalions pressed on most gallantly across No Man's Land, but were almost annihilated before they reached the German front trench. It was seen later from the position of the dead that some had crossed the front trench and moved on to the second before they were shot down, and that flanking parties had tried in vain to force an entrance into La Boisselle. The 25/Northumberland Fusiliers, advancing behind them, also lost heavily in its vain efforts to carry forward the attack across No Man's Land.

By now all the commanding officers of the 102nd Brigade, Lieutenant Colonels C.C.A. Sillery, A.P.A. Elphinstone, W. Lyle, and Major F.C. Heneker, had fallen and two seconds-in-command and two adjutants had been killed and the others wounded. In the 103rd Brigade, Lieutenant Colonel L.M. Howard had been killed, and Lieutenant Colonels J.H.M. Arden and M.E. Richardson wounded (the latter however continued with the 26/Northumberland Fusiliers till evening), and fifteen out of the sixteen company commanders were casualties.

At 10.00 hours the situation on the front of the 34th Division was that part of the right column had reached a position on the further side of the Fricourt spur about Round Wood and Birch Tree Wood in touch with XV Corps and in the latter's sector; the second column was lying out in No Man's Land held up by machine-gun fire both from Sausage Redoubt and from La Boisselle, although part of it had joined up with the first on Fricourt spur; the third was in possession of a small sector of the German defences around Schwaben Höhe, on the northern slope of Sausage Valley; and the left column, except for a few individuals, had failed to reach the German front trench north of La Boisselle, and had withdrawn to its starting place. Although this village was to all appearance obliterated, the Germans, safe in their deep dug-outs during the bombardment, were holding the ruins in strength, and bombing parties had been unable to enter.

So thick, however, was the smoke and dust, that until nearly 09.00 hours it was believed at divisional headquarters that the attack had made progress, and the close support field battery had actually begun to move forward.

All three brigades having been employed in the attack, Major General Ingouville-Williams had no troops available to clear the enemy out of Sausage Redoubt, or to press the attack on La Boisselle village from the south. At 11.25 hours, therefore, he telegraphed to III Corps headquarters asking for reinforcement for these purposes, and a battalion (9/Welch) of the 19th Division in corps reserve, was placed at his disposal. Any action by this battalion was, however, postponed, and an attack by the last available company of the 18/Northumberland Fusiliers (Pioneers) countermanded, as it was decided that the 19th Division should carry out an attack on La Boisselle with two brigades after dark. Measures were nevertheless taken in hand spontaneously by the troops nearby for the purpose of clearing Sausage Redoubt, but they were limited to the action of small parties. At 13.00 hours the redoubt and the adjoining trenches were bombarded until 15.20 hours, when a party from the 21st Division (XV Corps) was to bomb northwards along the German front trench to the redoubt, and another from the 34th Division southwards from the Lochnagar mine crater.

The bombardment, however, did not affect the German defence, and the attacks on the redoubt were a failure: the 21st Division party was too weak, and could make little headway, whilst of the 34th Division party, the leading line lost twenty-three out of thirty men killed or wounded almost immediately the advance began. Sausage Redoubt, which by checking the second column had been the chief factor in the delay of the advance of the 34th Division on Contalmaison, remained therefore in German hands.

By the evening, however, two communication trenches were available across No Man's Land into the German trenches held on either side of the redoubt. On the right, one had been dug in XV Corps' area, and touch was thus gained with the 15th and 16/Royal Scots at Birch Tree Wood – Round Wood; on the left one of the tunnels[18] constructed previously under No Man's Land to within a short distance of the German front line, formed a covered communication by which touch was gained with the party of the Tyneside Scottish holding the German defences south of La Boisselle. By these routes, bombs, ammunition, water, etc., were sent up by carrying parties of the 209th Field Company Royal Engineers and the 18/Northumberland Fusiliers (Pioneers), and the transport personnel of the 16/Royal Scots (who fed and re-equipped the troops near Scots Redoubt); it was due to the exertions of these parties that the men in the front line were able to hold on to the two small footings they had gained.

The survivors of the 10/Lincolnshire and 11/Suffolk who had been held up in No Man's Land throughout the day – when to move was to be shot at from the German parapet – got back under cover of darkness to the British front trench, which was later taken over by the 19th Division.

8th Division: The assault on the Ovillers Spur

The 8th Division,[19] which put all its three brigades in the front line, was to assault the Ovillers spur, the dominating feature immediately north of the Albert to Bapaume road, with the lower slopes inside the British lines. To the centre of the division fell the easiest part of a difficult operation: its advance against Ovillers, on the eastern slope of the spur, would be out of sight of the defenders except for the last three or four hundred yards. The flank brigades, however, were forced to move along the exposed and open slopes of the valleys on either side – Mash Valley to the south and Nab Valley to the north – and these were swept from the German positions on the far sides of the valleys, from La Boisselle in the 34th Division area, and from the Leipzig Salient in that of the 32nd Division area. In fact, it seemed to Major General Hudson that there was small chance of success unless the divisions on either side advanced a little ahead of his own. A proposal to postpone its zero hour slightly was, however, rejected by the commander of the Fourth Army, but the 8th Division was given a call on a battery of the 32nd Division to keep down flanking fire.

SLAUGHTER ON THE SOMME: 1 JULY 1916

The right brigade, the 23rd (Brigadier-General H.D. Tuson) was to attack up Mash Valley, its right gaining the Albert – Pozières road due south of Ovillers. Thence it was to advance astride the road over the mile of steadily rising ground to its objective, Pozières village. The centre brigade, the 25th (Brigadier-General J.H.W. Pollard), was to carry the sector of the German front defences in and about Ovillers village. The 70th Brigade (Brigadier-General H. Gordon), on the left, was to attack up the southern slope of Nab Valley on to that part of Ovillers spur north of the village, and thence advance over almost level upland to the German second position north of Pozières, the left of the brigade on Mouquet Farm (exclusive).[20]

For the last eight minutes before the infantry assault, that is from 07.22 hours onwards, the final artillery bombardment was supplemented by the fire of trench-mortar batteries from concealed positions near the front, three sections (twelve 3-inch Stokes mortars) to each brigade,[21] which fired eighty to one hundred rounds per mortar on the German front defences. During this period the leading waves moved out two or three hundred yards into No Man's Land, where it was wide (it varied from 300 to 800 yards), at once coming under machine-gun and rifle fire; in fact, from 07.00 hours, when the bombardment was intensified, at least two machine-guns constantly traversed the front line.

At 07.30 hours the artillery barrage lifted, the trench mortars ceased fire, and the leading battalions of all three brigades rose and moved forward, each battalion in four lines of companies at 50 paces' distance, and on a frontage of 400 yards. The enemy machine-gun and rifle fire immediately grew in volume: from La Boisselle and Ovillers and from the German second trench it poured into No Man's Land. Nevertheless, the advance over the greater part of this absolutely bare ground was carried out with great coolness and precision and in excellent order.[22]

When, however, the front wave was within eighty yards or so of the German trench the enemy fire rose to extreme violence along the whole front of the position. Almost simultaneously the German batteries behind Ovillers placed a barrage on No Man's Land and along the British front and support trenches, causing heavy losses. Instead of keeping the even walking pace intended, the lines of companies, on receiving this very heavy fire, tried to charge forward, as the ground in the centre of No Man's Land was uncratered and provided no cover. The original wave formation soon ceased to exist, and companies became mixed together, making a mass of men, among which the German fire played havoc. That they were moving quickly did not help them to escape, and for the most part only isolated detachments reached the German trench.

On the front of the 23rd Brigade, a number of the 2/Middlesex and 2/Devonshires[23] actually passed through the scattered groups of Germans in the front trench, and some reached the second trench, two hundred yards beyond, but further advance was completely checked by cross fire from the communication trenches and from shell holes on either flank.

The survivors, about seventy in all, were reorganized by Lieutenant Colonel R.

Bastard of the 2/Lincolnshire, in three hundred yards of the German front trench, which they held for nearly two hours, until, much reduced in numbers and having exhausted their supply of bombs, they were driven out by German counter-attacks from both flanks. Retiring as best they could, they occupied shell holes in No Man's Land, and found that the rear waves, unable to move forward, were lying out in the open behind them, and suffering so very heavily that the ground was covered by dying and wounded men.[24]

The 2/West Yorkshire, which moved forward in support at 08.25 hours, lost over two hundred and fifty men in passing through the German artillery barrage on the British front trench, while its subsequent advance was enfiladed throughout from La Boisselle and that side of the valley. Only small parties reached the German front trench.[25] The advance of the 2/Scottish Rifles beyond the front line was therefore stopped. About this time Lieutenant Colonel Bastard returned to the British front line to collect as many men as possible to support those in front of the German defences, but, by brigade orders, no further attempt was made to reinforce, and he went forward again and withdrew what men he could to the old front line.

On the front of the 25th Brigade the course of events was almost similar, the lines of the leading battalions, the 2/Royal Berkshire and 2/Lincolnshire[26] receiving the same heavy fire. Parties of the latter battalion, moving by short rushes from shell hole to shell hole, reached the German front trench about 07.50 hours, but this was so wrecked that it gave little cover, and attempts made to consolidate a position along it were of no avail. Some men pressed on to the second trench, but by 09.00 hours, enfiladed from both flanks and attacked by bombers from the shell craters, they were compelled to withdraw as best they could, Lieutenant Colonel A.M. Holdsworth of the Berkshire receiving wounds of which he died six days later, his successor, Major G.H. Sawyer, also being wounded.

The 1/Royal Irish Rifles, which had moved forward in support of the 25th Brigade attack, suffered very heavily from the German artillery barrage on the British front trench, losing Lieutenant Colonel C.C. Macnamara, who died of wounds; and its subsequent efforts to cross No Man's Land proved as costly in life and fruitless as had those of other units, only ten men getting over. Each of the three battalions of the 25th Brigade had now lost more than half its strength in the action.[27] Many of the survivors lay out in the shell craters in and about the German front line throughout the day, only returning to the British trenches at nightfall.

The assault of the 70th Brigade, on the left, was at first more successful. Aided by the attack of the 82nd Division on the left, which diverted from it some of the German flanking fire from the Leipzig Salient and works on the Thiepval spur, the two leading waves of the 8/King's Own Yorkshire Light Infantry and part of those of the 8/York & Lancaster[28] got across No Man's Land, and pressed straight over the front trench and on to the second one, leaving untouched the trenches north-east of "The Nab". Very few of the third and fourth waves, however, got across the four hundred yards of open grassland separating the two lines. At the second trench opposition stiffened and further progress of the first waves became slow, although some men entered the third trench, two hundred yards beyond. Owing to the heavy casualties the impetus of the assault was now exhausted; no reinforcements appeared, and time was given to the enemy to take measures for the defence of the gap which had been made in his line.

The 9/York & Lancaster, following the leading battalions, tried to get forward to support them, but the machine-gun fire from the Thiepval spur, which enfiladed the advance at a range of six hundred to eight hundred yards, now greatly increased. The battalion lost fifty per cent of its strength almost at once, and very few men reached the German front trench. Brigadier-General Gordon had now to make a decision. The 11/Sherwood Foresters, his fourth battalion, was moving up automatically towards the front line. Should he allow it to go on? In view of the situation on his flanks, where his neighbours seemed at this time to be progressing, he decided to do so. The Foresters had to pass a continuous stream of wounded on the way up, and literally step over the corpses of the York & Lancaster which had preceded them, but forward they went in two waves in a desperate attempt to join the remnants of the brigade still in the German lines. The first wave suffered heavily in No Man's Land, but parts of it got across to the wire, only to be shot down; for Germans almost immediately appeared in the front trench. The second wave was sent forward, but the machine-gun fire was too severe and hardly a man reached the enemy wire. A further effort was made by a party of fifty, chiefly bombers, to get across No Man's Land under cover of the sunken road leading from The Nab towards Mouquet Farm, but a heavy frontal fire down the road from a single German machine-gun checked it within eighty yards of the German trench. Later in the morning so intense was the fire sweeping the front of the Ovillers spur, that communication with the troops in the German position was completely cut off, even attempts at visual signalling being unsuccessful.

The losses of the 70th Brigade were the heaviest in the division, and it had very few unwounded men left: two commanding officers, Lieutenant Colonels B.L. Maddison and A.J.B. Addison, were killed, and the other two, Lieutenant Colonel H.F. Watson and Captain K.E. Poyser, wounded.[29]

At 09.15 hours the 25th Brigade asked that the barrage should be brought back on to the Ovillers line, and, after some discussion, this was done; it could not well be turned on to the front system, which the Germans had manned again at most places, as our men were lying close up to it, even where they were not thought to be in it.

About 09.30 hours the commanders of the 23rd and 25th Brigades were instructed by divisional headquarters to arrange mutually the hour for a half-hour bombardment prior to a renewed attack on Ovillers, but both Brigadier-General Tuson and Brigadier-General Pollard reported that, as the German defences were fully manned, they did not consider a fresh attack advisable with the few troops remaining in hand, and they pointed out that the bombardment would fall on our own men believed to be in the first and second lines. Brigadier-General Gordon made a similar reply when asked to renew the attack of the 70th Brigade – there was indeed little left of it, and its front was held by under a hundred of its men and the 15th Field Company Royal Engineers.

Major General Hudson informed III Corps accordingly, and at 12.15 hours General Pulteney placed the 56th Brigade (Brigadier-General F.G.M. Rowley) of the 19th Division at his disposal for another attempt, formal orders for it being issued at 12.35 hours. The 56th Brigade was directed to attack on a frontage of six hundred yards past the northern side of Ovillers, its right on the Ovillers – Courcelette road (which passes north of Pozières), so as to come up on the immediate right of those troops of the 70th Brigade, the 8/King's Own Yorkshire Light Infantry and 8/York & Lancaster, which were believed to be holding out. The assault was to be launched at 17.00 hours, after half-an-hour's artillery preparation. Wiser counsels, however, prevailed.

It was apparent that until the Thiepval spur was captured by X Corps, and the machine-guns there, as well as those in Ovillers, silenced, no further advance was possible. Up to 14.30 hours various observers reported seeing bomb fighting going on in the German front trench. Parties of our men, doubtless those who had been driven back from the second and third trenches, were seen standing on the parapet and throwing bombs. They were eventually overpowered by the enemy, who got at them from both flanks. Thus the Germans were again in complete possession of their defences opposite the 8th Division, and of most of their line opposite the 34th Division.

At 16.15 hours, in view of the poor prospect of success, the difficulty in getting the troops up owing to congestion in the trenches, and the fact that it appeared doubtful if any British troops were still alive and uncaptured in the German position, the order for the 17.00 hours assault was cancelled.

At 17.30 hours, however, orders were issued to proceed with the attack on La Boisselle at 22.30 hours with the 57th and 58th Brigades of the 19th Division. The movement did not, however, take place until the early morning of the 2nd. The 8th Division received instructions that it would be relieved by the 12th Division from Fourth Army reserve, which had been placed by General Rawlinson at the disposal of III Corps at 16.40 hours. Meantime the other field companies Royal Engineers, 2nd and 1st Home Counties (Territorial Force), of the division, which had not left their positions of assembly, were sent up to assist in holding the line. They actually spent the night bringing in wounded. The relief was carried out uneventfully during the night, which was extraordinarily quiet on III Corps' front, and completed by 05.40 hours on 2 July, the three brigades of the 8th Division being withdrawn to the north-west of Albert.

The losses of the 8th and 34th Divisions on 1 July were over 11,000, but Ovillers and La Boisselle were both still in the enemy's hands and III Corps had nothing as consolation for its heavy casualties but a success on the right by the 15/ and 16/Royal Scots next to XV Corps, and a holding of the 2nd and 3rd Tyneside Scottish at Schwaben Höhe.

Of the wounded, 5,605 were received in the field ambulances of III Corps in the twenty-four hours after 06.00 hours on 1 July, and 4,993 were evacuated thence to Casualty Clearing Stations in the same period. Once they got out of No Man's Land (and the enemy offered no opposition to their removal after the attack had completely died down), they were brought back with great rapidity, cases from as far forward as the third German trench, after first dressing, reaching the main dressing station in 2½ hours. In spite of the sudden rush of large numbers – a third Casualty Clearing Station had to be opened – there was never an undue accumulation at the field ambulances, although the numbers were too great for the stretcher bearers to carry off the field, and it was not until 3 July that all were got away.

The Germans opposite III Corps[30]

The section of the 110th Reserve Regiment opposite the 34th Division suffered greatly during the bombardment: "Trenches and obstacles, the slighter dug-outs and all the best observing posts were nearly completely battered in … The original position of the trenches was scarcely recognizable and only by the greatest exertions were they kept passable. The entrances of the few deep dug-outs not smashed up could only be kept open by constant attention."

The assault did not come as a surprise: "At 02.45 hours the 56th Reserve Brigade, from its battle headquarters at Contalmaison, reported to the 28th Reserve Division a fragment of an order of the 34th Division, picked up by the 'Moritz' overhearing post at the southern point of La Boisselle. It ran: 'The infantry must hold on obstinately to every yard of ground that is gained. Behind it is an excellent artillery.' This order, apparently the conclusion to an order of the Fourth Army, pointed to the beginning of the general enemy offensive in the morning."[31]

The mine (Y Sap) fired close to La Boisselle, it is stated, occasioned no loss, as the trenches there had been evacuated, but the large double one (Lochnagar) at Schwaben Höhe did much damage, and the defenders were delayed in getting out of their dug-outs. But it is claimed that, after many hours' hand-to-hand fighting with heavy losses, they managed to drive out the British who had penetrated the position. That Schwaben Höhe and the trench behind it were lost is admitted, but it is incorrectly stated in the official monograph that "only the great crater at Schwaben Höhe remained in the enemy's hands".

The 180th Regiment, defending the Ovillers sector opposite the 8th Division, lost seventy-eight killed and 124 wounded in the bombardment, and its defences, like those of the 110th Reserve Regiment, were badly damaged, only those of the right company opposite The Nab remaining in "tolerably good" condition.

The following is an account of the assault on this front by a German eye-witness:[32]

"The intense bombardment was realized by all to be the prelude to an infantry assault sooner or later. The men in the dug-outs therefore waited ready, belts full of hand-grenades around them, gripping their rifles and listening for the bombardment to lift from the front defence zone on to the rear defences. It was of vital importance to lose not a second in taking up position in the open to meet the British infantry which would advance immediately behind the artillery barrage. Looking towards the British trenches through the long trench periscopes held up out of the dug-out entrances there could be seen a mass of steel helmets above the parapet showing that the storm-troops were ready for the assault.

"At 07.30 hours the hurricane of shells ceased as suddenly as it had begun. Our men at once clambered up the steep shafts leading from the dug-outs to daylight and ran singly or in groups to the nearest shell craters. The machine-guns were pulled out of the dug-outs and hurriedly placed in position, their crews dragging the heavy ammunition boxes up the steps and out to the guns. A rough firing line was thus rapidly established.

"As soon as the men were in position, a series of extended lines of infantry were seen moving forward from the British trenches. The first line appeared to continue without end to right and left. It was quickly followed by a second line, then a third and fourth. They came on at a steady easy pace as if expecting to find nothing alive in our front trenches. Some appeared to be carrying kodaks to perpetuate the memory of their triumphal march across the German defences.[33]

"The front line, preceded by a thin line of skirmishers and bombers, was now half-way across No Man's Land. "Get ready!" was passed along our front from crater to crater, and heads appeared over the crater edge as final positions were taken up for the best view, and machine-guns mounted firmly in place. A few moments later, when the leading British line was within a hundred yards, the rattle of machine-gun and rifle fire broke out along the whole line of shell-holes. Some fired kneeling so as to get a better target over the broken ground, whilst others, in the excitement of the moment, stood up regardless of their own safety, to fire into the crowd of men in front of them.

"Red rockets sped up into the blue sky as a signal to the artillery, and immediately afterwards a mass of shell from the German batteries in rear tore through the air and burst among the advancing lines. Whole sections seemed to fall, and the rear formations, moving in closer order quickly scattered. The advance rapidly crumpled under this hail of shell and bullets. All along the line men could be seen throwing up their arms and collapsing, never to move again. Badly wounded rolled about in their agony, and others, less severely injured, crawled to the nearest shell hole for shelter.

SLAUGHTER ON THE SOMME: 1 JULY 1916

"The British soldier, however, has no lack of courage, and once his hand is set to the plough he is not easily turned from his purpose. The extended lines, though badly shaken and with many gaps, now came on all the faster. Instead of a leisurely walk they covered the ground in short rushes at the double. Within a few minutes the leading troops had advanced to within a stone's throw of our front trench, and whilst some of us continued to fire at point-blank range, others threw hand-grenades among them. The British bombers answered back, whilst the infantry rushed forward with fixed bayonets. The noise of battle became indescribable. The shouting of orders and the shrill cheers as the British charged forward could be heard above the violent and intense fusillade of machine-guns and rifles and the bursting bombs, and above the deep thunderings of the artillery and shell explosions. With all this were mingled the moans and groans of the wounded, the cries for help and the last screams of death. Again and again the extended lines of British infantry broke against the German defence like waves against a cliff, only to be beaten back.

"It was an amazing spectacle of unexampled gallantry, courage and bull-dog determination on both sides."

Where the British did break in, their efforts to extend right and left were limited by occupying the communication trenches, of which there were far more than in the British defences.

The defence was carried out by the two front battalions of the 180th Regiment unaided, only a part of one company of the battalion in regimental reserve being engaged. The casualties of the regiment on 1 July were four officers and seventy-nine other ranks killed and three officers and 181 other ranks wounded, and thirteen missing.

NOTES

1. III Corps (Lieutenant General Sir W.P. Pulteney): 34th Division (Major General E.C. Ingouville-Williams, killed in action 22nd July 1916) comprised 101st, 102nd and 103rd Brigades; 8th Division (Major General H. Hudson) comprised the 23rd, 25th and 70th Brigades; 19th Division (Major General G.T.M. Bridges) the 56th, 57th and 58th Brigades; and also G.O.C. Royal Artillery, Brigadier-General H.C.C. Uniacke; Heavy Artillery, Brigadier-General A.E.J. Perkins; Chief Engineer, Brigadier-General A.L. Schreiber.
2. Howitzers: One 15-inch; three 12-inch (on railway mountings); twelve 9.2-inch; sixteen 8-inch; and twenty 6-inch. Guns: One 12-inch, one 9.2-inch (both on railway mountings); four 6-inch; thirty-two 60-pounders; and eight 4.7-inch.
3. At the rehearsals of the assault, the artillery lifts had been represented by lines of men carrying flags.
4. This is admitted in Somme-Nord, i. p.18, but the time, stated vaguely as the evening of the 30th, is a mistake. A message picked up on the night of 1/2 July, notifying the change of headquarters, resulted in General von Stein being shelled out again next day. His final headquarters were in Beugny, 3½ miles behind Bapaume.
5. In two charges of 36,000 and 24,000, 60 feet apart, and 52 feet below the surface.
6. The tunnel was driven from the northern flank with a gallery 1,030 feet long, the longest ever driven in chalk during the war.

7. This tunnelling in close proximity to the enemy was carried out in silence, with bayonets fitted with a special spliced handle; the men were barefooted and the floor of the gallery was carpeted with sandbags. The operator inserted the point of the bayonet in a crack in the "face" or alongside a flint, gave it a twist, and dislodged a piece of chalk, which he caught with his other hand and laid on the floor. If for any reason he had to use both hands on the bayonet, another man caught the stone as it fell. The dimensions of the tunnels were about 4½ feet by 2½ feet. An advance of 18 inches in 24 hours was considered satisfactory. The spoil was packed in sandbags and passed out along a line of men seated on the floor, and stacked against the side, ready for use later to "tamp" the charge. There was no interference from the Germans, but as the charges were being loaded they could be heard quite plainly in their system at Lochnagar below and at Y Sap above the British.

8. This division arrived in France on 9/10 January 1916. Originally numbered 41st and nominally organized in December 1914, it actually came into being on 15 June 1915, when a single officer, the D.A.Q.M.G., arrived at Ripon. It consisted entirely of new men, raised mainly in the north of England by local effort. Two infantry brigades and the Pioneer battalion were Northumberland Fusiliers; the two battalions of Royal Scots came from Edinburgh. The artillery came from Sunderland, Staffordshire, Leicester and Nottingham; the engineers from Nottingham.

9. See German account at end of the introduction.

10. The original commander, Brigadier-General H.G. Fitton, had been shot by a sniper in January.

11. Brigadier-General Cameron was wounded soon after zero, and the brigade was commanded by Lieutenant Colonel G.R.V. Steward, 27/Northumberland Fusiliers, until 4 July, when Brigadier-General H.E. Trevor took it over.

12. The 34th Division was opposed by the German 110th Reserve Regiment on a similar frontage, two battalions holding the front defence system, the third battalion being in reserve in the intermediate lines and 2nd Position.

13. A company from the reserve battalion of the 110th Reserve Regiment.

14. The casualties in the two Scottish battalions on 1 July were: 15/Royal Scots, eleven officers killed, six wounded and two missing; 230 Other Ranks killed, 263 wounded and one missing. 16/Royal Scots six officers killed, seven wounded and none missing; 327 Other Ranks killed, sixty-seven wounded and fifty-nine missing.

15. There was no necessity for this wait.

16. Some, however, had started before the order reached them. The Lincolnshire lost fifteen officers and 462 other ranks; the Suffolks, fifteen officers and 512 other ranks. An artillery officer who walked across found "line after line of dead men lying where they had fallen".

17. An officer and thirty-five men were taken out of a dug-out just beyond the dangerous radius of the mine, thoroughly cowed. The officer stated that nine dug-outs equally full must have been closed in by the mine.

18. Three tunnels had been constructed on the III Corps front to provide covered communication across No Man's Land after the assault, one in the 34th Division area south of La Boisselle, and two in the 8th Division area, one north of La Boisselle and the other to a point opposite Ovillers. These tunnels were 8'6" high, 3'6" wide at the bottom, and 2'6" at the top. They had been dug through the chalk at a depth of 12 to 14 feet, the last 150 feet being excavated with bayonets to prevent any sound of working reaching the enemy. Owing to the construction having been kept secret, the tunnels were not taken into use as soon as they might have been.

19. This division, originally composed of troops of the old Army, arrived in France in November 1914. It had lost heavily in the Battles of Neuve Chapelle and Aubers Ridge in 1915. In the autumn of 1915, when certain old infantry brigades were sent to stiffen new divisions, its 24th Brigade was exchanged for the 70th of the 23rd Division. The division therefore went into battle with a large proportion of recruits lacking battle experience. Its Pioneer battalion, the 22/Durham Light Infantry, joined it only a fortnight before the battle.

20. The 8th Division was opposed by the 180th Regiment, with two battalions holding the front defences on the Ovillers spur and across Nab Valley, and its third battalion in reserve in the 2nd Position north of Pozières. Of the four lines of trenches comprising the front defences, the first two were held by three companies from each battalion, each company on a frontage of 400 yards, whilst the fourth

company, in reserve, was in the third trench. The fourth line was occupied by two companies from the reserve battalion, one in rear of each of the front battalions. There were thus ten infantry companies, approximately 1,800 men, to oppose the three brigades, roughly 9,600 men, of the 8th Division.

21. Except the 23rd, the width of No Man's Land in front of it being too great.

22. See the German account.

23. The 2/West Yorkshire was in support and 2/Scottish Rifles in reserve.

24. The 2/Middlesex lost twenty-two officers and 601 other ranks; the 2/Devonshire, seventeen officers and 433 other ranks.

25. The 2/West Yorkshire lost eight officers and 421 other ranks.

26. The 1/Royal Irish Rifles was in support and the 2/Rifle Brigade in reserve.

27. These losses were: 2/Royal Berkshire, twenty-seven officers and 347 Other Ranks; 2/Lincolnshire, twenty-one officers and 450 Other Ranks; 1/Royal Irish Rifles, seventeen officers and 429 Other Ranks; 2/Rifle Brigade, four officers and 115 Other Ranks.

28. The 9/York & Lancaster was in support and the 11/Sherwood Foresters in reserve.

29. These losses were: 8/K.O.Y.L.I., twenty-one officers and 518 Other Ranks; 8/York & Lancaster, twenty-one officers and 576 Other Ranks; 9/York & Lancaster, fourteen officers and 409 Other Ranks; 11/Sherwood Foresters, seventeen officers and 420 Other Ranks.

30. From *Schlachten des Weltkrieges: Somme Nord*, Reichsarchiv (Oldenburg), i. p.53. and M. Gerster, *Die Schwaben an der Ancre* (Heilbron).

31. In the monograph the message is given in German. It has been translated back into English. The actual message sent out by the Fourth Army to the corps, Reserve Army and IV Brigade Royal Flying Corps at 22.17 hours on 30 June ran: "In wishing all ranks good luck the Army commander desires to impress on all infantry units the supreme importance of helping one another and holding on tight to every yard of ground gained. The accurate and sustained fire of the artillery during the bombardment should greatly assist the task of the infantry."

32. Schwaben, *Ibid*, pp.108-9.

33. These "kodaks" were no doubt the pigeon baskets, "power buzzer" boxes and other experimental gear carried.

Index of Battalions

Cheshire Regiment, 9th (Service) Battalion
Devonshire Regiment, 2nd Battalion
Duke of Cambridge's Own (Middlesex Regiment), 2nd Battalion
King's Own (Yorkshire Light Infantry), 8th (Service) Battalion
Lincolnshire Regiment, 2nd Battalion
Lincolnshire Regiment, 10th (Service) Battalion (Grimsby)
Northumberland Fusiliers, 18th (Service) Battalion (1st Tyneside Pioneers)
Northumberland Fusiliers, 20th (Service) Battalion (1st Tyneside Scottish)
Northumberland Fusiliers, 21st (Service) Battalion (2nd Tyneside Scottish)
Northumberland Fusiliers, 22nd (Service) Battalion (3rd Tyneside Scottish)
Northumberland Fusiliers, 23rd (Service) Battalion (4th Tyneside Scottish)
Northumberland Fusiliers, 24th (Service) Battalion (1st Tyneside Irish)
Northumberland Fusiliers, 25th (Service) Battalion (2nd Tyneside Irish)
Northumberland Fusiliers, 26th (Service) Battalion (3rd Tyneside Irish)
Northumberland Fusiliers, 27th (Service) Battalion (4th Tyneside Irish)
Prince of Wales's Own (West Yorkshire Regiment), 2nd Battalion
Princess Charlotte of Wales's (Royal Berkshire Regiment), 2nd Battalion
Rifle Brigade (The Prince Consort's Own), 2nd Battalion
Royal Irish Rifles, 1st Battalion
Royal Scots (Lothian Regiment), 15th (Service) Battalion (1st Edinburgh)
Royal Scots (Lothian Regiment), 16th (Service) Battalion (2nd Edinburgh)
Sherwood Foresters (Nottinghamshire and Derbyshire Regiment), 11th (Service) Battalion
Suffolk Regiment, 11th (Service) Battalion (Cambridgeshire)
York And Lancaster Regiment, 8th (Service) Battalion
York And Lancaster Regiment, 9th (Service) Battalion

9th (Service) Battalion Cheshire Regiment

ALBERT (RAILWAY EMBANKMENTS OF)

Tools and bombs were issued in the Assembly trenches.

10.0 a.m. The Battalion took up its allotted position in the TARA-USNA line being the right front Battalion of the 58th Brigade.

7.0 p.m. Orders were dictated personally to the Commanding Officer, which were to take up a position from LOCHNAGAR St to INCH St to carry out an attack at 10.30 pm, the direction of the attack being given as N.E. The Battalion proceeded via NORTHUMBERLAND AVENUE, SCOURINBOURNE ST, ASHDOWN ST, LOCHNAGAR ST in the following order 'D' 'C' HQ 'B' and 'A' Coys. On arrival at DUNDEE AVENUE conflicting verbal orders were received resulting in part of 'B' Coy and 'D' Coy under Lieut A.V. Ward and Lieut C.F. King occupying the line as ordered, the remainder of the Battalion making its way to BECOURT WOOD where they were assembled by Capts T.L. Jackson and G.G. Symons. The Commanding Officer after attending the conference at the H.Q. 58th Brigade, proceeded to the front line to meet the Battalion. Here he could only find parts of the two Coys above specified.

9.40 p.m. At 9.40 p.m. he ordered this portion of the Battalion to reinforce troops of the 34th Division who were holding the GERMAN line adjacent to the new Crater. Capt. Jackson ordered the Battalion to proceed from BECOURT WOOD to the front line, where they arrived at about 3.30 a.m. on 2nd inst. where the Commanding Officer came in touch with them and all went to work repairing the line.

2nd Battalion Devonshire Regiment

Report on the part taken by the 2nd Battalion Devonshire Regiment during the attack on Pozières on 1st July 1916:

It was a comparatively quiet night and there was little fire on either side until 6.30 a.m.

At 6.35 a.m. our artillery which consisted of guns of all calibres opened an intense bombardment which lasted for one hour. The enemy front and support line came in for most of the shelling. The enemy's reply was not very vigorous, most of his fire being directed on our Support and Communication trenches.

During the last 7 to 10 minutes of the intense bombardment 'A' and 'B' Coy's left the "NEW TRENCH" and advanced in open order to within about 100 yards of the enemy trenches, closely followed by 'C' and 'D' Coy's, who moved down to the new line and advanced from there.

This advance was carried out in four successive waves in the most perfect order; the casualties were not very heavy during this advance. Lieut. Temp. Captain E.G. Roberts who was in command of 'A' Coy was badly wounded by shell fire while leaving our front line, 2/Lieut L.A. Carey also of 'A' Coy was killed at the same time.

Just before the advance began a mist drifted over from the enemy's line towards our own and made observation very difficult. Captain J.A. Andrews was in Command of the Front Line and it was due to him, to a great extent, that the advance from our front line was carried out with such remarkable coolness and precision. At the same time as our Coy's advanced towards the hostile trenches, the 2/Middlesex Regiment on our right and the 2/Royal Berks. Regiment on our left, advanced with remarkable coolness and order.

At 7.30 a.m. our artillery lifted from the enemy front line trenches on to the trenches in rear. During this pause the hostile artillery fire had gradually increased. As soon as the artillery lifted Captain J.A. Andrews got up and gave the order to advance, hardly had the order been given when he was killed by a hostile bullet which struck him in the head. As soon as the order to advance had been received, the four waves dashed for the German trenches opposite X.8.c.5.2. – X.8.c.8 ½ .3 ½. – X.8.d.2.4.

Immediately the troops advanced the enemy opened a terrific machine gun fire from the front and from both flanks, which mowed down our troops, this fire did not deter our men from continuing to advance, but only a very few reached the German Lines alive. Some of these managed to effect an entry into the German Lines, where they "put up" a determined fight against enormous odds and were soon killed.

At first and for some little time owing to the mist, and dust caused by our shell fire, it was difficult to realise exactly what had happened, although the heavy hostile Machine Gun fire told its own tale. The lines appeared at first sight to be intact, but it was soon made clear that the lines consisted of only dead or wounded, and that no one was there to support the few that had got in, and to carry on with the advance.

The cause of this was eventually discovered; the 2/West Yorks. Regt who were in support had been caught by hostile Machine Gun and Shell fire as soon as they advanced from their assembly trenches, and had been cut to pieces.

The Brigade was informed as to what had happened to the Battalion but no information could be given to them as to what had happened to the supporting Battalion, as our runners were unsuccessful in getting in touch with them, neither could any accurate information be given as to what had happened to the 2/Middlesex Regt on our right and the 2/Royal Berks Regt on our left. From observation it was soon ascertained that the Battalions on either flank had also been caught by the hostile Machine Gun fire and had been unable to take the German trenches. This information was communicated to the Brigade. This information was shortly corroborated by our wounded who began to crawl back to our lines in small numbers. None of the runners sent by Company's reached Headquarters, they were all either killed or wounded.

No accurate information could be ascertained as to the exact number of casualties the Battalion had suffered, although it was clear that there were very few left who had not been hit; the enemy began to snipe our wounded, it was quite clear that we were not holding the front line, the barrage was brought back on the German front line trenches, and the 2/Scottish Rifles were moved forward to the "New trench" and were told to hold themselves in readiness to advance.

During this time the hostile shelling had increased and the front line systems of trenches were very badly knocked about.

The enemy used a very high proportion of lachrymatory shells which caused a great deal of inconvenience to anyone not wearing gas goggles.

The enemy continued to confine his shelling practically entirely to our front line, support and communication trenches.

About midday orders were issued by the Brigade that no further advance would take place till further orders.

Our wounded still continued to crawl in to the "New Trench" but great difficulty was found evacuating the wounded to the Regimental Aid Post as the trenches were too narrow to allow a stretcher to pass and also the trenches had been so knocked about that in many places one was exposed to hostile Machine Gun and Shell fire.

The Medical Officer went down to the "New Trench" and bandaged all the wounded while the Stretcher Bearers and parties of Regimental Pioneers from Headquarters carried the wounded back to the Aid Post on their backs and in waterproof sheets. By this means all our wounded which it was possible to get at were removed to First Aid Post where the M.O. re-dressed their wounds. The supply of Orderlies for removing the wounded from the Aid Post was not good. Several messages had to be sent asking for Orderlies to be sent up to remove the wounded.

About 4 p.m. all Adjutants were ordered to report at Brigade Headquarters. The Brigade Major started to dictate orders to the effect that the Scottish Rifles would take over the front line and the remainder of the other Battalions of the Brigade would move into the support trenches. While taking down the orders the 8th Division informed the Brigade that the whole Brigade would be relieved that night, and that orders for the relief would be issued. Adjutants then returned to their Battalions and C.O's were ordered to re-organise their Battalions.

About 4 p.m. the artillery fire on both sides slackened down considerably.

During the day wounded and unwounded crawled in, in small numbers. The unwounded were organised into parties by Company's.

About 8 p.m. orders were received that the Brigade would be relieved and that in the meantime the 2/Scottish Rifles would hold the line and the remainder of the Battalions were to move into dugouts in HODDER and HOUGHTON Streets, in the vicinity of Bde Headquarters and that the Brigade would later move to bivouacs in MILLENCOURT. By this time about 40 men not including Headquarters had been collected.

By 10 o'clock all the men had been placed in dugouts.

The C.O. and Adjutant then proceeded to Brigade Headquarters where a conference was held by the G.O.C. 23rd Infantry Brigade, on the operations and the best methods of overcoming the difficulties which had been met.

The remnants of the Battalion moved off for MILLENCOURT about 11 p.m. The C.O. and Adjutant left Brigade Headquarters for MILLENCOURT about 1.30 a.m. on the 2nd July and arrived at MILLENCOURT about 3 a.m.

The following casualties were suffered during the action:

Captain J.A. Andrews	Killed (In Command of Front Line O.C.'B' Coy)
Captain A. Preedy	-do-
2/Lieut L.A. Carey	-do-
2/Lieut E.M. Gould	-do-
2/Lieut C.V. Beddow	-do-
2/Lieut M.C. Ley	-do-
2/Lieut E.A. Jago	-do-
43 Other Ranks	-do-
Captain E.G. Roberts	Wounded (O.C.'A' Coy)
2/Lieut C.O.R. Jacob	-do- (O.C.'D' Coy)
2/Lieut A.R. Newton	-do-
2/Lieut J.A. Rennie	-do- (since died of wounds)
2/Lieut G. Parker	-do-
2/Lieut A.H. Cornell	-do-
194 Other Ranks	-do-
2/Lieut J.S.McGowan	Missing, (since reported killed)
2/Lieut G.S.D.Carver	-do- (O.C.'C' Coy)
2/Lieut F.B.Coldwells	-do-
178 Other Ranks	-do-

Two Lewis Guns were lost the remaining 6 were brought in during daylight under heavy fire, 2 of these by Privates who were the only men left of their teams.

2nd Battalion Duke of Cambridge's Own (Middlesex Regiment)

TRENCHES

The Battalion in conjunction with the remainder of the 8th Division assaulted the German front line system between OVILLERS LA BOISSELLE and LA BOISSELLLE at 7.30 a.m. after an intense bombardment lasting 65 minutes. The assault was carried out in four waves – the leading wave consisting of 2 Platoons of 'B' Coy on the right and 2 Platoons of 'A' Coy: the second wave which followed at 50yards distance consisting of the remaining Platoons of 'A' & 'B' Companies. The third and fourth waves similarly composed of 'D' and 'C' Coys followed the preceding waves at 50 yards distance. The Battalion Bombers were distributed by squads amongst the four waves & the 8 Lewis gun teams amongst the 2nd, 3rd & 4th waves.

On the right were a battalion of the TYNESIDE SCOTTISH belonging to the 34th Division & on the left were the 2nd Devons R.

As soon as our leading wave left our trenches to assault it was caught by heavy machine gun fire and suffered heavy losses. As soon as the succeeding waves came under this fire they doubled forward and before anyone reached the German front line the original wave formation had ceased to exist.

About 200 of all ranks succeeded in reaching the German lines – passing over the front line they entered the 2nd line of trenches, but after a short fight, during which about half became casualties, they were forced to retire to the German front line. Here, under the leadership of Major H.B.W. Savile, Capt & Adj R.J. Young, 2/Lieuts P.M. Elliot, W. Spatz & H.C. Hunt the survivors proceeded to consolidate.

By 9.15 am the handful of unwounded men, numbering perhaps a dozen, were forced to retire to shell holes outside the enemy front line, where the majority remained until darkness enabled them to regain our lines.

Of the 23 Officers who took part in the assault only 2/Lieut H.C. Hunt regained our lines unwounded, of the 650 N.C.O.s & men who took part in the assault a bare 50 answered their names in the early hours of July 2nd.

The following Officers were reported as casualties:

Killed, Capt C.S. Hilton, 2/Lieuts P.M. Elliot, R.E. Grundy, W. Spatz, J. Wilson, Capt Meere.
Wounded: Lt Col E.T.F. Sandys,[1] Major H.B.W. Savile, Capt & Adj R.J. Young, Capt. G. Johnson, Lieuts W.J. Clachan & R. McD. Yorston, H. Peckham, 2/Lieuts C.H. Rawson, O.N.S. Dobbs.
Wounded and missing: 2/Lieuts C.S. Davis, W.F. Forge, G. Scott, T.J. McManus, F. Van-den-Bok, & H.D. Wood, A.I. Frost

1. Due to the nature of his wounds, Lieutenant Colonel Edwin Thomas Falkiner Sandys was evacuated back to the United Kingdom. It would seem that that he was never able to come to terms with the losses suffered by his battalion on 1 July. *The Daily Mirror* of 15 September 1916, carries the following account of his death:"A tragic story was told at a Westminster inquest yesterday on Lieutenant-Colonel E.T. Faulkner [*sic*] Sandys D.S.O., who died at St. George's Hospital as the result of a bullet wound. On September 6 he took a room at the Cavendish Hotel and was found dead in bed with a revolver in his hand. Captain Lloyd Jones said that Colonel Sandys, who resided at the Bath Club, had been wounded five times, and was greatly depressed and much distressed because in the attack on July 1, his battalion suffered severely. He had never threatened suicide, but said he wished he had been killed with his men. Witness received a letter from him, saying:'I have come to London today to take my life. I have never had a moment's peace since July 1.'The coroner said the case revealed a pathetic tragedy of a very distinguished soldier, who thought less of his own wounds than he did of the loss of his men." Born in Bareilly, India, 40-year-old Sandys died from his gunshot wound on 13 September 1916. A few days later he was awarded the DSO and he was Mentioned in Despatches by Haig in 1917. The Coroner recorded a verdict of"suicide whilst temporarily insane".

8th (Service) Battalion King's Own (Yorkshire Light Infantry)

TRENCHES NEAR OVILLERS

The Battalion attacked at 7.30 a.m. having on its left 8th Y&L, on its right 2nd Lincolns. In support to our Battalion were the 11th S.F.s. Below is set forth copy of statement made consequently in reporting action to 70th Brigade.

During the preliminary bombardment our losses from hostile shell fire were considerable. I estimate them at 10% of the whole strength. The first two waves leaving our trenches just before 7.30 a.m, reached the German Lines with only slight loss. The remaining waves lost heavily in NO MANS LAND from M.G. fire from both flanks, & I estimate their loss before they reached the German front line at 60%. No casualties occurred from our own Artillery. The German wire offered no obstacle. Our men were soon mixed up with those of the 8th Y&L, 9th Y&L, 11th S.F. and 2nd Lincolns, and severe fighting took place for the second German trench, which several times changed hands. Several of our men penetrated at one time the third line. At the second & third lines we were held up by Machine Guns. The enemy relied throughout almost entirely on Machine Guns and Bombs, very little on rifles and bayonets. At about 8.30 a.m. the order"Retire" was passed round, possibly originating from the enemy & our men were thereafter organised & rallied by officers of 2nd Lincolns, our own N.C.O.s & sometimes by men, & returned to the attack time after time, fighting for the second & third lines. The last men of this Battalion to have the German lines left at about 6pm, & it is thought that there were none of our men being then in the German second line. Very few of our officers reached the German trenches. The Germans were many times observed sniping & bombing our wounded. Our Battalion went into action with 25 officers, 1 M.O. and 659 other ranks, of these the M.O. & 110 other ranks have reported to the Battalion.

The above statement has been put together from evidence taken from N.C.O.s & men only, no officer taking part in the operations being available. *Signed G.L. Ryman, Captain Commanding 8th Battalion K.O.Y.L.I.*

During the night the Battalion was withdrawn to LONG VALLEY.

2nd Battalion Lincolnshire Regiment

IN TRENCHES OPPOSITE OVILLERS

Everybody was in their position by 3.30am. and the wire along the whole of our front reported cut by 2.30am. 2/Lt Eld and a few men got wounded doing this, and Lt Ross' party had trouble owing to continual hostile machine gun fire. Brigade time was checked at 5.30 a.m.

6.25 a.m.   The intensive bombardment commenced to which the enemy retaliated on our front line and assembly trenches with high explosive shrapnel.

7.25 a.m.   Companies started to move forward from their assembly positions preparatory to the assault. The three assaulting companies getting their 1st two waves out into No man's land, and their 3rd & 4th waves out at zero hour. These arrangements were carried out most excellently, no hitch occurring, but casualties were fairly heavy from machine gun fire. The support company got into our front line trench but suffered a lot of casualties from shell fire.

7.30 a.m.   As soon as the barrage lifted the whole assaulted. They were met with very severe rifle fire and in most cases had to advance in rushes and return the fire. This fire seemed to come from the German second line, and the machine gun fire from our left. On reaching the German front line they found it strongly held and were met with showers of bombs, but after a very hard fight about 200 yards of German line were taken about 7.50am. the extreme right failing to get in and also the extreme left where there appeared to be a gap of about 70 yards although bits of platoons of the 70th Brigade joined them. The support company by this time joined in. The few officers that were left gallantly led their men over the German trench to attack the second line but owing to the rifle and machine gun fire could not push on. Attempts were made to consolidate and make blocks but the trench was so badly knocked about that very little cover was obtainable. From the enfilade machine gun fire and continual bombing attacks which were being made by the enemy the whole line and one frontal attack from their second line which we repulsed.

9.00 a.m.   This isolated position became untenable, no supports being able to reach us owing to the intense rifle and machine gun fire. Our left being driven back the remainder which by now only held about 100 yards had to withdraw. On reaching our own line all the men that could be collected were formed up and tried to push on again but the heavy machine gun and rifle fire made the ground quite impassable.

1.00 p.m. Orders were received from the Brigade to withdraw to Ribble and Melling Streets and occupy the assembly dugouts there which was done.

12 We were relieved by the 6th West Kents and proceeded to Long Valley midnight. (O.R. 26 killed, 303 wounded, 89 missing, 25 wounded and missing.)

Officers present with the Battalion:
Lt Col R. Bastard D.S.O.[3]
Capt R.B. Leslie
" H.G.F. Wisemam, wounded and missing
" S.H. Jendwine, missing
" B.L. Needham, killed
" F.K. Griffith
Lieut B.G. Woodcock, wounded
" D.S. Ross, missing
" H.H. Shearman, died of wounds
" H.E. Sowerby, wounded
" J.H. Toolis, wounded and missing
" C.G. Shaw, missing
" H.G. Clifford, wounded and missing
" J. Shelley, wounded
2nd Lt G.W.H. Applin, killed
" A.W. Eld, wounded
" S.N. Carter, wounded
" J. Anstee, killed
" P.H. Gates, wounded
" C.C.W. [illegible], died of wounds[1]
" L.O. [illegible], killed[2]
" E.Q. Jemmett, wounded
" S.T. Stevens, wounded
Capt W. Fotheringham, Medical Officer.
2/Lt K.M.J. Ferguson (with 25th Trench Mortar Battery)
2/Lt J.D. Drysdale (with Brigade Bombers)

NOTES

1. Believed to be Lieutenant Constant Clifford William Meyer, killed in action 1 July 1916.
2. Believed to be Temporary Second Lieutenant Leon Owen Sharp, killed in action 1 July 1916.
3. By the time his battalion was finally withdrawn, Lieutenant Colonel Reginald Bastard had crossed No Man's Land under fire no less than four times, as well as having participated in the fighting in the German trenches. For his actions that day, he was awarded a Bar to his D.S.O.

10th (Service) Battalion (Grimsby)
Lincolnshire Regiment

BECOURT

7.30 a.m. At this hour the 101st Infantry Brigade, 34th Division delivered an assault on the German position south of LA BOISELLE. The 15th Royal Scots being the right assaulting battalion & the 10th Lincolnshire Regt the left assaulting battalion, the 16th Royal Scots right supporting battalion, the 11th Suffolks left supporting battalion.

The portion of the German front line trenches assaulted by the 10th Lincolns was known as the BLOATER & lay between the LA BOISELLE salient & the redoubt known as HELIGOLAND. The formation of the 10th Lincolns was as follows 'A' Coy on the right 'B' in the centre 'C' on the left. 'D' Coy less 1 platoon was employed as a carrying company & advanced in rear of 103rd Brigade which was in reserve. Two minutes before the attack was timed to take place a mine was exploded near the S.W. corner of the LA BOISELLE salient forming an immense crater about 100 yds in diameter.

On leaving their trenches, the 10th Lincolns who advanced in 4 waves on a 3 platoon frontage at a distance of 100 yds between the first & second waves & 150 yds between the others, with a platoon of 'D' Coy as a clearing platoon 50 yds in rear of the 4th wave & accompanied by 101/3 Trench mortar Battery were immediately exposed to a heavy shell fire, shrapnel & H.E. and the most intense enfilade machine gun fire from LA BOISELLE and HELIGOLAND Redoubt.

Advancing with the utmost steadiness & courage, not to be surpassed by any troops in the world, yet the distance they were away from the German trench 800 yds & the intensity of the machine gun fire did not allow of the possibility of reaching & penetrating the enemy's line.

Some few men were able to enter German trench from the NEW CRATER & bombing their way up blocked it & helped to protect the right flank of the 102nd Brigade which attacked on our left, others consolidated & held positions in the NEW CRATER with a like object. One Officer 2nd Lt Hendin with three men made his way on the right by way of the 21st Divisional front & consolidating a strong point in the German trench helped to protect the left flank of the 21st division.

It is doubtful if troops have since been subjected to a more intense machine gun fire than was experienced in this assault, a fire which made it absolutely impossible either to relieve or reinforce units during daylight. The 34th Division was relived by the 19th Division in the early hours of the morning of July 4th, moving for the night to ALBERT & subsequently on the 5th July to HENENCOURT. The battalion went into action with a total of 20 Officers (of whom 4 were killed, 10 wounded and 1 missing) and 822 other ranks of whom 66 were killed, 259 wounded and 162 missing.

The rank and names of those officers taken into action are as follows:

Lt Col	E.K. Cordeaux, (in command)
Major	E.H. Kendrick, (2nd in command)
Major	W.A. Vignoles, (wounded)
Capt	T. Baker, (killed)
Hon. Major	G.L. Bennett, (Adjutant)
Capt	C.H. Bellamy, (wounded)
Capt	J.F. Worthington, (wounded)
Lieut	H.L. Dent
Lieut	R.C. Green, (wounded)
2nd Lieut	H.P. Hendin
Lieut	E. Inman, (missing) K[2]
Lieut	R.P. Eason, (wounded) d of w 1/7/16
Lieut	J.K. Murphy, (wounded)
2nd Lieut	L. Cummins, (killed)
2nd Lieut	H.W. Bannister, (wounded)
2nd Lieut	J.H. Baines, (killed)
2nd Lieut	C.H. Jolin, (wounded)
2nd Lieut	R.G. Ingle, (killed)
2nd Lieut	J.H. Turnbull, (wounded)
2nd Lieut	J.R. Moore
2nd Lieut	A. Hartshorn

NOTES

1. Often referred to by its original name of "The Grimsby Chums" – this being the only Pals battalion to be called "Chums" – the battalion was initially formed by former pupils of Wintringham Secondary School in Grimsby.
2. The 'K' denotes that 21-year-old Lieutenant Edwin Inman was subsequently listed as having been killed in action on 1 July 1916. The son of Edwin and Alice Inman, of 5, Clifford Road, Sharrow, Sheffield, he is buried in Bapaume Post Military Cemetery which lies on the west side of Tara Hill, and south-west of Usna Hill.

18th (Service) Battalion (1st Tyneside Pioneers) Northumberland Fusiliers

CHAPES SPUR ALBERT

The Battalion was disposed as follows, at 7 a.m. this morning: Hd Qtrs, 'A' 'B' 'D' Companies in BECOURT WOOD 'C' Co holding the Crater area in immediate contact with the enemy from INCH to SCONE Streets both inclusive. Captain Dodsworth was in charge of 'D' in store in RUE PAPETRIE ALBERT, he had with him Lt. Hall and 2nd Lt. Caswell and 40 O.R. This party was to detonate all bombs & see to loading & unloading wagons. 2nd Lts Renton & Nicholson were in charge of the two Divisional Dumps in ST. ANDREWS AVE & BECOURT WOOD each had a small party of N.C.O.s & men.

Lt. Wood was in charge of 101st Bde. Dumps. Lt. McQuillan of 103rd Bde Dumps & 2nd Lt. Parry in charge of 102nd Bde Dumps.

7 a.m.	No.4 Column, to carry for 102nd Bde under comd Capt Fortune moved off to gain its position by passing in rear of the Reserve Brigade, which was formed up in the TARA-USNA Line. The other three columns formed up & then took whatever could be obtained at the edge of the wood.
7.28.	The mines exploded, & two minutes later the advance began there was a certain amount of shrapnel & rifle fire which most passed high over us but 2nd Lt. Nicholson & a stretcher bearer were wounded. The former remained in charge of his Dump, the latter went to the Dressing Station offering to assist there, though he could not carry a stretcher.
8.50 a.m.	No.1 Column moved off to 101st Bde. Dumps, under Major [*possibly Stephenson*].

No.2 column moved off to THE NOSE to dig the communication trench across NO MAN'S Land under Lt. Helsby & 2nd Lt.[*illegible*].

No.3 Column moved off to 102nd Dumps.

Hd. Qrts. moved to CHAPES SPUR, the progress of the columns to their destinations was obstructed by crowds of returning wounded. There was considerable shell & rifle fire. Lt. Coombs, was wounded (since died)[1]. Major Porch 2nd in comd did good service in finding portions of the different columns which got separated & leading them to their destination. Column No. never reached its destination. It moved in two parties 2nd Lt. Cook finding the trenches too obstructed with wounded got out & was at once wounded, & his party eventually found its way to Lt. Helsby who with his party was held up by crowds of wounded and when he reached the NOSE, it was evident that the M.G. fire & Artillery barrage was too heavy to make the digging of a communication possible & therefore this party informed Company Hd Qtrs at the 102nd Dump.

The SHALLOW GALLERY Lt. NIXON & his platoon of 'B' Company went down on the night of 30th-1st & stayed in this gallery or a mine shaft near by. He found 12 feet of earth above the end of the gallery instead of 2 as he had been led to expect. Starting work at midnight by 8.20 a.m. he had broken through sufficiently to let cables be passed through & by 10 a.m. there was a passage for men but work was terribly impeded by the passage of wounded back & stores forward. A communication trench was begun & pushed on to the enemy's front line reaching it 7 p.m.

It was soon evident that the attack had failed in places, & that the whole scheme of supplying the troops in advance of our front line would have to be rearranged.

1 p.m.   Captain Fortune O.C. 'D' Coy comdg the column carrying for 102nd Brigade got an urgent order to send Bombs to the mine crater south of LA BOISELLE, in which a party under comd of Captain Acklom, had established itself. This demand was promptly complied with Captain Fortune & 2nd Lt. Dodds taking a party laden with bombs direct to the Crater. 2nd Lt. Dodds remained on this duty till the evening of the 3rd, except during the afternoon of 2nd when he took a party to SCOTS REDOUBT.

The carrying column for the 103rd Bde. based in KERRIMUIR Street Dump also supplied this CRATER, with water, Rations S.A.A. & Bombs.

2 p.m.   An urgent order came to send 4 platoons to carry out a bombing attack in conjunction with a party of 10th LINCOLNS on HELIGOLAND & KINGSGATE, was organised for the attack, under Major Porch. The attack was subsequently countermanded at 6 p.m. as the LINCOLNS lost so heavily directly they left our front line. While waiting in MARESCHALL & other trenches near the front line, our men were heavily shelled with H.E. shells. Lt Wood was seriously wounded, several men were killed & wounded, & one Lewis gun, with nearly all its equipment was destroyed.

3.40 p.m. 'D' Coy was ordered to stand by for a bombing attack which was countermanded half an hour later, 7 p.m. The SHALLOW Gallery or Tunnel from KERRIEMUIR Street to the German front line was opened up and the communication trench completed.

'C' Company, was under orders of the 102nd Brigade, till 10p.m. on 1st, when it again came under orders of C.O. 18th North Fus, & was withdrawn from the front line to the Dugouts in PANMURE Street.

Before the attack was launched the company held the front line from SCONE to INCH Streets, so men were employed on lighting the smoke candles prior to the advance. The Company stood by till 3.30 p.m. when an order was received to attack LA BOISELLE. Bombs were drawn and the Company moved forward to head of SCONE Street, & was just ready to advance when an order was received, to abandon the attack & return to its former positions, where it remained till 10 p.m. & then moved to Dugouts in PANMURE Street.

1. The son of Arthur Henry and Mary Sophie Whitaker Coombs, of The Manse, Bratton, Wiltshire; 23-year-old Lieutenant Henry Whitaker Coombs B.A., C.C.C. – a junior master in Wellington College – died on 2 July 1916. He was buried in Corbie Communal Cemetery Extension, where some of those who died at Nos. 5 and 21 Casualty Clearing Stations, based nearby at La Neuville, were interred.

20th (Service) Battalion (1st Tyneside Scottish) Northumberland Fusiliers

ALBERT

7.30 a.m. (Zero). The Battalion took part in the General Offensive & formed the Left Assaulting Battalion of the 102nd Brigade (34th Division). The Corps Front was divided into Right, 21st Division; Centre, 34th Division; Left, 8th Division; Reserves 19th Division.

The 101st Brigade (34th Division) attacked immediately on the right of the 102nd Brigade & the 103rd Brigade was in support. The objective of the Battalion was from X.9.c.4.6. to X.15.B.2½.8. which was part of the 4th line of the GERMAN system of trenches.

The Battalion attacked up MARSH VALLEY in four waves, 100 yards between waves. A special Bombing Party was sent into LA BOISELLE. Prior to the attack, the bombardment which had been continuous for seven days became intense, and LA BOISELLE was subjected to a concentrated bombardment for the last twelve minutes. Two mines were also exploded at -2 minutes (7.28 a.m.) one on each side of LA BOISELLE. When the advance began at 7.36 a.m. the Battalion came under a heavy enfilade machine gun fire from OVILLERS–LA-BOISELLE partly due to the fact that the 8th Division had not been able to advance from their trenches. It is difficult to discover exactly what happened but though a few reached the 3rd GERMAN line the remaining survivors fell back to our first line under cover of darkness, not a single officer who went forward escaped becoming a casualty. The strength of the Battalion prior to the attack was [*left blank*] & the casualties amounted to:

Officers		Other Ranks	
Killed	10	Killed	62
Wounded	10	Wounded	305
Missing	7	Missing	267

The Commanding Officer Lieut Col. C.C.A. Sillery being among the killed, & the Adjutant Captain K.E. Kerr wounded. The advance was carried out in a most gallant way in the face of a deadly machine gun & artillery fire.

21st (Service) Battalion (2nd Tyneside Scottish) Northumberland Fusiliers

OVILLERS

7.30 a.m. The Bombardment was continuous throughout the night and at 6.25 a.m. increased in violence for 65 mins. At 7.28 a.m. a large mine was exploded by us at X.20.a.8.3. The advance commenced at 7.30 a.m., the Battalion moving forward in 4 lines at 150 yds interval followed by 22nd N.F. in similar formation.

The objective was a point X.15.C.3.4 and the remainder of the 103rd Brigade supporting us were to follow through to a line cutting POZIERES and establish themselves. The enemy bombardment, however, was severe, and as a result of heavy casualties we were unable to reach our objective. We were successful in establishing ourselves and in consolidating in the German lines at X.20.a.5.7 to X. 20. b.1.5 .The weather was warm and sunny throughout the day.

A notable feature was successive bombing attacks by the enemy on our left flank.

These were in all cases repulsed.

22nd (Service) Battalion (3rd Tyneside Scottish) Northumberland Fusiliers

ASSEMBLY TRENCHES

7.30 a.m. The Battalion together with the 21st NORTHD FUS, forming the 102nd BDE RIGHT assaulting column moved forward to the attack on the enemy trenches S of LA BOISELLE. Heavy enemy fire was experienced but the Bn less heavy casualties suffered reached ENEMY 2nd LINE.

A small party proceeded towards the ENEMY 3rd LINE but had to retire owing to heavy enemy fire, several casualties were suffered. Major Acklom had by this time taken command owing to Lt. Col. Elphinstone having become a casualty.

8.0 a.m. RIGHT FLANK of position held in ENEMY 2nd LINE extended to small party of LINCOLNS, trenches strengthened. Six separate attempts to rush our flanks were made by the enemy without avail.

12.45 p.m. Strength 7 Officers and 200 other ranks, a mixture of remnants of 22nd and 21st N.F. of which Major Acklom had taken command.

10.15 p.m. A patrol got in touch with other troops in the NEW CRATER caused by our mine, 100yds beyond our right flank.

23rd (Service) Battalion (4th Tyneside Scottish) Northumberland Fusiliers

TRENCHES. Z DAY.

The preliminary bombardment which had commenced on the 24th June and had continued throughout with varying intensity developed from 7 a.m. to 7.30 a.m. on this date to a hurricane bombardment concentrated on the German Trenches. At 7.30 a.m. the hour previously decided upon to launch the attack, the Battn proceeded to carry out its allotted task in the general scheme which was as follows:

The 102nd Brigade had been given as their objective a position of the first system of German trenches with a frontage of 1400 yds from X.13.a. to X.20.a. on which Battalions formed to attack LA BOISELLE from both flanks. 'C' Company 18th Northd. Fusl. being detailed to remain and hold the British front line trenches immediately opposite LA BOISELLE SALIENT, for a distance of 450 yds.

The 1st and 4th Battns Tyneside Scottish were detailed to attack from the left commencing with the trench running North from the ALBERT-BAPAUME road to the embankment in square X.14.a. and the 2nd and 3rd Battalions the German trenches on the right immediately S.E. of LA BOISELLE on a frontage of about 500 yds.

At 7.30 a.m. the artillery barrage lifted and the 1st and 2nd Battns advanced left and right of LA BOISELLE respectively over our front line parapet to attack.

Each line advanced without the least hesitation, and through and across "NO MANS LAND" the Battalion suffered very heavily indeed in all ranks. The losses principally being due to Machine Gun fire.

It was here that the following officers lost their lives namely, Lieut. Col. W. Lyle who was last seen alive with walking stick in hand, amongst his men about 200 yds from the German trenches. Major M. Burge who fell before he had gone many yards from our lines. Capt. J.G. Todd commanding 'B' Company, who fell immediately he reached our wire. Capt. J.B. Cubey Commanding 'A' Company was killed before he had gone 100 yds. Capt. H.A. Bolton, Lt. A.E. Shapley, Lt. S. Macdonald, Lt. J.H. Patterson, 2nd Lt. L. Williams also fell mortally wounded before reaching the German line. In addition Lieut W.B. Tytler, who was reported to have reached the German Trenches and to have been seen there badly wounded, is now missing and believed killed. 2nd Lt. R. Macdonald last seen wounded is now missing and believed killed.

The German first line was taken and the second line was also reached but owing to the heavy casualties it was impossible to hold on to these lines. A party of our men hung on for a time on to a portion of their front line trench a little to the North of the ALBERT-BAUPAUME ROAD. The Germans however launched a very strong counter attack against this party who fought gallantly but owing to being greatly outnumbered were obliged to fall back and take cover in "NO MANS LAND" where they lay all day and waited ready to go forward again with the next attacking force.

As dusk came on and as no further attack was to be made that day these men under cover of darkness made their way back into our lines in an exhausted condition through the want of food and water and remained there until the following morning. Many heroic deeds were performed during the day and though only about six came to special notice there were undoubtedly very many gallant deeds performed which will never come to light.

Our stretcher bearers were conspicuous by their daring in bringing in wounded men in daylight under fire. The dressing station and the trenches near were soon congested with casualties and only by continual and very exhausting work by Capt. J.M. Muirhead our M.O. and his staff were they able to gradually relieve this pressure which was not until the following day.

24th (Service) Battalion (1st Tyneside Irish) Northumberland Fusiliers

FIELD

7.40 a.m. The Battalion under Lieut Col L.M. Howard[1] left the assembly trenches as third wave in the attack to gain a point from X.17.A.10.7. to X.11.C.7.4. (ref Special Map A, scale 1/5000 sheet 1-2 'B' Trench Map OVILLERS.)

On leaving the trenches the enemy opened intense machine gun fire doing heavy damage to our troops. The Battalion objective (i.e. IIIrd objective) was not gained, so much assistance being needed for the Battalions in front taking the 1st & 2nd objectives. A few of the 24th N.F. managed to reach their objective moving with the Battalion on the right which had less resistance to cope with.

2nd Lieut T.W. Thompson & a handful of men almost reached CONTALMAISON but had to retire not having any support. 2nd Lt Thompson & his men took up a position in the German second line trenches, which he held successfully till reinforcements arrived. The left flank of the Division on our right was unprotected owing to meeting with little resistance and getting ahead of us.

NOTE

1. Wounded during the fighting on 1 July 1916, 37-year-old Lieutenant Colonel Louis Meredith Howard succumbed to his wounds the following day. Having served in the Boer War (1899 to 1902) as a Corporal with the Cape Mounted Rifles, during which he gained promotion to a commissioned rank because of an act of gallantry, Howard was buried in Ovilliers Military Cemetery.

25th (Service) Battalion (2nd Tyneside Irish) Northumberland Fusiliers

TRENCH AREA between ALBERT and LA BOISELLE

7.45 a.m. Battalion ordered to attack German positions north of and adjoining fortified village of LA BOISELLE. Intensive bombardment from 6.20 a.m. to 7.30 a.m. when artillery lifted to second German lines. Mines exploded at 7.30 a.m. in LA BOISELLE, which was also subjected to intense trench mortar bombardment and thought to be obliterated. But when our advance began, LA BOISELLE was found to be strongly held with machine guns and rifles, which completely held up our advance.

Battle order of battalion was 'B' Coy on right, 'D' Coy on left, each company in column of platoons at 150 paces distance, whilst 'A' Coy (on left) and 'C' Coy (on right) advanced in similar formation in support of and 150 paces behind leading companies. Battalion headquarters advanced in rear of last platoon. Heavy fire from machine guns and rifles was opened on battalion from the moment the assembly trenches were left also a considerable artillery barrage at 3 places on the line of advance. The forward movement was maintained until only a few scattered soldiers were left standing, the discipline and courage of all ranks being remarkable. Twenty officers and seven hundred and thirty other ranks took part in this advance.

10.30 p.m. The survivors of the battalion were collected in British front trenches near KEATS REDAN N.W. of LA BOISELLE, and the work of collecting wounded and stragglers went on all night. Bombing parties were posted on flanks and the trench held under a heavy fire. 16 officers were missing and 610 other ranks, the remainder of battn being commanded by Captain T.L. Williams.

26th (Service) Battalion (3rd Tyneside Irish) Northumberland Fusiliers

Battalion took part with 34th Division in assault on enemy's trenches S.W. of LA BOISELLE. Orders were for 101st Brigade to take and consolidate enemy first system of trenches, 102nd Bgde to take second system and 103rd Bgde to push on and build strong posts 500 yards short of enemy third system between POZIERES and CONTALMAISON.

Battalion started from trenches near TARA REDOUBT about 800 yards in rear of our front line, with 24th N.F. on right and 25th on left. At 7.30 a.m. advance commenced with 'A' and 'C' Coys in front and 'B' and 'D' Coys in reserve, all in columns of platoons.

Men advanced as if on parade under heavy machine gun and shellfire against part of German first line which had not been taken by 101st and 102nd Brigades as had been expected, these two Brigades having passed more to the right leaving part of German trenches still occupied. Two artillery barrages were passed through during this advance. Owing to heavy casualties Battalion was unable to proceed further and small parties remained consolidating shell craters in "No Man's Land" and remains of our first line trenches. Some small parties also reached German first line.

Battalion, relieved by troops of 19th Division were withdrawn from trenches and assembled at BELLEVUE FARM, having lost 19 officers and 470 men, killed wounded and missing. Only 2nd Lieuts Fortune and Downend, of the officers who went into action, remained at duty.

27th (Service) Battalion (4th Tyneside Irish) Northumberland Fusiliers

3 a.m. At 3 a.m. on 1st July 1916, the 103rd Infantry Brigade in position USNA TARA LINE ready to advance in support of 101st & 102nd Infantry Brigade – 27th (S) Bn. Northumberland Fusiliers on right supporting 15th & 16th Battalions Royal Scots, the Battalion objective, on support being unnecessary, being CONTALMAISON & Communication Trench 300yards SOUTH of it.

The hour of attack was 7.30 a.m. At 7.40 a.m. the 103rd Infantry Brigade, advanced, Battalion (in column of platoons) on two platoon front, platoons at 150 paces distance. The left of 103rd Infantry Brigade came under heavy machine gun & barrage fire from start, but the 27th Battalion on right suffered few casualties till crossing CHAPES SPUR, when heavy machine gun fire caused numbers to drop. They, however, continued to press on, although the left Battalions were held up, and about 70 per cent, dropped before German Front Trench was reached.

This Trench was in the hands of the Germans, as the Royal Scots had not left sufficient men to "mop up" the garrison. The 27th Battalion crossed this trench and some managed to reach CONTALMAISON, but had to retire to join the survivors of rear companies under Capt. J.V. Bibby – who at 10 a.m. were holding SHELTER WOOD. These in turn retired slowly before the Germans and eventually joined up with the Royal Scots holding German Support & Second Support Lines.

There they remained continuously attacking & attacked until relieved on the early morning of 4th July, total casualties being:

Officers: 5 killed and 15 wounded

Other Ranks: 99 killed (16 died of wounds), 373 wounded and 58 missing.

2nd Battalion Prince of Wales's Own (West Yorkshire Regiment)

The role of the Battalion in the attack was to support the Devons and Middlesex if required to, during the early stages, and the capture and consolidation of the village of POZIERES was allotted to it as a special task.

Heavy opposition in the early stages was not anticipated as OVILLERS and the enemy's front line system had been so heavily bombarded, it was however held probable that WHALLEY and RYECROFT STREETS would be sharply barraged as soon as the enemy discovered our forward movement.

The Brigade Orders to this Battalion were for each Company to file into RYECROFT STREET as soon as it was clear of 2nd Middlesex and then to climb ladders and advance in succession.

At 7.10 a.m. Battalion Headquarters moved to a previously selected and commanding position at the junction of RYRCROFT and WHALLEY STREETS from where a view of the enemy's front trenches could be obtained and the successive advance by Companies controlled.

The Battalion (21 Officers and 702 Bayonets) had breakfast at 5.30 a.m.

The hurricane bombardment commenced at 6.25 a.m.and was immediately replied to by the enemy who placed a light barrage of 5.9s on the junction of RYECROFT and WHALLEY STREETS (about 1 shell per minute).

The Company of the 2nd Middlesex Regiment in RYECROFT STREET advanced over the top at 7.35 a.m. and were followed by 'B' Company under Captain H. Freeman at 7.42 a.m.

The enemy increased his barrage on WHALLEY STREET at this hour to about 4 shells per minute.

'A' Company followed 'B' Company from RYECROFT STREET at 7.52 a.m. This Company was delayed 3 minutes and lost about 15 men by two heavy shells falling into the entrance to RYECROFT STREET.

The enemy at this hour began opening a barrage of shrapnel along the whole length of RYECROFT STREET.

'A' Company was led by Captain J.F. Ruttledge.

The fine way in which the right of this Company swung forward so as to correct the misalignment of RYECROFT STREET to the general direction of the advance was very noticeable.

These leading two Companies moved forward under the command of Captain P.Y. Harkness, Second-in-Command, who had orders not to proceed beyond our front line until OVILLERS was made good, unless asked for support by the leading Battalions.

'D' Company commenced filing into RYECROFT STREET at 7.52 a.m. The advance of this Company was not quite so accurate as the previous ones owing partly to the condition of WHALLEY STREET and RYECROFT STREET due to the enemy's heavy shells and partly to the very sharp shrapnel barrage which was now in full swing.

The head of this Company did not move fully up RYECROFT STREET before advancing out of it, and I took steps to see that the same mistake was not repeated by 'C' Company which followed.

At 8 a.m. BN HQ was informed by Brigade Headquarters that the front line had not been forced and in accordance with orders 'C' Company was directed to delay their advance out of RYECROFT STREET.

At 8.23 a.m. all enemy machine gun fire seemed to die down so this Company was ordered to advance and a message "All Clear" was sent to Brigade Headquarters.

Battalion Headquarters moved at the same time with a view of passing through OVILLERS up to the head of the Battalion in accordance with prearranged plans.

On arrival in front trench it was found that enemy front line had not been taken, and that all movement had ceased.

'B' the leading Company, had at the request of Major Saville supported the 2nd Bn Middlesex Regiment (about 8.5 a.m.). 'A' Company had similarly supported the right Devon Company. The remains of 'C' and 'D' Companies lay in the gap between the Devons and Middlesex the latter having swung round towards X.14.a.1.3. where their dead and ours lying on the parapet of the enemy trench could be identified.

The Battalion Headquarters were established where the road to OVILLERS joins the new front trench at X.13.a.6.6.

Touch was re-established with Companies. Companies lay approximately as follows:

'A' Company: X.8.c.1.4. to X.8.c.2.2.

Remains of 'C' and ½ 'D' Companies: X.8.c.2.1. to X.14.a.2½ .8 ½.

'B' Company: X.14.a.3.7. to X.14.a.1.5.

Battalion Headquarters withdrew at 12.30 a.m. on the 2nd July.

The head of 'B' company had apparently penetrated the enemy trench at X.14.a.3.5. where their helmets could be identified on the parapet.

This was confirmed by subsequent reports from wounded who came in.

At about 10.30 a.m. orders were received from Brigade Headquarters that no further advance was to be made.

During the day many wounded crawled back to our lines.

At 10.30 p.m. two patrols under 2/Lieuts C.A. Phillips and E.H. Matheson crawled down the Battalion Front and shouted to such men who could to crawl back.

Battalion Headquarters withdrew at 12.30 a.m. on 2nd July. The Battalion marched to MILLENCOURT at 1.45 a.m.

Out of the 21 Officers and 702 Other Ranks who went into action, 5 Officers and 212 men came out.

The failure of the attack was probably due to the numerous enemy machine guns placed in deep emplacements or tunnels in the slopes of the hill on the LA BOISELLE side of the valley.

Machine guns so emplaced could enfilade the whole Brigade attack.

After careful investigation the casualties of the Battalion between RYECROFT STREET and our front trench are estimated at about 250; 75% being due to machine gun fire; 200 of these were in 'C' and 'D' Companies, the last Companies to go over.

'B' Company which supported the Middlesex and penetrated the enemy trenches lost 146 out of the 169 who went into action.

The Battalion as a whole accurately carried out their orders to the best of their ability under the conditions which obtained.

2nd Battalion Princess Charlotte of Wales's (Royal Berkshire Regiment)

Attack on OVILLERS. The Battalion took up its assembly position in accordance with Brigade Operation Order No.100 – The 2nd Bn. Lincolnshire Regt was on the left and the 2nd Bn. Devonshire Regt on right.

Our own wire was not sufficiently cut and parties were immediately sent out by Companies to clear it. At 6.25 a.m. the intensive bombardment began as scheduled. At about 7.15 a.m. the enemy opened rifle and machine gun fire on our line; this fire was probably drawn by the 2nd Devon Regt which at about this time attempted to line up in front of their parapet. At 7.20 a.m. Companies began firing down trenches and getting ready for the assault.

At 7.30 a.m. the three assaulting Companies advanced to attack the German line. They were met by intense rifle and machine gun fire which prevented any of the waves reaching the enemy line. A little group on the left of the Battalion succeeded in getting in, but were eventually bombed out.

At about 7.45 a.m. the Commanding Officer (Lt. Col. A.M. Holdsworth)[1] and Second In Command (Major G.H. Sawyer DSO) were wounded in the sap on the left of our front, the Commdg Officer handed over Command of the Battalion to 2nd Lieut C. Mollet (Actg. Adjt.).[2] By this time the parapet was swept by rifle and machine gun fire which prevented any exit from our trenches. The enemy replied to our intensive bombardment by barraging the front line from about 6.35 a.m. onwards. No message was received from other Battalions in immediate vicinity.

At about 11 a.m. the order came from Bde Headquarters to "stand by" & await further orders.

About 200 men of the Battalion collected on the right of the front line and in the assembly trenches off ULVERSTON Street.

At about 12.30 p.m. news was received that the Brigade would be relieved.

NOTES

1. Lieutenant Colonel Arthur Mervyn Holdsworth's wounds proved fatal. The eldest son of Arthur Frederick and Florence Anne Holdsworth, of Widdicombe, Kingsbridge, Devon, the 40-year-old Commanding Officer, who was Mentioned in Despatches, died from his injuries at Etaples on 7 July 1916.
2. At this stage, the senior officer present was in fact Lieutenant Colonel Reginald Bastard of 2nd Battalion Lincolnshire Regiment.

2nd Battalion Rifle Brigade (The Prince Consort's Own)

OVILLERS-LA BOISELLE

At 6.25 a.m. a very intense bombardment was opened on the German trenches at Ovillers-La Boiselle lasting till 7.30 a.m. at which hour the 2nd Berks & 2nd Lincolns attacked with the R.I.Rs coming up in support.

The Battalion being in Reserve left the assembly trenches at 7.30 a.m. and proceeded up the communication trenches to the front line. The leading troops and about half the supporting troops were met with heavy machine gun, rifle and shrapnel fire and only succeeded in reaching the enemy's trenches at few points whence they were soon driven back. The Battalion being blocked in the trenches came under intense shell fire from guns of all calibres.

As it was decided to attempt no further infantry attack, 'A', 'B' & 'C' Coys were withdrawn to the support line, whilst 'D' Coy with details of the rest of the Brigade held the front line. Shortly before dark details of other Battalions were withdrawn and relieved by 'A' Coy in the front line. The Battalion was relieved by the Queens & West Kents of the 37th Brigade shortly after midnight and returned to Bivouac on the Long Valley. Casualties, nearly all shell fire, consisted of 5 Officers wounded, Capt. A.H. Curtis, Capt. W.G.K. Boswell, 2nd Lieut H. Daniels V.C.,[1] 2nd Lieut Etheridge, 2nd Lieut C.B. Sayer and 128 other ranks killed and wounded.

2nd Lieut S.W.P. Steen joined for duty.

NOTE

1. Harry Daniels was awarded the Victoria Cross for his actions on 12 March 1915, during the fighting at Neuve Chapelle. A Company Sergeant-Major at the time, Daniels's unit was ordered to attack the German lines. Whilst crossing No Man's Land, the men faced intense enemy machine-gun fire and imposing belts of barbed wire. Daniels and another man, Corporal Cecil Reginald Noble, voluntarily rushed forward with cutters and attacked the barbed wire. They were both wounded in this action; Noble died later of his wounds. Both men were subsequently awarded the Victoria Cross. Later awarded the Military Cross, and having attained the rank of Lieutenant Colonel, Daniels died on 13 December 1953.

1st Battalion Royal Irish Rifles

7.30 a.m. Zero hour for the attack was at 7.30am. The Brigade attached with the 2 R. Berks and 2 Lincolnshire Rgt in the front – 1st R.I. Rifles supporting and 2 Rifle Bde in reserve. The 23rd Brigade was on our right with its left flank on OVILLERS and the 70th Brigade on our left. The 34th Div was on 8th Div right and 32nd Division on the left. The Battalion crossed the Brigade front and if the attack had been successful would have gone through the two preceding Battalions to our objective which was allotted to it.

On moving from the assembly trenches the Company Positions were as follows:

'B' Company (Capt A. J. Rose) was on the right,

'C' Company (2/Lt Glastonbury) in the centre,

'D' Company (2/Lt Smith) on the left,

'A' Company (Capt G.J.Gartlan) in support.

'D' Company crossed the parapet and attacked and entered the German 1st and 2nd line but in order to conform with the movements of the troops on the left and right were forced to retire. 'C' Company advanced under extremely heavy fire but it is not clear as to whether they ever entered the German front lines at all owing to the severe machine gun fire. 'A' and 'B' Company were owing to the extremely heavy and accurate Barrage put up along the communication trenches and front line unable to leave our own trenches, 'A' Company especially losing very severely moving from the assembly trenches.

The German trenches had been completely bombed by our bombardment but excellent use had been made of the cellars in OVILLERS – the trenches were thickly manned.

11.50 p.m. The Battalion (whole Division) was withdrawn and returned to LONG VALLEY. 20 officers [*sic*]

Casualties on the 1st July. Officers:[1]

Capt & Adjt	D.A. Browns, (Killed)
Lieut Col	C.C. Mcnamara (Wounded died of wounds)[2]
Captain	A.J. Ross, (Wounded)
Captain	G.J. Gartlan, (Wounded)
Lieut	G. Lawlor, (Wounded)
Lieut	E.V. Banks-Murphy, (Wounded)
2/Lieut	E.A. Mahoney, (Wounded)
2/Lieut	J. Marshall, (Wounded)
2/Lieut	M.A. Palethorpe, (Wounded)
2/Lieut	W.S. Maitland, (Wounded)
2/Lieut	H.J. McConnell, (Wounded)

2/Lieut	W.G. Tyrell, (Wounded)
2/Lieut	A. McDowell, (Wounded)
2/Lieut	D.B. Hill, Norfolk Regiment (alc'd)
2/Lieut	H.M. Glastonbury, (Wounded & Missing)
2Lieut	S.D.J. Smith, (Missing)
2/Lieut	W.H. Grigg, (Missing)

NOTES

1. The War Diary also states that seventeen Other Ranks were killed in action, 348 wounded, twenty-seven were missing and that a further eight were wounded and missing.

2. The fatal wounding of 41-year-old Lieutenant Colonel Carroll Charles MacNamara (note this spelling of his surname is that used by the Commonwealth War Graves Commission) meant that the survivors of 1/RIR, along with the remnants of 2nd Battalion Princess Charlotte of Wales's (Royal Berkshire Regiment), were all under the overall command of Lieutenant Colonel Reginald Bastard of 2nd Battalion Lincolnshire Regiment. As the fighting drew to a close, this combined force, drawn from the remains of three battered battalions, was less than 100 men strong (see Martin Middlebrook, *The First Day on the Somme* (Penguin, London, 1984), page 144).

15th (Service) Battalion (1st Edinburgh) Royal Scots (Lothian Regiment)

TRENCHES
JUMPING OFF POSITION
Z day, Zero Hour 7.30 a.m.

Exactly on time the 15th Royal Scots jumped forward to the attack. 1st & 2nd waves had moved out to No Mans Land some few minutes previously. The men left with great heart & in grand form, with least hesitation or [*illegible*] 3rd & 4th waves got severely handled when quitting front line parapet mostly from M. Guns, one of which was in a bank astride S end of Boiselle – another believed to be higher up the Sausage Valley – Advance moved slightly more to the right than was intended – but this Machine Gun fire naturally forced their left flank over a bit - their left flank was "in the air" as 10th Lincolns on our left where not timed to assault until some minutes later with15th R.S. this undoubtedly caused considerable loss first to the 15th R.S. & later on to 10th Lincolns & 11th Suffolks as M. Gun could afford to play on each at separate times: from the start there can be little doubt all the units of the 101st Brigade started off to the right too much. News came back to me that at 7.48 a.m. Scots Redoubt was crossed – & about 3 p.m. that 'C' Coy (our right flank Coy) had made Peake Trench – but at same time the runner Pte. Quinn on being questioned said he had seen a few Suffolks &

some 12 men of the 16th R.S. in with our men in Peake Trench. Other news coming in from wounded returning & another runner from 'C' Coy (who delivered his note & returned) that where attacks had been forced on to extreme right of our objectives: also doubted later if Scots Redoubt had actually been crossed right astride. The left of attack no doubt clipped the S. end: not a single man I questioned ever saw any of our troops to the left of our 'C' Coy, which as pointed out was now on extreme right of our area: neither did those in Peake Trench see any troops pass over them towards Contalmaison: I heard that some 12 or so of 16th R.S. some Suffolks & 1 Lincoln & a few Tyneside Irish had been in Peake Trench, but after holding same for an hour or so were beaten back some 200 yards to S. Corner of the Horse Shoe. Also heard enemy were attacking on Peake Trench from the left front & M. Gun fire was strong, as soon as any extension to the left was attempted.

Major Starks (reported wounded & now missing) reformed his line on the road some 300 yds or so in front of Peake wood – no troops were then on his left, indeed I believe portions of B Coy & D Coy* (our extreme left) were among his men: which he filled with the troops on his left, made me sure only the extreme right of the 15th R.S. made their objective namely Peake trench. They were however in touch with the 21st Div – (the East Yorks) it was their block which prevented the enemy from rolling the left up still further, the East Yorks heard from several men from the men of the 15th R.S. extraordinary high praise for the fight they were putting up (R.S.M. Porteau was one of the men who told me) The later events are naturally more or less known now with the exception that no man holding the most advanced position was known to have been held by Major Starks 15 R.S. namely Peake wood ever saw any British troops go through them or troops fighting in their front as they were themselves counter attacked & driven back to the Horse Shoe would seem to establish the truth of this – no doubt when Advance is pushed forward the truth will be established beyond any question of doubt, losing practically every officer (except Lieut Robson) makes it somewhat difficult to get as much information as one would like.

*and I believe came in with other units of 101st Brigade showing that all got pushed over the extreme right.

NOTE

1. Also referred to as the 1st Edinburgh City Pals or Lord Provost's Battalion, the battalion was formed in 1914 by Robert Cranston (a Lord Provost of Edinburgh from 1903 to 1906). This was quickly followed by two further volunteer battalions: the 16th and 17th. Sir Robert was honorary commander in chief of all three battalions.

16th (Service) Battalion (2nd Edinburgh) Royal Scots (Lothian Regiment)

BECOURT WOOD

2.30 a.m. Breakfast issued to the men

5 a.m. Leading platoon left the wood to take up position of assembly.

6.16 a.m. Battn. reported in position.

7.30 a.m. Zero hour – first wave (15th Royal Scots) attacked.

7.35 a.m. Leading platoon (16th R.S.) left position of assembly succeeding waves following at 150 yds distance.

Attack reported by Brig to be developing satisfactorily.

11.3 a.m. Message received from Capt Coles – O.C. 'C' Coy – timed 8.45 a.m. stating that his men had reached point 400 yds on ALBERT side of PEAKE WOOD, that units were much scattered but that reorganisation was in progress.

1.50 p.m. Message received from 2/Lt Buchanan stating that 34th Div has taken up position in front of ROUND WOOD.

5.40 p.m. Message received from Capt Armit – O.C.'B' Coy – stating that he, four of his own men and 150 O.Rs of different units were holding position on German support trench and that enemy was present in neighbouring trenches.

9.20 p.m. Order from Brig to move H.Q forward.

9.25 p.m. Bn. H.Q moved forward in two parties: (1) CO, Maj Warden, Art. liaison off with observers & guides; (2) Adj, signalling off, signallers, runners and two Regt Policemen.

No.1 party was held up by heavy art. fire in WILLOW PATCH. No.2 party having no guide failed to reach SCOTS REDOUBT, but reached point held by Capt Armit. During the hours of darkness the enemy was quiet.

Document Attached to the War Diary

Account of the battalion's operations between 1 July and 3 July 1916:

The 16 R.S. following the 15 R.S. appear to have crossed No Man's Land with few casualties but the Battn. on the left (10th Lincs and 11th Suffs) suffered heavily – very few reaching the enemy lines. The Brig on the left the 102nd was also held up, as was the 8th Div on the left of the 34th. The Battn. left flank was therefore exposed.

The advance appears to have been pushed forward at good speed and despite the heavy casualties some of the 16 R.S. are said to have reached CONTALMAISON.[2]

The direction was somewhat lost owing to the exposed flank and the Battn. merged into the 21st Div area.

The enemy having withdrawn to neighbourhood of PEAKE WOOD rallied and counterattacked. A considerable body of British, composed of many regiments, and among whom no officers were seen, withdrew. Lt Rawson with a small party of 16 R.S. endeavoured to hold up the enemy and while being unable to push him back forced him to take cover: a Vickers gun team came up at this time and forced enemy back into PEAKE WOOD.

A rumour stated that the XV Corps had been joined by a party from PEAKE WOOD. It was hoped this party had been composed of 101st & 103rd Bde details but no confirmation of the report could be obtained.

Twenty Officers & 790 O.R.s took part in the assault.[3]

Officers being:	Lt Col Sir George McCrae[4]
HQ	Major H.R. Warden
	Capt W.B. Robertson (Adj)
	2/Lt J. Miller (Signalling officer)
	2/Lt W.J. Buchanan
A Coy	Capt P. Ross (Killed)
	2/Lt T.H. Bell, (Wounded)
	2/Lt W.A. McMichael, (Wounded)
	2/Lt W.L. Crombie, (Missing)
B Coy	Capt N. Armit
	Lt R.C. Lodge
	2/Lt G.J. Hamilton
C Coy	Capt L.G. Coles, (Killed)
	2/Lt F.M.W. Millar, (Wounded)
	2/Lt J.G.P. Stevenson, (Wounded)
	2/Lt G.S. Russell, (Missing)
D Coy	Capt A. Whyte, (Wounded and prisoner)
	Lt H.W. Rawson, (Wounded)
	2/Lt J. McKenzie, (Wounded)
	2/Lt R.M.F. Pringle, (Missing)

NOTES

1. Also known as the 2nd Edinburgh City Pals, McCrae's Battalion or the Scottish Sportsmen's Battalion, it was formed at Edinburgh by Sir George McCrae VD. It comprised sixteen playing members including entire first team squad members, a number of support staff and boardroom members from the Heart of Midlothian Football Club (more commonly known as simply Hearts). In November 1914, Hearts comfortably led the First Division, having started the 1914-15 season with eight straight victories. Following the outbreak of war, a public debate upon the morality of continuing professional football while young soldiers were dying at the front was started. A motion was placed before the Scottish Football Association (SFA) to postpone the season, with one of its proponents, Thomas Forsyth,

declaring that "playing football while our men are fighting is repugnant". Whilst the SFA waited for War Office advice, the noted East London philanthropist Frederick Charrington was orchestrating a public campaign to have professional football in Britain suspended. A prime tactic of the campaign was to shame football players and officials in to action through public and private denouncement. Meanwhile, the group from Hearts enlisted in Sir George McCrae's new volunteer battalion, joining en mass on 25 November 1914. The battalion was to become the 16th Royal Scots and was the first to earn the "footballer's battalion" sobriquet. The volunteers also included some 500 Hearts supporters and ticket-holders, 150 followers of Hibernian and a number of professional footballers from Raith Rovers, Dunfermline and Falkirk, along with amateur players from Dalkeith Thistle, Linlithgow Rose, Newtongrange Star, Pumpherston Rangers and West End Athletic.

2. The battalion was known to have managed to penetrate deeper into German territory than any other regiment on 1 July 1916.

3. Some accounts state that by the end of the First World War, seven of the Hearts' first team players had lost their lives. Three of these men are known to have been killed on 1 July 1916: 23-year-old Sergeant Duncan Currie, 30-year-old Private Ernest Edgar Ellis, and 23-year-old Private Henry Wattie. The bodies of all three men were never found or identified, and they are consequently commemorated on the Thiepval Memorial.

4. Knighted in 1908, McCrae had made his mark in the textile trade. He has been described variously as a draper or a merchant hosier and mercer. In 1909, after a successful career as the Liberal MP for Edinburgh East, he resigned from the House of Commons to take up a position in Scottish government service, accepting the appointment of Vice-President of the Scottish Local Government Board.

11th (Service) Battalion Sherwood Foresters (Nottinghamshire and Derbyshire Regiment)

Battalion formed part of the attack near OVILLERS. Return of casualties is herewith attached.

The Battalion took over the 70th Brigade Sector on the evening of the 26th June, being relieved on the following evening when the Brigade took up the final position of assembly.

Owing to the Attack being postponed 48 hours the Battalion again took over the front line on the evening of the 28th and held the Sector until position of assembly was taken up a second time on the evening of the 30th June.

During this time our casualties were comparatively slight, although we were unfortunate in losing 3 Officers including the Medical Officer wounded, and a platoon Sgt.

At 7.45 a.m. on the morning of the attack, 1st July, a message was received that the German First Line was taken, and shortly after the Battalion was ordered to take over our front line vacated by the 9th York and Lancaster Regiment. This was done independently by Coys by pre-arranged routes, under a fairly heavy shrapnel fire.

It had been arranged prior to the assault that the Left Centre Company 1st Wave was to file straight out of a sap and occupy a bank about 70 yards in front of our own front line. After considerable difficulty owing to the congestion of wounded in the sap an attempt to do this was made. A very heavy machine gun fire was brought to bear on this wave from the left flank and the enemy front line which had apparently been re-occupied by use of underground galleries from the enemy 2nd line after the assaulting Battalion had passed over. The same fire was directed on the remainder of the first wave when they attempted to advance from our front line.

The 2nd Wave, lead by Major G.H.W. Bernal DSO, the second in command, then pushed forward in support hoping to carry forward the 1st Wave.

Casualties along the whole line were very heavy, and a general attempt was made to crawl forward under intense machine gun and shrapnel fire, any available cover being made use of.

Headquarters, lead by Lieut. Col. H.F. Watson DSO, the Commanding Officer, then advanced, only Headquarters Bombers being left to hold out trenches.

Lieut. Col. Watson walking diagonally across the front collecting men as he went gave a fresh impetus to the advance by his personal example, but the advance died out before the 1st line was reached, Col. Watson himself and other H.Q. Officers being wounded.

Another attempt to reach the German trenches by the sunken road on the right flank was made by about 50 men under Captain C.E. Hudson, including the Battalion Bombers and details of other units collected in our line. This attempt was brought to a standstill by heavy frontal and flank fire as they came over the brow of the hill in the last 80 yards.

The casualties sustained by the Battalion during the day amounted to 21 Officers and 508 N.C.O's and men.

The strength of the Battalion on entering the trenches on the 26th June was 27 Officers and 710 men.

11th (Service) Battalion (Cambridgeshire) Suffolk Regiment

BECOURT

5 a.m. Bn commenced to leave BECOURT WOOD and proceeded to jumping off places in DUNDEE AVENUE and NEW CUT 'B' and in MONIKIE STREET.

7 a.m. Bn all in position with Bn H.Q. in a dugout near junction of DUNDEE AVENUE with ARBROATH STREET and NEW CUT 'B'. The Bn was considerably delayed in getting into position owing to the right of the 102nd Brigade extending too far to the right.

7.28 a.m. The mine opposite left of 101st Brigade was exploded.

7.30 a.m. The infantry assault was launched. The Bn followed the 10th Lincolns from our assembly trenches down into SAUSAGE VALLEY and across to the German lines. Owing to the failure of the 102nd Brigade on the left to capture LA BOISELLE, our advance from the moment it left our assembly trenches was subjected to a very heavy fire from machine guns from LA BOISELLE. In spite of the fact that wave after wave were mown down by machine gun fire, all pushed on without hesitation though very few reached the German lines.

Documents Attached to the War Diary

A letter, dated 5 July 1916, that was received from the G.O.C. 101st Brigade:

"Dear Colonel Somerset,
"Will you please express to your Battalion my admiration for their gallant conduct in the attack on July 1st, theirs was the hardest task of any, having the furthest to advance before crossing our own front line in face of a deadly fire, their courage was magnificent as in spite of wave after wave being mown down they fearlessly pressed forward towards their objective and got well into the German line but unfortunately their numbers were too few in the end to gain it. No troops could have done better and I am sure that their advance in this battle will go down to posterity as one of the most gallant actions of the war.
Yours sincerely,
[*signed*] R.C. Gore, Brig-General,
Commdg, 101st Infantry Brigade.

A Special Order of the Day that was issued by the G.O.C. 34th Division:

"The Divisional Commander congratulates his troops on the fine reputation they have earned for themselves. With them he mourns deeply for our absent comrades.
"The G.O.C. III Corps himself addressed the 101st Brigade and expressed himself as greatly pleased with their performance in the action.

The following wire, dated 6 July 1916, was sent by the G.O.C. Fourth Army to the G.O.C. III Corps:

"Please convey to the 34th Division my hearty congratulations on their successes. Whilst regretting their heavy casualties I desire to express my gratitude for and admiration of the determination and gallantry with which they carried out their difficult task."
G.L. Turle [*possibly Tuile*]
Capt & Adjt. 11th Suffolks.

8th (Service) Battalion York And Lancaster Regiment

TRENCHES AUTHUILLE WOOD (SOMME)

Being the leading Battalion on the left of the 70th Brigade, in the attack near OVILLERS the Battn assaulted as per APPENDIX I (attached to JUNE Diary). The attack was timed for 7.30 a.m. & for an hour previous to that hour the guns delivered an intense bombardment to which the enemy replied. At the time the assault commenced our front line trenches in the NAB were heavily shelled but the casualties were very few. No smoke was liberated on our front as the wind was unfavourable.

The first wave left our trenches in perfect order & to time & were at once met by an exceptionally heavy fire from front & both flanks. Most of the men were killed or wounded, but the remainder continued the advance. In spite of the heavy fire the remaining waves advanced to the attack but before getting halfway to the enemy trenches were mown down by the machine guns.

About seventy men reached the enemy trenches & some of these eventually reached the enemy's third line of his front system of trenches. Here they remained fighting for some time until all were killed or taken prisoners – one returned. The remainder were held up in the enemy front line & considerable fighting took place here until almost all were killed – only 3 returned. Many of the enemy were killed by our men both in his trenches & when he marched across the open to counter attack. The supporting Battn (9th York & Lancs) was also caught by the machine guns as they advanced to the attack & suffered so many casualties that only an odd man or two reached the German Line where our men so badly needed support. The same happened to the Reserve Battn (11th Sherwood Foresters).

The Battn as it went over the parapet numbered 680 NCO's & men & 23 officers. Of these only 68 men returned. All the officers were casualties. 18 Being killed & missing & 5 wounded. The C.O. & Adjutant were among the killed.[1] In the evening the Bde was withdrawn upon being relieved by the S.W.B.

Document Attached to the War Diary

Statement of operations by 8th (Service) Battalion York And Lancaster Regiment on 1 July 1916:

Before the assault commenced the enemy had opened a heavy barrage of shells between our front line and CHORLEY STREET and very heavy machine gun fire first swept our parapet from the enemy front line opposite the Battalion and also from somewhere on our left flank.

The Battalion advanced in four waves as intended but most of the men were shot down in No Man's Land including the C.O. and Adjutant. The remainder reached the enemy's wire. This was in places still uncut and many Officers and men were shot down whilst cutting it.

So far as can be gathered the first men who reached the enemy trenches got as far as the third line but they were not seen again. Our men in the first and second line were immediately engaged by the enemy who came out of dug-outs and what were supposed to be communication tunnels. Meanwhile our telephone wires had been laid across No Man's Land but were broken several times. The signallers then sent messages back (by disc and after the disc men had become casualties – by flags) for reinforcements but none arrived.

Bombing then continued between parties of the enemy and our men both second and first line and many of the enemy including several officers were shot who attempted to come over the top of the trenches. Eventually all the men in the second line became casualties. The men in the first line joined up with the Lincoln's on the right who had apparently come too far to the left. Shortly afterwards word came down from the right to retire and the Lincoln's left the trench. At the time fighting was not so heavy. An Officer was seen and heard trying to get the men on the right back again, but they were not seen to come back.

The enemy then attacked in stronger force and as ammunition and bombs were exhausted some of our men went out into No Man's Land and searched the casualties.

Further heavy fighting continued until only odd parties of two and three men were left. These were eventually driven out of the trenches and retired.

It is reported that an enemy machine gun was found in the front line with two Germans chained to it. Both were dead, one having been bayoneted and the other apparently killed with the butt of a rifle. The gun was destroyed. All the bombers except one man were casualties. Only two Lewis Gunners returned bringing back one gun, the remainder being lost.

All the signalling equipment is missing excepting one telephone instrument.

Out of a total of 680 N.C.O.s and men and 22 Officers who went over the parapet the following numbers returned unwounded: 1 Sergeant, 3 Corporals, 10 Lance Corporals, 54 Men, No Officers.

Major, Commanding 8th Battn York & Lancs Regiment.

NOTE

1. The CO was Lieutenant Colonel Bertram Lionel Maddison of the 2nd Battalion, attached to the 8th York and Lancaster Regiment. He is buried in Blighty Valley Cemetery.

9th (Service) Battalion York And Lancaster Regiment

On the 1st July the Bn. was in action. Nothing official as regards the casualties could be ascertained:

C.O. reported wounded (unofficial.)[1]
Major Lewis reported killed (unofficial).
Adjt Lt McCallum reported wounded (official).

Orders received that the Bn. was being relieved. About 7 p.m. arrangements being made for the comfort of the men who returned safely out of action. G.S. Wagons & Limbers were sent patrolling the roads between Long Valley & Crucifix Corner, under orders to pick up any men who were on their way to rejoin the Bn. in Long Valley. 180 returned up to 10 p.m. Strength of Bn. going into action, 25 Officers, 736 other ranks.

NOTE

1. The CO, 49-year-old Lieutenant Colonel Arthur Joseph Berkeley Addison, twice Mentioned in Despatches, was in fact one of those killed. He is buried in Becourt Military Cemetery.

XV Corps

1 July 1916

XV Corps[1], on the left of XIII, faced the head of the Fricourt salient, the corner stone of the German line between the Ancre and the Somme. The slopes of the Bazentin–Pozières ridge are here broken through by the Willow stream and its feeders, whose valleys before they unite to pass through the gap between the ends of Mametz and Fricourt spurs, have in plan roughly the shape of a trident. The centre valley runs up the western side of Mametz Wood, with Caterpillar Valley to the east and Contalmaison Valley to the north-west; the two latter formed as it were a "ditch" inside the German position from the neighbourhood of Montauban to Pozières.

The Willow stream made the boundary between the two divisions of XV Corps in the front line, the 7th on the right facing north, opposite Mametz village, on the lower slopes of Mametz spur, and the 21st on the left facing east along the western slopes of Fricourt spur. The 17th Division was in corps reserve.

The German defences about Mametz and Fricourt were of exceptional strength, a maze of trenches and communication trenches twelve hundred yards in depth, and the front trench, with its many salients and flanks, was particularly well sited for defence. The villages themselves had been developed into little fortresses; there were numerous strong machine-gun emplacements, and the dugouts were exceptionally fine, some of them with two storeys, lighted with electricity and, it was said, provided with every convenience except water. The front system was backed up by two intermediate lines: Fritz Trench – Railway Alley – Crucifix Trench and White Trench – Wood Trench – Quadrangle Trench, and also by the second and third positions, here three and six miles, respectively, behind the front line.

Opposite XV Corps was the centre sector of the German 28th Reserve Division, held by six battalions.[2] In this area the German artillery had also been practically silenced; there was no real barrage when the assault began, only a few shells fell intermittently, and the defence was maintained almost entirely by machine-guns, the crews with their weapons having remained in the dug-outs till the last moment, whence they emerged intact.

In the first phase of the battle the 7th and 21st Divisions were to clear the high ground on both sides of the Willow stream gap, including the villages of Mametz (in the first stage) and Fricourt (in the second). Then, passing over the spurs called

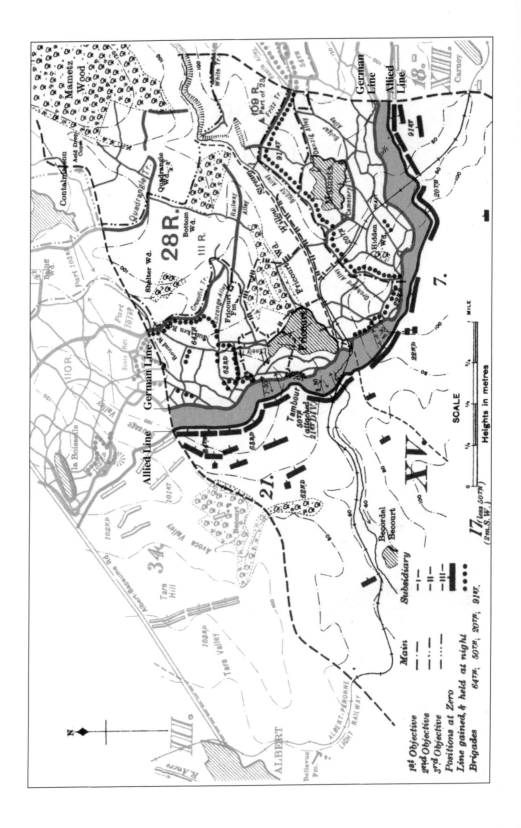

by these names and the German first intermediate line, they were to secure a position in the second intermediate line, astride the valley facing Mametz Wood, the right in touch with XIII Corps in White Trench and the left with III Corps in Quadrangle Trench, south of Contalmaison. This position appeared to be a favourable one for meeting a counter-attack, while it offered good observation posts and cover for artillery from which to bombard the German second position. Should all have gone well in the subsequent phases of the battle, XV Corps, using its reserve division, was to press on through Mametz Wood up the northern slope of Caterpillar Valley and capture the villages of Bazentin le Grand, Longueval and Ginchy.

In order to avoid the difficulties and losses which would be inevitable in a frontal attack against the strong defences of Fricourt village and Fricourt Wood, the triangular area covered by them was not to be dealt with in the initial assault, which was to be delivered on either side, thereby isolating it as a preliminary to its capture at a later stage. With this end in view, the right or outer brigade of the 7th Division was to capture Mametz and then press on to White Trench, whilst the centre brigade was to form a defensive flank along the southern side of the Willow stream valley facing Fricourt and its wood. Similarly, the left, or outer, brigade of the 21st Division was to cross the top of Fricourt spur, continue on to Bottom Wood, joining up there if possible with the right brigade of the 7th Division, whilst the centre brigade, with part of the right, formed a defensive flank facing Fricourt village and wood. The inner brigades of both divisions were to wait in the front trenches until the situation created by the advance of the others was favourable for the attack to be launched against Fricourt, the hour for which would be settled by the corps commander.

At 06.25 hours the intensive bombardment of the enemy's front system began,[3] and between 07.15 and 07.25 hours, in order to mislead the enemy, what remained of the gas was released from the centre of the corps front from which no assault was at first to be delivered.

At 07.22 hours a hurricane bombardment by Stokes mortars on the whole front of attack took place. At 07.26 hours smoke discharges were launched by the 4th Mortar Company of No.5 Battalion, Special Brigade Royal Engineers, in order to create barrages to screen the inner flanks of the attacking wings of the 7th and 21st Divisions, also to form a cloud on the German support line opposite the 7th Division, to mask the direct assault.

At 07.28 hours three mines of 25,000lbs, 15,000lbs and 9,000lbs, placed by the 178th Tunnelling Company Royal Engineers, were fired under the German line opposite the salient known as "The Tambour", facing Fricourt, against which no assault was to be made. The purpose of the mines was to distract the enemy's attention and form craters which would block enfilade fire against the 21st Division from the northern face of "The German Tambour" (just south of the Tambour).[4] Bulgar Point, a heavily wired strongpoint jutting out into No Man's Land (south of the south-east corner of Mametz), was completely destroyed by a 2,000lb mine, and a sap west of it by one of 200lb. Four small mines of 500lbs each were also exploded under the German line south of Hidden Wood, where much mining had already taken place and a frontal attack was not to be made.

The artillery orders of XV Corps for the assault are of special interest, as going further in the use of the creeping barrage than those of XIII Corps.[5] The instructions issued by the G.O.C. Royal Artillery of the Corps on 14 June laid down:

"When lifting, 18pdrs should search back by increasing their range, but howitzers and heavy guns must lift directly on to the next objectives." A map showing six proposed lifts from the German front line back to Caterpillar Valley and the west side of Mametz Wood was issued.

The divisional instructions went into detail. Those issued on 18 June by Brigadier-General J.G. Rotton of the 7th Division artillery[6] contained the following information:

"During the advance of the infantry a barrage of artillery fire will be formed in front of the infantry according to the timings shown on the tracings issued to those concerned. The lines shown on the tracings indicate the nearest points on which guns will fire up to the hour indicated. At the times shown heavy guns will lift their fire direct to the next barrage line. The divisional artillery will move their fire progressively at the rate of 50 yards a minute. Should the infantry arrive at any point before the time fixed for the barrage to lift, they will wait under the best cover available and be prepared to assault directly the lift takes place."[7]

The instructions of the infantry brigades repeated the paragraph given above, those of Brigadier-General C.J. Deverell (20th Brigade), who had collaborated in devising the procedure, adding: "The assault will be carried out steadily behind the artillery barrage. At the hour named for the barrage to lift, the leading line will be as close to the hostile position as possible, and on the barrage lifting will at once move forward steadily, keeping touch, and only halt or lie down when next compelled to do so by awaiting the lift of the artillery barrage."

The 21st Division artillery (Brigadier-General R.A.C. Wellesley) issued instructions that: "Batteries will search back to the next barrage in order that the whole ground may be covered by fire immediately before our infantry advance over it."

The explanation given in some of the battalions' orders reveals that the procedure was thoroughly understood. For example, those of the 15th Battalion Durham Light Infantry (Lieutenant Colonel A.E. Fitzgerald[8]), and dated 25 June, are particularly lucid: "The barrages will not exactly lift from one point and be put on to another; they will gradually drift forward, leaving certain lines at certain hours (which may be changed). The line of the barrage must be constantly watched by the infantry, whose front lines must keep close up to it."

The "drifting forward" of the 18-pounder barrage undoubtedly gave considerable assistance to the attack of the brigades of the 7th and 21st Divisions. The barrage, however, was "thin", fewer guns being employed than in later attacks, and only shrapnel was fired, while it moved too quickly for the infantry to keep up with it. After the first shoot, the infantry never again got near enough to the barrage to derive any benefit from it, one battalion (63rd Brigade) reporting that the intervening ground between its first wave and the barrage was full of Germans as safe from it as our own men.[9] Much further experience was needed before the creeping barrage became really effective.

The Entry into Mametz Village by the 7th Division

The right and centre brigades of the 7th Division were to attack on a front of eighteen hundred yards between the Carnoy–Mametz track and the quarry south of Hidden Wood. They assembled in the support trenches, leaving the front line empty, in order to avoid casualties. The 91st Brigade (Brigadier-General J.R. Minshull-Ford) was to capture the head of the Mametz spur, and the eastern half of Mametz village which lay on that spur. It was to consolidate as its first objective the line Fritz Trench, eleven to seventeen hundred yards ahead on the west of Pommiers Redoubt, with a left flank thrown back along Bunny Alley to the northern edge of Mametz village, its right connecting with XIII Corps in Beetle Alley.

In the centre, the 20th Brigade (Brigadier-General C.J. Deverell) was detailed to form the defensive flank facing Fricourt. It was to wheel left-handed during its advance and occupy a line with its right on the north-western edge of Mametz, its centre along Orchard Alley, astride the Maricourt road, and its left joining up east of Bois Français with the 22nd Brigade, which was to await in the British front trenches the order to advance through Fricourt.[10] On this sector also four Russian saps had been driven right up to the German front line, the ends of the saps being successfully opened up soon after zero.

The 22nd Battalion Manchester Regiment and 1st Battalion South Staffordshire Regiment, leading the assault of the 91st Brigade across No Man's Land which was only 100–200 yards wide, crossed the German front line with little loss, but, in spite of the creeping barrage, heavy machine-gun and rifle fire came from Mametz and from Danzig Alley, an eight-foot deep communication trench running through, and eastwards and southwards from, the village. Heavy casualties were inflicted upon the extended companies as they advanced up the slope on to the shoulder of the spur. Nevertheless, by 07.45 hours, an advance of seven hundred yards had been made, and the line of Cemetery Trench immediately south of Mametz had been rushed by the 1st Battalion South Staffordshire Regiment.

By 08.00 hours parties of the 22nd Battalion Manchester Regiment were entering Bucket Trench, only a couple of hundred yards short of their objective, and the leaders of the South Staffordshires were in the ruins of Mametz.

At this early stage of the movement, the enemy resistance was half-hearted. In a few places machine-gun detachments held on tenaciously and caused heavy casualties – especially near the south-western corner of the village, where a concrete machine-gun post in a house, with 4-inch armour-plate loopholes, was subsequently discovered – but elsewhere surrenders came freely as the British advanced.

From Danzig Alley and the western and northern part of Mametz, however, opposition continued, and in face of it the advance was gradually brought to a standstill. The South Staffordshires were forced back to Cemetery Trench and the hedges south of the village, leaving only a few small parties ensconced in the ruins. Soon after 09.30 hours the two supporting battalions were sent forward to reinforce and carry forward the attack. The two front companies of the 2nd Queen's reached those of the Manchester Regiment in Bucket Trench and Bulgar Alley, but, the creeping barrage having passed on, they were unable to enter Danzig Alley (East).

Similarly, the 21st Battalion Manchester Regiment reinforced the South Staffordshires, but could make no progress beyond Cemetery Trench. A re-bombardment for half an hour of Danzig Alley (East), Fritz Trench and Bunny Alley, forming a triangle north and east of Mametz, was ordered by Major General Watts, and was begun at 10.00 hours, but it seems to have been ineffective and did not lessen the resistance. Small parties which managed to enter Danzig Alley were counter-attacked from Mametz village and compelled to withdraw, and for the moment no further advance could be made.

At 11.15 hours the corps commander, having heard of the capture of Pommiers Redoubt by XIII Corps at 09.30 hours and of Beetle Alley at 10.15 hours, ordered a further effort to be made to capture Danzig Alley and Fritz Trench beyond it.

At 12.25 hours a further half-hour bombardment was carried out on the same objectives as before, at the request of Brigadier-General Minshull-Ford, who saw that a local counter-attack was developing, and following this the two remaining companies of the 2nd Queen's were sent forward to deliver an assault. The renewed artillery fire, following on the advance of XIII Corps to Pommiers Redoubt and Beetle Alley, across the enemy communications from Montauban to Mametz, broke down the resistance, but one forward section of German field guns remained firing over open sights until its detachments were all killed.

Soon after 13.00 hours Danzig Alley (East) was in British possession, its defenders disappearing into Mametz or falling back north-westwards along Fritz Trench. Bombing parties now moved westwards along Danzig Alley and thence northwards from it up Bright Alley, which was occupied by 13.40 hours. At the same time an entrance was made by the Queen's into Fritz Trench, in which a number of Germans still held out, from the eastern end of Danzig Alley. About seventy-five prisoners were taken by the bombing parties.

By this hour, too, the 1st Battalion South Staffordshire Regiment, supported by three companies of the 21st Battalion Manchester Regiment (the fourth was kept in brigade reserve) had crossed the two hundred yards of open ground between

Cemetery Trench and the southern houses of Mametz village, reinforced the small parties of the battalion still among the ruins, and occupied the western end of Danzig Alley (East), which lay along the main street of the village, thus completing the capture of the first objective. A number of Germans, however, still held out in the northern quarter of Mametz.

The fan-shaped advance of the 20th Brigade (Brigadier-General C.J. Deverell), intended to form the defensive flank, led it down the Carnoy valley, on either side of the light railway, and on the left over the top of the spur marked "Quarry" (south of Hidden Wood). Along the enemy front on this flank, between the 20th and 22nd Brigade lay 500 yards of cratered area, a warren of Germans, which required very thorough "mopping up", in spite of the four mines fired there just before zero.

The 2nd Battalion Gordon Highlanders on the right was to capture the western half of Mametz village and the northern slopes of the valley, whilst the 9th Battalion Devonshire Regiment overran the southern and steeper side, the two battalions joining hands about Mametz station (Halt).[11] Thence they were to move together on to the objective, Bunny Alley and part of Orchard Alley. On the left, the 2nd Battalion Border Regiment was to wheel left-handed over the Quarry spur, clear the cratered area, and occupy Apple Alley, which diverged southward from Orchard Alley.

The operation required of the brigade was complicated; it was delayed by the stout resistance of the Germans, particularly in the centre, and consequently soon lost the advantage of the creeping barrage.

The 9th Battalion Devonshire Regiment, in the centre on the steep side of the Carnoy valley, assembled some 250 yards behind the front trench, which, with the support trench, was too badly damaged to be used. From the moment its first lines entered No Man's Land, they suffered from a devastating machine-gun barrage, their movement being completely exposed to direct fire at long range from Fricourt Wood and at close range from ground about the level of the enemy support trench, and in enfilade from trenches south of Mametz. Fully half the casualties of the battalion occurred before Mansell Copse in the centre of No Man's Land, here 400 yards wide, was reached.[12] The extended lines of the companies nevertheless pressed steadily forward and entered the German front trench, small parties pressing on to the support trench, two hundred and fifty yards behind. By degrees they cleared these trenches and adjoining communication trenches, and sent back a number of prisoners.

By now all the officers had fallen; it was impossible to proceed, but the 9th Devonshires kept the enemy in front engaged in order to assist the battalions on right and left, which could be seen advancing. At 07.40 hours the fourth company was sent forward to reinforce, but it lost all its officers in No Man's Land, and although survivors of it joined the others in the German front system, no further progress could be made. Later two companies of the 8th Battalion Devonshire Regiment from brigade reserve were sent up. They, too, lost very heavily on entering No Man's Land, but parties gained touch with the Gordons and 9th Devonshires.

The 2nd Battalion Gordon Highlanders, on the right of the 9th Devonshires, advanced on a 400 yard frontage in close touch with the 1st Battalion South Staffordshire Regiment (91st Brigade) and assaulted the German front trench with great spirit, the German defenders, who were preparing to meet them with bombs, being overrun before they could throw them. The left company, owing to some uncut wire in a dip of the ground, was at first unable, however, to get through; suffered heavy casualties before the trench in front of it could be cleared from the flank; and lost touch with the barrage. Here, and along the whole Fricourt sector, the number of unexploded British shells, of all calibres, lying about was very great. From now onwards the losses of the battalion were severe, heavy fire being opened on it from "The Shrine", a strongly held post in front of Cemetery Trench, and from Mametz behind it.

By 07.55 hours however, the leading troops had attained Shrine Alley, a trench passing through the Halt 300 yards behind the front line and parallel to it, running into Cemetery Trench: in places they had passed over it and reached the Mametz–Halt road. The enemy now offered more stubborn resistance, heavy fire being also opened by him from a cutting beyond this road on the southern side of the Maricourt road (here parallel to the light railway), which should have been cleared by the 9th Devonshires. Supported by a company of the 8th Devonshires, the left of the 2nd Gordon Highlanders set to work to clear the dug-outs in the cutting, a task which occupied the greater part of the morning. In the meantime, the remainder of the Gordons had been unable to progress beyond Shrine Alley, though they maintained touch with the South Staffordshire on the right in Cemetery Trench.

On the left the 2nd Battalion Border Regiment had moved forward with less difficulty. After crossing the front line the battalion, helped by the barrage, had wheeled to the left successfully, and advanced on Hidden Lane (behind Hidden Wood) on the upper slope of the valley, one hundred and fifty yards short of its objective, Apple Alley. The lines had by now become broken into groups, which were bombing and bayoneting the Germans scattered about in the cratered area, in the remains of trenches, and in the entrances to the German mines, but by 09.30 hours Hidden Lane was occupied. Considerable loss was suffered at this period from machine-gun and rifle fire from Mametz, which enfiladed the trench, and also from the right rear from Hidden Wood. This wood was cleared by an attack across the open, combined with a bombing raid down Hidden Lane, and parties were then sent forward to Apple Alley. The 2/Border Regiment thus reached its objective, but its right was in the air, the 9/Devonshire not having come up. The Gordon Highlanders also being short of their objective, it was obvious that the defensive flank towards Fricourt could not be formed without reinforcements and a further effort.

The advance to the sunken road by the 21st Division

The 21st Division was formed up with three of its four brigades, the 50th (attached from the 17th Division for the assault), the 63rd and 64th, in the front line, and the 62nd Brigade in reserve. The greater part of the 50th Brigade (Brigadier-General W.J.T. Glasgow)[13] was to remain in the front trenches in readiness for the assault on Fricourt at a later stage of the battle, if the village were not "squeezed out" by advances on its flanks; its left battalion, the 10th Battalion West Yorkshire Regiment, was to form the defensive flank towards Fricourt. The 63rd and the 64th Brigades were to gain the German first intermediate line, Crucifix Trench, as the first objective, and Bottom Wood and part of Quadrangle Trench, the second intermediate line, as the second objective, joining up at the wood with the 7th Division.[14] No Man's Land was, in places, as much as three hundred yards but mostly about two hundred wide.

The attack of the 10th Battalion West Yorkshire Regiment (50th Brigade) was delivered on a frontage of six hundred yards. The lines of the two leading companies crossed into the German front trench with little loss, and pressed on towards "Red Cottage" at the northern end of Fricourt, the Germans in that quarter of the village and the neighbouring trenches not emerging from their deep dug-outs quickly enough to stop them.

By the time, however, that the third and fourth companies moved forward, the machine-guns in Fricourt and the German Tambour,[15] brought up out of the dug-outs which had not been blown in by the mine explosions, were in position.[16] With the barrage having passed on there was no fire to keep the Germans down in their shelters. The machine-guns which were causing most loss were firing from the northern edge of the Tambour, but although this information was at once passed back, they were still in action two hours later. As a result, the third and fourth companies were practically annihilated and lay shot down in their waves. Lieutenant Colonel A. Dickson and all the regimental staff, including the second-in-command and adjutant, were killed, and only small groups reached the German front trench.[17] The leading companies however, passed on along communication trenches and reached Red Cottage, but, being isolated, they were overcome later in the morning, except a few small parties who effected a junction with the right of the 63rd Brigade further north. Owing to the intense machine-gun fire opened from Fricourt on any sign of movement in the open, it was not found possible to reinforce the survivors of the third and fourth companies in the German front trench, and they remained there until dark, the battalion losing twenty-two officers and 688 other ranks in the day's fighting.

The 63rd and 64th Brigades had first to ascend the western slope and cross the Fricourt spur, and then advance across the depression down which ran the western of the two Contalmaison–Fricourt roads (Sunken Road) before they could reach their initial objective, Crucifix Trench, on the eastern slope of the Fricourt spur.

Their right was directed on Fricourt Farm and the left, thrown forward, on Round Wood, just south of Scots Redoubt.

Both the leading battalions of the 63rd Brigade (Brigadier-General E.R. Hill) lost very heavily in the assault of the German front trench. Two companies of the 4th Battalion Middlesex Regiment, on the right, in attempting to leave their own front trench five minutes before zero and crawl forward into No Man's Land, came under such heavy machine-gun fire that they had to return. So severe had been the casualties that they were then ordered to advance as one line only, and the survivors left the trench for the second time only a minute before zero.

They faced the fire in a most gallant manner. Though swept by six machine-guns, untouched by the bombardment – two in a small work between the front and support trenches and four in the northern part of Fricourt – they reached the German support trench. All the officers of the leading companies were now casualties, and the surviving men, about forty in all, pressed on in scattered parties after the barrage to the Sunken Road. The two rear companies of the battalion also incurred heavy losses in crossing No Man's Land from the machine-guns in Fricourt and only four officers and 100 other ranks reached the German front trench.[18]

Fearing a counter-attack against his right flank from Fricourt, where the Germans could be seen moving about in some numbers, the commanding officer, Lieutenant Colonel H.P.F. Bicknell, decided to remain for the time being in the front trench and there consolidate his position. He was thus able to check three consecutive attempts made by the Germans shortly afterwards to bomb northwards.

The 8th Battalion Somerset Light Infantry, on the left, also came under heavy fire when its front companies crept into No Man's Land before zero hour, but the assault was nevertheless delivered. The losses were severe, Lieutenant Colonel J.W. Scott being wounded, and all but three of the officers hit before the German front trench was reached. The battalion, however, preceded by a shower of grenades, succeeded in entering the trench, and thence parties of bombers led the way along the communication trenches to the support trench and beyond.

The orders given to the supporting battalions had been to start their advance at 08.30 hours, so as to be ready to pass through the leading battalions to the second objective, Bottom Wood and Quadrangle Trench on the southern end of the Contalmaison spur, as soon as the creeping barrage advanced. Owing to the opposition encountered by the leading units, it was judged necessary to postpone the movement indefinitely.

Soon after, on arrival of reports of the heavy losses in the first assault, it was feared at brigade headquarters that the two front battalions would be unable to maintain the positions gained unless reinforced, so at 08.40 hours the 10th Battalion York & Lancaster Regiment and 8th Battalion Lincolnshire Regiment were ordered forward. Both suffered heavily in crossing No Man's Land, but the survivors pressed on to the high ground on the top of the spur and reached the leading units.

On the right, the 10th York & Lancs advanced through the remnants of the Middlesex Regiment in the German front trench and got to the Sunken Road, beyond which the barrage was now put down, but there it was held up by heavy machine-gun fire both from Fricourt and Fricourt Wood on its right front. On the left, the 8th Lincolnshires reinforced the Somerset and, led by bombers, made further progress along the communication trenches, which were tenaciously held by a long line of enemy bombers. Lozenge Alley, running towards Fricourt Farm, was thus occupied as far as the Sunken Road and manned to secure the right flank. Small detachments moved northwards along the Sunken Road into Crucifix Trench, and others eastwards along Lozenge Alley towards Fricourt Farm, but these latter were compelled to retire.

Strong parties of German bombers now counter-attacked up Lonely Trench, in order to clear Sunken Road, but they were repulsed and parties of the York & Lancaster Regiment eventually constructed a sandbag barricade which effectually blocked Lonely Trench. The sections of the 98th Field Company Royal Engineers sent up to consolidate became involved in the fighting, and were utilized to strengthen the 63rd Brigade's right flank.

The original front of the 64th Brigade (Brigadier-General H.R. Headlam) had a salient at each end with a drop back of sixty or seventy yards in the centre, but the divisional engineers, without even the infantry knowing it, had mined a Russian sap from salient to salient. The top of this tunnel was knocked in on the night of 30 June/1 July, so that the first wave could start from a straight line in front of the British wire, which, however, was almost entirely removed.

The attack of the brigade was led by the 9th and 10th battalions King's Own Yorkshire Light Infantry. During the final five minutes of the intense bombardment,[19] the leading companies left the Russian sap and succeeded in crawling forward into No Man's Land. However, here the Germans, notwithstanding the heavy fire, also brought machine-guns out of dug-outs and, placing them on top of the parapet, opened rapid fire, whilst enfilade machine-gun fire from the trenches on the higher ground south of La Boisselle swept No Man's Land and the whole of the ground over which the subsequent advance of the brigade was made.

As soon as the bombardment ceased, the lines of both battalions of the King's Own Yorkshire Light Infantry rose and went forward, and, in spite of heavy losses, they pressed on, never wavering, the lines in rear coming up and filling the gaps. The German wire had been well cut, and the Yorkshiremen, although met by showers of stick-bombs, rushed in and overran the position. The two supporting battalions, the 15th Battalion Durham Light Infantry and 1st Battalion East Yorkshire Regiment, following up close behind, now reinforced the line, and all four battalions, intermingled, pressed forward at a rapid pace to the support trench, which was successfully occupied. Two hundred German prisoners were sent back under escort.

The capture of the two lines of trenches had been carried out within ten minutes from the start – but at great cost. More than half of the two leading battalions, including most of their officers, had fallen. Lieutenant Colonel C.W.D. Lynch (9th Battalion King's Own Yorkshire Light Infantry) – who had gone forward to lead his men when there was a check – was killed, and Lieutenant Colonel M.B. Stow (1st Battalion East Yorkshire Regiment) mortally wounded. Lieutenant Colonel H.J. King (10th Battalion King's Own Yorkshire Light Infantry) was wounded later in the day.[20]

When the creeping barrage moved forward and the advance was continued beyond the first position across the top of the spur below which lay the Sunken Road, a running fight developed; small parties of Germans attempted to offer resistance, but they were forced back or overcome with bomb and bayonet. At about 08.00 hours, after a mile of open ground had been covered, the Sunken Road was reached.

Here, where a mountain gun and some boxes of soft-nosed bullets were captured, a general halt was called. Parties of all four battalions, however, pressed on to Crucifix Trench and occupied it, when some hundred Germans in overcoats came forward from Shelter Wood and surrendered. The companies remaining in the Sunken Road were at once reorganized in Lonely Trench behind the road, and the further bank was consolidated for defence.

It was now obvious that machine-gun and rifle fire from three localities about five hundred yards ahead, Fricourt Wood, Shelter Wood and Birch Tree Wood, would, as the barrage had passed on, make any further advance very difficult. Brigadier-General Headlam came up at this time to the Sunken Road, placing what men he could find to cover the exposed left where the 34th Division (III Corps) should have been, as he did so. Parties were sent forward to gain touch with those in Crucifix Trench, and Lewis-gun detachments moved out to hold Lozenge Wood to the south. Learning that Round Wood to the north was still in German hands, Brigadier-General Headlam himself led a party towards it, but his brigade major, Major G.B. Bosanquet, was killed whilst reconnoitring for the advance and most of the party were knocked over by a machine-gun in the wood.[21]

As the 34th Division had not come up, the left flank was secured by a post at the corner where Crucifix Trench meets the Sunken Road. Round Wood, just to the north of this corner, and the trench running west by north from it were occupied by a company of the 1st Battalion East Yorkshire Regiment about an hour later (09.45 hours), just as the Germans were counter-attacking the parties of the 15th and 16th battalions Royal Scots (34th Division) which had now appeared. The Yorkshiremen took part in stopping this, driving the enemy back into Shelter Wood.

Lieutenant Colonel A.E. Fitzgerald, 15th Battalion Durham Light Infantry, the only surviving commanding officer, was put in charge of the captured line, with instructions not to continue the advance till further orders, as the troops on either flank were hesitating to do so and in fact were not yet up in alignment. Owing to the long communications and the congestion in the trenches, artillery support was difficult to arrange, and Brigadier-General Headlam now returned to report to divisional headquarters, reaching there at 11.00 hours. A message which he had previously sent off arrived one-and-a-half hours later, sufficient indication of the difficulties of intercommunication.

On his representation that both flanks of the division were in the air – for the small parties of Royal Scots on the left had seemed to disappear – two battalions of the 62nd Brigade, in reserve, the 10th Battalion Green Howards and the 1st Battalion Lincolnshire Regiment,[22] were sent up. They were, however, delayed by congestion in the trenches and by change of orders resulting from the improvement in the situation on the left. Eventually they took post on the right of the 63rd and left of the 64th Brigade respectively.

The assault on Fricourt

The messages which reached XV Corps headquarters at Heilly (eight miles south-west of Fricourt) by midday gave General Horne an optimistic impression of the situation on either side of him. From the right, XIII Corps sent news that the 30th Division had captured the whole of Montauban, that the 18th Division had taken Pommiers Redoubt and reached Beetle Alley on the further side of the Mametz ridge, and that the enemy was in full retreat on Bazentin le Grand, being shelled as he retired.

From the left, III Corps announced (11.45 hours) that its leading troops had pushed through Peake Woods and were moving on Contalmaison, which gave an utterly erroneous idea of the situation. Aeroplane observers reported (11.20 hours) that enemy guns were being withdrawn along the Pozières–Bapaume road and that the British infantry had been seen moving along the communication trenches between Fricourt and Contalmaison.

In view of this encouraging outlook, and because the preliminary bombardment of the Fricourt sector seemed to have been very successful, General Horne decided to order the initiation of the third phase of the battle, the attack up the Willow stream valley on Fricourt and Fricourt Wood.

As a matter of fact the units attacking on either side of these localities had not yet reached the whole of their first objectives or had even formed, except partially on the right, any defensive flank towards Fricourt. Moreover, the second phase, the advance beyond Mametz and Fricourt Farm towards the German second intermediate line covering Mametz Wood, had not yet been begun. At 12.50 hours orders were sent to the 7th and 21st Divisions – whose 22nd and 62nd Brigade with the greater part of the 50th Brigade, were still intact – and to the artillery concerned, that zero hour for the third phase would be 14.30 hours, and would be preceded by the usual half-hour bombardment.[23]

The 22nd Brigade (Brigadier-General J. McC. Steele) of the 7th Division, waiting in the front trenches on the end of the Maricourt spur south of Fricourt, accordingly sent the 20th Battalion Manchester Regiment, with two companies and the bombers of the 1st Battalion Royal Welch Fusiliers, to attack.[24] The leading companies of the Manchesters crossed No Man's Land and entered the German trenches with little loss, but the support lines came under severe machine-gun fire directed down the long gentle slope on the left, and suffered heavy casualties: Lieutenant Colonel H. Lewis of the Manchesters was killed, and, on the left of the line, the detachments, which, after crossing the front trench were to bomb down the two support trenches towards the valley and Fricourt, were practically annihilated.

In the centre a small party entered "The Rectangle", a strongpoint connecting the support lines, but was bombed out of it and forced back to a support trench which had been occupied by the right companies. An attempt was made to advance across the open from this trench, but heavy loss was suffered from fire from the left, so it had to be abandoned. A long bombing contest now ensued with varying fortune and no further advance was made.

The success of the Welch Fusiliers, who had bombed their way up Sunken Road Trench and both sides of the Rectangle until they reached Apple Alley, even entering Fricourt for a time, enabled the Manchesters to hold on. The line at nightfall, when the 54th Field Company Royal Engineers came up from reserve to assist in consolidating the ground gained, included the second support trench and the Rectangle, with advanced posts up the communication trench, the right in touch with the 20th Brigade in Apple Alley.

North of the Willow stream the attack on Fricourt by the 50th Brigade (Brigadier-General W.J.T. Glasgow) was even less successful. According to the original plan it was to be carried out by the 7th Battalion Green Howards, protected on the north by the 10th Battalion West Yorkshire Regiment, which should by this time have formed a flank towards Fricourt. However, the practical annihilation of the West Yorkshires in the morning had made such co-operation impossible, and the 7th Battalion East Yorkshire Regiment, in support, was moved up into the front trenches to take their place and assist the attack by keeping the enemy down by fire.

The Green Howards was only three companies strong, for, owing to an error, one company had attacked at 07.45 hours, soon after the first general assault, and was, like the West Yorkshires, practically destroyed in the first twenty yards by a single machine-gun.

On receiving the orders for the 14.30 hours attack, the 50th Brigade represented that it would be useless to attack with the 7th Battalion Green Howards until the objective originally assigned to the 10th Battalion West Yorkshires had been made good, but orders were, nevertheless, received for the attack to proceed.

The attack by the 7th Green Howards was delivered against the strongest part of the Fricourt defences, between Wing Corner and the German Tambour, still occupied in force. As regards the wire the short artillery preparation had been ineffective – owing to bad fuzes, so the infantry maintain – thus there were only four small gaps in it, and the deep dug-outs, the feature of the Fricourt defence, had not been touched.

When the three companies, covered by Lewis-gun fire from the railway embankment, crossed the parapet into No Man's Land they at once came under murderous machine-gun and rifle fire from front and left, some Germans standing on the parapet to fire. Whole lines fell in the first fifty yards, and within three minutes the battalion lost fifteen officers and 336 other ranks. A few men reached the village, but all these, except a handful who got into a cellar and there passed the night, were soon killed or captured.

The survivors of the attack lay out in shell holes until dark, when they returned to the British line. The advance of the 7th East Yorkshires, made on the initiative of its commander a little after that of the Green Howards, shared a similar fate. The two leading companies suffered casualties of five officers and 150 other ranks in the first few yards, and were unable to cross No Man's Land. Further operations of the 50th Brigade were therefore stopped.

Further advance of the 7th Division

Whilst the brigades on the inner flanks of the 7th and 21st Divisions had been making their fruitless efforts to reach Fricourt and the ground in the valley between this village and Mametz, on either side, the other four – the 91st, 20th, 63rd and 64th – were strengthening the line gained earlier in the day on the Mametz and Fricourt spurs. About 13.00 hours the last company of the 8th Battalion Devonshire Regiment was sent in to fill the gap between the Gordon Highlanders and the 9th Devons. Its leading platoon lost heavily, but the company commander, guiding it to the left to avoid the devastating fire from the Shrine, brought his men up, as will be seen, most opportunely.

Taking advantage of the assault on Fricourt at 14.30 hours, which attracted German attention to that sector, fresh efforts were made by the four brigades to get forward. Major General Watts (7th Division) had placed at the disposal of the 20th Brigade on the right two companies of the 2nd Battalion Warwickshire Regiment from divisional reserve with which to push on from the trenches facing Mametz through the village to Bunny Trench beyond. They were to co-operate with the 1st Battalion South Staffordshire Regiment (91st Brigade) which, with the help of the 21st Battalion Manchester Regiment, had already worked forward from the southern into the eastern part of the village and captured a number of prisoners.

With the two companies of the 8th Devons sent up in the morning, the two companies of the Warwickshires were organized into four lines. They advanced after half an hour's bombardment at 15.30 hours, the last company of the 8th Devons joining in. Before they had even reached the front line of the 2nd Battalion Gordon Highlanders in Shrine Alley, some two hundred Germans came forward from Mametz and the Shrine dug-outs, holding up their hands, a considerable number having been seen previously retiring northwards towards Fricourt Wood.

The 8th Devons cleared the deep dug-outs in Danzig Trench (South) at the bottom of the valley, reached Hidden Wood, and was able to take all the objectives allotted to the 9th Devons with comparatively few casualties. By 16.05 hours, after a few Germans had resisted to the last with the bayonet, the whole of the ruined village of Mametz was in British hands, and Bunny Trench along its north-western edge had been occupied. The first objective allotted to the 20th Brigade was consolidated, and the remaining two companies of the Warwickshires were moved up to Shrine Alley as a brigade reserve. By 17.00 hours, except for slight machine-gun fire from Fricourt Wood and a few long range shells, the situation was quiet and movement could be carried on in the open.

In the meantime the 91st Brigade had secured all its objectives and taken several hundred prisoners. On the right, east of Mametz, the 2nd Queen's had by 18.30 hours or earlier completely cleared Fritz Trench, the eastern end of which had been entered about 15.00 hours, and, after considerable opposition, Bright Alley. An hour later the South Staffordshires moved from Mametz up Bunny Alley to its junction with Fritz Trench.

By evening, therefore, the first objective of the right and centre of the 7th Division – Fritz Trench, beyond Mametz, and a flank facing Fricourt – had been secured, the line running from Beetle Alley, where junction had been made with XIII Corps, along Fritz Trench, and thence down Bunny Alley and Bunny Trench round the north-western edge of Mametz. Thence the 20th Brigade took it down the slope along Orchard Alley, across the Péronne road and railway by Apple Alley, up on to the Maricourt spur, joining with the left brigade (22nd), whose line on the right was partly in the German support line and partly in the front line.

As early as 18.00 hours the rear services of the division were well established, two roads via Carnoy and Wellington Redoubt having been repaired up to the German front line, and two duck-boarded communication trenches provided for each brigade for "up" and "down" traffic.

The enemy's resistance on the front of the 30th, 18th (of XIII Corps) and the 7th Divisions was completely broken. Everything was curiously quiet, localities beyond the first day's objectives – even Mametz Wood – could probably have been occupied with small loss, and they subsequently proved very costly both in time and life to capture. The battalions at the front reported that the enemy had cleared off, and that ground further to the front could be made good, but no orders for any further movement were issued by any of the higher staffs.

With the assistance of the 54th and 95th Field Companies Royal Engineers, which went up above ground about 16.30 hours, the 24th Battalion Manchester Regiment (Pioneers) and the 1/3rd Durham Field Company which went up later, the whole of the new front of the 7th Division was wired during the night: four strong points were constructed, and dumps of stores formed in shell holes. Mametz village was placed in a state of defence under the direction of Lieutenant Colonel W.W. Norman (21st Battalion Manchester Regiment). A wireless station was erected at its south-west corner, and two of its wells were cleared out, saving a long "carry" of two-gallon water tins.[25] Part of the advanced dressing station at Minden Post (500 yards west of Carnoy) was also sent up to Mametz.

Situation of the 21st Division

Although the 7th Division had greatly improved its position, the 21st Division hardly moved during the afternoon; it did, however, manage to establish a flank towards Fricourt. In order to take advantage of the 14.30 hours attack on that village, the 63rd and 64th Brigades had been ordered to press on at that hour from the Sunken Road and Crucifix Trench to Fricourt Farm and Shelter Wood, respectively, and the 63rd Brigade was to be ready to cut off the retreat of any Germans from Fricourt village. On the front of this brigade, however, any movement from Lonely Trench and Lozenge Wood was at once checked by machine-gun fire from Fricourt Farm and the northern side of Fricourt Wood.

The order to the 64th Brigade did not reach Colonel Fitzgerald, commanding the leading troops, till ten minutes after the preliminary bombardment of Shelter Wood had lifted, and the attack from Crucifix Trench, carried out by a mixed force of the 10th Battalion King's Own Yorkshire Light Infantry and 15th Battalion Durham Light Infantry, failed. At 16.35 hours, therefore, Major General Campbell ordered both brigades to hold and consolidate the trenches gained.

At that hour the line ran from the Willow stream along the British original front to opposite the German Tambour, the 7th Green Howards having failed to get forward. North of this work some of the survivors of the 10th West Yorkshires, the left of the 50th Brigade, were still in the German front trench, but the majority were in the British front line. On their left the units of the 63rd Brigade formed a flank towards Fricourt village and wood along Lonely Lane – Lozenge Alley – Lozenge Wood, where a message sent by pigeon brought them the ammunition and water of which they were badly in need. Further north, the 64th Brigade had gained and held the first objective from Lozenge Wood along the first intermediate line, Crucifix Trench, to Round Wood, where its left was in touch with the 34th Division (III Corps).

At 17.33 hours Major General Campbell had ordered the 62nd Brigade (Brigadier-General C.G. Rawling) to send up its two remaining battalions (12th and 13th battalions Northumberland Fusiliers) to take the place of the 64th Brigade, which had suffered the heaviest losses in the attack. The latter brigade was relieved at dawn on the 2nd and withdrawn to the old German support trench, where it organized a defensive flank facing north.

Three hours after this order (20.50 hours), following some conversation on the telephone, corps headquarters – in view of the heavy losses of the 21st Division – ordered the 17th Division, from corps reserve, to take over the front facing Fricourt, and the 51st Brigade (Brigadier-General R.B. Fell) with the 77th Field Company Royal Engineers relieved the 50th Brigade preparatory to a renewal of the attack on the village the next morning.

This relief proved unfortunate, and, in view of the situation, an appeal was actually made against it by the 50th Brigade; for before dusk it was evident from the observing posts that the Germans were weakening, and patrols then sent out established that they were going back. The 6th Battalion Dorsetshire Regiment had, indeed, been moved up and, with the remaining two companies of the 7th Battalion East Yorkshire Regiment, ordered to assault. This movement was now countermanded and the change of brigades took place. Owing to congestion in the trenches it was not completed until 05.00 hours on the 2nd, by which time the 51st Brigade, having marched from Morlancourt carrying fifty extra rounds of S.A.A. and three days' rations, was very tired; the opportunity had passed.

In the 21st Division area, as the enemy hardly fired a shot after dark, there was no difficulty in clearing the wounded – any delay being due to lack of sufficient stretchers and bearers – or in getting up supplies. Water proved the only exception, for the parties told to carry it were insufficient owing to the heavy demands. During the fighting there had been congestion in the communication trenches, due to the walking wounded who persisted in taking the nearest way instead of the trenches allotted to them. Then there had been straggling on the roads, which led to the Deputy Director of Medical Services of the corps, Colonel F.R. Newland, making the suggestion, later carried into effect, that lorries should be provided to carry walking wounded once they were clear of the communication trenches.

As a general result of the day's fighting, XV Corps had made considerable headway on both its flanks, the right wing having advanced 2,500 yards and captured Mametz, and the left 2,000 yards across the top of the Fricourt spur to beyond the Sunken Road. It had taken prisoner in all twenty-nine officers and 1,596 other ranks. In the centre, however, the attack had failed and, in spite of envelopment on three sides, there were still Germans in Fricourt.

The losses of XV Corps had been over 8,000 of all ranks, due almost entirely to machine-gun fire.[26]

The German account

The front opposite to XV Corps was held by the centre portion of the 28th Reserve Division. Opposed to the 7th Division was the greater part of the 109th Reserve Regiment (its eastern boundary was the Carnoy–Montauban road), with the I and III Battalions and fifteen machine-guns "in shell hole positions" in the line, and the II Battalion in support in and around Danzig Alley. The regiment should have been relieved on the night of 30 June/1 July by the 23rd Regiment, but, owing to the heavy British fire, only one company and a half of the relieving unit had been able to get up, and the rest, as already mentioned, had remained near Montauban.

The deep dug-outs in the front line had not been much damaged, but, as hardly any had been constructed in the other lines, the garrison was mostly crowded together in the front line and caught there; thus the defence had no depth.[27] The artillery of the 28th Reserve Division could give very little assistance, as "a great number of the guns had been smashed up", and it suffered badly on 1 July from further fire directed by aeroplane observation. The few guns still in action could not prevent the British reinforcements from coming up.[28] All telephone communication broke down. The machine-guns in Danzig Alley (East) and in the northern part of Mametz were either knocked out by direct hits or became unserviceable. It is claimed that Mametz was still held at 18.00 hours, and that the few men of the 23rd and 109th Reserve Regiments left alive only withdrew at 19.00 hours.[29]

At the first news of the attack the brigade commander sent the 55th Landwehr Ersatz Battalion and two battalions of the 23rd Regiment, with all available men of the 109th Reserve Regiment, as already mentioned, to occupy the second position. In view of the uncertainty of the situation at Montauban and the necessity for securing the second position, and for keeping back some troops to occupy Mametz Wood, he decided not to send forward reinforcements to recover the front lines which had been lost.

Opposite the 21st Division was the sector of the 111th Reserve Regiment, and it suffered "quite particularly" during the bombardment: "The trenches and obstacles, the weaker dug-outs and also the best observation posts were nearly completely destroyed ... Only by great exertions were the trenches, whose original course was hardly recognisable, kept passable. The entrances of the few deep dug-outs not smashed up could only be kept open by extemporized means."

The situation on Fricourt spur was the worst. There a company of the 110th Reserve Regiment, on the extreme right (north), had been reduced to eighty men by the bombardment, and another of the 111th was ordered to replace it. This company, however, did not go up to the front. It sent twenty men to Round Wood – who were no doubt there when a party of the 64th Brigade attacked the wood – to block the gap in the line by fire, and held the rest in reserve between the wood and Contalmaison.

SLAUGHTER ON THE SOMME: 1 JULY 1916

The success of the British, in spite of a warning of attack received by the 28th Reserve Division through its listening station at La Boisselle, is attributed to "the weak German artillery barrage being unable to stop the advance of the enemy", and to lack of hand-grenades. It is stated that a mine was fired which buried thirty British, but there is no mention of this in any British account. Only 3½ lines are given to the attack on Fricourt, to say that it failed with heavy loss. The German casualties for the day are not available.

NOTES

1. XV Corps (Lieutenant General H.S. Horne) comprised: 7th Division (Major General H.E. Watts), 20th, 22nd and 91st Brigades; 21st Division (Major General D.G.M. Campbell; from December 1915 to May 1916, Major General C.W. Jacob, then promoted to command a corps), 62nd, 63rd and 64th Brigades; 17th Division (Major General T.D. Pilcher), 50th, 51st and 52nd Brigades; G.O.C. Royal Artillery, Brigadier-General E.W. Alexander; G.O.C. Heavy Artillery, Brigadier-General W.J. Napier; Chief Engineer, Brigadier-General P.G. Grant. The heavy artillery consisted of five groups, the 3rd, 14th, 18th, 21st and 23rd, and the 44th Siege Battery, and comprised howitzers (two 12-inch, twelve 9.2-inch, twelve 8-inch, and twelve 6-inch) and guns (four 6-inch, twenty 60-pounders, and sixteen 4.7-inch). As corps artillery there were also the French 6th Field Artillery "Groupe" and a 4.5-inch howitzer battery. The front being a little over 5,000 yards, this gave about one heavy per fifty-eight yards, and one field gun or howitzer per twenty-five yards.
2. Part of the 109th Reserve Regiment (headquarters in Mametz village), with one company of the 23rd Regiment, held as far as Hidden Wood, south-west of Mametz, and the 111th Reserve Regiment carried on the line across Caterpillar Valley past the western side of Fricourt to about Round Wood on the top of the Fricourt spur. A battalion of the 55th Landwehr Regiment was in the second position.
3. One 18-pounder battery dug in close behind the front line opposite Wing Corner (a salient in the German front line immediately south of Fricourt) now opened fire for the first time, having been silent during the preliminary bombardment.
4. Fire from its southern face caused very serious loss to the left brigade of the 7th Division.
5. Major General E.W. Alexander, VC, who was G.O.C. Royal Artillery of the corps, stated that "to some extent this [the creeping barrage] was used by the 15th Division (of which he was C.R.A.) at the battle of Loos. ... I rather think that I got the tip from Budworth (the late Major General C.E.D. Budworth). " In the *Journal of the R.A. Institution* for April 1931 will be found an article "The Coming of the Creeping Barrage" by Major A.F. Becke, which deals with the subject as a whole.
6. He had three 18-pounder batteries of the 17th Division in addition to his own, and one of the 21st Division.
7. It must be understood that, at this experimental stage, the creeping barrage began at the enemy front trench and did not help the infantry across No Man's Land.
8. Wounded on 1 July 1916, Fitzgerald died of his wounds on 12 July 1916. He is buried in Twyford (The Assumption) Churchyard, Buckinghamshire.
9. There were plenty of forward observing artillery officers with the infantry, so many that, as one infantry officer said, he thought there was a tactical exercise in progress, but they could get no information back to artillery headquarters, and, as all batteries had the strictest orders to fire according to the programme until further orders, they continued to do so.
10. The Field Companies Royal Engineers (54th, 95th and l/3rd Durham – later 528th), with the Pioneer battalion (24th Battalion Manchester Regiment), were kept back in reserve, it being intended that they should go up at night to construct strong points and communication trenches. As far as possible, the companies were always sent to work in the zone of the same brigade; they were "affiliated", as it was called, but not "attached".

11. Here was found, untouched, a machine-gun emplacement cleverly sited low down in a bank parallel to the line of advance.

12. An officer of the 9th Battalion Devonshire Regiment who had made a plasticine model of the ground over which the 20th Brigade had to advance had forecast that this would be the case, and he himself was among the killed. That officer was Captain Duncan Martin.

13. The brigade had been holding the front of the 7th Division; it was then withdrawn into reserve, and had had no opportunity of becoming acquainted with the front from which it was to attack, patrolling being forbidden for fear of the enemy gaining vital intelligence or identification. A section of the 78th Field Company Royal Engineers was attached to it.

14. The Royal Engineers (97th, 98th and 126th Field Companies), and the Pioneer battalion (14th Battalion Northumberland Fusiliers) of the 21st Division were divided into working parties to construct strong and supporting points in the objectives when captured, and took position in rear of the leading or rear battalions of the 63rd and 64th Brigades, according to whether they were to consolidate the first or second objective.

15. So far as can be discovered, from one nest only in the village and one only in the Tambour.

16. The amount of damage done to Fricourt by the bombardment had been small on account of the failure of the 9.2-inch shells to explode, the fuzes having come out during flight.

17. Forty-one-year-old Lieutenant Colonel A. Dickson, 1st Battalion South Lancashire Regiment, attached 10th Battalion West Yorkshire Regiment, lies in Fricourt New Military Cemetery.

18. The total casualties of the 4th Battalion Middlesex Regiment that day were nineteen officers and 469 other ranks.

19. In this three 18-pounder batteries of the 95th Brigade Royal Field Artillery, dug in on the eastern edge of the southernmost strip of Bécourt Wood at 1,350 – 1,800 yards range, specially fired on the sector that the 64th Brigade was to attack: during the last minute with percussion instead of time shrapnel.

20. Thirty-five-year-old Lieutenant Colonel Colmer William Donald Lynch was buried in Norfolk Cemetery, Becordel-Becourt, whilst Lieutenant Colonel Montague Bruce Stow, aged 32, lies in Daours Communal Cemetery Extension. The casualties for the day were: 9th Battalion King's Own Yorkshire Light Infantry, twenty-one officers and 383 other ranks; 10th Battalion King's Own Yorkshire Light Infantry, twenty-one officers and 428 other ranks; 15th Battalion Durham Light Infantry, fifteen officers and 373 other ranks; 1st Battalion East Yorkshire Regiment, twenty-one officers and 478 other ranks.

21. Major G.B. Bosanquet MC, 1st Battalion Gloucestershire Regiment was buried in Gordon Dump Cemetery at Ovillers-La Boisselle.

22. To the 1st Battalion Lincolnshire Regiment was attached the first active service contingent of the Bermuda Volunteer Rifle Corps (one officer and eighty rank and file), which had arrived in France on 23 June 1915.

23. No creeping barrage was arranged for this attack: at zero the barrage was to lift 500 yards back, fifteen minutes later lift 250 yards and continue on this line for one hour and thirty minutes.

24. The remaining two battalions were in divisional reserve.

25. The work of discovering wells and improving roads was continued by the Royal Engineers on the following days.

26. The 7th Division suffered sixty-seven officers killed and sixty-nine wounded, along with 965 other ranks killed, 2,252 wounded and twenty-seven missing – a total of 3,380. The 21st Division suffered ninety-one officers killed, 103 wounded and one missing, along with 1,091 other ranks killed, 2,859 wounded and 111 missing (one was a prisoner of war) – a total of 4,256. The 17th Division suffered twenty-one officers killed and twenty-one wounded, along with 536 other ranks killed, 544 wounded and thirty-three missing – a total of 1,155.

27. This is certainly true of the portion south of the Carnoy –Fricourt road, where the front trench was found literally crowded with German dead and wounded.

28. According to British reports, there was hardly any shelling of XV Corps after 14.00 hours.

29. At 18.00 hours the only Germans in Mametz were a few badly wounded prisoners. The village was entirely in British hands soon after 16.00 hours.

Index of Battalions

7th (Service) Battalion Alexandra, Princess of Wales's Own (Yorkshire Regiment)

Trenches in front of FRICOURT VILLAGE.

The Batt H.Q. moved to a dug out at FRICOURT STATION in the evening, formerly occupied by H.Q. of 'C' Coy. Lt Col R.D. A'FIFE C.M.G. Commanding the Battn.

'A' Coy was commanded by Major R.E.D. KENT.

'B' Coy was commanded by Capt L.G. HARE.

'C' Coy was commanded by Capt R.W.S. CROFT.

'D' Coy was commanded by Capt H.L. BARTRUM.

A heavy artillery bombardment of the whole of the German position was maintained throughout the night. The enemy retaliating in a half hearted manner, mainly directing his fire on the front line trenches but doing little damage except to trenches in the "CEMETERY".

The attached Battn Operation Order No.63 gives the general and detailed orders for the offensive for which the Battn assembled in the trenches opposite FRICOURT VILLAGE on the afternoon of 27th June 1916. The first zero hour was 7.30am on July 1st when the troops on our left and right attacked, and the 2nd zero hour was at 2.30pm when the Battalion assaulted.

Owing to an unfortunate mistake on the part of the Officer commanding 'A' Coy, his company assaulted at 7.45am as soon as they began to climb over our parapet terrific machine gun fire was opened by the enemy and the company was almost at once wiped out. The survivors lay in crump holes some 25 yards in front of our wire until after dark. As soon as it was discovered that 'A' Company had assaulted by itself, 'D' Coy (the reserve coy) was brought up into the assembly trenches to take 'A' Coy's place.

At 2pm 1/7/16 our Artillery began the ½ hour preliminary bombardment of FRICOURT VILLAGE. This bombardment was feeble and did little damage to the enemy as the Battalion soon learned to its cost. At 2.30pm the Battn assaulted and were met by a murderous machine gun and rifle fire, officers and men were literally mown down and were finally brought to a standstill about half way across to the enemy's trenches. 13 Officers and over 300 men became casualties in about three minutes.

The survivors lay in crump holes until dark with a few exceptions who managed to crawl back. Many magnificent deeds of courage were performed especially in bringing in wounded and in carrying messages under fire.

The Battn was withdrawn after dark on 1/7/16 and marched some 5 miles behind the line to re-organise at VILLE continuing the march at 4pm 2/7/16 to HEILLY.

The Battn was relieved by 6th Batt Dorset Regt. Which was subsequently relieved the same night by 51st Bgde.

This Bgde. occupied FRICOURT VILLAGE on the morning of 2/7/16 without a shot being fired, the enemy having evacuated his trenches during the night. (about 11.30pm)

The casualties in the Battn amounted to:

5 Officers killed and 10 wounded.

O.R. 336 killed and wounded.

10th (Service) Battalion Alexandra, Princess of Wales's Own (Yorkshire Regiment)

In the Field

Took part in the Battle of The SOMME, and got as far as CRUCIFIX TRENCH, where we were relieved and marched back to DERNANCOURT into bivouac.

(More details cannot be given, owing to COL EDDOWES, being sent to England sick, & having taken the fuller details with him, a special report has been already sent to the 21st Division.)[1]

NOTE

1. One of those killed during the attack by this battalion on 1 July 1916, was 36-year-old Major Stewart Walter Loudoun-Shand. Loudon-Shand had been working as a tea merchant in Ceylon when war broke out in 1914. He immediately returned to the UK, finding a place on one of the first available sailings home to volunteer his services. He gained a commission with the 10th Battalion Alexandra Princess of Wales's Yorkshire Regiment - Green Howards. Promoted to Captain in June 1915, his battalion landed in France in early September of that year. At Zero Hour on 1 July 1916, Major Loudoun-Shand's "B" Company was soon in severe difficulty as the men tried to clear the trench due to the murderous machine-gun fire raining down on them. *The London Gazette* of 9 September 1916, provides the following account of what happened next:"When his company attempted to climb over the parapet to attack the enemy's trenches, they were met by very fierce machine gun fire, which temporarily stopped their progress. Maj. Loudoun-Shand immediately leapt on the parapet, helped the men over it and encouraged them in every way until he fell mortally wounded. Even then he insisted on being propped up in the trench, and went on encouraging the non-commissioned officers and men until he died."His company had gone into action with five officers and 117 men; they returned with just one officer and twenty-seven men. Major Loudon-Shand is buried in Norfolk Cemetery, Becordel-Becourt.

2nd Battalion Border Regiment

On the night of the 30th June/1st July 1916, the Battalion moved up from MORLANCOURT & took up a position in B.2. Sub-sector of the trenches. The move was completed at about 1.30am on 1st July 1916.

The Battalion was formed up as follows:

1st Line   Right: 'A' Company under Lieut G.M.F. PRYNNE occupying
              RESERVE TRENCH from 70 Street to 71 Street.
              Left: 'C' Company under Capt L.A. NEWTON occupying
              RESERVE TRENCH from 71 Street up to about 72 Street in
              ALBERT STREET.
2nd Line   Right: 'B' Company under Lieut R.F. MILLARD having 2 Platoons
              in ALBERT STREET on N.W. of 70 Street & 2 Platoons in
              WELLINGTON REDOUBT.
              Left: 'D' Company under Lieut P.N. FRASER, having 2 Platoons
              in ALBERT STREET from junction of WEBB STREET to the left.
              2 Platoons in WELLINGTON REDOUBT.

Battalion Head Quarters, Head Quarter Bombers, Signallers, 2 Lewis Guns in
Reserve, Battalion Aid Post all in WELLINGTON REDOUBT.

Whilst the Artillery Bombardment of the hostile line continued the Battalion
was subjected to a heavy bombardment in retaliation from the enemy but as this
was mostly directed at our front and support lines little damage was done.

At 7.27am. the Battalion advanced in 4 lines from our trenches in the following
order:

1st LINE   Right: 2 Platoons of 'A' Company.
                       Left: 2 Platoons of 'C' Company.
2nd LINE   Right: 2 Platoons of 'A' Company.
                       Left: 2 Platoons of 'C' Company.
                       Three Lewis Guns.
3rd LINE   Right: 2 Platoons of 'B' Company.
                       Left: 2 Platoons of 'D' Company.
                       Three Lewis Guns.
4th LINE or Reserve   Right: 2 Platoons of 'B' Company.
                       Left: 2 Platoons of 'D' Company.
                       Two Lewis Guns.

Just as our first line had cleared our front the head of the subway from 71 Street
towards DANUBE TRENCH was blown out. Zero hour.

The Battalion now moved forward until it reached its first objective DANUBE
SUPPORT TRENCH when the left wheel was commenced.

Up till now the casualties were small in the first and second lines and were
caused by a machine gun firing from our right in the direction of SAP 'A' in hostile
trench & also from one on our left in DANUBE SUPPORT. The wheel was now
gradually completed & the advance continued towards our objective, APPLE
ALLEY, which was reached by our 1st Line at about 8.30am. During this advance
our line was broken up into a line of groups bombing & bayoneting the enemy,

who when they found that their line had been entered formed a new front in shell holes & communication trenches facing us thus checking our advance.

On reaching SHRINE ALLEY the Battalion was temporarily checked through coming under heavy indirect machine gun fire from FRICOURT and enfilade fire from MAMETZ, but on the 1st & 2nd Lines being reinforced by the 3rd Line the advance was continued to HIDDEN LANE. Here the line was again temporarily held up by fire from a machine gun & hostile party in HIDDEN WOOD & another party at about the junction of KIEL SUPPORT & BOIS FRANCAIS SUPPORT. The latter were bombed out without very much difficulty by our party working along KIEL SUPPORT, but the former had to be attacked across the open as well as down HIDDEN LANE. This was done by a party organised & led by 2nd Lieut S.J.C. RUSSELL. The advance was now continued to APPLE ALLEY by parties being pushed forward by the 1st & 2nd Lines whilst the 3rd Line consolidated HIDDEN LANE.

At this time the right of the 4th Line moved up to HIDDEN WOOD so as to strengthen that flank as it was found that the DEVON REGT. had not kept up with the advance of the Battalion & this flank was very exposed. The left of the 4th Line was still in reserve in KIEL TRENCH, close up to the junction of HIDDEN LANE.

The Battalion was now checked in HIDDEN LANE with posts forward in APPLE ALLEY at junction of it & PEAR TRENCH – ditto BOIS FRANCAIS SUPPORT & also BOIS FRANCAIS TRENCH.

At 2.30pm. the 20th MANCHESTER REGT. advanced across our front and bombing parties of the BORDER REGT. worked along APPLE ALLEY without any opposition.

At about 5.00pm. APPLE ALLEY was occupied by 'A' and 'C' Coys of the Border Regt. with a party of 8th DEVON REGT. on the right. 'B' and 'D' Coys BORDER REGT held HIDDEN LANE as a support line. Head Quarters were established in an old Company dugout in SUPPORT Trench at its junction with 75 Street.

This position was maintained until 8.00am. on 3rd July when the Battalion changed its position to BOIS FRANCAIS SUPPORT which was held by 'B' and 'D' Coys with 'A' and 'C' Coys in BOIS FRANCAIS TRENCH. Battn. Head Quarters remaining in the same position.

Here the Battn. remained until the evening of 3rd July when it moved down to POST 71 SOUTH in Reserve.

The casualties in the attack were not as heavy as they might have owing, firstly, to the splendid way the wire had been cut by 'T' Battery R.H.A. & secondly to the fact that the advance was very close behind the artillery barrage the whole time. During the latter half of the attack the Battn. was subjected to a heavy sprinkling of hostile shrapnel which in addition to rifle and machine gun fire & bombs caused the casualties mentioned.

The whole Battalion behaved with their usual steadiness & coolness under fire

& all orders were strictly carried out. No mistake was made in the advance & the wheel was carried out without any gaps being left in the line, which is entirely due to the care taken by all Officers in instructing their NCOs & men in all fronts regarding the operation and the interest taken by all ranks in it.

The Battalion captured 3 Machine Guns, 2 Trench Mortars, 1 Projector, 5 Canister Throwers.

The casualties were: Officers 3 Killed, 6 Wounded, 1 Died of Wounds.

Other Ranks 79 Killed, 240 Wounded, 10 Died of Wounds, 4 Missing.

Documents Attached to the War Diary

Letter addressed to the Adjutant, 2nd Border Regiment, written by Lieutenant G.M. Prynne, O.C. 'A' Company, 2nd Border Regiment, at 10.30 hours on 5 July 1916:

Sir – On the 1st July 1916 I was in command of 'A' Company, 2nd Border Regt. At 9.15pm of the previous day, I moved the Company into position in RESERVE TRENCH between 70 trench & 71 trench. The order in which I posted the platoons from right to left was No's 3,1,2,4.

At 7.27am. No's 3 & 4 platoons moved forward forming part of the front line, with 'C' Company on the left & the 9th Devons on the right. About 100 yards in rear of them I came up with No's 1 & 2 platoons. The lines advanced in quick time, only losing at the most, two or three men before reaching the enemy's front line. This was crossed with comparative ease, & a few of the enemy showed themselves first in the SUPPORT LINE. Some of these were killed or taken prisoners & a few fled down the communication trenches & disappeared. Between the FRONT & SUPPORT lines I passed Lieut O'BRIEN walking back wounded.

From this point the enemy appeared to be scattered all over the field, in small groups or singly, bombing or firing from shell holes or pieces of trench. This had the immediate effect of completely breaking our lines into small parties formed of 1st, 2nd & 3rd lines. These sections had great difficulty in keeping direction & soon I noticed the right of our line was going to the right slightly, while the left wheeled round so far as to be advancing at an angle towards our own lines. I immediately ran & warned an officer leading them, & we returned to find the line distinctly thin on the left. From here we advanced in short rushes, all companies & lines by this time mixed up. I saw 2nd Lieut LUCAS leading one section here.

By the time I had advanced another 50 yds, I found myself with a party of about 20 men held up by a party of Germans to our left & front. We proceeded to advance down a trench towards them, as a bombing section & soon found ourselves in contact with them, & both parties started bombing. We advanced 20 or 30 yds, when bombs began to run short & as there was no sign of anyone on our right flank or in support the position seemed to be rather serious. Then our shells which had been falling just in front, began to fall short, so I immediately lit some flares on the parapet. This only had the effect of apparently drawing the enemy's fire, which soon grew very intense.

I then sent one man back to fetch more bombers & bombs, I also ordered 2nd Lieut MARSH, who joined up with a few men, to man a shell hole to our left which could command a view of the trench from which the enemy were bombing us. I also got a rifle grenade into action from a shell hole on the right. This was soon answered by a small aerial torpedo gun which fired incessantly, & also a "Cannister" battery. Several casualties were caused by this fire, but the enemy although they continued to bomb, did not attempt to advance, & some minutes later a reserve of bombs came up & the trench was cleared & held by a bombing section. I then went round to the right to find connection, & came across a large number of men under 2nd Lieut Holland and 2nd Lieut RUSSELL, holding HIDDEN LANE.

From here we could see the DEVONS on the further side of HIDDEN WOOD, but there were a few German's apparently in the WOOD itself between our right & the DEVON'S left. 2nd Lieut RUSSELL volunteered to clear them out, & organised two bombing sections who worked down two trenches leading to the front & rear of the wood, & cleared the wood taking a few prisoners, & connecting up with the DEVONS.

This completed our new front line, & we set of to consolidate the trench from BOIS FRANCAIS TRENCH down HIDDEN LANE through HIDDEN WOOD, joining up with the 9th DEVONS.

I also sent forward three bombing sections into APPLE ALLEY one by BOIS FRANCAIS TRENCH, one by LUKE TRENCH & one by HIDDEN WOOD, who found the trench clear.

At 2.30pm. we saw the 22nd Brigade pushing past our front. They took the part of BOIS FRANCAIS TRENCH to our front & attempted to push on but were held up & made strong the old German FRONT LINE.

We then worked round & connected up with them, occupying APPLE ALLEY by 'A' & 'C' Companies, & also two Machine Guns which were shortly afterwards brought up. 'B' & 'D' Companies continued consolidating HIDDEN LANE for a SUPPORT LINE.

While this was being carried on, a hostile Machine Gun suddenly opened enfilade fire from the valley, causing several casualties.

This was dealt with by 2nd Lieut LAWLEY who took a bombing party & a Machine Gun, & drove the enemy's gun away causing several casualties.

In this position we remained all night losing a few men through the enemy's heavy gun fire, which fired incessantly on HIDDEN LANE.

This fire ceased in the morning & all day (July 2nd), we strengthened our lines & reorganised the Coys, & collected & dumped ammunition, bombs etc.

The following morning we took over the lines BOIS FRANCAIS SUPPORT &

BOIS FRANCAIS TRENCH by 'B' & 'D' Coys & 'A' & 'C' Coys respectively. In the evening the battalion was withdrawn to the CITADEL, in Divisional Reserve.

Report on the part taken by 'C' Company "in the recent operations", dated 6 July 1916 and written by Second Lieutenant E. Holland, O.C. 'C' Company:

For the attack which was to be launched on the morning of the 1st July the Company was put into position in RESERVE TRENCH between 71 STREET & ALBERT STREET, reaching this trench about 12.30am. on the 1st July without casualties. The order of platoons from right to left was No.11 platoon under 2nd Lieut E.L. Holland, No.9 platoon under 2nd Lieut L. Marsh, No.12 platoon under Sgt. Knox & No.10 platoon under 2nd Lieut Ewshaw. There were two Lewis gun teams with the Company. Captain A.E. Newton was in command of the Company, which was on the extreme left flank of the Division.

At 6.30am. began the intense bombardment of the enemies front trenches, which was to last an hour, & at 7.27 the two platoons on the right, left RESERVE TRENCH & advanced over the open, followed at a hundred yards by the remaining 2 platoons, the Lewis gun teams advancing in the interval between the two waves.

The forward end of a shallow gallery which had been mined towards the German parapet from our front line at 71 STREET had been timed to be exploded at 7.30 am. & as 11 & 9 platoons reached our own front line this was blown, & the barrage lifted from the German front trench.

It is attributed to the Company's having advanced so near its first objective under cover of our own artillery fire that up to this point not a single casualty had occurred.

Machine gun fire, however now opened from the right & [illegible] of small [illegible] as were [illegible] causing [illegible] men to fall, but the first & second German lines were crossed with hardly any other opposition, & the leading platoons wheeled to the left making the line of SHRINE ALLEY their new front line.

No.10 platoon, on the left of the Company's second wave wheeled to the left at the first German trench & drove out some hostile bombers who were throwing their grenades from behind the right craters, the Lewis gun under L/Cpl Clarke greatly assisted in this act, but unfortunately the entire team coming under machine gun & rifle fire was shot down. Sgt Knox also fell dead at the same spot shot through the head. [illegible] platoon, No.12, following in rear of the other three, which owing to their wheeling were now in one line, came under the command of Sgt. Gronow. All four platoons soon after became merged into one line.

The first serious show of resistance by the opposing infantry began as the Company attacked the two communication trenches, SHRINE ALLEY & KIEL

LANE, & from these onwards to our final objective enemy riflemen & bombers, hiding in the innumerable large shell holes, put up a good fight, breaking up our line to a certain extent, but not checking our advance as the occupied shell holes were worked round, and their holders shot or bombed.

Captain Newton was well in the lead, encouraging a party of men to oust some Germans as above, & was in the act of shooting one of the latter when he was hit by a bullet in the left hand. The wound was a serious one, half the hand being blown away, & the command of the Company fell to 2nd Lt Holland.

The advance of the line on the left was slower than on the right, German bombers made stubborn stands in the KIEL TRENCH, but our bombers drove them out & some 25 of the enemy were captured as they emerged from dug-outs. Other dug-outs were bombed.

At 8.45am. parties of our men reached our final objective, APPLE ALLEY, & smoke candle flares were lighted there. Bombing posts were established as follows:

(1) At the junction of JOHN TRENCH & APPLE ALLEY under Sgt. Gronow. The remaining 'C' Coy Lewis gun was placed here & did excellent work.

(2) At the junction of BOIS FRANCAIS SUPPORT & APPLE ALLEY, under 2nd Lt Holland. It was attempted to block the BOIS FRANCAIS SUPPORT trench forward, but this trench had been so badly knocked about by shell fire & had become so shallow that the men on this work were shot as they exposed themselves, & this post were employed in firing at the enemy who were holding the un-named trench joining BOIS FRANCAIS & BOIS FRANCAIS SUPPORT trenches about 40 yards to their front.

(3) At the junction of HIDDEN LANE & BOIS FRANCAIS trenches, with a party of three bombers pushed up BOIS FRANCAIS trench (which was blocked) under 2nd Lieut Marsh. This post did very excellent work & was made a target by aerial torpedoes & canisters. It constantly repulsed enemy bombers who attempted its dislodgement.

In the mean time the remainder of the battalion had reached HIDDEN LANE, which they were consolidating. HIDDEN WOOD had not been captured, but 2nd Lt Russell lead down a party of bombers who cleared the wood & a Lewis gun was put into position to fire down the HIDDEN WOOD valley from HIDDEN LANE protecting the right of the trench. Touch with the battalion on our right seemed to be lost, & it was decided to make HIDDEN LANE as strong as possible & to wait until our right was secure before holding APPLE ALLEY in strength.

At 2.30pm. the 22nd Inf Brigade attacked across our front, and while a party of the Border Regt advanced down LUKE TRENCH & along APPLE ALLEY, another party of 6 bombers & 10 men under 2nd Lt Holland proceeded down BOIS FRANCAIS TRENCH & along the un-named trench mentioned above. There was no opposition but about 20 Germans surrendered. Touch was now gained with the 20th Manchester Regt at F10C43.80. The un-named trench was watched by 2nd Lt Holland's party & orders were issued for APPLE ALLEY to be garrisoned. Unfortunately the intended garrison was led astray, & being informed by the 9th Devon Regt which had now come up on our right that they were holding APPLE ALLEY, it returned to HIDDEN LANE.

However this error was soon after put right, APPLE ALLEY occupied & work was done to put it in a state of defence.

With the exception of apparently only one heavy gun, which fired at our position at about one minutes interval till the next morning there was no molestation by the enemy.

The Company remained in APPLE ALLEY, from its junction with MARK TRENCH & BOIS FRANCAIS SUPPORT until 8.00am. on the morning of the 3/7/16 when it proceeded to BOIS FRANCAIAS TRENCH & the same evening to the CITADEL.

I consider the bearing of the Company was at all times most praiseworthy.

The Casualties were: Killed, 31; Wounded, 40; Missing, 14.

A narrative of 7th Division's operations from 1st to 5th July 1916:

Heavy fire was maintained during the night by all arms, a concentrated bombardment lasting for one hour and 5 minutes being opened at 6.25am.

At 7.30am the Division moved to the assault. The 22nd Bn. Manchester Regiment on the right, in close touch with the 1st Bn. South Staffordshire Regiment, had little difficulty in passing over the first line of German trenches.

In the centre, the 2nd Bn. Gordon Highlanders, in touch with the 1st Bn. South Staffordshire Regiment, came under very heavy Machine gun fire after crossing "NO MAN'S LAND", but succeeded in advancing, with the exception of their left company, who were held up by uncut wire.

At 7.50am. The road running N.E. from the HALT was occupied, close touch being continuously maintained on the right. On the left, however, the 9th Bn. Devonshire Regiment failed to keep touch.

This Battalion on reaching our front line near MANSEL COPSE suffered very heavily from Machine gun and Artillery fire, the leading companies losing all their officers. They remained near TIRPITZ Trench and SHRINE ALLEY and failed to establish touch either to the right or left, or to clear the dug-outs in the wooded bank West of the Railway, this task being carried out by one company of the 8th Bn. Devonshire Regiment who were sent forward from Brigade Reserve to assist the 2nd Bn. Gordon Highlanders. In the meanwhile the 2nd Bn. Border Regiment had reached DANUBE SUPPORT with but little trouble, and wheeled to the left, as ordered; reaching their final objective, but not consolidating it, by 9.30am. During its advance the Battalion was temporarily held up at SHRINE ALLEY and again at HIDDEN LANE by indirect and enfilade Machine gun fire from FRICOURT and MAMETZ respectively. Small parties of the enemy were disposed of by bombing parties in KEIL SUPPORT and by direct attack across the open. The advance was then continued, APPLE ALLEY and HIDDEN LANE being consolidated. On the right a defensive flank, rendered necessary owing to the inevitable failure of the 9th Bn. Devonshire Regiment to maintain touch, was established.

Meanwhile the 91st Infantry Brigade had continued its advance with varying success. The 22nd Bn. Manchester Regiment took BUCKET Trench and entered DANTZIG ALLEY at 8.15am the 1st South Staffordshire Regiment having entered the outskirts of MAMETZ at 7.45 a.m. where they were hold up by Machine gun fire from houses. During these operations casualties were very heavy and two companies 21st Bn. Manchester Regiment were sent up in support.

On the right a counter-attack from FRITZ Trench drove the 22nd Bn. Manchester Regiment out of DANTZIG ALLEY. It was therefore impossible to launch the 2nd Bn. "Queens" Regiment to their objective. This Battalion had occupied a position of readiness in our old front line when the assaulting troops moved to the attack. The General Officer Commanding 91st Infantry Brigade at once ordered one company 21st Bn. Manchester Regiment to support the 22nd Bn. Manchester Regiment in an attack on DANTZIG ALLEY, so as to enable the 2nd Bn. "Queens" Regiment to advance through FRITZ Trench, to their final objective, the necessary artillery barrages being arranged.

At 12.0 noon the XV Corps reported that the whole of MONTAUBAN had been captured, and that the enemy were in full retreat to BAZENTIN-le-GRAND. In view of this information the Divisional Commander ordered the 91st Infantry Brigade to attack as soon as possible and the times of barrages were adjusted as necessary.

At 1.0pm the situation was approximately as follows:

On the right, the 22nd Bn. Manchester Regiment after very severe fighting had been reinforced by one company of the 21st Bn. Manchester Regiment and were moving into DANTZIG ALLEY, which they occupied at 1.30pm. The 1st Bn. South Staffordshire Regiment supported by 2 companies 21st Bn. Manchester Regiment were holding the line of DANTZIG ALLEY through MAMETZ and were in touch with the 2nd Bn. Gordon highlanders. The 2nd Bn. "Queens" Regiment in support had two companies in our original front line and two companies in that of the enemy's in readiness to move to their final objective as soon as MAMETZ was won.

In the centre, the 2nd Bn. Gordon Highlanders with 2 Stokes Mortars were held up in front of MAMETZ, in touch with the 91st Infantry Brigade but not in touch with the 9th Bn. Devonshire Regiment who had been unable to advance and had suffered heavy casualties. The 2nd Bn. Border Regiment had reached, but had not yet consolidated, their final objective, as they were waiting for the 9th Bn. Devonshire Regiment to come up on their right flank.

On the left, the 22nd Infantry Brigade were in a position of readiness preparatory to their subsidiary attack at 2.30pm.

The 91st Infantry Brigade carried out the instructions previously issued. The General Officer Commanding 20th Infantry Brigade ordered two companies of the 2nd Bn. Royal Warwickshire Regiment already attached to him, to report to Officer Commanding 2nd Bn. Gordon Highlanders and to attack and capture MAMETZ. The Officer Commanding 9th Bn. Devonshire Regiment was ordered to gain touch with the 2nd Bn. Border Regiment and to capture the trench near HIDDEN WOOD and to press on to his objective. The Officer Commanding 2nd Bn. Border Regiment was ordered to consolidate APPLE ALLEY and to co-operate with the 22nd Infantry Brigade. The 8th Bn. Devonshire Regiment was moved up in support, by HIDDEN WOOD to PLUM LANE. The 22nd Infantry Brigade was ordered to move to the attack at 2.30pm.

At 2.0pm the 2nd Bn. "Queens" Regiment in touch with the 54th Infantry Brigade (18th Division) began their advance towards their final objective and reached the eastern edge of FRITZ Trench at about 4.0pm. On their left the 22nd Bn. Manchester Regiment, reinforced by one company of the 21st Bn. Manchester Regiment, advanced on the western half of FRITZ Trench and on BRIGHT ALLEY; the 1st Bn. South Staffordshire Regiment advancing simultaneously on the N. and N.E. corner of MAMETZ. This line was taken and touch established with the 20th Infantry Brigade by 5.0 p.m.

In the centre, the 20th Infantry Brigade carried out their orders, and, as soon as the 2nd Bn. Royal Warwick Regiment advanced to support the Gordon Highlanders, 600 of the enemy at once surrendered and at 4.5pm the N.W. corner of MAMETZ was occupied.

By 5.0pm the work of consolidating the day's objective was started. The remaining two companies 2nd Bn. Royal Warwickshire Regiment were attached and formed the Brigade Reserve near SHRINE ALLEY.

At 2.30pm the 20th Bn. Manchester Regiment, 22nd Infantry Brigade, advanced to the attack and captured BOIS FRANCAIS SUPPORT and SUNKEN ROAD Trench with little difficulty. Their supports, however, suffered heavy casualties by Machine gun fire from the RECTANGLE SUPPORT and FRICOURT, which held up the advance. The Officer Commanding the left company moved to his right to gain touch with the troops in BOIS FRANCAIS SUPPORT and at once organised a bombing party which advanced down ORCHARD ALLEY and made a block in LINE Trench. It was, however, held up at PAPEN Trench and forced back to BOIS FRANCAIS SUPPORT.

At about 3.30pm touch was established with the 20th Infantry Brigade and during the rest of the afternoon there was a considerable amount of Bomb fighting round the RECTANGLE and the adjoining trenches. The situation was eventually cleared up by a company of the 1st Bn. Royal Welsh fusiliers who consolidated the RECTANGLE – SUNKEN ROAD Trench – BOIS FRANCAIS SUPPORT and part of ORCHARD ALLEY.

As the 21st Division, and the 50th Brigade, (17th Division), had found it impossible to advance and to maintain touch on our left at the N.E. corner of FRICOURT WOOD, and at WILLOW Trench respectively, a defensive flank was consolidated and wired from our original line South of FRICOURT to the ORCHARD. At nightfall the situation was as follows:

On the right, the 2nd Bn. "Queens" Regiment held FRITZ Trench with one company of the 21st Bn. Manchester Regiment on their left. The 22nd Bn. Manchester Regiment with one company 2nd Bn. Royal Irish Regiment, who had been sent up to strengthen the line, were in BRIGHT ALLEY and the 1st Bn. South Staffordshire Regiment in BUNNY Trench with two companies 2nd Bn. Royal Warwickshire Regiment in BUNNY ALLEY.

In the centre, the 2nd Bn. Gordon Highlanders occupied the S.W. portion of BUNNY Trench and the SUNKEN ROAD as far as ORCHARD Trench. The 8th and 9th Bns. Devonshire Regiment held the line from that point along SUNKEN ROAD to ORCHARD ALLEY, to its junction with APPLE ALLEY, with the 2nd Bn. Border Regiment in APPLE ALLEY.

On the left, the 20th Bn. Manchester Regiment with one company of the 1st Bn. Royal Welsh Fusiliers on their flank held BOIS FRANCAIS SUPPORT up to the RECTANGLE inclusive.

8th (Service) Battalion Devonshire Regiment

The battalion arrived in trenches and were in the following positions at 3.45am, 1-7-1916. 'B' Company in PERONNE AVENUE. 'D' Company LUDGATE CIRCUS. 'A' and 'C' Company in LUCKNOW REDOUBT. Two Platoons of 'C' Company rejoined the Battalion at 6.25am.

At Zero hour 7.30am, 'B' Company moved from PERONNE AVENUE to RESERVE TRENCH via 68 STREET their left on 69 STREET, their right in touch with 'D' Company. 'D' Company occupied 67 SUPPORT.

'A' and 'C' Company moved from LUCKNOW REDOUBT to LUCKNOW LANE, 'C' Company picking up their Two platoons at ESSEX AVENUE. 'A' Company with their right on LUCKNOW AVENUE. This was the situation at Zero hour.

8.40am.   'A' Company moved up into RESERVE TRENCH having 'B' Company in touch with their right. This made Two Companies in RESERVE TRENCH, One Company in 67 SUPPORT and One Company in LUDGATE LANE. At 8.6 am O.C. 'B' Company reports 91st Brigade are on East of MAMETZ. Parties of GORDONS can be seen in MAMETZ but seemed to be bearing off to the East of our objective.

10.30am.   'B' Company were moved from RESERVE TRENCH and sent forward to support the left of the GORDONS and right of the 9th DEVONS O.C. 'B' Company moved his troops via MANAEL COPSE in-to the hollow on the BRAY–FRICOURT Road. This Company did not move again as a whole until 4.0 pm. when all its Officers had been wounded and C.S.M. [*illegible*] Helwill assumed command.

10.10am. 'C' Company took up position in reserve trench vacated by 'B' Company at 10.15 am. O.C. GORDONS was lent 'D' Company 8th DEVON REGT to use as support to his battalion if required.

10.45am. Officer Commanding 'D' Company reports two of his platoons sent forward to support the right of the GORDONS.

10.20am. Colonel STOREY of 9th Devon Reg ordered the advance of 'A' Company to support the right of the 9th DEVONS.

This Company was in position in RESERVE TRENCH. No information of this move was given to Battalion headquarters. They moved in the direction of the HALTE. The four officers of this Company were either killed or wounded and I got no information as to the whereabouts of this Company until late in the evening when 2/Lieut DUFF reported to me he had picked this company up.

3.30pm. 'C' Company my last company in RESERVE TRENCH were given orders to proceed to HIDDEN WOOD via MANSEL COPSE. This company sent Two Platoons over the top of RESERVE TRENCH but Lieut SAVILLE seeing numerous casualties took remainder of the company via 70 STREET and proceeded to his objective with practically no casualties at all.

4.0pm. I sent out 2/Lieut Duff to collect 'B' Company and push on in support of 'C' Company to HIDDEN WOOD.

4.20pm. 2/Lieut DUFF report having found remnants of 'B' Company in MAMETZ TRENCH and working through trench with GORDONS in direction of DANTZIG SUPPORT and HIDDEN WOOD.

5.10pm. This same Officer reported having joined up with 2/Lieut JOSEPH of 'C' Company also 'A' Company men under C.S.M. MELHUISH also some 9th DEVONS, we have worked under the bank to HALTE and beyond, are now working round to HIDDEN WOOD. I have taken and sent back many prisoners from under the bank including four Officers. (Bank referred to is F.11.c.2.9. MONTAUBAN MAP).

At 8.6am 91st Brigade were reported to have reached their objective E. of MAMETZ. On the left of Brigade no advance was made. The nature of the engagement was affected by mopping up parties not clearing the trenches, leaving Machine Guns and Snipers who caused practically all their casualties.

The Bank by the HALTE was entirely disregarded and all dug-outs in DANTZIG TRENCH were found occupied; the enemy using the bank above could concentrate an enfilade fire on troops advancing to HIDDEN WOOD or MAMETZ. Also the traverses being fire-stepped, they could shoot down the valley to our lines. A machine gun was found at the HALTE which had fired a great quantity of rounds. The enemy had taken advantage of this high bank to make it an impregnable position advanced on by a bombing party down to COMBE ALLEY or along the bottom of the bank.

The result of the engagement was entirely successful.

In the aid post in DANTZIG TRENCH the O.C. 109th RESERVE REGT was found wounded on a stretcher with a broken thigh.

At night fall the brigade occupied the original objective assigned to it.

9th (Service) Battalion Devonshire Regiment

Trenches

The first line left RESERVE TRENCH at 7.27 am and GERMAN PRISONERS were brought back from SHRINE ALLEY at 7.50am. At 9.30am a message was received that "The right is being held up and bombed back by parties of the enemy from MAMETZ".

At 9.30am a message was sent by runner to O.C. No 3 Coy: "The BORDERS are consolidating in front of HIDDEN WOOD and our Batts are consolidating on the right, there is a gap between 9th Devon Regt. and the Border Regt. No 3 Coy, will fill this gap and consolidate it". At this point owing to the right flank of the Bn. being held up, a message was sent verbally to Brigade asking for a Coy of 8th Bn. Devonshire Regt. to reinforce the right, and orders were given to send 'A' Coy 8th Devons who were then in RESERVE Trench. At 10am 'A' Coy 8th Devons under Capt. Tregellis started out to reinforce our right. Later in the morning (all communication having been cut and Runners failing to get through) the Commanding Officer decided to proceed to MANSEL COPSE and investigate the situation. He found that No 4 Coy had been held up by heavy machine gun fire and that all officers and senior NCOs of this Coy had become casualties.

One Lance Corporal was found and sent forward with some men from MANSEL COPSE to collect the remainder of the Coy who were lying in the [*illegible*] ground in front of the COPSE. He was given orders to take them forward and join up with 'A' Coy 8th Devons. This N.C.O (Lce Cpl BEAL) pushed on with his men and joined up. During the afternoon Lieut Saville brought up 'C' Coy 8th Devons and attempted to reinforce through MANSEL COPSE. His leading platoon having been badly punished he decided to try further to the left and succeeded in getting over with few casualties from F.11.8 Trench.

6pm. In the meantime as all officers of the Battn. except 2nd Lieut G.E. PORTER has become casualties the reserve officers – 9 in number – were brought up from Echelon 'B', also 72 N.C.O's & men who had also been left in Reserve, these men taken over by the C.O. together with a few details of 'C' Coy 8th Devons at 6pm and proceeded to the final objective where the remainder of the Battn. were consolidating the position. No enemy counter attacks developed during the night.

Casualties 1st-3rd July 1916:

Killed: Capt. Martin[1]; Lieut. Hodgson[2]; 2/Lieut. Holcroft; 2/Lieut. Riddell; 2/Lieut. Raynes; 2/Lieut. Adamson; 2/Lieut. Sheppard; 2/Lieut. Hirst; 133 other Ranks

Wounded: Capt. Bridham; 2/Lieut. Freeland; 2/Lieut. Lewis; 2/Lieut. Butland; 2/Lieut. Ellis; 2/Lieut. Webber (since died of wounds); 2/Lieut. Walniot (Royal Sussex Attached); 2/Lieut. Howe; 2/Lieut. Dines (since died of wounds); 259 other Ranks. 55 other Ranks missing.

Document Attached to the War Diary

Extract from a despatch received from the Adjutant, 9th Battalion Devonshire Regiment, Lieutenant H. Hearse, to the Adjutant, 3rd Battalion Devonshire Regiment, dated 8 July 1916:

The 9th Battalion were one of the assaulting Battalions detailed to go over and attack the German lines at Zero. Zero was fixed at 7.30am. Our men were unable to occupy the two first trenches owing to heavy shell fire and accordingly had to leave their assembly trenches 3 minutes before Zero (7.27am).

At 7.27am we left our trenches in four lines and advanced on the enemy position and were immediately met with an artillery barrage which was most intense. Our Devon men walked through it in perfect line, only losing their dressing when closing in to cross trench bridges. As soon as the bridges were crossed they, immediately opened out again and assumed their dressing.

The Battalion were given three definite objectives and the first two were taken earlier than was expected, a certain amount of difficulty was experienced in gaining the 3rd objective owing to enemy machine gun fire, and reinforcements had to be asked for.

These were supplied by the 8th Battalion who sent up 'A' Company and 'C' Company and in due course the first objective was captured and consolidated. Our men behaved splendidly throughout in spite of the fact that all Company Officers except one, and all senior NCOs had been killed or wounded.

This speaks well for the individual training of the men as the remains of the Companies and Platoons were led to their final objectives by Lance Corporals and in some cases Privates. A great deal of credit is due to those Officers and NCOs at home who have trained the reinforcements which have arrived from time to time.

Our losses were: Officers, 8 killed, 9 wounded.

Other ranks, 141 killed, 323 wounded.

I don't think it will be giving away a State secret to say that we attacked on the left of the 2nd Gordons.

NOTES

1. It was during a period of leave in the UK prior to 1 July 1916, when Captain Duncan Martin studied a large-scale map of the area which his company was to attack. He also constructed a model of the battlefield from plasticine. "The longer he looked at the model," wrote historian Martin Middlebrook, "the stronger his feeling grew that if and when his company advanced over a small rise by some trees called Mansel Copse, they would come under fire from a German machine-gun position built into the base of a wayside shrine in Mametz." Located in the area of Shrine Alley, this machine-gun position survived the British bombardment and did indeed wreak havoc amongst the 9th Devons on the morning of 1 July. One of the men reported killed by its withering fire was Martin himself.

2. Another young officer who died alongside Captain Martin was Lieutenant William Hodgson. Hodgson was the Bombing Officer of 9th Devons and had been awarded the Military Cross for his gallantry during the Battle of Loos. Known as "Smiler", he was the son of the first Bishop of St. Edmundbury and Ipswich and was educated at Durham School and Christ Church, Oxford, where he was awarded a First in Classical Moderation. By the Battle of the Somme, Hodgson had already become a published writer of short stories and poems about his war experiences. As he prepared to go into action on 1 July 1916, the 23-year-old penned his last poem. It contains the following verse:

> I, that on my familiar hill
> Saw with uncomprehending eyes
> A hundred of Thy sunsets spill
> Their fresh and sanguine sacrifice,
> Ere the sun swings his noonday sword
> Must say good–bye to all of this;
> By all delights that I shall miss,
> Help me to die, O Lord.

4th Battalion Duke of Cambridge's Own (Middlesex Regiment)

1st July

6.25am. The intense preliminary bombardment commenced at 6.25am: this caused some retaliation by the enemy's artillery which caused considerable casualties among the two companies occupying the front line, especially 'A' Coy.

7.25am. The leading Platoons attempted to have the trenches at 7.25am in accordance with instructions, but suffered severely from machine gun fire & had to get back. Two mines were exploded at 7.28am on our right near the German TAMBOUR.

7.30am. The leading Platoons left the front trenches again slightly before 7.30am the actual hour of assault, & were met by intense rifle & machine gun fire. The remainder of 'A' & 'B' Companies followed in lines of Platoons at 100 yards distance: 'C' Coy followed them in two lines, two Platoons in each line, at the same distance: 'D' Coy in the same formation came last: the rear line carrying the Battn reserve of ammunition & grenades. Battn Head Quarters moved with the rear line of 'C' Coy.

The leading Companies reached & passed over the German front line. By this time all the officers, with the exception of 2 Lt Simpson, and most of the NCOs had been hit: the survivors pushed on in small groups beyond the support line: between this line & the SUNKEN ROAD in spite of severe fighting they were able to maintain themselves until the arrival of the supporting Battns. They attached themselves to the 8th Lincoln Regt on their arrival & remained with them until the morning of 3rd July when they were brought back to Bn. Hd. Qrs. by Sgt. Millwood.

'C' & 'D' Companies & Battn Hd. Qrs. similarly lost very heavily from machine gun fire in crossing "No Man's Land" & by the time they reached & had established themselves in the German front line trench were reduced to a strength of four officers & about one hundred other ranks.

Owing to the failure of the 50th Inf. Bde. on the right to hold the German trenches in front of FRICOURT the right flank of the Battn. was exposed & considerable parties of the enemy with machine guns were able to work up between the remnants of the leading companies & the support companies from the direction of FRICOURT. At this time the situation was extremely critical, the leading Coys were disorganised & had lost the whole of their officers; the supporting Coys were holding & had only partly consolidated their position in the German front line trench.

At this time most valuable services were rendered by Capt. Willis and 2 Lt's. Lofts and Barnett also by Sgt. Warboys, Sgt. Wright & Sgt. Millwood. About this time three determined bombing attacks were made by the enemy from the right all of which were repulsed. It was realized that owing to the severe losses & strong opposition of the enemy any attempt to advance further without support would be impossible: it was decided to consolidate & hold the ground won & at 8.15am a message to this effect was sent to Brigade Hd. Qrs.

9.15am.   At about 9.15am the supporting Battns began to arrive: the 10th York & Lancaster Regt. pushed through the left of the Battn. & drove the enemy from his supporting lines which they occupied and the 8th Lincolns went through the 8th Somersets & occupied LOZENGE ALLEY and eventually the SUNKEN ROAD.

11am.   At about 11am orders were received from Brigade to protect the right flank of the Brigade as the York & Lancaster & Lincolns Regts. were going to make a further advance. The bombing posts which had already been established were strengthened & Lewis guns added and all enemy trenches leading to FRICOURT were blocked. To form this defensive flank absorbed the whole strength of the Battn. and this position was held till mid-day 3rd July. The Lewis guns were able to bring a most

375

effective fire to bear on the enemy in FRICOURT & inflicted severe casualties on parties seen moving about.

15th (Service) Battalion Durham Light Infantry

LA CHAUSSEE

The Battalion moved up into the ASSEMBLY TRENCHES on the night of the 30th June as per Operation Orders, [*not attached*]. Battalion moved off from BUIRE at 8pm and took up their allotted position in the ASSEMBLY TRENCHES in support of the 9th K.O.Y.L.I.

Battalion Headquarters took up a position in a dug out in SHUTTLE LANE. The bombardment was terrific. The German retaliation was surprisingly feeble, and the allotted positions were reached with but few casualties.

The time fixed for the assault was 7.30am on the morning of the 1st of July. The hour immediately preceding this was marked by an intense bombardment by all available guns and mortars on the German first line system. About 3 minutes from 7.30am i.e. 7.27am three mines were sprung in the TAMBOUR. The day itself was beautifully fine and clear and our aeroplanes were scudding about overhead. Promptly at 7.30am the first assaulting Battalions the 9th and 10th K.O.Y.L.I. supported by the 15th Durham L.I. and the 1st E. Yorks Regt respectively, clambered up the assaulting ladders and with magnificent dash made straight for the German line. The Germans opened up a heavy Machine Gun and Rifle fire, and many officers and men were wounded soon after mounting the parapet.

But there was no hesitation. All were eager to get across and meet the enemy at close quarters.

Among the officers who were wounded quite early were Capt. F.P. [*name unclear, possibly Stamper*] and 2nd Lieut C.S. Haynes, the former in the leg, the latter slightly wounded in the arm. The latter gallantly continued and subsequently met his death as the head of his men.[1]

What opposition that survived was quickly overcome by grenade and bayonet and the prisoners who came up from their deep dug-outs were sent to the rear to QUEEN'S REDOUBT under charge of slightly wounded cases.

The attack now proceeded along the German communication trenches bombing from trench to trench. There was little cover for those Germans who remained, for the trenches paid eloquent tribute to the power of our guns, being smashed up entirely and in some cases being quite unrecognisable as trenches. Led by the Commanding Officer – Lieut Col A.E. FITZGERALD – and their respective Coy and Platoon officers the men fought their way forward to the SUNKEN ROAD, and from there to CRUCIFIX TRENCH. These positions were immediately consolidated. M. Guns and Lewis Guns were put in position and all arrangements made to hold the position against counter-attack.

Battalion Headquarters were established at the head of a German dug-out in Sunken Road – the interior being used partly to confine some wounded prisoners, and partly to shelter our own wounded – and here the C.O. assumed Command of the various parties of different regiments – 9th & 10th K.O.Y.L.I. some Lincolns, some 1st E. Yorks, and our own men who had now become intermingled. The casualties among the officers of the different regiments had been severe and some little difficulty was experienced in bringing these remnants under direct control from the H.Q. dug-out.

With the aid of such officers as remained this was ultimately effected and word was sent by runner to Bde H.Q. in SHUTTLE LANE advising them of the situation and asking for advice. Any further attempts at a forward movement was rendered extremely hazardous by the fact that enfilade M.G. fire from both flanks swept the area between CRUCIFIX TRENCH and SHELTER WOOD. Our next objective – FRICOURT – on our immediate right still held out and Germans in BIRCH TREE WOOD enfiladed us from our left. Moreover with the effectives at the disposal of Lieut Col FITZGERALD an attack across the open on SHELTER WOOD was considered out of the question.

Word came from Bde H.Q. however to re-organise and press on to SHELTER WOOD and if possible reach QUADRANGLE TRENCH, the last objective.

Parties accordingly pressed on in this direction and two parties in particular deserve special mention – one under 2nd Lieut F.J. CARTMAN, and one under 2nd Lieut A.S. MORLEY who both reached positions between 30 and 40 yards from the edge of the wood. The smallness of their numbers made it impossible for them to proceed further as they took up a precarious position in shell-craters and proceeded to snipe any of the enemy who showed themselves.

One incident in connection with this is worthy of note, Capt. D.H. ELY though wounded slightly in the foot, pressed on with his men towards SHELTER WOOD. He showed a magnificent example to his men and until his death by a sniper's bullet he was full of enthusiasm and courage. That sniper's time was short. One of our men, Pt J. JOLLEY saw him. They saw each other and fired. The German's bullet grazed Jolley's nose. Jolley's bullet struck fair and square in the head.[2]

The two parties under 2nd Lieut's. MORLEY and CARTMAN maintained their position until the Battn. was relieved.

Meanwhile SUNKEN ROAD and the German system back from there to the original German front line had come under heavy shell fire from heavy artillery.

SUNKEN ROAD was enfiladed by M. Gun fire and any movement along it was extremely precarious. The men had dug themselves in on the far side i.e. nearest the Germans, and had consolidated the position so as to form a line of resistance should the parties who had advanced in SHELTER WOOD have to withdraw.

About 5pm word came into the C.O. in the dug-out in SUNKEN ROAD that the Germans had been seen massing on the left of SUNKEN ROAD, presumably with a view to counter-attacking. The C.O. hurried out to supervise arrangements to meet them. Machine Guns and bombers were moved up to the left. A party of about 300 Germans actually did appear on the left but were mowed down by our Lewis Guns.

It was while supervising these arrangements that the C.O. was wounded, a M.G. bullet striking him full in the leg about half way between knee and the thigh. It was roughly dressed there and then and he was carried back to his Headquarters in SUNKEN ROAD – a place of only tolerable safety. He refused to be carried downstairs as this would mean moving a badly wounded man from the only stretcher on the place.

He stayed here – tended by his servant – until it was possible to remove him – nearly 14 hours later.

About 10pm word came from Bde H.Q. that two regiments of the 63rd Bde – the 1st Lincolns and the 4th Middlesex Regt – would relieve us in SUNKEN ROAD and CRUCIFIX TRENCH. The relief was partially completed by 12 midnight on the 1st July. Major Johnson taking over command of the Battalion at 10pm.

The remnants of the Battn – with its compliment of officers by now increased by reserve officers left with Echelon A – took up a position in our original front line trench, the Battalion was relieved from here on the evening of the 3rd July.

NOTES

1. The body of 25-year-old Second Lieutenant Clifford Skemp Haynes was never found or identified. The son of the Reverend and Mrs. W.B. Haynes, husband of L. Abbie Haynes, of The Cabin, Grimsby Road, Louth, Lincolnshire, he is commemorated on the Thiepval Memorial.
2. Captain Denis Herbert James Ely is also remembered on the Thiepval Memorial.

1st Battalion East Yorkshire Regiment

FRICOURT AND VICINITY

The battalion moved up to the assembly trenches on the night of 30/1. The following officers moving up with the Btn: Hd Qrs CO Lt Col M.B. Stow, Adjt Capt G. Willis, Bombing Officer 2/Lt J.B. Bailey, Signalling Officer 2/Lt H. Reeder, Lewis Gun officer Lt T.F. Smith, M.O. Capt Winfield R.A.M.C.

'A' Coy: Capt J.L.J. Hawksworth, 2/Lt D.V. Black, 2/Lt Boncker.

'B' Coy: Capt C.J. Huntriss, 2/Lt's J.S. Cracknell, [*illegible*] Moore, Sawyer, English.

'C' Coy: Capt D.F. [*name unclear*], 2/Lt's J.S. Baltifude, Peregrine, Smith & Gatrell.

'D' Coy: Capt T.L. Besant, 2/Lt's [*name unclear, possible Trounle*], Cooper, Lanson.

The following were left behind as first reinforcements, Lewis Major: Major H.E.R. Saunders, Lts Rhodes, Marshall, 2/Lt's Eames, Dennis, Benson, Stockham, Collin, Williams, Sheffield & Box.

Captain E.F. Pipe who had been appointed acting Bde Transport officer remained with the 1st line transport.

On the way up 2/Lt Gatrell was killed & 3 other ranks wounded while in the communication trenches, the battalion getting into place at 3.30am in its position of Assembly. A heavy & continuous shelling was maintained throughout the night, which at 6.30am became intense & continued until 7.30am when the artillery barrage lifted off the German front line & the Infantry moved forward to the assault.

The 64th I.B. attacked in the following order; 9th K.O.Y.L.I. on the Right,10th K.O.Y.L.I. on the left, supported by the 15th D.L.I. right & the E York R on the left, the 64th Bde M.G. Coy advanced as follows; half the Coy behind the 9th & 10th K.O.Y.L.I. & half behind the supporting battalions.

The Battalions attacked in the following formation 'B' & 'D' Coys in column of platoons at 100 yards distance, then Btn Hd Qrs, their 'A' & 'C' Coys in a similar formation to the two leading Coys. Although our bombardment had been very severe & the German trenches were badly damaged, there were still a few machine guns untouched and these took a heavy toll of the battalion. In spite of heavy losses the Bde pushed on & seized the first objective i.e. the CRUCIFIX Trench & the SUNKEN Road, though the SHELTER WOOD & BIRCH TREE WOOD on the N. flank still remained in German hands. This object line was reached at about 8.5am all the units of the Bde had become considerably intermingled, on our left the line was continued N. by the 34th Divn, the 15th and 16 Royal Scots & 27th N.F. being the regts in our immediate vicinity, while the 63rd Bde was on our right.

At about 2pm the German's counter-attacked in a half hearted manner from the direction of SHELTER WOOD, but were repulsed. It was impossible to advance further owing to the heavy casualties the Bde had incurred & all efforts were directed towards consolidating the position & holding the ground already won. Our artillery vigorously bombarded SHELTER WOOD & its vicinity to which the enemy replied on the SUNKEN RD, but his range was not good & although the fire was at times hot, few casualties resulted. At about 7.30pm Major Saunders together with Lt Marshall, 2/Lt's Eames, Benson & Stockham arrived & took over command from Capt Willis, who had been in charge of operations since the early morning, when Col. Stow had been wounded. Orders were now received that the 62nd Bde would relieve the 64th's & the 1st LINCOLNS & 10th YORK R. arrived, owing however to delay on the part of the 12th N.F. the relief was not completed until about 6.30am 2nd.

7th (Service) Battalion East Yorkshire Regiment

7.15am.   2 Lieut Cleaver & 50 men 'D' Coy passed H.Q. 7.15am. 7.16am. Lt [*name unclear*] & 2 Lewis Guns passed H.Q. 7.16am.

7.25am.   'C' Company passed 7.25am.
[*The two above lines appear to have subsequently been crossed through*]
Wire to 'D' Coy at 7.45am. ordering up South Avenue to junction with Bn H.Q.

7.52am.   Major King reported 'C' Coy all in Surrey Avenue 7.52am.
Captain Heathcock arrived at H.Q. at 8.15am. 'D' Coy then having position in South Avenue.

8.20am.   It was reported that West Yorks had taken prisoners.
'D' Coy ordered up Surrey Street at 8.20am. This Coy passed H.Q. a few minutes later.

8.26.   Last of W.Y. gone over. 'C' Coy in front line. Our aeroplanes flying low, giving light signals to artillery. Wood on left being heavily shelled. Forward guns in action.

8.30.   'A' Coy report casualties NIL.

8.35.   'A' and 'B' Coys ordered to remain in BONTE until 2nd Zero hour of which earliest possible notice will be given. Os.C. ordered to then keep in touch with 7.Y. and move into KINGSTON ROAD & hold front line with one platoon and 2 Lewis guns and await further instructions. Ordered to acknowledge and report all moves.

9.0.   All W.Y out & E.Y. hold front line, 1 platoon and 2 LEWIS Guns, J.M. carrying party in front line.
'D' Coy in SURREY STREET, 2 platoons 'C' Coy in front line.

9.50.   First batch of wounded (W.Y's) brought down.

10.06.   Yorks report first Coy has attacked, & is now in front of FRICOURT.

10.15.   'A' Coy ordered up in support of YORKS. Lewis Gun Officer reports impossible to post gun on crater so long as German M.G's remain active. He has mounted a gun on parapet.

10.44.   W.YORK H.Q. now in KÖNIG Trench. The Battn. on their left hung up in Dark Trench.

11.am.   1 Officer and 25 other ranks detailed from 'B' Coy to carry bombs to W.Y. Dump at junction of left T TANGIER front line.

11.15.   From O.C. 'B' Coy "I have sent 'A' Coy forward to support YORKS. Guides say one Coy went over without orders & were cut off by our own rifle fire. This is only a rumour. I have moved 'B' Coy towards RUNDEL AVENUE ready to go up, awaiting orders."
2 Lieut Thomas and 2 men left trench at PURFLEET to get in touch with W.Y.'s report.

11.15.   Following from Major King. "Have sent good N.C.O and 3 men to patrol to touch up with W. Yorks and bring back information quickly. Thomas has not yet returned."

11.55.   'A' Coy in position in Kingston Road. Casualties NIL.

12.10.   2/Lieut G.D. Thomas brought in wounded. His servant got across & found no W.Y's in front trench. He helped his master back on his return.

12.15pm Following message received at Battalion H.Q. from Major G.E.King; - "Have sent out Lt Cpl Frost and 2 men to get in touch with West Yorks Line and gain all information. Cpl Wright's patrol not yet returned."

1.15.   Battalion ordered to move to attack in support of WEST YORKS at second Zero hour, which was announced as 2.30pm. 'B' Company ordered to move at once to SURREY ROAD. Left of Company on DORSET DRIVE. Ready to move from there at 2.30pm.

1.45.   Written orders received as follows:
"Zero for second phase of assault is at 2.30p.m. aaa LAKE, less one Company, will advance in support of LADY, and will gain touch with SLAYon left. One Company of LAKE will support LAMB aaa. First objective of LAKE is from RED COTTAGE to LONELY COPSE inclusive. LAMP will move one Company to SURREY from SUNKEN ROAD."
Battalion H.Q. moved immediately on receipt of above message to SURREY ROAD.

2.33pm.   'C' and 'D' Companies advanced over the parapet to attack towards RED COTTAGE, but owing to heavy casualties from machine gun fire it was found impossible to reach enemy front line, and 'B' Company did not advance beyond our front line.

3pm.   Two Companies of 6th DORSET Regt arrived in SURREY ST.

3.15pm.   Following wire sent to 50th Brigade:
"Have had probably 150 casualties out of first six platoons going over, West Yorks appear all to have come back aaa. Think you can safely shell GERMAN front trench to opposite PURFLEET aaa. Am moving more to left of PURFLEET to gain touch with 63rd Brigade. One cause of failure was the short notice aaa. Major King had only just time to get to front line by Zero, and I had not then reached the Reserve Company aaa. There was only a ladder here & there so men started out in file. The whole GERMAN trench opposite us appeared to be occupied by the enemy. Some WEST YORK officers who have come back admit this is probable aaa. Have explored our front trench 300 yards to left of PURFLEET without touching 63rd Brigade. Have two Companies in front line extending beyond PURFLEET 100 yards aaa. One Company in DORSET DRIVE. One Company DORSET REGT. in SURREY ST."

4.20.   O.C. 'A' Company wired:
"Am now in our front line awaiting orders to advance. The C.O. 7

Yorkshire Regt has informed Brigade that a further advance is impossible without another bombardment. Killed: 2nd Lieut A.K. KIPPAX."

5.pm.   Following wire sent to 'C' Company:
"You must get in touch with Battalion on your right at once aaa. They are in our front line on right of TAMBOUR. O.C. 7 E. York R."

5.5pm.   The Commanding Officer wired as follows to Major King:
"We are in touch with Brigade, but have received no orders yet, and am ordered to stay near telephone. Please dig out trench where possible, and do all you can to re-organise trench before dark."

5.25pm.   Brigade informed that up to 5pm. Casualties as follows:

'C' Coy   Missing: CAPT. J.B. RUTLEDGE.
2nd LT. F. THORNTON.
2nd LT. C.W. PERRY.

OTHER RANKS: Estimated killed, wounded and missing 178.

5.40.   O.C. 'B' Coy ordered to move his Company along SURREY ROAD till in touch with Company of DORSETS, who were there.

5.45.   Following wire sent to Brigade:
"Rations and water carts to bottom of SUNKEN ROAD tonight. Can you wire time we might expect."

6.35.   The Officer in charge of the 10th WEST YORKS was wired as follows:
"Please send statement of Officers & men of your Regiment at present in SURREY STREET" aaa. The reply received stated that the number was 3 officers and 124 men.

6.40.   Brigade advised Battalion H.Q. that rations & water carts would arrive at QUEENS REDOUBT about 10.30pm.

7.30.   Following order sent to 'C', 'B' and 'D' Coys by Battalion orderly:
"'C' and 'D' Coys will be relieved about 11.30 tonight by 'B' Company, thus giving you time to make careful search for wounded & dead. They will come back to SURREY STREET. The front to be held is from PURFLEET to TAMBOUR, both inclusive, but touch must be kept with Battalion on left by a system of patrols."

8.45.   Brigade notified that there was a considerable gap between the right of the TAMBOUR, which was held by the Battalion, and the machine gun at head of ROYAL AVENUE, and again a wider gap before reaching 7th YORKSHIRE REGT.

9.45.   Brigade informed that Battalion did not require any rum.

10.30.   Two parties of GERMAN PRISONERS brought in – first party of 5 & second of 9. Only one could speak English. They belonged to the LANDSTURM, & some of their number were machine gunners. Their papers were collected at H.Q, and prisoners, under escort, were marched to Brigade H.Q. Papers found in their possession were also forwarded to Brigade H.Q.

10.45.   Patrols went out in front of GERMAN trench, to report on enemy's disposition.

11pm.   Wire received from Brigade stating that 50th Brigade would be relieved that night.

10.55.   O.C. 'A' Company asked to send stretcher bearers to KING'S AVENUE, where TAMBOUR joins.

11.20.   The Commanding Officer reported to Brigade that LIEUT MARSDEN (10th W.Y.) was wounded. He reported to H.Q. of this Battalion. He had been lying in 'No Man's Land' since morning, & returned to our lines at dusk.

11.40.   Os.C. 'C' and 'D' Companies were ordered to make a dump of all bombs in excess of 2 per man and 40 per squad.

12mn.   Patrols reported they had been to GERMAN trench, and it was apparently unoccupied. No firing took place from front line, But machine guns were firing from close support.

2nd Battalion Gordon Highlanders

7.30am.   The battalion attacked at 7.30am in four lines.[1] 100 yards between lines. 'B' and 'D' Coys 1st & 2nd lines (2 platoons each in each line) 'A' & 'C' Coys 3rd & 4th lines. The advance was carried out under a very heavy barrage of machine gun and rifle fire. 'D' & 'C' Coys were held up by the barbed wire and suffered very heavy losses whist 'A' & 'B' Coys pushed on steadily. Three lines of trenches had to be crossed before nearing the village of MAMETZ, which was the final objective.

7.55am.   'A' & 'B' Coys who had lost heavily during the advance had reached the SUNKEN ROAD immediately in front of MAMETZ VILLAGE. All the officers of 'B' Company were wounded except Lieut K.S. Gordan. The 1/5th Staffords were on our right and the 9th Devons on our left. The objective of the Staffords was the East half of MAMETZ VILLAGE & the 9th Devons to prolong the line to the left of MAMETZ.

8.00am.   Message Received from Captain A.N. Davidson commanding 'A' Coy:m "Am rallying in SUNKEN ROAD N. of CEMETRY trench preparatory to rushing MAMETZ".

9.00am.   A second message was received form O.C. 'A' Coy:" Am in touch with party of 50 1/5 Staffords on right – they are in SHRINE ALLEY – cannot get any touch on left which is at present in the air. MAMETZ being heavily shelled – reinforcements badly needed" – On receipt of this message two runners were sent forward to find 'C' & 'D' Coys. They returned stating that 'C & 'D' Coys were still held up in front of the German wire and unable to advance owing to the heavy machine gun fire & snipers.

9.30am.   3rd message from O.C.'A' Coy:"Situation more normal MAMETZ being
           still heavily shelled – Left flank still in the air and valley west of SHRINE
           held by enemy's machine guns – [*illegible*] officers & N.C.O with party
           of S. Staffords on my right".

           A message received from Captain G.H. Gordan:"Am held up by wire,
           am going to try and work round on the left".

11.05am   4th message from O.C 'A' Coy "Left flank by SHRINE still in the air –
           Patrols cannot find 'D' or 'C' Coys and have met with serious opposition
           from enemy's machine guns in the valley W. of SHRINE. Am occupying
           from SHRINE to point F.11.a.7.9 along bank of road – Propose
           advancing to objective when Devons and Gordons on left get into line".
           The 9th Devons suffered v. heavy losses in their initial advance & right
           company being wiped out & never getting to the first line German
           trench, the result being that our left was v. much exposed.

1.45pm   5th message from O.C.'A' Coy:"Situation grave – being bombed by large
           parties at SHRINE. Reinforcements absolutely necessary".

2.40pm.   A reply to the 5th message was sent:"2 Coys of 2/Warwicks are coming
           up to support you at once, hold onto your position at all costs".

3.45pm.   The two companies 2/Warwicks arrived at 3.40 & advanced in 4 lines
           with little opposition.

4.05pm.   The enemy surrendered as soon as the 1st line 2/Warwicks approached
           the SUNKEN ROAD & MAMETZ was captured & 600 prisoners – 2
           platoons of the 8th Devons who had been sent up previously in support
           joined up, they had been held up by the barbed wire.

4.45pm.   The force now consisted of 2 Coys Gordon Highs, 2 Coys 2/R. Warwicks,
           2 platoons 8/Devons & 3 machine gun sections – they were re-organised
           at [*illegible*] other defence of the village at once taken in hand – 2 Coys
           2/Warwicks were in touch with 1/5 Staffords left, 2 Coys 2/G.H
           prolonged to the left of 2/Warwicks & 8/Devons (2 platoons) prolonged
           to left of 2/G.H. Three strong points were made & a machine gun
           section placed in each point.

10pm.   2 more Coys, 2/Warwicks came up & formed a close support, the whole
           force being under command of Lt Col B.O.R. Gordon DSO
           commanding 2/The Gordon Highlanders.

10.30pm   95th Coy R.E arrived & assisted in consolidating the position – during
           the hours of darkness a large number of high explosive shrapnel was
           burst over the VILLAGE of MAMETZ but little damage done. Captain
           Gordan & about 50 of his men joined up about this hour but nothing
           was known of 'D' Coy less 1 N.C.O. & 18 men.[2]
           Special notes of battle of 1st July.
           A party of Bombers under 2/Lt Lawrence bombed all the dug outs up
           the valley accounting for a large number of killed. The trophies captured

besides 600 prisoners, one machine gun, one anti air craft machine gun, one trench mortar & large supplies of rifles, ammo and bombs, R.E. stores etc.

1. The strength of the battalion at the time of going into action was twenty-four officers and 783 other ranks.

2. Casualties are given in the War Diary as being seven officers killed and nine wounded, with 119 other ranks killed, 287 wounded and thirty-nine missing. The War Diary lists the following officers as being killed: Second Lieutenants White, McMil [sic], W. Fearnley, King, Gordon, Giles, and Davidson (died of wounds). It also lists the following officers as having been wounded: Captains Brooke, Murray, Cross, and Fiennes; Lieutenants MacDonald, Cookson, Pyper, Guild and Ferguson.

9th (Service) Battalion King's Own (Yorkshire Light Infantry)

TRENCHES

7.25am.   During eight minutes intense bombardment, No.1 platoon, 'A' company and No.9 platoon 'C' company under 2/Lt N.L. ALEXANDER and 2/Lt S.S.F. OLDERSHAW respectively, left the Russian Sap at 7.25am, five minutes before Zero hour (7.30am); they were to crawl forward as far as possible under our barrage, and then advance in quick time when the barrage lifted at 7.30am. They were followed by each successive wave at 1 minute's interval. When the leading platoons had crawled forward about 25 yards into NO MAN'S LAND, they were greeted by a hail of Machine Gun and Rifle Fire; the enemy, in spite of our barrage, brought his Machine Guns out of his dug-outs and placing them on the top of his parapet, opened rapid fire. 'A' and 'C' companies suffered chiefly under this, while 'B' and 'D' companies endured chiefly a heavy artillery barrage. When the leading troops were close enough, the enemy also employed cylindrical stick bombs against them.

The battalion suffered heavily in NO MAN'S LAND, and the waves in rear were soon up with the leading platoons; in spite of heavy losses, the battalion carried the front line with little delay; when it had passed the front trench the 15th D.L.I. came up to reinforce it magnificently; and within ten minutes or a quarter of an hour of the start the whole Brigade was united, irrespective of battalions, and driving the enemy rapidly out of his support trenches. From here to the SUNKEN ROAD the attack became a running fight or series of small fights; much work was done with bomb and bayonet, and some prisoners were taken. It was during this first stage, more especially in NO MAN'S LAND, that the battalion suffered most; out of the 24 officers who left our trenches, only 5 (Lt B.L. GORDON, 2/Lt's A.E. DAY, G.F. ELLENBERGER, R.F. FRAZER and G.H. FEATHERSTONE) succeeded in passing the German front trench; of these 5, 2/Lt G.H. FEATHERSTONE was hit later in the morning and died in the afternoon in LOZENGE ALLEY, on the right of the battalion's frontage.[1]

The Brigade re-organised in the SUNKEN ROAD and proceeded to consolidate the further bank of the road. Brigadier-General HEADLAM was present himself, but eventually was forced to return to Brigade Headquarters in our own lines in order to get telephonic communication; he left Lt Col. FITZGERALD of the 15th D.L.I, the only surviving Commanding officer, in charge, with orders to await instructions from the Brigade before advancing to CRUCIFIX TRENCH. Meanwhile attempts were made to get into trench with troops on our flanks; it was soon found that the left flank was in the air, and all connection with the 34th Division lost, nor was this established again during that day. No.19970 Pte. KEARFORD J. ('B' Coy) of this battalion performed a risky and invaluable piece of work by proceeding down the SUNKEN ROAD towards FRICOURT, not knowing upon what he might chance, until he found and established communication with the 4th Middlesex Regt, 63rd Brigade.[2]

It was also soon discovered that there were a few of our troops right ahead in CRUCIFIX TRENCH; there were men of each battalion of the Brigade there, under 2/Lt A.E. DAY of this battalion, who had continued the advance so far in spite of shrapnel wounds received in the right leg while crossing NO MAN'S LAND; he continued moreover to hold on to CRUCIFIX TRENCH with the few men he had until orders were eventually received from the Brigade for the troops in SUNKEN ROAD to advance to and consolidate CRUCIFIX TRENCH.

1.30pm. These orders arrived at about 1.30pm. Immediately the troops in the SUNKEN ROAD advanced to CRUCIFIX TRENCH in 3 waves under the 3 remaining officers of this battalion (Lt B.L. GORDON, 2/Lt's G.F. ELLENBERGER and R.F. FRAZER). Having arrived they proceeded to consolidate the trench. 2/Lt A.E. DAY'S wound was by this time becoming worse and threatened shortly to incapacitate him; he refused however to go back until ordered to do so by Lt GORDON. Shortly after this a Captain of the NORTHUMBERLAND FUSILIERS (Pioneer battalion) arrived and took charge of the troops in the trench. Consolidation continued throughout the afternoon. Steps were taken to secure the flanks, both of which were completely in the air; the right was secured by two Lewis Guns and the left by a bombing squad placed where the trench leading to BIRCH TREE WOOD (held by the enemy) joined CRUCIFIX TRENCH. During the afternoon Capt SANTAR of the 10th K.O.Y.L.I. arrived and took command of the trench.

6pm.   At about 6pm. 2/Lt R.F. FRAZER was hit in the head by shrapnel and had to go out. Shortly afterwards Capt. SANTAR, who had been wounded in the chest a few hours previously, was also compelled to go out. About this time messages were received stating that the 62nd Brigade were to relieve the 64th in CRUCIFIX TRENCH that evening. Lt Col FITZGERALD was also reported wounded and Lt B.L. GORDON was detailed by the N.F. Captain to return to the SUNKEN ROAD for information and orders from the Adjutant of the 15th D.L.I. who had been left in charge there.

About   Shortly afterwards an officer of the 62nd Brigade came across to take
8.30pm.   over. Communication with the rear now became frequent. A runner arrived for 2/Lt ELLENBERGER with information that Lt L.D. SPICER, the Adjutant (2/Lt W.F. KEAY), and other officers from Echelon "B" of this battalion were waiting in the SUNKEN ROAD to arrange for the relief of the battalion.

About   2/Lt ELLENBERGER leaving Regimental Sergt. Major CROSSLAND in
9.15pm.   charge of the remnants of the battalion, proceeded to the SUNKEN ROAD and reported to Lt SPICER.

BUIRE

3.30.   Orders received from Brigade addressed to Senior Officers of 9th K.O.Y.L.I. in "B" Echelon to detail four officers and report with them to Bde HQs MEAULTE. LIEUT L.D. SPICER being the senior officer detailed the following officers: LT. B.H.L. HART, 2.LIEUT. W.F. KEAY, 2.LIEUT. H.F. KINGSTON and 2.LIEUT. W.W. SHEPHERD, who reported Bde HQrs MEAULTE.

5p.m.   These officers were ordered by STAFF CAPTN BUCKLEY to report to Advanced Battle HQ of Bde for further orders. Information was given that there had been heavy officer casualties and the five officers detailed were urgently required to take command of the Battalion.

7.30pm.   Party of officers reported at Brigade Battle HQ and were ordered to join the battalion in the SUNKEN ROAD (from FRICOURT) and collect all the remaining men of the Battalion and withdraw after being relieved to SOUTH SAUSAGE SUPPORT where battalion was to act as battalion in Reserve. The five officers proceeded across the old "No Man's Land" into old German front line and eventually reached the SUNKEN ROAD about 8.45pm. LT. B.L. GORDON was in command of the Battalion part of which was in CRUCIFIX TRENCH under 2/LT. G.F. ELLENBERGER and the remainder in the SUNKEN ROAD where LT. B.L. GORDON had established Btn HQs. The Battalion numbered about 150 O.R. On being relieved by a battalion of the 62nd Bde (1st LINCOLNS) the party in CRUCIFIX TRENCH with drew to the SUNKEN ROAD which was strongly held by battalions of the 62nd Brigade and the remnants of the 64th Bde. As the whole of the 62nd Bde did not arrive in SUNKEN ROAD and CRUCIFIX TRENCH, COL. GRANT of the 1st LINCOLNS the senior officer present would not allow the 64th Bde to withdraw to SOUTH SAUSAGE SUPPORT.

9pm to 10pm.
CRUCIFIX TRENCH was rather heavily shelled with 5.9s and on the flanks of the Battalion front in the SUNKEN ROAD but no counter attack was made and the whole the night passed quietly and without incident. The opportunity to re-organise and collect the Battalion was made good use of. The Battalion dug themselves in and made quite good trenches. A number of shovels were found at a German Dump in the SUNKEN ROAD also a large quantity of sandbags which was most useful in the work of digging trenches. Large quantities of food were found in German Dug-outs.

11pm
LT. B.L. GORDON who had been slightly wounded on the chin went back to Dressing Station and handed over the command of the Battalion to LT. L.D.SPICER.

NOTES

1. The War Diary contains a list of those officers killed in action: Lieutenant Colonel C.W.D. Lynch DSO; Captains G. Griffen (CWGC records state Griffin), W. Walker, G. Haswell, and L.D. Head; Second Lieutenants C.W. Howlet, C.W. Ellis, N.L. Alexander, C.E. Vassie, J.J.F. Oldershaw, A.D. Maconachie, F.W. Golding, and G.H. Featherstone. The following are listed as wounded: Second Lieutenants R.A. Stokes, A. Hardman, D. Williams (subsequently died of wounds), G.A. Kemp, A.E. Day, R.F. Frazer, J.R. Wood, F.G. Morris, and I.R. Nott (subsequently died of wounds). It adds that casualties amongst the other ranks numbered 475, of whom some 145 were killed.
2. Private J. Kearford's award of the Military Medal was gazetted on Wednesday, 23 August 1916 (*The London Gazette*, Issue 29719, page 8362).

10th (Service) Battalion King's Own (Yorkshire Light Infantry)

TRENCHES

The British offensive commenced, this battalion leading the 64th Brigade assault. They left the trenches at 7.30am and took CRUCIFIX TRENCH that morning & held it till early the next when they were relieved by the 1st LINCOLNS.[1]

1. The War Diary states that there were nine officers killed and wounded, and fifty other ranks killed, 292 wounded and 135 missing.

1st Battalion Lincolnshire Regiment

The first day of the attack launched by the British in conjunction with the French at the Battle of the Somme. The 62nd Infantry Brigade being in reserve to the 21st Division, the Battn. was ordered to carry S.A.A. Mills Grenades and Stokes Mortar Bombs to a Dump immediately N. of the EASTERN end of PATCH ALLEY on the SUNKEN ROAD (x 27.b.2.8.).

At 8.00am billets at MEAULTE were evacuated and the Battn. proceeded as detailed to a position at BON ACCORD ST. and MARESCHALL ST. where loads were picked up. Battn. H.Qrs. was established in ABERDEEN AVENUE.

At 1.30pm carrying parties proceeded across the open to the first line captured German trenches and thence to the Dump. Parties then returned to the first line captured position and the work of consolidation began in the sector x 20.d.7. 2. on the left to x 26.d.7. 8. on the right. Owing to the terrific effect of our artillery fire during the bombardment of this position, the task proved a very arduous one and was rendered more difficult owing to the fact that the Battn. was subjected to heavy machine gun fire and artillery fire.

During the work of consolidation, Battn. H.Qrs. was moved to the captured front line at x 26.d.7. 9.

At 6pm. we were ordered to reinforce the 64th Brigade and proceeded as follows:

'B' Coy to CRUCIFIX TRENCH (x 27 b – x 28a) with 'D' Coy & B.V.R.C. on their right, 'A' and 'C' Coys in support at SUNKEN ROAD, the latter Coy joining up with the 34th Division on our left. Battn. H.Qrs. was established on the SUNKEN ROAD at the DINGLE (x 27.b.2.8.).[1]

The position taken over did not appear to have been consolidated at all, thus necessitating working continuously until 3.0am on the morning of 3rd July.

The weather was fine and night quiet.[1]

The total strength of the Battalion, including employ with transport on the morning of 1st July stood as follows:

Officers 40

Other Ranks 994

The following casualties were sustained: Wounded (officers): Capt. H. Marshall, Lieut [*illegible*] E.A. Kirk, 2nd Lieut E.Y. Edwards, 2nd Lieut T.S.H. Jacques, 2nd Lt G.M. Rowland, 2nd Lt J.J. Taylor, 2nd Lt E.H. Catton, 2nd Lt F.H. Robinson, 2nd Lt P.T. Pryce.

Other Ranks: Killed 3, Wounded 105, Missing 2.

Total All Ranks: 119.

NOTE

1. The Bermuda Volunteer Rifle Corps (B.V.R.C.) was formed in 1894 as a reserve unit for the British Regular Army infantry component of the Bermuda Garrison. In December 1914, the B.V.R.C. formed a detachment to send overseas. This contingent was composed of volunteers who were already serving, as well as those who enlisted specifically for the front. The Contingent trained at Warwick Camp through the winter and spring. It consisted of Captain Richard Tucker and eighty-eight other ranks. As there was a shortage of officers, the Governor and Commander-in-Chief, Lieutenant-General Sir George Bullock, filled the role of Adjutant, a position normally filled by a Captain. As a consequence, the contingent was popularly known as "Bullock's Boys". The Contingent left Bermuda for England in June 1915, travelling to Canada, then crossing the Atlantic in company with a much larger Canadian draft. It had been hoped that the Contingent could be attached to the 2nd Battalion, Lincolnshire Regiment, which had been on garrison in Bermuda when the war began. However, when the B.V.R.C. arrived at the Lincolnshire Regiment's Depot in Grimsby, the 2nd Battalion had already been despatched to France and the men were consequently attached to 1st Battalion, Lincolnshire Regiment. Although commanders at the Regimental Depot had wanted to break the Contingent apart, re-enlist its members as Lincolns, and distribute them as replacements, a letter from the War Office ensured that they remained together as a unit, under their own badge. The contingent arrived in France in July 1915, the first colonial volunteer unit to reach the Front, as an extra company attached to the 1st Battalion Lincolnshire Regiment, and remained as such until the following summer, by when its strength had been too reduced by casualties to compose a full company, having lost 50% of its remaining strength at Gueudecourt on 25 September 1916.

8th (Service) Battalion Lincolnshire Regiment

TRENCHES FRICOURT

Battalion in attack in support to 8th BN. SOMERSET LIGHT INFANTRY.

Report upon operations and attack see Appendix X by Cmdg officer Lt. Col. R.H. Johnston DSO.

Report upon medical arrangements during the attack by Capt H.D. Smart R.A.M.C.

Casualties:

Officers

Killed, 2nd Lts. J.F. Cragg, W. Swift, R.L. Courtice, J.H. Parkinson.

Missing (believed died of wounds) Capt A.C. Jones

Officers wounded Capt R.G. Cordiner, Lt (tempry Capt) E.R. Devonshire, Lt G.G. Lafferty, Lt M.G. Rowcroft, 2nd Lt J.S. Boadle, 2nd Lt W.J. Haward, 2nd Lt E.G. Mitchell.

Other Ranks:

Killed 30,

Wounded 197,

Missing 12.

Total O.R. Casualties 239.

Document Attached to the War Diary

Appendix A, a report written at Vaux on 5 July 1916, and signed by Lieutenant Colonel R.H. Johnston, Commanding Officer, 8th Battalion Lincolnshire Regiment:

In reply to your no 6783 of 4th July.

'D' Company was detailed to advance behind 8th Somersets & clear out German trenches. This they did. 'B' Company coming up into position in their place. The advance of the remainder of Battn was timed to start at 8.30am. At 8.20am I received message from Brigade not to start till ordered.

I was unable to stop the leading platoons of 'A' & 'B' Coys in time. The remainder I stopped; & telephoned to Brigade for instructions. Receiving orders to advance with the Battn I started the remainder of the leading Coys & got messages back to our rear line in MARISCHAL Street.

I advanced to point X27C49 the advance was progressing on the left. There was a good deal of Rifle & Machine Gun fire here. There were some men of all Battns in 63rd Brigade & of 2 Battns of 64th Brigade. I sent parties down DART LANE to the right with bombing squad, and strung out the rest to the left along BRANDY Trench, telling them to get up to the Sunken Road.

Men were meantime getting forward up LOZENGE ALLEY, up which I advanced trying to find out the situation on the right.

I could not see any advance here. It was therefore necessary to watch our Right Flank. I pushed up men to Lozenge Wood and along Sunken Road, getting touch with 64th Brigade on Sunken Road, & in left (North) portion of CRUCIFIX Trench. Those advancing up Lozenge Alley meeting Germans coming from FRICOURT Farm. The Germans made 2 bombing attacks up LONELY TRENCH both of which were repulsed. Though at one time the Germans got a few men into LOZENGE ALLEY here. They used Rifle Grenades as well as bombs and so could out distance our bombers until we got up Rifle Grenades. The Germans left at least 20 dead in LONELY TRENCH close up to LOZENGE ALLEY & some in LOZENGE ALLEY.

I asked also for Stokes guns to repel these bombing attacks but all were out of action until later, when we got four Stokes guns to help us, but the bombing attacks were not repeated.

We then received orders to hold the trenches we were in; & consolidated LOZENGE ALLEY as our Right Flank with bombing posts up LONELY Trench & LOZENGE ALLEY & joining up with 64th Brigade up Sunken Road.

During the night our Artillery Barrage prevented any counter attack from Fricourt Wood.

In the morning our patrols reconnoitred LONELY TRENCH to RED COTTAGE and LOZENGE ALLEY to FRICOURT FARM and found all clear.

We saw the attack advance through FRICOURT Wood & occupy FRICOURT FARM & CRUCIFIX Trench.

As our Right Flank was then secure, prepared LOZENGE ALLY for Defence facing North in case of emergency owing to the firing we heard between LA BOISELLE & SAUSAGE REDOUBT. This trench was made quite strong, being worked on until we got order to move - meantime we had to pass up all our S.A.A. reserve, Rifle Grenades & STOKES Mortar ammunition to the 62nd Brigade & our hand grenades & a squad of bombers were sent up to 62nd Brigade together with supplies from the Rear.

We then received orders to move to PATCH ALLEY facing north with our Right on Sunken Road. Arriving there we continued work of preparing the trench for defence; until we were relieved about 2am on the 4th, when we marched to DERNACOURT.

20th (Service) Battalion (5th City) Manchester Regiment

'B' Echelon transport and draft of 82 Other ranks at BOIS-DE-TAILLES.

On the morning of the 1st July, 1916 word was received from Bde. H.Q. that the ZERO hour for MAIN ATTACK would be 7.30am and that the 20th Manchesters would attack on the right of FRICOURT at 2.30pm. Promptly at this hour the Battalion attacked as follows;

'C' Company   Over the Craters.
'A' and 'B' Companies   From the New Front Trench.

'A' and 'B' Companies were supported by 2 Platoons of 'D' Company.

'C' Company were supported by 2 Platoons of 'D' Company.

The Commanding Officer, Adjutant and Headquarters accompanied the 2 Platoons of 'D' Company who were in support of 'A' and 'B'.

Heavy Machine Gun Fire was encountered from WING CORNER in FRICOURT – and the rear of 'B' Coy and the 2 Platoons of 'D' Company suffered many casualties in the Sunken Road from this Gun.

The 2 leading Companies reached SUNKEN ROAD Trench and were met by heavy Machine Gun Fire from somewhere in the region of ZINC Trench. Here 'A' and 'B' suffered very heavily.

2 Officers, Sec. Lieut A.G.N. DIXEY and Lieut H.S. BAGSHAW reached the RECTANGLE and found that they had no men near to them; they worked along to the right and Lieut Bagshaw collected a party of Bombers to get into touch with 'C' Company in BOIS FRANCAIS SUPPORT WHICH had been reached by this Company without much serious opposition. 'C' Company then advanced over BOIS FRANCAIS SUPPORT Trench and suffered very heavily from Snipers and Machine Gun Fire.

'A' Company Bombers proceeded down ORCHARD ALLEY Trench; made a BLOCK at its junction with ZINC Trench and proceeded as far as PAPEN Trench. This they found held in force by the enemy and a Machine Gun was opened on them from behind in ZINC Trench. The party of Bombers very much reduced in strength retraced their steps along ORCHARD ALLEY and when in BOIS FRANCAIS SUPPORT touch was established with the MOBILE RESERVE under Lieut DADDS 1st R.W.F. who at once organised a party to bomb down ZINC Trench from the South end.

The Commanding Officer, Lieut Colonel H. LEWIS, was killed before reaching SUNKEN ROAD Trench, thus leaving the Adjutant, Captain F. BRYANT in command of the Battalion at 2.45pm.

The Adjutant (Captain F. Bryant) and Lieut DENTON-THOMPSON reached SUNKEN ROAD TRENCH with 9 men, and after a sharp fight with Snipers in RECTANGLE SUPPORT and also from the direction of FRICOURT, Headquarters were established in SUNKEN ROAD Trench, 4 of the party meanwhile having been shot. During this fight Lieut B.J. DENTON-THOMPSON was Wounded. He endeavoured to obtain touch on the Right but found the Headquarters entirely surrounded.

No.18417 Lce. Cpl. F. BARNES, who was one of the party of Headquarters, volunteered to go over the open in the face of heavy Machine Gun Fire to report the situation to O.C. 1st Royal Welsh Fusiliers, who were in support – as up to this time no telephone communication had been established. He successfully went across the open, delivered his message and returned still in the face of heavy Machine Gun Fire.[1]

About 5.10pm Telephone wire was carried up by means of the "Daisy Cutter" and no.17822 Pte. BATESON, J. (Signaller) arrived with the telephone instrument.

Communication was then established with Brigade H.Q. and reinforcements of Bombers were asked for.

Headquarters party, under the Adjutant, remained in SUNKEN ROAD Trench and were the only men on the left flank of the Brigade, which was otherwise exposed towards FRICOURT.

About 7.15pm 2 sections of Bombers of the R.W.F. arrived, and proceeded to bomb down SUNKEN ROAD Trench. The Left flank having been thereby secured, the Adjutant, having learnt that the Companies were in BOIS FRANCAIS SUPPORT, proceeded to join them there.

The only Officers remaining with the Battalion in BOIS FRANCAIS SUPPORT were:

Captain F. BRYANT. (Adjt.)
Lieut H.S. BAGSHAW.
Lieut B.J. DENTON-THOMPSON. (wounded)
Sec.Lieut A.G.N. DIXEY. (slightly wounded)
Sec Lieut T.H. CLEGG.

The work of consolidating BOIS FRANCAIS SUPPORT was proceeded with and Fire Steps were dug in the Parados.

Orders were then received that BOIS FRANCAIS SUPPORT was to be held by the Battalion during the night 1st/2nd July. The Battalion frontage was from APPLE ALLEY exclusive, to ZINC TRENCH exclusive, with the BORDER Regt. on the Right and 1st R.W.F. on the Left.

Note: The actual Fighting Strength of the Battalion on the 1st July, was as follows: Officers 20, Other Ranks 670.

The total Casualties 1st to 5th July were:

Officers:

Killed	10
Wounded	5
	15

Other Ranks:

Killed	110
Wounded	171
Missing	29
	310

Note: The 50th Brigade of the 17th Division was timed to attack at 2.30pm opposite FRICOURT, but up to 2.45pm no sign of this attack was seen.

1. For his actions on 1 July 1916, Lance Corporal F. Barnes was awarded the Military Medal (gazetted on Thursday, 10 August 1916). It is also known that the same award was made to Major F. Bryant and Lieutenant B.J. Denton-Thompson.

21st (Service) Battalion (6th City) Manchester Regiment

Bois de Tailles B1 Subsector

12mn.	Battn marched to forming up trenches in B1 Subsector. Strength 20 Officers 796 O.R.
7.30am	Attack commenced – Battn in Brigade reserve. 'A' Coy followed first Battns over to clear up German front lines and send back prisoners. 2/Lieut P.J. RAM Killed.
9.40am.	'B' & 'C' Coys sent to reinforce 1st South Staffords attacking Mametz. Mametz Captured and trenches gradually taken on the far (North) side.
3.50pm.	'D' Coy sent to reinforce 2nd Queens in their attack on Queens Nullah.
4.30pm.	Bn H.Q. moved to Mametz – Col Norman takes Command of 1st South Staffs & 21st Manchesters and prepares for defence of Mametz – 2/Lieut G.F. WILSON & H.H. COWIN Killed. Capt T.I.W. WILSON, 2/Lieut FAIRCLOUGH wounded.

22nd (Service) Battalion (7th City) Manchester Regiment

The Battn was on the right of the 91st Bde assaulting line. The Battn. was formed up in our own Trenches and at 7.30am moved forward to the assault in 4 lines, 'B' and 'D' coys forming the first 2 lines ('B' on the Right and 'D' on the left) and 'C' and 'A' the second 2 lines ('C' on the right and 'A' on the left). Each Company occupied a 2 Platoon frontage. Bombers, Lewis Guns etc; went forward in the positions allotted to them in the various lines.

The leading companies reached the 1st objective – line BUCKET TRENCH – DANTZIG ALLEY – with heavy casualties and the supporting companies with the remainder of the leading companies then pushed on towards the final objective (FRITZ TRENCH) but owing to still heavier casualties (principally from M.G. & shell fire) were unable to reach it. There were still large numbers of the Enemy in dug-outs in DANTZIG ALLEY and this trench was now cleared by a bombing party of the 2nd QUEEN'S Regiment assisted by 2nd Lt. RILEY of this Battn.

Arrangements were then made with the 2nd QUEENS Regt. for them to clear FRITZ Trench by bombing down it from the direction of POMIERES TRENCH which we bombed through BRIGHT ALLEY toward the junction of BRIGHT ALLEY and FRITZ Trench. This was done and about 75 prisoners fell into our hands at this point.

FRITZ Trench & BRIGHT ALLEY then occupied by the 2nd QUEENS Regt, whilst this Battn held DANTZIG ALLEY, the 1st S. STAFFORDS holding BUNNY Trench and BUNNY ALLEY. This was the situation on the night of 1st/2nd July.

The total casualties of the Battn. during the assault were 18 officers and 472 other Ranks, 10 officers being killed and 8 wounded, whilst of other Ranks 120 were killed, 241 were wounded and 111 were missing (i.e. unaccounted for and probably killed or wounded). Officer reinforcements sent up.

24th (Service) Battalion (Oldham) (Pioneers) Manchester Regiment

GROVETOWN.

12 mn. Weather: Fine wind light, still N.W.

Situation: The 7th Division attacked the enemy at 7.30am Artillery barrage and smoke attacks were carried out as per operation orders in June War Diary.

As the attack progressed 'B' and 'D' Coys were employed as follows:

'B' Coy made strong points on to N.E. of MAMETZ after its capture from the enemy.[1] 'D' Coy less two platoons opened up enemy trenches blown in by our bombardment. As the attack was successful these companies were at once put into clearing roads and removing enemy wire. Troops were able to proceed through MAMETZ over the open ground.[2]

Our A Echelon transport parked at GROVETOWN and B Echelon at K.6.a.5.7. (ALBERT combined sheet)

Casualties: Our casualties were Officers nil – O.R. 8 including one who returned to duty.

NOTE

1. Mametz was the second village to be captured in the fighting on 1 July 1916.
The capture of Mametz extended the earlier success on the British right flank to a frontage of three miles, for the 18th (Eastern) Division had also taken all its objectives between Mametz and Montauban – the latter being the first village to fall.

13th (Service) Battalion Northumberland Fusiliers

Document Attached to the War Diary

The War Diary entry is represented by a report dated 8 July 1916, and signed by the Adjutant, Captain W.T. Massiah-Palmer:

REPORT ON MOVEMENTS AND OPERATIONS FROM 30th JUNE 1916 TO 4th JULY 1916.

The report is necessarily somewhat disjointed owing to the Battalion being split up into several parties, and the actions of Companies must be detailed to keep a clear account during the first two days of the Attack.

1st July the Battalion was disposed as follows:

3 Officers and 100 Other ranks of 'B' Company and 3 Officers and 100 Other Ranks 'D' Company were in BECOURT VALLEY under orders of O.C. 178 Tunnelling Company R.E. and O.C. 'B' Coy 14/Northd. Fusrs (Pioneers) respectively. The remainder were in MEAULTE.

At 5.0am 1st July 3 Officers and 100 Other Ranks of 'C' Company moved to BECOURT VALLEY and came under orders of O.C. 98th. Fd. Coy R.E.

At 5.30am 3 Officers and 100 Other Ranks of 'A' Company moved to BECOURT VALLEY and came under orders of O.C. 196th Fd. Coy R.E. The remainder of the Battalion consisting of Headquarters, Lewis Gunners, Company Bombers, Battalion Bombers and Signals moved from MEAULTE to position of Assembly in SHUTTLE LANE and MARISCHALL STREET leaving MEAULTE at 9.0a.m. Position of Assembly reached at 11.45a.m.

At 12 noon the Enemy were pressing on Right flank of attack endeavouring to get in behind 63rd Inf. Bde. from FRICOURT WOOD. The Battn. (less 12 Officers and 400 O.R.) moved to position of assembly in captured German trenches vis:

BRANDY TRENCH and SOUTH SAUSAGE SUPPORT TRENCHES where it remained until 9.30.am on the 3rd of July carrying supplies and ammunition forward to troops in front. Two squads Bombers and one Lewis Gun were sent forward to hold up attack from FRICOURT WOOD which was made on 3 occasions during the afternoon of 1st July.

The work of the Companies was as follows:

'A' Company (less Company Bombers) consisting of 3 Officers and 100 other ranks were ordered to cross "No Man's Land" as soon as our Second Objective had been gained, and assist R.E. in making of Strong Points in consolidating. The Company crossed "No Man's Land" at 12.30am on the night 1/2 July. As the work of consolidation could not yet be done Two parties were formed of 50 O. Ranks. One of these was sent forward with Stokes Gun Ammunition to SUNKEN ROAD where it was detained as Support to 1/Lincoln Regt. On the 3rd July during the attack on SHELTER WOOD when reinforcements were called for to repel a Counter Attack this party was sent up under Command of Sergeant Sinclair R. (the Officer Commanding the party having been previously wounded).

The party outflanked the enemy on the right and captured 30 prisoners, they consolidated position gained in SHELTER WOOD and held on until relieved by the Battalion of 17th. Division which relieved 1/Lincoln R. during night 3/4 July.

The other party of 50 was sent to and fro with Rations and finally joined the Battalion in BRANDY TRENCH, where work of consolidation was carried on. At 9.30am on July 3rd. this party under Company Commander moved up to SUNKEN ROAD was used for escorting Prisoners and more especially for carrying up Ammunition and Bombs, Food and Water to Front Line in SHELTER WOOD. Two Squads of Company Bombers were sent as Reinforcements to 'D' Company in SHELTER WOOD. Of these Squads Corpl. Skinner volunteered to go out Single handed over the open and endeavour to silence a Machine Gun that was holding up the Advance of 'D' Company. He was with difficulty restrained and subsequently led his Bombers round on the flank and silenced the gun. The remnants of 'A' Company were relieved by the 12/Manchester Regt. at 3.30am on July 4th.

'B' Company (less Company Bombers) consisting of 3 Officers and 100 Other Ranks moved at ZERO from position given above to Assembly position in DINNET STR. losing heavily on the way. One Officer and 50 other Ranks were detailed to dig Communication Trench across "No Man's Land" from DINNET STREET to SOUTH SAUSAGE TRENCH. This task was completed about 3.0pm 1st July. Several casualties were sustained from Machine Gun fire from the direction of La BOISELLE. Remainder then assisted in clearing SOUTH SAUSAGE SUPPORT TRENCH.

The second party consisting of Two Officers and 50 Other Ranks was detailed to bridge captured German Trenches. Owing to heavy shelling all the Bridges save one were smashed before the German Trenches were reached, the party was therefore ordered to clear up S. SAUSAGE SUPPORT TRENCH. This work of consolidating and clearing was carried on until 6.0pm 2nd July. During the time 7 unwounded and Two wounded prisoners were made. On completion the party returned to QUEENS REDOUBT under orders from R.E. and rejoined Battalion in BRANDY TRENCH at 11.0pm on same day.

The one Bridge which was not destroyed was placed in position. Whilst engaged in this work a strong German Bombing Party attacked the men engaged, the Corporal in charge ordered a Counter Attack which was so successfully carried out that several of the enemy were killed and 9 wounded prisoners made.

On July 3rd at 9.30am the Company was moved up to SUNKEN ROAD to take part in the Attack on SHELTER WOOD. One half Company was sent up to reinforce the 1/Lincoln Regt. in SHELTER WOOD – The other half was used entirely as carriers for Brigade Troops in front line of the Attack taking up Ammunition and Bombs, Food, Water & R.E. material. Relieved at 9.30am 4th July by 12/W. Riding Regt.

'C' Company (Less Bombers) consisting of 3 Officers and 100 O. R. moved as stated above. At Zero the Company took up position of assembly in advanced Saps before "GUILDFORD" with intention of going forward to make strong points when first objective had been secured. They remained in position until 11.0pm when they were ordered to return to BECOURT VALLEY and formed Ration Parties for 1/Lincoln Regt. during night 1/2 July. On completion about 4.0am on July 2nd some 40 men joined Battalion Headquarters in SOUTH SAUSAGE SUPPORT TRENCH and a similar number proceeded to forward Saps before GUILDFORD subsequently joining remainder of Company at 4.0pm 2nd July. The Company (less one Platoon) was detailed to make Strong Points at Junction of SODA TRENCH with BRANDY TRENCH, - SODA TRENCH with SOUTH SAUSAGE SUPPORT TRENCH, with orders to protect Left Flank of Divisional Attack at that point as position on 34 Div: front was obscure. Bombing Patrols were sent out towards SAUSAGE REDOUBT and SCOTS REDOUBT. One Platoon moved to SUNKEN ROAD and came under orders of O.C. 1/Lincoln Regt. and took part in the attack on SHELTER WOOD on 3/7/16 taking 20 prisoners. Remainder of Company held on in Strong Points until 9.15am on 4 July then proceeded to SUNKEN ROAD and acted as Ammunition carriers until 11.0am when it was ordered to clear the Western edge of SHELTER WOOD which was still held by the enemy. After this operation the Company consolidated making Strong Points at N.E. and N.W. corners of SHELTER WOOD and held them until relieved at [illegible].30am by 12/W. Riding Regt. Two Squads Company Bombers were sent to assist 12/Northd. Fusrs. Bombers in clearing Trench running through BIRCH TREE WOOD and SHELTER WOOD.

'D' Company (less Company Bombers) consisting of 3 Officers and 100 O.R. moved as stated above. It moved across "No Man's Land" in rear of 9th and 10th Battalions K.O.Y.L.I. and gradually worked up to SUNKEN ROAD by about

8.45am. The men were carrying materials for consolidating but were ordered to Dump these and take part in the assault. About 11.15am the remnants advanced with 64th Infantry Brigade mixed troops – a total of some 5 Officers and 250 O.R. – and took possession of CRUCIFIX TRENCH and consolidated as far as possible. About 11.40am three Officers and about 100 O.R. of 15th D.L.I. advanced against SHELTER WOOD and were not seen again. This left about 150 O.R. with Two Officers to hold CRUCIFIX TRENCH. Both flanks so far as could be ascertained were in the air and the position was heavily shelled during the time 9.0 to 11.0pm 2/7/16.

Captain Godber organized the Defence and held on until reinforcements arrived. Entire touch was lost with 64th Infantry Brigade but touch was obtained through Battalion Headquarters with 62nd Infantry Brigade. During the night 2/3 July the Company was relieved by 10th Yorks Regt. and rejoined Battalion Headquarters in SOUTH SAUSAGE SUPPORT TRENCH. The Company Bombers with all that were left of the Company, about 30 men, moved up at 9.30am on July 3rd. as part of Battalion Reserve to SUNKEN ROAD. At 10.45am reinforced by Two Squads of 'A' Company Bombers they moved up and attacked the N.N.W. corner of SHELTER WOOD where they were held up by Machine Gun Fire and partly driven back. The Machine Gun Team or most of the men were put out of action by our Snipers and Bombs were also thrown at them, and the Company was able to advance. On relief by 12/W.Riding Regt. and 12/Manchester Regt. the Battalion marched back to DERNACOURT via FRICOURT.

14th (Service) Battalion (Pioneers) Northumberland Fusiliers

VILLE.

5am   'A' & 'C' Companies moved from VILLE up to their points of assembly in the trenches namely Queens Redoubt
The following are the reports of the Company Commanders as to the work accomplished by their Companies from 65 minutes before zero (7.30am) until the Battalion was relieved from the trenches.

'A' Company
65 minutes before zero the Company marched from L. Dump to Queens Redoubt via NEAULTE & PIONEER AVENUE, sustaining on the way 2 casualties.
Queens Redoubt.

8.30pm   Orders were issued for the Company to proceed to consolidate a position about X.21.d.4.8. We arrived at our old front line at midnight under heavy shell fire when I discovered that most of the men had lost touch owing to the bad condition of BON ACCORD and the front line trench through which we had to pass being in several places almost completely blocked by scaling bridges which in many cases could not be removed owing to being half buried and as we had some distance to go before arriving at our objective and were under orders only to work until dawn. I ordered the Company back to Queens Redoubt.

'B' Company

1am   I reported to Hqs 64th Inf. Bde. on being sent for by the Brigadier and was instructed to take over command of 'B' Coy vice Capt G.S.McPherson who was unable to proceed with the Company. He instructed me to follow the 9th & 10th K.O.Y.L.I. at 200 yards interval and to send one officer to their Hqs to enquire exact time they would assault. This I did. I also informed the Bde that my men were in their assembly trenches namely MARECHAL STREET excepting No 7 platoon and the Machine Gunners. These however turned up later.

7.32am   The time of assault. Marechal Street being roughly 200 yards behind front line my time for going over was fixed at that hour, which was carried out, the Company taking part in the assault. We were mixed up with KOYLI owing either to there going to slow or us going to fast. Parties having become mixed up it was difficult to find them.

8am   On arrival at SUNKEN ROAD I saw the Brigadier and he ordered me to collect my men and wire ROUND WOOD. This I did by using all the wire I could find and I succeeded in wiring the front and northern sides. I eventually found another party of my Company in CRUCIFIX TRENCH and later a portion of 1 section of RES under a Sgt. the officer having been wounded.

7pm   I received communications from the other sections of RE's under Lieut Clarke also of 2nd Lieut Hilton and one officer of 13th N.F. I gave instructions to carry on the improvement of trenches as we were unable to reach positions of strong points. We were standing to on several occasions assisting the Infantry both in CRUCIFIX TRENCH, SUNKEN and DINGLE TRENCH.

'C' Company

5.35am   The Company left camp at VILLE each man carrying about 30lbs of material and tools en route for Queens Redoubt via [*name unclear*]Av. and LINDUM ST.

8.30am   The first platoon reached Queens Redoubt the other three platoons were blocked in [*name unclear*] Avenue by 62nd Inf Bde and did not reach the dugouts until 10.30am.

8.30pm   I received orders which were new owing to the Infantry having failed to reach their objective, as follows: No 9 & 11 platoons to proceed to trench junction at X.27.c.4095 following one section of 98th Field Coy R.E. No 10 platoon to consolidate Trench junction at ROUND WOOD. No 12 platoon to carry up materials and dump it for R.E.s. E of Sunken Road. The orders were issued to me somewhat late and further time was lost in getting together material. No 9 platoon under Lt G.J. Jackson arrived on the work about 12.30am and worked until dawn. No 11 Platoon under 2nd Lt H.C. Kirsopp lost connection and after picking up some stray Pioneers and Engineers was set to work by O.C. 97th Field Coy R.E. on a communication trench in No Mans Land in X.2b.d. The reason why this platoon failed to reach its objective is that while the party consisting of 98th Field Coy R.E. No 9 & 11 platoons were proceeding up HUNTLEY ST. they unavoidably got detached from each other owing to troops blocking the passage.

Lt. Kirsopp was unable to take a compass bearing of the particular objective owing to that particular objective only being allotted to him during the hours of darkness immediately prior to his proceeding on the way up. No 12 Platoon accomplished its task. No 10 Platoon which I accompanied proceeded via ABERDEEN AV. to the front line which was not reached until 2am. The exceptional delay was due to the fact that NEW ABERDEEN AV. was being used by the Division on our left as an up and down communication trench. On arrival at the German support line the light had got very bright and as the mens endurance had already been severely tried and there was no prospect of doing any work before daybreak I ordered the material to be dumped in S. SAUSAGE support and returned to our own front line which was reached at 3.45am.

'D' Company

8am   The Company started from Queens Redoubt with 98th Field Coy R.E. and two platoons of Infantry (13th Northd. Fusrs.) one being attached to the R.E.s, towards the front line via LINDUM STREET, the Coy then being under the command of Lieut Appleyard. On the way up LINDUM ST. Lieut Appleyard was wounded.

1pm   Owing to delay caused by (1) people using up trench as a down trench (2) wounded coming down (3) parties making in from branch trenches we reached the front line at about 1pm and then awaited orders from O.C. 98th Field Coy R.E.

11pm   I received no orders to advance until about 11pm and I was then informed that our destination had been changed from Crucifix Trench and that we were going to construct a strong point at a point on LOZENGE ALLEY about 50 yards from the Western End of the wood. As neither the Engineers or the Infantry were going with us we had to change our loads which had been made up for our original destination. This caused a certain amount of delay and the Infantry being mixed up with the Company caused more delay. I gave the order for the Company to file out waiting myself to see the Company off. Passing the Infantry the Company got disconnected and one part finally joined up with 'C' Coy. The remainder with myself to the point given via RUM LANE. BRANDY TRENCH. LOZENGE ALLEY and across the SUNKEN ROAD into LOZENGE ALLEY, thence to the proposed strong point, which was reached at 1am.

8th (Service) Battalion Prince Albert's (Somerset Light Infantry)

TRENCHES
6.30am   Trench ladders & bridges were put in place and an intense Artillery barrage was opened.

7.30am   Was Zero time for assault.

7.25am   Front waves of 'B' & 'C' Coys crawled out.

The Battalion was ordered to attack in the following formation 'B' & 'C' Coys in front 'B' on the right & 'C' on left were to advance in 4 lines of Platoon at 2 paces interval, about 100 yards between lines - supported by 'A' Coy in 2 lines of ½ Coys. 'D' Coy coming on in rear in Artillery formation e.g. in lines of platoon in file as a carrying party for S.A.A. Bombs, picks & shovels – Trench stores etc.

Directly the Artillery barrage lifted our men advanced in quick time. They were met by very heavy machine gun fire and although Officers & men were being hit & falling everywhere the advance went steadily on, and was reported to by a Brigade Major who witnessed it to have been magnificent.

The leading platoons lost quite 50% going across "No mans land".

On arrival near the enemy's front line they were momentarily held up by a machine gun, but as the successive supporting lines came up they soon got in.

Already the enemy had opened an Artillery Barrage on "No mans land" & our front line trench – which carried heavy casualties among the supports. The only enemy found alive in this front line were a few machine gunners, who were immediately killed.

Our men worked their way down the german communication Trenches Bombing Dugouts which contained live germans, then on to where the trenches had been battered out of all recognition, and only consisted of a mass of craters.

They were supported by our STOKES gun but the officer in charge & the team were soon knocked out; Then a Lewis gun team of ours got up & lent considerable help; enabling our men to make a further advance. This party was under 2/Lt Kellett and worked its way from crater to crater until it got to LOZENGE ALLEY which had not been straffed by our Artillery, here they consolidated – making fire steps etc because it was only a communication Trench. The enemy's barrage of shrapnel prevented further advance.

In LOZENGE ALLEY 2/Lt KELLETT'S party joined up with 2/Lt A.H. HALL'S party making a total of about 100, who had been doing much the same work – They held this position all night – during which time they repulsed a bombing attack coming from the direction of FRICOURT.

10th (Service) Battalion Prince of Wales's Own (West Yorkshire Regiment)

O.A.S.

At 7.30am the Battn took part in the grand assault. On the right were the 7th Divn & on the left the 21st Divn. The Battn assaulted in 4 lines. 2 lines got through the German position to the 4th line & were cut off, the attack on our left having failed. Casualties were very heavy chiefly caused by machine guns which enfiladed our left flanks & were so deadly that the 3rd & 4th lines failed to get across "no mans land". 27 officer casualties including Lt Col Dixon cmdg & Major J. Knott 2nd in command both killed & approximately 750 O.R. The Battn was then withdrawn to VILLE.

2nd Battalion Queen's (Royal West Surrey Regiment)

12.5am. En route from BOIS DES TAILLES to position of Assembly – halted for about 30 minutes, men given water & 2 bandoliers S.A.A, after which Bn. proceeded by Companies via NORFOLK AVE & MINDEN POST to their positions.

Support Trenches.

4.00am. From left to right –
'A' Coy in LONDON ROAD W.
'B' Coy in LONDON ROAD E of Francis Ave.
'C' Coy in CROSS ST.
'D' Coy in CROSS ST. & PORTLAND ROAD.
Hd.Qrs. CROSS ST. near junction of HIGH ST.

Situation of other units from left to right –

Front line   1st S. Staffords – 22nd Manchesters.
Support line   21st Manchesters – 2nd Queen's.
91st Bde HQ DURHAM TRENCH 250 yards S. of MINDEN POST.
20th Inf. Bde on left, 11th R. Fus. (18th Div) on right.
1st Objective, MAMETZ village & high ground East along MONTAUBAN-MAMETZ road.
2nd - do - FRITZ Trench, BRIGHT Alley, BUNNY Alley. (Strong & well made German trenches)
3rd - do - High ground 150 yards South of MAMETZ WOOD. (S. 25. b 45 to x 29.b.5.6)
21st Div attacking on N.W. side of FRICOURT to establish their front line on N. side of BOTTOM WOOD with a strong point just W. of x 29.b.5.6. to protect our left flank.

2nd Battalion Royal Irish Regiment

The Battalion assembled at 1am in a position in rear of the 20th and 91st Brigades who were in position to attack at ZERO hour (7.30am). Orders were received that a new position was to be taken up in close support of the 91st Brigade at 7.30am, which were carried out, the Battalion moved into trenches vacated by 22 Bn Manchester Regt under a heavy fire.

As the 91st Brigade had reached its final objective for the day the Battalion was not used in the attack, but at 10pm. 'A' Coy was sent to MAMETZ to consolidate a position for the 21st Manchester Regt and 'D' Coy reinforced the 22/ Manchester Regt with the object of repelling counter attacks. Both these companies withdrew at Dawn the following morning and reformed the Battalion which was still in Divisional Reserve. On this day our casualties were 50 men all.

2nd Battalion Royal Warwickshire Regiment

BOIS de TAILLES
Strength of Battn, officers 38, o. Ranks 1,049.
7.30am   Moved up to assembly trenches vacated by assaulting troops in rear of 20th Brigade.
         Companies in the following order: 'B' Coy occupied DUKE ST.
                                           'C'   "   "   LORD ST.
                                           'D'   "   "   BOLD ST.
                                           'A'   "   "   LUDGATE LANE.
                                           Bn Hd Qrs with 'B' Coy.
Strength – officers 20, o. Ranks 760.

2.30pm 'B' & 'C' Coys moved up to re-inforce the Gordons who were held up opposite MAMETZ & assisted them to take the ruins capturing 200 prisoners, 2 Machine Guns & 1 Automatic Rifle. Lt Hodgkinson and Lt Martin were killed during these operation & several men wounded.
'D' & 'A' Coy occupied trenches vacated by 'B' & 'C' Coys.

6.30pm Hd Qrs with 'D' & 'A' Coys moved up to DANTZIG ALLEY & occupied the trench during the night in support of 8th & 9th Devons.
'B' & 'C' Coys & remainder of Gordons held a line from MAMETZ to the Craters along ORCHARD ALLEY facing FRICOURT WOOD.

1st Battalion Royal Welch Fusiliers

The attack of the 4th Army in conjunction with a French Army to the south commenced at 7.30am being preceded by a bombardment of extreme intensity.

The action of the 22nd Infantry Brigade was subordinate to the action of the rest of the 7th Division on its right and the 21st Division on its left.

The task set to the Brigade was, to assault and take the system of German trenches known as the BOIS FRANCAIS TRENCH & support – SUNKEN ROAD trench – The Rectangle and Rectangle support – its final objective being ROSE TRENCH.

The attack was to be carried out in conjunction with an attack by 2 Battns of the 50th Brigade on FRICOURT, thus prolonging the line to the left.

A Zero hour was to be fixed when touch had been established between the rest of the 7th Division and the 21st Division at BOTTOM WOOD which would cut off the sector to be attacked.

The attack was ordered to be carried out by the 20th Bn. Manchester Regt., assaulting from NEW TRENCH against SUNKEN ROAD and from the western Craters against BOIS FRANCAIS TRENCH.

The 1st R.W.F. were ordered to support the principal attack against SUNKEN ROAD, moving forward as the assaulting Battn pushed on until the Battn stood as follows:-

'A' Coy – SUNKEN ROAD TRENCH, 'B' Coy – NEW TRENCH, 'D' Coy – in Reserve in QUARRIES, 'C' Coy was at the disposal of the Brigde as a carrying party. A brigade mobile reserve under 2/Lt E.H. Dadd consisting of 2 Sections Infy, 2 Sections Bombers, 2 Lewis Guns & 2 Stokes Guns was established in the QUARRY.

9am. Verbal message received from B.H.Q. that Zero hour would be at 10.30am.
Companies were ordered to move to their positions of readiness and stood as follows;
2 Platoons 'B' Coy on the left of the 20th Manchesters in front line.
2 Platoons 'B' Coy CEMETERY ROAD & 2 Sections Bombers & 1 Lewis Gun.

'A' Coy & 1 Platoon Bombers & 1 Lewis Gun 71 NORTH.
Reserve – 'D' Coy & 2 Sections Bombers & 1 Lewis Gun in the Deep
Level Shaft at the QUARRY.
1½ Platoons of the Bombing Coy. 4 Lewis Guns.

10am   Owing to a check to the attack on the right the necessary junction between 7th & 21st Divisions was not established and the Zero hour postponed.

1pm   Zero (subsidiary) hour 2.30pm.

2.30pm   At 2.30pm the 20th Manchesters assaulted; the Brigade on their left failed to assault. They came under severe enfilade M.G. fire from WING CORNER, lost direction and finally reached BOIS FRANCAIS TRENCH & BOIS FRANCAIS SUPPORT. Very few reached SUNKEN ROAD TRENCH and the Battn. owing to loss of Officers became disorganised.

4.20pm   Support called for from 20th Manchesters. 'A' Coy pushed up via Craters to BOIS FRANCAIS, this flank movement being necessary owing to the activity of the M.G. at WING CORNER.

'A' Coy got mixed up with the 20th Manchesters but succeeded in establishing communication with the 20th Bde on the right and in stopping the activity of the German bombers in the vicinity.

The position at this time was dangerous, the enemy's main position at the RECTANGLE being still in their hands. FRICOURT was also untaken and our troops were jammed up in BOIS FRANCAIS TRENCH & BOIS FRANCAIS SUPPORT.

'A' Coy made little progress to their left. The Brigade Mobile Reserve was called up to co-operate and clear ZINC TRENCH and safeguard our exposed flank.

7.45pm   The Bombing reserve ordered to cross by the craters, seize and block SUNKEN ROAD, seize and block RECTANGLE and place it in a state of defence.

10.30pm   By 10.30pm, these orders had been admirably carried out by Lt. STEVENS in charge of the bombers. Immediate steps were taken to consolidate the position. A block was established at WING CORNER from which the M.G. was so harassed that it withdrew. The Bombers had done splendidly, the Mobile Reserve ably co-operating.

The position was occupied as follows:

'A' Coy & Bombers – SUNKEN RD & RECTANGLE.
'B' Coy in our front line.
'D' Coy in QUARRIES.
The Reserve Lewis Guns were pushed up to the position.

During the night it was reported that the Germans were demoralised and withdrawing and the Brigade was asked to permit an attack on WING CORNER, but this was refused.

Casualties: 4 Killed. 35 Wounded. Prisoners taken about 200. Also a large amount of booty in the shape of canisters & heavy trench mortars etc. One canister machine which for months had made itself a nuisance was claimed as a trophy, the detachment being all killed by the Bombers. 2 Rifle grenade machines were also claimed.

1st Battalion South Staffordshire Regiment

MAMETZ

7.30am   Attack launched. The attack was pushed forward very successfully and with very few casualties until the whole battalion was in MAMETZ, where a large number of Germans were encountered. At 9.8am a message was received from C.O.'D' Company stating the Battn was held up on South side of MAMETZ, and required reinforcements, the enemy being in strong numbers in the village. 'A' Company of the 21st Manchester Regiment was sent to our support and at 11.20am we received a message stating that we had advanced to the North East corner of the village and were consolidating. We also held BRIGHT ALLEY with a small force.

Noon   The position of companies was: 'C' Company on the Right, making a strong point, 'D' Coy. in DANTZIG ALLEY making a strong point with two Stokes Guns. 'B' Company on the Left Front.

2.0pm   Battalion had gained and was consolidating the whole of its objective with the exception of BUNNY ALLEY.

3.10pm   Battalion had to withdraw in line with the church as FRITZ TRENCH had not been captured.

5.30pm   Battalion Headquarters moved up into MAMETZ and on reaching the village found that the Battalion's final objective had not been captured. Major Morris, with great skill, at once reorganised all the troops in the village and allotted each a task, and sent the following message to Brigade at 6.0pm. "On reaching MAMETZ I found 80 men of the 2nd Gordons, two Companies of the R. Warwicks and about 1½ Coys. of Manchesters with 500 South Staffords – The Colonel of the Gordons had not arrived and the general line held by the units was, DANTZIG ALLEY from East to West, running through the village. After a short conference I ordered the whole force to reorganise and advance to final objective and forthwith consolidate – this is now in progress. The final objectives were taken and held at about 7.40pm. During the operations 150 prisoners and two Machine Guns were captured."

The following casualties occurred during the day's fighting:

Killed: Captain Charles Roy Limbery, 2nd Lieut (?Capt) George White, 2nd Lieut Stanley Albert Webber, 2nd Lt Percival Harvey Emberton.

Died of wounds: 2nd Lieut Warwick Hall.

Wounded: Lieut Eric Hindsley, Lieut Reginald Lockyer Hibberdine, 2/Lieut John Percival Lloyd, 2/Lieut Godfrey Edward Holdsworth, 2/Lieut William Henry Ratcliffe, and 300 Other Ranks.

Most of our casualties occurred after we had taken DANTZIG ALLEY. During the action the Battalion captured Machine Guns and Automatic Rifles, Portable Telephones and a great quantity of stores of all kinds. During the night all was quiet and work of consolidating was carried on under the command of Colonel Norman of the 21st Manchester regiment – Patrols and listening posts were out in front all night.

10th (Service) Battalion York And Lancaster Regiment

Trenches

Reference 10th York and Lancs. Operation Orders dated 23/6/16: Z-day. Attack was commenced at 7.30am by 4th Middlesex Regt. and 8th Somerset L.I. on 21 Div Sector. At 8.30am 10th York and Lancs and 8th Lincoln Regt. advanced from Assembly Trenches and passed through 4th Middlesex Regt. and 8th Somerset L.I. respectively, coming under very heavy machine gun fire from FRICOURT and FRICOURT WOOD. After very hard fighting (in which heavy casualties occurred) the Battalion consolidated in LOZENGE ALLEY and later in DART LANE. Battalion remained in this position till about 2.00pm third day when it moved.

Document Attached to the War Diary

Appendix II: A report of the battalion's operations from 1 July to 4 July 1916, signed by the Commanding Officer:

The Battalion advanced through 4th. Middlesex Regt, who were in German front line, and came under heavy machine gun fire from FRICOURT and FRICOURT WOOD. The leading waves got some distance in advance of DART LANE, when they were held up by machine gun fire from FRICOURT WOOD.

At the same time three large parties of Germans attempted to bomb their way up all the trenches South of DART LANE. Also at the same time the Battalion Bombers were having a hard struggle with a large bombing party in LONELY TRENCH. They had three barricades in this, which we destroyed. We then placed a barricade at North end of LONELY TRENCH near junction of LOZENGE ALLEY. A party of 'D' Company with stragglers from other Units were sent into ARROW

LANE to protect that flank, with the assistance of one gun of Machine Gun Corps. This party came under heavy fire from the South, the enemy making several strong attempts to bomb up EMPRESS SUPPORT and the remains of EMPRESS TRENCH.

The remainder of Battalion were then in LOZENGE ALLEY with the Lincolns and parties of other Units. This we were consolidating. About 5.0pm I re-organized the Battalion to take them to DART LANE, which I consolidated. I had also a holding party of Bombers at corner of DART LANE, EMPRESS SUPPORT and LONELY LANE. I had also a party in ARROW LANE: with this party were about 50 men of 10th Yorkshire Regiment. The Battalion remained in this position till about 2.0pm on the second day, during which time the Battalion was working very hard in passing up S.A.A. Bombs, etc, to 62nd Brigade, who were calling for supplies very urgently. This work went on continuously till about 2.0pm. when I was ordered to move up and join 62nd Brigade.

I took Battalion up SUNKEN ROAD and put them in DINGLE TRENCH from D21 Central to about junction of DINGLE TRENCH and PATCH ALLEY, with my headquarters in SUNKEN ROAD at South end of ROUND WOOD.

Whilst here we were under fire from two heavy enemy guns. We remained here till relieved by one Company of 12th Manchester Regt at about 4am on morning of 4th. The blocking party ordered to follow immediately in rear of 4th Middlesex Regt did not reach their objective, as all the men were knocked out with the exception of about six men, the Officer being wounded just after getting over the parapet. I also collected what spare bombers I had and sent them up to 52nd Brigade, who were calling for more men. The party protecting our right collected a fair number of prisoners from the dug-outs in DART LANE, EMPRESS SUPPORT and various small communication trenches.

One officer and a small party of men actually reached the hedge running on outside of FRICOURT FARM, but were compelled to fall back owing to a large bombing party coming down LOZENGE ALLEY from FRICOURT FARM.

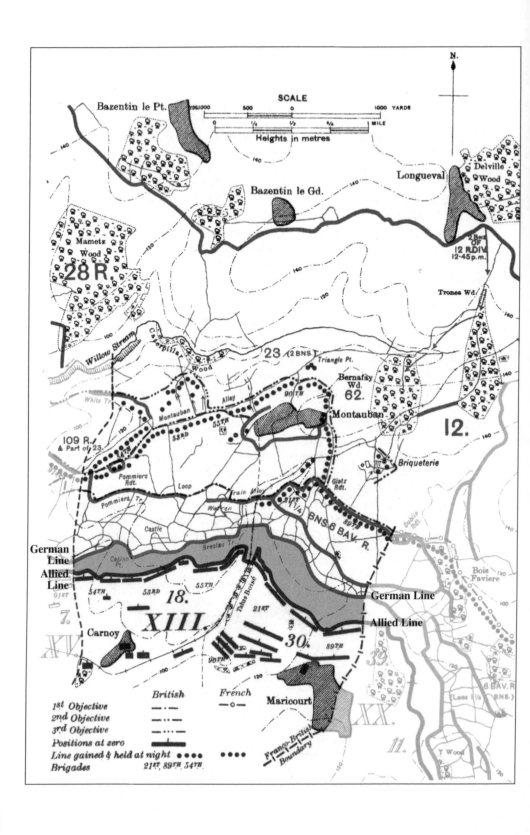

N.

SCALE

500　　　　　　0　　　　　　　1000　YARDS

0　　　1/4　　　1/2　　　3/4　　　　MILE

Heights in metres

Bazentin le Pt.

Bazentin le Gd.

Longueval

Delville Wood

Mametz Wood

28 R.

2 Bns. OF 12 R.DIV. 12·45 p.m.

Trones Wd.

Willow Stream

Caterpillar Wood

23 (2 BNS.)

Triangle Pt.

Bernafay Wd. 62.

Montauban

12.

White Tr.

Alley

90 TH

109 R. & Part of 23.

Montauban

53RD

55TH

14TH

Briqueterie

Pommiers Rdt.

Loop

Train Aley

Glatz Rdt.

Pommiers Tr.

Warren

21ST 1/4

BNS 6 BAV. R.

89TH

Dublin Rdt.

Castle

Breslau Tr.

Bois Faviere

German Line

Allied Line

Casino Pt.

91ST

54TH

53RD

55TH

18.

Talus Boisé

21ST

German Line

Allied Line

7.

XIII.

30.

89TH

39.

6 BAV. R. (Less 1 1/4 BNS.)

Carnoy

90TH

Maricourt

Bois Faviere

Y Wood

11.

1st Objective

2nd Objective

3rd Objective

Positions at zero

Line gained & held at night

Brigades 21ST, 89TH, 54TH

British

French

Franco-British Boundary

XX.

XIII Corps

1 July 1916

The front line of XIII Corps,[1] which was on the right of the British line next to the French, extended from Maricourt to beyond Carnoy. It lay near the bottom of the northern slope of the valley between the Maricourt and Montauban ridges, in which the village of Carnoy is situated. The German front line was higher up on the same slope.

Both the ridges take off near Guillemont from the Ginchy – Pozières ridge and are really spurs from it. The Maricourt ridge drops on its eastern side into the Hardecourt valley, in which are the two woods, Bois d'en Haut and Bois Favière, where the French were to have severe fighting. Between the Montauban ridge, on whose crest the red roofs of the village were a conspicuous landmark before the bombardment, and the Ginchy – Pozières ridges is a long valley known from the shape of a wood it contains as Caterpillar Valley. The Carnoy valley bifurcates; the northern branch, which provided good cover and in which ran a pre-war light railway line, was known as Railway Valley, and on its steep eastern slope stretched a long plantation called Talus Boisé. The ground over which the advance of the divisions of XIII Corps must proceed was therefore a long gentle slope, on the right almost flat, cut into by Railway Valley and other depressions, the spurs between being known by the names of the adjacent villages as Carnoy and Mametz spurs. There was splendid observation over the ground as far as the Montauban – Mametz road from Maricourt ridge, on whose reverse slopes the mass of the artillery of the corps, heavy and field, was deployed.

The German position was held by about nine battalions of the 12th, 28th Reserve and 10th Bavarian Divisions.[2] The German defences consisted of a front position of several trenches, with a recently dug reserve line, Dublin Trench – Train Alley – Pommiers Trench, 700 to 1,000 yards behind it. A communication trench (called Montauban Alley) running from Montauban to Mametz on the reverse slope of Caterpillar Valley, formed a further retrenchment. The second position, some 3,000 yards behind the first, extended past Maurepas to Guillemont, Longueval and the two Bazentins. The third position was under construction. The front system was strengthened by numerous strong points formed as a rule by isolating a sector of the trenches by means of all-round wire and trench-blocks. Among these self-contained defences were Glatz and Pommiers Redoubts, and

"The Castle". The village of Montauban had been put in a state of defence, and on its southern side outside its perimeter ran a continuous trench.

The plan of attack of XIII Corps, issued on 15 June, divided the operations into three "phases". In the first phase, the first day's work, Montauban, in the centre, on the top of the ridge, was to be secured. East of the village the advance was to reach the German trenches Nord Alley and Dublin Trench, in order to form a long flank to connect with the French at Dublin Redoubt. On the west, the line was to be pushed forward so as to capture Montauban Alley and gain observation into Caterpillar Valley. The German reserve line Dublin Trench – Pommiers Trench, over 1,000 yards distant, was to be the first objective, but from this line only the centre and the left of the corps were to go on to the second objective, Montauban and the top of the Montauban – Mametz ridge, and only the left to a third objective, a short distance ahead, in order to obtain better observation. As soon as the plan was settled, the 30th Division dug a new front trench, 150–200 yards nearer the enemy, with six communication trenches, across the re-entrant then existing between the Maricourt road and Talus Boisé.

The second and third phases, dependent on the success of the attack of the corps north of Fricourt, were to consist of a right wheel, pivoting on Favière Wood and Dublin Redoubt followed by a general advance eastwards through Bernafay Wood and Trônes Wood to the German second position, Falfemont Farm and Guillemont, the French on the right capturing Hardecourt and Maurepas.

As regards assistance from artillery XIII Corps' plan laid down that: "The advance of the infantry will be covered by a heavy barrage from all natures of guns and mortars. The heavy artillery barrage will lift direct from one line on to the next. The field artillery barrage will creep[3] back by short lifts.[4] Both will work strictly according to timetable. The lifts have been timed so as to allow the infantry plenty of time for the advance from one objective to the next, on the principle that it is preferable that the infantry should wait for the barrage to lift than that the latter should lift prematurely, and thus allow the enemy to man his parapets. The infantry will follow as close behind the barrage as safety permits."

The 30th Division was to attack on the right, the 18th on the left, Talus Boisé and then the track to Montauban, allotted to the 30th, forming the boundary between them. The 9th Division was to be in corps reserve, assembling in and around Billon Wood (two miles behind the front), Trigger Wood,[5] and localities where it would be sheltered from view by the crest of the Maricourt ridge.

The two leading brigades of the 30th Division were to capture the first objective, Dublin Trench – Glatz Redoubt, between Maricourt ridge and Montauban, in two stages, by 08.28 hours. The right brigade moving along the flat top of the ridge was in the first stage to go only as far as Casement Trench, a switch trench running westward from Dublin Redoubt. The left brigade, passing along the western slope, was, in the first stage, to secure the trench 150 yards west of Glatz Redoubt, Train Alley, and next Glatz Redoubt. The third brigade, moving up Railway Valley, was then, at 09.30 hours, to pass through the leading ones and capture Montauban, the second objective. The artillery lifts were timed to fit in with the three stages, a barrage map showing six lifts being issued by the divisional artillery commander, Brigadier-General G.H.A. White. During the pause at the first objective the second was to be bombarded.

The 18th Division, moving up the Carnoy spur and the southern slope of the Mametz spur, was to capture the first objective, Train Alley and Pommiers Trench, using its three brigades in line. These, continuing abreast, were all to go on to the second objective, Montauban Alley, from Montauban to Pommiers Redoubt a commanding point on the Montauban – Mametz road. The total advance was nearly 2,000 yards. The division was then, if possible, to push on to its third objective, a short distance only on the right but four hundred yards or more on the left, in order to gain possession of a projecting portion of the Montauban spur above Caterpillar Wood, which gave observation into the valley.

The arrangements of the 18th Division artillery (Brigadier-General S.F. Metcalfe) were similar to those in the 30th Division, with the important addition that the advance to the second and third objectives, when the formidable front trench system on the forward slope had been passed, was to be covered by a shrapnel barrage"moving in front of the infantry by increments of range[6] until final barrage is established on line H": that is beyond the objective for the day. Arrangements were also made with XV Corps on the left to enfilade Pommiers Trench with 60-pounder shrapnel, which was done most effectively.[7]

On reaching the final objectives, the new line was to be consolidated by the formation of strong points. The 30th Division attached one section of a field company Royal Engineers to each brigade, and the 18th Division two sections, for this purpose, besides detachments of the pioneer battalions (11/South Lancashire Regiment and 8/Royal Sussex). As soon as possible, detachments of infantry and machine-guns were to be pushed forward from the final objective to seize important points. Thus the 30th Division was to secure La Briqueterie, a brick factory with a prominent chimney used as a German observation post, north-east of Glatz Redoubt, and the 18th Division was to raid Caterpillar Wood and to secure other points along the northern slope of Montauban ridge, from which Caterpillar Valley could be effectively commanded, while the escape of enemy guns from the valley would be prevented.

Points beyond the new position suitable for artillery observation during the subsequent phases of the battle were also to be occupied. Certain specified field batteries (two brigades in all) were to be pushed forward to positions from which they could cover the ground between the new front and the German second position, special attention being paid to the establishment of a strong"box"barrage round Montauban to deal with probable German counter-attacks on the salient which would be created if XIII Corps was successful.[8]

The corps' heavy artillery,[9] which, combined with that of the French XX Corps on the right, was greatly superior in numbers to the German in this sector, being nearly four to one,[10] had already obtained the mastery of the enemy, and during 1 July it practically destroyed its opponents, so that there was almost a complete absence of artillery reply. Indeed, so well had it done its work that, as will be seen, there was little resistance except from a few of the strong points, and machine-guns, not artillery, were responsible for the British casualties.[11] Like the field artillery, the heavies were to be moved forward to positions from which the German second position, especially about Bazentin le Grand, could be effectively engaged.

It was decided not to attempt to cover the assault across No Man's Land by smoke, as the infantry commanders who had experience at Loos were opposed to its use, and the wonderful observation – almost every strand of wire could be seen – from the high ground near Maricourt, which ensured very accurate artillery barrages, would have been sacrificed. Some 4-inch Stokes mortars, however, were held in readiness to fire smoke bombs against machine-guns and flanks of the line should this be required, and six Russian saps, to provide covered communications, had been mined by the 183rd Tunnelling Company Royal Engineers right across No Man's Land ready to be connected to the German front line by blowing small charges at the ends.[12]

There was hardly any enemy shelling during the night on XIII Corps' area, except a little by 5.9-inch howitzers on Carnoy, and the troops had no difficulty in getting to their assembly positions. Although the morning of 1 July was fine, the low ground near Carnoy, where the British and German front trenches lay, was at first hidden in mist, which cleared about 07.00 hours.

Capture of its first objective (Dublin Trench) by the 30th Division

The assault by the right brigade of the 30th Division,[13] the 89th (Brigadier-General Hon. F.C. Stanley), the right of the British line, starting from four lines of assembly trenches, was carried out with complete success. At 07.22 hours there was a hurricane bombardment by six Stokes mortar batteries[14] distributed on the divisional front at the end of special Russian saps, opened up during the previous night.[15]

At 07.30 hours through the mist and smoke the two leading battalions, the 17/King's and 20/King's, left their trenches and advanced in quick time, with rifles slung, across No Man's Land – which averaged 500 yards in width – in extended lines of companies at 100 paces' distance. To ensure good liaison, the officer commanding the 17/King's, Lieutenant Colonel B.C. Fairfax, and Commandant Le Petit of the 3rd Battalion of the 153rd Regiment, the left battalion of the French 39th Division, stepped over the parapet together with the second wave, at the point of junction, and, pushing forward, eventually led the advance arm-in-arm. The last companies started somewhat in advance of schedule time, in order to avoid the German barrage, which was almost immediately, though very feebly, put down on the assembly trenches which they had just left.

The wire of the front line was found to have been exceedingly well cut,[16] one account saying "there was none left".

The German defenders, cowed perhaps by the bombardment and certainly depressed by want of food, no rations having reached them for six days, were not out of their dug-outs in time to man the trench, and offered little resistance. Three hundred prisoners, chiefly of the 62nd Regiment, and four machine-guns were subsequently captured in the dug-outs by the "mopping-up" parties of the 2/Bedfordshire, the supporting battalion. The two leading battalions passed on, after a pause, to Casement Trench and Alt Trench, the goal of the first stage, a party of thirty Germans in a small copse, German's Wood, surrendering to them on the way. Thence, after a short pause for the artillery barrage to lift – for the advance had been so rapid that the infantry were actually held back by it – the 89th Brigade pressed on with the utmost steadiness to Dublin Trench, the first objective, which was reached at 08.30 hours. It was found unoccupied.

Simultaneously the 3rd Battalion 153rd Regiment entered Dublin Redoubt at the eastern end of the trench, where Commandant Le Petit embraced his British confrère. The new position was now consolidated, picks and shovels being brought up by carrying parties of the supporting battalions, the right in close touch with the French and the left in the eastern end of Glatz Redoubt[17] where the 21st Brigade was about to arrive.

Dublin Trench had been so battered by artillery that it was unrecognizable, and at least one battalion passed over it and dug new trenches by connecting shell holes some fifty to a hundred yards on the German side of where Dublin Trench had been, a circumstance which saved many casualties later when the Germans shelled the old position. Three batteries of the 149th Brigade Royal Field Artillery (Lieutenant Colonel Hon. G.F. Stanley) were pushed forward north-west of Maricourt; one was immediately knocked out, but the other two were left undisturbed by the enemy.[18]

The 21st Brigade (Brigadier-General Hon. C.J. Sackville-West[19]) achieved similar success. The German front line was crossed with few casualties. The defenders, here too, were mostly caught in their dug-outs and taken prisoner by the "moppers-up". The leading battalions, the 19/Manchester and 18/King's, following the eastern slope of Railway Valley, went steadily forward until held up by the British barrage on Alt Trench, the first stage.

Moving close up behind the barrage, the leading companies waited till it lifted, at 07.45 hours and then occupied the trench. The Manchesters had suffered little loss, but the King's, stopped by some Germans in Train Alley covered from view by a hedge, had been severely handled by enfilade machine-gun and rifle fire from the western side of Railway Valley, where the 18th Division was in difficulties. A party of Germans in a network of trenches known as "The Warren", projecting from the German reserve line just inside the 18th Division boundary, threatened indeed to hold up any advance towards Glatz Redoubt. The majority of the five hundred casualties sustained by the 18/King's during the day were incurred at this time. The 2/Green Howards, which were in support, suffered two hundred casualties from machine-gun fire in No Man's Land, and only a small number managed to cross it.[20] Two small parties which had followed the leading battalions as "moppers-up" were at once sent along the trenches to the left to deal with enemy bombers who, emerging from dug-outs, had begun to push eastwards.

After some delay, these opponents were killed or scattered, mainly through the exertions of one officer who out-threw the Germans. This cleared the way for a party of the 18/King's who ran up Train Alley, killed the defenders holding the line of the hedge, and took prisoner an officer and thirty men, the others retiring towards Montauban. The Germans in the Warren, however, still held out in front of the 18th Division.

The 21st Brigade, relieved by the action of the 18/King's, advanced without further incident to Glatz Redoubt, which was reached at 08.35 hours and made junction with the 89th Brigade. The 30th Division, thanks mainly to the artillery preparation and covering fire, had thus attained its first objective in little over an hour.[21]

Capture of part of its first objective (Pommiers Redoubt) by the 18th Division

Major General Maxse attacked with his three brigades in line,[22] from right to left, the 55th (Brigadier-General Sir T.D. Jackson), the 53rd (Brigadier-General H.W. Higginson) and the 54th (Brigadier-General T.H. Shoubridge).[23] Having been in the area since March, the units knew it well. There had been mine fighting in May on the Carnoy front, resulting in a mass of small craters which covered a width of about a hundred and fifty yards in No Man's Land close to the Carnoy – Montauban road. The Germans here had withdrawn from the front line after filling it with barbed wire and spiked stakes, and held the support line, but they continued to occupy some of the craters, in which they had built dug-outs, with a few machine guns and snipers. The 55th and 53rd Brigades were to pass on either side of the crater zone, which was to be cleared and occupied by a party from the 55th Brigade, assisted by a large flame projector.[24]

At 07.27 hours two mines (one of 5,000lbs and the other of 500lbs), laid by the 183rd Tunnelling Company Royal Engineers, were fired with success under the enemy's parapet, at the salient Casino Point and at the western end of the enemy front to be attacked, in order to destroy flanking machine guns and blow in dug-outs. Taking advantage of the explosions – the debris from the larger mine caused a few casualties in the 6/Berkshire – the leading lines of the three brigades started forward from old trenches cleaned out for the purpose and from taped positions.[25]

Under cover of the barrage and machine-gun fire, the parapet was crossed into No Man's Land, which was only about 200 yards wide. The bombardment of the crater area had not, however, destroyed its garrison,[26] and, although the flame projector on the western side of it successfully stifled resistance there, the eastern side was not affected, and the clearing party (a company of the 7/Buffs less two platoons) was unable to force an entry.

A German machine-gun firing eastwards along No Man's Land from the craters, and some others just east of the crater area, were therefore able to rake the line of the 7/Queen's, on the left of the 55th Brigade,[27] causing it, and the following troops of the 7/Royal West Kent, heavy casualties. The confusion and delay which ensued gave the Germans time to man the support trench – held as the front trench – and the trenches and strong points behind seemed to be already garrisoned. When therefore the barrage lifted and the advance was continued, there were over three hundred Germans ready in position, and their rifle fire for a long time was very heavy. The barrage had gone on to the next line and all advantage of it was lost, but, fortunately, the enemy's artillery fire was slight, chiefly shrapnel bursting high.

The check to the 7/Queen's delayed the advance of the 8/East Surrey on the right, and at 08.37 hours, although this battalion had crossed the enemy front line, it had been unable to get beyond the support line, being held in front by the enemy in the Warren, and enfiladed from the left. It was not until half-an-hour later, when the establishment of the 30th Division in Glatz Redoubt and Train Alley, together with the advance of the 90th Brigade, threatened the line of retreat of these Germans, that the defence began to weaken, a number of men retiring by the communication trenches to and through Montauban. The 8/East Surrey, supported by two companies of the 7/Buffs, was then able to get bombing parties forward into the enemy trench just short of its objective, Train Alley, but by this time its three leading companies had lost all their officers but one, and it was difficult to organize a further advance. The 7/Queen's, on the left, was still held up in front of Breslau Support Trench.

The 53rd Brigade,[28] west of the Carnoy road, with the 8/Norfolk on the right and the 6/Berkshire on the left, was able to get forward more easily. This was due to the effect on its right of the flame projector, which cleared resistance off the western edge of the Carnoy craters, and on its left, of the mine under Casino Point, which destroyed the flanking arrangements, blowing one machine gun into the air. The moral effect, too, of this mine was considerable; for a number of Germans ran out into No Man's Land and surrendered to the Berkshire.

The wire having been almost completely cut, the battalions crossed the enemy front and support lines, meeting little opposition, except on the right, where first

Germans in "The Castle", a small work behind the support line, and then a party holding out in Back Trench, behind Breslau Support Trench opposite the 55th Brigade, delayed the right of the Norfolks. The Castle was quickly brought to surrender, but Back Trench continued to resist stoutly. This, however, did not affect the left of the Norfolks and the Berkshire, which proceeded to attack the next objective, Pommiers Trench, the German intermediate line, which lay on the high ground of Montauban ridge.

In spite of the enfilade fire of XV Corps which had assisted the barrage, three German machine-guns opened from this trench, and the advancing lines were checked until a bombing party working up Popoff Lane, a communication trench, succeeded in surprising one of the gun crews and rushing it. The crew of the other two guns, taken in flank, did not show further fight, and retired with their guns along a communication trench towards Pommiers Redoubt.

The lines then moved on again, and at 07.50 hours, Pommiers Trench was occupied without further incident. The consolidation of this trench, facing north, was at once taken in hand. "The Loop", a strongpoint at the eastern end of the trench, had still to be captured, fire from it causing heavy losses (the greater part of the day's casualties of the 6/Berkshire, twelve officers and 339 other ranks, were incurred at this period), and a company of the 10/Essex was sent to reinforce. Bombing squads with Lewis guns were sent towards the Loop, but found the trench blocked. A strong party with a Stokes gun was sent up Pommiers Lane towards Pommiers Redoubt, 400 yards ahead, but here, too, the trench was found blocked by a mass of barbed wire, and it was clear that the redoubt would not be easy to take.

Meantime the 54th Brigade, the left of the 18th Division, attacking up the southern face of Mametz spur between the craters formed by the two mines which had been fired, with the 7/Bedfordshire and 11/Royal Fusiliers leading, had crossed both the German front and support lines with little loss. Moving as if at manoeuvres, they continued on, until a single machine-gun in "The Triangle", a strongpoint in the third trench, swept the two leading companies of the Bedfordshire and caused heavy losses before it could be rushed.

The advance of the Royal Fusiliers over the top of the Mametz spur was so rapid that a halt had to be made in front of Pommiers Trench as the artillery had not yet ceased firing on it. At 07.50 hours, on the lift of the guns, this trench, the first objective, was at once assaulted and entered almost simultaneously with the left of the 53rd Brigade, which had been much assisted by two of the brigade machine-guns.

During this advance, bombing parties of the 11/Royal Fusiliers, told off beforehand, moving ahead of the line, did splendid work in overcoming the resistance and clearing the dug-outs in Black Alley, a communication trench leading back to Pommiers Trench. Their instructions were to stay in the alley until every German in it was dead, and they did not very long delay there.

Preparations were at once begun by the 53rd and 54th Brigades for the further advance across the top of the ridge against Pommiers Redoubt, Maple Trench and Beetle Alley, the next objectives.

At 08.28 hours, therefore, when the artillery was due to lift to the second objective, the situation of the 18th Division was that the extreme right had nearly, and the left had completely, reached their first objective, but, in the centre, the 7/Queen's and the right of the 8/Norfolk were held up by the enemy in Breslau Support Trench and in the maze of trenches behind it. Meanwhile the left of the Norfolks, owing to the resistance in the Loop, where the 6/Berkshire was still engaged, could not move eastwards to help them.

The advance against Pommiers Redoubt[29] was carried out at 08.30 hours, by the 10/Essex (53rd Brigade) and the 7/Bedfordshire and 11/Royal Fusiliers (54th Brigade). With a good field of fire over the flat top of Montauban spur, and with its wire entanglements only imperfectly destroyed, the redoubt made a stout defence. Immediately the bombardment lifted from the second objective, the creeping barrage"by increments"was fired, and the attack developed, the leading lines encountering heavy machine-gun and rifle fire. Several times men reached the wire, but all frontal attempts to penetrate further broke down. Parties were therefore sent to try to approach the redoubt from the flanks.

A detachment of the Royal Fusiliers with Lewis guns was despatched along a communication trench to attack from the west, and succeeded in entering Maple Trench. From here it was able to enfilade the southern face of the redoubt, and put out of action the Germans who were lining it, head and shoulders above the parapet, firing on the infantry lying out in front. Before the enemy had recovered from this surprise, the bulk of the Royal Fusiliers and the leading men of the Bedfordshire, who had worked round the eastern flank of the redoubt, rushed through the gaps in the wire. With the assistance of the companies left in front of the work, and after hand-to-hand fighting in which quarter was neither asked nor given, the remainder of the garrison was killed or taken prisoner. Maple Trench was also secured.

The fight for the redoubt lasted an hour. The casualties incurred were heavy, units were considerably intermingled, and the barrage was well ahead, but, in spite of this and although the troops on either flank – the left of the 53rd Brigade on the right and the 91st (of the 7th Division) on the left – had not reached the level of the redoubt, the Bedfordshire and Royal Fusiliers, reinforced by the 6/Northamptonshire, pressed on to Beetle Alley, beyond which the barrage was now falling.

This trench was entered at 10.15 hours, any resistance being overcome by bombing parties. Attempts to push eastwards along it and along Montauban Alley were, however, strongly resisted; the fight became a bombing contest, but, the German trenches being well blocked, for some time no further progress was made by the centre and left brigades of the 18th Division, whilst on the right movement was only just recommencing.

Capture of its second objective (Montauban) and La Briqueterie by the 30th Division

The occupation of the Dublin Trench – Glatz Redoubt – Train Alley line, the whole of the first objective of the 30th Division, by the 89th and 21st Brigades, had prepared the way for the advance, through the 21st, on Montauban of the 90th Brigade (Brigadier-General C.J. Steavenson). This brigade had been in readiness in the assembly trenches in the deep valley about Cambridge Copse, west of Maricourt, since 02.30 hours.

At 08.30 hours, one hour after zero, as previously arranged, its two leading battalions, the 16/Manchester and 17/Manchester, moved forward in lines of companies, each company in line of half-platoons in file, followed by the 2/Royal Scots Fusiliers in close support, Lieutenant Colonel R.K. Walsh of this battalion being in command of the attack.

The advance along the east side of Talus Boisé was sheltered, being in Railway Valley, while forward of this a smoke candle barrage was formed by the battalions of the 89th and 21st Brigades in Dublin Trench. The Germans put down a light barrage directly the movement began, but it did little damage, owing to the formation adopted and because the ground, in addition to being soft, was ploughed and pulverized by previous shelling; Lieutenant Colonel H.A. Johnson of the 17/Manchesters was wounded.

The advance of the Manchesters was carried out with remarkable steadiness and enthusiasm, in spite of the fact that severe casualties were soon inflicted on the brigade by a German machine-gun which held out in a position behind the old German front line trench, about the point where it was joined by Breslau Alley. This machine-gun had taken toll of the advance of the 18th Division and had then swung round on to the 90th Brigade, which, however, continued its advance undeterred.

Train Alley and the 21st Brigade line was reached fifteen minutes before scheduled time and before the barrage, with its final intensive five minutes, was timed to lift. A halt had therefore to be made, the front lines waiting in Train Alley, the remainder of the brigade lying down in the open.

It was not till this moment that it was possible to locate the German machine-gun, firing in enfilade on the left flank, which was entirely left open. It was then destroyed by a Lewis gun of the 16/Manchesters, its gallant crew standing to their posts to the end. There was a question at corps headquarters as to whether the advance should be stopped until the 55th Brigade (18th Division) on the left, most of which was still held up, had won all of its first objective. But, in the expectation that an advance on Montauban would do much to weaken the opposition being offered to the right and centre of the 18th Division, the 90th Brigade was allowed to proceed.

The enforced wait lengthened. All the commanders of the leading companies of the 16/ and 17/Manchesters had been killed or severely wounded, but there was little delay when at last the artillery lifted. A sudden burst from a solitary machine-gun in Montauban decided the situation and the front wave sprang forward and swept up the slope to the village followed by the rest of the brigade.

Owing to the heavy casualties, companies had become intermingled and they presented from the rear the appearance of two dense lines of men four hundred yards apart. Fortunately arrangements had been made by the 30th Division to screen the advance forward of Glatz Redoubt by a smoke barrage launched by two sections of the 4th Mortar Company of No.5 Battalion Special Brigade Royal Engineers (twelve 4-inch Stokes mortars), which had been sent to the redoubt for the purpose.[30] Although the trench outside the southern edge of Montauban was well-sited, the Germans made no effort to defend it, and the village was entered by the Manchesters and Scots Fusiliers at 10.05 hours without opposition.

It was deserted – except for a fox – and a scene of complete devastation, although, the houses having been small, the alignment of the main streets was quite plain.[31] The front line pressed on through the ruins, with the second line hurrying up close behind from the determination of the men to be in at the finish. By 11.00 hours, as the last of the smoke cloud dispersed, the part of Montauban Alley beyond the northernmost houses, the second and last objective, was entered. The Germans still there, some hundred in all, mostly surrendered without a fight.

Across Caterpillar Valley beyond could be seen several hundreds more streaming northwards along the Bazentin le Grand road, and the forward artillery observing officers, who had been provided with lettered panorama sketches to enable them to direct fire on enemy concentrations, at once got the British guns turned on to these fugitives. The last to leave were the German field artillerymen, driven from their guns in Caterpillar Valley by men of the 16/Manchesters, who rushed the batteries and captured and brought back the first three guns taken in the Somme battle. The others had to be left and some of them were removed by the Germans during the night.[32]

The consolidation of the northern side of Montauban was at once taken in hand, and strong points as previously arranged constructed by the 201st Field Company Royal Engineers and the 2/Royal Scots Fusiliers. A hot meal for the troops was brought up by carriers from the cookers, which had been pushed forward to the old British line in Maricourt. From 13.45 hours onwards, however, work in Montauban itself was carried on with difficulty and considerable loss, the 201st Field Company Royal Engineers, the whole of which had been now sent to the 90th Brigade, having many casualties, for the enemy began an accurate and methodical bombardment of the village from the north and east, which continued throughout the afternoon.

With the fall of Montauban, the way to the capture of La Briqueterie, with the important German observation post in its chimney stack, was clear.

At 11.30 hours orders had been issued from divisional headquarters for the heavy artillery to open on it, and to lift at 12.30 hours, at which time the attack was to be delivered by No.4 Company of the 20/King's. This enterprise was entirely successful.

The company moved forward northwards in open order from Dublin Trench under cover of the bombardment to within close range of the buildings, whilst simultaneously a bombing party which had moved up Nord Alley, a communication trench leading from Glatz Redoubt, advanced eastward to cut off the retreat of the garrison. At 12.34 hours the buildings, which had suffered severely in the bombardment, were rushed, and many German dead were found, but no opposition was encountered until the far side was reached. There a machine-gun was being hurriedly brought into action from a dug-out, and a few casualties occurred before resistance was overcome. A number of officers and men in the deep dug-out nearby, surrendered.[33] Two machine-guns and a quantity of documents, orders and material were taken.

Thanks to very efficient artillery support and careful rehearsals, the 30th Division had most successfully and expeditiously accomplished the first phase of its task, reaching and holding its second objective. It had cleared the Germans off a frontage of 1,500 yards to a depth of 2,000 yards, captured twelve officers and 489 other ranks, and three field guns, and established a firm footing soon after midday on the Montauban ridge overlooking Caterpillar Valley – although, as the 18th Division was not yet up, its left was exposed.

The French XX Corps on the right, there being eight hours more of daylight, was prepared to go on;[34] the men of the 30th Division were not tired, nor had the losses been heavy, and XIII Corps' reserve, the 9th Division, was available, besides higher reserves. However, failure on other parts of the British battle line led to Major General Shea being ordered to delay the initiation of the further phases of the battle of the 30th Division: the advance through Bernafay and Trônes Wood to Guillemont. He was, however, instructed to give a helping hand to the 18th Division.

Patrols were sent out, including some into Bernafay Wood which was found empty except for a few men who were taken prisoners,[35] but no other steps were taken to keep touch with the enemy; for the day's programme of advance had been carried out, and it had been impressed upon all at rehearsals that the enemy would counter-attack to recover Montauban as surely as night follows day.

The energies of the troops were therefore devoted to consolidation, which proved no easy matter, as the chalky ground was so broken and cracked by shell fire that sandbags had to be built up to obtain cover. Strong points in the area between Montauban and Dublin Trench – Train Alley were built by the battalions and engineers in support. Four communication trenches were dug across No Man's Land by the 11/South Lancashire (Pioneers), and by 18.00 hours the road from Maricourt towards Montauban was repaired by the engineers to a point two hundred yards beyond the old German front line.

XIII CORPS

Capture of the whole of its objectives by the 18th Division

By the original time-table, the objective of the 18th Division, the northern face of the Montauban ridge, should have been reached by 10.00 hours; although the left of the division had got there by that hour, the right was still short of Train Alley, while the centre – the inner wings of the 55th and 53rd Brigades – was still near the German old front trench. It was not till 09.30 hours that the clearing party of the 7/Buffs was able to overcome the unexpectedly strenuous opposition in the Carnoy crater area, which had proved a regular warren of Germans.

The enemy in Breslau Support Trench and the Loop continued, however, to hold on. The urgent need of pressing forward the advance was fully realized by Brigadier-General Jackson (55th Brigade); for the attack on Montauban, just related, of the 90th Brigade, on the right, was due to cross the line of Glatz Redoubt by 10.00 hours, and furthermore the barrage might be lost, for it was impossible to get in touch with the artillery and change the times of the lifts. At 09.45 hours therefore he ordered the 7/Royal West Kent, which he supposed to be in the British old front trench, to reinforce and carry forward the attack to the Pommiers line, but the officer commanding, having heard that the 8/East Surrey was held up, had already ordered his companies forward.

Continuous machine-gun and rifle fire from the direction of the Loop interfered greatly with getting this movement under way. The runners sent to the two left companies were wounded, and there was a delay until the adjutant himself got through with the message. Meanwhile the two right companies, under cover of the Carnoy spur, managed to reach the East Surrey, who were close up to Train Alley. The two left companies of the West Kent now came up and both battalions eventually reached the Montauban road about noon. Their presence was signalled to a contact aeroplane which soon afterwards flew low over the ridge blowing a Klaxon horn.

The progress of this advance, together with the occupation of Montauban by the 30th Division, and Pommiers Redoubt by the 53rd and 54th Brigades, had an unsettling effect on the Germans holding out about Breslau Support Trench and the Loop for it seriously threatened their line of retreat. Many, following the earlier example of those in the Warren, began to leave the position, and shortly after 10.00 hours, the 7/Queen's, sending forward parties along the communication trenches, was able, although only about ten grenades were available, to rush and clear it.

The Queen's captured ninety men of the 62nd and 109th Regiments, and entered the western end of Train Alley, held by part of the East Surrey.[36] Whilst the eastern flank of the German resistance was being dealt with, the 8/Norfolk, the right battalion of the 53rd Brigade, was overcoming it on the other side, and at 10.20 hours – after a sniper who had caused many deaths had been shot by a company sergeant-major of the 6/Royal Berkshire in single combat – some sixty Germans holding the Loop surrendered to this battalion.[37]

There then remained only the enemy hanging on in a strongpoint in Back Trench,[38] near where Breslau Alley crossed it. This was at once approached by bombing attacks from three sides, but it was not until about 14.00 hours that the garrison stood up on the parapet and surrendered; it included two officers and 150 other ranks, chiefly Bavarians.[39] Back Trench was then occupied by the 7/Queen's and the 8/Norfolk, both of which battalions had suffered heavily.[40]

The Queen's, now numbering little more than a hundred all told, reinforced by a company of the 7/Buffs, moved on without further incident to the Montauban – Mametz road, where, about 15.00 hours, it joined up with the 8/East Surrey, 7/Royal West Kent and other Buffs on the right. Stokes mortars were brought into action against a party of Germans in front of Montauban Alley, and, under cover of this fire, this further sector of the alley was occupied by 17.15 hours without difficulty, the Germans retiring to Caterpillar Wood. Thus the right half of the second objective of the 18th Division was secured.

Meantime the rest of the alley had been captured, and the assistance which XIII Corps directed the 30th Division to give the 18th was found unnecessary. Working from Pommiers Redoubt, a bombing party of the 10/Essex cleared 400 yards of it as far as White Trench, reached by 15.30 hours. Here, at 17.40 hours, it met parties of the 6/Royal Berkshire and 8/Norfolk, which had made their way up Loop Trench from the Loop with considerable difficulty, owing to the presence of a number of snipers with automatic rifles, who prevented any movement above ground near the trench. The Norfolks and Berkshire then took over the sector of Montauban Alley between the 7/Queen's (55th Brigade) and the 54th Brigade, and the whole alley, the second objective of the 18th Division, was in British possession.

The Norfolks now sent parties forward along Caterpillar Trench, double-blocking it in front of Caterpillar Wood, to which it led, without meeting any enemy. Both Norfolks and Berkshire established advanced parties in the third objective, the advanced line overlooking Caterpillar Wood, the right in touch with the 55th Brigade west of Montauban. On the front of the 54th Brigade, the 7/Bedfordshire and 11/Royal Fusiliers had worked forward to White Trench, their third objective, along the northern face of Montauban ridge, parties of both battalions occupying it at 16.00 hours.[41]

Strong points were sited in and behind the third objective, and constructed during the night. The supporting battalions of all three brigades set to work consolidating the front line and positions in rear and repairing the old German trenches; the 2/Wiltshire (21st Brigade) was sent for the same purpose to Montauban. Six field batteries were pushed up abreast of Carnoy, and single guns told to enfilade certain lines. Towards 22.00 hours two battalions (12/Royal Scots and 6/King's Own Scottish Borderers) of the 9th Division were placed by the corps at the disposal of the 18th Division for carrying and digging.

XIII CORPS

As a result of the successes of the 30th and 18th Divisions, XIII Corps had driven the Germans from the entire sector of the Montauban ridge allotted to it as the objective in the first phase of the battle. The corps attributed the successes of its divisions to their training in open warfare; to thorough "mopping up", so that no Germans sprang up behind the lines to shoot the attackers in the back; and to the preliminary ascertainment, by feints, of where the German barrages would fall, and rapid movement of the troops over the belts of ground involved. The losses, in spite of the comparatively easy advance, had been over 6,000.[42]

The late afternoon was extraordinarily quiet: the bombardment of Montauban ceased and only a single German 5.9-inch gun shelled Montauban Alley at extreme range slowly and inaccurately. From the air some infantry was seen advancing between Trônes and Bernafay Woods.[43] There was no difficulty in getting up supplies or removing wounded. The Germans being fully occupied by the attacking troops, the clearance of the wounded, indeed, had been begun soon after the first advance, and was carried on steadily all day across the open, motor ambulances coming up as far as Carnoy. All wounded were evacuated within twenty-four hours.

Once Montauban had been reached, the long slope between it and the old front line was dotted with groups of carrying parties, and of engineers repairing the roads and the light railway, which was made available for pushing trucks by hand. Even the field batteries trotted forward without molestation.

In the evening light the outposts of XIII Corps, looking across Caterpillar Valley to the broad southern slopes of the Ginchy – Pozières plateau, could see the villages of Longueval, with Delville Wood on its eastern side, Bazentin le Grand and Contalmaison, half hidden and separated by the Bazentin and Mametz Woods, and, further behind, High Wood. The names of these localities, when discovered from the map, meant nothing to the watching groups, though all were soon to become for ever memorable in the annals of the British Army.

As the light failed, all fighting ceased; even the British guns which had been shelling fugitives were silent. Activity behind the front line, however, increased and intensified: the machinery by which food, water[44] and ammunition reached the troops was soon in full swing, and aided by reinforcements; the work on defences and improvement of communications was redoubled.

An attempt made at 21.30 hours by a small party of Germans to approach Montauban from a quarry in Caterpillar Valley north of it was driven off by fire,[45] and night fell with XIII Corps in solid occupation of its conquests.

The complete success of the French on 1 July

The French Sixth Army (General Fayolle), astride the Somme, on the British right, in the Group of Armies of General Foch, obtained all its objectives and more on 1

July. North of the Somme, alongside the British XIII Corps, was XX Corps (General Balfourier);[46] next to it, across the river, were the I Colonial Corps (General Berdoulat)[47] and the XXXV Corps (General Jacquot).[48] The French II Corps (General Duchene)[49] was in reserve.

XX Corps, with two divisions in the front line, made the assault at the same time as the British – 07.30 hours. Favoured by a river mist which allowed the French to reach the front trenches unseen, the 39th Division (General Nourrisson) on the left, like the British 30th Division next to it, attained its objectives without any difficulty, although, according to German accounts, there was severe hand-to-hand fighting in Bois Favière, the north-eastern corner of which remained in German hands for some days. The situation at midday was so satisfactory that General Nourrisson, as already mentioned, proposed to attack Hardecourt, opposite his front, but, as the British XIII Corps was not proceeding to the second phase of its programme, he abandoned the idea. Four counter-attacks from Hardecourt were repulsed by fire.

The 11th Division (General Vuillemot) had a stiffer task; in the first rush, however, it was right over the German first position, including the great Y Wood salient, but it failed to break into Curlu on the extreme right, and therefore formed a flank there. The village was captured by a second effort in the evening. "At the end of the day the XX Corps was in occupation of the entire German first position; it had suffered very few losses, and had not employed any reserves, not even partially."

The French corps south of the Somme, whose heavy artillery was in overwhelming preponderance – eighty-five batteries against eight – did not assault until 09.30 hours, two hours after the British and XX Corps, and this postponement enabled them to take the Germans by surprise. On the left flank the village of Frise, captured from the French in January, held out – it was protected on one side by the Somme – but the I Colonial Corps carried the German first position including the large villages of Dompierre and Becquincourt.

By midday was installed in its first objective, and General Berdoulat commenced preparations for the attack on the second, pushing his advance towards Herbecourt and Assevillers, so that by nightfall the corps was entrenched within assaulting distance of the German second position. XXXV Corps was equally successful, although, being on the flank, it suffered considerably from fire from the unattacked German sector further south. "Thus by the evening of 1 July the Sixth Army had reached all its objectives, it had gone beyond them at certain points, and engaged the German second position. It had taken more than 4,000 prisoners, of whom 2,000 were the share of the Colonial Corps."

The Germans opposite XIII Corps and the French XX Corps on 1 July 1916

In consequence of the heavy losses in officers suffered by the Germans, the account of the fighting opposite XIII Corps and French XX Corps given in the German official monograph is somewhat meagre. There is, for instance, no mention of the British mines or flame projectors. Owing to all labour being required to keep the first position in some sort of defensible condition, the second position of the 12th Division consisted only of a single shallow trench. The third position had been barely commenced.

The artillery of both the 12th and 28th Reserve Divisions suffered greatly in the preliminary bombardment, and more seriously still on 1 July. According to one reliable history, the German batteries in the valleys north of Mametz and Montauban were destroyed with the greater part of their ammunition, and very few guns could be withdrawn to the second position.

The official monograph goes into some details:"One battery in the 12th Division had lost a gun on 30 June. Gradually the other three were put out of action." Another"lost two guns before midday. The other two followed in the afternoon." In a third battery, two were lost, and in a fourth,"all the howitzers became gradually unserviceable. The greater part of the other batteries of the Group had considerable losses. Their fighting power fell off more and more." In the 28th Reserve Division "the batteries had suffered severely in the artillery battle, and could give little assistance. A great number of the guns were smashed up ... Particularly the batteries in the Caterpillar Valley had lost numerous guns. When the British attacked there were only ten field and thirteen heavy batteries in readiness, and these had numerous unserviceable guns."All the field guns of the 28th Reserve Division were "rendered unserviceable by British fire or other causes."The British artillery fire on 1 July in this part of the field is described as"devastating".

By midday on 1 July 1916, four of the heavy batteries on XIII Corps'front were completely unserviceable, and later another is mentioned as sharing the same fate.

Opposite the 30th Division, most of the garrison and nearly all the machine-guns had been put out of action by gun fire, and the rear defences could not be manned in time owing to the rapid British advance.

Opposite the left of the 18th Division, in the sector of the 109th Regiment, there were no deep dug-outs except in the front trench; the whole garrison congregated in these, and there was no defence in depth. Opposite the right, where the previous mine explosions had forced the garrison to defend the support trench, new dug-outs had been made.

Opposite the French XX Corps"nearly all the deep dug-outs in the first position were blown in, only a few specially deep ones were still partly serviceable. The garrison lay mainly in shell and mine craters."Under protection of a thick morning mist, the French overran the whole front line.

SLAUGHTER ON THE SOMME: 1 JULY 1916

As usual in the case of disaster, the information that came back was "inexact", and the greatest confusion seems to have arisen on the German side. The British were reported before midday to have occupied Bernafay and Trônes Woods – as they might have done – and "the situation was uncertain".

In view of the small reserves and great loss of artillery, counter-attacks appeared useless; in fact there were few troops at hand to oppose a further advance of XIII Corps if boldly pushed, and orders to collect all available men, including clerks, cooks, batmen, etc., and 200 recruits, to occupy the second position were issued.[50] The 12th Reserve Division, in rest in the Cambrai area, which already had some troops in the third position, had, at 13.35 hours, been ordered by XIV Reserve Corps to Rancourt – Bouchavesnes (about six to seven miles east of Montauban). Various detachments were hurried up to weak places, and about 13.30 hours the division was directed to be prepared to attack the ridge between Montauban and Mametz at dark. At 21.00 hours this was postponed to 23.30 hours, but at midnight the leading regiments detailed had only just reached the second position.

NOTES

1. XIII Corps (Lieutenant General W.N. Congreve) comprised: 30th Division (Major General J.S.M. Shea), 21st, 89th and 90th Brigades; 18th Division (Major General P.I. Maxse), 53rd, 54th and 55th Brigades; 9th Division (Major General W.T. Furse), 26th, 27th and South African Brigades; G.O.C. Royal Artillery, Brigadier-General R.St. C. Lecky; G.O.C. Heavy Artillery, Brigadier-General L.W.P. East; and Chief Engineer, Brigadier-General E.P. Brooker.

2. The 6th Bavarian Reserve Regiment (10th Bavarian Division) held from the Somme to the Montauban – Carnoy road, with the 63rd (opposite the French) and 62nd Regiments (12th Division) in support, and the 109th Reserve Regiment (28th Reserve Division) from that road to Mametz (inclusive). Attempts had been made on the night of 30 June/1July to relieve the 109th by the 23rd Regiment (12th Division), but, on account of heavy fire, only 1½ companies had got up to the line, the others remaining at Montauban. The history (published 1931) of the 16th Bavarian Regiment (10th Bavarian Division), pp.156-160, shows two companies in the second position, at Longueval and Bazentin le Grand, and the whole of the 6th Bavarian Reserve Regiment in the front position. The rest of the regiment was near Bapaume under orders to relieve the 99th Reserve Regiment, shattered by the bombardment, in the Ovillers – Thiepval position. The third infantry regiment (9th Bavarian Reserve) of the division was in the Thiepval – St. Pierre Divion sector. The division, which had been resting since May, had been sent up to the Bapaume area on 12 June.

3. The official history states that this was apparently the first use of the word "creep" in this connection.

4. This part of the operation was of the nature of a creeping barrage in that it was formed by a succession of short lifts, but by request of the infantry brigadiers the lifts were made on to previously registered points in the enemy's trench system. Thus the advance of the barrage was not continuous: it was dropped in turn on every piece of trench blocking the way, each battery keeping to its own "lane".

5. The quarries in the valley between these woods were full of French batteries.

6. Defined in one War Diary as "50 yards every 1½ minutes".

7. In return, XIII Corps permitted XV Corps to put an 8-inch battery in its area in the Carnoy valley.

8. This barrage had been accurately registered with air observation during the bombardment. It was called for by a special visual (blue lamp) signal, and was put down in thirty seconds. The infantry was specially informed of this, and it gave the men great confidence.

9. This consisted of the 29th, 31st and 33rd Heavy Artillery Groups, and four French batteries of mortars: Howitzers were two 12-inch, eight 9.2-inch, four 8-inch, and twenty-four 6-inch; the guns were two

6-inch, sixteen 60-pounders, and four 4.7-inch; and mortars were sixteen 240-mm. This gave one heavy gun or howitzer for every forty-seven yards, with a field gun or howitzer to every seventeen yards of front.

10. The French XX Corps had thirty-two heavy batteries, including some very ancient and noisy mortars, the British XIII Corps eighteen; the German 12th Division had ten, to which must be added a third of those of the 28th Reserve Division, which had thirteen.

11. One account describes the "devastating effect" of the British and French fire on the German batteries.

12. The ground being hard chalk, the tunnellers were forced to work with push-picks to avoid being heard; when close to the enemy progress was continued by boring holes in the face with carpenters' augers. Vinegar was poured into the holes and, thus softened, the chalk surrounding each hole was then scraped out. One auger actually penetrated into a German officers' dug-out unnoticed by the enemy.

13. The 30th Division, formed in November 1914, under Major General W. Fry, was recruited in Lancashire (largely Liverpool and Manchester) by Lord Derby, two of whose brothers served in it, commanding an infantry and an artillery brigade respectively. It embarked for France in November 1915, Major General Shea taking command in May 1916. The infantry brigades were originally the 89th, 90th and 91st, but the last was exchanged after arrival in France for the 21st Brigade (7th Division), two battalions of which were then exchanged, one with the 89th and the other with the 90th Brigade. Except these battalions, the units of the division had not taken part in any previous battle, although the 90th Brigade had suffered considerably from shelling during the action in which the French lost Frise on 28 January 1916. The 149th Brigade Royal Field Artillery had been in action on the same occasion, and had sunk row-boats carrying Germans across the Somme.

14. Space does not admit of the mention of every trench-mortar battery and machine-gun company; they all had their specific tasks and places, and generally were to cover the advance to the first trench, then lift, and, later, go forward.

15. An accident in one of the emplacements, due, it is believed, to a shell striking the embrasure as it left the mortar, exploded hundreds of rounds stacked behind the sap.

16. Mainly by the medium trench mortars, it was said.

17. A heavy shell had penetrated a deep dug-out in this redoubt, killed a regimental staff and apparently scattered its defenders.

18. The total losses of the two leading battalions of the 89th Brigade, reported at noon, were: 17/King's, three officers and 100 other ranks; 20/King's, three officers and forty-nine other ranks.

19. Later to be Major General Lord Sackville.

20. The 2nd Battalion Wiltshire Regiment, employed mainly as carriers, lost just under a hundred men.

21. The captured diary of Lieutenant Colonel Bedall, commanding the 16th Bavarian Regiment, states: "The troops who had so far held the lines south of Mametz and south of Montauban had sustained severe losses from intense enemy bombardment, which had been maintained for many days without a pause, and for the most part were already shot to pieces."

22. The 18th (Eastern) Division was formed in October 1914 from the "Second Hundred Thousand", mostly from men of the home counties and East Anglia, with one Northamptonshire battalion. It trained near Colchester and arrived in France on 24/25 July 1915. It had not taken part in any previous battle.

23. The 8th Battalion Royal Sussex Regiment (Pioneers) and the Field Companies Royal Engineers were divided amongst the brigades.

24. This flame projector was under the direction of Major W.H. Livens, Royal Engineers, subsequently the inventor of the Livens projector. The range of the flame was limited by its being in a fixed emplacement at the end of a Russian sap.

25. It was considered that freshly dug assembly trenches would probably give the enemy warning of the assault.

26. A proposed bombardment of the area by heavy howitzers on the previous day was abandoned because it involved withdrawing the troops in the front line during its execution. According to German accounts, the area was held by portions of the 109th Reserve and 23rd Regiments, but most of the

prisoners eventually taken belonged to the 6th Bavarian Reserve Regiment, who said they had only arrived during the night, so possibly the original garrison was destroyed.

27. Front line 8/East Surrey and 7/Queen's; in support 7/Royal West Kent and 7/Buffs. The last-named battalion was much divided during the attack to reinforce the others.

28. Comprised the 8/Norfolk and 6/Royal Berkshire in front line; 10/Essex Regiment and 8/Suffolk in support and reserve, and providing carrying parties.

29. It was the headquarters of a battalion of the 109th Regiment, and had a garrison of a whole company.

30. German diaries state that the smoke cloud at this time was so thick in Montauban and Caterpillar Valley that one could only see two or three yards ahead.

31. One of the French 240mm mortar batteries had fired on Montauban for the whole seven days of the bombardment. The German dug-outs in the village were very deep, but one shell had entered the artillery command dug-out and killed the occupants. This no doubt disorganized the control of fire. Maps of the enemy communications and "reconnoitred battery positions" were found by the British troops. One dug-out was full of dead whom there had been no opportunity for a week to bury.

32. The 54th Brigade brought in two undamaged guns from south of Mametz Wood on the night of 2/3 July. The records of the German Field Artillery Regiment No.21 state: "The infantry had retired behind the battery positions of 4/21 and 4/29. Colonel Pietsch thereupon gave the order to evacuate the position. In their retirement the men came under a heavy fire both from machine-guns in Montauban and from airmen, who came down to within 150 feet … The loss of the guns, however, gave the men no peace, and all volunteered for the dangerous task of recovering them. The same evening the battery leader of 4/21 and nine men went forward with three of the limbers through the front line of infantry to the old battery position. Three of the guns were limbered up under fire and brought back successfully to Longueval, although the battery leader was killed during the action." According to the Bavarian Official Account, four more of these guns, undamaged, were recovered from between the opposing lines by No.4 Company 16th Bavarian Reserve Regiment on the night 3/4 July.

33. Including the headquarters (colonel and adjutant) of the 62nd Regiment and two artillery officers (commander and observer) of No.2 Group Field Artillery Regiment No.21.

34. On the following days, when the British wished to go on, it did not suit the French to do so.

35. At 15.00 hours German artillery observers found there was no infantry in Bernafay Wood. About the same time, however, pilots from the Royal Flying Corps reported that enemy infantry was moving from Trônes to Bernafay Wood.

36. One German machine-gunner, a "grey-headed, elderly man, with a pile of empty cartridge cases nearly as high as the gun, was found dead, still holding on to its handle".

37. A wounded Bavarian who had chained himself to his machine-gun was found.

38. Located midway between Breslau Trench and Train Alley.

39. Of the 6th Bavarian Reserve Regiment. The diary of this regiment contains the following entry: "1st July – Regimental staff moves from Ginchy to Bois de Bernafay, 1km east of Montauban, to battle headquarters. 2nd July – nothing known of the regiment." The Bavarian Official Account states: "Placed at the disposal of the 12th Division, the 6th Bavarian Reserve Regiment on the night of 29/30 June was spread out over the whole of the divisional sector, and sent forward as working parties into the front trenches. During the attack of the French and English on the morning of 1 July, the regiment was practically wiped out, losing 35 officers and 1,775 men."

40. The casualties suffered by these two battalions were: 7/Queen's, fifteen officers and 463 other ranks; 8/Norfolks, eleven officers and 292 other ranks.

41. The casualties suffered by these two battalions were: 7/Bedfordshire, fifteen officers and 306 other ranks; 11/Royal Fusiliers, five officers and 222 other ranks.

42. During the fighting, the 30th Division suffered thirty-six officers killed, along with seventy-six wounded, and 792 other ranks killed, along with 2,042 wounded, fifty-three missing and twelve taken prisoner – a total of 3,011. The 18th Division, for its part, suffered forty officers killed, with a further seventy wounded, and 872 other ranks killed, along with 2,087 wounded and forty-six listed as missing – a total of 3,115.

43. No doubt elements of the 12th Reserve Division arriving.

44. A water main had been laid up to Carnoy before the battle, and a water point was now opened there.

45. This party of 150 men of various regiments had apparently hidden in the quarry until night.

46. General Foch's first command in the war, and now composed of the 11th, 39th, 72nd and 153rd Divisions, with thirty-two batteries of heavy artillery.

47. This comprised 2nd Colonial, 3rd Colonial, 16th Colonial and 99th Territorial Divisions, with sixty-five batteries of heavy artillery.

48. 51st, 61st and 121st Divisions, with twenty batteries of heavy artillery.

49. 3rd and 4th Divisions, with four batteries of heavy artillery.

50. The losses of only two of the regiments engaged are available: the 109th Reserve lost forty-two officers and 2,105 other ranks. The 6th Bavarian Reserve Regiment lost thirty-five officers and 1,775 men. In the Bavarian Official Account it is said that this regiment"was practically wiped out", and the captured diary of Lieutenant Colonel Bedall states that it"was completely destroyed; of 3,500 men only 500 survivors remain, and these for the most part are men who have not taken part in the battle, with two regimental officers and a few stragglers who turned up on the following day. All the rest are dead, wounded or missing."

Index of Battalions

2nd Battalion Alexandra, Princess of Wales's Own (Yorkshire Regiment)

BRITISH TRENCHES OPPOSITE MONTAUBAN.

7.30.   At 7.30am, the hour fixed for the attack on the German system of trenches, the Battn was in "Headquarters Avenue" trench, with the exception of 2 platoons of 'D' Coy under 2/Lieut's PARRISOTTI and DICKINSON which were detailed as "cleaning" platoons and were with the 18th Bn Kings (L'pool) Regt and 19th Battn Manchester Regt respectively.

The strength of the Battn was 24 Officers, 688 other ranks – The remainder of the Battn was left with the 1st line transport in BOIS DES TAILLES as first reinforcements.

The Brigade had as the front to be attacked & taken, the German trenches from junction of the GLATZ redoubt with DUBLIN TRENCH, on the right, to the railway A 3 c 8.6 on the left. The 89th Bde (30th Div) was attacking on the right & the 55th Bde (18th Div) on the left.

The assaulting Battns were the 19th Manchesters on the right, & the 18th Kings on the left – The Battn was in support of these and was responsible for occupying and consolidating the German front and support lines – Its advance was to be made in 2 lines, each of columns of sections and with this in view companies were arranged in the line in alternate half companies.

At 7.30am the leading line ('A' Coy under 2/Lieut BROOKE D.S.O. and 'B' Coy under Capt WYLDE) advanced, followed about 3 minutes later by 'C' Coy under Capt MAUDE and 'D' Coy under Lt ROWLEY.

7.50am.   The leading line crossed "No man's land". 'A' Company came under heavy machine gun fire from its left front & suffered very severely. 2/Lt BROOKE D.S.O. 2/Lt's Henderson & COLK were wounded, the former dying at the dressing station; 2/Lt Denman was killed; only a party of about 30 reached the German trench under a Corporal. 'B' Coy also suffered, 2nd Lieut's MYERS was wounded and BENNETT was killed, Capt WYLDE was wounded – 2nd Lt FRASER was left in command. The second line also suffered, 2nd Lt NIBLETT being wounded: the German artillery barrage was very heavy; altogether the Battn sustained about 200 casualties in crossing "No man's land" the remainder reached the portions of the German trenches allotted to them and at once commenced the work of consolidation.

9.15am.   A German machine gun which had escaped notice by the advancing waves opened fire from the German front line – It was located by Lce Cpl W. PARKIN who singlehanded made for its position, killed the 2 men serving it and captured the gun which was then handed over to the 21st Bde M.G. Coy and mounted for use against the enemy.

11am.   Battn Hd.Qrs. crossed over and was established in a German dug-out near the bottom of SILESIA ALLEY. It was not until 1.30pm in spite of gallant efforts by the linemen, that telephone communication was definitely established with Bde H.Q.

3pm.   The C.O. after going round the Battn, decided to hold the front German line only and withdraw 'B' Coy into it. The line was then held firm left to right by Companies in the following order A,B,D,C – of Lewis guns 'A' Coy had lost one and 'B' Coy both guns, all from shell fire . The remaining 5 were dispersed with a view to covering the flanks – Touch was maintained with the 89th Bde but with no unit of the 55th Bde.

The 90th Bde had passed through about 9am. & occupied MONTAUBAN – of the 2 "cleaning" platoons, one, 2/Lt Parrisotti, had been practically exterminated in the crossing. One or two men under Cpl PEAT who succeeded in reaching the Germans trench did very good work and held up a party of Germans who were bombing their way up from VALLEY TRENCH until the other platoons under 2/Lieut DICKINSON came to their assistance. 2/Lt DICKINSON with commendable promtitude & decision, on seeing the state of affairs, at once got his men onto the top and overwhelmed a considerably superior number of Germans who threw up their hands.

9pm.   The work of consolidation was continued till dusk. The trenches had been so completely battered by the British bombardment that communication was difficult - in many cases it was impossible to locate the line of the original trench – at 9pm sentries were posted & ordinary trench routine resumed – There were frequent alarms from MONTAUBAN but no counter-attack really developed.

2nd Battalion Bedfordshire Regiment

JULY 1st 1916

During the night of June 30th the Battalion which was in support formed up in the Trenches of Z.1 Subsector as shown in attached copy of Operation Order No.76.

The early morning of July 1st was hazy and from our positions we could not see the GERMAN positions. At 7.30am (ZERO Hour) the general advance commenced, led by the 17th and 20th Bns KINGS LIVERPOOL Regt, the 2nd Battalion Bedfordshire Regiment being in support and the 19th Bn. Kings Liverpool Regiment in RESERVE.

The bombardment had been so successful that very little resistance from Rifle Fire took place, but most of the casualties were sustained from shell fire.

The Headquarters of the Battalion were in the CHATEAU dug-outs during the preliminary advance.

By 8am the GERMAN 1st Line Trenches were taken (including FAVIERE and SILESIA Fire Trenches) the leading Battalions pushing on to CASEMENT TRENCH – ALT ALLEY – GLATZ ALLEY.

'B' and 'C' Companies, commanded by Captain R.A.W. PEARSE and Captain R.O. WYNNE respectively, followed 100 yards in rear of the attacking Battalions and established themselves in FAVIERE SUPPORT and SILESIA SUPPORT trenches whilst the Artillery bombarded DUBLIN TRENCH. 'A' and 'D' Companies during this period occupied our old front line trenches.

At 8.28am the leading Battalions assaulted and captured DUBLIN TRENCH.

The 21st Brigade on our left assaulted GLATZ REDOUBT and the French on our right assaulted DUBLIN REDOUBT.

During this advance 'A' and 'D' Companies, commanded by Captain C.G. TYLER and Captain L.F. BEAL respectively, advanced and occupied FAVIERE SUPPORT – SILESIA SUPPORT and 'B' and 'C' Companies supported the advance to DUBLIN TRENCH occupying CASEMENT TRENCH.

At 12.30pm the 20th Battalion Kings Liverpool Regiment assaulted and took the BRIQUETERIE.

Besides supporting the advance of the Brigade the Battalion had special duties allotted to it.

2nd Lieutenant A.M.B. GAZE, 2nd Lieutenant A. YOUNG and 60 Other Ranks of 'D' Company followed the 3rd wave of the attacking battalions for the purpose of cleaning up the GERMAN dug-outs and trenches. These were split up into small parties of an N.C.O. and 5 men, each told off to work up defined sections of enemy trench. This was successfully accomplished and about 300 prisoners and 4 Machine Guns were taken, this work completed the men rejoined their Company.

No. 1,2,5 and 6 Strong Points as on Map Appendix 'A' were made by the Battalion under heavy shell fire during the day and night.

At 8.15am Battalion Headquarters moved up into LEXDON STREET in our old Front Line Trenches and remained there during the operations of July 1st to July 4th

2nd Lieutenant R.F.C. BALLARD rejoined from Hospital.

2nd Lieutenant's H.G. FYSON and J.B. PRIMROSE-WELLS proceeded from Reserve of Officers to 89th Brigade Hd.Qrs for duty.

7th (Service) Battalion Bedfordshire Regiment

CARNOY TRENCHES
At about midnight on night of June 30/July1st 1916 the whole of the 54th Brigade was concentrated on its Battle Front ready for the assault on morning of 1st July.

Assaulting Battalions were 7th Bedfords and 11th R. Fusiliers, in support – 6th Northants, and in reserve – 12th Middlesex.

An artillery bombardment waged heavily all night and increased in intensity up till 7.30am Zero hour, when the assaulting Battalions stormed the German first line trenches.

Operation Orders appended.

A special account of the events is being compiled by the Commanding Officer and will be appended hereto also.

Document Attached to the War Diary

The account of the fighting prepared by the battalion's Commanding Officer:

Sir,
I beg to forward herewith report on the operations carried out by the Battalion under my command on 1st July 1916.

In a report of this nature, in order to arrive at a clear understanding of the various incidents that took place, where the advance was held up, and where it progressed, it appears advisable to divide the front allotted to the Battalion into the right and left attack. The dividing line between the assaulting companies ran roughly through the TRIANGLE and left of POMMIERS REDOUBT. The right started on BAY POINT, then swinging half right on to POPOFF LANE, kept in touch with the 53rd Brigade. The left was directed on AUSTRIAN JUNCTION to a point about 50 yards west of POMMIERS REDOUBT.

ASSAULTING COMPANIES:
Right attack   'B' Company under Captain W.H. Bull
Left attack   'C' Company under Captain E. Clegg

SUPPORTING COMPANY:
'D' Company under Captain T.E. Lloyd supported the attack of the two assaulting companies.

RESERVE:
'A' Company under Captain A.E. Percival was held in Battalion Reserve.

FORMATIONS:
The Battalion was formed up in four forming up trenches each company of the assaulting companies on a two platoon frontage of 175 yards, with one platoon in support and one on Company Reserve.

No.3 Company acted as support to the two leading companies, No.4 Company was in Battalion Reserve.

The first three waves of each company moved in extended order, the fourth wave in sections.

No.3 Company moved in sections, in Artillery formation.

No.4 Company moved in platoons in Artillery formation.

I would here call attention to the fact that although Nos.3 and 4 Companies moved in what would appear to be close formation, yet their losses while remaining in these formations were extremely small.

Their losses really began when called into the final stages of the attack.

As this formation is more mobile and infinitely more under the control of their leaders, it is one that might be adhered to on future occasions, and the fact that they are not so vulnerable as would appear at first sight might with advantage be made more widely known.

Touch was maintained from rear to front. The result was good especially as regards the 3rd and 4th Companies, and permitted the leaders of the assaulting companies to devote all their attention to the forcing of the enemy's position, in addition to keeping the largest numbers of rifles in the front waves. The vital responsibility of keeping touch with units on right and left remained with the leader of the assaulting companies.

RIGHT ATTACK:

At 7.28am the Right Attack started to move out, Zero being 7.30am I considered this most necessary as it had some distance to traverse before reaching the 1st line German trenches, secondly in order to get straighten its first line of advance it had to move half left before the right of the company could rest on BAY POINT; thirdly, previous to the intense bombardment enemy machine guns had been particularly active and I wished to get the men through our wire whilst this bombardment continued; fourthly, it seemed of vital necessity not to run any risks in being late for the pre-arranged barrage up to the POMMIERS REDOUBT.

As the machine gun fire, even on cessation of intense bombardment, was still very galling, the waves hurried through the gaps in the wire and doubled down the slope. It was on the gaps and the top of the slope that the machine gun fire was principally directed. There was practically none at foot of slope. Here the right attack formed up in deliberate fashion, making absolutely certain of its line of advance. It then advanced as if on parade. The waves were perfectly dressed, intervals and distances, as it seemed to me from our trenches, were kept extraordinarily well.

The machine gun fire still continued very active and casualties were seen to occur before AUSTRIAN TRENCH was reached, but the waves still continued on their way, seemingly without a check.

Between the Austrian Trench and EMDEN TRENCH the company was practically leaderless as regards officers, all having been either killed or wounded. There was practically no opposition except from machine gun fire; this principally came well away from our right flank which from the early commencement of the fight was most exposed owing to the Battalion of the 53rd Brigade on our right being unable to advance at the same rapid rate as our right attack. Severe machine-gun fire seemed to come from POPOFF LANE which did considerable execution. It was not until reaching the ground between BUND and POMMIERS Trench that a real check occurred. Here the wire in front of POMMIERS was not cut and a mixed party of the right attack with men of the BERKSHIRE Regt. proceeded to cut the wire in a most methodical way.

In the words of Captain Bull in a letter to me "The ½ hour outside that trench will be a nightmare for years to come, and this was our expensive time. There were about 20 Berkshires and about that same number of my lot; the way they cut the wire just as if nothing was doing was splendid."

The Company Sergeant Major of the right attack states that the German front line where he crossed it was filled with barbed wire and spiked stakes. From previous reports it would appear as if the Germans only held parts of the front line and these parts are defended with machine guns only, which this statement confirms. As their second line was so close and contained deep dugouts, this method appears to be quite possible and has it advantages in the event of a sudden raid. The C.S.M. further states that the wiring and spikes seemed to him recently put in. This may have been the case as a guard against our continual raids during the preliminary bombardment.

The left of the right attack was held up by a machine gun in the right corner of the triangle, firing across front of right attack, and was put out of action by the bombers of the left attack and by men of the right attack crawling up the right side of the Triangle.

I would here call attention to the close co-operation of the assaulting companies; from The Triangle to the Redoubt this was from all accounts most marked; it enabled all engaged to keep to the time table laid down. The right attack or at all events the larger portions of it, arrived at POMMIERS REDOUBT roughly at 8.30am.

As regards the actual storming of the redoubt, this was carried out piecemeal, elements of 'B', 'C' and 'D' Companies, the latter having pushed in sections here and there, all taking part. It is quite clear that the front face was forced by parties swinging round to the flanks. Here many individual acts of great gallantry and devotion to duty were performed, as the German front trench which was held very tenaciously by the enemy was filled with their dead. Here too our losses were heavy; many of the dead lay round the front and flanks of the redoubt. It is unquestionable that the Germans who remained in the redoubt were either ordered or fully prepared to defend this last vital point in their line of defence to the last.

The fight at this point was therefore extremely obstinate and costly to both sides, for the redoubt was not in our hands entirely until roughly about 9.30am, our first elements having arrived at 8.30am which hour was the scheduled time. Before the redoubt was taken men of all 3 Companies had pushed on to the MAPLE Trench which was subjected to a heavy shrapnel fire, and here it was that Captain BULL who had done splendid work, was wounded severely and had to retire.

BEETLE ALLEY was next to be occupied; by that time, though platoons had been reorganised and men were under the control of very junior NCOs. the Companies were still mixed. This applied especially to the right attack whose losses had been very heavy in the taking of part of POMMIERS TRENCH and The REDOUBT.

Those that were left were used in bombing attacks along the MONTAUBAN ALLEY and the eastern part of BEETLE ALLEY and during the latter part of the day were among those who occupied WHITE TRENCH until the relief of the Battn. on the morning of the 2nd July.

From all reports it would appear that the taking of the REDOUBT was made by elements of all three companies and it is impossible to follow closely the operation of the right attack as such from the time of their leaving the POMMIERS TRENCH.

LEFT ATTACK:

The left attack crossed our lines on the stroke of Zero. It was straight opposite its line of advance and as regards direction had not the same difficulties to contend with as the right attack. It has been difficult to get exact details of what happened to the first two waves. From observation it appeared as if the lines of both assaulting companies were moving on at exact intervals. From a sergeant in the 4th wave who eventually took command of the company, it seemed to him that the 1st and 2nd waves became merged before reaching the EMDEN Trench. It is certain that the left attack passed quickly through our wire and doubled down the slope – reforming in the valley below.

It is equally certain that their losses were heavier in the initial stages of the attack than the company on the right, for between AUSTRIAN and EMDEN a section of the company reserve had to be thrown in to make good a gap. Somewhere in the vicinity of EMDEN this part of the attack came under the German barrage but the men dashed through it, suffering very few casualties as they put it behind them. After EMDEN Trench the left attack was left without an officer. Between BUND and POMMIERS the line became very ragged and there was some difficulty in keeping the formation as the fire was very heavy. The barrage on POMMIERS TRENCH was so hot that the left attack pressed on and lay in the open beyond it and the MAPLE TRENCH.

Whilst waiting there this attack came under fire of machine guns and snipers. Men were lying in shell holes and any cover they could get, and there was again some difficulty in re-organising the line. Relief eventually came from the right which had got ahead of the left attack, for the latter were able to get at those that were holding up the left. As the Germans fell back the left attack followed closely on them and some made their way into the Redoubt and some outside. The bulk of the left only remained about 20 minutes in the Redoubt and being scattered had once more to be reformed and came under shell fire which was avoided by their pressing on, but unfortunately they ran into our own barrage which compelled them to fall back. Thus they waited and on the barrage lifting rushed forward and took BEETLE ALLEY without opposition at the place they entered it. Patrols were pushed forward then, and the work of consolidation proceeded with. Those of the left attack who got into BEETLE TRENCH apparently remained there, for from EMDEN TRENCH they were without officers, the company being under command of a sergeant.

It is to be regretted that no one, either officer or NCO, who could be relied on was left with the first three waves, for further details explaining the reasons of their losses and cause of there being behind the right attack would have been of very great value, and a more concise view of the situation from the beginning obtained.

SUPPORTING COMPANY:

This went over two minutes after zero. The losses in parts were nil for there was no barrage and no machine gun fire at the time it crossed our wire.

Their losses commenced at German 2nd line Trench from a machine gun in the EMDEN Trench, brought up after first waves had passed from a dugout. This gun was actually put out by the 3rd Company. An officer was with it, who shot Sergeant Laughton and was in turn killed just a second too late by Serge. Slough. Between EMDEN and BUND Trench the right flank of the Fusiliers overlaps our left platoon. Before reaching BUND TRENCH all the officers of this company were out of action.

In the advance between BUND and POMMIERS TRENCH the Fusiliers eased of to their left, leaving our front free and here it was that a machine gun from left of POMMIERS held up the whole attack. It was being used on the parapet and moved about. This gun must apparently have been taken on by the Fusiliers for it stopped firing, and when the men rushed forward after being reinforced they found heaps of ammunition but no gun. It was here that the elements of all three companies became mixed up, before taking the Redoubt and getting into MAPLE Trench. There is no doubt that the supporting company carried on these elements of 'B' and 'C' that had been severely handled. It is also quite certain that between the edge of POMMIERS and MAPLE Trench certain parts of the line ran into our own artillery barrage and came under heavy German barrage.

Flares were lighted which were acknowledged by an aeroplane and five minutes afterwards our fire ceased. Here as far as possible the elements of the companies were re-organised and Serge. Slough took charge of the 3rd company.

On reaching BEETLE TRENCH bombing parties were organised and they proceeded to clear the eastern edge of same, while others went on with work of consolidation. About 4pm parties of Fusiliers and Bedfords occupied the White Trench, the latter remaining until recalled on the morning of July 2nd.

RESERVE COMPANY:

The Reserve Company went through our wire at 7.40am. This company came under quite a heavy barrage of the shrapnel and machine gun fire of the enemy. This latter seemed to come from the direction of BLACK ALLEY. Half of the losses of this company occurred while getting through the wire and two officers were put out of action before crossing our own fire trench. Times of reaching the German trenches were as follows:

Austrian Trench 7.50am.

Emden Trench 7.55am.

Bund Trench 8.00am.

Between AUSTRIAN SUPPORT and EMDEN a German barrage was encountered. Company was reorganised in BUND TRENCH, leaving it at 9.15am and moved up towards POMMIERS Trench. At 9.30am I gave orders while in the TRIANGLE for the reserve to push through and make for final objective as word was brought that the REDOUBT was taken.

Before reaching the Redoubt this company went through a 3rd barrage. The statement of Captain Percival on his arrival at Redoubt as follows:

"On arrival at Redoubt a great state of confusion reigned. Men of four different Battalions (Bedfords, Fusiliers, Essex and Berkshire) – no Officers, no NCOs.

"As the Fusiliers were making for the BEETLE TRENCH I at once sent forward 3 platoons under 2/Lieut. Colley with instructions not to go beyond it until arrival of 53rd Brigade on our right flank. I then set about the consolidation of Redoubt, and told off men of the 53rd Brigade into bombing parties to clear up MONTAUBAN ALLEY. At 10.15am there were no signs of the main attack of the 53rd Brigade. A strong party of Germans was holding MONTAUBAN ALLEY at this time. The first attempt to clear it was not successful but a fresh party of men of the ESSEX Regt. accomplished the clearing of it by 2.30pm. About 3.30pm the same platoon of the Essex Regt. cleared MONTAUBAN ALLEY as far as LOOP TRENCH. About 6pm the NORFOLK Regt. made good the remainder of Montauban Alley. Our machine guns assisted very materially during the whole time by flanking fire. At 6.15pm this trench was occupied by one platoon of Bedfords and 2 platoons Fusiliers. At 10pm the construction of strong points S.W. of New Trench was commenced. At 10.30pm covering party reported advance of Germans coming over ridge. These were fired on and retired. The Coy was brought out of the line at 3.15am."

The above is a description of what happened as far as can be gathered from the most trustworthy sources now available. Had the losses in officers and senior

NCOs not been as heavy further details would have been available.

On my arrival at the Redoubt the confusion mentioned by Captain Percival was still very evident; my time of arrival was about 9.50am.

POMMIERS LANE was chocked with men, principally 53rd Brigade and I had considerable difficulty in thinning the men out as at any moment there was danger of heavy shell fire from the Germans.

The consolidation of our right flank especially was being rapidly put in hand and was strongly held by Vickers and Lewis Machine Guns.

The situation at this time was critical. On our right the 53rd Brigade seemed solidly held up with no signs of any advance of their main attack though considerable numbers of the Essex and Berkshires had in some manner made their way into the Redoubt.

Similarly on our left flank, the advance of the 91st Brigade had not made headway beyond FRITZ Trench. The two assaulting Battalions of the 54th Brigade had made good as far as BEETLE Trench which was being consolidated. The Northamptonshire Regt. was close up in support. We were thus in a salient, on our right neither MONTAUBAN nor CATERPILLAR Alleys were clear of Germans and these appeared to be heavy fighting in the direction of MONTAUBAN Village. On our left Fritz Trench was held but to our left flank there was the wood of MAMETZ which might easily have harboured a large force for counter attack. Under these circumstances I deemed it more prudent to consolidate the positions already gained and to endeavour as far as possible to clear MONTAUBAN ALLEY in order to relieve the pressure on the 53rd Brigade.

The NEW TRENCH was therefore not fully occupied until our right flank had been made good – roughly about 6pm, though elements had reconnoitred it some time previously.

Strong points were at once put in hand at the places previously ordered.

The chief reasons of the success of the operation are in my opinion as follows:

1. The work of the Artillery; with very few exceptions the wire was beautifully cut and the trenches filled up.

The sheeting was wonderfully accurate.

2. The training of the Battalion at PICQUIGNY. The time and attention to every detail that was carried out there was repaid a thousand fold. As an example I may quote that only three officers in the entire Battalion got beyond EMDEN Trench, most of the platoon and very many section leaders had gone; yet so thorough was the training beforehand that the men carried on entirely by themselves, knew where to go and what to do when they got there.

3. The clear and concise orders that were received. Nothing had been forgotten and provision was made for all emergencies.

4. The good work done by the clearing up parties. The work done by the Northampton Regt. was splendid and we had no shooting from behind. I would suggest that these parties, so absolutely necessary, should be increased in strength.

5. The good work of the carrying up parties. In addition to those provided under Brigade arrangements, another party made up from odd men in the Battalion, about 30 in number, carried up with the 4th Company a supply of S.A.A. and Bombs. This party then returned to the most advanced dump and continued during the whole day to maintain this supply. A large number of bombs were used in clearing MONTAUBAN ALLEY and without this supply furnished by the advanced party; matters would have come to a standstill. They did most excellent work and never ceased carrying until a large stack of bombs and S.A.A. had been accumulated. I would suggest this advanced carrying party going with the 4th Company whenever possible.

6. The quickness with which the assaulting Battalion left our trenches. Where a pre-arranged time table barrage is arranged it seems imperative that the men should be quick off the mark. In the assault the two companies left our trenches before cessation of intense bombardment. They were thus able to take full advantage of the artillery barrage and consequently arrived at the POMMIERS REDOUBT at 8.30am. It would thus appear safer to risk a few casualties from our own guns than to miss the effect of the barrage and so come under the fire of enemy machine-guns which are without doubt kept in dugouts until the barrage has stepped forward. This point has continually been insisted by all those who were in the first waves.

7. The close co-operation of all units in the assaulting waves. This was very marked, both between our own companies and the company of the Fusiliers on our left. With regard to the latter, both at the POMMIERS Trench and Redoubt they rendered most invaluable assistance at very critical times. Their help was very deeply appreciated and remarked on by the men of my Battalion. I would suggest also that in clearing MONTAUBAN ALLEY as far as the LOOP TRENCH considerable assistance was given to the 53rd Brigade which enabled them to make good their final objective.

8. A sustained and continued advance. This seems highly important and exemplified in the taking of the REDOUBT. Those immediately facing it were held up but elements which outflanked it pressed on, made use of their bombers and machine guns – either killing or forcing the defenders to fall back. Those held up immediately pressed forward and allotted the lines to maintain their formations. An advance of this nature has no doubt a big effect on the morale of the enemy.

COMMUNICATIONS:

Though minute and detailed arrangements were made for visual signalling and communications by runners neither were very successful. Messages took a very long time in getting through, and the varying aspect of the operation could not be brought quickly enough to the notice of the higher authority. Perhaps some form of portable wireless telegraphy might be arranged for in future operations.

LOSSES:

Officers:

Killed	2
Wounded	13

Other Ranks:

Killed	79
Wounded	212
Missing	6
Died of Wounds	9

In conclusion I would bring to your notice the wonderful steadiness and coolness of all ranks under heavy shell and machine gun fire. As before mentioned from EMDEN TRENCH to the taking of the REDOUBT the men were practically without officers and the majority of their senior platoon and section commanders – a truly wonderful performance when it is taken into consideration that their training had not reached its second year. Both during the preliminary bombardment when the weather was very bad and the men were living in trenches filled with water day and night, and during and after making good their final objective, the cheeriness and high morale of all ranks was remarkable.

7th (Service) Battalion Buffs (East Kent Regiment)

CARNOY

By midnight 30 June/1st July Battalion was disposed as follows:

'B' Coy – Assembly trenches – near Crater area.

'D' Coy – In shelters in MERCHISTON AVE. 'A' and 'C' Coys – Assembly trenches, just North of PERONNE Road and east of LA PREE Wood.

Bn Report Centre – PRINCES St.

7am.   'A' Coy followed by 'C' Coy commenced to move down into CARNOY Valley.

7.30am.   'D' Coy (less 2 platoons) moving into assembly trenches.

'B' Coy (less 2 platoons) moved to attack Crater area.

2 platoons 'B' Coy – distributed between 7th Queens and 8th E. Surrey R. (assaulting Bns) for clearing up trenches.

2 platoons 'D' Coy – To Dumps in our line, for duty as carrying parties forward.

'A' Coy moving to assembly trenches vacated by 8 E. Surrey R. in A.9.a.

'C' Coy moving to assembly trenches vacated by 7 Queens in A.8.d.

7.30am.   ZERO Time – Assaulting Battalions and Crater party went over the parapet.

7.35am.   Leading waves could be observed from Bn Report Centre moving forward.

German rifle and machine gun fire heavy.

Heavy hostile shelling of our front line system.

8am.	Message recd. from 'C' Coy that 2 platoons had lost heavily in moving into assembly trenches.
8.25am.	Message recd from 'C' Coy detailing casualties and asking if POMMIERS line taken.
8.30am.	Message to 'C' Coy – no news re POMMIERS. No.13 platoon placed at disposal of 'C' Coy to replace No.12 platoon (heavy casualties).
8.30am.	Message recd from 'A' Coy – Captain BLACK wounded. – Casualties slight.
8.40am.	Message to 'A' Coy – Two platoons to reinforce left of E. Surreys at once.
8.45am.	Message recd from Bde as follows: Queens report Eastern crater still holding out get touch with Queens and give help they require to take craters, and push on to POMMIERS Line to support E. Surreys.
8.50am.	Orders sent to 'C' Coy to support Queens & E. Surreys and capture POMMIERS, working in conjunction with left of 'A' Coy.
8.55am.	Orders sent to 'D' Coy to support Crater party and get in touch with Queens.
9am.	Message to Brigade giving situation and orders issued.
9am.	Message from Capt KENCHINGTON (O.C. Crater Party) timed 8.35am. Craters reported clear except one machine gun 8.30am. considerable resistance offered.
9.3am.	Message to Capt KENCHINGTON – 'D' Coy ordered to support you.
9.5am.	Acknowledgment recd from 'D' Coy as regards supporting crater party.
9.7am.	Messages to Queens and E. Surreys stating 7 Buffs were supporting them.
9.10am.	Message recd from Capt KENCHINGTON that machine gun and snipers still holding out in chalk dump at Craters.
9.10am.	One platoon 'A' Coy advised to support E. Surrey's at WARREN Trench.
9.15am.	Message recd from Capt KENCHINGTON – one platoon urgently needed for craters.
9.20am.	Message recd from E. Surreys – Company urgently required to work along railway and valley where enemy is still holding out between our right and left of 21st Inf. Bde.
9.23am.	Message to R.W. Kent – repeating E.Surrey message and asking them to take it on as have only one platoon in hand.
9.25am.	Message to E. Surreys – have passed your message to R.W. Kent.
9.43am.	Message recd from E.Surreys – our latest messages are F.O.O. reports Train Alley taken – also verbal report POMMIERS LINE occupied by us.
9.45am.	Message repeated to Brigade.
10.5am.	Message recd from Bde – E. Surreys in WARREN – Germans reported bombing down valley – support E. Surrey right.

10.8am.   Message to 'A', 'C' and 'D' Coys – Report situation.

10.10am.   Conversation with Brigadier on telephone – he says R.W. Kent will undertake consolidation of POMMIERS Line.

10.15am.   Message to R.W. Kent. Brigadier asks me to refer to you for company to consolidate POMMIER LINE.

10.15am   No information of situation.

to

11.15am.

11.15am.   Message from 2/Lt DYSON commanding 'A' Coy – Am at DUGOUT Trench with 2 platoons and 1 platoon 'C' Coy – Am bombing up BRESLAU ALLEY and MINE ALLEY to take MILL Trench.

11.15am.   Message from R.W. Kent. Am sending 2 Coys to push home the advance – one other Coy will follow behind them to consolidate POMMIER LINE.

11.30am.   2 Coys 8th Suffolks arrived in our front line system of trenches to support 55 Inf. Bde.

           From 11am. Bn. Report Center heavily shelled with 15cm howitzers.

12.30pm.   No definite information – C.O. with Lieuts BURNSIDE and McCOLL moved forward via Craters – moved up MINE ALLEY as far as two left hand houses of MONTAUBAN trying to find O.C. E. Surreys but without success – Parties of E. Surreys, W. Kent seen, also a few Buffs. Returned down MINE ALLEY and met O.C. Queens near junction of MINE ALLEY with CARNOY – MONTAUBAN Road.

           Advance H.Q. of both Battalions established at this point.

           Ascertained that situation as regards Queens was as follows:-

           They had lost heavily & [*illegible*] on the line of the MAMETZ – MONTAUBAN Road with their right on the orchard. As O.C. Queens was doubtful if he was strong enough on his left O.C. Buffs ordered 2 platoons of 'D' Coy under Capt NEAME to reinforce the left of the Queens & to fill the gap existing between the 55th & 53rd Bdes – This they did & the whole line advanced & occupied MONTAUBAN ALLEY, Capt NEAME being unfortunately killed.

           Capt KENCHINGTON & the remains of 'B' Coy came to Battn H.Q. (No.2 strong point) shortly after this – also a few men of 'D' Coy.

           O.C. 7th R.W. Kent Regt. arrived at No.2 Strong Point & asked 7th Buffs to undertake consolidation of POMMIERS Line.

           This work was handed over to 'B' Coy.

           Later Capt TAIT arrived with 1 platoon of 'C' Coy.

           The distribution of the Battn. at this time was roughly as follows:

           'A' Coy 2 platoons under 2/Lt DYSON in MONTAUBAN ALLEY.

           1 platoon under 2/Lt CHANT in POMMIERS Line.

           1 platoon (No.1) in rear of POMMIERS Line.

'B' Coy No.2 Strong Point.

'C' Coy 1 platoon MONTAUBAN ALLEY.

[*illegible*] collected at No.2 Strong Point.

'D' Coy 2 platoons MONTAUBAN ALLEY on left of Queens.

2 platoons Carrying party.

Advanced Battn. H.Q. No.2 Strong Point.

Rations arrived during the evening 2/Lt KEOWN (Transport officer) doing excellent work in getting them up.

Intermittent shelling by the enemy on MONTAUBAN Alley, MINE ALLEY and POMMIER trench. There was no difficulty with the water supply – carrying parties were working well.

Document Attached to the War Diary

A report on the operations of 1 July 1916, by Captain A.G. Kenchington, 'B' Company, 7th (Service) Battalion Buffs (East Kent Regiment):

1. TWO PLATOONS DETAILED TO TAKE CRATER AREA.

Before "Y" day I had collected and stored in No.10 sap necessary bombs and apparatus. I had put notice-boards directing runners to this point at the end of all saps and trenches in the crater area.

At Zero the three sections of each platoon advanced as arranged round the flanks and the other sections with snipers went over the craters which were very muddy.

The left hand party entered the enemy trenches with only one casualty, the platoon Commander Lieut E.H.A. GOSS, who was killed instantly by a shell. This platoon found the rear portion of the crater area quite knocked out of recognition, and soon overcame two bombing parties and three or four snipers who opposed them.

By 8.15am this party had reported clear and were directed to work across to the help of the other platoon who had sent no news.

The R platoon, leaving No.3 sap and our front line, were met with M.G. fire from a gun at the base of the large chalk dump opposite and from rapid fire from about 10 Germans in BRESLAU TRENCH just W. of the craters.

They suffered severely, quite 40% being knocked out as they crossed. The remainder led by the Platoon Commander (2/Lieut V.G.H. TATAM) doubled half left into the craters and entered the enemy trenches by twos and threes from inside the craters.

The M.G. was firing across the Brigade Front, so this party worked round to get it from inside, two or three snipers with the M.G. harassing them badly. Only 12 men were still attacking.

Formed German bombing parties defended the approaches to this strong point and fierce hand to hand fighting went on for an hour. The M.G. was put out of action by 8.45am, by our men sniping at close quarters but the snipers still held out.

During this hand to hand fighting the benefit of properly organised parties was seen as our party killed at least 3 to 1. At this stage apparently only 8 or 9 men were left yet they continued fighting in the trenches and bombing dugouts. 2/Lieut. V.G.H. TATAM and SERGT. UPTON P.C. jumped into one trench containing 5 germans. They despatched these and also 7 more who came out of a side trench one by one to the fight. Afterwards these two (supported by 3 of their men), who had joined them by now, accounted for another party of 6.

The smallness of the party prevented any message being sent back till 9.10am, when reinforcements and bombs were asked for. Meanwhile, judging from reports on my Observer who reported what he could see from the end of the Russian sap; and from what I myself could see when I crossed at 8.30am to try to get news. I had sent an extra bombing party, and three more snipers to their help with instructions to work round to the far side of the enemy snipers.

My No.1 LEWIS GUN which had secured a good target of enemy running up the MONTAUBAN ROAD during the first 10 minutes was now with-drawn and the spare men used to take over more bombs.

At 8.50am I warned the party in the area as far as possible and turned the STOKES gun for 10 minutes on to the strong point where the enemy were sniping.

This had excellant [sic] results, a concerted rush on the part of the men remaining (with 4 more bombers sent by Major KEMP-WELCH commanding the 7th QUEENS) carried the dump and the snipers were bayoneted. They died splendidly with heaps of cartridges round them. The M.G. emplacement was found to be concreted. The gun we kept.

By this time it was 9.30am, I had previously asked for howitzers to re-bombard the dump if this failed, but, on receipt of report "crater clear" from R platoon at 9.35am. I cancelled this and reported clear.

At 9.40am I established my H.Q. just near the dump and started on a final tour of the crater trenches to ensure that they were quite clear. Three more Germans were found and killed but otherwise all was clear, and every dugout we could find was bombed.

I re-organised what men I had left and found 18 and one Officer. 1 Platoon of 'D' Company (No.13) had come to reinforce me by now. I organised (1) My own 18 men to clear across Brigade front in BRESLAU TRENCH. (2) No.13 Platoon to clear BRESLAU SUPPORT.

Each party was to send back any groups of prisoners left in their lines and to send off parties up communication trenches to keep touch.

We found that practically all of the other platoons detailed to accompany the leading waves of the QUEENS and EAST SURREYS had been absorbed into these waves and finding a number of Germans still in dugouts we carried on clearing right across the Brigade Front.

I reported to Battalion Headquarters at 11.45am when clear right across to No.4 sap. Then finding 2/Lieut. CARMANS platoon (No.13) had also been absorbed either taking back prisoners or reinforcing the line, we cleared back across BRESLAU SUPPORT.

At 12.30pm I reported from the crater area that the Brigade front was cleared, gathered together more of my men (10 of the 18 from original crater party) had been used escorting back our captures.

I now had 1 Officer and 20 men. With these I made my way up MINE ALLEY and reported to O.C. 7th BUFFS.

He instructed me to collect available men and consolidate No.2 strong point.

We dug a new trench on what remained of an old one for the left face, cut fire steps on the N.W. face, cleared and firestepped that part of POMMIERS TRENCH and put out some wire.

As far as can be ascertained No.7 platoon lost about 30% going over and most of the rest were absorbed into the firing line (except 8 men who escorted prisoners back).

No.8 Platoon disappeared in much the same way, Sergeant RUSSELL (in command) and Lance Corporal Gettins killed the crew of an enemy M.G., but left the gun.

Lance Corporal Matthews did excellent work in the rallying stragglers of various units and leading them into the line.

12th (Service) Battalion Duke of Cambridge's Own (Middlesex Regiment)

First World War Service:

Went out to France with 54th Brigade, 18th Division, during July 1915; disbanded in February 1918.

Casualties:

Officers killed in action: 0
Other Ranks killed in action: 2
Officers died of wounds: 1
Other Ranks died of wounds: 3

CARNOY

The 54th Brigade went into action as follows; Right Assaulting Bn. 7th BEDFORD REGT. Left Assaulting Bn. 11th ROYAL FUSILIERS. Supporting Bn. 6th NORTHAMPTON Regt. Reserve 12th Bn. MIDDLESEX Regt. The Bn. went into action 21 Officers and 820 Other Ranks. Officers as follows;

Bn Hd Qrs.	Lt Col F.A. Maxwell VC, CSI, DSO, Commanding; Major M.C. Scarborough 2nd in Command; Lieut H.Corner Adjutant. 2/Lieut G.B. Borth Signalling Officer; 2/Lieut A.J. Keith M.G. Officer.
'A' Coy	Capt. I.H. Methuen; 2/Lt Alexander; 2/Lt Corbett; 2/Lt A.W. Souster.
'B' Coy	Capt. G.L. Harrison; Lt C.E. MacDonnell; 2/Lt Wellstead; 2/Lt Knight.
'C' Coy	Lieut A.E. West; Lt H. Mackenzie Rogan; Lt B.L. Franklin; 2/Lt L.N.B. Odgers.
'D' Coy	Capt. A.C. Dennis; 2/Lt E.J.L. Garstin; 2/Lt Stubbs; 2/Lt Cooke.

As soon as it was light our artillery started a heavy bombardment which became intense at 7am.

At 7.30am the assaulting Bns. moved out, the Bn. remaining in their Dug outs at CARNOY. At 8.30am the Commanding Officer and Adjutant moved up to the Bn. Hd. Qrs. at PICCADILLY in our front line. The Bn. remained in the Dug outs until 12.45pm when they went up into the forming up trenches shortly afterwards crossing to the enemy's front line and taking up the following positions:

'A' Coy; 2 Platoons in BUND Trench. 2 Platoons in EMDEN Trench on the Right of the Triangle.
'B' Coy; 2 Platoons in BUND Trench. 2 Platoons in EMDEN Trench on the Left of the TRIANGLE.
'C' Coy; in AUSTRIAN Support Trench.
'D' Coy in AUSTRIAN Front Line.
Bn. Hd. Qrs. PICADILLY.

Going over the open in Artillery formation, an enemy barrage was put upon our front line Trench at the commencement of the attack and kept there but was weak and not very accurate. As soon as the Coys were in their positions they started consolidating. The German Trenches were very much damaged and in places almost obliterated. There were many German dead in the Trenches and prisoners taken appeared very dazed and shaken, testifying to the intensity of our Bombardment. Weather was warm and clear.

Casualties.
Officers: 2/Lt. Huddleston killed. Wounded; Lt. Mackenzie Rogan, 2/Lts. Alexander & Cooke.
Other Ranks: Killed 3, Wounded 27, Missing 4. The surplus officers returned to GROVETOWN where the Transport and Specialists were left.

2nd Battalion Duke of Edinburgh's (Wiltshire Regiment)

GILLSON STREET.

The assault by the army in conjunction with the French on our right. 21st Brigade attacking with the 19th Manchester Regt, and 18th Kings Liverpool Regt in front. 2nd Yorkshires in support and 2nd Wiltshires in reserve, three companies supplying organised carrying parties, and one Company ('D') advancing to old British front line and halting to be ready in case of need .Our Brigade takes the whole of its objective i.e. GLATZ REDOUBT, and our 'D' Coy advanced to old British front line vacated by attacking troops, during which 2/LT J.MCWHANNEL is wounded fatally. The 90th Brigade then pass through us and take MONTAUBAN. 'A" B' & 'C' Companies work hard through the rest of the day and night carrying water rations, and material to the forward troops under shell fire.

8th (Service) Battalion East Surrey Regiment

A.1. SUBSECTOR.

From midnight on, the enemy shelled our front line and the assembly trenches mostly with 10.5cm and 15cm shells, knocking in the trenches in several places and several small dugouts, causing a total of 13 casualties, 3 killed and 10 being wounded.

Enemy artillery was less active from about 5am until 6.30am when he started an intense but distributed bombardment, a large amount of which fell round the Right Battalion Headquarters.

At 5.30am Companies reported that they were in position and that all the necessary stores etc. had been issued.

At 7.15am Adjutant left the Headquarter Dugout to observe the attack from our parapet.

At 7.27am 'B' company started to move out to their wire, Captain Nevill strolling quietly ahead of them, giving an occasional order to keep the dressing square on to the line of advance. This Company took four footballs out with them which they were seen to dribble forward into the smoke of our intense bombardment on the Hun front line.

The first part of 'B' Company's advance was made with very few casualties, but when the barrage lifted to the second Hun trench, a very heavy rifle and machine gun fire started from our front and left, the latter coming apparently from the craters and the high ground immediately behind them.

At 7.50am the Adjutant reported that the Battalion was in the German trenches. Hand to hand fighting went on for a long time in the German Trenches and news received that both Captains Flatau and Pearce had been killed and later it was known that Captain Nevill, Lieuts Soames, Musgrove, and 2/Lieuts Kelly and Evans had also been killed.

At 8.5am the Battalion Bombing Section was sent forward and at 8.7am 2/Lieut P.G. Heath i/c two Stokes Guns was sent out with orders to proceed as far as he could with reasonable safety, and report to the nearest East Surrey Officer and find out how best his guns could be used.

At 8.10am and again at 8.25am the Adjutant returning from our front line trenches reported heavy machine gun and rifle fire from the left and that apparently the craters and the high ground immediately behind them had not been successfully dealt with by the Battalions on the left.

Owing to reports of heavy casualties the C.O. sent to O.C. 7th Buffs for reinforcements.

At 8.40am the Adjutant again reported heavy fire from the left causing us a large number of casualties. O.C. 7th Queens was asked whether the craters had been taken, and the reply received at 8.47am was that he believed the craters had been taken, but as it turned out later this was not the case.

At 9.am 2/Lieut Stimson, who had been wounded in the arm reported at Battalion Headquarters. He said that the Germans were along the Railway Line and advancing along the Valley TRENCH and VALLEY SUPPORT TRENCH.

At 9.8am a message was sent to O.C. 7th Buffs asking him to send 2 Platoons to proceed along the Valley and into TRAIN TRENCH.

At 9.20am this message was acknowledged O.C. 7th Buffs sending one Platoon forward and keeping one Platoon in reserve.

At 9.21am an intercepted message on the telephone told us that the Queens were held up in BACK TRENCH, and at the same time, Private BILLSON one of the Battalion orderlies, who had been sent forward to remind Companies to wave their Artillery flags, returned with the report that our men were now in the POMMIERE LINE, and a few minutes afterwards information was received from the F.O.O. that the Surreys were in TRAIN ALLEY.

At the same time an Orderly from 2/Lieut Wightman brought in a report that the Brigade on the right were getting up reinforcements splendidly, and going ahead well.

A few minutes earlier 2 Huns ran into the Trench near our Battalion Headquarters crying for mercy.

At 9.44am Major Irwin handed over command at Report Centre to the Adjutant, and went forward to ascertain and if possible to bring back, news as to the actual position.

At 9.49am a message was intercepted from the craters that the enemy was still holding out in the craters and the high ground. Strong point at the end of Craters.

At 9.55am the Commanding Officer, and Adjutant 7th Royal West Kents, and a numerous staff, reported at Battalion Headquarters.

The Adjutant sent 2/Lieut Wightman forward with 2 Signallers and a telephone line to proceed to POMMIERE and try to get in touch with Major Irwin.

At 10.10am Lieut Thorley reported that the Brigade on the right were advancing well, but that nothing could be seen on our front.

The Adjutant reported the position to the Brigade which was that we had taken POMMIERS, but had suffered extremely heavy casualties in doing so and that the line was too weak to advance without reserves being put in.

Thereupon at 10.30am a message from the Brigadier ordered 3 Companies 7th W. Kents to advance and push the line forward. Their position in A.1. Subsector would be taken by the Suffolks. The 7th W. Kents to detail 1 Company to consolidate the POMMIER LINE.

At 10.30am a message was received from Lieut Griffin F.O.O. through Lieut Carver, liaison Officer, that the enemy were leaving Mill TRENCH and MINE ALLEY and converging on the MILL and the ORCHARD, also that they were seen to have machine guns with them. We ordered an immediate intense bombardment on these two points, and this was done practically at once.

At 10.45am the Adjutant with the remainder of Headquarters left Battalion Report Centre to find the wire which had been laid forward, and to establish a forward Report Centre.

Some difficulty was experienced in finding the wire and it was not until 10.45am that the forward end of the wire in the German third line trench was found. The Signallers here reported that Major Irwin was in the POMMIERS LINE, and that he would be returning to the telephone shortly. From this point a splendid view of the whole slope of MONTAUBAN could be obtained and the dispositions of our troops could be clearly seen. They had advanced from POMMIERE and lined the parodos of BRESLAU ALLEY.

The position was reported by telephone to the Brigade, and also the urgent necessity for hurrying the West Kents and pushing the attack home. At about noon the 1st of the West Kents appeared in BACK TRENCH.

Major Irwin returned to the telephone at 12 Noon and gave orders for 2/Lieut Wightman to see Captain Bowen who was still engaged on the left, and tell him if possible to disengage and go forward with all men he could collect. The Adjutant was ordered to carry the line on from BRESLAU ALLEY to MILL TRENCH and either consolidate there or carry on to MONTAUBAN as he thought best, according to the situation.

The bombardment of the MILL and the ORCHARD continued most satisfactorily, and when the line went forward from BRESLAU ALLEY and MILL TRENCH at 12.10pm not a shot was fired from our immediate front, and it was decided to carry on from MILL TRENCH to MINE ALLEY and after a short halt there and finding that the Artillery evidently having seen our men go forward had lifted, the whole of the East Surreys advanced to the Road West of MONTAUBAN, which they reached at 12.22pm with their right resting on the two Westerly houses of MONTAUBAN, their left about 100 yds East of the Orchard.

MONTAUBAN RIDGE

There was no sign of any troops on the left so Sgt. Willis was sent with half a dozen men to the WINDMILL too watch the left flank, and as other men came up from time to time reinforcements were sent him until the line stretched from the Windmill across the road and along the road from the small copse to MONTAUBAN ALLEY.

When Sgt. Willis first got to the MILL he took prisoners 1 Officer and 2 men.

At 12.35pm Major Irwin arrived with Headquarters and took command of all troops of the 55th Brigade West of MONTAUBAN. A number of Buffs and West Kents had arrived by this time and were ordered to hold on in MONTAUBAN ALLEY with the E. Surreys in close support.

When Lieut Heaton 7th Queens arrived he was ordered to extend the line to the left so that the whole Brigade objective was reached by 1.30pm.

Captain Gimson had arrived close behind Major Irwin, and later L/C Brame turned up with a bottle of Champagne to be drunk in MONTAUBAN "ON DER TAG". This bottle was sent round from Officer to Officer, those who shared in it being Major Irwin, Captain Gimson, Captain Bowen, 2/Lieut Derrick, 2/Lieut Janion, Lieut Thorley, 2/Lieut Wightman, 2/Lieut Alcock and Captain Clare, in fact all the East Surrey Officers engaged in the attack who had not been killed or wounded.

Major Irwin having fully reported the position to the Brigade, and having satisfied himself as regards the dispositions moved Headquarters and 'B' and 'C' Companies down MINE ALLEY, putting Headquarters in MILL TRENCH and 'B' and 'C' Companies in MINE ALLEY, either side of MILL Trench in a position where they would be able to resist any counter attack from the left, where our flank was still in the air.

Headquarter Officers and 2/Lieut Janion put their kit on the firestep in MILL TRENCH, and had only just finished tea when the first of a number of 5.9 shells landed almost on MILL TRENCH. A rapid decision was arrived at, and Headquarters were moved further away to the right. One of the next few shells landed plumb on the firestep on which all the Officers had been sitting. The shelling was also on MINE ALLEY. At the junction of MINE ALLEY and MILL TRENCH where the Brigade had ordered a strong point to be made we suffered several regrettable casualties, both Sgt. Simons and Sgt. Abrey being killed, and a number of men wounded. It was hard to know where to put the men for safety, but as the top of MINE ALLEY seemed to be suffering somewhat less all men were moved forward.

At 9pm a party of Suffolks reported with 25 canvas buckets of water, which were extremely welcome.

Major Irwin left for a Conference of Commanding Officers with the Brigadier at No.2 Strong Point, where POMMIERE LINE joins MINE ALLEY and returned later with news that the Battalion would be relieved at daylight, but must remain till then in a position forming a defensive flank on the left.

At midnight 2/Lieut DERRICK was carried down from the front line a large piece of shrapnel having torn through his right foot.

There was great difficulty in attending to this and all other casualties in the crowded communication trench and Captain Gimson got no rest that night.

Document Attached to the War Diary

A "report on the attack on the Montauban Ridge from the two westerly houses in Montauban inclusive to the Orchard Copse exclusive on the 1st July 1916", written by Major A.P.B. Irwin, Commanding 8th (Service) Battalion East Surrey Regiment:

Orders were received that the Battalion was to assault at 7.30am on the morning of the 1st July 1916 with the 18th LIVERPOOLS on the right and the 7th QUEENS on the left.

The Battalion moved into the assembly trenches on the afternoon on the 30th June and the relief was complete by 7.30pm.

From midnight 30th June/1st July until 5am 1st July the trenches in which the Battalion was assembled was shelled mostly with 10.5cm and 15cm shells, killing 3 men and wounding 10, and knocking in the trenches in several places.

At 5.30am all Companies reported that they were in position, and that all extra ammunition, grenades, rations, water etc had been issued.

The disposition of the Battalion was:

Right Assaulting Company	'C' Company
Left Assaulting Company	'B' Company
Support Company	'D' Company
Reserve Company	'A' Company

'B' and 'C' Companies had each 2 Platoons in our Firing Line and 2 Platoons in the Second Assembly Trench.

'D' Company was in the 3rd Assembly Trench, and 'A' Company in the 4th Assembly Trench.

The frontage occupied by the Battalion was from the RAILWAY on the right to point A.8.B.8510 on the left.

At 6.30am the enemy started an intense bombardment of our trenches most of which was on the right of the 2nd Assembly Trench.

At 7.27am the leading platoons of the Left Assaulting Company in the re-entrant left our trenches and moved out to the enemy wire, and were followed by the 2 remaining Platoons. As the Left Company came level with the Right Assaulting Company it also moved forward to the attack, and by 7.45am all Companies had left our trenches.

SLAUGHTER ON THE SOMME: 1 JULY 1916

The Germans were strongly holding their trenches, especially BRESLAU SUPPORT and BACK TRENCH, and hand to hand fighting took place in all of them so that it was impossible for the pre-arranged programme of advance to be adhered to.

At 8.30am the position was that we had taken the German Trenches on the whole Battalion frontage up to and including BACK TRENCH.

On the right the 21st Brigade appeared to have reached their objective, but on our left a very heavy rifle and machine gun fir was coming from the Craters, and the Germans were still holding out in BRESLAU SUPPORT and BACK TRENCH.

The whole Battalion was engaged, but had suffered such heavy casualties that reinforcements were asked for from O.C. 7th BUFFS, and at 9.7am a message was received from O.C. 7th BUFFS that he was supporting us with 4 Platoons.

At 9.30am some of our men were in the right of POMMIERE but it was not until 10.15am that this trench was occupied along our whole frontage.

On the right the 90th Brigade were advancing, but on our left the Germans were still holding out in BRESLAU SUPPORT and the trenches in rear.

At 9.45am Major Irwin went forward to find out the actual position, re-organise the Battalion, and push the attack forward from POMMIERE. At 10.30am it was reported that the enemy with machine guns were gathering in the MILL and in the ORCHARD COPSE, and a re-bombardment of this point was ordered, and this was most promptly and effectively carried out.

At 11am Major Irwin had completed his arrangements and all men on the right of the Battalion had advanced and lined the parapet of BRESLAU ALLEY close up to where it joins with MILL TRENCH, but our left were still engaged in hand to hand fighting and bombing with the Germans in BACK TRENCH and POMMIERE.

At 11.45am orders were sent to Captain Bowen on the left to disengage and collect all men of the Battalion and advance to MILL TRENCH.

An officer was sent forward to BRESLAU ALLEY to carry the advance on from there to MILL TRENCH, and if possible to the MONTAUBAN RIDGE. The advance was carried steadily forward to the top of MINE ALLEY, where a short halt was made to reconnoitre, and the results of the reconnaissance proving satisfactory the advance was carried forward to the MONTAUBAN RIDGE to a point about 100 yds West of the two Westerly Houses in MONTAUBAN, along the road and across the road to the WINDMILL. This position being reached by 12.22pm.

By 12.35pm nearly all that was left of the Battalion was on the MONTAUBAN RIDGE and proceeded to consolidate the position.

The arrival of other troops of the Brigade gave more men than were required on that frontage, and at 4p.m. Headquarters and 'B' and 'C' Companies moved down MINE ALLEY to MILL TRENCH.

At 6pm the enemy started a bombardment of MILL TRENCH and MINE ALLEY which continued throughout the afternoon and night.

At 2am 2nd July 'A' and 'D' Companies on the MONTAUBAN RIDGE were relieved by the 7th R. WEST KENTS, and at 4.30am the Battalion left the top of MINE ALLEY and moved down to that part of it which forms part of POMMIERE LINE.

Our casualties amounted to 8 Officers and about 125 Other Ranks KILLED, and 5 Officers and about 400 Other Ranks WOUNDED.

These casualties were nearly all incurred in 'No Man's Land' and the ground between BRESLAU TRENCH and BRESLAU SUPPORT, and a great part of them were due to the extremely heavy enfilade rifle and machine gun fire from the Craters.

10th (Service) Battalion Essex Regiment

CARNOY

The Battn. was accommodated during the night 30/1st in trenches of CARNOY defences with the exception of 2 platoons each of Nos. 2 & 3 Coys, which were with 8th Norfolks & 6th R. Berks in the Assembly Trenches. Bn H.Q. was at R.C.2. in front line trenches throughout the night.

The morning was fine.

5.30am. The men were served with a substantial breakfast of hot tea & rum, bacon, & bully beef – The Battn went into action with approximately 645 rifles (excluding Lewis Gun teams.)

7.27am. Mine under KASINO POINT was blown – This was near the surface & threw up a great deal of chalk which was widely scattered and wounded many men of the Berkshires & Essex.

7.30am. Zero time – Infantry attack launched – Men went over splendidly & full of eagerness. Our clearing platoons went over with the leading waves.

7.40am. First prisoner arrived at R.C.2 – He belonged to the 6th Res. Regt – Many others followed. BUND SUPPORT was soon taken.

8.48am. BDE observation officer reported POMMIER TRENCH taken. The Norfolks did not confirm this but reported that they could get no news of their leading Coys.

9.30am. Remainder of Nos. 2 & 3 Coys and No.4 Coy went forward in accordance with orders – O.C. No.2 Coy having had 2 runners put out of action came back to report that although BUND SUPPORT was taken the enemy was still strongly holding the LOOP, BACK TRENCH, & BOCHE TRENCH. No information as to this had been received from the Norfolks.

11.30am. Telephonic Communication established with BUND SUPPORT. This forward telephone was of great use. O.C. No.4 Coy reported that LOOP was taken but that BACK TRENCH was still holding out.

12.2pm.	Norfolks reported LOOP taken and that their 2 Leading Coys were making their way up LOOP trench.
12.35pm.	G.O.C. 53rd Bde called for bombing parties for MONTAUBAN ALLEY. These were to go up via POPOFF LANE and POMMIER LANE.
12.39pm.	These were sent by No.4 Coy from BUND SUPPORT.
12.55pm.	O.C. No.3 Coy reported that his Coy was constructing Strong Points Nos. 9 & 11.
1.5pm.	6th R. Berks. wired that they now had MONTAUBAN ALLEY up to its junction with LOOP TRENCH. The right if the Bde was still somewhat hung up.
1.55pm.	8th Norfolks reported pushing up MINE ALLEY to Strong Point 6, & up BOCHE TRENCH to LOOP. These places were gradually cleared and won by bombing parties. No.2 Coy lent a good deal of assistance in this.
3.5pm.	Berks called for help to deal with enemy at N. end of LOOP TRENCH – No.4 Coy sent up 2 platoons.
	About 4.30pm Bn. H.Q. moved from R.C.2. to BUND SUPPORT near its junction with MINE ALLEY. C.O. & Adjutant visited all the Coys in the line and also BERKS and NORFOLK H.Qrs. which were then in POMMIER TRENCH and the LOOP respectively. No.3 Coy was working hard on its Strong Points in POMMIER TR. and No.2 Coy in LOOP whilst remainder of No.4 Coy was in BUND SUPPORT.
About 7pm.	G.O.C. Bde visited the line, & went round with the C.O.
8.30pm.	The 2 platoons of No.4 Coy which had been helping the Berks returned, & were put into the left of POMMIER TRENCH. The Berks spoke in glowing terms of the help these had afforded them.
10.20pm.	Norfolks and Berks reported that Bde was holding its furthest objective.
11.40pm.	Bde rang up to say that S.O.S. had been sent up from CATERPILLAR TRENCH. No further message was received with regard to this but Battn was fully prepared to defend its line.
	Touch was established with the 'C' Battns of the 55th and 54th Bdes on right & left respectively (7th Buffs & 12th Middlesex).
	Rations came up CARNOY-MOMTAUBAN Road on pack animals – This method proved very satisfactory.
Midnight.	Orders re Defence of ground gained received from Bde – Our role was to hold the POMMIER LINE to the last man.
	During the early part of the night our new Report centre in MINE ALLEY received all the messages for the Berks.

17th (Service) Battalion (1st City) King's
(Liverpool Regiment)

Bn in position in assembly trenches – Bn frontage from MARICOURT-BRIQUETERIE RD to 100 yds WEST of MARICOURT MONTAUBAN RD – 1st wave 2 platoons of 'A' Coy on the right & 2 platoons 'B' Coy on the left – 2nd wave remaining platoons of these companies – 3rd wave 'C' Coy & 4th wave 'D' Coy in parallel trenches at about 100 yds distance.

3rd Bn 153rd Regt French Infantry on our right & 20th Bn K.L.R. on our left. The Bn's objective was DUBLIN TRENCH from DUBLIN REDOUBT exclusive to a point 400 yds west.

'Zero Hour', the assault commenced, some shelling but very slight infantry resistance & but little machine gun fire encountered, the work of our artillery having been very effective on the German trenches.

The objective was taken at 8.30am, the French on our right gaining theirs at the same hour, Lt Col B.C. FAIRFAX & COMMANDANT LE PETIT cmdg 3rd Bn 153rd Regt arrived together in DUBLIN TRENCH. 'A' & 'B' Coys dug in about 100 yds North of DUBLIN TRENCH which the Germans shelled intermittently all day hardly touching the new trench.

Casualties up to 12 noon: CAPT E.C. TORREY cmdg 'C' Coy, Lt D.H. SCOTT cmdg 'A' Coy & 2nd Lt P.L. WRIGHT wounded. 100 O.R.

Later in the day the 90th Bde took MONTAUBAN & the 20th K.L.R. captured the BRIQUETERIE.

LT SCOTT died of wounds in a French hospital at CERISY where Capt MIRASCOU cmdg the left Coy of the French also lay wounded.

Perfect liaison existed between the French and ourselves, the above two officers commanding respectively our right company & the French left Coy being in constant touch.

Shortly after the attack commenced Bn HQ moved up to a German dugout in FAVIERE SUPPORT under BRIQUETERIE RD where COMMANDANT LE PETIT also established his HQ.

During the remainder of the day there was intermittent bombardment of DUBLIN & CASEMENT & FAVIERE SUPPORT trenches.

Rations were brought up safely at night.

Disposition of Bn, 2 Coys in DUBLIN and 2 in CASEMENT TRENCH.

18th (Service) Battalion (2nd City) King's
(Liverpool Regiment)

TALUS BOISE

6.30am.   Artillery commenced intensive bombardment of enemy's trenches.

7.30am. Zero – Battalion commenced to leave their trenches and attack commenced – the attack was pressed with great spirit and determination in spite of heavy shelling and machine gun enfilade fire which caused casualties amounting to 2/3rd of the strength of the Battalion in action – the whole system of German trenches including the Glatz Redoubt were captured without any deviation from the scheduled programme.

Document Attached to the War Diary

An account of the fighting of 1 July 1916, written by Lieutenant Colonel E.H. Trotter DSO, Commanding 18th (Service) Battalion (2nd City) King's (Liverpool Regiment):

The Battalion was formed up in the assembly trenches by 7.20am. At 7.20am I went down the line & saw all was in order and then returned to Battn. Headquarters. I tried to observe the advance of the Battalion at 7.30am but I was too late by about a minute in seeing the front line getting out of their trenches, but I saw the enemy attempting to barrage our front line just after our 3rd line left and before our 4th line reached the barrage. The enemy barrage did not appear to do much harm to our men before they left our front line as I saw our 4th line who were in section columns pass successfully through the shell area but I heard afterwards there were casualties from the enemy's artillery on the racecourse. There are very few officers left now from No.1 Company, the leading Company on the left and none from No.4 Company, the Support Company, but from the narratives of the survivors, officers and men, I think the following is a pretty accurate story. In many places our men could leave the trenches without being seen by the enemy's front line trench, this was on the Fleche side and to deal with them the enemy had, on the 18th Division front, well back, machine-guns in the open which it was impossible to locate before the action commenced.

The hedge running in front of MONTAUBAN which was the apparent place was under barrage from our own artillery. These Machine Guns dealt with men unseen leaving the parapet. On the right where the men were more on the high ground there was a Machine Gun firing directly on our men advancing from the front line trench. This was afterwards captured and its team, who fired up to the very last minute and then attempted to surrender, were shot. A CO had one hand on the gun and one hand in the air.

The front line seems to have been taken with a certain amount of opposition and 1 officer & some men surrendered, but previous to this on our advance [*illegible*] men were seen to leave the back trenches and retreat towards MONTAUBAN. A certain amount of bombing took place in the 2nd line trench and 30 men surrendered after being forced into dugouts by our clearing parties.

The line was not held by the barrage on the front 2 trenches or ALT TRENCH and reached that.

Here a difficulty arose and the officers who remained alive with the men had difficulty in stopping their forward rush. The barrage was on as ordered at schedule time and the Battalion had to wait until it lifted during which time they were subjected from the left flank in the 18th Divisional area to Machine Gun fire which enfiladed them, besides which on our own front, on the part of TRAIN ALLEY running North East which looks like a communication trench and was filled with dugouts and very little touched by our artillery, being in the valley, the enemy had placed a flanking party under cover of a rough tree hedge with its right running into ALT ALLEY, covered by a bombing party. Captain A. de Bels Adam who was in the 2nd line and whose duty it was to keep intercommunication with the 18th Division and cover our left flank, immediately saw the situation and as agreed attempted to deal with it by the bombing parties told off for this object. The bombing parties were however shot down by sniper. The gallantry of the men and officers and the foresight and battle knowledge of Captain Adam is beyond all praise for at this point and at this moment I think the whole of the operations for the taking of MONTAUBAN were in the balance. Our forward bombing parties had all been shot down by sniper, & 2nd Lieut G.A. Herdman who had come forward to deal with the situation was blown to pieces by an enemy bomb. 2nd Lt E. FitzBrown who led his Company and was the first man to enter the enemy's front line trench, where he had emptied his revolver, seeing the situation took two bombs in his hand and attempted to bomb TRAIN ALLEY and the hedge, and immediately met with the same fate as other bombers had done who had tried to do the same thing, from the enemy's snipers. Here it was that Captain Adam's battle knowledge and determination saved the situation.

He immediately sent to Lieut Watkins of the clearing party for more bombers who came up.

Men whose names deserve mention, reconnoitred at the risk of wounds (which they received) and death also located the enemy bombing party and reported to Lieut Watkins that ALT TRENCH was held by an advanced bombing party which covered the enemy's snipers in TRAIN ALLEY with rifles fixed on ALT TRENCH.

Lieut Watkins attempted to go down and found the body of 2/Lieut Herdman, and threw a bomb which failed to reach the enemy bombing guard. Lieut Watkins acted as one of Captain Adams' subalterns would act and grasping the situation immediately, he told off his longest thrower who with the greatest luck threw a bomb into the German bombing guard killing two and pushing the rest back into TRAIN ALLEY, thus making the advance possible and the bombing of Lieut Watkins party drove the enemy into their dugouts, many including an officer were shot in the hedge by riflemen and 30 including a Medical Officer surrendered to Lieut Watkins on their dugouts being bombed but the bombs do not appear to have done much damage to the dugouts.

SLAUGHTER ON THE SOMME: 1 JULY 1916

This action relieved any enemy pressure on our left and enabled the 18th Battalion to carry the GLATZ REDOUBT when the barrage lifted in conjunction with the 19th Manchesters who were slightly intermixed.

The fire from the GLATZ REDOUBT on the enemy retiring into MONTAUBAN caused us to take cover in dugouts and folds in the ground and they served very well as the 90th Bde advanced towards MONTAUBAN.

I had reported to Brigade that I considered the 18th Division were slow on our left. This I consider was not an unmixed blessing for the German for when I reached the GLATZ REDOUBT I came into touch with Lieut Colonel Sir Henry Hill Commanding 19th Manchesters and the situation seemed favourable.

We both went forward and considered the consolidation of the position which was much hampered by the 90th Brigade being in our GLATZ REDOUBT trenches waiting to assault MONTAUBAN.

Even then 1.15 after Zero I could see we were behind the enemy on the 18th Divisions front, but our men & our Lewis Gunners who had been told off to guard our left flank had apparently seen the opposing lines fighting and had enfiladed the enemy trenches which looked to me to be the wired part of TRAIN ALLEY and trenches in its vicinity. The enemy's retreat from the front of the 18th Division was raked by us and stopped down TRAIN ALLEY and was probably diverted to BRESLAU ALLEY causing the enemy heavy casualties from the 18th Division. On the 90th Brigade moving forward consolidation along the GLATZ REDOUBT to TRAIN ALLEY was completed by the remnants of the fighting Battalion. No.1. Strong Point and Trench was held by Headquarters 18th Ser. Battn. K.L.R. and a working party from R.E.

The enemy shelled these places intermittently during the night inflicting about 12 casualties. Activity against MONTAUBAN beyond our line took place. The Stretcher Bearers whose ranks were thinned by casualties worked incessantly on the wounded of every Battalion they came across. Many of our men and the wounded of the 90th Brigade remained on the field for 40 hours. The Medical Officer and every available officer went out to deal with them and marked their positions and the 2nd Wiltshire Regt. over worked as they were gave valuable help in clearing the racecourse into our front trenches. I cannot help mentioning that I never heard a man of my Battalion make a single complaint or request that he should be moved but seemed to look upon it as a kindness that Officers and the Medical Officer should come out and do their best for them when they were helpless.

Every fighting Officer was hit by enemy's bullets or shells except one and he was accidentally bayoneted as he crossed a trench.

The officers of the Battn. Staff alone were untouched.

I estimate our casualties at about 500.

I told both officers and men that there were to be no S.O.S. messages and the REDOUBT was to be carried by themselves without causing the Brigadier to use his reserves, so during the battle the estimates were put at a lower figure than the actual number.

I cannot speak too highly of the gallantry of the Officers and men. The men amply repaid the care and kindness of their Company Officers who have always tried to lead and not to drive. As laid down in my first lecture to the Battalion when formed, in the words of Prince Kraft"Men follow their Officers, not from fear but from love of their Regiment where everything had always and at all times gone well with them".

20th (Service) Battalion (4th City) King's (Liverpool Regiment)

MARICOURT

7.30a.m. After 65 mins intensive bombardment the Battalion advanced to the attack of the German trenches. The Battn advanced in four lines each of the two leading Companies on a frontage of 2 platoons – No.1 and 2 Co. (in that order from the right) leading. No.3 Co in 3rd wave, No.4 Co in 4th wave, there being a distance of about 100 yds between each line.

The lines advanced thro' the enemies' artillery fire as tho' on parade in quick time. The leading waves went on without a pause to ALT TRENCH and CASEMENT TRENCH which were secured at [gap in text] am the casualties up to this being small, on our barrage lifting DUBLIN TRENCH (the 1st objective) was captured and consolidation immediately proceeded with, Captain WHITING with 3rd wave entrenching about 150 yards in rear. Captain ROBINSON was wounded and No.2 Co was commanded during the rest of the day by 2/Lieut C.P. MOORE. Casualties up to now were: Killed 2 Officers & 1 wounded – 49 O R casualties killed and wounded.

At 11.50am orders were received for the assault of the BRIQUETERIE, Battn Operation orders for this were issued from N.W. of GERMANS WOOD – our barrage lifted at 12.30pm and No.4 Co under Captain E.C. ORFORD assisted by a Section of bombers under 2/Lieut BAKER who went up NORD ALLEY and CHIMNEY TRENCH to secure his left flank, who had got right forward under cover of the fire of our guns rushed it almost without opposition – on the far side a party of the enemy were found in deep dug-outs they brought a machine gun into action and some close fighting ensued in which Lieut GOOCH and 2/Lieut WILLIAMS were wounded.

Opposition was however speedily overcome and the garrison consisting of the H.Q. of a Regt, 1 Colonel and 4 other officers, 40 rank & file, 2 Machine Guns together with maps, orders, documents and material fell into our hands. Steps were immediately taken for consolidating the ground won, which however owing to the destruction wrought by our"Heavies"was a matter of great difficulty, what had been trenches being almost unrecognisable as such and the earth so pulverized that cover could only be made by aid of Sandbags. The garrison was heavily shelled thro' afternoon and most of the night and casualties were many. Bn. H.Q. were at the junction of GLATZ ALLEY and CASEMENT TRENCH N.W. of GERMANS WOOD and this together with DUBLIN TRENCH received considerable attention from the enemies' guns.

Casualties during the day: 2 Officers killed, 2/Lieut's F. BARNES and J.C. LAUGHLIN, and 3 wounded – Captain H.H. ROBINSON, Lieut S. GOOCH, 2/Lieut F.J. WILLIAMS

75 O.R. killed and wounded.

6th (Service) Battalion King's Own Scottish Borderers

FIELD

Battn paraded 11.10pm night of 30th June/1st July at cross roads GROVETOWN and marched by X road to TRIGGER WOOD VALLEY. All in 12.45am. Men in splendid condition and very keen. Bombardment by us all night; very intensive from 5 to 7.30AM. Our infantry attacked on large front 7.30am.

At 12NOON objective reported taken in immediate front – MONTAUBAN. Weather splendid. Wind S.W.

'D' Coy out 7.15pm back 5.30am (2-7-16) carried R.E. Stores to LOOP TRENCH for Essex Battn of 53rd Bde.

'A' Coy out 11.50pm to 6.30am (2-7-16) carried stores to forward Dump of 54th Bde near POMMIERS REDOUBT.

16th (Service) Battalion (1st City) Manchester Regiment

Left Assembly trenches 8.30am information as previously practised. Moved up as close as possible to our artillery barrage and halted about 9.20am. Maintained communication with the 17th Manchester Regt. on our right, but were under heavy machine gun and rifle fire from our left rear, being unsupported by troops on our left.

At 9.55am on the artillery barrage lifting, no supporting troops still appearing on our left and the hostile machine gun fire still being very severe, the advance could not be continued. At 10.5am on the appearance of the leading troops attacking on our left, continued the advance and without a check passed through MONTAUBAN and seized and occupied MONTAUBAN ALLEY at 10.30am and immediately proceeded to consolidate as follows: 'A' 'B' and 'C' Companies MONTAUBAN ALLEY; 'D' Company edge of village also Keeps F. and D. and established H.Q. in Valley trench immediately S. of D. Keep.

About 9.30pm enemy attacked against our front and left, S.O.S. sent, barrage placed on our right front (a few shells too short), attack held up by M.G. and rifle fire, and eventually withdrawn under cover of darkness.

During night 1st/2nd continual bombardment from E. and N. with heavy shells.

At 3.30am on the 2nd enemy counter-attack along the whole front, S.O.S. sent, but no reply for 15 minutes; brought to a standstill along front at 250 yds distance.

Number of attacking troops estimated at two battalions; front attacked about 800 yds.

Enemy entered MONTAUBAN ALLEY on our right and a bombing encounter ensued with our right flank. Asked O.C. MONTAUBAN for support and one company immediately placed at my disposal, and two platoons sent up to reinforce. About 5am Headquarters and two leading companies 2nd Wilts arrived to relieve. The enemy counter-attack having been withdrawn about 4a.m. having suffered heavily from M.G. L.G. and rifle fire, but their bombing party left in our trenches.

Relief commenced about 8am and Battalion withdrawn by 1.30pm.

Captured two guns and 16th Manchester Regt written on them, also names of men who captured them – and about a hundred prisoners.[1]

NOTE

1. This text appears in the War Diary under the heading"Brief Report of Operations carried out by 16th Manchester Regiment on July 1st/2nd (In accordance with Bde Operation Order No.23.), July 3rd 1916". The text is signed by Lieutenant Colonel C.L. Petrie, Commanding 16th (Service) Battalion (1st City) Manchester Regiment.

17th (Service) Battalion (2nd City) Manchester Regiment

8.30a.m. The Battalion attacked E. of MONTAUBAN. Casualties: 8 Officers, 340 O.R.

Document Attached to the War Diary

Report on the actions of 17th (Service) Battalion (2nd City) Manchester Regiment on 1-2 July 1916, signed by Major C.L. MacDonald, Adjutant:

8.30am The Bn left assembly trenches according to programme in 8 waves. Order of Company's 'A' 'B' 'C' 'D' and proceeded by prescribed line towards MONTAUBAN – formation lines of ½ platoon's in file.

Slight shrapnel & indirect M.G. fire met with, 100 yds in advance of assembly trenches. The C.O. Col. JOHNSON was hit about 400 yds from the assembly trenches & Major MACDONALD assumed command of the Bn.

The leading waves were held up by our own barrage N. of GLATZ REDOUBT. Rear waves closed up to shorter distance and became to a small extent intermingled.

During this check the advance was harassed by rifle and M.G. fire from left flank.

10am   Shelter was taken in trenches & shell holes, the losses at this point were slight.

At 10am approximately barrage lifted from trench on to N. end of MONTAUBAN and the advance was continued.

Shells were still falling short of MONTAUBAN on our left flank during the advance up the Southern slope. By this time the first 4 waves had practically amalgamated & had extended.

At the point when the advance was resumed the rear waves were held up by a wide trench which could only be crossed at one or two points & traffic in this trench was obstructed by a downward flow of prisoners. The result was that the rear waves became intermingled & had to shake out again on emerging from the trench.

The general appearance of the Bn. now was two large waves at a distance of 400 yds.

10.20am The first waves entered MONTAUBAN under Capt. MADDEN who had pushed forward from 'C' Coy after most of the officers of the leading company had fallen. There was no opposition to the entry. Bombing parties proceeded to clear NORD & TRAIN ALLEY & C.T. in orchard N.E. of B. strong point, the enemy met with in these places surrendered without opposition and the leading waves pushed on through the town. The near waves consisting partly of carrying parties, arrived in rather an exhausted state, due chiefly to their desire to be "in at the finish". The town was practically deserted & was completely in ruins. It was almost impossible to trace even the run of the streets. All enemy met with surrendered immediately. The Coys then proceeded to their allotted places in the previously arranged defence scheme. 'A' Coy to N.E. 'B' Coy to S.E. 'C' Coy to strong point C & 'D' Coy to strong point B.

About 100 of the enemy were seen streaming northwards along the road to BAZENTIN-LE-GRAND.

A party of about 40 endeavoured rally & organised a small counter attack but this attempt was broken up by rapid fire.

A small party from 'A' Coy was pushed out to "TRIANGLE POINT" - this point was found to be non-existent and the party cleared a portion of MONTAUBAN ALLEY and proceeded to establish themselves there.

Hostile M.G. fire was opened on the village immediately on our entry & about 2pm a heavy bombardment of 15cm & 77mm was opened on the town, which continued almost without cessation until the Bn was relieved about 40 hours later.

Parties were set to work at once to consolidate Strong points & the perimeter. The digging of trenches was very difficult owing to the fact that the village was a mass of shell holes & loose crumbling earth. The total inadequacy of trenches in such a soil was abundantly proved in the next 48 hours. The prearranged line on the E side of N1. was found to be untenable as it was commanded by direct enfilade from the high ground S of BAZENTIN-LE-GRAND & a new line was taken up to the W of N1. Practically no dug-out shelters were available for the men & casualties were heavy from the commencement of the bombardment.

The enemy was making accurate observation of the village during the whole of our tenure of it & his shooting was extraordinarily good. No sooner did a working party commence to work on a new bit of trench than shells rained upon them.

At night when work was able to proceed unobserved the eastern side of the village was shelled with impartiality & was searched from N. to S. in a very thorough fashion. Evidently the most methodical arrangements had been made for rendering the village uninhabitable – special attention being paid to Strong points B & C and the middle of the Orchard, on East Side.

Bn Hqrs. were established in a well constructed dug-out just South of Strong point B, and a dressing station in a good cellar just in rear. Fortunately both these shelters withstood the bombardment.

Throughout the operations our own Artillery support was all that could be desired. Retaliation was almost invariably prompt. At the same time they failed to silence the enemy batteries which were causing us such heavy loses.

Barrage were always prompt & effective. It was noticeable that when an aeroplane was making observations enemy's artillery fire almost ceased. This gave us two lulls of ½ an hour each in the course of our tenure of the village. Possibly if an aeroplane had been kept in continual observation casualties might have been reduced & hostile batteries might have been located.

COUNTER ATTACK

At 3.15am on the 2nd the detached post in MONTAUBAN ALLEY near "TRIANGLE POINT" was attacked & bombed out. They held out until their supply of bombs was exhausted, & then endeavoured to retire, only 3 got back, 2 of whom were wounded.

Germans to the number of 100 then massed on the W side of the MONTAUBAN – BAZENTIN-LE-GRAND Rd just N. of MONTAUBAN ALLEY.

1 platoon of 'C' Coy advanced up N.1. under Capt. MADDEN and took up a position on the Rd. just E of VALLEY TRENCH. Artillery were informed & the enemy suffered heavy casualties from shrapnel & rapid rifle fire; they then dashed into MONTAUBAN Alley. The heavies then opened on MONTAUBAN ALLEY and the enemy became demoralised & dashed back across the road to the dead ground towards LONGUEVAL, they also suffered casualties from the platoon across the road N.1.

Some of them remained in MONTAUBAN Alley and a bombing party was sent up N.1. to bomb them out. This party could not get near enough owing to the barrage by the heavies. The relief of 16th MCHRS on the left interrupted the operations and the C.O. of the WILTS undertook the clearance of MONTAUBAN ALLEY.

COMMUNICATIONS
It was found impossible to establish any system of communication N. of Bn. Hqrs. except by runner. Communication with the rear was obtained sometimes by wire, sometimes by visual means, & was practically uninterrupted.

ATTACHED PARTIES
Nothing was seen of attached R.E. parties who were detailed to assist in consolidation of strong points.

M.G. COY.
Communication with this unit was not entirely satisfactory. 2 guns were placed in position on Northern perimeter of E orchard under the orders of O.C. M.G. Coy. Of the other 2 guns detailed nothing was seen.

STOKES MORTARS
Sgt of the Stokes Mortar Batty reported at Bn Hqrs. about midday on the 1st & was shown the position (strong point C) to which to take his guns. He returned to KEEP "A" to bring up his guns but nothing further was seen of the party.

18th (Service) Battalion (3rd City) Manchester Regiment

MONTAUBAN
The battalion took part in the operations which led to the capture of MONTAUBAN, acting as carrying battalion to the 90th INFANTRY BRIGADE.
Total casualties: 6 officers wounded (CAPT S.E. WOOLLAM, Lt H.B. HARRISON,

2nd Lt A. COOPER (died of wounds) 2nd Lt F.A. ESSE and 2nd Lt. G.H. DOUGHTY) and 170 other ranks, killed wounded and missing.

Document Attached to the War Diary

Report to the G.O.C. 90th Infantry Brigade signed by Lieutenant Colonel W.A. Smith, Commanding Officer of the 18th (Service) Battalion (3rd City) Manchester Regiment:

Sir,

I have the honour to report that the Brigade having begun to advance one hour after Zero as ordered the various detachments of the battalion under my command left their assembly trenches between 1 hour 15 min and 1 hour 30 min after Zero.

1. I had two platoons attached to the field Company R.E. to carry stores for them to MONTAUBAN.
2. Two platoons carrying R.E. stores to keep 'A' at MONTAUBAN.
3. Two platoons carrying S.A.A. and bombs to MONTAUBAN.
4. One platoon carrying S.A.A. between dumps within our own lines.
5. One platoon carrying ammunition for the Stokes Mortar Battery.

There were left to me two companies to form the Brigade Reserve, but half of one of these companies had to carry equipment up for the Brigade Machine Gun Coy. to MONTAUBAN.

Generally speaking all the carrying parties and the Brigade Reserve moved off in rear of the other three battalions of the Brigade, but as the leading battalions halted for some time these parties closed up and in one case (No.1) arrived there before some of the party for whom they were carrying and the others practically on the heels of the assaulting troops.

All carrying parties had casualties on the way up caused by machine gun fire and shells, but showing admirable devotion to duty, every man arrived at his destination with his load – excepting casualties – and among them individuals who through no fault of their own became detached from their units on their way up. The loads were found to be very heavy especially in view of the heat and most men arrived in an exhausted condition, but all parties went back for more loads and no time was lost. Many casualties occurred in subsequent journies owing to shell fire.

As regards the Brigade Reserve one company started to advance about 500 yards in rear of the 2nd R.S.F. but as the leading battalion halted for some time and it became difficult to distinguish different units the company passed through the units in front and went straight to a front about 600 yards south of MONTAUBAN and commenced digging in. During the advance the company suffered many casualties from shells and rifle and machine gun fire on our left. The platoon on the left touching the railway, crossed over and disposed of some cunning snipers.

Our other company of the reserve together with the Brigade Machine Gun Coy. and battalion H.Q. advanced close in rear of the other company but finding the battalions in front halted, it remained for about thirty minutes in the vicinity of the enemy VALLEY SUPPORT trench. Up to and during this time there was a lot of machine gun and rifle fire from the left and a fair amount of shelling which caused some casualties. During the halt I got a machine gun and Lewis gun into position in order to bring fire to bear on the trenches on our left, but as the exact spot where the fire came from could not be located and the adjoining brigade appeared to be advancing in the trenches instead of above ground I was afraid of shooting into them and had to abandon the idea but was able to fire with effect into a party of the enemy retreating on our left.

As the leading battalions advanced I moved up to my intended advanced position in ALT TRENCH but as we were heavily shelled decided to go forward to the trench S. of MONTAUBAN when I joined the two companies of R.S.F. the other company being in rear in the ravine. The half company with me then commenced digging a new trench but shortly afterwards I was ordered by O.C. MONTAUBAN to send it to reinforce the 16th. Battn. Manchester Regt. in the meantime the Brigade Machine Gun Coy. had advanced into MONTAUBAN and the O.C. that Coy ordered the two platoons of the reserve Coy. attached to him to assist in making emplacements and to go to MARICOURT for ammunition. I was afterwards ordered by O.C. MONTAUBAN to send my remaining reserve company to reinforce the 17th. battalion Manchester Regt. in MONTAUBAN.

Later in the evening I was ordered to withdraw the reserve companies and I sent them back to the ravine. The following morning I moved my H.Q. back from S. Trench to TRAIN ALLEY.

During the morning of the 2nd inst. nothing of note occurred but I was able to increase the reserve Coy. by the addition of some of the carrying parties.

Our total casualties during the operations were 6 officers wounded, and about 170 other ranks killed and wounded.

19th (Service) Battalion (4th City) Manchester Regiment

OBJECTIVE – THE GLATZ REDOUBT

After an intense bombardment by guns and trench mortars of all calibres and also by Stokes Mortar placed in Russian saps, the first wave went over the parapet at 7.30am – successive waves followed at about 100 yard interval.[1]

8.35.   The only checks to our advance were our own artillery barrages and these pauses were utilized for reorganisation of the lines. The final objective was gained at 8.35am and at this time 2 sections only of the Support Company had been used as reinforcements.

The positions taken up by the companies are shown on the attached map.

The Lewis guns were not used in the actual advance.

The cleaners examined all trenches and dug-outs, but found little opposition from the German Infantry left behind. A little bombing opposition was met by C Company in Alt Trench, but it was quickly overcome. The casualties were heaviest on the left and were chiefly occasioned by a machine gun well on the left flank. 2 machine guns, 3 trench mortars and many prisoners were taken.

Immediately the Northern face of the Glatz Redoubt was attained, smoke candles and red flares were lighted. The smoke barrage was very effective in concealing the approach of the 90th Brigade towards MONTAUBAN. Consolidation was immediately begun. Picks, shovels and smoke candles were immediately sent to front line by the Support Company. Other materials arrived by the 2nd Yorks Regt. Wire was put out, T head saps dug, and manned by Lewis guns, pending the arrival of Vickers guns, fire steps were made, deep and narrow trenches dug in the old ones, rifles were cleaned, water bottles filled from petrol cans brought by carriers. Tools and sandbags were the chief shortage.

12.45.   When the Briqueterie was taken at 12.45pm MONTAUBAN having been previously captured, No.5 strong point was consolidated and Nord Alley was taken over by 2 Platoons of D Company.

All day and night shrapnel and time fuze H.E. was used intermittently, but no work was interfered with. Nord Alley suffered most.

2.30.   D Company (1 Platoon) under Capt. Gevere moved into TRAIN ALLEY as support to the 2 platoons in Nord Alley at 2.30pm and the rest of D Company moved up there the following morning (July 2nd).

No.6 strong point was started at dawn.

8.30.   Headquarters moved into Alt Trench one hour after the battle began & established a position near No.1 Strong Point. Communication was well maintained by runners and later by disc and telephone. Scouts and runners did exceptionally good work and the linesmen were notable for their work also. When not otherwise engaged, all men attached to Headquarters consolidated Alt Trench. Smoke from shell fire interfered for a long time with visual signalling. All companies were in telephonic communication with advanced H.Q. in the afternoon of July 1st.

Total casualties for this day, 2nd Lt. A.W. ATKINSON and 40 O.R. killed, 2nd Lt. E. OUTRAM missing, believed killed. Missing 11 O.R., Wounded 2/Lt. K.H. ALLEN & 136 O.R. Died of wounds 1 O.R.

NOTE

1. The War Diary also contains a table that illustrates the battalion's formation of attack. The first wave consisted of two platoons from each of 'A' and 'C' companies. The second and third waves, meanwhile, each comprised one platoon from 'A' Company and one from 'C' Company. The following "cleaners" consisted of two groups, one which comprised thirty men from 'D' Company and a platoon from 2/Yorks, the other thirty men from 'B' Company and a platoon from 2/Yorks. The fourth wave involved men from two platoons of 'B' Company; the fifth two platoons from 'B' Company; and the sixth and seventh waves both being made up of two platoons from 'D' Company ordered to advance "in lines of half platoons in file". The breadth of the battalion's front was "between 250 and 300 yards".

8th (Service) Battalion Norfolk Regiment

ASSEMBLY TRENCHES
The Battalion took part in an assault on the German trenches North of CARNOY, and S.W. of MONTAUBAN.

The 7th Battalion The Queens Royal West Surrey Regiment of the 55th Brigade were on our Right and the 6th Battalion Royal Berkshire Regiment, of our own Brigade, were on our left.

In the early hours of the morning the Battalion was in position in the four assembly trenches, i.e., in their battle position ready for attack.

The early hours of the morning were passed in comparative quietude.

5.30am. Teas were bought up from CARNOY and served out in the Assembly trenches.

7.20am. Our artillery commenced the intense bombardment and the enemys retaliation on our Fourth line Assembly trench became more apparent.

7.27am. A mine and two Russian saps were exploded on our front.

7.27am. The first wave of 'C' and 'D' Companies deployed from our firing line and laid out in the open about 30 yards in front. This movement was accomplished without loss.

7.30am. The assault commenced. The remainder of the two assaulting Companies left our trenches and moved forward in four successive waves.

MINE TRENCH was reached and crossed by these two Companies with practically no opposition, and without loss on our side. All Germans remaining alive in this trench after our artillery barrage had passed were thoroughly cowed and at once surrendered. 'C' Company on our right took about 30 prisoners from the West edge of the Mine craters.

MINE SUPPORT was taken about 7.40am. The wire entanglements in front having been completely demolished by our artillery.

Up to this point the Battalion suffered very few casualties.

BUND SUPPORT was reached and taken at 8.00am. where a halt was made.

The two assaulting Companies on leaving BUND SUPPORT came under very heavy enfilade machine gun fire from the direction of BRESLAU SUPPORT and BACK TRENCH and suffered heavily, Captain B.P. Ayre being killed and Captain J.H. Hall being seriously wounded. By this time the following Officers had been wounded:-
Capt & Adjt H.P. Berney-Ficklin., 2nd Lieuts, J.G. Hampson, C.T. Blackborn, L. Padfield, S.A. Wharton, G.R. Ironmonger and E. MacLean, (At Duty). There now remained no Officer with the Left leading Company and two subalterns in the Right leading Company, which were reduced to about 90 and 100 respectively.
The Left leading Company under C.S.M., A.F. Raven, reached our first objective – POMMIERS TRENCH – and took it about 10.30am. A portion of the Right Leading Company also got into POMMIERS TRENCH near the East side of THE LOOP at the same time, but the remainder of this Company was held up by Machine Gun fire and a strong point at the junctions of BOCHE TRENCH and BACK TRENCH with MINE ALLEY.
After this Company had been reinforced by a platoon from the Support Company under 2nd Lieut. G.E. Miall-Smith, and the Battalion Bombers under Sergeant H.H. West had also been sent up to this point, this strong point fell and the garrison of about 150 Germans and 2 Officers of a Bavarian Regiment surrendered, and right leading company was then able to push forward in to the East portion of POMMIERS TRENCH which up to then had not been taken, At this point in the attack 'A' Company which had been in Reserve and had advanced from the assembly trenches in artillery formation, at 7.45am and had been consolidating MINE SUPPORT, now advanced to BUND SUPPORT and commenced the consolidation of this trench: at the same time 'B', the Support Company, advanced with three platoons (1 already having been sent to reinforce 'C') to POMMIERS TRENCH.

3.00pm. 'D' Company had now taken THE LOOP and both assaulting companies advanced to take the MONTAUBAN ALLEY line – the final objective of the Battalion.
Owing to machine guns firing from this line and from N.W. of MONTAUBAN, 'D' Company on the left suffered heavy casualties, and 'C' Company, led by 2nd Lieut J.H. Attenborough made repeated attempts to get into MONTAUBAN ALLEY, but did not succeed until a bombing party, under 2nd Lieut L.A. Gundry-White gained an entrance by way of LOOP TRENCH on the left.
Unfortunately, just before this had been effected, 2nd Lieut J.H. Attenborough with C.S.M. J. Coe had both been killed in the attempt to get into this trench.

473

5.45pm. The MONTAUBAN ALLEY line was taken and the Battalion was in touch with the 7th Queens on our right and the 6th Royal Berks on our left.

6.00pm. The whole of 'B' Company having been used to support 'C' and 'D' Companies who were now reduced to, respectively, 70 and 80 Other Ranks and 1 Officer, the work of consolidation of MONTAUBAN ALLEY was commenced at once and patrols were sent forward to reconnoitre along CATERPILLAR TRENCH and EAST TRENCH.

The Reserve Company, whom in the meanwhile had advanced and consolidated POMMIERS TRENCH and THE LOOP, were now bought up and sent forward to take up the advanced post known as the GREEN LINE.

The Green Line was taken up and the strong points commenced at about 8.00pm and patrols were sent forward in the direction of CATERPILLAR WOOD.

8.00pm. From now onwards the enemy commenced a heavy and continuous bombardment with 5.9 and a few 77mm Shells on the West end of MONTAUBAN ALLEY held by the Battalion, generally in the vicinity of the junction of LOOP TRENCH with MONTAUBAN ALLEY, a few shells falling in the LOOP itself, but practically none in rear.

Our Casualties for the days fighting were:

Officers:	Killed	2
	Died of Wounds	1
Wounded	8 including 2 At Duty. These being 2nd Lieut S.N. Cozens-Hardy (who was wounded just outside Battalion Headquarters, which were at the S.W. end of THE LOOP, were they had been moved up to as soon as the MONTAUBAN ALLEY line had been reached) and 2nd Lieut E. MacLean.	
Other Ranks:	Killed	102
	Wounded	219
	Missing	13
TOTAL CASUALTIES:		
	Officers	11
	Other Ranks	334

6th (Service) Battalion Northamptonshire Regiment

Narrative of the part taken by the 6th (Service) Battalion, Northamptonshire Rgt. in the attack on the German position between MAMETZ and MONTAUBAN:

The 54th Brigade were the left brigade of the 18th Division, which attacked the German position between MAMETZ (exclusive) and MONTAUBAN (inclusive) with three brigades in the front line. The first objective of the 54th Brigade was from POMMIERS REDOUBT (inclusive) on the right to the junction of BEETLE ALLEY and MAPLE TRENCH (inclusive) on the left. The final objective was a ridge overlooking CATERPILLAR WOOD and WILLOW BROOK, demarcated by a blue line on attached map [*not present*]. The 91st Brigade, 7th Division were on our left and the 53rd Brigade, 15th Division on our right.

The 11th Royal Fusiliers on the left and the 7th Bedfordshire Rgt on the right formed the front line of the 54th Brigade.

The 6th Battalion Northamptonshire Rgt (less six platoons) were the 3rd or supporting battalion and also found one company as "dug-out" clearing parties, which were attached to the Royal Fusiliers and Bedfords and cleared the "dug-outs" in the German trenches. The three remaining platoons acted as carrying parties to the brigade.

The 12th Middlesex regiment were in Brigade Reserve.

The Brigade had undergone a week's previous training over ground laid out on the plan of the German trenches to be attacked and were in fine fettle when the day arrived.

The German trenches and wire entanglement had been battered for seven days by our intense artillery bombardment.

On the night preceding the launching of the attack (June30th-July 1st) the two battalions in the front line were accommodated in our four front line trenches. The 6th Northamptonshire Rgt (less six platoons) moved from BRONFAY FARM about 11.30pm on 30th June and occupied their forming-up trenches as follows:- 'A' Coy right Coy supporting the Bedfordshire Rgt in trenches N. & N.W. of CARNOY.

'B' Coy left Coy supporting the Royal Fusiliers in trenches in CAFTET WOOD. 'D' Coy (less 2 platoons) with a portion of Battalion Hqrs. were in reserve and were concealed in trenches in the same wood.

It was no easy matter for these companies in such a restricted area to debouch from the wood and get into position for the advance, as there were many trenches to cross and gaps in our wire entanglements to be negotiated. The terrain however had been carefully reconnoitred by officers and section commanders on previous nights, and trenches had been bridged and wire cut.

At half-an-hour after zero hour (8am) the regiment in lines of half platoons at about 60 paces interval and 150 paces distance found themselves launched to the attack. They had to change direction slightly to the right and open out, soon after moving off, but this was successfully accomplished. The battalion advanced as steadily as if they were on the parade ground, their instructions being, that it was not to halt until the enemy second trench AUSTRIAN SUPPORT was reached.

All companies came under a heavy artillery barrage before our rear trench

HYDE ROAD WEST was reached, but they continued to move forward with admirable coolness, 'A' Coy even checking in "no man's land" to correct their direction. The two leading companies arrived simultaneously at the EMDEN and AUSTRIAN support trenches. A halt of 40 minutes here took place, during which the left Coy and bombing parties were detached and sent up BLACK ALLEY. At the same time (8.20am) the right platoon of 'A' Coy had reached BUND TRENCH, and were followed 20 minutes later by the 2nd platoon, who moved to avoid artillery fire.

From BUND TRENCH to POMMIER TRENCH both companies came under a heavy artillery fire and suffered considerably and here Captain Neville commanding 'B' Coy was wounded. 'A' Coy on reaching POMMIER TRENCH immediately began making strong point VI, the three remaining platoons proceeding to POMMIERS REDOUBT and consolidated that on evacuation by the Bedfords. 'B' Coy moved up at the same time and started to consolidate their allotted strong points as follows:

```
1 platoon to No. III Strong Point
1     "      " MAPLE TRENCH
1     "      " No.IV Strong Point
1     "      " No.V    "      "
```

On ascertaining that the 91st Brigade had been held up on our left, which was thus exposed, the officer commanding 'B' Coy asked for further help and 2 platoons of 'C' Coy, who had been bombing "dug-outs" but had rejoined Hqrs. went sent forward and eventually occupied MAPLE TRENCH – 'D' Coy in reserve had followed 'B' Coy and detached one platoon to garrison Strong Point II, placing the remaining platoon in POMMIER TRENCH – This Coy and part of Hqrs. came in for heavy shell fire and suffered severely. By about 10.15am all Strong Points in the first objective had been occupied and were being placed in a state of defence, and the task allotted to the Battalion had been accomplished.

The two platoons of 'C' and two of "D' Coys who went over with the Royal Fusiliers and Bedfords worked through the 3 front lines of the enemy trenches on a set plan and carried out their work thoroughly & well. Three sections of 'D' Coy however suffered very heavily from machine gun fire and were practically wiped out.

Liaison was well maintained between the battalion and the companies in its right and left.

All company commanders carried out their orders correctly and handled their companies with gallantry & skill. Platoons were well led both by officers and NCOs.

Signalling was perhaps our weakest point - Runners & bearers worked splendidly.

2nd Lt. Price distinguished himself by the excellent and reliable information which he obtained.

Bn. Hqrs. was first established at PICADILLY and afterwards moved to a point in BUND TRENCH about 100 yards W. of the TRIANGLE.

The following casualties occurred on this day:

Officers wounded:	Capt. Neville, Frank Septimus	
	Lieut. Shankster, George	
	2nd Lieut. Hamilton, Noel Crawford	
Other ranks:	Killed	29
	Wounded	123
	Missing	4
	Shell Shock	1
Total:	3 Officers	
	Other ranks	157

11th (Service) Battalion (St. Helens Pioneers) Prince of Wales's Volunteers (South Lancashire Regiment)

The Battalion took part in the offensive carried out by the 30th Division on the right of the British front. Hour of Zero 7.30am 1st July, 1916.

The duties and objectives allotted to the Battalion as above were carried out to time. At 2.45pm on 1st July, 2 Communication Trenches were through to German Front Line to a depth of 4 feet. (Nos. 2 and 4 from right of Sector). At 3.43pm No.1 Communtn [*sic*] Trench was open to a depth of 5 feet. All these 3 were immediately continued and work progressed favourably.

No.3 was not ready till much later owing to heavy casualties from shell fire. At 9.20pm Russian Saps were opened by Trench Communication Parties. Saps from A.P. 3 and 4 and A.P. 5 and 6. Parties also provided on MONTAUBAN-MARICOURT ROAD.

6th (Service) Battalion Princess Charlotte of Wales's (Royal Berkshire Regiment)

CARNOY

12mn.	Battn in forming up trenches – A2 subsector – Carnoy.
7am	Coys report all ready and everything in order.
7.28	CASINO POINT mine exploded – some casualties caused by debris thrown back into our first two assembly trenches.
	First wave advanced into NO MANS LAND.

7.30	Attack launched – first wave takes MINE TRENCH and CASINO POINT.
7.32	Second wave advanced from forming up point in NO MANS LAND.
7.35	First batch of 6 prisoners brought in – shoulder strap – [*illegible*] – and all papers sent by special runner to Brigade Advanced Report Centre. 3rd wave moved forward from our line.
7.50	First wave reached POMMIER TRENCH having suffered heavy casualties. 2/Lt Hollis went forward to BUND SUPPORT and reported Capt LITTEN killed – no officers left with leading Coy – (B Coy) Capt McArthur wounded. Capt LONGHURST has ordered 2/Lt COURAGE to move up and take command of 'B' Coy. As far as known Capt FENNER still with 'A' Coy but 2/Lt COLLOT and Lt TRAILL killed. Bombardment of POMMIER Redoubt continued. Bombers of 'B' Coy and Bn Bombers start bombing up POPOFF LANE. Vickers Guns sent up to get in position near junction of POPOFF LANE and POMMIERS TRENCH. Norfolks held up round the LOOP – right flank exposed. Work of consolidation started. Suffering severe casualties from M.G. in the LOOP.
9.30	POMMIER REDOUBT assaulted and taken – line starts to advance towards MONTAUBAN ALLEY.
9.35	Bn H.Q. moved to POMMIERS TRENCH. 2/Lt HOLLIS remained in Old Report Centre. No communications except by visual – all wires broken in many places.
9.40	Adjt sent to reconnoitre and report on situation as Brigade calling for information.
10.0	Adjt reports: "Norfolks on our right not advancing – 'A' Coy have made a succession of bombing posts with L.G's to protect their flank and are working up LOOP TRENCH – strong opposition against them here – our right is very exposed. On left we are in touch with Bedfords – and are advancing up MONTAUBAN ALLEY by bombing. Have suffered heavy casualties especially among officers." Reported verbally to Brigade.
10.40	Reported that Norfolks have taken LOOP. Pi/3 sent to Brigade.
10.50	Norfolks still held up at BACK TRENCH and BOCHE TRENCH. Bombing attacks at MONTAUBAN ALLEY and LOOP TRENCH progressing slowly.
10.55	Collected about 30 scattered men and pushed these into attack at MONTAUBAN ALLEY – two Stokes guns bought up to assist. Pi/4 sent to Brigade.
11.10	Situation reported to Bde in Pi/5
12.15	Situation reported to Bde in Pi/74. Small reserve of about 30 men collected Pi/73 sent to O.C. 'A' Coy.

12.50	Bombing attack on MONTAUBAN ALLEY progressed well and half the line taken. Attack up LOOP TRENCH has cleared up to the MONTAUBAN-MAMETZ Road. Slow progress continuing at both points. Essex have arranged to support us with 30 bombers for LOOP TRENCH. Pi/75 to Brigade by Pigeon.
1.30	C.O. and Adjt visited whole line. Position – The Norfolks still not up on our right. Capt Fenner with about 50 men hold LOOP TRENCH to the point where it crosses the MONTAUBAN-MAMETZ Road and are bombing on but are meeting with desperate resistance. Line from there runs across open to MONTAUBAN ALLEY about 100 yds from its junction W of LOOP TRENCH. Essex bombers not yet arrived and urgently called for again. Advance held up by several M.G.s and snipers and bombers.
3.15	Right report repeated attacks fail to effect advance – can reinforcements be sent up. Norfolks in touch on right but not yet advancing. Pi/78 sent to Norfolks. Reinforcements – 1 Capt, 2 subalterns and 2 O.R arrived.
3.20	Essex bombers arrive and sent up to MONTAUBAN ALLEY.
4.0	Advance appreciably increased at MONTAUBAN ALLEY. Two unemployed Stokes Guns found and sent to support attack in LOOP TRENCH.
4.45	Situation reported to Bde in Pi/80.
4.50	Brigade report verbally a re-bombardment of CATERPILLAR TRENCH and MONTAUBAN ALLEY. We urgently request them to cancel this as our two bombing attacks are advancing successfully.
5.20	Bde report verbally re-bombardment put off 30 minutes. Our advance has progressed considerably and the two parties only separated by 50 yds.
5.40	Rebombardment cancelled. MONTAUBAN ALLEY and LOOP TRENCH taken – line pushing on to final position & objective.
5.45	LOOP TRENCH handed over to NORFOLKS who were advised to bomb up CATERPILLAR TRENCH.
6.10	Situation reported to Norfolk H.Q. see Pi/85.
6.15	Bn H.Q. moved up into MONTAUBAN ALLEY. Communication by wire with Bde H.Q. established.
6.30	Final objective reached – work of consolidation progressing satisfactorily. Supplies of ammunition, food, water, bombs, grenades and a flame projector brought up.
8.30	Situation reported to Bde in Pi/86. Heavy shelling of POMMIERS REDOUBT and MONTAUBAN ALLEY with 5.9s.
8.50	Wires to Bde H.Q. all broken. Work of consolidation progressing well, strong points completed.

SLAUGHTER ON THE SOMME: 1 JULY 1916

Document Attached to the War Diary

A report on operations undertaken by the battalion between 27 June 1916, and 2 July 1916; signed by Captain S. Fenner, Commanding 6th (Service) Battalion Princess Charlotte of Wales's (Royal Berkshire Regiment):

The 6th Bn. Royal Berkshire Regt. entered the trenches and held the Brigade front during the bombardment of the German line. During the period 27th June to 7am 1st July the Battalion lost 50 NCOs and men from shell fire, of these many would have escaped uninjured had adequate dug-out accommodation been provided.

At 3am on the morning of July 1st the Battn. formed up into the assembly trenches. Although somewhat crowded here losses were small as the enemy only shelled the 3rd trench and this was left vacant and the men put in the 4th trench and the men originally to have gone into the 4th trench were in the open about 50 yards in rear of the 4th trench.

At 7.30am the attack started. The mine at CASINO POINT which was exploded at 7.27am threw some debris on to our first two waves but the loss sustained from this was not serious. A machine gun was actually heard firing before the mine went up and was blown up in it and actually seen at about 40 yards from the mine crater. This alone would have caused considerable losses. The moral effect of the mine on the Huns was also very noticeable and many rushed out towards our men holding up their hands.

The waves advanced to time and the clearing up parties of ESSEX attached to the Battalion did their work well.

The NORFOLKS on our right failed to advance and our right flank was in the air. Bombing squads were formed on this flank but losses were heavy from enfilade and rifle fire from the LOOP.

The Battn. Bombers and two Stokes Guns co-operated with the BEDFORDS up POMMIER LANE in the taking of POMMIER REDOUBT.

The O.C. Right assaulting Coy, as the NORFOLKS failed to advance determined to clear LOOP TRENCH and bombed up this and finally made good this trench and MONTAUBAN ALLEY.

LOOP TRENCH was handed over to the NORFOLKS at 5.30pm and the whole of the 6th ROYAL BERKS worked on consolidating – strengthening the position.

The Battalion lost heavily during the day – 13 officers and 337 other ranks chiefly due to lack of support on our right flank. Even after the LOOP fell a considerable time elapsed before any NORFOLKS attempted to advance to our support on the right.

The Battn. held the line until relieved on the 2nd July with only small losses.

The success of this operation was due to the thorough grounding everyone had in this work. The whole scheme had been explained to the men and even when the majority of the officers had been knocked out the N.C.O's and men carried on according to programme.

Every man knew the ground from the excellent maps that were received and this assisted in the successful attainment of the objective.

Bombers were found a good flank guard and once the LOOP TRENCH was taken it was held facing the right with two M.G. – two Lewis Guns – and bombers – and formed a good defensive flank.

Stokes Guns co-operated in the taking of MONTAUBAN ALLEY and POMMIERS REDOUBT. At both places they were effective, and they greatly assisted the Battn. in taking MONTAUBAN ALLEY without a re-bombardment.

Communication was difficult. Visual was most effective and as we were attacking uphill at the start was easy, but once the crest was passed separate receiving and forwarding stations had to be formed.

The Artillery barrage was very successful and the wire had been well cut.

7th (Service) Battalion Queen's (Royal West Surrey Regiment)

ASSAULT

A.1 Subsector

At 7.30am the Battn assaulted the German trenches to the front of left half of A1 subsector on a front of about 400 yards. After 12 hours fighting the final objective west of MONTAUBAN was reached and consolidated on a front of about 280yards.

Casualties:

Killed:	Capt J.R. WALPOLE, Capt G.H.H. SCOTT, LIEUT. H. CLOUDESLEY, LIEUT O.E. SALTMARSH, 2/Lt. F.J. MILLER, 2/Lt. G.S. DANDRIDGE, 2/Lt. R.C. HERBERT.
Wounded:	Lt. C.A. HAGGARD, Lt. A.J.R. HAGGARD, 2/Lt. E.F. BENNETT, 2/Lt. M. SHULDHAM-LEGH, 2/Lt.J. FARREN, 2/Lt. M.J.PENROSE-FITZGERALD, Lt. V. HOOK (attached 55th T.M.B.), Lt. D.R. HEATON and 2/Lt. H.J. TORTISE were both slightly wounded but remained at Duty.
O.R.	Killed: 174
	Wounded: 284
	Missing: 58.

Battn. held objective during night establishing touch with 8th E. Surrey Regt on its right and 8th Norfolk regt on its left.

SLAUGHTER ON THE SOMME: 1 JULY 1916

Document Attached to the War Diary

A short report on the action of 1 July 1916, written by Major Kemp-Welch, Commanding 7th (Service) Battalion Queen's (Royal West Surrey Regiment) and dated 9 July 1916:

While holding the Brigade battle front for two days immediately before the assault, the battalion had lost 40 casualties and had become somewhat exhausted owing to enemy shelling and lack of sleep owing to constant clearing of front trenches owing to our bombardment and other activities.

During the night previous to assault, the enemy intermittently shelled assembly trenches of the Battn. particularly in the vicinity of BATTY ROAD and N and S ends of PRINCES STREET. The shelling increased in from 6.am.to the hour of assault. The Battalion suffered four casualties only during the night. These were in the front line trench.

7.27am.   First wave left our trenches, and after a short wait in NO MANS LAND, advanced to the assault at 7.30am. At zero the whole Battalion moved forward. Havy [*sic*] rifle and Machine Gun fire was at once opened on the Battalion, coming chiefly from the E. end of the CRATER area, and BRESLAU SUPPORT and BACK TRENCH. 'D' Company, left leading Company of the Battalion, suffered very severely from Machine Gun fire from the CRATERS, only about twenty men of this Company reaching BRESLAU SUPPORT. The two sections that went round W. of the CRATERS were also decimated, and therefore failed in their mission of keeping touch with the Norfolk Regt. on our left.

7.35am.   'B' Company, finding that the two leading Companies had suffered heavily, pushed on without waiting and joined 'A', and 'D' in BRESLAU SUPPORT. Three platoons on the left of this Company suffered very severe casualties from rifle and Machine Gun fire in the CRATERS. Few of these ever reached BRESLAU SUPPORT. 'A', 'C' and 'D' Companies, were, from this time onward, hotly engaged in BRESLAU SUPPORT. About twenty men under 2nd Lieut A.B. Marston were in position in shell holes and disused trenches about S. end of MIDDLE AVENUE and were engaged with enemy in a strong point at A.2.d.91. which they finally neutralised.

7.50am.   'C' Company advanced from our front line trenches, forming line in NO MANS LAND ready to advance. Up to this time they had suffered few casualties. On advancing beyond the cover supplied by the CRATERS and the formation of the ground in NO MANS LAND, the two right platoons suffered very severely, particularly from Machine Gun fire from point 91.

7.55am.   'C' Company joined remainder of Battn. in BRESLAU SUPPORT, the remnants of No.12 platoon being employed in clearing BRESLAU TRENCH. By this time the Artillery barrage had lifted from both BACK TRENCH and POMMIERE LINE leaving the Battalion with no Artillery Support. The severe loses suffered by the left flank of the Battalion, had caused a wide gap on the left of the Battalion which was not filled till late in the afternoon. The right of the Battalion at this time was in touch with the East Surreys. From now onwards, the Battalion being unsupported, either by Artillery or by reinforcements, was definitely held up by BACK TRENCH. The East Surreys, on the right, moving on at about 8.45am the connection was not maintained to either right or left.

8.30am. No news received at Battalion Report Centre from any Company. Captain G.H.H. SCOTT, commanding fourth Company, went forward to attempt to find his Company and report situation, but was unfortunately killed before reaching German lines.

9.15am. Message received at Battalion Report Centre that E. end of CRATERS remained untaken. Stokes Gun brought into action and CRATERS reported to be cleared of the enemy at 9.40am.

10.30am. Pte. Anscombe volunteered and went forward to find an Officer of the Battalion and get situation. He found 2nd Lieut H.J. Tortise in BRESLAU SUPPORT, and obtained situation from him, returning with a fairly accurate report of the situation at 11.30.am.

11.45am. The C.O. moved forward to find out the situation and get in touch with Battn. at junction of BRESLAU SUPPORT and CARNOY-MONTAUBAN ROAD. The situation was then as follows:

About 100 men of the Battn. were in BRESLAU SUPPORT between CARNOY-MONTAUBAN ROAD and MIDDLE AVENUE. They were not in touch on either flank, the East Surreys having moved up towards DUGOUT TRENCH and no reinforcements having been received to fill the gap between the Battn. and 8th Norfolk Regt. on the left. The advance of the Battalion was being held up by enemy holding BACK TRENCH from A.2.d.13. They appeared to be of considerable strength with Machine Guns and kept up continuous rifle fire at any man who showed himself in BRESLAU SUPPORT. A Stokes Gun under Lieut V.Hook was with the Battalion, but out of action, owing to missing base plate. This gun was not ready for action until after 1.pm. Except for a few men of the Buffs under Capt. Neame no reinforcements had been received in this locality. A few men of the Battalion had got mixed up with the East Surreys and moved up with them to POMMIERE LINE.

12.45pm. A platoon of the Royal Sussex Pioneers who had been sent forward with a view to the consolidation of the POMMIERE LINE, was brought in line with the Battn.

1.0pm. Lieut D.R. Heaton collected a bombing party of the Royal Sussex

Pioneers and the Battalion and advanced up MIDDLE AVENUE. On reaching point 91 they bombed the junction of BACK TRENCH and MIDDLE AVENUE and simultaneously the Battalion with the platoon of Sussex Pioneers and a few men of the Buffs under Capt. Neame advanced to the attack from BRESLAU SUPPORT. The Germans holding BACK TRENCH at once left their trenches and surrendered, numbering about 160. Previous to this time 2nd Lieut A.B. Marston led a party of about 15 men along BACK LANE and reached MINE ALLEY about point A.2.d.78. at 1.pm.

1.15pm.   Lieut C.A. Haggard and Lieut D.R. Heaton collected all available men of the Battn. and led them on towards the Battalions final objective. BLIND ALLEY was found to be occupied and 2/Lieut H.J. Tortise and three men attacked it with one bomb and drove the twelve occupants of the trench out.

2pm.   The Battalion reached MONTAUBAN-MAMETZ ROAD on its allotted front. A number of men now rejoined from 8th East Surrey Regt and stray parties coming up from behind and brought the strength of the Battn. up to about 200. The situation this time was as follows: MONTAUBAN ALLEY and trench running round N. side of MONTAUBAN was held by the East Surreys and Royal West Kents. The rest of the Battalion was completely in the air, no connection whatever being obtained with the right of the 53rd Brigade until much later in the day. MONTAUBAN ALLEY was held by the enemy from about S.26.d.87. to the left by Machine Guns which made further advance over a very open bit of ground impossible without reinforcements or Artillery Support.

2.30pm.   The C.O. met C.O. 7th Buffs in MINE ALLEY and explained the situation and asked for support to attempt to connect left of Battalion with 53rd Brigade. The C.O. 7th Buffs sent up all the men he had left at his disposal (2 platoons) to prolong left of Battalion.

5.0pm.   Lieut V. Hook with Stokes Guns came into action at N. end of BLIND ALLEY and MONTAUBAN ORCHARD.

5.15pm.   The F.O.O. of 51st Brigade R.F.A. put about four rounds on to MONTAUBAN ALLEY between CATERPILLAR TRENCH and 67 TRENCH. Stokes Guns also fired on this area. Immediately after this bombardment a party of the Battalion under 2nd Lieut H.J. Tortise and C.S.M. King assaulted and occupied this section of trench establishing connection with the R. W. Kent Regt. on the right. Except for the presence of a small party of the 8th Norfolks, no real connection was yet established with 53rd Brigade.

6.45pm.   Touch was established with the 53rd Brigade who appear to have moved up in LOOP TRENCH and along MONTAUBAN ALLEY, a procedure which probably accounts for their delay in reaching this objective. The Battalion now consolidated the length of MONTAUBAN ALLEY which it had gained and occupied it during the night.

7th (Service) Battalion Queen's Own (Royal West Kent Regiment)

7.30am (Zero) The attack by 55th Bde commenced. 8th E. Surreys were leading Battn on the right and 7th Queens on the left; the 7th Buffs were third Battalion, in support covering the whole Brigade frontage, & 7th R. W. Kent Regt, less two platoons detached for carrying forward material from Brigade Dump to our front line, in Brigade reserve. The 8th Suffolk Regt of 53rd Brigade were in Divisional Reserve in rear of 55th Brigade.

8.10am A message was received from 8th E. Surreys Report Centre that all was going well, but they had not heard whether the POMMIER LINE was taken.

8.12am The Brigade informed us by telephone that all appeared to be going well, but that the leading Battalions had met with more opposition than was anticipated, and had suffered considerable casualties.

8.35am I ordered [*illegible*]. Companies to move up to the forming up trenches as they became vacated by 7th Buffs. Each Company had patrols out to keep in touch with the Buffs. 2nd Lieut Tindall had been sent as Liasion Officer to H.Q. 7th Buffs. The weather became decidedly hot.

8.47am The leading platoon of 'C' on the right, 'A' in the centre, and 'D' on the left started moving forward.

9.30am Bn. H.Q. started moving forward up COKE AVENUE to right Report Centre, leaving the Signalling Officer and Battalion Report Centre in its initial position.

9.42am The whole Battalion was clear of RAIL AVENUE. Captain Waddington intercepted a message from the Buffs to us, asking for help for the E. Surreys who were held up at TRAIN ALLEY and stating that the whole Battalion (Buffs) had been thrown in less one platoon. This message actually reached Bn. H.Q. at 10.40am, but at 9.45am a message to that effect had been received from 2nd Lieut Tindall. Therefore at 10.8am a message was sent to the 8th Suffolks informing them that in the event of our being thrown into the fight they would have to move up to our original front line.

Sent 2nd Lieut Tindall to the Suffolks as Liaison Officer. Between 10am and 10.30am an officer of each of 'A', 'C' and 'D' Companies reported personally to me I issued to them verbally orders to move forward vide my Q.O.G.487(app10) and at 10.25am I issued these orders in writing by runner. Of the above mentioned officers, 2nd Lieut Heaton of 'A' Co was wounded, and 2nd Lieut Phipps of 'D' Coy was temporarily knocked out by shell shock, and owing to the runner going to 'D' Coy becoming a casualty, that Company never got the orders.

'C' Coy and 'A' Coy were ready to move by 11.10am and actually moved at 11.20am. Very shortly after this Captain Latter and 2nd Lieut Woodhouse were wounded. The advance of 'A' Company was much slower than that of 'C' Company, the platoons lost touch and became separated, but three platoons were collected and re-organised by C.S.M. Klien in the POMMIER LINE between 12noon and 12.20pm, and the 4th platoon was at No.5 Strong Point about this time, under 2nd Lieut Fale, who was not aware that he was at the time the only officer left in this Company. By this time, (actually 11.45am) two platoons of 'C' Coy with Captain Waddington had reached the final objective, passing through elements of E. Surrey and Buffs, and two platoons were still in the POMMIER LINE.

10.30am Battalion Report Centre moved to Right Bn Report Centre.

11.25am One platoon of 'B' Coy was sent to carry up S.A.A. and bombs to the final objective.

11.45am A message from the Brigade informed us that the 90th Bde had taken MONTAUBAN.

12noon The Adjutant was sent out to find out where 'D' Coy was, as they did not appear to have moved. He found Capt Camden and his Coy still in our trenches, central, and it was only then discovered that the orders to move (app.10) had not been received by him. They were delivered to him personally by the Adjutant at 12.15pm.

12.25pm A message was received from Capt Waddington that he had reached MONTAUBAN Alley at 11.45am with two platoons of his own Coy, with one platoon 7th Buffs and one platoon 8th E.Surrey in rear, and that he was at work consolidating the line.

After leaving our lines, (11.20am), he met with no opposition at all, but two platoons under Lieut Innocent got left behind for some reason that has not been explained, (this officer having been since killed in action) and they did not arrive in MONTAUBAN Alley until 3pm, more than three hours after the leading two platoons. In the meantime the 3 platoons of 'A' Coy under C.S.M. Klein moved forward to the junction of MINE Alley and the end of MONTAUBAN, where they stopped at 12.45pm to consolidate, and engaged in German machine gun firing from MONTAUBAN Alley about S.26.b.13.

3pm C.S.M. Klein reported to Capt Waddington in MONTAUBAN Alley about 5pm. Captain Waddington ordered him to bring his 3 platoons up into Montauban Alley, which he did, arriving about 6pm. The platoon of 'A' Coy under 2nd Lieut Fale, passed over the POMMIER Line at 11.50am and proceeded over the open close to MINE Alley, and got in touch with Capt Clare and Lieut Thorley of 8th E. Surreys at the MILL and on the MAMETZ-MONTAUBAN road at 12.15pm. He then moved up into MONTAUBAN Alley, on the left of a platoon of 7th Buffs, who were on the left of the two platoons of 'C' Coy where they started consolidating. It was not until 6pm that C.S.M. Klein and 2nd Lieut Fale eventually met, and then 2nd Lieut Fale took over command of 'A' Coy. Meanwhile 'D' Coy had moved up to the POMMIER Line which they reached between 12.30pm and 1pm. Number 15 platoon under 2nd Lieut Wills appears to have received orders to carry S.A.A. to the firing line, which they did, and did not return to the POMMIER Line until 4pm.

2.20pm	Battalion H.Q. moved up to the POMMIER Line, to the junction of that line and BRESLAU ALLEY, running a wire out from the right report centre.
3pm	Colonel Feinnes went forward to confer with O.C. 8th E. Surreys and to review the situation. He found the situation as follows: A mixed force of all four Battalions holding MONTAUBAN ALLEY, length of frontage about 600 yards, amounting to about 400 rifles, 4 Vickers guns and 8 Lewis guns, they were in touch with the 30th Division on the right, but the left flank was in the air. The men were much exhausted, and S.A.A. and water urgently required. Tools and a carrying party were much needed.
4.43pm	Colonel Feinnes returned to Bn. H.Q. and sent this information to Bde H.Q.
7.33pm	After a further review of the situation, and consultation with O's. C. 7th Buffs and 7th Queens, report vide app.11 (Q.O.G.4) was sent to Brigade H.Q.
7.30pm	Report Centre joined Battn H.Q. in the POMMIER LINE.

During the evening the Brigadier came forward and after consultation with D and C battalions decided that the line should be re-organised at once and that it should be taken over by 7th R.W.Kent Regt as far as possible. Therefore at 10pm Battalion H.Q, 'D' Co. and 'B' Co. less 2 platoons, moved forward via BRESLAU ALLEY, MILL Trench, and MINE alley to a point in MINE alley about 100 yards S. of the western house in MONTAUBAN where Capt.Waddington was sent for to meet Col. Feinnes. After consultation with him, it was decided that it was impracticable to carry out the relief by night owing to enemy shelling and the locality being unknown. All through the night MINE Alley was heavily barraged. A telephone cable was run out from Battn report centre as far as MILL Trench, but was broken several times by shell fire; each time 2nd Lieut Lewin took a party out to repair the breaks.

11th (Service) Battalion Royal Fusiliers
(City of London Regiment)

7.30 a.m.
Attack on the German 1st Line trenches was carried out: (See special Report attached). Casualties in the attack were as follows:

  47 Killed
    6 Died of Wounds
148 Wounded
  17 Missing
    4 Shell Shock.

Document Attached to the War Diary

A report on the attack on 1 July 1916, dated 6 July 1916, and signed by Lieutenant Colonel P.P. Carr, Commanding 11th (Service) Battalion Royal Fusiliers (City of London Regiment):

The Battalion formed the left assaulting Battalion of the 54th Brigade, the 7th Bedfordshires being on the right. The Manchesters of the 91st Brigade were on our left.

By 1.0am the Battalion was ready in the forming-up trenches, in the following order: 'A' Coy., 'B' Coy, [in front wave], 'C' Coy., 'D' Coy.

At 7.30am (Zero hour) 'A' and 'B' Coys led off, advancing in four waves in extended order, the Supporting and Reserve Coys following up in artillery formation. The intervals between the advancing waves from 100 to 150 yards. In comparison with the hurricane bombardment which had been opened by our concentrated artillery, 2" and Stokes Mortars, the enemy's reply was feeble, so that the casualties that we suffered in crossing no man's land were few. Some machine guns, however, opened on the flanks, and these knocked out a few, but in no way held up the steady advance. One of these guns was rushed and captured with great dash by L/Cpl Payne of 'B' Coy.

The enemy's front line offered no opposition, and EMDEN TRENCH was reached bang up to time. In BUND TRENCH a few Bosch were encountered, but were easily dealt with. At this point it was possible to look round and see how things stood. The 7th Bedfordshires on our right had kept touch perfectly with us; on the left the Manchesters seemed to be rather hung up. It was, therefore, imperative to watch the left flank, and this fell to Major Hudson, in command of 'A' Coy, who was most careful on this point, and was kept well backed up by Capt. Hoare, in command of 'C' Company.

It was on the advance from BUND to POMMIERS TRENCH that 2/Lt Parr-

Dudley dealt so effectively with a party of 30 Germans who were attempting to counter-attack from the direction of MAMETZ. He wheeled his platoon half-left and charged them, using rifles, bayonets and bombs. Not one of the enemy escaped, but unfortunately Parr-Dudley was killed – the only one of the party.

The POMMIERS TRENCH was manned to some extent by riflemen, and a machine gun in a bedded emplacement kept up a steady fire even after the first two waves had got into the trench, but the man behind the gun was soon dealt with and his gun captured.

As, according to scheduled time, there was a [illegible] minutes' wait in this trench, some hand-to-hand fighting took place, as the dugouts contained a lot of Bosch. Many were bombed effectively before they had time to make a bolt into the trench.

The REDOUBT and MAPLE TRENCH line was a tougher nut to crack, and, as the first waves of the Bedfordshires and our men got out of POMMIERS, rifles and machine guns opened fire from the REDOUBT and mowed them down.

On the East face of the REDOUBT the wire was much damaged, but on the West it was in sufficiently good repair to enable the enemy to hold us. Several times the men reached the wire only to be shot. As the frontal attack on the REDOUBT was not progressing, Capt. Johnston, commanding 'B' Coy, decided to take his men up BLACK ALLEY with the intention of bombing up MAPLE TRENCH and so into the REDOUBT, but the last 60 yards of this trench is straight and a machine gun held him up. He then decided he would attack the REDOUBT in the rear over the open, but was bothered by German snipers who were established in BEETLE ALLEY, so he asked 2/Lt Savage , who was with 'A' Coy, on the left, to rush them out of the trench. He carried out this operation so thoroughly and quickly that Capt. Johnston was able to get his men up to the REDOUBT without a casualty.

The Germans were very thick in the REDOUBT, and were firing head and shoulders over the parapet. Capt. Johnston put his Lewis guns at the end of BLACK ALLEY so as to enfilade the front of the REDOUBT, and they successfully wiped out all the Germans who were in the trench, which enabled the Bedfordshires and ourselves to dash in and finish the rest. This is practically the story of the Right Company.

The Left Company were unfortunate in losing Lt. Nield, who was killed near the German front line. The POMMIERS line was reached easily, and the dug-outs in BLACK ALLEY received many bombs. At the junction of POMMIERS and BLACK ALLEY there was some hand-to-hand fighting, a German officer suddenly appearing from a dug-out followed by some men - they were all killed. This Company's task was difficult and dangerous, as the Battalion on our left had not secured DANTZIG ALLEY, and the left was consequently in the air. 2/Lt. Savage was helping 'B' Coy by clearing BEETLE ALLEY of snipers, and it was then that he was killed by a sniper while trying to see how things were going on the left. He had been hit in the foot from the very start at 7.30am but had stuck on and led his men gallantly the whole time.

Some good work was done by the Lewis Guns with this Coy, who got their guns in position to command the approach from FRITZ ALLEY, which was full of Bosch, and it was entirely due to the way in which the machine guns and Savage's platoon dealt with the situation that our left remained secure. Capt. Hooke, with his Stokes mortars, rendered great assistance by pounding FRITZ TRENCH and causing the Germans to bolt, presenting a splendid target to our Lewis guns, who bowled them over in the open.

The Support and Reserve Coys, supported closely and did excellent work in repelling small counter-attacks which had been launched from the flanks. The programme was that they should pass through the assaulting Coys at BEETLE TRENCH and secure the final objective at WHITE TRENCH, but, on consultation between the Commanding Officers, it was decided that it would be a dangerous undertaking while the Brigades on the left and right were so hung up.

The Battalion set to making its strong points and making fire steps, and parties from the Dumps soon came up with wire, stakes, bombs, ammunition and water. The men were all in the best of spirits and seemed delighted with the fight. Later on in the afternoon a reconnaissance was made to WHITE TRENCH, which was found to be unoccupied – so a small garrison was put here.

Communication:

It was very seldom that the telephone worked satisfactorily, but admirable work was done by our Signallers, who, by means of shutter and flag, succeeded in getting our messages through. One of the finest things witnessed was the performance of Pte. Hughes, who, knowing his message to be important, selected the white signalling flag, mounted to the top of the parados in spite of shot and shell which were all round him. He did not give in till a shell dealt him a terrible injury.

It is difficult to pick out any one incident of gallantry and devotion to duty when every man behaved with such dash, but such episodes as the following give an idea of individual pluck:

1. Pte. H.R. Wheeler found himself alone in EMDEN TRENCH, in which were 7 Germans. Three of these he managed to shoot before his bolt got jammed by the sock breech cover. He retired behind a traverse and jumped on to the top of the trench, shooting the remaining four with a revolver he had found.

2. Sgt. Brisby was called upon for assistance by a bombing section who had run into some German bombers in BLACK ALLEY. He went over from his position in the open on the left of BLACK ALLEY, and shot one of the Germans who had thrown bombs at him from the fire step. He then jumped into the trench and bayoneted the remaining three.

Mention must be made of the fine way in which the dug-out clearing parties of the 6th Northamptonshires behaved. They did not scruple to enter dug-outs whether they contained live arms or not, and in this way secured many prisoners.

At the end of the day the Battalion was disposed as follows:

1 Coy in MAPLE TRENCH and garrisoning No5 Strong Point.

3 Coys in BEETLE TRENCH and 1 platoon pushed out as an outpost to the WHITE TRENCH.

On the night of July 2nd the Battalion was relieved by the 12th Middlesex Regt.

2nd Battalion Royal Scots Fusiliers

ASSEMBLY TRENCHES

The Bn. reached its Assembly Trenches between midnight and 1a.m. having left ETINEHEM CAMP in two half's at 6.10 and 7.10pm (30.6.16) and joined the rest of the Brigade which moved from BILLON WOOD in two parallel columns.

Only waterproof sheets and rations for one day – besides emergency rations – were carried and on each man's pack was a yellow patch – 30th DIV – and a metal disc. Every man – with exception of bombers who carried 10 – carried 2 No.5 grenades and 200 shovels, 100 picks and a quantity of sandbags were distributed over the Bn.

7.30am	Zero was fixed for 7.3am. and an intensive bombardment started apparently at 6am.
8.30am	The Bn. left its trenches behind CAMBRIDGE COPSE at 8.30am in the following order: Three platoons of NETTOYEURS from 'B' 'C' and 'D' Coys – marked by yellow shoulder strap – behind the third waves of 16th MANCHESTERS on the left and 17th MANCHESTERS on the right. The remainder of the Bn. moved in two lines of columns of half platoons, 150 yards between Coys – 'C' and 'B' Coys on right and 'A' and 'D' on left – with its right on the W. end of GLATZ REDOUBT and its left on TALUS BOISE.
	There was very little shell fire and hardly any casualties occurred before reaching BRITISH Front Line – 1000 yards – after reaching the German lines there was considerable rifle fire from the left flank which increased as the Bn. advanced causing numerous casualties in 'A' and 'D' Coys.
	The 18th DIV. who were operating W. of the TALUS BOISE appeared to be held up and to be keeping to the trenches while the enemy could be plainly observed firing on our men. The Bn. however kept its formation perfectly.
9.20am	The Bn. halted in conformation with the leading Bns. the Bde. having covered the ground too quickly, the barrage being on MONTAUBAN till 9.55am owing to the mass of shell craters the ground was difficult to manoeuvre over but no trouble was experienced from uncut wire.

9.30am   The Bde. moved again but halted at 9.45am when the advance seemed to waver. The barrage lifted off the village and both 'B' and 'C' Coys caught up the 17th MANCHESTERS and 'A' and 'D' the 16th MANCHESTERS on the right and left respectively, about 400 yards from the village. Our field guns again put a barrage on the village.

10am   The whole Bde. advanced again, our NETTOYEUR platoons and most of the Bn. being in the assaulting line. There was no rifle fire from the village itself but it was still heavy from the left flank.

10.15am   'A' Coy had reached the centre keep and the remaining three Coys had occupied the trench S. of the village (SOUTH TRENCH) by 10.30am and the whole started consolidating. The casualties during the advance were:

Officers Killed: LIEUT J.W. TOWERS-CLARK (Commdg 'A' Coy). 2nd LT. J.H.L. GRIERSON ('C' Coy).

Wounded: CAPT & ADJT. M.B. BUCHANAN. CAPT. M.J.N. LAW (O.C. 'D' Coy). Lt.J.S. CRAIG ('A' Coy). 2.Lt. A.G. LOCHHEAD ('D' Coy). W.M. KNOX ('C' Coy). CAPT. G.D. FAIRLEY R.A.M.C. att. Total 8.

O.R. Killed: 18. Wounded: 94. Missing: 58. Total 170.

Only 20 Officers had been taken into action and fighting strength was 743 O.R.

LT.COL. R.K. WALSH Commdg. 2/R.S.F. had been previously appointed O.C. MONTAUBAN. The Adgt. duties were taken over by LT. M. CARR. All strong points and trenches – so far as recognisable were occupied as practised but touch was not obtained with the 18th DIV. on the left. The NETTOYEUR platoons after clearing the village rejoined their Coys one platoon taking 28 prisoners.

Several batches of prisoners including an Artillery Brigadier and his Staff were conducted to the rear.

The Bn. was disposed as follows: 'A' Coy holding KEEP A, one platoon of 'D' Coy just S. in KEEP E. Rest of 'D' Coy W. end of SOUTH TRENCH, Bn. H.Q. 'C' Coy & 'B' Coy at E. end of SOUTH TRENCH. The 16th and 17th MANCHESTERS holding MONTAUBAN ALLEY Trench N. of the village – with the N. perimeter and the E. perimeter of the village respectively. Touch with 21st Bde. in CHIMNEY TRENCH was established.

12noon   The enemy commenced bursting heavy shrapnel over KEEP A and this with the shortage of tools severely held up the work of consolidation.

12.30pm   Enemy guns turned their attention to other parts of the village and heavy enfilade fire from 5.9s and 4.2s was brought to bear on NORD and TRAIN ALLEYS. The carrying parties of MANCHESTERS which had been retained at A KEEP now returned to obtain more stores from forward Bde. Dump.

2.45pm   One platoon of 'C' Coy was sent to reinforce KEEP B, held by 17th M, which was being heavily shelled. The remaining two companies of the 18th MANCHESTERS had previously moved into SOUTH TRENCH – their H.Q. adjacent to those of 2/R.S.F. – to strengthen the garrison.

5pm 'D' Coy's platoon was withdrawn from point E. owing to the heavy and continuous shell fire and the impossibility of consolidating that position.

8pm Enemy shelling increased and continued throughout the night grew from the direction of BERNAFAY WOOD enfilading SOUTH TRENCH causing several casualties. One of our own batteries was also putting shells into the village.

10.30pm One platoon of 'B' Coy was moved to NORD ALLEY to reinforce the 17th M. whose ranks were being thinned by the continual shell fire.

12th (Service) Battalion Royal Scots (Lothian Regiment)

BILLON VALLEY
Bn. arrived in BILLON VALLEY 12.30am and settled down in dugouts. Bn. under 40 minutes notice to move – News received that the attack has commenced and that MONTAUBAN has fallen into our hands. At 10.30pm all coys proceeded to POMMIERES LINE to help the 18th Divn to consolidate it.

8th (Service) Battalion (Pioneers) Royal Sussex Regiment

CARNOY
7.30am The DIVISION Attacks.

The Platoons attached to Brigades moved off between 7.30am and 8.30am. The Platoons for opening communications over "NO MANS LAND" left Hqts at ZERO time(7.30am) in order to be in position to commence work, 1 hour after assault.

'B' Coy marched from BRAY at 8.30am arriving at Bn Hqts 10.30am. The following is a short summary of action of each coy during the day.

'A' Coy No's. 2 and 4 Plats attached to 55th Bde.

No.2 followed the assaulting Battn to MONTAUBAN and consolidated strong points marked A and B on the map (app XXXI) These Platoons reached MONTAUBAN ALLEY very shortly after Infantry had got in and were to some extent involved in the actual fighting. They worked throughout the day and night returning to Batt Hqts at 3am on 2nd inst. having completed both strong points.

No.4 Platoon moved to 7th QUEENS Report Centre for orders as to where the POMMIER LINE was taken when they were to consolidate strong point marked C on map. The Infantry were however held up at the LOOP and the Plat was called upon by O.C. Batt to assist in the capture. This they did subsequently moving off to their allotted task. At this they worked till 10pm when they were relieved by a platoon from 'B' Coy in reserve.

Nos.1 and 3 Platoons commenced work on Nos.1 and 2 Communications across "NO MANS LAND" and worked till 10pm when they were relieved by the Plat of 'C' Coy in reserve. The Saps were open for traffic by 4pm.

'D' Coy   No's. 13 and 16 platoons attached 53rd Bde. These platoons left Hqts at 7.30am following the attack and at 10am commenced consolidating on POMMIER TRENCH Line sending their Bombers to assist in capturing the LOOP. The LOOP having been captured they commenced work on strong point D. These Plats returned to Batt Hqts at 11.45pm on completion of the LOOP strong point. Nos.14 and 15 Plats left Hqts at 7.45am and proceeded to frontline between LOTHIAN ST and YORK Road where they commenced opening up saps 5 and 6 across "NO MAN'S LAND". These platoons worked till 2am on 2nd inst. by which time practicable comms was opened up through both saps and they returned to Hqts.

'C' Coy   No's.11 and 12 Platoons attached to 54th Bde.

These platoons moved out after the assaulting troops.

No.11 proceeded to BLACK ALLEY and commenced work on strong points E.F.G.H. The platoon worked on these points till 2am on the 2nd when it moved back to the TRIANGLE for food and rest. Work commenced again 3pm. on 2nd and continued till 8.15am on 3rd when platoon returned to Batt Hqts at CARNOY.

No.12 Platoon followed the attack to POMMIER redoubt where they consolidated a strong point in the redoubt. They worked at this till 5am on 2nd when they went back to the TRIANGLE for food and rest commencing work again at 3pm on 2nd and continuing till 10am on 3rd when they rejoined Batt Hqts at CARNOY.

No.10 Platoon was employed repairing the CARNOY-MONTAUBAN Road as soon as the attack had got as far as the POMMIER LINE. They worked till 8.30pm. by which time the road was practicable for wagons up to the BRESLAU Support trench. At 8.30pm this platoon was relieved by a platoon of 'B' Coy from the Batt reserve.

No.9 Plat formed part of the Batt reserve. It remained in CARNOY till 9pm. on 1st when it moved out and relieved Nos.1 and 3 Plats of 'A' Coy on Saps1and 2. It worked till 8.20am on the 2nd when it was again relieved by No.3 Plat of 'A' Coy.

'B' Coy   This Coy formed part of the Batt reserve. It marched from BRAY at 8.30am arriving at Bn Hqts at CARNOY at 10.30am. At 6.30pm No's 5, 7 and 8 Plats proceeded to work on repairing the CARNOY-

MONTAUBAN Road where they worked till 1-30am. Work much interrupted by heavy shelling.

No.6 Plat moved out at 9pm to relieve No.4 plat of 'A' coy at strong point C.

Casualties during this day:

3 Officers Wounded (Lt. A.D. FOSTER 2/Lt. F. NORRIS, Lt. W.H. SAINTON)

11 O.R.'s Killed, 79 O.R's Wounded (18 of whom slightly at duty) 2 O.R's reported missing.

8th (Service) Battalion Suffolk Regiment

CARNOY

5.30am.   Battalion reported "ready" for the attack.

6.0am.   Breakfast served.

Battalion in reserve to 55th Bde until capture of MONTAUBAN complete.

7.20am.   Our bombardment most intense.

Close touch kept with 7th R.W.Kent Regt, who were the 4th Battn in 55th Bde attack.

8.30am.   German prisoners started to come down from the front. All looked pale & haggard and were apparently very hungry and thirsty. One prisoner stooped to drink from cesspool.

11am.   Battalion moved from shelters in CARNOY to Assembly trenches of 55th Inf Bde, 'A' Coy to original front line of 55th Bde, 'C' Coy to No.2 Assembly trench, 'D' Coy to No.3 Assembly trenches and 'B' Coy to No.4 Assembly trench. Enemy shelled the troops as they crossed the open with 4.2" & 5.9" H.E. shells but did very little damage.

Battn H.Q. moved to 'C' Battn H.Q. of 55th Bde in PRINCES ST.

1pm.   'B' Coy detailed to carry R.E. Material from forward dump to W. houses of MONTAUBAN.

2.35pm.   'A' & 'C' Coys moved to the left and occupied Nos.1 & 2 assembly trenches on 53rd Bde front.

During afternoon enemy's shelling considerably diminished.

Casualties for the day 2/Lt Williams wounded, 7 O.R. killed, 13 O.R. wounded.

Document Attached to the War Diary

An account of the Battle of the Somme:

From June 10th. to 18th. two Companies of the Battalion were billeted in CORBIE and employed entireky [sic] upon loading ammunition on to barges and lorries.

SLAUGHTER ON THE SOMME: 1 JULY 1916

During this period one Company was employed at the 18th Divisional School and another also at loading work at AILLY-SUR-SOMME.

On the evening of the 19th. the Battalion was concentrated in a comparativeky [*sic*] small number of tents at GROVETOWN CAMP BRAY.

On the 20th. and 22nd. Inckusive [*sic*] the Battalion was employed day and night on working parties chiefly in the vicinity of CARNOY.

The Battalion left GROVETOWN CAMP on the evening of June 23rd. to relieve the 6th. Royal Berkshire Regiment in the trenches at CARNOY.

We took over the Attack Frontages of both our own and the 54th. Bde. with Battalion Headquarters at Report Centre No.3.

Everything was very quiet with the exception of a certain amount of Machine Gun Fire at night.

June 24th. (1st day of the Bombardment).

'D' Company who were holding the attack frontage of the 53rd. Bde. remained on this frontage but 'B' Company holding the 54th Bde. frontage were relieved during the course of the morning by the 7th. Bedford Regiment and settled down as best they could in No.3. Assembly Trench, 'C' Company being in No.4. Assembly Trench and 'A' Company in shelters about the North end of CARNOY.

The bombardment was almost entirely confined to Field Guns cutting the enemys wire and throughout the night firing intermittently on the gaps they had made. Both the Brigadier and the Divisional Commander visited our line during the course of the morning and early afternoon. At 4 o'clock in the afternoon a conference of Commanding Officers was held at the Brigade Office which had now taken up its battle position in BILLON WOOD. Later in the afternoon Battalion Headquarters were moved forward to Report Centre No.1. on the CARNOY-MONTAUBAN ROAD.

During the night the Regimental Scouts and one patrol from both 'D' and 'B' Companies patrolled almost the entire length of the enemys wire opposite the front held by the Battalion with a view to ascertaining what damage had been done and in what strength the enemy was holding his front trench.

June 25th.

Our bombardment was far more severe, Heavies, Field Guns and Trench Mortars all starting on their separate tasks. Selected Officers N.C.O's and men were posted at various places of vantage in order to give reports on the effect of the Trench Mortar Fire on the enemy's front line wire; and from all observations the effect was extraordinarily good. The enemys fire in retaliation to the almost incessant stream of shells fired against his various defences was extraordinarily little especially during the day, but at night when our fire decreased his seemed to increase. Starting at 10.30pm. we had patrols out almost continually until 1.30am. At 12midnight 'A' Company carried out a small raid on the enemys front trench.

(A separate report of which is attached) Appendix No.2.

During the night and the early hours of June 26th. Parties were out from all Companies starting the removal of all wire in front of our own front and rear trenches.

June 26th.
Our bombardment still continued with an intense display between 9-10.30am. The enemy shelling was somewhat heavier on our lines than the previous day and appeared to be largely concentrated around the vicinity of No.3. Assembly Trench and the MONTAUBAN ROAD. Patrols were out as before, practically throughout the darkness and at 12midnight'C' company carried out a small raid on the enemys front trench. (A separate report of which is attached) Appendix 3.

June 27th.
The weather on the evening of the 26th. turned wet and remained so for several days. June 27th. was from our point of view much the same as the two previous days except that the enemys artillery fire was a good deal more severe and did us a considerable amount of damage especially around Battalion Headquarters and No.3. Assembly Trench.

During the course of the night we were relieved by the 6th Royal Berks Regiment and marched down by Companies to Billets in Bray where the Battalion arrived at about 4am. on the 28th. About 11 o'clock on the morning of the 28th. there was slight enemy shelling on BRAY, only one shell doing us any damage. Our Casualties between June 23rd. and 28th. Both days inckusive [sic] are shewn [sic] in Appendix No.4. [not present].

Our original orders to move up to CARNOY on the night of the 28th. were now cancelled (presumably on account of the bad weather) for probably 48 hours.

June 29th. The Battalion remained in BRAY.

June 30th.
At 10pm on June 30th. the Battalion left BRAY by Companies for CARNOY where they were accomodated in Shelters in the vicinity of BRICK ALLEY. Battalion Headquarters being at Report Centre No.3.

The weather had now taken a change for the better.

July 1st.
Hot Breakfast was served to the men at 6am in CARNOY.

At this hour there was nothing but a continuous roar of Artillery fire and up till about [illegible]. (Zero hour being 7.30am) there was a thick mist. At this hour there appeared to be little enemy Shell, Machine Gun or Rifle Fire.

7am   B.M.444 was received:

"Following from 4th. Army begins. In wishing all ranks good luck" the

Army Commander desires to impress on all Infantry Units the supreme importance of helping one another and holding on tight to every yard of ground gained. The accurate and sustained fire of the artillery during bombrdment [sic] should greatly assist the task of the Infantry. Ends".

8.22am   448 received:

"6th Royal Berks report they have taken Bund Support and are working up Popoff Lane. Two Battalions 7th. Division entered MAMETZ 7.45am. 54th Bde. report they have taken Pommiers Trench. Battalion on our right doing well".

8.55am   B.M. 451 received:

"Brigade Observation Officer reports our troops have taken Pommiers Trench and are not being shelled much. Addressed 18th. Div. repeated 54th. Bde. 55th. Bde. 10th. Essex Regiment 8th. Suffolk Regiment.

9.23am   B.M.452 received:

"No further news from Battalions. 6th. Royal Berks report heavy casualties from falling debris of the Mine Explosion. Addressed 18th. Div. repeated 55th.Bde. 54th.Bde 8th.Suffolks 10th.Essex.

9.48am   B.M. 453 received:

"Get in touch with West Kents at once and be prepared to move up into the 55th.Bde. trenches when ordered".

10.25am   Q.O.G. 486 received:

"You may have to take over our original front line (i.e.) 55th.Bde. frontage in the event of our having to move forward. I am sending a liaison Officer to you and will let you know when I move forward. My present headquarters are forwrd [sic] in Coke Avenue (Right Battalion Headquarters)".

10.45am   B.M. 459 received:

"East of the craters still holding out. French have taken NAMELESS WOOD and FAVIERE WOOD and CLAPHAM FARM CURLU. Troops of the 7th. Div. have been seen N.E. corner MAMETZ. Third Corps have taken strong post N. of OVILLERS. 21st. Div. are doing well near RED COTTAGE N. of FRICOURT. Our troops have been seen advancing up the slopes of CONTALMAISON HILL. 30th. Div. have taken DUBLIN TRENCH. GLATZ REDOUBT. ALT ALLEY, and CASEMENT TRENCH".

10.58am   B.M. 458 received:

"You will move up and relieve the West Kents at once in front line system, and come under orders of G.O.C. 55th. Bde. Addressed 8th. Suffolks repeated 55th.Bde. Acknowledge."

11am   Q.O.G. 488 received:

"We are moving forward to push home the attack on 55th. Bde. frontage. Will you move up to our original front line at once."

Immediately on receipt of B.M 458 the Battalion started to move by Companies in the order 'A'. 'C'. 'D'. 'B'. to occupy Nos.1.2.3. and 4 Assembly Trenches respectively in the 55th. Bde. Area. During the process of crossing the open from Carnoy to these Assembly Trenches we suffered some casualties owing to the enemy barrage (largely 5.9") in the vicinity of Nos. 3 and 4 Assembly Trenches. At 11.28am the Battalion with its Headquarters in Princess Street [*probably means Princes Street*] were assembled in these trenches and P.C./A/1 was sent to both the 55th. and 53rd. Bdes.

8th. Suffolks now in 55th. Bde. assembly trenches. H.Q. at present at C Battn. Shortly moving to A Battn. H.Q.

From this point onwards any reliable information was extremely difficult to get although telephone communication to the rear appeared to be very good. At these Headquarters we were not in telephone communication with any battalion of our own Brigade nor for that matter with any battalion of the 55th. Bde. At 1.7pm two platoons of 'B' Coy were sent to the Western Houses of Montauban carrying R.E. material.

1.29pm   Q.O.G. 495 was received:
"Message from 55th. Bde. begins. Instruct O.C. 8th. Suffolks Regt. To send two Companies to report to the 53rd. Bde. in original front line system at once. H.Q. and 2 remaining Coys to remain where they are. Ends. Please acknowledge."

'A' and 'C' Coys were immediateky [*sic*] instructed to move to 53rd. Bde. Area. At 1.57pm 1 N.C.O. and 12 men from 'B' Coy were ordered to report to the 55th. Bde. left Dump at the top of Batty Road as a carrying party with ammunition and Bombs.

2.49pm   Q.O.G. 500 was received:
"G.O.C. 55th. Bde. has ordered me to ask you for a carrying party or one platoon to take ammunition and some picks and shovels and wiring material to the junction of Mill Trench and Mine Alley reporting to O.C. 8th. E. Surreys. S.A.A. particularly is urgently required."

1 Platoon of 'B' Coy was immediately sent off to carry out the task asked for.

4.40pm   B.M. 473 was received.
"Following from 18th. Div. Areoplane [*sic*] report 12.30pm. Enemys guns being taken away on all roads to the rear of Poziers and Contalmaison and Fricourt. Ends."

5pm   The remaining platoon of 'B' Coy plus those who had returned from other carrying parties together with one platoon of 'D' Coy started to carry forward water to Battalions of the 55th. Bde.

10.2pm   P.C. 215 was sent to O.C. 'A' Coy.

"Detail two platoons to report Bde.Forward Dump at junction Liverpool Street and Leeds Avenue by 10.30pm to carry ammunition and water to Loop.

11.25pm B.M. 488 was received:

"Following from Ho. 18th. Div. begins. GENERAL CONGREVE wires please convey to all ranks my intense appreciation of their splendid fighting which has attained all asked of them and resorted in heavy losses of the enemy nearly 1000 have already passed through the cage. Ends. From GENERAL MAXSE 18th. Division. Well done its what I expected now hold on to what you have gained so splendidly. Ends."

Index

MILITARY FORMATIONS

INDEX

PLACES

INDEX